The Humor of the Old South

The Humor of the Old South

Edited by
M. Thomas Inge
and Edward J. Piacentino

THE UNIVERSITY PRESS OF KENTUCKY

Scholarly publisher for the Commonwealth,
serving Bellarmine University, Berea College, Centre
College of Kentucky, Eastern Kentucky University,
The Filson Historical Society, Georgetown College,
Kentucky Historical Society, Kentucky State University,
Morehead State University, Murray State University,
Northern Kentucky University, Transylvania University,
University of Kentucky, University of Louisville,
and Western Kentucky University.

Editorial and Sales Offices: The University Press of Kentucky
663 South Limestone Street, Lexington, Kentucky 40508–4008

05 04 03 02 01 5 4 3 2 1

Library of Congress Cataloging-in-Publication Data

Inge, M. Thomas.
The humor of the Old South / M. Thomas Inge and Edward J. Piacentino.
p. cm.
Includes bibliographical references (p.) and index.
ISBN 0-8131-2194-9 (acid-free paper)
1. American wit and humor—Southern States—History and criticism. 2. American wit and humor—Southwest, Old—History and criticism. 3. American wit and humor—19th century—History and criticism. 4. Southern States—In literature. 5. Southwest, Old—In literature. I. Piacentino, Edward J., 1945- II. Title.
PS261 .I55 2000
817.009'975—dc21
00-012286

This book is printed on acid-free recycled paper meeting
the requirements of the American National Standard
for Permanence in Paper for Printed Library Materials.

Manufactured in the United States of America.

For Jack Kennon—EP

For Larry Mintz, a congenial fellow traveler through the comic groves of academe—MTI

Contents

Preface

The purpose of this book, the first of its kind since co-editor Inge's *The Frontier Humorists: Critical Perspectives*, is to address the enduring importance of the humor of the Old Southwest. Since the publication of *The Frontier Humorists* in 1975, over four hundred separate critical and scholarly works, as well as many new editions and reprints of antebellum southern humor collections, have appeared—an indication that interest in Southwestern humor has not seriously waned. This volume's nine new essays and introduction, representing some of the premier scholarship on the subject, reexamine Southwestern humor and offer insightful and illuminating perceptions about its influence and continuing significance to American (and in particular southern) literature and culture. We have also included several previously published essays (three of which have been revised) that still stand as important contributions to the large volume of scholarship published in the last twenty-five years about the humor of the Old South. Our comprehensive bibliography, the most extensive compilation of Southwestern humor criticism ever published, includes, among other things, critical materials on five writers who have not been represented in earlier bibliographies and provides an essential starting point for anyone interested in this brand of humor, its practitioners, and its legacy to modern southern writing.

Our gratitude goes out to David Bryden and Pat Sager of the reference staff of Smith Library at High Point University for securing copies of numerous essays on Southwestern humor written over the last twenty-five years; to Keith Auman, who scanned some of the previously published essays; and to Professor Shirley Rawley, the English Department chair at High Point University, who provided funding for the scanning services. We also wish to thank Bill Lenz for revising his essay for this collection, Jim Justus for his perceptive introduction, and the other contributors for their original essays.

We would like to thank the following for permission to reprint previously published essays: The *Southern Literary Journal* for R.J. Gray's "Southwestern Humor, Erskine Caldwell, and the Comedy of Frustration," *Southern Literary Journal* 8.1 (1975): 3–26; Duke University Press for Leland Krauth's "Mark Twain: The Victorian of Southwestern Humor," *American Literature* 54.3 (1982): 368–84; the *Southern Literary Journal* for J.A. Leo Lemay's "The Origins of the Humor of the Old South," *Southern Literary Journal* 23.2 (1991): 3–13; the *Mississippi Quarterly* for William E. Lenz's "The Function of Women in Old Southwestern Humor: Rereading Porter's *Big Bear* and *Quarter Race* Collections," *Mississippi Quarterly* 46

(1993): 589–600; the *Southern Literary Journal* for Ed Piacentino's revised "Contesting the Boundaries of Race and Gender in Old Southwestern Humor," *Southern Literary Journal* 32.2 (2000): 116–40; the *Southern Literary Journal* for Ed Piacentino's revised "'Sleepy Hollow' Comes South: Washington Irving's Influence on Old Southwestern Humor," *Southern Literary Journal* 30.1 (1997): 27–42; *Studies in the Novel* for Stephen M. Ross's "Jason Compson and Sut Lovingood: Southwestern Humor as Stream of Consciousness," *Studies in the Novel* 8.1 (fall 1976): 278–90; the Southern Historical Association for Johanna Nicol Shields's "A Sadder Simon Suggs: Freedom and Slavery in the Humor of Johnson Hooper," *Journal of Southern History* 56 (Nov. 1990): 641–64.

Introduction

James H. Justus

What do we talk about when we talk about humor of the Old Southwest? Like cult buffs in other forms of popular culture, those among us who have long read and taught this writing have sometimes enjoyed thinking that this particular favorite has never been fully appreciated. The truth is that since its emergence in the 1830s, antebellum newspaper humor has never wanted critical attention. It may have been fitful and wrongheaded; it sometimes became the occasion to illustrate unfortunate turns in American literary history—the tribute that popular culture must often pay to the custodians of high art. But, as the bibliographies show, the commentary has been with us almost as long as the humor itself.

Most of us of a certain age who were first introduced to this body of writing (probably in graduate school) read Longstreet and his followers almost as glosses on a handful of critical pieties about nineteenth-century American literature: this antebellum newspaper writing celebrated an ungenteel population who spoke bad colloquial English yet was also colorful and energetic; it exploited in some detail the rich resources of frontier geography; it chronicled the folk wisdom and lore of an oral culture; it contained the first stirrings of literary realism; it became a vehicle for Jacksonian egalitarianism and related values (no, it was really a subversive defense of Whiggish hierarchy against political chaos). Perhaps the longest-lasting truism was that these writers were "gifted amateurs," dilettantes whose corporate project was stronger on social history than literary art.

Not all generalizations are critical whoppers (just as there was some validity to the Eleven Characteristics of British Romanticism that some of us once had to memorize); but a few are what Huck Finn would call "stretchers." M. Thomas Inge addressed some of the shortcomings of Kenneth Lynn's Whiggish theory about this humor a quarter-century ago; James Meriwether, Richard B. Hauck, James M. Cox, Lewis P. Simpson, and others have found revisionist dimensions in this humor that go beyond the half-truths of generalizations. Like the truisms we settle for when we talk about the sentimental novel, detective fiction, and other specialty genres in popular writing, those about Southwestern humor are plausible enough to elude public reprimands from academic critics impatient about everything not measuring up to Mark Twain's *perpendicular.* But the commonplaces we feel most at home with are at best *slantindicular*. As we move further and further from the three decades in which Southwestern humor flourished, it deserves the reclamation—by fresh approaches and from alternate premises—that other forms of popular art have begun to enjoy in recent years.

The successful model for the newspaper sketches we now term Humor of the Old Southwest was A.B. Longstreet's *Georgia Scenes* (1835). Written by males for an appreciative masculine audience, other sketches by lawyers, planters, editors, and preachers characteristically appeared anonymously or pseudonymously in local newspapers and (through the journalistic exchange system) distributed nationally in such lively sheets as the *New Orleans Picayune* and the *St. Louis Reveille.* The best of them were published in William T. Porter's popular, influential, and long-lasting weekly, the *New York Spirit of the Times*. Indeed, it is Porter who encouraged contributions from all the newer settlements in the South and West, giving them editorial readings, prodding responses from writing rivals, and in due time making a personal tour of his favorite region, cultivating the goodwill of old contributors and making contacts with new ones. Porter's agenda resembled that of a social anthropologist. He wanted to preserve both the ordinary flow of life in these newer regions and the spectacular oddities that always seemed to outnumber the ordinary types. The premise behind Porter's calculations (and it is repeated by many of the authors who issued book-length compilations of their pieces) was that the rapid filling up of former Indian lands was providential, a necessary stage in the continental empowerment of America; in this scenario, the period of settlement, with its lawless standards and chaotic governance, was a fleeting moment. What would surely follow the catch-as-catch-can opportunism was consolidation—of society, of the economy, of political values. The task of the correspondents from the Old Southwest, then, was to capture the transition—to record for posterity the stage of primitive exuberance before the softening work of civilization began to make its people like everybody else in the older sections of the nation.

Porter's project was successful in part because a vast readership, entertained as it was, was also willing to be the entertainer—in pieces ranging from brief letters to the editor to multicolumned accounts of bear hunts or practical jokes among the Jacksonian "democracy." Formally, the humorous sketch from 1835 to the end of the Civil War boasts a hodgepodge lineage—a museum of types including the topographical description, the almanac entry, the historical sketch of specific places, the public letter, the gentleman's essay on outdoor sports, the turf report, the profile of local heroes and colorful characters, and the "Character" itself (descended from Webster and Overbury through Addison, Irving, and Paulding). Although a few of the pieces retain marks of older utilitarian forms, all of these professionals who took up their pen responded to their literary promptings through humor, thus freeing themselves from the great American cultural expectation that literature be socially responsible. Even more importantly, they freed themselves from the faintly disreputable burden of "serious" authorship that at one time or another nagged their mainstream contemporaries of the American Renaissance. The diverse prior forms of respectability and prestige were sufficiently flexible to allow the humorists individualized shaping even as they dictated the gentlemanly style—allusive, balanced, complex, witty—with which the amiable "amateur" could maintain his authority without being an "author."

Nineteenth-century readers certainly enjoyed this newspaper humor as a source of amusement, receiving it in much the same spirit as its authors offered it; and for those later readers who expect nothing socially redeeming to come from ephemeral popular writing, amusement is its only excuse for being. True, eye-gouging fights, inept nostrums for assorted internal ailments, practical jokes that are painful as well as humiliating, and hostility to outsiders may require footnotes or a patient teacher to explain cultural shifts in what makes us laugh. Today we are just as likely to temper our amusement with disdain at the frequent cruelty to animals and the cavalier harassment of widows, matrons, and nubile girls. We often find hurdles in the transcription of dialects, sesquipedalian words, inflated images, and typesetting conventions that bestow on the texts more flavor than enjoyment. But, seen in the light of better writing of the era, those who are willing to be amused usually find the humor refreshing and surprisingly vigorous.

As we all know, however, the critical enterprise founders on literary transparency. Amusement is rare enough, and even popular forms require depths that need plumbing. For much of the twentieth century—after the flush of literary realism and its bumptious, more doctrinaire variants—the reading of Longstreet and his contemporaries was usually justified, because their writing heralded the compositional practice of Mark Twain and the aesthetic principles of his more genteel contemporaries, Howells and James. As protorealism, the humorous sketches ignored the relational sentimentalism of the plantation novel (a regional version of the dominant school, domestic fiction) and transcribed, more or less faithfully, the grittier surfaces of antebellum life in the dialectal idioms heard in the margins and backwoods of the lower South. Southwestern humor became a crude foreshadowing of the local color movement, a tonier if no less formulaic body of writing exploiting the characters, customs, costumes, scenery, and speech patterns of a designated region. Within a generation, purged of their more barbarous inelegancies, the linguistic scofflaws of A.B. Longstreet, Johnson Jones Hooper, and George Washington Harris modulate into the better-behaved colloquialists of Sherwood Bonner, Mary Noailles Murfree, and Joel Chandler Harris, who endearingly violate the rules with dignity and homespun fluency. With this narrative justification—the prestige of provenience—we would thus make space for Southwestern humor in a vital, if narrow, room in the house of fiction.

By the 1950s these newspaper sketches ceased to be simple amusement, a string of texts about colorful backwoodsmen who talked funny; and, however important to the development of realistic modes in literary history, in the latter half of the century, when we talked about Southwestern humor we did so in terms of nineteenth-century social and political history. Beginning with Lynn's *Mark Twain and Southwestern Humor* (1959), the sketches became subversive weapons in the historical struggle for political power. The premise behind this influential reading was that the ideological differences between Whig gentlemen (who mostly wrote the sketches) and Democratic yeomen (who mostly served as subjects) prohibited sympathetic mingling—the very condition we had earlier assumed to be necessary for the production of the humor. For a half-century now we have tended to conceive of the humor as a textual manifestation of Whiggery vs. "the Democracy" in antebellum politics and society: the sketches stand as veiled warnings to all good men to resist the chaotic leveling notions of ignorant Jacksonians who spurn the civilized order implicit in law, custom, progress, hierarchy, and elite leadership.

One general article of faith in the critical commentary on southern writing has been its "sense of place." That much-vaunted characteristic was born in the post-Reconstruction era, itself an aesthetic plank in the platform for the Myth of the Ruined Homeland. Its greatest pertinence has been in the authors of the Southern Renascence, who produced the region's finest writing between the two world wars. The texts of vernacular humor, however, show little evidence of such sentiment; rather, they constitute a collective unsentimental profile of one vast *region* in an even vaster geography that William T. Porter called the "Universal Yankee Nation."

It is not that the vernacular storyteller disregards his home turf. A recurring motif in the sketches is the often bellicose trumpeting by quasi-literates of their particular spot of earth—sometimes a state or district, but often a specific settlement: not just Arkansas, but the "Devil's Fork of the Little Red River"; not just Mississippi, but the town of Satartia in the Yazoo hills. Yet these garrulous identifications with place are rhetorically perfunctory: pride in being able to live in the most fertile region anywhere, where unsurpassingly rich soil and water raise up prodigal harvests of corn, cotton, buxom girls, and fearless fighters. Likewise, most of the correspondents, in their pose as disinterested observers (modeled on the sketchbook-carrying visitor of travel discourse), feel little compulsion to individualize their own locales, even when—as in the case of Thorpe, Noland, Baldwin, and others—they lived a semi-backwoods life for substantial stretches of their careers. From the first, the not-so-reluctant authors wrote and sent in their dispatches datelined Tuscaloosa; Greeneville, East Tennessee; Baton Rouge; Hawkins County, Kentucky; Little Rock, as if the geography mattered; but like many of the backwoods figures that the sketches celebrated, the woods and villages in which their verbal and physical exploits are set all look the same. If geography happens to be relevant, it is geography of the most generalized forms: streambeds and rivers, hunting camps deep in the bush, clearings with cabins, dogs, and "worm fences." Except for Henry Clay Lewis's bizarre, Poesque scene-painting of Louisiana swamp country, the texts betray few topographical peculiarities. Longstreet's Georgia is intended to represent the sparsely settled, raw, and morally unenlightened counties west of Augusta and Savannah; Baldwin's Alabama and Mississippi are geographically interchangeable; and Cobb's Mississippi could be any of those states below the Ohio and north of Louisiana.

Despite the authors' habit of giving names of states to their gathered collections, what we remember in the humorous sketches is not a specific site of action, nor the substance of the narratives, nor even the vernacular storytellers, who, except for Harris's Sut and perhaps Hooper's Simon, are mostly types. The most memorable aspect is the so-called demotic style that gave headaches to linguistic custodians, dictionary men, and New England schoolmarms of both sexes. But how much is even this mode—an efflorescence of overdetermined extravagance—an expression of the common people in the Old Southwest?

The best of the authors knew from the beginning that the *said* things—the way backwoods men and women recounted their often less than spectacular deeds—were the primary interest. Yet one of the several fictions about the humorous sketch is the assumption that backwoods vernacular has been rendered in some kind of transparent medium meant only to reveal its spokenness. It is easy to overlook the central irony at the heart of Southwestern humor: a body of writing that valorizes speech only emphasizes writing itself as the originating mode. Only writing can celebrate oral culture. What we are expected to regard as an innocent transparency is a calculated, composed, hyperconscious system that draws attention to itself as a vehicular agent.

The writers of the Old Southwest were not merely literate; most of them were well-read. If these preachers, doctors, lawyers, actors, and planters could only incidentally parade their learning in the conduct of their primary callings, they were more than eager to exploit it when they took up their pens. Beginning with Longstreet, these writers produced a discourse that reflects less the raw, overheard, spoken language in the Old Southwest than an older turn-of-the-century written language, with its full arsenal of linguistic and rhetorical conventions.

The sway of convention governed not merely the "genteel" portions of the humorous sketch—those featuring the narrator as detached observer and man of the world—but the depiction of the vernacular protagonist, especially the way he dressed and the way he sounded. Such convention governs all the work descended from *Georgia Scenes*. But the discoverer of the backwoods individualist was not A.B. Longstreet. The seaboard colonists in both New England and the South acknowledged his existence and described his eccentricities; and some, notably Timothy Dwight, even made an effort to render his odd speech in certain regularized forms. By the 1830s, then, the literary tradition of how regionalisms were reproduced was already well established; their forms were conventions that Longstreet and his contemporaries freely drew upon.

Most of the humorists have a good enough ear for picking out the words, phrases, and striking imagery that made backwoods speech different from their own usage; but they have an even better eye for how previous writers rendered oral delivery in print. Thanks largely to William T. Porter, who encouraged a kind of competitive camaraderie among the stable of contributors to his *Spirit of the Times*, the authors mutually enriched their sketches not only in subject matter and characterization but also in the journalistic devices for making regional sounds effective. (Even today there is no consensus about how *natur* or *natur'* actually sounded, but the dialectal rendering of *nature* had the prestige of, among others, Cooper's Natty Bumppo behind it, and the Southwestern authors showed little inclination to alter it.)

Another abiding fiction about Southwestern humor is that the backwoodsman's *natural* tongue was a perpetual tour de force—a logorrheic stream of *ramstugenous* here, *slantindickler* there, and a considerable sprinkling of *homogification, prognostics,* and *exflunctoficated* all cluttering up the narratives. Such flashy diction is in fact the exception in the humor because (presumably) it was not the common currency. Codswallop words begin with Davy Crockett and Mike Fink, but they are rare enough even there (and conspicuous mostly in the faux Crockett *Almanacs*). Some commentators have speculated that this extravagant linguistic foolery is nothing more than mockery of school-learning, directed perhaps at the genteel pretentiousness of some of the authorial narrators.

Nevertheless, whatever its motivation, backwoods speech quickly becomes vernacular set-pieces: verbal displays of folk idioms, malapropisms, neologisms so striking, so rhetorically revved up that they virtually become material objects. And it is well to remember that they are not really *found* sounds but *made* sounds, and that the maker of such displays is finally the author, an aural poacher fashioning sounds into marvelous patches of wordplay.

Although speech is a privileged mode, according to certain theories, it achieves that status *after* the advent of a text-centered culture. The dialect, the exaggerated images, the fabricated words are the mixed gifts of the humorist authors. What we are really getting from the narrator, and from the author whose mouthpiece he is, is a showy gesture of skill: *I'm talking like him now*, which of course celebrates the *I*, not the *him* he mimics. The illusion of a spoken English is paradoxically reinforced by textual tricks possible only in a print culture: the aural effects corralled in italic type or encased in quotation marks; authorial aids to clarify meaning tucked intrusively within parentheses. For all the editorial pieties from Porter and other editors about capturing the flavor of native culture before the natives disappear into a homogenized population, the native speakers themselves have no control over how they sound once their speech has been appropriated by the writers. What we read is a literary construct at least two removes from actual vernacular. Jim Doggett and Pete Whetstone of Arkansas sound like Jim and Chunky of Mississippi, Daddy Biggs of Alabama, and Yellow Blossom of Georgia. Typography serves equally for speakers in any of the fictionalized sites of the Old Southwest.

The genius of the humorists was not in devising in print an oral style that would suggest characterological differences between, say, Major Jones and Pete Whetstone, nor in reproducing apparent idiolects of surpassing invention to demonstrate imaginative richness among the folk. (The exception here, as it is in so many ways, is George Washington Harris, whose Sut Lovingood is absolutely unique in how he speaks, acts, and thinks.) Most of the Southwestern authors, even those who mangled their own stories by irrelevant exposition and uncertain narrative pacing, made backwoods orality memorable by speech *rhythm*.

That is the real source of energy and authenticity in Southwestern vernacular, the same principle of rhythm that makes a difference in later American style. In capturing the distinctive flow of English as it is spoken by (often) renegade users of the language, the humorists anticipate not only Mark Twain but also such modernist writers as Ezra Pound, Gertrude Stein, Ernest Hemingway, and Eudora Welty. Richard Poirier once declared that literature recreates itself by troping received language. In the case of Longstreet and his fellows, that received language is spoken, a tribal tongue that transformed written English and continues to dominate not merely popular writing but what passes as contemporary high art.

To return briefly to Lynn's subversive theory of the humor: the once-fashionable view of this writing, clabbered up in its inapt hygienic metaphor, is that the Southwestern authors were Whig moralists who tempered their amusement of Democratic hijinks by constructing cautionary tales of warning against the uppity illiterates. As a cue for reading this humor, *cordon sanitaire* has scant textual support. The vernacular characters are not quarantined, and the writing that features them is neither a medical detention camp nor a house of correction. Although we readily spot condescension in the stand-in narrators, it is of the garden-variety type, a familiar sign of the bias that permeates the entire nineteenth-century social order. Only a single major sketch, Taliaferro's "Ham Rachel, of Alabama," can be said to betray the supposed scorn and distaste of the Whig gentleman forced into the company of yeomen. Moreover, many of the sketches recount how willingly the educated figure falls in with high-talking illiterates; indeed, some of the narrators actively seek them out.

I would suggest that the authors, associating themselves with all other ambitious men in the opportunistic Southwest, think of themselves more as Moderns than as partisan Whigs. And if the humorists are Moderns who have cast their lot with the future, the characters who dominate their writing are unambitious yeomen and marginal settlers, whose quirky, complacent individualism resists the progressive program of the time: Manifest Destiny, economic enterprise, order, civilization.

And how could it be otherwise? In the competitive games between the aggressive settlers and the less favored people whom they encountered in the drive to fill up the newly opened lands, the winners were always confident of their success. The squatters and marginalized settlers, the riverboat hustlers, the hunters poaching in Choctaw and Cherokee lands, even the reclusive and suspicious loners in the deep bush were, like their socially privileged betters, interested in their own economic survival; but unlike the settlers, they had no economic stake in seeing either the backwoods or the frontier space transformed into Deep South versions of Virginia or Carolina. What these prior residents of the region were up against were determined and ambitious emigrants, the kind noted in travelers' accounts as *go-ahead* types. The term derives from Davy Crockett, that quintessential misfit whose "philosophy" was widely circulated: *Be sure you're right—then go ahead.* The final clause became a universal recipe for action, even as the first clause was a burdensome condition to be ignored. Visitors to the flush-times crossroads and villages applied the term to middle-class artisans, displaced professionals, and shrewd entrepreneurs, but especially to the restless, risk-taking planters trekking in from the old seaboard states, usually with an extended family and a few slaves. The competitive spirit in the backwoods was more modest—or at least it was played in a different key. The activities of rural Georgians that first prompted Longstreet to a writing career were by and large intramural competitions: eye-gouging, ear-biting fights; horse-swaps; bouts of marksmanship; practical jokes—a tendency we see in most of the sketches that followed *Georgia Scenes.*

The Georgians of Longstreet's Lincoln County, the Arkansawyers of Noland's Devil's Fork, Hooper's Simon Suggs and Harris's Sut Lovingood: these iconic figures harken back to the Lubbers and farmers of William Byrd and St. John Crevecoeur, contrarian poor whites more content with the margins than with the mainstream. In their attributed ignorance, recalcitrance, and sloth, they are imaginatively frozen in these clusters denoting all values that are antimodern. Wherever he shows up, in whatever area of the vast region known as the Southwest, he is the avatar of the *then*, an unfortunate reproach to the (always) unfinished business of the *now.*

We can speculate that one of the reasons why Longstreet, Alexander McNutt, John S. Robb, William C. Hall, Thomas Bangs Thorpe, and many others were found so engaging was that they were not only largely confined to rivals within the same marginalized groups, but they also offered no threats to the planter and professional classes: their truculent deeds, their explosive games, their extravagant displays of independence were in fact shadow versions of the larger games ongoing among the privileged classes. Of course, there is no evidence that these backwoodsmen thought of themselves as a kind of surrogate, second-best version of their betters—illiterates leave few records—but they were not stupid. They knew as early as the 1820s that the wielders of power were the literates—Indian agents, land commissioners, legislators, judges—many of whom were also planters eager to expand their holdings. In the context of such larger games, mere bear hunts, fights, and courting rivalries must have been perceived by the participants as local and harmless and quaint—as they certainly were perceived by the authors. Even the backwoodsmen's hardy encroachment on and dispossession of the original inhabitants are half-hearted, frail, and desultory compared to the official program of dispossession undertaken by the shrewd Moderns, the efficient and educated purveyors of governmental civilization.

The authors, who are also purveyors of that civilization, safely celebrate the games of a marginal people who will become even more marginalized in the years just before the Civil War. What these authors celebrate is the voice of the backwoods, but the celebration is on civilization's terms: writing rather than speech. The theater of the oral performance—on the decks of steamboats, in courtrooms, on village streets—has limited occupancy; the theater of the oral performance rendered in writing reaches beyond those shabby local sites into other local sites, into law offices, parlors, smoking rooms, in every region of the country, into the offices of the *New York Spirit of the Times*, even into the salons of connoisseurs in England. The authority lies not with those primitives who speak with vernacular bite but with the Moderns who mimic those idioms in writing.

In that writing the Southwestern author has the satisfaction of control over all the disparate elements of his world, if only in a symbolic way. He unobtrusively mimics the gentleman, even if he is only a hard-scrabbling newspaperman or an actor or a middling lawyer in a crowded field, just as he mimics all those vernacular heroes who are not as socially aspiring as he and whom he chooses to see as amiable agents of disorder. Seeing himself in one light and the backwoods subject in another, he uses his power of literacy to assert the priority of order, measure, reason, the virtues of a civilized community, even when the text he produces is laced with irony, self-mockery, and the frequent temptation to succumb to the anarchic freedom he imagines the backwoods to be.

One of the interesting aspects of Southwestern humor is how its subject—the grittier social scene of antebellum life—seems to unfold within a framework of romantic projection. Simon Suggs is no New World leech gatherer, of course, but the generic backwoodsman functions less as an object lesson for a political agenda than as a figure of nostalgia, a residual reminder of the *folk* that American progress is steadily assimilating into an undifferentiated whole. The attraction of the Moderns to the Primitives occurs in this curious suspension of crisply defined boundaries. Indeed, one of the strengths of the humorists' moment is its *in-betweenness.*

With the ejection of the native tribes by Jacksonian fiat, the Old Southwest is no longer one thing; and with the process of filling up still continuing, it is not yet what it is destined to be. In that interval are the chroniclers—guidebook writers, travelers, diarists and letter writers, and those scribes most gifted with in-betweenness themselves—the professionals-turned-humorists. Their time is a transitional one of remaking, reformulating, repossessing; their place is a transitional territory of mobile boundaries and shifting landmarks in which the making, formulating, and possessing are still provisional attempts. The Southwestern humorist—himself an exile, an emigrant, committed to the party of civilization and tempted continually by the party of individualism—is defined by what historians once called the "frontier paradigm," with its concept of neutral space as stage for all the assorted dramas of free will and determinism. But such choices are never permanently made in the writing of the humorists. The in-betweenness is a psychic space as well as a geographical one, and within the flexible boundaries of that kind of frontier, they play out the game of their own moral amphibiousness.

Although the signal motif of Southwestern society as the humorists depict it is competition, the party of the Moderns is not visibly privileged. Although destined ("fixed aforehand" in Simon-speak) as the big winners of all the games in this antebellum world, the high-profile politicians and the planter elite whose interests they served are nowhere to be seen. And in the authors' gallery, so crowded with canvases of confidence men, the most conspicuous and successful confidence man in the antebellum South—the land agent—is only hinted at in the transparent schemes of Hooper's Simon Suggs and Baldwin's Simon Suggs Jr. A number of the authors delight in "scoundrel time," but their principals are small-bore tricksters, political hacks of unsurpassing density, bumbling birds of prey, inept victims of inept schemers. It is true that Baldwin ventures to touch on a handful of real and disguised makers and shakers, lawyerly gentlemen who, from the retrospective of 1853, worked toward stability and integrity in the Flush Times of nearly twenty years earlier; but even these are compassed about with such cloudy witnesses that not a single one of them escapes the taint of moral ambiguity.

There is a political dimension to this humor that is far more implicative of our national history than the partisan scenario popularized by Kenneth Lynn. What, for example, does it mean that Southwestern humor lacks figures of real importance? The readiest answer of course is that this writing concerns an unambitious yeomanry, who, as postbellum historiography assiduously taught us, had no significant roles to play. But as we learn from another popular genre, detective fiction, what is missing in the humorous sketches may be as significant as what is present. As discourse, this humor is a calculated image of southern life in the thirty years before the Civil War. It is a specialized construction that freely omits certain actualities of political and economic importance while cheerfully stressing others that were not conducive to the definition of a future separate nation. Like other kinds of antebellum imaginative writing—the sentimental novel, reform fiction, genteel verse, sensation and adventure thrillers—the humor does not fairly reflect a real society taking shape in a specific time and place.

The humor is a refracted image of the society that generated it—a cluster of narrative scenarios that only obliquely suggest the larger antebellum story of competition and appropriation. While much of the action in Southwestern humor is largely physical, a straightforward and unsubtle series of "Best Man" contests, it still functions in that larger world of rival political and economic currents. It is no accident that impersonation is the ruse of choice among the authors' casts of characters. In a new country, the remaking of identity—a new name or gussied-up past—is a useful strategy of quality and rabble alike. The humorists' Southwest is a proving ground for counterfeit gentlemen, imitation planters, and professional quacks. Stripped of any commanding source of power, the humor happily makes do with what passes for power: down-home poseurs with impromptu assertions of office and claims of connections, all verbalized in bloated idioms that implausibly are meant to inspire confidence.

The absence of any sustained experience of power in the humor suggests something more than the authors' assessment of the poorer whites' role in the making of the southern nation; it anticipates the frightening prospect of irrelevance for men of importance in the tumultuous and unstable society of the lower South. Although the authors modestly pride themselves as Moderns among the Primitives, their work dramatizes the fragility of governance even as the planter class and its allies begin to triumph internally. But in the external competition for power, when the regional politics of coercion in the late 1850s supersedes national party thresholds, the proud Moderns will prove to be not modern enough. Indeed, in the national binary, it will be the fate of southerners to be cast as Primitives struggling against the real Moderns, the technologized market capitalists of the North.

Origins and Influences

1

The Origins of the Humor of the Old South

J.A. Leo Lemay[1]

The best humor of the Old South is *sui generis*, inexplicable, a product of the individual genius of the creator. Yet the writings clearly are part of local tradition, and a host of contemporaries throughout the South in the 1840s and 1850s influenced one another. Writers like George Washington Harris grew up admiring the best writings appearing in the newspapers and periodicals. Such writings challenged aspiring authors who tried to excel and to exceed in the characteristic subjects and techniques of their predecessors. The language, characters, settings, and plots of the stories of Harris are all comparable to numerous other earlier writers in the tradition, though he, finally, is distinctive. But as soon as we begin comparing him to his contemporaries, we can also think of antecedents—not only in important works and traditions in English literature of the seventeenth, eighteenth, and nineteenth centuries but also in a series of colonial American writings that anticipate in many ways the best humor of the Old South. The English or American background will never explain the genius of a particular work like T.B. Thorpe's "The Big Bear of Arkansas" or the creation of an extraordinary character like Sut Lovingood, but it will make a contribution to our understanding of the background and the important place of the humor of the Old South in American literary history.

The emergence of the Old South's humor remains a puzzle that will never be completely explained. More pieces, however, are constantly being discovered, so that the whole design is gradually taking on an elusive shape. Outstanding features of the humor's origins may be found in several traditions of English literature from the seventeenth, eighteenth, and nineteenth centuries; in traditions of folk and popular culture, including rituals, story-telling, and popular anecdotes;[2] and in the eighteenth century's increasing fascination with folk culture, as manifested by Bishop Thomas Percy's *Reliques of Ancient English Poetry* (1765) and by the theoretical suggestions of the significance of folklore and folkways by Johann Gottfried Herder and the American Joel Barlow.[3] The seventeenth- and eighteenth-century English literary works most important to the humor of the Old South were Charles Cotton's burlesques of Virgil (1664) and Lucian (1665);[4] Samuel Butler's extremely popular mock-heroic *Hudibras* (1663, 1664, 1678);[5] the anti-Petrarchan and anti-pastoral burlesques by Sir Walter Scott and John Gay;[6] and the traditions of low comedy found in Aphra Behn's *Widow Ranter*, in Gay's *The Beggar's Opera*, and in the afterpieces of eighteenth-century English drama.[7] These literary works, along with the English sporting literature of the early nineteenth century,[8] are all reflected in various writings of the Old South.

In this paper I will focus upon a hitherto unknown author who adds to our understanding of the American background of ante-bellum Southern humor. First, though let me recapitulate the Southern colonial background. A newly discovered early eighteenth-century poem by the Delaware poet Henry Brooke, entitled "The New Metamorphosis, or, the Fable of the Bald Eagle," adds an interesting burlesque of the American success story from the late 1720s[9] (Immersed in the literary traditions of the Old South, William Gilmore Simms wrote one of the great satires of the American Dream[10]). So now in Southern colonial literature, we have at least ten key works anticipating the humorists of the Old South: first, Ebenezer Cook's hudibrastic satire of frontier American culture and especially of English ideas about America, *The Sot-Weed Factor* (1708);[11] second, Henry Brooke's rollicking, anapestic burlesque of the American success story (1727, just mentioned above); third, Richard Lewis' fine translation of a Latin mock-heroic poem, *The Mouse-Trap* (1728);[12] fourth, William Byrd's satirical passages about low-life frontier types in *The History of the Dividing Line* (written during the 1730s);[13] fifth, Dr. Alexander Hamilton's great prose satire of the early and mid-1750s, "The History of the Tuesday Club," which has just appeared in Robert Micklus' elaborate, three-volume edition, containing, among innumerable other typically American motifs, a memorable version of the wonderful hunt;[14] sixth, John Mercer's mock-illiterate prose and poetic satires in the "Dinwiddianae" of the mid-1750s, lampooning Virginia's governor, Robert Dinwiddie;[15] seventh, Robert Bolling's grotesque poem "Neanthe," of around 1762, based upon folklore concerning seventeenth-century Virginia, and reflecting both the techniques of English low burlesque and Italian anti-Petrarchan verse (I might incidentally note that Bolling was the most knowledgeable native American student of French and Italian literatures in colonial America);[16] eighth, Thomas Cradock's "Maryland Eclogues in Imitation of Virgil's" a poetic travesty featuring slaves, transported felons, whores, crackers, planters, and other Southern types;[17] ninth, Charles Woodmason's backcountry journal of the late 1760s and early 1770s, containing ferocious diatribes against the manners, morals, and unbelievable acts of his frontier parishioners, as well as the earliest mock-sermon in American literature;[18] and tenth, Jonathan Boucher's idiomatic tour-de-force of a mock pastoral from about 1770.[19]

These ten precursors generally contain a mixture of native American characteristics and English traditions. Cook's *The Sot-Weed Factor* models its basic structure upon a popular anti-American ballad and uses numerous echoes of Butler's *Hudibras;* but it is really a proudly American poem, satirizing the pretensions of the foolish greenhorn narrator who is bested by the local yokels, using a number of American folklore motifs and locating the work precisely within the historical and cultural traditions of early Maryland.[20] Similarly, Robert Bolling's "Neanthe," a mock-elegy using Italian anti-Petrarchan traditions and the English form for low verse satire, hudibrastics, is set soundly within Virginia's seventeenth-century history, its eighteenth-century folklore, and the places and way of life of Eastern Shore Virginia. Like *The Sot-Weed Factor,* it depicts a frontier more rough and tough than any that every actually existed, and its description of a fight between Neanthe's lovers anticipates a major subject of the humor of the Old South.[21] At the same time, its burlesque of the elegy satirizes the sentimental and doleful motifs and moods so common to mid-eighteenth-century English graveyard verse, while anticipating the satires of the genteel and romantic viewpoints so common to the realistic humor of the Old South.

So we can document a continuous tradition of Southern colonial precursors of the ante-bellum South's humor. The trouble is, these writers were, as far as any evidence reveals, completely unknown to the writers of Southern humor who flourished from the 1830s to the 1860s.[22] The latter writers use the same settings, character types, and motifs—like hunts, fights, revival meetings, and poor whites simply because these types and events existed as commonly in the ante-bellum South as they had in the colonial period. Now into the vacuum that seemingly existed between the Revolution and appearance of Augustus Baldwin Longstreet's *Georgia Scenes* in 1835, I want to introduce another hitherto unknown piece of the puzzle—the Charleston poet William Henry Timrod, who was born in 1792 and died in 1838. If the name William Henry Timrod seems vaguely familiar, that is because his son was the South's fine Civil War poet Henry Timrod (1828–1867).

William Timrod wrote poetry, published a volume entitled *Poems on Various Subjects* (which remains almost unknown to bibliographers of poetry and of imprints) in 1814,[23] and was well known in Charleston's early nineteenth-century literari.[24] William Timrod's son Henry Timrod sent a selection of five poems by his father together with a brief biographical account to Everet A. Duyckinck in 1855 for inclusion in Duyckinck's *Cyclopedia of American Literature* (New York, Duyckinck 1856). Duyckinck printed only the poem that William addressed to his son as an infant and ignored the biographical information. A fellow Charlestonian, William Gilmore Simms, knew and admired Timrod. Simms twice wrote appreciative reminisces of the older writer, remembering Timrod as "a good talker, full of life and geniality, with no small share of humor," and lamenting that "scores" of his periodical "poems and essays" were never collected and "are now probably lost."[25] Both Simms and the printer James McCarter recalled Timrod's club. Timrod talked to the Charleston literateurs as he worked in his bindery. McCarter recalled that "so constant was their attendance on Mr. Timrod's workshop that the name of Timrod's club was finally bestowed on it, and he was seldom during the day and often late in the evening without one or more members of the club in his shop eagerly listening to his delightful conversation."[26]

Two of Timrod's poems in *Poems on Various Subjects* are similar to the characteristic writings of the Southern humorists. They are Timrod's mock eclogues, "Morning, An Eclogue" (pp. 25–30) and its companion piece, "Noon, an Eclogue" (pp. 31–38). When William Timrod published his volume of poetry, he was twenty-one; and Longstreet, whose *Georgia Scenes* (1835) is often considered the most important book in the humor of the Old South, was nineteen. Timrod's two mock pastorals are similar to writings by such colonials as Ebenezer Cooke, John Mercer, Robert Bolling, Thomas Cradock, and Jonathan Boucher. Timrod's eclogues prove that the same traditions that underlie the work of the Southern colonial satirists also influenced works by writers of Longstreet's generation.

Walter Blair defines the characteristics of the humor of the Old South as a framework story, with an educated speaker narrating the opening and closing and with a colloquial speaker narrating the body of the story. He has argued that this structure reveals the influence of oral traditions upon the ante-bellum Southern writers.[27] Kenneth Lynn added his belief that the framework structure typically indicates a distancing by the author/narrator from the tale's subject. He maintained that the distancing grew out of the conservative political convictions of the writers and their scorn for the colloquial speakers who are the ostensible heroes of the stories.[28] But the framework structures used by the Southern colonial writers and by William Timrod cast doubt upon Blair's and Lynn's theses. Indeed, I and other scholars have already refuted Lynn's thesis, though it is still cited by some critics.[29]

Timrod's poem "Morning, An Eclogue" portrays the lament of a poor white female farmer, Dolly Dumpling, whose lover, Dickey Gosling, has left her for the superior charms of Hester Bull. It has a framework structure. The poet-speaker narrates the opening and closing verse paragraphs, but the body of the poem consists of Dolly Dumpling's lament. The obviously belittling names—Dolly Dumpling, Dickey Gosling, and Hester Bull—dehumanize the characters, so that the reader feels no temptation to sympathize with them. Each of Dolly Dumpling's verse paragraphs concludes with a refrain on the falseness of male lovers (a nice reversal of the poet's usual complaint of the falseness of women): "Fly from the swains, ye maids, as from Old Nick; / Heed not their vows, they all are false as Dick." The sexual meiosis whereby the male lover becomes merely "Dick" and the implied complaint about the sexual inadequacy of the quickly spent lover add to the bawdy humor.

In the body of the poem, Dolly Dumpling tells of Dickey Gosling's courtship, of his abandoning her, and of his insults. The subject matter of the poem is so filled with references to food and eating that it (like the names of the characters) reduces the individuals to animals. Here is the grotesque fourth stanza:

"Oh Dickey Gosling, can you hear me cry,
"And, basely, perjured, leave thy Doll to die?
"How oft the maiden, now a prey to care,
"Has filled your belly with delicious fare?
"To please your appetite, full many a slice
"These hands have cut of bacon, fat and nice;
"Then, I remember well—(O! times of bliss!)
"You'd kiss and eat, and eat again, and kiss!
"Think of those days, false Swain! And tell me why
"You scorn me? Think you I've no more to fry!
"Indeed you're wrong—in shoulder, ham, and flitch,

"Spite your hate, your Dolly still is rich.
"Return, return—and, then, no more forsaken
"I'll stuff you to the throat with greens and bacon! (pp. 27–28)

The poem's penultimate stanza describes Dolly Dumpling's alternating urges to beat Dickey Gosling or to kill herself. The final stanza reverts to the poet-speaker's educated voice and mock popular clichés of gothic fiction, as well as sentimental motifs:

In vain her guardian angel's hand essay'd
To snatch the goblet from the frantic maid!
Deeply she drank! Loud screams the boding owl:
The oxen bellow, and the mastiffs howl!
The frightened sun looks as it did before!
She drains the goblet, the deed is o'er!
Her limbs relaxing, to the ground she sunk—
And faithless Gosling found her dead—dead *drunk*! (p. 30)

The fine humorous poem mocks the sententious literary traditions of the past and present. Charles Cotton's burlesques and John Gay's anti-pastoral *Shepherd's Week* are clearly in the background of William Timrod's mock eclogue. The structure, subject matter, motifs, and voices in "Morning, An Eclogue" are similar to and anticipate the humorous and realistic writers of the Old South—Augustus Baldwin Longstreet, Thomas Bangs Thorpe, George Washington Harris, Joseph Baldwin, Joseph M. Field, Johnson Jones Hooper, and others. Like the later and better-known writers, William Timrod portrays low-life poor whites, emphasizes their animality (Robert Bolling's "Neanthe" characters are more grotesque), and dwells upon local folk-ways. Thus his mock eclogue at once both celebrates familiar life in the Old South and satirizes pastoralism and other highfalutin literary traditions (especially sentimentalism and romanticism). With the exception of Joseph Glover Baldwin's *Flush Times in Alabama and Mississippi*, the literary origins of Timrod's "Morning" are more obvious than those of the later Southern humorists. Like many American works from the earlier period, Timrod's "Morning" suggests that the literary traditions are more important to the framework structure of Southern humor than either the oral folk story (Blair's emphasis) or the political opinions and supposedly superior posturings of the writers (Lynn's thesis).

Timrod's second mock-pastoral, "Noon, An Eclogue" (pp. 31–39), imitates the fourth and fifth idylls of Theocritus and especially Virgil's third Eclogue. Featuring a boasting contest between the slaves Sampy and Cudjoe, "Noon" consists entirely of dialogue between them and the contest's judge, Quasheboo. Because it burlesques the same source, "Noon" is similar to the third of Thomas Cradock's "Maryland Eclogues in Imitation of Virgil," which features a boasting contest between two transported felons[30] But there is a key difference in the authors' voices.

The Rev. Thomas Cradock, who had recently emigrated from England, held America and its native fools and local customs in contempt. He hoped soon to return to England. Like his fellow Maryland clergyman Jonathan Boucher, and like his countryman in South Carolina the Rev. Charles Woodmason, he believed himself superior to Americans.[31] But William Timrod, like Ebenezer Cook, Henry Brooke, John Mercer, and Robert Bolling, identifies with America and Americans. Although Timrod's molk-eclogue contains obvious elements of condescension and satire, it also expresses appreciation for and identification with the native plants and folkways of South Carolina. The literary tradition (Theocritus, Virgil, the English burlesques by Cotton and Gay) may be more important than the influences of patriotism, folklore, and local custom, but the poem nevertheless fondly celebrates local characters and scenes while satirizing the highfalutin traditions.

The poem opens with three slaves sneaking off for a break when the overseer goes to sleep. Alternately, Sampy and Cudjoe both boast of their loves' beauties, comparing her attributes to familiar local objects. They wage a jug of rum against a pipe of good tobacco, with Quasheboo to decide the winner. At the end, however, Quasheboo, disgusted with their poetry, awards Sampy back his jug and Cudjoe his pipe but drinks the rum and takes the tobacco himself. The poem ends when "the Driver" awakes and comes "to spoil our fun." One of my favorite exchanges concerns the girlfriends' teeth:

> Cudjoe
> Hast thou not mark'd how smooth and white appear
> The grain first forming on the milky ear?
> But may full thirty lashes mark my back,
> If with her teeth compared the corn appears not black.
>
> Sampy
> When first at spring those snowy flowers appear'd
> Call'd by the learned Buckras old man's beard,
> Of them a wreath Jemimah's temples grac'd
> And 'tween her teeth a fragrant branch she plac'd,
> Believe me, Cudjoe, to my wond'ring view,
> Her teeth were far the whitest of the two! (pp. 35–36)

The descriptions of the earliest tassels on the ear of corn and the spring appearance of Spanish moss on the South Carolina oak trees arouse fond appreciations of characteristically local, familiar objects.

The slaves' last exchange is a riddle contest. Cudjoe says, "Solve thou this riddle, and I will be dumb / Ee come, ee come, ee come." And Sampy replies, "Explain thou this, and be the triumph thine / Ee shine, ee shine, ee no shine, ee shine." Timrod appends a note explaining, "*These riddles are given literally as they are spoken by the Negroes. They must be rendered, 'If the Crows come, the Corn will not—*

If the Sun shines the Stars will not, and vice versa" (p. 37). The corn–crow riddle is native to America, turning up in several versions in the late nineteenth and early twentieth centuries, but the earliest recorded example dates from Joel Chandler Harris's Uncle Remus in 1881.[32] Timrod's version is sixty-seven years earlier. The sun–star riddle descends from a sixteenth-century English popular proverb, but no other riddle form of it is recorded. Augustus Baldwin Longstreet said that he wrote *Georgia Scenes* to capture and preserve the folkways of the Old South; obviously Timrod wrote his mock pastorals partly for the same reason.[33]

Timrod, then, is another precursor of the humor of the Old South. Indeed, his dates are such that he can almost be made a member of the school; however, the publication of his *Poems on Various Subjects* (1814) is so much earlier than the publication of Longstreet's *Georgia Scenes* (1835) that Timrod almost seems to belong to an earlier generation than Longstreet. Since, however, he wrote in poetry rather than prose, and since his writings did not immediately spawn a number of imitators, he must be considered a precursor rather than a founder of the school. If we could compare the creation of the humor of the Old South to the creation of the novel, then Timrod would be in the position of Daniel Defoe, a forerunner, rather than Samuel Richardson, whose great novel *Pamela* ushered in a dozen major novels as imitators and successors within a decade.

As more sustained research on the manuscripts and the periodicals of the period from the Revolution to the 1830s is completed, additional unknown interesting poems and stories—as well as additional unknown writers—will surely turn up.[34] But I suspect that they will reinforce the continuous series of Southern colonial writings from 1708 to the Revolution that use the subjects, themes, characters, structures, and vocabulary of the humorists of the Old South. Now we know that at least one hitherto unknown writer, William Henry Timrod, early in the nineteenth century, reflects those same impulses and traditions.

Notes

1. I am greatly indebted to my friend James B. Meriwether, Professor Emeritus of the University of South Carolina, for calling the work of William Henry Timrod to my attention and for supplying me with a xerox of Timrod's *Poems on Various Subjects*. Brief versions of this essay were delivered as lectures at the Modern Language Association, San Francisco, December 28, 1987, and at Montpelier, France, to Professor Michel Bandy's seminar, on June 10, 1990. My research assistant Darin Fields has helped in numerous ways.

2. Joseph Strutt, *Sports and Pastimes of the People of England* (1801; rpt. London: Chatto and Windus, 1876). Richard M. Dorson surveys the beginnings of the movement in *The British Folklorists: A History* (Chicago: U of Chicago P, 1968).

3. Robert T. Clark, *Herder: His Life and Thought* (Berkeley: U of California P, 1969). J.A. Leo Lemay, "The Contexts and Themes of 'The Hasty Pudding.'" *Early American Literature* 17 (1982): 3–23.

4. Franklin testified that Dr. Jon Browne (1667–1737), a New Jersey physician, travestied the Bible "in doggerel Verse as Cotton had done Virgil." *Benjamin Franklin's Autobiog-*

raphy: A Norton Critical Edition, ed. J.A. Leo Lemay and P.M. Zall (New York: Norton, 1986), 19.

5. Richard Pugh Bond, *English Burlesque Poetry, 1700–1750* (Cambridge, MA: 1952). William Byrd recorded that Major William Mayo read aloud from *Hudibras* on October 28, 1728, during the dividing line expedition (*The Prose Works of William Byrd of Westover*, ed. Louis B. Wright [Cambridge: Harvard UP, 1966], 130). Ebenezer Cook, John Mercer, and Robert Bolling all used the hudibrastic form in the poems mentioned below. *Hudibras* appears both in the *Catalogue of the Library Company of Philadelphia* (Philadelphia B. Franklin, 1741), 46, and in the *1764 Catalogue of the Redwood Library Company*, ed. Marcus A. McCorison (New Haven: Yale UP, 1965), no. 821.

6. See commentaries in *Poetry and Prose of John Gay*, ed. Vinton A. Dearing and Charles E. Beckwick, 2 vols. (Oxford: Clarendon Press, 1974). Robert Bolling used the anti-Petrarchan and anti-pastoral traditions in "Neanthe." See J.A. Leo Lemay, "Southern Colonial Grotesque: Robertr Bolling's 'Neanthe,'" *Mississippi Quarterly* 35 (1982): 97–126, esp. 104. *The Library Company Catalogue* (1741) records Gay's *Moral Fables* (1732), p. 33, Gay's *Poems*, 2 vols. (London, 1737), p. 53. *The Redwood Library* records Gay's Poems, 2 vols., #669.

7. Leo Hughes, *A Century of English Farce* (Princeton: Princeton Up, 1956). Victor Clinton Clinton-Baddeley, *Burlesque Tradition in the English Theatre after 1660* (London: Methuen, 1952). Ian Donaldson, *The World Upside-Down: Comedy from Johnson to Fielding* (Oxford: Clarendon Press, 1970).

8. Walter Blair, "Traditions in Southern Humor," *American Quarterly* 5 (1953): 132–42, esp. 137.

9. David S. Shields, "Henry Brooke and the Situation of the First Belletrists in British America," *Early American Literature* 23 (1988): 4–26.

10. Ian Marshall, "The American Dreams of Sam Snaffles," *Southern Literary Journal* 18.2 (Spring 1986): 96–107.

11. See the chapter on Cook in J.A. Leo Lemay, *Men of Letters in Colonial Maryland* (Knoxville: U of Tennessee P,1972), 77–110.

12. See the discussion in Lemay, *Men of Letters*, 127–31.

13. Discussed by Kenneth S. Lynn, *Mark Twain and Southwestern Humor* (Boston: Little, Brown, 1959).

14. Dr. Alexander Hamilton, *The History of the Tuesday Club*, ed. Robert Micklus (Chapel Hill: U of North Carolina P. 1990), 1–79. Nicholas Scull, "The Son of Old Moor of Moor Hall," tells of the son's killing twelve ducks and a deer with one shot (Manuscript Am. 1359 [c. 1733], Historical Society of Pennsylvania). I am indebted to David S. Shields for a transcript of the poem, and I have used the title that he gave it.

15. Richard Beale Davis, ed. *The Colonial Virginia Satirist* (Philadelphia: American Philological Society, Transactions, pt. 1, 1967), 57. See J.A. Leo Lemay, review of The *Colonial Virginia Satirist* in *Virginia Magazine of History and Biography* 75 (1967): 491–93, for additional evidence that Mercer wrote "The Dinwiddianae." See also Richard Beale Davis, *Intellectual Life in the Colonial South 1585–1763*. 3 vols. (Knoxville: U of Tennessee P, 1978), 3:1378; and J.A. Leo Lemay, "John Mercer and the Stamp Act in Virginia, 1764–1765," *Virginia Magazine of History and Biography* 91 (1983): 179–200.

16. J.A. Leo Lemay, "Southern Colonial Grotesque: Robert Bolling's 'Neanthe,'" *Mississippi Quarterly* 35 (1982): 97–126.

17. David Curtis Skaggs, *The Poetic Writings of Thomas Cradock*, 1718–1770 (Newark: U of Delaware P, 1984), 138–200.

18. Charles Woodmason, *The Carolina Backcountry on the Eve of the Revolution: The Journal and Other Writings of Charles Woodmason*, ed. Richard J. Hooker (Chapel Hill: U of North Carolina P, 1953).

19. M.M. Mathews, ed. "Boucher's Linguistic Pastoral of Colonial Maryland," *Dialect Notes* 6 (1933): 353–63.

20. See the discussion in Lemay, *Men of Letters*, 78–91.

21. Besides Lemay, "Southern Colonial Grotesque," see Joseph J. Arpad, "The Fight Story: Quotation and Originality in Native American Humor," *Journal of the Folklore Institute* 10 (1973): 141–72.

22. Perhaps Charles Fenton Mercer Noland (1816–1858) knew or heard about the writings of John Mercer, the grandfather of the person for whom he was named, Charles Fenton Mercer.

23. Though not in the standard poetry or imprint bibliographies, it appears in Robert J. Turnbull, *Bibliography of South Carolina, 1563–1950*, 6 vols. (Charlottesville: U of Virginia P, 1956–60), I:503.

24. [Judge George S. Bryan?], "William Henry Timrod," Charleston *Evening News*, March 28, 1848; William Gilmore Simms, *Southern Society*, October 12, 1867 (I:18–19); Simms, "Early Writers of South Carolina," *The XIX Century* 2 (February 1870), 695–97.

25. Simms, "Early Writers," 696.

26. Mr. Carter's reminiscence of December 2, 1867, is printed by Jay B. Hubbell, *The Last Years of Henry Timrod* (Durham: Duke UP, 1941), 174–75.

27. Walter Blair, "Traditions in Southern Humor," *American Quarterly* 5 (1953): 132–42.

28. Lynn, *Mark Twain and Southwestern Humor*, 64–65.

29. John Q. Anderson, "Scholarship in Southwestern Humor—Past and Present," *Mississippi Quarterly* 17 (1963–64): 67–84, esp. 69–80; J.A. Leo Lemay, "The Text, Tradition, and Themes of 'The Big Bear of Arkansas,'" *American Literature* 17 (1975): 321–42.

30. Cradock, *Poetic Writings*, 159–65.

31. See Lemay, "Southern Colonial Grotesque," 97–98 and above, notes 3 and 4.

32. Burton Stevenson, *Home Book of Proverbs, Maxims, and Familiar Phrases* (New York: Macmillan, 1948), 34, notes that "Crow en corn can't grow in de same fiel" is found in Joel Chandler Harris, *Uncle Remus' Plantation Proverbs*, 1881. Though listed in Stella Brewer Brookes, *Joel Chandler Harris—Folklorist* (Athens: U of Georgia P, 1950), 109, it is not recorded in Archer Taylor and Bartlett Jere Whiting, *A Dictionary of American Proverbs and Proverbial Phrases 1820–1880* (Cambridge: Harvard UP, 1958), nor in Whiting's *Early American Proverbs and Proverbial Phrases* (Cambridge: Harvard UP, 1977).

33. "Preface" in Augustus Baldwin Longstreet, *Georgia Scenes* (Augusta: Sentinel Office, 1835).

34. One wonders, for instance, what else Oliver Hillhouse Prince (1787–1837), a Connecticut native who moved to Georgia at the beginning of the nineteenth century, wrote beside "The Militia Muster" sketch that Longstreet included in *Georgia Scenes* and that Thomas Hardy copied in his novel *The Trumpet Major;* Carl J. Weber, "A Connecticut Yankee in King Alfred's Country," *The Colophon*, n.s., 1 (1936): 525–35.

2

"Sleepy Hollow" Comes South:

Washington Irving's Influence on Old Southwestern Humor

Ed Piacentino

Near the end of Washington Irving's "Rip Van Winkle," Rip, noticeably unnerved by the startling changes he observes upon returning to his native village after a twenty-year nap, exclaims in desperation: "'Does nobody here know Rip Van Winkle?'" (Irving 38). While it becomes clear that Rip has doubts about his identity—his desire to be recognized for who he is—his creator, Washington Irving, especially after the publication of *The Sketch Book* in 1820, never experienced any difficulty with recognition. In fact, the first printing of two thousand copies enjoyed brisk sales, and with this book and others that would soon follow, Irving became one of the most popular American writers of his time (Hart 83).

In attempting to account for Irving's widespread appeal, Haskell Springer writes: "his work was narrative and descriptive without being seriously analytical, . . . his aesthetics were not tied to deeply held political or religious convictions, . . . [and] he did not address metaphysical questions. [In short] he could produce work of delightful and moving superficial qualities in response to his readers' interest and out of his own eclectic experience" (230). If one focuses more narrowly on the popularity of one of Irving's best-known tales, "The Legend of Sleepy Hollow," not only among general readers but also among American writers of the nineteenth century, it becomes apparent that this story offered a usable paradigm for a significant number of works that would follow. Yet why did this happen? One explanation lies in Irving's conscious use of elements of traditional folklore associated with the Dutch culture of New York.

In a seminal study on the subject, Sara Puryear Rodes has demonstrated Irving's indebtedness to the folklore of the Dutch who settled along the shores of the Hudson River. Acknowledging materials such as "folk attitudes," "homey descriptions," "ghost lore," the "practical joke," and the overall humorous texture of "Sleepy Hollow," Rodes rightly claims that this tale follows the "spirit of American folklore," more so than any of Irving's other Hudson Valley stories, except "Rip Van Winkle" (147, 149). Daniel J. Hoffman, who may have been the first to advance an explanation for the potential adaptability of "Sleepy Hollow" to similar materials other American writers would find suitable for appropriation, notes that Irving's tale "helped to popularize the conflict of cultures which the rest of our literature has adumbrated ever since" (94). Going a step further than Hoffman, Cecil D. Eby Jr., in an article demonstrating William Faulkner's use of the "Sleepy Hollow" scenario in *The Hamlet* (1940), the first novel in the Snopes trilogy, sees the significance of Irving's Hudson Valley tales for American literature in "their discovery of a vein of indigenous folk materials that were suitable for the artist" (465).

In regard to nineteenth-century southern frontier humor, we do know that in addition to the oral tradition of the region, the writers who penned backwoods sketches (usually only authors by avocation) were, for the most part, well educated and knowledgeable of literary trends. Cohen and Dillingham, in their introduction to *Humor of the Old Southwest,* generally note that besides having familiarity with and assimilating somewhat the influences of British and continental writers such as Goldsmith, Addison, Steele, and most particularly the German Rudolph Raspe (the author of *The Travels of Baron Munchausen),* these humorists likewise knew and assimilated American materials, most notably Irving's "The Legend of Sleepy Hollow" (xx–xxi). James M. Cox, who observes that "it is no small wonder that 'The Legend of Sleepy Hollow' was imported by Southern humorists, disguised in one form or another, and retold along 'native' lines," regards this importation as "inevitable"—in that "it was just what Irving himself had done to German stories he had read" (103). While generally speaking, "Sleepy Hollow" contains, Cohen and Dillingham point out, "most of the ingredients of a typical sketch of Old Southwestern humor: the physically awkward, ugly, and avaricious Ichabod; the good-natured but rowdy Brom Bones and his friends, who love a practical joke; the desirable plum, Katrina Van Tassel," and while they mention a few selected authors— Joseph B. Cobb, William Tappan Thompson, and Francis James Robinson—who, in varying degrees, seem to draw directly on "Sleepy Hollow" subject matter—neither Cohen and Dillingham nor anyone else has really investigated the extent to which nineteenth-century southern practitioners of backwoods humor adapted "Sleepy Hollow" to a southern setting (xx–xxi).[1] My intent, then, is to examine a series of tales in the tradition of nineteenth-century southern backwoods humor, tales that represent modifications or reworkings of Irving's "Sleepy Hollow," and to offer possible explanations concerning why these humorists seemed to find these materials readily adaptable to southern settings and situations.

One of the familiar patterns assimilated by southern frontier humorists who seem to have been influenced by "Sleepy Hollow" involved the adaptation of the conflict of cultures theme and humorous pranks, the latter a device the countryman or backwoodsman typically employed to humiliate and sometimes to oust outsiders, often vain and pretentious persons who threatened his way of life. A sketch in this vein is William Tappan Thompson's "The Runaway Match; or, How the Schoolteacher Married a Fortune," initially published in the *New York Spirit of the Times* on 25 March 1848, and subsequently reprinted as "The Runaway Match; or, How the Schoolmaster Married a Fortune" in the *Southern Sentinel* on 6 February 1851, and in the revised and enlarged edition of *Major Jones's Courtship* (1872). Set in Pineville, Georgia, this sketch features a Yankee schoolmaster named Ebenezer Doolittle, who, like Ichabod Crane, is obsessively ambitious and determined to marry Nettie Darling, the daughter of a wealthy southern planter, hoping to acquire her father's property in the process. Though this bears a resemblance to the economic conflict in "Sleepy Hollow" when Ichabod Crane desires the Van Tassel farm so that he can sell it and invest the proceeds in western frontier land, Thompson does not suggest that Ebenezer poses a formidable threat to the economic security of Mr. Darling, the southern planter whose daughter he seeks to marry. Still, there is conflict here, because Nettie's parents oppose the union of Doolittle and their daughter; but Nettie, rather than her parents, becomes the major factor in foiling the schoolmaster's designs. Mischievous, shrewd, and deceptive, Nettie—"sich a tormentin' little coquet that the boys was all afraid to court her downright yearnest" (Thompson 215)—seems adept at arousing Ebenezer's feelings for her and then humiliating and rejecting him by making him a victim of a practical joke. What seems interesting about the new twist that Thompson gives to the "Sleepy Hollow" plot is that Nettie engages her slave girl Silla as an accomplice by using Silla, whose face has been veiled to impersonate her mistress, to dupe Ebenezer into thinking he has married Nettie, only to discover he has married her slave instead. With this collaboration of two female tricksters—one white and privileged, the other black and enslaved—the prank preserves the social status quo of the local community by ridding it of an outsider who has avaricious designs. In his alteration of "Sleepy Hollow," Thompson seems to be favoring attitudes and social practices amenable to the conservative nineteenth-century male gentry, northerners as well as southerners, regarding the courtship and marriage etiquette appropriate for women in a rural, provincial culture (women were expected to date and marry men who met their parents' approval).

Orlando Benedict Mayer, a South Carolina physician and author of backwoods humorous sketches featuring the folkways and traditions of the Dutch Fork, an area located between the Broad and Saluda Rivers in central South Carolina, knew Thompson and seems to have known some of his humorous sketches.[2] Like Thompson, Mayer also recognized viable material in "The Legend of Sleepy Hollow," seeing that it might be readily adapted to the traditional culture of the Dutch Fork. "The Corn Cob Pipe: A Tale of the Comet of '43," published initially in the *Columbia South Carolinian* on 8 December 1848, and subsequently acclaimed Mayer's "single best work of short fiction" (Kibler 215), contains many parallels to "Sleepy Hollow" and, like Thompson's "The Runaway Match," employs the conflict-of-cultures theme, humorous situations, a practical joke executed by a local farm girl, and characters who closely resemble Irving's. Again, a genteel and refined schoolmaster with romantic aspirations becomes the victim of a humiliating prank that foils his plans for matrimony to the daughter of a Dutch Fork farmer. Mayer's schoolmaster, Isom Jones, an outsider from Arkansas, Iowa, or Ohio (there is no agreement among the locals on exactly where), desires to marry Susy Elfins, a Dutch Fork farm girl; but the feeling is not mutual, even though her parents favor the union. Susy's own preference for a spouse, Abram Priester, a "young man of athletic proportions" (119), bears a resemblance to Irving's backwoods ruffian and prankster Brom Bones. Along with this, Mayer develops a conflict between Abram and Isom, terminating in the schoolmaster's humiliation in the eyes of the local community and his subsequent withdrawal from the region.

While the ensuing conflict between the schoolmaster and the backwoodsman for the hand of the farmer's daughter follows in much the same manner as the courtship plot in "Sleepy Hollow," Mayer adds a comical twist in his handling of the prank that makes up the denouement of the sketch. In "The Corn Cob Pipe," as in Thompson's "The Runaway Match," the farmer's daughter only partially resembles her prototype, Irving's Katrina Van Tassel. Like Thompson's Nettie Darling, Susy Elfins is a schemer. As such, she subverts her father's authority, and in collaboration with her backwoods beau, cleverly masterminds a gunpowder plot to discredit the schoolmaster as an eligible suitor and in so doing to embarrass her father publicly when the pipe Isom Jones has brought as a gift to Mr. Elfins blows up in his face.

Despite Susy's audacity in contesting her father's plans for her to wed an educated and cultured outsider, perhaps even more daring than Nettie Darling's duplicity against Ebenezer Doolittle in "A Runaway Match," Mayer's authorial narrator makes it clear that while he admires Susy, he does not condone her actions to undermine patriarchal intentions. Mayer's ambivalence toward Susy's brash actions is best expressed when the narrator clumsily interrupts the story line on a frequent basis, reasserting authorial control over the plot, over just how far he will permit Susy to carry her transgressions against authority. At one point, for example, Mayer interjects contrived sentiment, showing Susy acting in a more traditional feminine manner. With tears in her eyes—the result of having been berated by the narrator for angrily striking her cat with a fire poker—Susy displays unexpected sensitivity by picking up the hurt and frightened feline and rubbing its head against her neck. After Susy's demonstration of compassion, Mayer softens his tone toward her, addressing her directly: "Good hearted Susan! the old cat has forgiven you, and I will swollow [*sic*] my pen before you shall marry the school master; that is—if you do not blow up your father" (123).

Such overt intrusions, which annoy the modern reader, nevertheless serve a distinct function insofar as satisfying the expectations of Mayer's contemporary readers. As storyteller, as the one in total control of what happens in "The Corn Cob Pipe," Mayer will allow Susy Elfins to go only so far to sabotage her father's marital plans for her. To be certain that he keeps Susy within respectable bounds, Mayer exercises his narrative prerogative by exerting his authorial control. Mayer's direct and commanding presence functions in preventing Susy from further challenging patriarchal authority and extending her female privilege beyond limits that his male readers could comfortably tolerate. Still, in contrast to Irving's Katrina Van Tassel, Susy Elfins provides effective constraints to prohibit the forces of change, progress, and refinement, embodied in pretentious and ambitious schoolmaster, Isom Jones, from supplanting the folkways and traditions of the rural community. And it is the marriage of Susy Elfins to the burly backwoodsman Abram Priester that reaffirms Mayer's preference for the preservation of traditional culture.

Of the Southwestern humorous sketches thus far considered, perhaps the one most closely approximating Irving's classic tale is Joseph Beckham Cobb's "The Legend of Black Creek," which one critic has aptly labeled "a localized version" of "Sleepy Hollow" (Rogers 141). Cobb, Georgia-born and subsequently lawyer, planter, newspaper editor, Whig politician, and sometime author of humorous sketches, is best known for his collection of backwoods humorous pieces, *Mississippi Scenes; or, Sketches of Southern and Western Life* (1851). Interestingly, in 1850, Cobb wrote an appreciative review of G.P. Putnam's revised edition of Irving's works for *The American Whig Review, a* direct indication of his knowledge of Irving. In it, he significantly devotes considerable attention to *The Sketch Book*, with emphasis on "The Legend of Sleepy Hollow." Concerning "Sleepy Hollow," he appreciably wrote: it "stands . . . inimitable and unrivalled as regards any or all the various excellences which make up the sum total of a master-piece" (607). Noting more particularly the tale's attributes, he cited "its simple, undefiled Saxon elegance of language, the beautiful intonation of short paragraphs, the melody of smooth-flowing sentences, the tasteful touches of refined sentiment, the chaste ebullitions of humor and satire, the choice specimens of descriptive eloquence, and the delightful train of associations evoked by its lovely pictures of quiet domestic life, [pointing out that they] constitute an entirety of rare and unequalled excellences that must long uphold 'The Legend of Sleepy Hollow' as one of the most cherished literary *heirlooms* of the country" (607–8).

In "The Legend of Black Creek," Cobb seems to have borrowed all the familiar ingredients of Irving's tale, including characters closely resembling Ichabod Crane, Brom Bones, and Katrina Van Tassel; a provincial town whose residents are superstitious and who believe and delight in recounting tales of ghost lore; and the successful execution of a prank based on a local ghostly legend that follows a scenario similar to the one Brom directs against Ichabod to frighten him from the region, making Cobb's sketch a near reenactment of "Sleepy Hollow."[3]

Being that "The Legend of Black Creek" is set in antebellum times, Cobb acknowledges the presence of black raconteurs in Simstown, the secluded Mississippi hamlet where the story is set. Numbering them among the ranks of the town's superstitious and fearful, Cobb notes that the "wonder-loving sons of Africa would charm and excite their masters' children with tales of Jack-o'-the-lanterns, and swamp owls and whippowils [*sic*], all of which were, with them, beings of speech and thought" ("Black Creek" 99). In describing the black slaves in this manner, Cobb, a proslavery Whig, supports popular stereotypes promoting social stability and suggesting social and cultural inferiority as well as the notion that the function of blacks was to serve and entertain whites. While Cobb has clearly borrowed the element of ghost lore from "Sleepy Hollow," he has gone beyond his source, transforming this to fit local circumstances of time and place.

Tony Randall, Bob Bagshot, and Charity Plainlove—all of whom figure prominently in the conflict that informs the plot of "The Legend of Black Creek"—seem near reincarnations of the familiar Ichabod Crane, Brom Bones, and Katrina Van Tassel of "Sleepy Hollow," and their respective roles and functions closely correspond to those of their literary prototypes. Though not a schoolmaster, Tony Randall, who makes a living selling produce and doing various odd jobs for local farmers in nearby towns, resembles Ichabod in his fondness for singing religious hymns, belief in superstition and the supernatural, and being the victim of a prank executed by a vengeful backwoods native of the place, who Cobb describes as a "roaring, rattle-brained, rumpussing character of a fellow—the very counterpart of Brom Bones" ("Black Creek" 107). Charity Plainlove, a farmer's daughter with a "pretty face," "plump limbs," and "ripe charms" ("Black Creek" 110), traits presented in sumptuous imagery closely paralleling Irving's description of Katrina Van Tassel, becomes the object of romantic conquest, not of Tony Randall, but of the robust outdoorsman Bob Bagshot. This is yet another of the alterations of "Sleepy Hollow" matter that Cobb weaves into "The Legend of Black Creek." Because Cobb chooses not to make the love triangle the primary focus of his sketch, Charity Plainlove assumes far less importance than does Katrina in "Sleepy Hollow." Her function becomes that of an accessory, who, partly because of her secretive romantic affair with Bob Bagshot, prompts Bagshot's execution of vengeful trickery against Randall. Unlike "Sleepy Hollow," however, Randall, who at the time is in the temporary employ of Mr. Plainlove, Charity's father, and who consequently boards at their farm, has no overt romantic interest in Charity himself. Instead, what arouses Bagshot's ire and subsequent prank is that Randall has inopportunely observed Charity and himself "most amorously embraced" one evening, and he believes that Tony Randall may have informed Mr. Plainlove about this.

Bagshot, who represents the Brom Bones of Cobb's sketch, is the quintessential frontiersman, engaging in the masculine pursuits of hunting, fishing, frolicking, and practical jokes and who leads a gang of neighborhood rowdies who share his same fun-loving interests. In fact, the notorious Bagshot, Cobb reports, kept "the country, for miles around, in a constant stew for fear of his frolics or pranks" ("Black Creek" 107), but even so remains well liked by the rural inhabitants whom he often voluntarily assists in times of need or difficulty. The prank that Bagshot plays on Tony Randall and the slave Ned, who accompanies him at the time, seems well planned and skillfully executed. Like Brom Bones, Bagshot waits patiently until an opportune moment to execute his mischievous trick, knowing as he does that the success of a prank usually depends on the jokester knowing the weaknesses of his adversary (the victims, Randall and Ned, are superstitious, afraid, and aware of the legend of Black Creek and thus believe that ghosts lurk in the vicinity). Moreover, the time is the "awful anniversary" of a murder and robbery of a traveler that had occurred at Black Creek many years before, and Simstown residents believed that the ghost of the man who murdered the traveler still frequented the vicinity, reenacting on this occasion the crime in all its grisly detail. Bagshot's prank follows so closely the details surrounding the murder and other legends associated with the haunted Black Creek that like Ichabod Crane, Randall and Ned believe they see the apparition of the murdered traveler. As a consequence, their frightened mules run, and Randall, who is thrown from the wagon, is never seen in the region again.

Another of Cobb's frontier humorous sketches, "The Bride of Lick-the-Skillet," published in *Mississippi Scenes,* likewise consciously borrows "Sleepy Hollow" subject matter, this time adding a few new dimensions. Like "The Legend of Black Creek," this sketch depicts a backwoods community, the inhabitants of which show "strong tendencies to the marvelous and supernatural" ("Bride" 208); includes a popular legend of local ghost lore; features three characters whose actions and manner approximate those of Ichabod Crane, Katrina Van Tassel, and Brom Bones; and uses a bawdy prank to frighten a superstitious, pretentious, rustic militia leader on his wedding night. To this, Cobb adds a love triangle in which the rejected lover becomes the instigator of the practical joke against the rival suitor and several comical scenes approaching a level of sexual suggestiveness well ahead of their time. Concerning the latter, in the 1969 article on Cobb, Tommy Rogers may be overstating the handling of the sexual references in "The Bride of Lick-the-Skillet" in claiming that the sketch "reads like a vignette in a contemporary *Playboy*" (142). Yet, interestingly, unlike most of the other southern renditions of "Sleepy Hollow" we have examined, "The Bride of Lick-the-Skillet" does not feature in its present action an outsider or intruder who threatens the rustics or their way of life, which suggests that Cobb did not wish to emphasize this particular motif.

Despite this omission, the echoes to "Sleepy Hollow" are numerous, which indicates that the subject matter of Irving's tale was still of significant interest to Cobb and, more importantly, still applicable to the southern backwoods experience. Interestingly, in "The Bride of Lick-the-Skillet," Cobb employs, as he had done in his description of Charity Plainlove of "The Legend of Black Creek," imagery that establishes a close physical resemblance between his heroine, Sophie Pomroy, and Katrina Van Tassel. In introducing Katrina, Irving poignantly describes her as a "blooming lass of fresh eighteen; plump as a partridge; ripe and melting and rosy cheeked as one of her father's peaches" (278). Similarly, Cobb figuratively describes Sophie as a "nice, buxom, blooming girl of seventeen . . . her complexion . . . fairer than a lily, and her cheeks as red as the roses which blushed from amidst her mother's rude, but tasteful trellis work" ("Bride" 192). Unlike Katrina, Sophie is tomboyish, free-spirited, and highly competitive, especially in regard to swimming races. Later, when Cobb introduces Captain Lafayette Mantooth, an old bachelor and leader of a local militia company, the man who eventually marries Sophie, he intentionally disparages him, assigning to Mantooth physical traits, strikingly like those of Ichabod Crane. In Cobb's words, Mantooth is a "tall, gangling, long-limbed, water-jointed figure of man with long bushy red hair and broad projecting teeth, which it was his habit now and then to gnash fiercely and with an air of ludicrous gravity" ("Bride" 194–95).

Dr. Hop Hubbub, the third participant in the love triangle of "The Bride of Lick-the-Skillet," has loved Sophie for a long time before Captain Mantooth begins his active pursuit. Hop, however, only resembles Brom Bones as a jealous lover and prankster. Yet the prank he and a friend execute in terms of the motive that precipitates it and the effect it has on the victim parallels closely enough to the Headless

Horseman scenario in "Sleepy Hollow" to suggest Irving's probable influence. Knowing that Mantooth has a penchant for the supernatural tales popular in the region, and that "no one believed them more devoutly and unqualifiedly" ("Bride" 210) than the Captain, Hop, like Brom Bones, plays on his weakness, concocting a "most cruel and wicked prank" (210), which he carries out on Mantooth's wedding night. Like Brom Bones, who impersonates the Headless Horseman, thereby precipitating Ichabod Crane's rapid flight from Sleepy Hollow, Joe Morehead and Hop Hubbub impersonate the ghosts of Hans Von Tromp, whose mysterious death had been the source for local ghost lore, and of the giant Negro who legend held supposedly murdered the Dutchman. As ghosts, they successfully frighten the hysterical Mantooth to abandon Sophie and his marriage bed by jumping out of the window, spending the remainder of his wedding night in his "own quiet home" (223). This disruption only proves temporary, for at the end of the sketch the newlyweds are reconciled.

While Thompson's "The Runaway Match," Mayer's "The Corn Cob Pipe," and Cobb's "The Legend of Black Creek" and "The Bride of Lick-the-Skillet" exhibit enough identifiable parallels to "The Legend of Sleepy Hollow" to claim unquestionable influence, several other sketches in the tradition of antebellum southern backwoods humor, though less obtrusively imitative, also still bear a direct connection to Irving's classic story. One of these, William Tappan Thompson's "Adventure of Sabbath-Breaker," initially published in the *Augusta Mirror* on 14 December 1839, and subsequently in the *New York Spirit of the Times* and in *Major Jones' Chronicles of Pineville* in 1845, features the motif of the intruder plot Irving uses in "Sleepy Hollow." Thompson's central character, Eugenius Augustus Van Scoik, an outsider of Dutch extraction, closely resembles Ichabod Crane. A Down East Yankee—genteel, congenial, and with good upbringing—Eugenius, once a professional salesman, becomes a store clerk and resident of Pineville, Georgia. Almost from the outset of the sketch, Thompson, following the manner of Irving's ridiculing of Ichabod Crane's physical appearance, similarly describes Eugenius in disparaging language: "He was a tall, chalky-complexioned, crane-built, gosling-looking youth, with a very prominent beak, and eyes askew. The nose stuck 'right out,' and there was no help for it, but he managed to hide the slight obliquity in the setting of his visual organs, by means of a pair of large-bowled silver spectacles, with green glasses, which he wore under the pretext of weakness" ("Adventure" 86–87). Interestingly, Thompson employs some of the same unflattering details to describe Eugenius as Irving uses in describing Ichabod. Both are tall, lank, bear a resemblance to a crane, and have excessively long noses—Crane's "long snipe nose . . . look[ing] like a weathercock" (Irving 274). Moreover, Eugenius, like Ichabod, sings psalms and is a favorite among the ladies of the community. In short, both Irving and Thompson seem to regard outsiders with contempt, their presence being viewed as a threat to stability and harmony of the traditional values of the rural hamlet. After all, in Eugenius's case, he had once been a salesman, one who brings in wares from the outside to sale to local inhabitants, which, as in Stephen Crane's well-known story, "The Bride

Comes to Yellow Sky," is symbolic of the changing social order concomitant with the influx of commercial progress.

To further ridicule Eugenius, Thompson, again echoing Irving's portrayal of Ichabod Crane, shows the young outsider as having an unceasing passion: the desire to hunt robins. Breaking the Sabbath to pursue his passion, a clear violation of the community's practice of Sunday church attendance, Eugenius becomes an object of self-deprecation. Not only does he miss the robins he tries to shoot (obviously Eugenius is no marksman), but in a subsequent encounter with a bear that pursues him—an incident similar to Ichabod's confrontation with the Headless Horseman—Eugenius runs in fright, humiliating the outsider and making him look ridiculous in the eyes of the townspeople, and ultimately resulting in his presence being a less formidable threat to the traditional ways of the rural community.

Francis James Robinson's "The Frightened Serenaders; or, the B'hoys in a Fix," published in his humorous collection of frontier sketches *Kups of Kauphy* (1853), also draws on and alters a familiar element of the "Sleepy Hollow" story—the exploits of rural youthful pranksters. "Amongst other things," Robinson writes, "they would take delight in pelting a drunkard with *stale eggs,* disfigure his countenance with lampblack and oil, sometimes with an extra finish of black varnish—or frighten him nearly to death by charging theft or some other crime upon him—feigning themselves officers of the law and intending to execute its justice upon the unfortunate wight" (17–18). These displays of fun and frolic resemble, of course, the kinds of hijinks Brom Bones and his gang engage in in "Sleepy Hollow." Unlike Sleepy Hollow, however, which accepts and tolerates the mischief of Brom and his gang, Robinson's Georgian villagers are not so accommodating of the "Tugmuttons," as this youthful, mischievous band calls themselves. Creating widespread pandemonium on one of their noisy nightly rampages through the countryside, the "Tugs" experience armed resistance from the victims of their disturbance and therefore become victimized themselves. Frightened for their lives, the rowdy "Tugs" retreat to the village and reform their behavior. The twist that Robinson has brought to his rendition of "Sleepy Hollow" shows that the forces of disruption in a stable southern village do not always intrude from the outside but are sometimes associated with irresponsibility and mischief from within—in this instance, the conflict ensuing between two generations of locals of different levels of maturity and with different priorities.

Both Augustus Baldwin Longstreet, the author of *Georgia Scenes* (1835), and William Gilmore Simms, the antebellum South's most versatile and prolific professional writer, likewise authored tales echoing "Sleepy Hollow." In "The Turn Out," first published in the *Southern Recorder* in December 1833, and subsequently as one of the sketches included in *Georgia Scenes* (1835), Longstreet seems to have Ichabod Crane in mind in his portrayal of the schoolmaster Michael St. John. The sketch involves a clash between St. John and a feisty group of rural schoolboys determined to break the routine of daily school attendance and to be granted an Easter "holyday." Longstreet's schoolmaster, pompous, refined, and educated, is like his counterpart Ichabod Crane in that he represents an outsider, a disrupting force in a settled and traditional society. Moreover, St. John loses in his struggle against the recalcitrant boys, who successfully managed to shut him out of the schoolhouse, and he eventually succumbs to their demands for vacation from school.

Simms, who reviewed G.P. Putnam's revised edition of Irving's works in the *Southern Quarterly Review* in 1851, expressed a special fondness for *The Sketch Book*, which he regarded as Irving's best work.[4] Also, in the 1840s, Simms had a high regard for southern frontier humor, which he felt was the only genuine humor being produced in America at this time, and was especially appreciative of Augustus Baldwin Longstreet, Joseph Glover Baldwin, Johnson J. Hooper, and William Tappan Thompson, all humorists of this ilk (Parks 96).[5] Simms's possible appropriation of "Sleepy Hollow" may best be seen in "How Sharp Snaffles Got His Capital and Wife," regarded as Simms's most notable story in the backwoods humorous vein,[6] a tale probably conceived in the autumn of 1847, when Simms and some friends journeyed to the Balsam Range in the North Carolina mountains for a hunting trip (Guilds 798–99), but not published until 1870 in *Harper's New Monthly Magazine* after Simms's death. The connection between "Sleepy Hollow" and "Sharp Snaffles" lies in Simms's unflattering portrayal of Bachelor Grimstead, who in his manner and demeanor seems a character in the mold of Irving's Ichabod Crane and of Sam Snaffles, a poor backwoodsman and hunter, a southern counterpart of Brom Bones.

As in "Sleepy Hollow," Simms employs a humorous tone and structures his tale, which Sam Snaffles recounts in the best tall-tale manner, around a conflict between the refined, established, and respected John Grimstead, a prosperous farmer and old bachelor, and the uncouth, uneducated Sam for the hand of Merry Ann Hopson, whose father initially prefers the older, more respectable, and more financially secure Grimstead as a suitor and potential husband for his daughter. Unlike Brom Bones, Sam does not resort to pranks against his adversary to win the hand of Merry Ann, who clearly desires him over Grimstead. Instead, he becomes the beneficiary of a beautiful young woman who appears to him in a dream; and as he would have those listening to his tale believe, who encourages him to secure "capital," thereby enabling him to gain a fortune. Now rich and financially secure, having acquired an economic status that Merry Ann's father must acknowledge, Sam, who has purchased the mortgage to the Squire's farm, returns to Squire Hopson, proceeds "to give him a mighty grand skeer" (Simms 451), a vengeful ploy that humbles the Squire and teaches him a valuable lesson. As in "Sleepy Hollow," the rival suitor is discredited and the backwoodsman marries the farmer's daughter. Simms, however, adds an ironic variation to his story line by having Sam Snaffles first attain respectability and social mobility, both of which were dependent upon his securing economic credibility before doing so. In this respect, Simms, who was of a conservative persuasion, shows in Sam Snaffles's miraculous transformation a poor hunter-backwoodsman who has become an entrepreneur, a role in which he seems to become a potential despoiler of natural resources (part of this capital, so he claimed, consisted of twenty-seven hundred geese he snared in a net) and therefore a threat to the way of life of the traditional frontier community where the story is set.

In 1961, commenting on "The Legend of Sleepy Hollow," Daniel Hoffman raised an interesting query concerning whether the pumpkin killed Ichabod Crane at the end of the tale, which he then also answered in an insightful and suggestive manner. In responding to his own question, Hoffman went on to say: "Of course not! Our folk heroes never die. Wearing the magic cloak of metamorphosis, they stave off death forever by simply changing their occupations" (93). Hoffman's response seems especially relevant to the numerous southern renditions of Irving's masterpiece we have examined in backwoods humorous sketches by Thompson, Mayer, Cobb, Robinson, Longstreet, and Simms. In various ways, each of these writers seems to have been inspired by "Sleepy Hollow." Concerning the themes, plot elements, and character types they appropriated from "Sleepy Hollow" and modified or transformed for use in their own humorous sketches and tales, we may draw several conclusions.

A unifying characteristic of the six southern writers who turned to "Sleepy Hollow" is that they were conservative, educated gentlemen and staunchly loyal supporters of the South's traditions and way of life. For these reasons, they predictably promoted in their works a stable society predicated on distinctions in gender, social class, race, and suspicion of outsiders—basically the same kind of fixed society Irving also celebrates in "Sleepy Hollow." The interesting point about this connection is that both rural northerners and southerners of the first half of the nineteenth century seemed to share a solid respect for tradition, fondness for a settled and fixed society, and a guarded distrust of persons or institutions that might threaten their way of life. As we have seen in some of the more representative southern descendants of "Sleepy Hollow"—Thompson's "The Runaway Match" and "Adventures of a Sabbath-Breaker," Mayer's "The Corn Cob Pipe," and Robinson's "The Frightened Serenaders"—outsiders, almost always persons better educated, more sophisticated, and more refined and cultured than the local settlers of the frontier or rural communities where they resided, and occasionally even rowdy insiders, like Robinson's "Tugmuttons," are discredited. Not only were such persons often greedy and self-serving but also, because of their ambitions, they sometimes threatened the natural environment and the way of life associated with rural and provincial regions. Like Irving, his southern counterparts were skeptical of forced progress, which was often initiated by outsiders who did not share the same attitudes revered by rural southerners. Such outsiders in many of the southern renditions of "Sleepy Hollow" we have examined become outcasts—deserving victims and objects of disparagement—who, more often than not, are forced to depart from the regions they threaten. In "Sleepy Hollow," southern writers discovered a paradigm for treating this scenario. Almost always in the nineteenth-century versions of "Sleepy Hollow," the authors, consciously aware of the changes threatening the frontier, tended to favor exemplars of traditional rural virtues, as embodied in the backwoodsman, Brom Bones kind of character, who is physically strong, clever, defensive, and practically adept in the practice of frontier masculine activities of horsemanship, practical joking, hunting, and fighting. Mayer's Abram Priester ("The Corn Cob Pipe") and Cobb's Bob Bagshot ("The Legend of Black Creek"), represent this type and tend to be portrayed favorably by their creators. Generally, the authors of southern backwoods sketches typically wrote their humorous pieces for well-educated professional gentlemen like themselves, providing for them in the likes of the Brom Bones types, free-spirited and likable characters who epitomized masculinity and whose shenanigans and exploits male readers could accept vicariously without openly acknowledging they had done so. In sum, "The Legend of Sleepy Hollow" provided the practitioners of southern backwoods humor with a ready-made recipe for perpetuating a popular image of the antebellum southern frontier, an image favoring sectionalism, social stability, masculinity, and traditional and conservative values.

Notes

1. Hilton Anderson's "A Southern 'Sleepy Hollow,'" *Mississippi Folklore Register* 3 (1969): 85–88, which focuses on parallels between Irving's tale and Joseph B. Cobb's "The Legend of Black Creek" is the only study I know that addresses the impact of "Sleepy Hollow" on a southern backwoods tale.

2. In early 1848, sometime before the publication of "The Corn Cob Pipe," Mayer dined in Columbia, South Carolina, with Thompson, William Gilmore Simms, and A.G. Summer (at the time, the editor of the *Columbia South Carolinian*)—all of whom had an interest in southern frontier humor and who wrote sketches and tales in this tradition. On this occasion they seemed to have swapped with each other tales of a backwoods humorous variety. See the letter from Mayer to Paul Hamilton Hayne, 4 Feb. 1886, Paul Hamilton Hayne Papers, Special Collections Library, Duke University, Durham, N.C., and my article, "Letter from O.B. Mayer to Paul Hamilton Hayne: Some Notes on Literary Relationships," *Mississippi Quarterly* 50 (1996–1997): 117–23.

3. Anderson, 85–88, to which I previously alluded in note 1, provides a brief commentary on similarities between "Sleepy Hollow" and "The Legend of Black Creek." While I am indebted to Anderson's findings, I will, whenever possible, add several of my own insights concerning the connections between these two pieces.

4. Simms, 571, in favorably commenting on Irving's *The Sketch Book*, wrote: "The quiet grace of his style, the delicacy and simplicity of his taste, his happy sense of propriety, and his view of fancy, at once pleasing and yet unobtrusive, all combine to render the essay his most favourite province." Subsequently, in a letter dated 17 March 1860 to the members of the committee planning a commemorative birthday dinner for Irving to which Simms was invited but had to decline because of failing health, he bestowed further accolades on the author of *The Sketch Book*. He noted that Irving was the "earliest and most successful of our Literary Pioneers, as an Historian of large research; a Biographer of rare truthfulness; an Essayist of exquisite simplicity; a Romancer of equal freshness, fancy and purity; a writer whose style recals [*sic*] the freedom & grace of Goldsmith, his archness and sweetness, with the classic propriety and delicacy of Addison;—the claims of Washington Irving, simply as a Literary man, are beyond dispute, and should commend the veneration of his people" (*Letters* 5:429). In an earlier letter to Everet A. Duyckinck, 15 July 1845, Simms was less enthusiastic about Irving. In it, he claimed that Irving was "little more than a writer of delicate taste, a pleasant unobtrusive humour, and agreeable talent" (*Letters* 2:90). See Wimsatt, 25–

37, for a discussion of Irving's influence on Simms's *The Book of My Lady*, *Martin Faber*, *The Damsel of Darien*, *Count Julian*, and *Charlemont*.

5. See Parks 138, note 26, for references to Simms's knowledge of these humorists.

6. In notes to "How Sharp Snaffles Got His Capital and Wife," Guilds, 794–96, also mentions several source studies acknowledging the influences of Raspe's Baron Munchausen and of traditional American folk motifs on this tale; however, he makes no reference to "Sleepy Hollow."

Works Cited

Anderson, Hilton. "A Southern 'Sleepy Hollow.'" *Mississippi Folklore Register* 3 (1969): 85–88.

Cobb, Joseph B. "The Bride of Lick-The-Skillet." *Mississippi Scenes; Or, Sketches of Southern and Western Life and Adventure.* Philadelphia: A. Hart, 1851. 185–231

———. "The Genius and Writings of Washington Irving." *The American Whig Review* 73 (1850): 602–16.

———. "The Legend of Black Creek." *Mississippi Scenes.* 97–123.

Cohen, Hennig, and William B. Dillingham. Introduction. *Humor of the Old Southwest.* Eds. Cohen and Dillingham. 3rd ed. Athens: Univ. of Georgia Press, 1994. xv–xl.

Cox, James M. "Humor of the Old Southwest." *The Comic Imagination in American Literature.* Ed. Louis D. Rubin Jr. New Brunswick, N.J.: Rutgers Univ. Press, 1973. 101–12.

Eby, Cecil D., Jr. "Ichabod Crane in Yoknapatawpha." *Georgia Review* 16 (1962): 465–69.

Hart, James D. *The Popular Book: A History of America's Literary Taste.* Berkeley: Univ. of California Press, 1963.

Hoffman, Daniel. *Form and Fable in American Fiction.* New York: Norton, 1961.

Irving, Washington. "The Legend of Sleepy Hollow." *The Complete Works of Washington Irving. The Sketch Book of Geoffrey Crayon, Gent.* Ed. Haskell Springer. Vol. 8. Boston: Twayne, 1978. 272–97.

———. "Rip Van Winkle." *The Complete Works of Washington Irving. The Sketch Book of Geoffrey Crayon, Gent.* Ed. Haskell Springer. Vol. 8. Boston: Twayne, 1978. 29–42.

Kibler, James E., Jr. "O.B. Mayer." *Antebellum Writers in New York and the South.* Vol. 3. *Dictionary of Literary Biography.* Ed. Joel Myerson. Detroit: Gale Research, 1979. 213–18.

Longstreet, A.B. "The Turn Out." *Georgia Scenes, Characters, Incidents, &c., in the First Half Century of the Republic.* Gloucester, Mass.: Peter Smith, 1970. 62–70.

Mayer, O.B. "The Corn Cob Pipe: A Tale of the Comet of '43." *Fireside Tales: Stories of the Old Dutch Fork.* Ed. James Everett Kibler Jr. Columbia, S.C.: Dutch Fork Press, 1984. 117–31.

Oliphant, Mary C. Simms, Alfred Taylor Odell, and T.C. Duncan Eaves, eds. *The Letters of William Gilmore Simms.* 6 vols. Columbia: Univ. of South Carolina Press, 1952–1982.

Parks, Edd Winfield. *William Gilmore Simms As Literary Critic.* Athens: Univ. of Georgia Press, 1961.

Piacentino, Ed. "Letter from O.B. Mayer to Paul Hamilton Hayne: Some Notes on Literary Relationships." *Mississippi Quarterly* 50 (1996–1997): 117–23.

Robinson, Francis James. *Kups of Kauphy: A Georgia Book, in Warp and Woof, Containing Tales, Incidents, &c. of the "Empire State of the South."* Athens, Ga.: Christy & Chelsea, 1853. 17–23.

Rodes, Sara Puryear. "Washington Irving's Use of Traditional Folklore." *Southern Folklore Quarterly* 20 (1956): 143–53.

Rogers, Tommy. "Joseph B. Cobb: Antebellum Humorist and Critic." *Mississippi Quarterly* 22 (1969): 131–46.

Simms, William Gilmore. "How Sharp Snaffles Got His Capital and Wife." *The Writings of William Gilmore Simms: Stories and Tales.* Ed. John Caldwell Guilds. Vol. 5. Columbia: Univ. of South Carolina Press, 1974. 421–65.

———. Rev. of *Works*, by Washington Irving. *Southern Quarterly Review*, April 1851: 571.

Springer, Haskell. "Irving and the Knickerbocker Group." *Columbia Literary History of the United States.* Ed. Emory Elliott, *et al.* New York: Columbia Univ. Press, 1988. 229–39.

Thompson, William Tappan. *Major Jones' Chronicles of Pineville: Embracing Sketches of Georgia Scenes, Incidents, and Characters.* Philadelphia: T.B. Peterson and Brothers, 1858. 86–98.

———. *Major Jones's Courtship: Detailed, with Other Scenes, Incidents, and Adventures in a Series of Letters by Himself.* Atlanta: Cherokee, 1973. 214–21.

Wimsatt, Mary Ann. "Simms and Irving." *Mississippi Quarterly* 20 (1966): 25–37.

3

The Function of Women in Old Southwestern Humor

Rereading Porter's *Big Bear* and *Quarter Race* Collections

William E. Lenz

Old Southwestern humor flourished from approximately 1830 to 1860 in local papers such as the *La Fayette East Alabamian*, in widely read regional publications such as the *New Orleans Picayune*, and in that national clearinghouse for frontier writers, the *New York Spirit of the Times*. Numerous sketches of backwoods life were contributed to these publications primarily by professional men who enjoyed adopting the title of "Correspondent" to record the manners, morals, and odd customs of the inhabitants of the Old Southwest—Georgia, Alabama, North and South Carolina, Louisiana, Mississippi, Tennessee, Kentucky, and Arkansas. Lawyers, doctors, politicians, and editors translated into print the American ritual of swapping stories, at their best retaining the energy, exuberance, and excitement of the oral tradition. "Hurra for the Big Bar of Arkansaw!" shouts the vernacular narrator of Thomas Bangs Thorpe's quintessential Southwestern sketch, urging a cheer for the "creation bear,"[1] introducing his own boasting persona, and winning acceptance for himself among the riverboat's passengers (and the story's readers). Constance M. Rourke maintains that "these stories are as coarse-grained as poplar wood and equally light as timber."[2] M. Thomas Inge muses that "perhaps the best adjective which has been suggested to convey the quality of this humor is 'masculine.'"[3] Walter Blair, singling out the *Spirit of the Times* as "more important than any other publication," observes that it "had a racy masculine flavor."[4] William T. Porter, for most of its life the *Spirit's* editor and driving force, defined his ideal audience: "We are addressing ourselves to gentlemen of standing, wealth and intelligence—the very corinthian columns of the community."[5]

What these gentlemen enjoyed were stories of frontier fights, hunts, contests, swaps, lawsuits, tricks, and physical pranks. Kenneth S. Lynn asserts that the narrative frame technique, by means of which a cultured frame-narrator introduces rough vernacular language, characters, and actions, serves as "a convenient way of keeping . . . first-person narrators outside and above the comic action."[6] The very structure of these tales reminds the reader that he—like the frame-narrator—is linguistically, socially, and morally superior to the rude or eccentric characters described. Part of the reader's enjoyment depends on the incongruity between his world and that of forty-pound turkeys, "creation bears," savage fights, shifty confidence men, and brutally butchered grammar and spelling. And, it almost goes without saying, the Southwestern world constructed in these tales is decidedly male.

In *American Humor,* Constance Rourke contends that "women had played no essential part in the long sequence of the comic spirit in America" (142). Although she refers most specifically to an absence of female writers in antebellum American humor, she might also have had in mind women as characters in American humor. For at first glance the role of women in Old Southwestern humor would seem to be minimal. There are no women in Thorpe's catalogue of travelers aboard the Mississippi steamboat the *Invincible,* and the only reference to the gentler sex occurs when the creation bear magically transforms himself into a she-bear to make good his escape.[7] Nancy A. Walker asserts that "humor is aggressive; women are passive. The humorist occupies a position of superiority; women are inferior."[8] Zita Dresner notes "the generally acknowledged antifeminine bias in what has been labeled 'native' American humor," visible not only in "the relative absence of women as primary humorous characters, but also in their functions as negative stereotypes in masculine humor."[9] Linda A. Morris contends that "male humorists' attitudes toward women varied, from innumerable stories in which women do not figure at all . . . to traditional romanticization of women, to extreme instances of outright misogyny."[10] And Alfred Habegger sadly laments, "Where are the women among the Southwestern humorists?"[11]

Neil Schmitz writes that "William T. Porter's *Spirit of the Times* . . . effectively became the home journal for Southwestern humor in the 1840s."[12] From 1831 to 1861 the *Spirit of the Times* formed what Porter called "the nucleus of a new order of literary talent" *(Big Bear* 7), publishing the work of C.F.M. Noland, Thomas Bangs Thorpe, Johnson Jones Hooper, John S. Robb, George Washington Harris, and other prominent Southwestern writers. At the height of the *Spirit's* popularity, Porter edited *The Big Bear of Arkansas, and Other Sketches* (1845) and *A Quarter Race in Kentucky, and Other Tales* (1847), collections of stories most of which had appeared in the *Spirit. The Big Bear* went through five quick editions and *A Quarter Race,* four, evidence of their appeal. As selected by the "father of the Big Bear School," these fifty-four pieces function as a limited yet representative sample of the genre. Porter certainly had a broader readership in mind than the then-current subscribers to the *Spirit,* but it seems clear that he wished to convey without adulteration the characteristic flavor of Southwestern humor. Linda A. Morris asserts that "Porter himself did not believe the humor tales were meant for the eyes of the gentler sex; when he was editing his two humor anthologies, he 'banned' the proverbial prude, Mrs. Grundy, from his office" (20). With one exception, Porter reprinted materials directly from the *Spirit.* In an attempt to reach a national audience, he certainly would have chosen stories that had proven themselves popular at their first printing. That Porter reprinted them in nationally distributed books argues inferentially for their representativeness.

Do women figure prominently in *The Big Bear* and *A Quarter Race*? Although no female writers are represented, women *do* have central roles in eleven of the fifty-four sketches: "Billy Warrick's Courtship and Wedding," "Life and Manners in Arkansas," "Going to Bed Before a Young Lady," "Taking the Census," "Dick Harlan's Tennessee Frolic," "French Without a Master," "India Rubber Pills," "A Murder Case in Mississippi," "Somebody in My Bed," "A Day at Sol Slice's," and "Cupping on the Sternum." Representation of approximately 20 percent in these sketches is itself a surprise. Yet are women included only to become the victims of male humor? Of course, this is a trickier question, for *all* of the characters in Southwestern humor—often including the protagonist, the narrator, and the reader—are objects of fun. To formulate a series of sharper questions, we might ask if women are consistently victimized. Is Southwestern humor simply misogynistic, as Morris and other critics contend? Does it reveal a larger cultural pattern of male dominance and female submission? Or are there stories in which stereotyped gender roles are destabilized?

"Billy Warrick's Courtship and Wedding" retells the story of Billy's developing relationship with Miss Barbry Bass. Divided into three chapters represented as letters, the form itself creates a familiar kind of orthographic humor as the semiliterate "Wm. Warrick" tries to structure his experiences in his own idiom for a more sophisticated magazine audience: "Mr. Porter—Sir:—Bein' in grate distrest, I didn't know what to do, till one of the lawyers councilled me to tell you all about it, and git your opinion" (*BB* 90). Billy introduces Mr. Porter to the blooming Barbry Bass, a proud and intelligent local Piney Bottom girl, in vivid vernacular terms: "I tho't how putty she *did* look last singin' school day,—with her eyes as blue as indiger, and her teath white as milk, and sich long curlin' hare hangin' clear down to her belt ribbun, and sich butiful rosy cheaks, and lips as red as a cock Red-burd in snow time." (*BB* 91). In making his preparations for proposing, Billy exposes his male view of women as commodities and courtship as a costly but necessary investment: "It tuck one bale of good cotting and six bushils of peese to pay for my close. Dod drot it, it went sorter hard; but when I tho't . . . how she squeased my hand when I gin her a oringe than I gin six cents for—I didn't grudge the price" (*BB* 91). Billy also defines the characteristics he desires in a Piney Bottom wife: "'Well,' says I, 'she's bout the likeliest gal in this settlement, and I rekon mity nigh the smartest—they tells me she kin spin more cuts in a day, and card her own rolls, and danse harder and longer, and sing more songs outer the Missunary Harmony, than any gal in the country'" (*BB* 91). Screwing up his courage, Billy offers himself in a conventional formula: "'Barbry,' ses I, takin of her hand, 'aint I many a time, as I sot by the fire at home, all by my lone self, ain't I considerd how if I *did* have a good wife how I could work for her, and do all I could for her, and make her pleasant like and happy, and do every thing for her? . . . Barbry, if that sumbody that keard was only *you,* I'd die for you, and be burryd a dozen times'" (*BB* 95).

Although Billy's description disassembles Barbry into desirable parts while his evaluation assigns a woman value in terms of her domestic functions, what is most clearly revealed is not so much explicit victimization as the implicit acceptance of cultural conventions and gender-based stereotypes. Yet Billy does not exemplify a domineering male culture. He seems virtually powerless in this situation. "Mr. Porter . . . sich streaks and cold fits cum over me worse than a feller with the Buck agur, the furst time he goes to shute at a dear. My kneas got to trimblin,' and I could hardly holler 'get out' to Miss Basses son Siah's dog, old Troup, who didn't know me in my new geer and cum out like all creashun a barkin' amazin'" (*BB* 91–92). Billy has become unmanned, turned into a frightened child, and his clearly defined male identity disappears: when he changes his manly work clothes for the effeminate store-bought courting clothes—women's clothes, as it were—even the dog does not recognize him and treats him like an outsider. Billy is even mistaken for the dog (is reduced to the status of an animal) by Mrs. Bass because Billy's rude kissing of Barbry sounds like a dog drinking from the milk pan.

In truth, it is the women who are in control. As Billy reports to Mr. Porter in chapter 2, his second letter, " . . . Miss Bass and Miss Collins come back . . . and ses she, 'Good bye, Billy! Good luck to you! I know'd your daddy and mammy afore you was born on yerth, and I was the furst one after your granny that had you in the arms—me and Miss Bass *talk'd it over! you'll git a smart, peart, likely gal!* So good bye, Billy!'" (*BB* 101) Barbry's mother confirms their control. "Billy! Miss Collins and me is a bin talkin' over you and Barbry, and seein' you are a good karickter and smart and well to do in the world, and a poor orphin boy, I shan't say *no!*" (*BB* 101) Are women in charge of relationships and marriage? Do women have a kind of temporary cultural authority over men? Or does "Billy Warrick's Courtship and Wedding" suggest a sublimated male anxiety about which sex truly rules the roost?

Characteristically, "Mr. Porter" and the reader are superior to both the male and the female inhabitants of Piney Bottom. In addition, the role of fool is played first by Billy, a youth befuddled by love and passion, and second by Nancy Guiton, the girl Billy had left for Barbry Bass. The concluding section, chapter 3, is written from Nancy Guiton's point of view in the form of a letter to her friend Polly Stroud. This technique disrupts and replaces the male narrative with an authoritative, first-person female voice. Although she bemoans her jilted condition and the faithlessness of Billy Warrick—"And then to say I were too old for him and that he was always conceited I was a sort of a sister to him!" (*BB* 103)—she enthusiastically records the festivities and the antics of the participants with good humor, concluding with a list of marriages, births, illnesses, and a plea for news. Her predicament is not exactly funny (unrequited love never is), but the assertiveness and authority of her narration imply her ability to recover fully. As she insists, "Well, its all over, but I don't keer—theres as good fish in the sea as ever come outen it. Im not poor for the likes of Bill Warrick, havin now three sparks, and one of them from Town, whose got a good grocery and leads the Quire at church." (*BB* 105). She is, however, a reminder of the traditional necessity of marriage for nineteenth-century women. Mrs. Bass and Mrs. Collins, having entered the adult community through marriage, are wise, knowledgeable, and powerful. In a very real sense, these women are in control of Billy Warrick. Although they speak a low vernacular, drink, smoke, and chew tobacco, they command authority. The author reveals as if by accident a world of backwoods domesticity that runs parallel with yet counter to the male world of the hunt. In the eyes of men, this female world has its own rules and its own rewards. To get married, a man must enter it as carefully as he would a bear den; all men, in this situation, are, like Billy Warrick, orphans, cut off from the safety of male comradeship and the security of public dominance. Like Billy, men view this territory as a locus of female power. Although this may not be true in fact, and although even if true it does not appreciably alter the status of women in American culture, it does suggest an area of male unsureness and insecurity. That Mrs. Bass and Mrs. Collins appear to control the first two chapters of the story and that the third is told by Nancy Guiton in her own voice suggests an instability in cultural stereotypes of male dominance and female submission. And the author, Billy Warrick, and this reader admire the sureness and artistry that these women demonstrate as they construct Billy's future as if they were blowing smoke rings: "The way she rowl'd the smoke out was astonishin.'" (*BB* 93.)

A second tale, "Life and Manners in Arkansas," forgoes the vernacular narration of "Billy Warrick," establishing a clear distance between the self-controlled narrator and the inhabitants of Washita Cove, where he stops overnight at the Widow Gaston's. "At the Widow's I found her daughter, who was to be married, waiting for the groom. She was really a beautiful girl, with bright eyes, long black hair, a white band round her head, white dress, red shoes, and no stockings" (*BB* 155). Despite the narrator's obvious superiority to the local doings, he reveals no hint of condescension to the bride. He expresses only amusement at the desire of the reluctant groom to stay up all night playing public, social kissing games rather than to go to bed alone with his new wife. The groom's rebellion humorously admits a male suspicion of the dominance of female-enforced social institutions. He can resist their authority momentarily by refusing the marital bed tonight—insisting on an all-night backwoods bachelor party, as it were—but he must submit himself tomorrow. The conventional honeymoon humor in this situation is overtly at the expense of the groom. His reluctance expresses a male anxiety about male sexual performance and reinforces male uncertainty about the terra incognita of the female body and female sexuality. As opposed to the appreciative portrait he paints of the bride, the narrator describes the groom as "a great, clumsy, hulking, cur-dog looking fellow" (*BB* 155). If the bride is a victim, she is a victim of the groom's inexperience, ignorance, and fear. To be a little more critical, we might also see her as a victim of her environment: Arkansas is so rough that this "Big Bear" is the best it can offer. In addition, a single girl must marry in order to create an adult life for herself; Nancy Guiton in "Billy Warrick" recognizes that there is no other way out. Taking this view, the bride is trapped by language, convention, and circumstance in ways that local color writers including Harriet Beecher Stowe, Mary E. Wilkins Freeman, and Sarah Orne Jewett would later make explicit.

"French Without a Master" is typical of sketches that broadly satirize the pretensions of rural men and women to Eastern refinement. Despite the deeply ingrained American penchant for self-help manuals, it is clear that this family will neither learn to speak French nor learn to improve their socioeconomic status. What ultimately rivets their attention is a potentially fatal accident of a man and his horse outside their window.[13] "Oh, look there, daddy—there's the *hommy* off and he's smashed his *taty 'gainst* the *pavy!* The *roo* is full of *puples*—only look—" *(A Quarter Race* 102).

In "A Murder Case in Mississippi," the reader's laughter is also triggered by social incongruity. The rude constable, Jones, "a tall, thin man, with the nether ends of his trousers thrust into the legs of his horse-skin boots, without any coat, unshaven" (*AQR* 155), with his mouth overflowing with tobacco juice, mistakenly believes that Mrs. Granger has been murdered by her husband. Although we are led to suppose that husbands who argued constantly with their wives would not infrequently murder them, when the living Mrs. Granger enters the courtroom, we see that she appears less the victim than the victimizer: "Consarn you, Bill Granger, is it there you be, instead of hoein' the taters!" (*AQR* 159). At the very least, Mrs. Granger seems if not in control of her husband, at least able to hold her own. Like Washington Irving's Dame Van Winkle, Mrs. Granger seems quite capable of terrorizing her husband. While this image suggests a version of female power, it recasts the female in the male mold, either masculinizing Mrs. Granger or, as the allusion to Dame Van Winkle reminds us, reinscribing the powerful female in the male construction of the shrew. Or does it?

Susan V. Donaldson and Anne Goodwyn Jones suggest in "Haunted Bodies: Rethinking the South through Gender" that "seemingly stable categories of manhood and womanhood, invoked and repeated though they may be in numerous cultural texts, are everywhere inevitably susceptible to destabilization and alterity."[14] Mrs. Granger does invade and destabilize the public arena of patriarchy made visible—the law court—and, in just a few words, shatters the authority of the court, making clear the limits of sovereignty: "The court was dismissed. Granger and his wife went home, arguing, as usual, by the way; the spectators were convulsed with laughter at the termination of the awful murder case; the judge and the district attorney attributed the mistakes of the morning to that 'fool, Jones,' and Jones swore he would never make another arrest as long as he'd live" (*AQR* 160). Mrs. Granger does literally throw into chaos the public male world of privilege and dominance and, as Judy Elsley insists for Celie and her friends in Alice Walker's *The Color Purple,* "these women are disrupting the patriarchal world with their laughter to make room for themselves."[15]

The same disruption can be seen in the humor of the Irish country matron in "Taking the Census." The male census-taker, representing patriarchal big government and big taxes, is no match for the quick-witted woman he attempts to interrogate. He asks, "Who is the head of the family?" She names herself, "Ann Phelim, yer honor." "How many Males in the family?" Immediately she quips, "Three *males* a day with prateys for dinner." (*AQR* 80), deflating the importance of the male census-taker in particular and maleness in general. The "maternal head" of the house fences with the agent for a while and then, when he asks what she takes to be a question about the racial makeup of her family, she dismisses him entirely: "Out wide ye, and niver ask for me *senses* agin—don't ask about me *senses*—whither I have nagers in the family? Yer out of yer senses, yerself, begone and don't bother me" (*AQR* 181). Ann Phelim makes cultural room for herself and a mockery of the census.[16]

In "A Day at Sol Slice's," a country belle finds herself lifted airborne from the dance floor to reveal "a red petticoat, and . . . this 'pair of revolvers'" (*AQR* 180). As in many humorous sketches, however, the victim reasserts her identity and control through violence, as if she were a man. "The 'gall' arose to her feet, dealing blows, right and left, upon poor Bill—'Take that, and that, for histin' me up before all these people, you onmannerly, ugly piece of deformity.'" Sall reacts violently against the public display of her sexuality, lashing out at Bill Lever, the male who controlled her and thereby exposed her, as its physical embodiment. "'I beg pardon, Sall,' pleaded Lever, 'I couldn't help it—I wouldn't a done it ef I had knowed! You knows I was on this eend of you and couldn't see nuthin'" (*AQR* 181). Although he "couldn't see nuthin'," Bill Lever is felled by Sall's "revolvers" (as if she had hidden "guns" under her female apparel): "I turned in time to see Lever stretched on the floor, and his gal just 'settling upon him.' Old Mrs. Spraggs,—kind-hearted old soul—ran up to her assistance, and while picking her up *whispered,* as all old ladies do, so as to be heard by all—'Git up, Sall, all these fellers couldn't a seed more ef you was married to 'em all'" (*AQR* 180–81). Angry and embarrassed, she hurls a chair at her partner: "The Amazon . . . seemed perfectly satisfied with this manly effort at redress; and in a short time looked as if nothing had happened to disturb her peace of mind" (*AQR* 181).

Though some of the humor results from the girl's exposure, initially, from her powerlessness to prevent the gaze of the male and female onlookers and the fantasies of the tale's (male) readers, and then from her decidedly unladylike behavior, the sketch ultimately punctures the conventional image of proper feminine deportment and confers upon "the Amazon" a heroine's mythic stature. But to call Sall an Amazon is not necessarily positive or empowering; the author pigeonholes her in a safe cultural category, that of manly warrior-woman. It denies her independent female power as it subsumes it into a previously constructed patriarchal stereotype. In order to be powerful, Sall must give up her femininity and act like a man, by fighting and brawling. She becomes powerful by becoming a man—the female role, which she inverts, remains powerless.[17]

George Washington Harris in "Dick Harlan's Tennessee Frolic" tells of another dance that culminates in a free-for-all. As in "A Day at Sol Slice's," the social activity of the dance turns into an opportunity for men to compete with one another for status and dominance; dancing, eating, drinking, sparking, telling stories, all blur into the traditional male activities of fighting, brawling, vanquishing, and dominating. Susan V. Donaldson speculates that "Strangely enough, though, status and even gender identity were never quite a sure thing for white men in the antebellum South, where personal and social standing rested largely on the good opinions of one's fellows. If white men were to maintain their position among men and above women and black slaves, they had to prove their mettle over and over again, in duels and in appallingly brutal, eye-gouging brawls."[18] In the Old Southwest, women are the rough and ready equals of their backwoods beaux. "Jule Sawyer was thar, and jist annexed to her rite off, and a mity nice fite it was. Jule carried enuf har from hir hed to make a sifter, and striped and checked her face nice, like a partridge-net hung on a white fence. . . . Jule licked her gall, that's some comfort, and I suppose a feller cant *always* win!" (*AQR* 89, 90) Some women are tougher than their men and, as wildcats, explode traditional stereotypes and command admiration. But Harris limits these women and their power; stereotypically, Jule pulls out her opponent's hair, and the narrator puts a stop to Jule's aggression before anything more serious occurs. Significantly, the narrator reasserts his complete control over his female: "so when I thought Jule had given her a plenty I pulled hir off and put hir in a good humour by given hir as many kisses as would cover a barn door" (*AQR* 89). Playing with the image of the barn door, we might imagine that Harris is slamming the door shut on this lively lady, barring it tightly with the forced sexuality of unsought-for male kisses. The sketch seems to make a place for the momentary expression of male uneasiness about female aggressiveness—Are women like Jule more manly than the vernacular narrator? Are they more manly than the story's male readers?—yet rejects that possibility by concluding with the male narrator again in apparent control: "I'm agoin to marry Jule, I swar I am, and *sich* a cross! Think of a locomotive and a cotton gin! Who! whoopee!" (*AQR* 90). The need to control Jule, the representation of himself as a manly (consuming) locomotive and Jule as a female (productive) machine, and the disintegration of his style into a set of whoops seems forced and artificial. Jule's energy, once unleashed, creates male anxiety and stylistic chaos.

In "Going to Bed Before a Young Lady," Stephen A. Douglas writes of his own early misadventures. As a young man of political ambition, he found himself one midnight still talking with the daughter of his rural host. As in "Life and Manners," the narrator is superior in language to the vernacular characters, yet he likewise describes appreciatively an image of country beauty: "Did you ever see a Venus in linsey-woolsey? . . . Then you shall see Serena L——s. They call her the 'White Plover': seventeen:—plump as a pigeon, and smooth as a persimmon" (*AQR* 53). However, despite the narrator's voyeuristic images, she is no passive, tasty morsel for male consumption. Though she appears an idealized, titled, public, sexual object, he, ironically, becomes the passive object of her acute, unflinching, all-too-public examination. His difficulty is how to remain a gentleman and yet undress for bed. "How the devil, said I to myself, soliloquizing the first night I slept there, am I to go to bed before this young lady?" (*AQR* 53). Douglas casts himself as the focus of Serena's humor, for "those large jet eyes seemed to dilate and grow brighter as the blaze of the wood fire died away." (*AQR* 54). Serena has Douglas treed. "Bright as the sun, the merry minx talked on. It was portentously obvious to me at last, that she had determined to outsit me. By repeated spasmodic efforts, my coat, waistcoat, cravat, boots and socks were brought off. During the process, my beautiful neighbor talked to me with unaverted eyes, and with that peculiar kind of placidity employed by painters to imbody their idea of the virgin" (*AQR* 53–54). She obviously enjoys his discomfort, delighting in her power to prolong and intensify the moment. As Douglas sees, part of the story's humor derives from the reversal of traditional gender roles; conventionally, it is the female body that must remain hidden and modestly protected from the male gaze. "Certain it was, she seemed rather pleased with her speculations; for when I arose from a stooping posture finally, wholly disencumbered of cloth, I noticed mischievous shadows playing about the corners of her mouth. . . . 'Mr. Douglas,' she observed 'you have got a mighty small chance of legs there'" (*AQR* 55). He, rather than the "White Plover," has become the object of sexual humor. The male has been disassembled into a disparate pile of physical characteristics, reduced in a cutting phrase to "a mighty small chance of legs." That he perceives Serena to have been unmalicious (if not unmanipulative) he demonstrates when he replies to the first-person narrator's question: "But was the young lady modest?" The question communicates a prurient desire, as if the narrator is trying to recast Serena as a wanton woman. "Modest, sir!—there is not in Illinois a more modest, or more sensible girl! (*AQR* 56). Stereotyped sexual roles have been inverted, but Serena has not been corrupted. This woman retains her femininity and resists the objectification of male sexual desire. Serena is a powerful female, though she seems to gain this power by performing the male gaze. Can she put on male power without donning male perversity?

"Going to Bed" concludes with a parallel sketch of a Missouri politician. Expressing his concern about disrobing before the four daughters of the family that is hosting him, the candidate is able to disrobe successfully after his matronly hostess tells the gals to turn their backs to him. And, "stranger, as you aint used to us, you'd better *kiver up* till the *gals* undress, hadn't you?" (*AQR* 58). In a much more traditional manner, the candidate steals "sly glances" at the young women, while his hostess tells him that "You can un*kiver* now, stranger; I'm *married folks,* and you aint afeared o' me, I reckon!" (*AQR* 59). Without putting too much pressure on her comment, we might perceive a certain amount of fear expressed explicitly and implicitly. To be a male exposed to female scrutiny creates the fear of being unmanned, especially when the females are exuberantly adolescent and the male is significantly more mature; the usually dominant male becomes the passive, vulnerable object of their gaze, and the candidate's public authority is deflated. In addition, the candidate in a sense regains his youth and his vigor by peeping on the young women like a boy: "with regard to the 'gals,' he declares that his half-raised curiosity inspired the most tormenting dreams of *mermaids* that he ever experienced" (*AQR* 59). Hélène Cixous is more direct in her speculations about male desire: "Undeniably (we even verify it at our own expense—but also to our amusement), it's their business to let us know when they're getting a hard-on, so that we'll assure them (we the maternal mistresses of their little pocket signifier) that they still can, that it's still there."[19] Both stories in "Going to Bed" convey male insecurities about male potency, male importance, and male attractiveness, and most surely about female sexual appetite, female self-sufficiency, and female ridicule. The men who read these sketches will not sleep soundly in their gendered cultural superiority but will have "the most tormenting dreams." Once cultural categories have been destabilized, it is difficult to return them to their original positions of relationship.

With "India Rubber Pills," "Cupping on the Sternum," and "Somebody in My Bed," there is no doubt that women are deliberately victimized. The "tall, lanky factory girl" (*AQR* 152) of "India Rubber" scoops and swallows pills she fashions of the coat-covering compound she has purchased to cure her cough. The humor turns on the superiority of the male druggist and the male reader to the girl and her sister workers. They are ignorant of the use of India rubber, thinking it literally medicinal. The reader laughs at the girl because he does not see her as human; that she is a young, female, factory worker intensifies the social gulf between her and the reader, perversely increasing her objectification. She is, as it were, a type of ignorance. In "Cupping," the situation has a greater complexity, for both the black female patient and the white male medical student are ignorant of the meaning of the term "sternum" and assume that the blister should be applied to the woman's stern. Again, the reader is meant to enjoy his position of superiority; again, the woman is similarly dehumanized, the pain and embarrassment she feels perversely adding to his pleasure. That the patient is a black woman who must present her naked posterior to the white medical student for a painful surgical procedure that is both unnecessary and ineffectual suggests a malicious amusement—misogynistic and racist—with which the modern reader feels extreme discomfort.[20] This effect is reinforced with an accompanying illustration depicting a cowering, passive black woman in her bed being menaced by a towering, fully-clothed Roger Chillingworth figure clutching what appears to be a medical book (the symbol of male authority) and standing before a chair on which are his medical cups (the symbolic instruments of male dominance). To increase the reader's amusement, on the wall over the woman's bed is tacked a crayon drawing of a black funeral procession. Without question, the humor in both sketches depends on the exploitation of women. As cultural artifacts, the sketches confirm conventional stereotypes of male superiority and female inferiority.

U.J. Jones's "Somebody in My Bed" contains another striking example of the woman as victim in Southwestern humor. It is also a trick upon the audience, a story that raises pornographic expectations that it then refuses to satisfy. In part because of its apparently explicit nature, it is a story told by a doctor, who is introduced to the reader by the frame-narrator, keeping the action at three removes: narrator, doctor-as-narrator, and retold story. The doctor recounts his "adventure with a woman at my boarding house," an establishment "in which there were no females, but the landlady and an old coloured cook" (*AQR* 169). Disrobing for the night, the doctor notices a woman's frock, petticoats, stockings, and shoes near his bed. In it he discovers "a young girl—I should say an angel, of about eighteen." (*AQR* 170). In careful stages he describes the steps by which he begins to examine the intruder, appreciating her hair, neck, shoulders, bust, and waist, all the while working up his audience (most noticeably the captain) to a crescendo of excitement: "'She had on a night dress . . . softly I opened the first two buttons—. . . And then, ye gods! what a sight to gaze upon—a Hebe—

pshaw! words fail! Just then—. . . I thought that I was taking a mean advantage of her, so I covered her up, seized my coat and boots, and went and slept in another room!' 'It's a lie!' shouted the excited captain, jumping up and kicking over his chair. 'IT'S A LIE!'" (*AQR* 170–71).

"Somebody in My Bed" operates on multiple levels. On one it can be seen as a classic smoking-room story that creates and then denies pornographic expectations. The captain's repeated shout—"It's a lie!"—suggests two interpretations: the doctor did not retire to leave the girl further unmolested; or, the doctor made up the whole story. In assembling *A Quarter Race,* William T. Porter substantively edited only this sketch, omitting from its collected form its final line: "'I'll bet you fifty dollars that you got into the bed!'"[21] In either version, the sketch's intended victims are the doctor's audience and the reader, who of course desire the crass fulfillment of their sexual fantasies. To focus on audience, "Somebody" is in large part about the delicate relationship between the doctor and the captain. Mary Crawford argues that for many men, humor is competitive—a way of demonstrating dominance over other males. To tell a successful joke, and especially to spring a successful joke on another male, is to gain status.[22] David Leverenz concludes in his analysis of Virginia gentry that "To rise higher up the ladder built on that floor of natural and human property, a man had to display his status publicly, particularly through rituals of virility. . . . Southern men lived their code of honor as a constant test of manhood."[23] In these terms, the story is actually a verbal duel between two men competing for social advantage. The doctor, a man whose profession is still an inchoate trade, attempts to trap the captain, a man with an ancient and honorable professional pedigree. That it is a symbolic hand of poker the story's omitted last line reinforces—it is all about betting, bluffing, calling, and winning. The doctor clearly wins this game, for the captain, on his eleventh repetition of the explicative "WELL!!!!" is brought to a point of symbolic climax: "'WELL!!!!' said the captain, hitching his chair right and left, and squirting his tobacco juice against the stove that it fairly fizzed again" (*AQR* 171). He has been had.

On another level, the story functions as an example of incongruity: the girl is where she should not be; she appears to have miraculously materialized in the male boardinghouse and have even dropped into the hands of the doctor for his own personal use. On yet another level, the tale projects an idealized image of female passivity. The "young girl" appears completely available; beautiful yet unconscious, voiceless and completely vulnerable, reduced to the status of a sexual object, she is the archetypal victim. In her influential essay, "The Laugh of the Medusa," Hélène Cixous argues that in men's writing, the female body "has been turned into the uncanny stranger on display—the ailing or dead figure, which so often turns out to be the nasty companion."[24] Jones projects in like manner a male fantasy of dominance and submission—without doubt, one that in its retelling within a community of men reinforces negative stereotypes. At its center is the female body—"ailing or dead," sleeping or unconscious—it matters little so long as the female body is unresisting and mute. The violence to the young angel—or at least the imaginative violence done to her image in the men's minds—suggests a latent hostility to or at least an ambivalence toward women. The men apparently need to violate her, perhaps because women—and women's bodies—seem powerful and threatening. At the expense of the girl's dignity, personality, and humanity, the sharing of the tale creates a community of men—participants, listeners, and readers.[25] Last, we should not entirely overlook that she is also simply a pornographic image, an autoerotic device that has no reality beyond the narrator's words. This is not to deny the voyeuristic quality of the sketch but to suggest that, like Hebe, this angel inadvertently excites the prurient passions of the doctor, the captain, and the (male) reader. That of course is to attribute a reality to her that the sketch strives for; her only reality, such as it is, is on the page and in the minds of the doctor, the captain, the author, and the reader. And we must note that the young angel's female body disrupts the world of the male boardinghouse merely by its static presence: the passive female body arouses the captain and displaces the doctor from his bed. Even a corpselike female body overpowers the "b'hoys."[26]

Given this sample of Old Southwestern humor, we can fairly confidently make several generalizations. First, women do figure in this male-oriented genre with more frequency than commonly supposed. Although fights, swaps, hunts, contests, and tricks are recurring subjects, dances, home life, social occasions, courtship, marriage, and male-female relationships do have a significant representation. Second, if we accept as a structural element of the genre the humor generated by the low language, circumstances, and behavior of vernacular characters, viewing their depiction as essentially gender-neutral, then of the eleven sketches from *The Big Bear* and *A Quarter Race* that feature women, only three overtly cast women as victims ("India Rubber," "Cupping on the Sternum," and "Somebody in My Bed"). Third, in five of these pieces—in "Life and Manners in Arkansas," "Dick Harlan's Tennessee Frolic," "A Murder Case in Mississippi," "French Without a Master," and "A Day at Sol Slice's"—both men and women are equally satirized. Fourth, in "Dick Harlan," "A Murder Case," and "Sol Slice's," women who appear initially as victims reestablish themselves as equal to or tougher than their male counterparts. Finally, in "Billy Warrick's Courtship and Wedding," "Going to Bed Before a Young Lady," and "Taking the Census," women are in control of the men they encounter. As opposed to other character types—Irish, French, Yankee, Indian, black—women are portrayed in Old Southwestern humor as occasionally getting the best of white men. And even when they are represented as objects of humor, they are far less likely than men to be presented as amusing because they are physically brutalized; with much less regularity are women's eyes poked out, their teeth pulled, their flesh clawed, their necks stretched, and their nudity roughly revealed. The Southwestern humorists, professional men of culture and breeding, might naturally uphold gentlemanly standards of decorum and might feel uncomfortable overtly victimizing women even in their accounts of backwoods behavior. A more speculative reason to explain why surprisingly little "outright misogyny" appears in these sketches might be that male writers could not admit to themselves the authority they believed women to possess over them (an authority that victimization of women would make explicit). If this is so, it would go a long way toward explaining the idealized portraits of innocent female beauty that appear as set pieces in so many sketches.

Southwestern humorists also recognized as part of their culture a separate sphere of social institutions over which women ruled. These writers understood that men in social situations entered what they perceived to be the province of women. Once they entered a dance, a woman's home, or pursued a relationship with a woman, they often imagined themselves as ignorant, isolated, and relatively helpless before the collective identity of women and submitted themselves to women's authority.[27] However, we should not imagine that women actually possessed such authority in nineteenth-century American society. These sketches seem to reveal an uncertainty on the part of their male authors of their own cultural authority. Do the authors of Southwestern humor admire not only the enthusiasm of their vernacular characters but also their overt manliness? And do these writers—and their book-buying readers, as well—feel a little anxious that backwoods gals like Sall and Jule are themselves more manly than they are? Eye gouging and cheek biting may be impolite, but they do suggest vitality and virility. Alternately, Southwestern humorists may have felt so secure in their manliness and confident in their superiority to women that they had little repressed hostility to express. Comfortable in and confident of their dominant role in reality, in their fiction, they could afford to allow women a certain degree of power and could play the fool themselves without losing actual control.

To think of Old Southwestern humor as portraying numerous women who rule a domestic sphere that overlaps and competes with the roustabout world of the "b'hoys" is, to say the least, novel. The conventional assessment of this genre—that Southwestern humor reveals a clear-cut pattern of male dominance and female submission—appears reductive. In specific circumstances, women do have power. If we consider the sketches in which women exercise authority—"Billy Warrick," "Going to Bed," "Taking the Census," "Dick Harlan," and "Sol Slice's"—we can see that in each case men enter a social situation. As they cross the threshold of a home, join a dance, or sit with a family in conversation, men empower women and acknowledge their authority. Or, they become feminized, or lose the confidence of collective male action. An extreme exception is "A Murder Case," in which Mrs. Granger invades the law court—clearly the jurisdiction of men—to drag her husband home. Mrs. Granger succeeds brilliantly in thwarting the constable and the male court, severely disrupting the patriarchal world. In "India Rubber" and "Cupping on the Sternum," women alternately enter the public world of professional men and suffer the consequences. That public world is constructed specifically through the authority accumulated by professional accreditation to reinforce and enhance male superiority. Finally, the angelic girl who graces the bed of the doctor in "Somebody in My Bed" is obviously out of place, isolated and unaware of her predicament, stranded in the boardinghouse of men. She is anything but real, a male fantasy in sharp contrast to the spirited women who populate these volumes.

It is clear that women form an essential part of the tradition of Southwestern humor. They are presented most often in familial, domestic, or social situations, contexts in which the men feel alien or unsure; as a result, the women have and use power over men. When Southwestern writers place women in the male domain, women become susceptible to victimization and to its corollary, idealization. Analysis of the roles and functions of women in other key Southwestern texts—Augustus B. Longstreet's *Georgia Scenes* (1835), William Tappan Thompson's *Major Jones's Courtship* (1843), Henry Clay Lewis's *Odd Leaves from the Life of a Louisiana "Swamp Doctor"* (1843), Johnson J. Hooper's *Some Adventures of Captain Simon Suggs* (1845), Joseph G. Baldwin's *Flush Times of Alabama and Mississippi* (1853), and George W. Harris's *Sut Lovingood's Yarns* (1867)—can only add to our understanding of Southwestern humor and antebellum culture. What appears true from this limited sample is that Southwestern humorists are not simply misogynists but more complex creatures, writers who regularly portray women who seem to control a distinct world in which conventional perceptions of male superiority and cultural dominance prove illusory, or who are by definition powerful enough to disrupt the patriarchal world and its conventionally gendered roles.

As so often happens in Southwestern humor, the reader's laughter echoes that of the characters' and signals a destabilization of cultural conventions. More often than formerly thought, the comedy disrupts the patriarchal world and radically critiques cultural constructions of gender. Although their sketches certainly reflect masculine cultural ambivalence toward women, the Southwestern humorists often picture the relationships between men and women as complicated phenomena that are as intense, as exhilarating, and as satisfying as hunting a bear, fighting a "hoss," or tricking a Frenchman. No matter how much or how often they liquor up, the men in these tales ultimately cannot seem to resolve the anxieties released by the appearance of powerful women. In this sense, Southwestern humor is even more radically subversive than its authors intended.

Notes

1. William T. Porter, ed., *The Big Bear of Arkansas, and Other Sketches* (1845; rpt. New York: AMS Press, 1973), 15. Future references to tales in this collection will be from this edition, page numbers noted parenthetically in the text.

2. Constance M. Rourke, *American Humor: A Study of the National Character* (New York: Harcourt Brace Jovanovich, 1931, 1959), 69.

3. M. Thomas Inge, ed. *The Frontier Humorists: Critical Views* (Hamden, Conn.: Archon, 1975), 5.

4. Walter Blair, ed. *Native American Humor (1800–1900)* (1937; rev. ed. San Francisco: Chandler Publishing, 1960), 82.

5. Quoted in Lorne Fienberg, "Spirit of the Times," in *American Humor and Comic Periodicals,* ed. David E.E. Sloane (New York: Greenwood Press, 1987), 272.

6. Kenneth S. Lynn, *Mark Twain and Southwestern Humor* (Boston: Little, Brown, 1959), 64.

7. In "The Big Bear of Arkansas," the only female figure represented appears as the

result of the male Big Bear's supernatural powers, a transformation that allows him to escape, leaving in his place the dead carcass of a female (castrated? powerless? passive?) bear.

8. Nancy A. Walker, *A Very Serious Thing: Women's Humor and American Culture* (Minneapolis: Univ. of Minnesota Press, 1988), 12.

9. Zita Dresner, "Women's Humor," in *Humor in America: A Research Guide to Genres and Topics,* ed. Lawrence E. Mintz (New York: Greenwood, 1988), 138.

10. Linda A. Morris, *Women Vernacular Humorists in Nineteenth-Century America: Ann Stephens, Francis Whitcher, and Marietta Holly* (New York: Garland, 1988), 18.

11. Alfred Habegger, "Nineteenth-Century American Humor: Easygoing Males, Anxious Ladies, and Penelope Lapham," *PMLA* 91 (Oct. 1976): 884.

12. Neil Schmitz, "Forms of Regional Humor," in *Columbia Literary History of the United States,* ed. Emory Elliot (New York: Columbia Univ. Press, 1988), 316.

13. At the lowest level of humor, the author does disparage women in his wordplay, almost offhandedly: a mother is a *mare,* while sister is a *sewer* and *sour.* "French Without a Master" appears in William T. Porter, ed. *A Quarter Race in Kentucky, and Other Sketches* (1847; rpt. New York: AMS Press, 1973), 100. Future references to tales in this collection will be from this edition, page numbers noted parenthetically in the text.

14. In Anne Goodwyn Jones and Susan V. Donaldson, eds. *Haunted Bodies: Gender and Southern Texts* (Charlottesville: Univ. of Virginia Press, 1997), 6. Other recent interesting humor studies include Gail Finney, ed. *Look Who's Laughing: Studies in Gender and Comedy* (Newark: Gordon and Breach, 1994); Jeannie B. Thomas, *Featherless Chickens, Laughing Women, and Serious Stories* (Charlottesville, Va.: Univ. of Virginia Press, 1997); Karen L. Kilcup, ed. *Nineteenth-Century American Women Writers: A Critical Reader* (Malden, Mass.: Blackwell Publishers, 1998); and David E.E. Sloane, ed. *New Directions in American Humor* (Tuscaloosa: Univ. of Alabama Press, 1998).

15. "Laughter as Feminine Power in *The Color Purple* and *A Question of Silence"* in Regina Barreca, ed. *New Perspectives on Women and Comedy* (Newark: Gordon and Breach: 1992), 196.

16. There is undeniably some cultural anxiety about race expressed in this sketch beneath the overt humor resulting from empowering an Irish woman. See Susan V. Donaldson's fine discussion in "Gender, Race, and Allen Tate's Profession of Letters in the South," in *Haunted Bodies,* 492–518.

17. To my undergraduate research assistant, J. Belle Lenz, I am indebted for the insights in this paragraph on the persistence of female powerlessness despite the adoption of aggressive male behaviors.

18. Donaldson, "Gender, Race, and Allen Tate's Profession of Letters in the South," 495–96.

19. "The Laugh of the Medusa," rpt. in *Critical Theory Since 1965,* eds. Hazard Adams and Leroy Searle (Tallahassee: Univ. Presses of Florida, Florida State Univ. Press, 1986), 318.

20. Race in Southwestern humor also deserves serious analysis. As I noted in the text, I found myself very uncomfortable with the explicit racism in "Cupping on the Sternum." See Donaldson, "Gender, Race, and Allen Tate's Profession of Letters in the South," 496, and David Leverenz, "Poe and Gentry Virginia: Provincial Gentleman, Textual Aristocrat, Man of the Crowd" in *Haunted Bodies,* 91.

21. See Norris Yates, *William T. Porter and the Spirit of the Times: A Study of the Big Bear School of Humor* (Baton Rouge: Louisiana State Univ. Press, 1967), 83–86.

22. See "Just Kidding: Gender and Conversational Humor" in *New Perspectives on Women and Comedy,* esp. 32–33.

23. "Poe and Gentry Virginia," 84.

24. "The Laugh of the Medusa," 312.

25. See Caroline Gebhard's analysis of male relationships in "Reconstructing Southern Manhood: Race, Sentimentality, and Camp in the Plantation Myth," especially her discussion of Eve Kosofsky Sedgwick's "triangular structure of desire," in which "female bodies only exist to serve or to connect men" (in *Haunted Bodies,* 134).

26. This revised essay has profited greatly from a reading by my colleague Lynne Dickson Bruckner, who suggested that even this corpselike representation of the feminine overpowers men.

27. In contrast, the aside told by "'Old Sense' of Arkansas" (*AQR* 145–46) of a wife beaten for adultery suggests the need for patriarchal culture to enforce its dominance over females who violate the cultural conventions surrounding marriage. Despite the age-old male fear of being cuckolded, the narrator condemns the punishment as too severe—an easy condemnation to make as a male after the fact.

4

Contesting the Boundaries of Race and Gender in Old Southwestern Humor

Ed Piacentino

As has been generally acknowledged, the humor of the Old Southwest has often featured African American and female characters but most typically in secondary roles. And the portrayal of blacks and women has usually reaffirmed popular nineteenth-century sociocultural attitudes and assumptions regarding race and gender, thereby sustaining the marginalization of women and blacks. Still, there are a number of tales and sketches in southern frontier humor that seem to challenge, intentionally or unconsciously, the racial and gender status quo. Granted, the authors of southern antebellum humorous pieces were typically conservative gentlemen of Whig persuasion, who not only publicly supported the patriarchal and proslavery stances of the region, but who in doing so also wrote exclusively for a male audience that enjoyed patrician status. Even so, for reasons unknown, the antebellum backwoods humorist would occasionally slip from behind the mask, creating situations and portraying characters who through their words and/or actions seemed to exhibit distinctly human attributes. And these qualities did not always coincide with the sociopolitical dictates of the Old South, which tended to support stereotypical notions concerning race and gender. Yet in general Southwestern humor, according to Stephen Railton, there "was a counterattack upon the spirit of times, a deeply rooted motivated repudiation of the contemporary surge of democratic impulses most conveniently represented by Jacksonianism" (100). Though writings that challenge racial and gender assumptions, as some of the Southwestern sketches do, may seem subversive, actually they are not as radical as they appear to be. While selected tales and sketches of John S. Robb, Hardin Taliaferro, Francis James Robinson, George Washington Harris, Sol Smith, and Henry Clay Lewis sometimes deviate from the proscriptive racial and gender politics of their times, it is unlikely that the issues raised in the portraiture of blacks and women would have been offensive to their contemporary readers. Generally, the humorous manner in which these writers handled their material and the usually safe, non-offensive context in which they treated it often camouflaged or provided a buffer or safeguard for what they were doing.

Admittedly, African American characters appear with some frequency in old Southwestern humor. Even though virtually every humorist of this school included some black characters, most often their portrayal never transcended the level of stereotypes. In 1958, James H. Penrod, in commenting on black portraiture in southern frontier humor, generally and accurately claimed that these humorists "emphasized the stereotyped traits that have prevailed in the minds of Americans for generations" ("Minority Groups" 121) and that the roles of blacks "were those of comic characters in support of the principal actors" (128). Perhaps the two most prevalent black stereotypes featured in antebellum southern humor are the loyal contented slave and the comic black. Such stereotypes, which Seymour L. Gross terms the "fantasy construct" (25), are, he further points out, "marked by exaggeration or omission" and tend to emphasize "the Negro's divergence from white Anglo-Saxon norms, and are consciously or unconsciously pressed into the service of justifying racial proscription" (10).

John S. Robb, printer, reporter, and editor and best known for his association with the *St. Louis Reveille* and as author of humorous sketches collected in *Streaks of Squatter Life and Far-West Scenes* (1847), made significant overtures toward contesting the boundary of race. One such sketch is "The Pre-Emption Right," which features a black slave named Sam, whom critics often simply dismiss as an embodiment of the devoted servant stereotype.[1] Yet, whether Robb intended it or not, he portrays Sam as somewhat transcending this stereotype, as being a human being with compassion and capability, even though the author uses various means to attempt to mask this. Though Robb initially portrays Sam as conforming to the contented and loyal slave, "who was at once his master's attendant and friend" (118), he adds that "the bonds of servitude were . . . moulded [*sic*] into links of friendship and affection, securing to them a feeling of confidence in their lonely habitation in the wilderness" (118). Sam performs two humane and compassionate acts during the course of the tale.

The first of these is when, without being commanded to do so, Sam defends a woman from her physically abusive husband. Indeed a noble gesture, an act beyond the obligatory service to his master, Sam's behavior is more than a chivalrous response to a woman in distress; it is an unselfish display of genuine concern for a person in need of assistance. Expectedly, Robb tries to discount what Sam has done, and in the process even manages through the words of Dick Kelsy, Sam's master, to reduce the significance of the slave's individuality as an African American. Therefore, rather than acknowledge Sam's personhood, Kelsy half humorously tells his slave: "'Sam . . . *you're* a nigger, but thar's more real white man under your black skin than could be found in an acre of such varmints as that *sucker*'" (123). Because of Sam's magnanimity, his master extends to Sam obligatory praise—but not as a black man. Moreover, in what seems a rhetorical gesture, both for his slave and perhaps for his reader, Kelsy adds, "'Give me your fist, old fellar; while Dick Kelsy's got anythin' in this world, you shall share it!'" (123) Kelsy's choice of words seems to diminish Sam's personal dignity and act of kindness, because what he says attributes whatever qualities the slave possesses to his whiteness. For this reason, his master's words seem gratuitous, given that Robb's gesture seems to be done to reaffirm white superiority in accordance with the apologetics of slavery. In doing this, Robb attempts to placate his reader, who may fear that the author has overstepped his bounds in his portrayal of Sam's humanity.

The second occasion reflecting the slave's genuine compassion occurs when he actually saves Dick Kelsy's life after Kelsy, while homeward bound, has been stabbed by the same unfriendly squatter who earlier had assaulted his wife. Even though Robb foreshadows this event early in the tale, noting that Kelsy and Sam "had imbibed a lasting affection for each other,—each would have freely shed blood in the other's defence" [*sic*] (118), still one gets the impression that Sam's care of his master is not something that he feels obliged to do because Dick is his master. Rather, it seems an act motivated out of sincere kindness and concern for a fellow human being. In describing Sam's administering first aid to his master's wounds, Robb writes: "The faithful negro had staunched the blood, and applied every restorative his rude knowledge could devise. . . . The natural strength of the patient, together with Sam's careful nursing, soon restored him to his legs" (125). In saving his master's life, Sam becomes more than a faithful retainer, however; he shows that he is responsible and fully capable of making right decisions without being commanded or forced to do so.

In short, what Robb has done here is to create a black character who displays through his humanness a complexity that exceeds the limits of stereotyped portraiture. But at the same time, he seems to play on his reader's penchant for sentiment and uses the good-heartedness and other-directedness reflected in Sam's action to accomplish this purpose. Even so, Robb fails to sustain Sam at this level of characterization. And perhaps for reasons of political and social expediency, concerning the moral acceptance of black inferiority at this time, he again casts Sam in the mold of a stereotype—this time as a slave who has no individualizing identity. Thus at the end of the tale, Sam, who becomes a mere extension of his master, expresses great delight, praising Dick Kelsy's triumph over the despicable squatter who not only tried to kill him but also to cheat him of his land claim: "'Dat's Massa Dick's signature to his land claim—*dat is*!'" (132)

An even better illustration of a humorist who wrote several sketches that undercut the racial politics of the antebellum period, but within an apparent innocuous perspective, is in Hardin Taliaferro, Baptist minister, journalist, editor of religious periodicals, and author of *Fisher's River (North Carolina) Scenes and Characters* (1859), a collection of backwoods humorous sketches. This is seen in Taliaferro's portraiture of the Reverend Charles Gentry, the only black character to whom the author gives a narrative voice in his book *Fisher's River*. In fact, in the authorial frame to the Reverend Gentry's two folk sermons, Taliaferro displays no condescension or sarcasm in introducing Gentry, an actual slave preacher in Surry County, North Carolina, Taliaferro's birthplace and the setting for many of the humorous sketches in *Fisher's River*. In presenting Gentry, Taliaferro is mainly complimentary, and in the frame, he singles out the slave preacher for such attributes as goodness, cleverness, originality, and the "force of his cataract voice and rail-mauling gestures, if not by argument" (187). Coupled with this, Taliaferro shows respect for and understanding of the revisionist slant of Gentry's theology. In so doing, he closes the frame acknowledging, if only somewhat offhandedly, that Gentry's theory about the origins of the black and white races is as sound as anybody else's: "When men leave the plain teachings of the Bible and go into vague speculations, one man's hypothesis is nearly as good as another's" (187).

Gentry's two folk sermons, "The Origin of Whites" and "Jonah and the Whale," contain brief introductions rendered mainly in formal literary English, the familiar strategy the Southwestern humorist employed to create comic distance for himself and his audience from the vernacular voice and the free-wheeling subject matter of the tale. The illusion that Taliaferro creates for his audience of presumably white readers is that of overhearing a black preacher deliver—in a seemingly deadpan manner—sermons in dialect before a congregation of black faithful. While the doctrines Gentry espouses clearly deviate from the more widely accepted and orthodox beliefs contained in the Bible, such distortions afforded Taliaferro's readers amusement and at the same time enhanced their sense of racial superiority. For example, Gentry's inventive views, to quote him, that "'Adam, Abel, Seth, was all ob 'um black as jet'" (Taliaferro 188), clearly challenge beliefs regarding white racial origins that many conservative white southerners and even some northerners of the 1850s, who accepted the inferiority of blacks, would likely have held. Given the language Gentry uses to articulate his radical position and the associations of ignorance, illiteracy, inferiority, and primitiveness that African American dialect likely evoked in the minds of a white audience, his ideas probably would have been comfortably dismissed as ridiculous but also entertaining, and as such, amusing and non-offensive.

Yet underlying the stereotyped associations the black dialect had conditioned nineteenth-century white readers to image is a different perspective that probably would have been noticed and appreciated only by a black slave audience who listened to sermons like Gentry's. From the slaves' perspective, what the black preacher says, and even more so *how* he says it, seems comically original and liberating—an expression of an imaginative, yet subversive, black folk viewpoint. Rather than relying on abstract and intellectualized theories concerning the origin of whites, Gentry uses the familiar story from Genesis of Cain's murder of his brother Abel, but enlivens it with a humorously new twist, involving a dialogue between God and Cain. Gentry's God is anthropomorphic, very down to earth in his gestures and language. And the verbal exchanges between Cain and God, as the black slave preacher fabricates them, seem natural, lyrically repetitive, and concretely visual: "Cain he kill his brudder Abel wid a great big club—he walk-in-stick—and God cum to Cain, and say, 'Cain! Where is dy brudder Abel?' Cain he pout out de lip, and say, 'I don't know; what ye axin' me fur? I ain't my brudder Abel's keeper.' De Lord he gits in airnest, and stomps on de ground, and say, 'Cain! you Cain! whar is dy brudder Abel? I say Cain! whar is dy brudder?' Cain he turn white as bleach cambric in de face, and de whole race ob Cain dey bin white ebber since." (188–89)

In "Jonah and the Whale," Gentry uses an even more expansive, flexible range of language conventions than he did in "The Origin of Whites." Yet this practice would have made an entirely different impression on untutored slaves than on white readers. To Taliaferro's contemporary southern white readers (and to many northern readers as well), such strategies as repetition and incongruous comparisons coming from the mouth of an uneducated black preacher would be taken as entertaining and would have reinforced the notion of black inferiority, thereby diminishing the image of Reverend Gentry as well as the credibility of what he says. The black slave's reaction would have probably been somewhat different. Consider that in Gentry's account of the Jonah story, he creates amusing visual images by employing vivid incongruous comparisons. For example, in Gentry's words, "'de Lord he raise a mighty whirlygust, and de ship he rock to and fro like a drunkard man,'" (190) or "'But bless the Lord! whar Jonah? A great big fish cum up and lick him down like salt—hardly a bug moufful fur sich a big whoppin feller'" (190–91). Also, in Gentry's version of this familiar Bible story, we find a dialogue between Jonah and the whale, featuring the whale's comical repetitive response to Jonah's question, "'Hush yer mouf!'" (191) or a similar variation. It is likely that the black slaves would have felt comfortable with Gentry's sermons because they were consciously tailored to their backgrounds and needs and employed folk language that included familiar references they could understand and with which they could identify. The sermons also gave the black preacher the opportunity to discover and express his own voice and in so doing to create an original text rather than one endorsed by the white man. Under the surface of Gentry's lively and inventive accounts, "The Origin of Whites" and "Jonah and the Whale," one may find Taliaferro's affirmation and appreciation of the black man's capability as a storyteller, and at the same time one may observe the slave preacher as a formidable solidifying and influential force in the black community.

A third example of transgressive black portraiture in old Southwestern humor that discernibly challenges, but within relatively safe bounds, the prevailing racial attitudes and assumptions of the antebellum South is Francis James Robinson's "'Old Jack' C—,"a tale based on a real-life character who was a hotel waiter in Madison, Georgia (Cohen and Dillingham 377). More so than Robb's "The Pre-Emption Right," Taliaferro's "The Origin of Whites" and "Jonah and the Whale," or any other tale or sketch of southern backwoods humor with which I am familiar, Robinson's "'Old Jack' C—" portrays a slave as the central character and prominently keeps him in the foreground almost continuously throughout the sketch. Near the outset, Robinson describes Jack as being "possessed of quick perceptive faculties; a lover of the ridiculous; cunning and smart" (85), in short, gifted with qualities that elevate him to a distinctively human level and that enable him to function in a slave-holding society where the black man was regarded as contentedly inferior and subordinate. Yet even after celebrating Jack's attributes, Robinson, perhaps realizing he may have been too generous in his initial characterization of Jack, abruptly alters this image, reducing Jack to the restrictive stereotype of the loyal and devoted slave:

> To the superficial observer, Jack has the appearance of being too impudent for a *slave*, but those who know him best, and who can thus better

> appreciate his eccentricities by this knowledge, know him to be an obedient and industrious servant; contented in his station in life, and with not the shadow of a wish to change it. Attached to his master's family, and always acting—not as a mere servant, but as a person deeply interested in all that concerns them—none can be more gay and lively when pleasure is the order of the day; and should sorrow bring clouds, none evince more disinterested grief than *Jack*—thus ready "to laugh with those who laugh, and weep with those who weep"—though, no doubt, like all of his race, he'd rather "be merry than sad." (86)

This depiction suggests that Jack possesses no individualizing identity, his personhood being essentially an extension or shadow of the white people who own him. After somewhat crossing the boundaries of racial prejudice in his early description of Jack, Robinson, a staunch and outspoken advocate of slavery, seems to have realized that such an overture might antagonize his white readers, especially those who supported slavery and believed in the inferiority of the black man. Perhaps as a gesture of reassurance, Robinson interjects the stereotype and then offers an obligatory apologia espousing the benevolence of slavery: "Without a care for to-morrow, who but a fool, would sigh and cry to-day? With food and raiment, and comforts of all other kinds necessary, regular hours to work, to eat, to sleep and to play, there is not on the broad earth a happier set of mortals than the Uncle Tom's and Aunt Philis's of the South—the lies and slanders of the fanatics of New and Old England to the contrary notwithstanding!" (87) Robinson even echoes the principle of the noblesse oblige, observing that "it is a strong evidence of the humanity of slave-owners, that they every day become more and more rigorous in the exercise of their rights over the person of the slave. Thus endeavoring, by retaining him in the position designed him to occupy, to prevent the certain degradation and often total destruction of the human beings intrusted [*sic*] to his keeping by an all-wise Providence, should they once pass Mason and Dixon's line" (87). This kind of intrusive polemic was common in antebellum southern writing, especially among writers who felt compelled to defend the South's "peculiar institution."

Despite Robinson's editorializing, interestingly and importantly when he returns to his sketch, his subsequent portrayal of Jack contradicts the stereotype. His portraiture of the slave shows Jack's enviable capability to manipulate white people through verbal wit and cunning. Though many of Jack's interactions with white people are tempered by humor, still the author's treatment of his black slave does not really conform to the notion that his character is inferior or submissive. One of the more interesting anecdotes featuring Jack's ability to dupe a white man focuses on a character named Wills, a Yankee tenderfoot of Dutch extraction who comes to Georgia from Pennsylvania and is employed by Jack's master as a bartender and superintendent. Jack takes advantage of Wills' naiveté, providing the Dutchman with a gun that he has deliberately overloaded with powder to kill a cow. Yet when Wills, who has not the slightest clue that Jack has duped him, fires the gun, the recoil knocks him down. In describing Wills' humiliation, the victim of a prank a slave has skillfully engineered, Robinson writes: "The musket was uninjured, but it had *pirouetted* through the air in imitation of a *French danseuse*, as it passed from *Wills* to *Jack*. The latter soon picked himself up, more scared than hurt, and assisted poor *Wills* to the house, taking good care as he went along to attribute the catastrophe to *Will* [*sic*] *awkwardness in holding the gun!* never once alluding to the outrageous load he had placed in it" (92). While Jack's act emphatically shows his superiority to a white man—suggesting that Jack is smarter and shrewder than Wills—still the details of the anecdote make clear that the victim is not a white southerner, but an inept northerner. I would argue that what Robinson seems to be doing here in using an outsider as a victim of a slave's prank is Yankee baiting, and thereby possibly a gesture for appeasing his southern white readers.

But as "'Old Jack' C—" continues, Robinson becomes more daring in his portraiture of Jack's attributes, especially his ingenuity and ability to dupe white men, both reliable indicators of his superiority. In a confrontation with an overzealous white clergyman who reproves Jack for purchasing a bottle of whiskey and urges him to give up drinking, Jack shows his intelligence and quick wit by spontaneously contriving a simple but clever comeback, an amusing justification for imbibing spirits: "'Well, mas John, de fact is, I been thinking ober de matter, an' weighing ob de subject myself, sir: an' hab come to dis conclusion; whisky serves my friends very badly, makes 'em fight an' quarrel, lie an' steal, makes man an' wife quarrel and fight, an' I'm gittin old as you say; *darfore, sir, I b'lieves it to be my duty to distroy as much of it as I kin while I lib!*'" (Robinson 94). Again, Jack triumphs; he gets in the last word, this time using his knowledge of human nature to forge in colorful dialect a well-timed, witty, and hilarious response to upstage and ridicule the self-righteous and meddlesome clergyman. As Robinson writes, "This was a *settler*; and our parson turned away, while Jack, with his peculiar wink and smirk of the face, checked over his success in flooring his antagonist" (94). It seems doubtful many of Robinson's white readers, southern or otherwise, would have found Jack's retort to be offensive. The humorous dynamics of the anecdote reinforce Jack's outward pose of simplicity and good-natured outlook on life. In fact, many of Robinson's readers probably felt that the victim deserved the verbal put-down he receives. Furthermore, some of the apparent boldness of Jack's action is also diminished by the slave's dialect, which reinforces his apparent inferiority in the white reader's mind, and his witty punch line. Both the slave's primitive dialect and the well-timed comical comeback work effectively together in defusing the potential subversive nature of what of he says.

One other instance of Jack besting a southern white man occurs when the slave again, in his usual good-humored way, astutely exercises his verbal wit. This time Jack's victim is an itinerant peddler, a con artist of sorts popularly known as the "Razor Strop man." Significantly, the "Razor Strop man," Robinson insinuates, is disreputable since the wares he tries to sell are not what he promotes them as being. One strategy the peddler customarily uses as he hawks his razor straps through the streets of a town is loudly and repeatedly to exclaim, "*a few more left of the same sort!*"

(95). Later the peddler stops at the hotel for dinner where Jack served as a waiter. And Jack, in serving the peddler his food, turns entertainer, humorously mocking him publicly by presenting him with a single waffle and exclaiming: "'Master, have a square-toe'd warfle, sir? Don't be scared, sir, there's a *few more left in the kitchen of the same sort*!'" (95). Rather than to retaliate angrily or violently to Jack's prank, "Razor Strop" reacts in a good-natured manner, with an occasional "fit of uncontrollable laughter" (96), and even admits that Jack has gotten the best of him, another indication of Jack's capability and superior talents. Jack, Robinson observes, continues to triumph in bouts of verbal wit with the peddler. Yet the crowning touch in Jack's display of verbal ingenuity at the expense of "Razor Strop" takes place at the tea table when finding a "cambric needle" on his plate, he inquires of the slave "'what does this mean?'" (96). Relying on some well-timed wordplay, Jack responds: "'Well, Master, I thought you needed *sharpening up*, and ef you would eat de needle, perhaps in de morning you hab more *pint* about you, for I notice you gitting bery *dull*!'" (96). As the narrator points out, while the peddler had "*gulled* a good many '*white folks*' throughout the country with his 'wonderful, magical, tragical razor strops'" (96), he is unsuccessful in getting Jack to buy one. Though Jack wears the mask of a jokester and punster throughout this sequence, he actually shows himself to be keenly perceptive and practically smart—key weapons in his arsenal in humiliating the peddler. And in so doing, he not only recognizes that this white man is a fraud but independently opts to take advantage of him through calculated verbal wit and humor. Craftily delivering a series of humorous puns in rapid succession, Jack launches his final assault on the itinerant peddler's already badly damaged integrity. In Jack's words to the peddler, he exclaims: "'Dat de strop make *everything so sharp, even to the man who sold 'em*! he was 'fraid ob de consequences to himself!' 'De fact is,' continued Jack, 'dem *strops* makes heap o' people cut' dere eye-teeth jis by lying on a table in de rooms dey sleeps in, an' I'm 'fraid dey'd make me *cut* a whole new sett!'" (96–97).

To make doubly certain that his reader would not misconstrue Jack's portraiture as being too brash, near the end of the sketch Robinson turns once again to editorializing, emphatically defending and reaffirming his own position as a stolid supporter of the system of slavery, an ardent critic of the abolitionists, and finally reiterating that the duty of the slaveowner is to care for his slaves. What Robinson says, of course, is pure polemics and a convenient means for overtly providing a rationale for the sketch he has written about "Old Jack" C—. Yet his concluding discourse does more than this. It also may be the author's stratagem for diverting the reader's mind from concentrating too closely on the fact that while he apparently intended to write a story based on the notion that slaves were not human beings, he actually seems to have done somewhat very different. In creating Jack C— as an intelligent and cunning human being fully capable of getting along successfully in a world that regarded him as inferior, Francis James Robinson does not, however, insinuate that Jack, with his many delightful attributes, should not be a slave. Rather, he demonstrates through various anecdotes in "'Old Jack' C—" that given what

Jack is able to accomplish within the system of slavery without offending the white people whom he comes into contact with, being a slave was not so bad after all.

Like transgressing racial barriers, contesting the restrictions of gender, especially the narrowly circumscribed, marginal existence of women and the limited roles to which women were consigned in nineteenth-century American society, was not uncommon in old Southwestern humor. The so-called "cult of true womanhood," which was popular during the first half of the nineteenth century, the time period when most of the sketches examined here were published, professed that a woman should be pious, pure, passive, submissive, and humble and that she should restrict herself to the domestic sphere (Welter 152). As Barbara Welter notes, "Woman, in the cult of True Womanhood presented by the women's magazines, gift annuals, and religious literature of the nineteenth century, was the hostage in the home" (151). Moreover, in nineteenth-century literature generally—and, for the most part, in American literature of this period as well—the portrayal of women, as Cynthia Griffin Wolff points out, was in accordance with "the prevalent social attitude toward women; and since this attitude so often values men and masculine pursuits over women and feminine hobbies, women's concerns seem devalued" (205). Furthermore, a prevalent stereotype of the time was that of the sentimental woman, valued by patriarchal culture for her helplessness, physical weakness, incompetence, submissiveness, suffering, and emotionality (but only in connection with private or domestic domain) (Wolff 210–12).

The important scholarship that has already been done on female portraiture in Southwestern humor has challenged somewhat the nineteenth-century ideal of womanhood and has partially refuted the notion acclaiming the "generally acknowledged antifeminine bias in what has been labeled 'native' American humor," seen both in "the relative absence of women as primary humorous characters," as well as "in their functions as negative stereotypes in masculine humor" (Dresner 138). James H. Penrod, in a pioneering overview on the portrayal of women in nineteenth-century southern frontier humor, observed that the humorists of this school typically "avoided the stereotypes of womanhood" ("Women" 41); instead of focusing on the rigors of the frontier in respect to women's lives, they "emphasized the more humorous aspects of their life and character" (42). One of the more interesting areas of critical inquiry is the portrayal of women in the Crockett almanacs—"riproarious shemales," as Michael J. Lofaro calls the "half-horse, half-alligator" kind of women featured there, women "whose adventures and abilities are sometimes indistinguishable from those of their male counterparts" (135). Tales featuring women in the Crockett almanacs—the counterpoint to the sentimental woman described previously—Lofaro persuasively argues, provide both a "clear subtext of the secondary status of women by praising traditional roles" and likewise "break women loose from those confining patterns to act out male adventures and fantasies with a freedom that only life in a wilderness state can allow" (116). Crockett almanac characters like Lotty Ritchers; Sally Ann Thunder; Ann Whirlwind Crockett (Davy's wife);

and Sal Fink, "the Mississippi Screamer," are women whose strength, physical exploits, and independence replicate those of the legendary men also featured in the Crockett tales (Lofaro 135).[2] In a more recent essay on the gender dynamics of old Southwestern humor, William E. Lenz takes issue with the contention of some earlier critics that southern backwoods comedy is misogynistic. His examination of selected sketches from William T. Porter's two collections of frontier humor, *The Big Bear of Arkansas and Other Sketches* (1845) and *A Quarter Race in Kentucky and Other Tales* (1847), convincingly demonstrates that in a number of these pieces there is "some cultural ambivalence toward women" and that "Southwestern Humorists often picture the relationship between men and women as complicated phenomena" ("The Function of Women" 600). And in his revisionist perspective, Lenz goes on to show that in some of the sketches women actually display power, a corrective to the conventional view that Southwestern humor "reveals a clear-cut pattern of male domination and female submission" (599).

As was true in the sketches of Taliaferro and Robinson featuring black characters who stepped outside their stereotypical roles by somewhat transcending the restrictions on free speech imposed on their race, other Southwestern humorists occasionally challenged the popular view of male dominance and female submission by giving women characters voices—providing them with "word power," a weapon of verbal empowerment. A woman with a voice, often an assertive one, represents a clear deviation from the typical Southwestern sketch, which tends to suppress women's voices. In "The Consolate Widow," Sol Smith—a theatrical manager, actor, and author of humorous sketches and anecdotes, many of which were collected in *Theatrical Management in the West and South* (1868)—provides a lively and amusing demonstration of how female voice empowerment works. In this sketch, a drunken man and his horse have been killed in a quarter race (the race having been occasioned by a wager for a gallon of whiskey), after the horse has run full speed into a building. The authorial or frame narrator, a gentlemanly, sensitive, and compassionate observer who is passing through the region just after this disaster has occurred, curiously inquires about what has happened. Unexpectedly, the onlookers seem indifferent. When he asks what will the deceased man's widow feel when she learns of her husband's unfortunate accident, a woman (actually the man's wife, though the narrator is unaware of this), coldly responds: "'Yes . . . it *was* an unfortunate race. Poor man! he lost the whisky" (Smith 73). This prompts the narrator to ask this woman two additional questions—"'Did you happen to know his wife?'" and "'Has she been informed of the untimely death of her husband?'" (73) Then, when the woman to whom he has been talking (a woman of few words up to this point) informs him that she is the unfortunate widow, he, noticeably shocked, remarks: "'*You*, madam. *You* the wife of this man who has been so untimely cut off?'" (73). By this time, it has become apparent that the widow, both through her nonchalant manner and callous words, is not a person of sentiment or sensitivity. In fact, so far as she is concerned, the death of her husband is no great personal loss, as her final words to the narrator attest: "'Yes, and what about it. . . . Untimely cut off?

His throat's cut, that's all, by that 'tarnal sharp end of a log; and as for it's being *untimely*, I don't know but it's as well now as any time—*he warn't of much account, no how*!'" (74). Her response is, of course, unconventional and shocking. And the image of the widow Smith has created here becomes a blatant denial of the sentimental stereotype. Still, her words (she forthrightly says what is on her mind) have empowered her, and her final show of indifference reinforces that the widow is exactly the kind of person she appears to be. Although Smith has clearly traversed gender boundaries in "The Consolate Widow" and in doing so may have taken a risk of possibly horrifying and alienating a refined reader (the assumed reader being someone perhaps of the same class and background as the authorial narrator), we need to remember that the words of the widow are those of an independent frontier woman. And her unorthodox reaction to death clashes with the view of the authorial male narrator, who, obviously more cultured and sophisticated than she, regards her insensitivity as a disgusting social aberration. Because, in all likelihood, the so-called assumed masculine reader of this sketch shares the author's (and authorial narrator's) ambivalent feelings of revulsion and amusement; and probably because the reader feels superior to and therefore comically distanced from the kind of crudity the tale exposes, laughter takes precedence over indignation. Furthermore, since the incident the storyteller has related in the sketch is outrageous as well as ridiculous, the reader is prevented from concentrating too prominently on the female empowerment exhibited by Smith's widow.

Another sketch featuring the empowerment of a woman, a woman who challenges the male world by speaking her voice, is "The Curious Widow." Authored by Henry Clay Lewis, a country doctor and sometime writer of backwoods humorous sketches, several published initially in the *Spirit of the Times* and subsequently in *Old Leaves from the Life of a Louisiana "Swamp Doctor"* (1850), his only book, "The Curious Widow," begins with a distinctively biased male viewpoint predictably supporting the superiority of men. Dr. Madison Tensas, the narrator, in recalling his medical school days when he boarded with several other medical students at the house of a "curiosity-stricken" widow, opens the sketch with an outright attack on women. In describing the daughters of the landlady, he writes: "the quartette [*sic*] possessing so much of the distinguishing characteristic of the softer sex, that I often caught myself wondering in what nook or corner of their diminutive skulls they kept the rest of the faculties" (Lewis 75). Tensas's and his fellow students' disgust with the widow's excessive nosiness (she examines their personal belongings when they are not in their room) fuels their misogynistic attitude. In retaliation, the students contrive a prank to terrify the widow by sewing the deformed and horrifying face of an albino cadaver to an oil cloth, packaging it in numerous separate wrappers, and placing it in their room to await her curious tampering. Expectedly, the widow falls for the trap, opening the package as the students secretly watch, but her reaction is not what the students, or for that matter the readers of Lewis's sketch, had anticipated. As she gazes at the deformed and hideous face of the albino, Tensas writes, "She did not faint—did not vent a scream" (80). Apparently entranced by what she has found, she laughs hysterically, incessantly, feigning madness. Her uncontrollable laughter arouses attention in the lower quarters of the house and even on the street, attracting the curiosity of onlookers and bewildering the student pranksters, who see that their scheme has gone awry. Clearly, the widow has successfully foiled the cruel trick of the students, who have not only underestimated her ability but that of women generally. Adhering to what proves to be a false notion regarding male superiority, the students, who seem to have been conditioned to view women stereotypically, are eventually forced to confront the truth behind the widow's mask of pretense, but the full impact is not felt until she verbally berates them before all who have gathered in the room to find out the cause of the commotion and insane laughter. The widow's caustic words become the culmination of what has been a well-orchestrated display of histrionics, and the resulting humiliation of the students an appropriate way to disarm them. In Tensas's words, "the widow ceased her laughter, and putting on an expression of the most supreme contempt, coolly remarked: 'Excuse me, gentlemen, if I have caused you any inconvenience by my unusual conduct. I was just *smiling aloud* to think what fools these students made of themselves when they tried to scare me with a dead nigger's face, when I had slept with a drunken husband for twenty years'" (81).

As in Smith's "The Consolate Widow," a woman becomes empowered by the words she utters, the end result in Lewis's sketch being shaming and embarrassing the foolhardy young men who had tried to frighten her. In getting the best of her male adversaries, the widow also demonstrates that with age comes experience and that knowledge is power. In fact, it is the revolting knowledge about her past marital life that she employs skillfully to her advantage. Yet the widow's verbal attack on the male students, a sharp deviation from the ideals associated with the nineteenth-century "cult of true womanhood" and the sentimental stereotype, lacks the essential seriousness to be taken as an outright attack on male domination and thereby probably did not offend the male sensibility. Perhaps offense does not occur because the humor of the occasion defuses the potential volatility of the widow's brief tirade, or as Alan Rose puts it, "the humorous perspective is reasserted in a manner which . . . effectively transforms the disorder into a joke. . . . Equating the hideous Negro face with an everyday source of domestic irritation brings the story from the archetypal to the mundane" (30).

In "A Tight Race Considerin'" Lewis again, within safe limits, challenged the gender status quo in his portrayal of Mrs. Hibbs, whom her son describes as "a shrewd, active dame, kind-hearted and long-tongued" (43). Mrs. Hibbs, in what turns out to be an impressive display of horsemanship, steps out of her domestic role by triumphing over a new circuit preacher in a horse race, an activity in the southern backwoods usually regarded as a masculine pastime. As storyteller and therefore the controlling voice of this unconventional episode about his mother, Mrs. Hibbs, the son shares with Dr. Tensas, the authorial narrator of the frame, his contempt for the preacher—a deserving victim, who, in the son's words, is "a long-legged, weakly sickly, never-contented-onless-the-best-on-the-plantation-war-cooked-fur-him sort of man" (48). Unknown to the preacher but known to young Hibbs, the preacher's horse is a former race horse, a situation that Hibbs uses to his advantage to actuate a race between this horse and the family horse, Colt, the latter ridden by Hibbs's mother on her way to church. What seems interesting about all of this is the self-confidence and capability that Mrs. Hibbs displays when thrust into a situation where she clearly crosses the boundaries of gender as well as of respectability. In the race that ensues between his mother's horse and the preacher's, young Hibbs, in graphically amusing language, describes the determination, practicality, and skill his mother shows in carrying out her strategy to win, a strategy characterized by a touch of the risqué:

> "she commenced ridin' beautiful; she braced herself up in the saddle, and began to make calkerlations how she war to win the race, for it war nose to nose, and she saw the passun spurrin' his critter every jump. She tuk off her shoe, and the way a number ten go-to-meetin' brogan commenced given' the hoss particular Moses, were a caution to hoss-flesh—but still it kept nose to nose. She found she war carryin' too much weight for Colt, so she gan to throw of plunder, till nuthin' was left but her saddle and close. . . . The old woman commenced strippin' to lighten, till it wouldn't been a clean thing for her to have taken off one dud more." (52)

Though Mrs. Hibbs wins the race, besting a man in a generally acknowledged masculine activity, Lewis diminishes her triumph in several ways, perhaps to placate his male readers who may have felt a little unsettled by Mrs. Hibbs's success in the masculine domain. Although she wins, this happens only because a man, her husband, assists her by slapping Mrs. Hibbs's horse, thereby frightening it to jump ahead of the preacher's mount. Furthermore, the risqué slapstick antics at the race's end in which Mrs. Hibbs is pitched over her horse's head as it slams into the meeting house, and she flies through the church window, landing naked among the mourners, "her only garment flutterin' on a nail in the sash" (53), convert her into a laughingstock.[3] In short, Lewis makes Mrs. Hibbs look ridiculous, a victim of embarrassment (recall she has lost her last stitch of clothing). In what may be regarded as a subtle act of authorial privilege exercised to effect male revenge, Lewis, at the tale's end, humorously sabotages Mrs. Hibbs's accomplishment in the masculine domain of horsemanship, diverting his assumed male reader's attention by discrediting a woman's capability through the interjection of a perfectly timed anticlimax.

Critic Nancy Walker once observed that "humor is aggressive; women are passive. The humorist occupies a position of superiority; women are inferior" (12). Yet this is typically not true when measured against tales of old Southwestern humor focusing on courtship and featuring female tricksters, who always overstep the traditional boundaries defined by their gender. One of these humorists who effectively portrayed a female trickster is George Washington Harris, best known as a chronicler of the folkways and traditions of East Tennessee mountaineers and most significantly as the creator of Sut Lovingood, one of the most uninhibited and rascally characters in Southwestern humor. Harris addressed the subject of courtship and occasionally employed sensual women to challenge and undermine the prevailing notion of male superiority. In taking this stance, Harris may have been reacting to the narrowly defined roles and capabilities that a patriarchal society had imposed on the women. One of the best demonstrations of how Harris did this, but without likely arousing adverse reactions from his predominantly male readership, may be seen in "Blown Up With Soda," published initially as "Sut Lovingood Blown Up" in the *Nashville Daily Gazette* in July of 1857 and subsequently in *Sut Lovingood's Yarns* (1867). In this sketch, Harris humorously shows a male victimized by a woman primarily because of his own inherent weaknesses.

The victim of the prank in "Blown Up With Soda" is Sut Lovingood, though the extent to which he suffers as the result of Sicily's trick is negligible and certainly not long term. Sicily embodies in some ways what William E. Lenz sees as Sut's ideal woman, for she possesses in full measure the traits of "sensuality, vitality, and forcefulness" ("Sensuality, Revenge, and Freedom" 173).[4] No doubt, as becomes clear to Sut, Sicily is more than just a "handsome girl." And this is what gets him into trouble in his awkward attempt to win her favor, for he assumes that she is as attracted to him as much as he is to her. But this is not the case, and because of the absence of mutual feeling and attraction, Sut makes himself vulnerable to Sicily's prank, an action that gains for her much personal amusement at Sut's expense. Because Sut on this occasion is primed for physical love and assumes that Sicily is as well, she has no difficulty in convincing him that the soda powder, which she entices him to take, is a love potion whose effects will give him a new sensation.

While it appears that the power reversal resulting from Sicily's successful execution of her prank contradicts the familiar assumption in nineteenth-century American culture that the male is superior and that he usually obtains what he desires when women are involved, the humorous style of Sut's monologue (he describes the events of the tale retrospectively) actually creates a different impression, thus restoring the balance of power in Sut's favor. Milton Rickels, in the first book-length study of Harris's work, offers a partial and somewhat generalized explanation of Sut's reempowerment, focusing on Sut's amusingly graphic description of his departure from Sicily's presence as the soda powder foam streams from his nose and mouth. According to Rickels, "by telling the joke, Sut objectifies it, reduces its power to crush; instead, he turns it back into the fun it began with for Sicily. By his ability to see the comedy as well as feel the disappointment of his life, Sut expresses the power of humor to restore the balance of existence after defeat" (50). What Rickels implies here is that as a jokester, as a comic raconteur, Sut has found an effective way to play down Sicily's embarrassing emasculation of him, doing so by redirecting the reader's attention from a woman's capabilities in taking advantage of a man's vulnerability to focusing instead on his own ludicrous manner of description.

But I would contend that Harris actually places Sut in the role of jokester, whose attention-arousing exaggerations make him the center of attention, much earlier in the narrative than Rickels acknowledges—in fact, almost from the moment Sut begins to describe Sicily's duplicitous plan to snare him. For example, in describing how Sicily's kiss—a gesture to hold his interest so that she can entice him to take the soda powder—affects him, Sut employs humorous and visually incongruous comparisons: "'My toes felt like I wer in a warm krick wif minners a-nibblin at em; a cole streak wer a racin up an' down my back like a lizzard wif a tucky hen arter 'im'" (Harris 72). Also, shortly after Sut consumes the soda powder, and Sicily mockingly taunts him, telling him, "'Hole hit down, Mister Lovingood! Hole hit down! Hits a cure fur puppy luv'" (73), Sut craftily diverts the focus of humor from himself to Sicily: "'Now warnt that jis the durndes' onreaonabil reques' ever on o'man mad ove man? She mout jis es well ax'd me to swaller my hoss, an' then skin the cat on a cob-web'" (74). Sut's one-upmanship here at Sicily's expense is a well-executed display of comic mastery. And because of the class differences between Sut and Harris's assumed readers, likely educated and cultured gentlemen, they would have found instant amusement in *how* Sut said something in such passages rather than being caught up in the social ramifications of a woman daring to cross gender lines. Moreover, as Sicily is obviously lower class and lacking in cultural refinement, Harris's contemporary readers would not have found her emasculation of Sut to be personally threatening.

And finally, there is the matter of the sequel to "Blown Up With Soda," "Sicily Burns's Wedding." In this tale, Harris allows Sut to exact painful vengeance against Sicily through a prank of his own, coercing the Burns's bull into a beehive, which causes the bees to swarm and sting everybody, including Sicily and her new husband. This vengeful prank afforded the author the opportunity to restore the gender status quo, reaffirming the societal standard of male dominance.

Several pertinent questions arise from this extended analysis of selected texts of old Southwestern humor, texts that discernibly contest the restrictive and biased portraiture of race and gender. Were their authors consciously aware that they were defying convention? If they were cognizant of what they were doing, then why were they being rebellious? Of what significance were their transgressions, deliberate or unintentional, of prevalent attitudes endorsed by southern society? And lastly, how might one account for these humorists' ambivalence in characterization and attitude? Regarding authorial intention, it is difficult, if not impossible, to provide a definitively accurate response because little evidence, if any, exists to recover and determine explicitly and accurately the writer's purpose. Still, we may offer several tentative explanations for what the humorists we have examined here may have been doing.

In their deviations, which feature both transgressive content as well as character portraiture, these frontier humorists plainly violated prominent nineteenth-century societal assumptions and attitudes regarding race and gender. In doing so, Robb, Taliaferro, Robinson, Smith, Lewis, and Harris were first and foremost humorists, whose writings were intended to showcase comical incongruity, thereby accentuating deviations from accepted norms, standards, and expectations of nineteenth-century society. And as humorists, their major objective was to entertain an assumed audience of men, often by exaggerating situations and the actions of characters to effect surprise, a sudden reversal of expectations, and sometimes even shock. Therefore, at least on one level the subversive nature and purpose of the backwoods variety they were employing may offer a partial rationale for their transgressive depiction of race and gender. A more important angle to consider is that several of these humorists may be viewed as outsiders who did not always feel compelled to adhere strictly to societal assumptions held by proslavery southerners as well as white northerners who condoned black inferiority or conventional notions about the subservience of women. Robb, for example, the author of "The Pre-Emption Right," and Smith, the author of "The Consolate Widow," traveled widely, and as a consequence did not establish solid societal roots—a factor that likely prevented them from becoming consumed with attitudes regarding black inferiority and patriarchal convictions regarding gender. At different times, in fact, Robb, a printer, reporter, and editor by trade, resided in Philadelphia, Detroit, New Orleans, St. Louis, and California; and Smith, a cosmopolite of sorts, worked as a roving actor and stage manager in the small towns of the Ohio and Mississippi river valleys and places in the lower South such as Mobile and New Orleans. Perhaps because both were transients, Robb and Smith were expectedly alienated, never actually becoming a part of the southern frontier community, or *any* community for that matter. Because neither was a proslavery advocate, they could more comfortably take liberties in their portraiture of blacks and women. Moreover, Lewis, the author of "The Curious Widow" and "A Tight Race Considerin,'" has been acclaimed by a recent critic as a "serious writer" who placed a high premium on his art and who dared to use his humorous writing to examine "the disturbed, the deformed, and the dispossessed, the physical and psychological 'monsters' who inhabit the borderlands between solid earth and liquid swamp, and between the rational world and the world of madness" (Arnold xiv). And by critical consensus, Lewis has usually been acknowledged as an upstart, a subversive who had an independent and individualistic personality. Like Robb and Smith, Lewis was somewhat of an outsider as well, never closely sharing in the attitudes and beliefs of the people of northeastern Louisiana, where he practiced medicine briefly (Cohen and Dillingham 416), and as such, he seems to have felt free to satirize, among other things, the patriarchal narrow-mindedness and racial conservatism of the region.

While Hardin Taliaferro, Francis James Robinson, and George Washington Harris were all avowed conservatives and proslavery in their convictions, each, from time to time, did stray outside the bounds of conventionality, portraying in selected sketches blacks and women who do not stay within the marginalized behavioral molds where they had been consigned. Characters like Taliaferro's Reverend Gentry, Robinson's Old Jack' C—, and Harris's Sicily Burns are outspoken, individualistic, clever, and demonstrably capable. In short, these characters represent a level of ability and achievement that one would not have expected to see in sketches authored by loyal southern traditionalists. While Robinson objected vehemently to northern criticism of and interference in southern life, he concluded his book of humorous sketches *Kups of Kauphy* by noting the South's constitutional right to follow a lifestyle that the region deemed appropriate (Cohen and Dillingham 376). He also advocated verisimilitude in character portraiture (advice he practiced himself) and noted in particular that characters should be allowed to speak in their own voices: "Wherever it has been possible, we have let our characters use their own language in portraying their *individuality*! No *painter* desirous of success, or escaping righteous censure, would dare leave out an ugly feature in a *portrait*, or ignore a gnarled and crooked oak in a *landscape*" (vi). Desiring as he says "to be true to nature" (vi), Robinson would not only sometimes allow his characters the liberty of speaking in their own voices but also of saying what conceivably was really on their minds. At least in his public life as a Baptist minister and editor of Baptist periodicals, Taliaferro, like Robinson, may not have been as cautiously orthodox in his racial attitudes as he apparently intended to be. In 1869, Taliaferro was among only a few white ministers in Alabama who responded to the appeal of the Home Mission Society of Boston, an organization widely despised by southern Baptists, to aid in the training of black candidates for the Baptist ministry. In fact, of the small minority who volunteered, Taliaferro was one of three ministers actually appointed to undertake this responsibility. And between 1869 and 1873, he seems to have carried out this duty diligently and even helped to organize the first Baptist State Convention for black Alabamians (Piacentino 257). No records exist to indicate exactly how his fellow southern white ministers and the white Baptist faithful regarded Taliaferro's active role in the ministerial training of blacks. In all likelihood, they either condemned and ostracized him because of his willingness to help the newly freed slaves or they were indulgent toward his work with blacks because they may have regarded it as paternalistic. My guess is that the first possibility is nearer to what may have actually occurred, for in 1873, Taliaferro, who had lived in Alabama and had served as a Baptist minister there for thirty-eight years, abruptly and without explanation left the state and returned to Loudon, Tennessee, where he still had family connections (257). This same ambivalence can also be seen in Harris. Despite his avowed pro-southern attitudes and politics, Harris, as we have seen, was not totally consistent and therefore did not always conform to traditional notions regarding female portraiture in some of his humorous sketches, such as "Blown Up With Soda."

Whether or not the Southwestern humorists whose sketches we have explored here deliberately intended to contest the parameters that defined the racial and gender status quo is an issue that may never be adequately resolved. Still, what they did in this area was significant, even though they were severely handicapped by a repressive social climate, conservative racial politics, and the patriarchal circumstances of the times. My feeling is that Robb, Taliaferro, Robinson, Smith, Lewis, and Harris—all writers only by avocation—did not always consciously try to limit how they portrayed some of their marginal characters. But if perchance they became aware that they may have gone too far in delineating genuine human qualities in their portraiture of African Americans and women, they probably allowed sociopolitical considerations to influence their decisions concerning how they would ultimately handle these potentially controversial materials in their work. And this may help to account for the claim of ambivalence in their handling of characterization and situation. Perhaps desiring to comply with the political and/or social attitudes of their male audience, their subliterary sketches, despite the occasional transgressions in the portraiture of blacks and women, ultimately defended, if only in a roundabout way, the prevalent views on race and gender. What has been said of Thomas Bangs Thorpe, author of "The Big Bear of Arkansas," in this context may likewise be applicable to the backwoods humorists whose sketches we have discussed: "Since he was not prepared to challenge the expectations of his audience, he ultimately had to confirm their prejudices" (Railton 99).

Like their contemporary, William Gilmore Simms, these writers found themselves from time to time in a quandary. In his 1835 novel *The Yemassee,* Simms created in the African American slave Hector a character whose human qualities plainly contradicted southern assumptions and beliefs that a black man was subordinate and subhuman, but whose humanity his creator subsequently clumsily tried to destroy by recasting the slave in the mold of a stereotype (Rubin 1012–14). Realizing that they had veered outside the comfort zone in their portraiture of African Americans and women, and therefore may possibly offend their masculine readership, they seemed to have been willing to compromise what artistic integrity they may have exerted in honest and consistent characterizations by submitting to the demands of political and social expediency. Indeed, as we have seen, Southwestern humorists like those we have discussed, in their portrayal of African Americans and women, did occasionally create characters who exhibit complex human dimensions contrary to the views of nineteenth-century southern society. And like Simms, and also to a certain extent like Joel Chandler Harris, Charles W. Chesnutt, George Washington Cable, Mark Twain, and other southern writers who were their immediate literary successors, many of the Southwestern humorists had to face the dilemma of whether they should be true to their integrity as writers (albeit all of them were amateurs in the profession of authorship) or should be loyal to the popular convictions regarding race and gender espoused by and consonant with the southern communities where most of them resided or about which they treated in some of their humorous works. Thus, the southern frontier humorist who may have found himself portraying blacks and women with believable human traits, freeing them from demeaning strictures by giving them flexibility they rarely enjoyed in real life in the antebellum South, and showing them to be compassionate, caring, brave, intelligent, manipulative, resourceful, individualistic, self-expressive, capable, and shrewd and witty, ultimately failed to sustain their humanity. Yielding to the expectations of his assumed audience of conservative male readers, the Southwestern humorist always seemed to find ways to make certain that his sketch or tale featuring blacks or women remained within a noncontroversial framework. In every sketch we have examined, the writer cautiously skirted potential sociopolitical controversy, creating built-in concessions or useful diversionary tactics through such means as the dynamics of humor, inconsistent characterization, the manipulation of his audience's feelings through sentimental language and gestures, and even overt editorializing. While, then, these humorists occasionally did find themselves at variance with the racial and gender politics of their times—intentionally or unintentionally—it would not be until the twentieth century that southern writers the likes of Faulkner, Warren, Porter, Welty, and Richard Wright, among numerous others who felt that they could stand apart from their community and its loyalties and prejudices, would confidently traverse the boundaries of race and/or gender to portray African Americans and women with graphic honesty and complexity.

Notes

1. See Penrod, "Minority Groups in Old Southern Humor," 123, and Rose, *Demonic Vision,* 22.

2. Lofaro, 146, further claims that these "shemales . . . are at least in part the result of the projected comic fantasies of eastern male writers who saw the frontier as an almost equal opportunity experience regardless of the sexual stereotypes and roles."

3. Arnold, xxxvi–xxxvii, in speaking of male-female relations in "A Tight Race Considerin,'" sees Mrs. Hibbs, the mother, as the "dominant figure," who "in the throes of excitement, . . . divests herself of clothes, of religion, of propriety, and inspires the other women in the church to do the same. Thus the church is paganized; the Christian service (a funeral) becomes a bacchanalia, and the men flee from the nakedness—and the implied sexual ferocity—they see in the women."

4. Lenz, 179, goes on to note that Harris's women characters realize that "sex is a power before which men are helpless" and that this "suggests a tradition of American women characters who flaunt their inheritance in a popular male-dominated genre, one that Harris had the good fortune to discover and exploit."

Works Cited

Arnold, Edwin T. Introduction. *Odd Leaves from the Life of a Louisiana Swamp Doctor,* by Henry Clay Lewis. Baton Rouge: Louisiana State Univ. Press, 1997. xi–xlviii.

Cohen, Hennig, and William B. Dillingham. "Francis James Robinson." *Humor of the Old Southwest.* Eds. Cohen and Dillingham. Athens: Univ. of Georgia Press, 1994. 376–77.

———. "Henry Clay Lewis." 415–16.

Dresner, Zita. "Women's Humor" in *Humor in America: A Research Guide to Genre and Topics.* Ed. Lawrence E. Mintz. New York: Greenwood, 1988. 137–62.

Gross, Seymour L. "Stereotype to Archetype: The Negro in American Literature." *Images of the Negro in American Literature.* Eds. Seymour L. Gross and John Edward Hardy. Chicago: Univ. of Chicago Press, 1966. 1–26.

Harris, George Washington. "Blown Up With Soda." *Sut Lovingood's Yarns.* Ed. M. Thomas Inge. New Haven, Conn.: College & University Press, 1966. 69–75.

Lenz, William E. "The Function of Women in Old Southwestern Humor: Re-reading Porter's *Big Bear* and *Quarter Race* Collections." *Mississippi Quarterly* 46 (1993): 589–600.

———. "Sensuality, Revenge, and Freedom: Women in *Sut Lovingood's Yarns.*" *Studies in American Humor* 1 (1983): 173–80.

Lewis, Henry Clay. "A Curious Widow." *Odd Leaves,* 75–81.

———. "A Tight Race Considerin.'" *Odd Leaves,* 42–53.

Lofaro, Michael A. "Riproarious Shemales; Legendary Women in the Tall Tale World of the Davy Crockett Almanacs." *Crockett at Two Hundred: New Perspectives on the Man and the Myth.* Eds. Michael A. Lofaro and Joe Cummings. Knoxville: Univ. of Tennessee Press, 1989. 114–52.

Penrod, James H. "Minority Groups in Old Southern Humor." *Southern Folklore Quarterly* 22 (1958): 121–28.

———. "Women in the Old Southwestern Yarns." *Kentucky Folklore Record* 1 (1955): 41–47.

Piacentino, Ed. "H.E. Taliaferro." *DLB 202: Nineteenth-Century American Fiction Writers.* Ed. Kent P. Ljungquist. Detroit: Gale Research, 1999. 251–58.

Railton, Stephen. *Authorship and Audience: Literary Performance in the American Renaissance.* Princeton, N.J.: Princeton Univ. Press, 1991.

Rickels, Milton. *George Washington Harris.* New Haven, Conn.: College & University Press, 1965.

Robb, John S. "The Pre-Emption Right." *Streaks of Squatter Life and Far-West Scenes.* Ed. John Francis McDermott. Delmar, N.Y.: Scholars' Facsimiles & Reprints, 1978. 117–32.

Robinson, Frances James. "'Old Jack' C—." *Kups of Kauphy: A Georgia Book, in Warp and Woof, Containing Tales, Incidents, &c. of the "Empire State of the South."* Athens, Ga.: Christy & Chelsea, 1853. 84–107.

Rose, Alan H. "Blackness in the Fantastic World of Old Southwestern Humor." *Demonic Vision: Racial Fantasy and Southern Fiction.* Hamden, Conn.: Archon, 1976. 19–38.

Rubin, Louis D., Jr. "Southern Local Color and the Black Man." *The Southern Review,* n.s., 6 (1970): 1011–30.

Smith, Solomon Franklin. "The Consolate Widow." Cohen and Dillingham, 73–74.

Taliaferro, Hardin E. "Jonah and the Whale," *Fisher's River (North Carolina) Scenes and Characters, By "Skitt," Who Was Raised Thar.* New York: Harper & Brothers, 1859. 189–92.

———. "The Origin of the Whites." *Fisher's River,* 188–89.

———. "Rev. Charles Gentry." *Fisher's River,* 186–87.

Walker, Nancy. *A Very Serious Thing: Women's Humor and American Culture.* Minneapolis: Univ. of Minnesota Press, 1988.

Welter, Barbara. "The Cult of True Womanhood: 1820–1860." *American Quarterly* 18 (1966): 151–74.

Wolff, Cynthia Griffin. "A Mirror for Men: Stereotypes of Women in Literature." *The Massachusetts Review* 13 (1972): 205–18.

5

Darkness Visible

Race and Pollution in Southwestern Humor

Scott Romine

In "The Horror and the Glory," the second section of the restored *Black Boy*, Richard Wright describes working at a Chicago restaurant, where he discovers that a Finnish cook named Tillie spits into the food. Revolted, Wright informs his employer, who upon verifying his account fires the cook on the spot. But as Tillie leaves the restaurant, Wright recalls a former employer who had fired him for not liking his "looks." "I wondered," Wright muses, "if a Negro who did not smile and grin was as morally loathsome to whites as a cook who spat into the food" (326). As usual, Wright is dead on. In connecting black dissent and tropes of contamination, Wright identifies an intricate relation with a long history in southern culture and literature. This essay attempts to trace one thread of that history back to the genre of Southwestern humor—a genre often associated with beginnings. In the official narrative of southern literature, Southwestern humor is typically cast as a seedbed for later writers such as Mark Twain, Erskine Caldwell, William Faulkner, Flannery O'Connor, Harry Crews, and others. Too often this is emphasized as the genre's *main* virtue: Southwestern humor existed, it appears, so that later writers could make something literary out of the raw material—a colorful frontier culture and a vernacular form—that the genre first mined in a distinctly subliterary way.[1] Although this teleological bent has often obscured the considerable achievement of these writers, this essay repeats the pattern—with a twist. In examining the genre's conflation of racial blackness and tropes of pollution, contamination, and abjection, I reveal the seminal nature of Southwestern humor in terms of more fundamental—and altogether less admirable—cultural work.

In *Purity and Danger*, the anthropologist Mary Douglas observes that the presence of dirt presupposes a system. "[I]f uncleanness," Douglas says, "is matter out of place, we must approach it through order. Uncleanness or dirt is that which must not be included if a pattern is to be maintained. To recognize this is the first step toward insight into pollution" (40). If we conceive of uncleanness in this way, Douglas suggests, we are led directly to the symbolic schema by which communities mediate, organize, and standardize the experience of individuals. Douglas's observation that a culture's concept of defilement and pollution speaks directly to its regulation of social order is especially apropos of the world of Southwestern humor, a decidedly dirty world subject to a pervasive grammar by which themes of abjection, filth, deviance, horror, and death are displaced to groups and character types outside the normative social domain. Although my focus here is on how blackness absorbs these themes, social categories based on gender and class often serve a similar function; women and poor whites, that is, are often defined as contaminants in the masculine world that dominates these texts. Although race is by no means a common subject in Southwestern humor, a number of sketches make explicit attitudes toward blackness that tend to be elided elsewhere in antebellum southern writing.[2] Thus, Southwestern humor provides a rich opportunity to examine what Toni Morrison has called the "dark, abiding, signing Africanist presence" that haunts American literature (5), the "denotative and connotative blackness that African peoples have come to signify" (6).

Before attempting to demonstrate this thesis, it might prove useful to examine a humorous sketch that represents race in a way perfectly typical of antebellum southern writing. As Leonard Cassuto observes in *The Inhuman Race: The Racial Grotesque in American Literature and Culture*, the exigencies of slavery and the ever-present threat of slave revolt necessitated the "novelistic manufacture of bucolic Southern fantasies . . . peopled with Sambos because only they can fit within its parameters" (164–65). When slaves in the more polite plantation tradition indicate any resistance to white authority—and most do not—they tend to be cast as mischievous tricksters; Tom in William Gilmore Simms's *Woodcraft* and Carey in John Pendleton Kennedy's *Swallow Barn* are typical examples of the type.[3] So is "'Old Jack' C—," a slave who appears in Francis James Robinson's 1853 *Kups of Kauphy*. From the beginning of Robinson's sketch, Jack's verbal dexterity allows him to deflect, evade, and resist authority. For example, when a white minister warns Jack of the evils of alcohol, the slave concurs wholeheartedly and therefore, he relates, "'b'lieves it to be my duty to destroy as much of it as I kin while I lib'" (94). "This," says the narrator, "was a settler; and our parson turned away, while Jack, with his peculiar wink and smirk of the face, checked over his success in flooring his antagonist" (94). The sketch contains several incidents of a similar kind, and while Jack triumphs in them all, his pranks, sharp rejoinders, and evasions of authority are decidedly circumscribed. As the narrator affirms in an introductory frame, "To the superficial observer, Jack has the appearance of being too impudent for a slave, but those who know him best, and who can thus better appreciate his eccentricities by this knowledge, know him to be an obedient and industrious servant; contented in his station in life, and with not the shadow of a wish to change it" (86). While the trickster figure allowed white writers to stylize the resistance that slavery produced, the trickster's impudence is typically contained by this kind of rhetoric, although usually in a less explicit form. However mischievous he may appear, there is nothing especially threatening about Old Jack. In the end, he's just joking.

In contrast, John S. Robb's "The Pre-Emption Right," a sketch included in his 1847 *Streaks of Squatter Life*, tacitly defines blackness in a more symbolically complex way. The story involves a sturdy frontiersman named Dick Kelsy who lives with a "negro slave, who was at once his master's attendant and friend. Kelsy and the negro had been raised together, and from association, although so opposite their positions, had imbibed a lasting affection for each other,—each would have freely shed blood in the other's defense. The bonds of servitude were, consequently, moulded into links of friendship and affection, securing to them a feeling of confidence in their lonely habitation in the wilderness" (118). But as with Huck and Jim on the Mississippi, this scene of interracial harmony is disrupted by contact with an inharmonious world, which arrives in the form of a brutal squatter who savagely beats his wife and later makes two cowardly attempts on Kelsy's life. Four decades before Huck Finn could think of no higher praise than "I knowed [Jim] was white inside" (341), Kelsy makes an identical assertion minus the authorial irony. "Sam," he tells his slave, "*you're* a nigger, but thar's more real white man under your black skin than could be found in an acre of such varmints as that *sucker*" (123). Where the "sucker" forfeits his whiteness through moral corruption, Sam's fidelity permits his blackness to be voided, thereby earning him the status of honorary white. It is an oblique equation of blackness and depravity—all the more subtle for its apparent claim that skin color means nothing. But while "blackness" does not automatically attach itself to persons of African descent, it remains intimately linked to degradation; simultaneously, Kelsy provides the meaning of blackness and declares it arbitrary. Yet as an impurity, blackness (wherever it is found) demands purgation, which the community of backwoodsmen brings about by lynching the squatter.

A strikingly similar structure informs Joseph M. Field's "A Lyncher's Own Story," an 1845 sketch published in the *St. Louis Reveille*. The white stranger in this story is, if anything, even more depraved than the one in "The Pre-Emption Right." Not only does he beat the woman believed to be his wife, he attempts to drown her in a swamp; and in fact she is not his wife at all but instead a simple Tennessee schoolmarm whom he has seduced and ruined. Moreover, the unnamed stranger is an abolitionist who accepts the hospitality of southern planters so that he may free their slaves. The internal narrator, designated only as the "Colonel," describes such deceit as "treachery"; "it's not a white man's act," he informs his audience (228). Suspicious when the stranger arrives at his plantation, the Colonel formulates a plan: "I put my own servant, Jake—a very good boy, gentlemen—a perfect *white man*, and whom I never said a cross word to, in my life—I put Jake to 'tend on them, and, sure enough, after I was in bed, back came the boy to say that the gentleman had come to run him off" (228). When the Colonel later discovers the stranger, he "blushe[s] that he was a white man" (229). The parallels between the two sketches are striking. Again, the slave is declared an honorary white, while the white man forfeits his race. Again, the woman is rescued from heterosexual degradation, while the homosocial bond between master and slave is affirmed. And again, the community is purified through the ritual of lynching—this time in a particularly gruesome form. The mob fastens a noose around the culprit's neck and attaches it to a bent sapling. The sapling is released and the "nigger thief, with a jerk that snapped his neck, flew into the air, describing a half-circle as spanned by his halter, and swinging back to us again from the other side!" (232).

The interracial homosocial relationships in these two sketches are variations on the trope as it appears throughout nineteenth-century American narrative: Natty Bumppo and Chingachgook, Ishmael and Queequeg, Huck and Jim. And as Leslie Fiedler, who first called attention to this manner of writing in *Love and Death in the American Novel*, observes, the "other face of Chingachgook is Injun Joe . . . Jim is also the Babo of Melville's 'Benito Cereno'" (6). For Fiedler, the benign racial other implies the latent presence of a malignant double. Arguing in a similar vein, Cassuto follows Eugene Genovese and John Blassingame in suggesting that the pervasive stereotype of Sambo, the carefree and contented slave endemic to plantation fiction, existed in an organic tension with the more threatening type usually designated as "Nat Turner." "Sambo," Cassuto writes, "was never separate from the rebel, a shadowy figure in the back of the slaveowner's mind whose existence could never be fully denied" (163). A similar dynamic exists in the sketches by Robb and Field, where the malignant double of the respective Sambos is coded "black" despite the presence of white skin. It is significant, moreover, that pollution is displaced not only across racial lines, but displaced to sexual—and specifically heterosexual—relationships: the abjection of the two female victims *absorbs* themes of contamination and pollution. But in both cases there's a catch: sexual degradation is itself designated "black," and "black" in an explicitly racialized sense. Both strangers are, in a manner of speaking, lynched as black rapists, deeply encoded as that figuration may be. Robb and Field thus provide the cultural grammar by which sexual pollution is designated as a black racial trait, a grammar that would be articulated more explicitly in the postbellum era, when black dissent was invariably figured as a sexual threat to the purity of white women. Here it is white men who pose the threat to female purity, but in so doing, they assume blackness. Indeed, in both sketches the women stand between the men and vigilante justice, and it is only when the community can symbolically protect their purity that the lynchings can proceed.[4]

Likewise, the communal response to threatened sexual purity takes on a disturbingly prescient cast. "A Lyncher's Own Story," which begins with a conversation on the propriety—even necessity—of lynching abolitionists, bears witness to a historical circumstance noted by James E. Cutler in his seminal 1905 study of the institution. Cutler shows that shortly after 1830, lynching entered settled communities throughout the slave states as a specific response to abolitionist agitation. According to Cutler, lynching itself was therefore associated with racial structure in a specific way, although African Americans themselves were not often victimized until after emancipation. The incoherent rage white southerners directed toward abolitionists predicts the same emotion later directed at the carpetbagger, who follows his antebellum precursor in being represented not merely as the *catalyst* but the *cause* of black dissent. What is at stake in both cases is the perception of a paternalistic racial order at once hierarchical and consensual. Recalling Douglas's definition of dirt as "matter out of place," we might conceive of racial pollution as *blackness* out of place—or, to use a more southern idiom, as blacks out of *their* place. Just as soil is not "dirty" in the yard, so blackness is not a contaminant in its "proper place."

As James McBride Dabbs ironically said in 1958, white southerners "like the Negro in his place. The liking is a bonus for his staying there" (177). Thus, a political valence surrounds the representation of blackness as contamination, even in such a rudimentary form as we find in these two antebellum sketches. It is not only that attitudes toward race permit the institution of slavery but that attitudes toward slavery necessitate the concept of racial pollution. Implicitly, it is the consent of the two slaves to their inferior social position that voids them of their blackness, thereby transforming the "bonds of servitude" into "links of friendship and affection." And while "The Pre-Emption Right" contains no overt political dimension, it is no coincidence that the wife-beating stranger of Field's sketch is an abolitionist. Herein lies a certain symmetry: if the transformation of black to (honorary) white requires interracial consensus, it should not surprise us that the opposite transformation involves the disruption of interracial consensus—precisely, that is, the action of abolition. Indeed, two of the abolitionist's predecessors have abused the welcome extended by the Colonel to any "honest looking white man" and made off with two "valuable servants" (228). Nor is it a coincidence that the lynching (as purgative act) recuperates an idealized image of consensual racial hierarchy, since it is a slave who turns in the abolitionist. As he awaits his death, the abolitionist becomes, literally, an abject black body: "the man—a mighty small figure any how—shrunk to half his natural size; *discolored as if the last corrupting change had anticipated the grave* . . . like a thing too abject, even to *hang*—awaited the selection of a crotch for him to swing from" (first emphasis added, 230–31). A tale strewn with references to slavery and skin color thus concludes with a symbolic expulsion of racial disorder and physical blackness. If blackness as pollution accrues in the absence of black consent, the narrative work of Field's tale is to displace blackness from slave to abolitionist.

It is likewise suggestive that both "The Pre-Emption Right" and "A Lyncher's Own Story" place racial disorder (displaced racial content, threats to the slave order) in a kind of metonymic contiguity with threats to "normal" femininity. This association is in fact quite common in Southwestern humor: where there is racial disorder, gender trouble is likely to be found in close proximity. The connection may be more organic than coincidental. According to Julia Kristeva in her important work on abjection, societies with prominent pollution taboos usually display rigid gender divisions as well. "In societies where it occurs," Kristeva writes, "ritualization of defilement is accompanied by a strong concern for separating the sexes, and this means giving men rights over women" (70). In the homosocial world of Southwestern humor, threats to normal femininity come not only from sexual predators (as we have already seen), but from women who fail to fulfill the domestic imperatives of marriage and motherhood. "Samuel Hele, Esq.," a sketch contained in Joseph Glover Baldwin's 1853 *The Flush Times of Alabama and Mississippi*, shows how a language of deviant femininity corresponds in a relatively lighthearted way to the discourse of slavery and abolition. The sketch is occasioned by the arrival of an abolitionist schoolteacher, Miss Charity Woodey, from New England. When Miss Charity's "bilious" piety becomes too much for the townsfolk to bear, the misanthropic title character is sent to regale her with stories of the community's moral depravity. He accepts with gusto, and focuses especially on the treatment of slaves, who are, he claims, blown up with gunpowder, marked with "a slit in one ear and an underbit in the other," fed to dogs, drowned in creeks as infants, and publicly hung and burned to prevent slave uprisings (298–301). Such is the carnivalesque logic of Baldwin's world that the abolitionist is purged not as a contaminant, but as a morally "pure" outsider in a corrupted town. Unfortunately for the town, the plan backfires: Miss Charity writes to "Mrs. Harriet S—" on her way out of town, and Hele's outrageous stories provide the basis for *Uncle Tom's Cabin.* But amid the humor of the sketch, disruptions of normal femininity are once again linked to racial disorder. "Miss Charity," we are told, was "one of that fussy, obtrusive, meddling class, who, in trying to *double-sex* themselves, *unsex* themselves, losing all that is lovable in woman, and getting most of what is odious in man" (291). Likewise, *Uncle Tom's Cabin* is described as a "very popular fiction, or rather book of fictions, in which the slaveholders are handled with something less than feminine delicacy and something more than masculine unfairness" (303).[5]

At the other end of the sexual spectrum lies Evelina Smith, the title character of Augustus Baldwin Longstreet's "The 'Charming Creature,' as a Wife." Where Miss Charity is unsexed, Evelina is oversexed: she is a beauty, a flirt, and a coquette, whose sole desire—both before and after her marriage—is to attract the attentions of as many beaux as possible. Evelina is vain, affected, and socially dangerous, and one of her signal faults is her flat refusal to manage properly her domestic servants. In direct contrast to her mother-in-law, whose domestic virtue is marked by her ability to manage servants, Evelina flatly refuses to heed her husband's injunction to "regulate your servants with system—[to] see that they perform their duties in the proper way and the proper time" (68). The long-suffering fellow becomes exasperated when Evelina treats as her "superior" an "infernal black wench" named Clary (69); he is further disgusted by the slaves' "idleness, their insolence, and their disgusting familiarities with his wife" (70). The operative phrase here is "disgusting familiarities"; while contact within hierarchy is permissible, contact outside of hierarchy is contamination. The sketch's misogynist and racist tendencies thus converge—not surprising, perhaps, coming from an author who upon selling his slaves in 1829 commented on his relief at being rid of "the eternal torment of negroes" (qtd. in Fitzgerald, 47).

A similar association of racial disorder and the polluting black body appears in Robb's "Letters from a Baby," a series of letters written by a precocious infant named Bub. Like Longstreet, Robb satirizes fashionable women eager to follow the latest styles; indeed, both stories show racial pollution being enabled by women who fail in their domestic roles. Both Longstreet and Robb posit roughly symmetrical "purities" (racial and sexual) that work to preserve the boundaries and prerogatives of white male identity. "My ma," Bub informs his reader, "is what you would call a fashionable woman, and although she loves her baby, yet she says it is not fashionable for mammas in the southern states to nurse their own babies; I am, consequently, turned over to the care of nigger Molly, and Lord preserve me, such nursing as I get would kill a young *Indian*" (169). Where the homosocial bond of "The Pre-Emption Right" produces interracial pleasure, the misogynistic thrust of "Letters from a Baby" produces interracial contact of a highly disturbing nature. When Molly drops him because she is drunk, Bub relates a horrific scene: "she clapped her black lips to mine, smelling horribly as they were of whiskey, and kept in my breath until I was as black in the face as herself" (170). Matters do not improve until Bub lies near death and his mother resumes nursing; his health improves, and he becomes a leader of a convention of southern infants at which the following resolution is passed: "*Resolved,* That the introduction of negro nurses among white babies was a *dark* era in infantile history" (176). For readers accustomed to hearing white southerners wax poetic over the emotional and physical nourishment provided by their Negro nurses, "Letters from a Baby" comes as something of a shock, but it is fully consonant with a sporadic pattern of imagery found throughout Southwestern humor in which black bodies are rendered grotesque and bodily contact is rendered disgusting.

Although, as Milton Rickels points out in a 1984 essay, Southwestern humor abounds in grotesque bodies, more than a few of those bodies are black. No work exemplifies this pattern more than Henry Clay Lewis's 1850 *Odd Leaves from the Life of a Louisiana Swamp Doctor.*[6] Lewis's profession as a "swamp doctor" and plantation physician put him in direct contact with not only a number of black bodies but a pervasive medical discourse that situated and monitored the black body within a carefully controlled system of power relations. The quasi-medical disciplines of phrenology and craniology, for example, fixed black inferiority at the level of the physical body, while a southern physician named Samuel Cartwright famously diagnosed slave "diseases" such as "drapetomania" (running away) and "rascality" (qtd. in Gould, 70–71). As in the medical discourse of the day, the black bodies of Lewis's work gravitate toward a pathological condition. Sometimes the subject appears clothed in lighthearted humor, as in "Cupping on the Sternum," an early sketch in which Madison Tensas, Lewis's narrative persona, confronts a grotesquely obese female slave whom he unwittingly tortures by treating her posterior ("stern") instead of her sternum. In a similar vein, "How to Cure Fits" finds Tensas confronting a female slave who fakes seizures to escape work. Threatening to have her thrown into a river during one of her fits, Tensas effects a miraculous "cure." While the slave woman performs pathology as a way of evading authority, Tensas's diagnosis restores her body to its proper function laboring in the fields. Medicine appears—albeit in a lighthearted way—as a technique of discipline, a point Tensas himself suggests in noting that a "liberal flagellation completed the cure" (191).

But if the grotesque black body is sometimes the subject of humor, on other occasions it provides a horrific image of abjection. Both "Stealing a Baby" and "The Curious Widow" follow the pattern already noted in which racial pollution—the black body as abject image—accrues around sexual themes. And yet in both cases, the trope of black pollution is divested of political resonance. Unlike the insolent slaves of "The 'Charming Creature,' as a Wife" or the loathsome nurse of "Letters from a Baby," blackness is not aligned with a form of transgressive behavior, mainly because these black bodies—cadavers in both cases—lack the ability to act. However, Lewis's choice of the cadaver as the vehicle of black pollution is suggestive. According to Kristeva, abjection accumulates around boundary violations that do not permit a neat subject/object separation: the abject "disturbs identity, system, order. . . . [it] does not respect borders, positions, rules"; it is "something rejected from which one does not part, from which one does not protect oneself as from an object" (4). The corpse, consequently, "is the utmost of abjection. It is death infecting life" (4). "Stealing a Baby" describes how, as a medical student, Tensas steals the cadaver of a black infant to dissect at home. Already violating the boundary between life and death, the cadaver also violates the boundary between subject and object: despite being object of scientific dissection, "something," Tensas relates, "formed a bond of association between that dead nigger baby and myself, which held me to my place, my gaze riveted upon it" (134). Upon encountering his beloved, a woman named Lucy, Tensas is attacked by a bulldog, which dislodges the cadaver he has hidden inside his cloak: "out, in all its hideous realities, rolled the infernal imp of darkness" (137). Tensas never sees Lucy again, and as he relates in the closing lines of the sketch, "my haggard features and buttonless coat testify that I am still a bachelor" (137). Although Tensas here presents his loss of Lucy as (mock) tragedy, Edwin Arnold acutely observes of Lewis's work that "[w]omen and the idea of sex are generally couched in terms of disgust, violence, and death" (xxxi). Passages like the following necrophiliac fantasy suggest how Lewis presents the female body through images of corruption and decay. "Even when," Tensas relates, "my audacious lips were stealing a kiss from the pulpy-mouth of my lady-love, instead of floating into ecstasies of delight, my anatomical mind would wonder whether, even in death, electricity, by some peculiar adaptation, might not be able to continue their bewitching suction" (133).[7] Lewis's black and female bodies similarly gravitate toward a condition of corruption, thereby preserving the integrity of racial and sexual boundaries. If, as Arnold suggests, *Odd Leaves* is structured as a series of cathartic moments, blackness and femininity provide roughly symmetrical objects of purgation.

This implicit connection between race and gender is extended in "The Curious Widow," which places in suggestive proximity themes of sexual degradation and the grotesque image of the black body. The sketch begins with Tensas annoyed at being spied upon by his prying landlady. To teach her a lesson, he removes the facial skin of a hideous albino cadaver and conceals it in a package that he suspects she will open in his absence. Like the cadaver in "Stealing a Baby," the "white negro" (77) here violates a series of boundaries—between life and death, white and black, human and animal. He was, Tensas says, "one of the most hideous specimens of humanity that ever horrified the sight. . . . Every feature was deformed and unnatural; a horrible hare-lip, the cleft extending half way up his nose externally, and a pair of tushes projecting from his upper jaw, completed his bill of horrors" (77). The young man's plan comes to naught, however, when the landlady opens the package, laughs maniacally, and remarks on "what fools these students made of themselves when they tried to scare me with a dead nigger's face, when I had slept with a drunken husband for twenty years!" (81). Not even the horrors of the grotesque black body compare with the sexual degradation suffered at the hands of a drunken husband.

A nearly identical black body—this one alive—appears in Lewis's final sketch, "A Struggle for Life," where it belongs to a "negro dwarf of the most frightful appearance." His diminutive body, Tensas continues, "was garnished with legs and arms of enormously disproportionate length; his face was hideous: a pair of tushes projected from either side of a double hare-lip; and taking him altogether, he was the nearest resemblance to the ourang outang mixed with the devil that human eyes ever dwelt upon" (193). Unfortunately for Tensas, the dwarf is charged with leading him through a desolate swamp, and upon becoming drunk with brandy Tensas gives him, he grows hostile. Tensas refuses his request for more liquor, threatening to whip him if he does not cease his demands. Uncowed, the slave attacks and nearly strangles Tensas to death, leaving the erstwhile master in a nightmarish limbo between life and death. Tensas later awakens to find that the slave has fallen into the campfire and burned to death; only a "charred and loathsome mass" is left; "nothing of the human remained" (202). As in "Stealing a Baby" and "The Curious Widow," death itself is displaced to the abject black body, leaving Tensas—himself only recently a "corpse . . . [as] dead as human ever becomes" (200)—to detach himself from the "loathsome mass" as he reenters life. For sheer horror and brutality, "A Struggle for Life" surpasses anything in Poe.[8] As Alan H. Rose observes, Lewis's concluding sketch "reveals the intensity of the underlying impulse to associate the Negro with primal forces of destruction," thereby revealing "the depth of the racial tension in the ante-bellum South" (262). The necessity of rendering the black rebel as a physical grotesque is perhaps self-evident: the dwarf does not rebel because he is loathsome but is loathsome because he rebels. More than any other text of the antebellum period, "A Struggle for Life" defines racial disorder as racial pollution; the grotesque body is, quite clearly, a way of figuring the pathology of insurrection.[9]

As Toni Morrison observes in *Playing in the Dark,* it is essential to understand not only the traditions of resisting racism but the traditions of perpetuating it (9–12). And there is no question that the dynamics this essay has traced—the association of racial pollution and social disorder, the association of racial pollution and gender trouble—endured much longer than the school of Southwestern humor. In his 1905 novel *The Clansman*, for example, Thomas Dixon Jr. reifies the degradations of the Reconstruction era in the rape of a white woman by an animalistic Negro named Gus, who approaches his white victim "with an ugly leer, his flat nose dilated, his sinister bead eyes wide apart, gleaming apelike." "A single tiger spring," the novel continues, "and the black claws of the beast sank into the soft white throat and she was still" (386). The line of descent from "A Struggle for Life," whose protagonist similarly feels the "gripe [*sic*] of [the dwarf's] talons about [his] throat"

(200), could hardly be clearer. William Faulkner's *Light in August* likewise associates racial pollution and sexual disorder in its numerous references to miscegenation, menstruation, homosexuality, and blurred gender boundaries. *Light in August* is, of course, an elaborate examination of abjection and transgressed boundaries. Although race and sexuality provide abstract structures by which deviance and impurity can be defined, the content of impurity is located at a somatic level in black blood and menstrual blood, respectively. As Joseph Urgo observes, Christmas's early experiences with menstruating women cause him to conceive of black blood as the "secret, irremovable 'filth' of his own existence" (395). In a novelistic space where the "the original quarry, the abyss itself" (116) of Freedman town, Jefferson's black community, is aligned with "the lightless hot wet primogenitive Female" (115), blackness accumulates around sexuality in almost every conceivable way. In *Killers of the Dream,* Lillian Smith recognizes the interrelationship of racial and sexual prohibitions, the intimate connection between the uncleanness of black and female bodies as viewed through the lens of patriarchal white supremacist ideology. That examples of this kind could be multiplied almost endlessly suggests the pervasive capacity of the South's dominant white culture to recast dissent in the pathological, somatic language of pollution: black dissent especially has historically tended to terminate in the grotesque black body. Rituals of abjection, lynchings especially, have served to exorcise blackness (to use Trudier Harris's phrase) in a way that preserves the coherent boundaries and symbolic cleanliness of white identity. Abjection, Kristeva observes, exists "[o]n the edge of non-existence and hallucination, of a reality that, if I acknowledge it, annihilates me. There, abject and abjection are my safeguards. The primers of my culture" (2). In offering a disturbing primer of racial codes elided by the plantation tradition, Southwestern humor offers insight into a culture whose conception of blackness went well beyond contented Sambos to a nightmarish reality lurking beneath.

Notes

1. Even more sympathetic critics such as Kenneth Lynn and Allen Tate tend to locate Southwestern humor at the beginning of something. Lynn's *Mark Twain and Southwestern Humor,* still the most substantial single-author study of the genre, configures Southwestern humor so that Mark Twain will adopt its forms while breaking its rules. Ranking Augustus Baldwin Longstreet's *Georgia Scenes* alongside *Adventures of Huckleberry Finn,* Tate claims that these two works "made all the difference, or were eventually to do so . . . . [they] are the beginning of modern Southern literature" (146–47).

2. Rose makes a similar point specific to Henry Clay Lewis; see 255–56.

3. For an extended discussion of Carey as trickster, see Romine, 71–77.

4. One of the key proofs of the "real white man" lurking under Sam's skin is that, like the vigilantes, Sam defends female purity. When the stranger "twice, with his fist, fell[s] the woman to the earth" (122), Sam stands, knife drawn, ready to defend her. When Kelsy arrives, only the woman's intercession saves the squatter's life—at least temporarily.

5. Directed at Harriet Beecher Stowe, the charge was not an uncommon one. Writing

in the October 1852 issue of the *Southern Literary Messenger,* an anonymous reviewer of *Uncle Tom's Cabin* makes "a distinction between *lady* and *female* writers," before going on to excoriate Stowe, who, by her "shameless disregard of truth and of those amenities which so peculiarly belong to her sphere of life," had "forfeited the claim to be considered a lady, and with that claim all exemption from the utmost stringency of critical punishment" (630).

6. For further discussions of this theme, see Israel and especially Rose. In a provocative examination of race in Lewis's work, Rose argues that the "demonic Negro" acts as a psychological double on which Lewis displaces his own self-destructive tendencies.

7. Arnold extends his argument to include "A Tight Race Considerin'," a sketch in which a woman of propriety and manners is abjected by having her clothes torn off during a horse race. As Arnold says, Tensas's closest and most comfortable relations are with men.

8. As Rose notes, Lewis's representation of the "demonic Negro" has analogs in Poe, especially *The Narrative of Arthur Gordon Pym* and "Hop-Frog" (to which I would add the encoded Negro-as-ourang-outang in "The Murders in the Rue Morgue"). But as Rose says, "It is only in the stories of Henry Clay Lewis that one finds . . . the completely formed image of the demonic Negro, effecting his hideous destruction *in a realistic Southern context"* (emphasis added, 263).

9. It is striking to observe how many black revolutionaries—coded or otherwise—are physically misshapen, a list that would include, besides Lewis's dwarf and Poe's "Hop-Frog," Melville's Babo.

Works Cited

Arnold, Edwin T. Introduction. *Odd Leaves from the Life of a Louisiana Swamp Doctor,* by Henry Clay Lewis. Baton Rouge: Louisiana State Univ. Press, 1997. xi–xliv.

Baldwin, Joseph Glover. *The Flush Times of Alabama and Mississippi: A Series of Sketches.* 1853. Baton Rouge: Louisiana State Univ. Press, 1987.

Cassuto, Leonard. *The Inhuman Race: The Racial Grotesque in American Literature and Culture.* New York: Columbia Univ. Press, 1997.

Cutler, James E. *Lynch-Law: An Investigation into the History of Lynching in the United States.* 1905. New York: Negro Univ. Press, 1969.

Dabbs, James McBride. *The Southern Heritage.* New York: Knopf, 1958.

Dixon, Thomas, Jr. *The Clansman: An Historical Romance of the Ku Klux Klan.* New York: Grosset and Dunlap, 1905.

Douglas, Mary. *Purity and Danger: An Analysis of the Concepts of Pollution and Taboo.* New York: Praeger, 1966.

Faulkner, William. *Light in August.* 1932. Corrected text edited by Noel Polk. New York: Vintage, 1990.

Fiedler, Leslie A. *Love and Death in the American Novel.* New York: Dell, 1960.

Field, Joseph M. "A Lyncher's Own Story." 1845. *Old Southwest Humor from the St. Louis Reveille, 1844–1850.* Ed. Fritz Oehlschlaeger. Columbia: Univ. of Missouri Press, 1990. 226–32.

Fitzgerald, O.P. *Judge Longstreet: A Life Sketch.* Nashville: Publishing House of the Methodist Episcopal Church, 1891.

Gould, Stephen Jay. *The Mismeasure of Man.* New York: Norton, 1981.

Harris, Trudier. *Exorcising Blackness: Historical and Literary Lynching and Burning Rituals.* Bloomington: Indiana Univ. Press, 1984.

Israel, Charles. "Henry Clay Lewis's *Odd Leaves*: Studies in the Surreal and Grotesque." *Mississippi Quarterly* 28 (1975): 61–69.

Kristeva, Julia. *Powers of Horror: An Essay on Abjection.* Trans. Leon S. Roudiez. Columbia Univ. Press, 1982.

Lewis, Henry Clay. "Cupping on the Sternum." In *Humor of the Old Southwest.* Ed. Hennig Cohen and William B. Dillingham. 3rd ed. Athens: Univ. of Georgia Press, 1994. 417–18.

———. *Odd Leaves from the Life of a Louisiana Swamp Doctor.* 1850. Baton Rouge: Louisiana State Univ. Press, 1997.

Longstreet, Augustus Baldwin. *Augustus Baldwin Longstreet's Georgia Scenes Completed: A Scholarly Text.* Ed. David Rachels. Athens: Univ. of Georgia Press, 1998.

Lynn, Kenneth. *Mark Twain and Southwestern Humor.* 1959. Westport: Greenwood, 1972.

Morrison, Toni. *Playing in the Dark: Whiteness and the Literary Imagination.* New York: Vintage, 1992.

Rickels, Milton. "The Grotesque Body of Southwestern Humor." *Critical Essays on American Humor.* Ed. William Bedford Clark and Craig W. Turner. Boston: Hall, 1984. 155–66.

Robb, John S. *Streaks of Squatter Life, and Far-West Scenes.* Philadelphia: T.B. Peterson, 1858.

Robinson, Francis James. *Kups of Kauphy: A Georgia Book, in Warp and Woof, Containing Tales, Incidents, &c. of the "Empire State of the South."* Athens, Ga.: Christy and Chelsea, 1853.

Romine, Scott. *The Narrative Forms of Southern Community.* Baton Rouge: Louisiana State Univ. Press, 1999.

Rose, Alan H. "The Image of the Negro in the Writings of Henry Clay Lewis." *American Literature* 41 (1969): 255–63.

Smith, Lillian. *Killers of the Dream.* Rev. ed. New York: Anchor, 1963.

Tate, Allen. "Faulkner's *Sanctuary* and the Southern Myth." In *Memoirs and Opinions, 1926–1974.* Chicago: Swallow, 1975.

Twain, Mark. *Adventures of Huckleberry Finn.* Ed. Walter Blair and Victor Fischer. Berkeley: Univ. of California Press, 1985.

Rev. of *Uncle Tom's Cabin: Or Life among the Lowly. Southern Literary Messenger* 18 (October 1852): 630–38.

Urgo, Joseph. "Menstrual Blood and 'Nigger' Blood: Joe Christmas and the Ideology of Sex and Race." *Mississippi Quarterly* 41 (1988): 391–401.

Wright, Richard. *Black Boy (American Hunger): A Record of Childhood and Youth.* 1945. New York: HarperPerennial, 1993.

Perspectives on Earlier Authors—1830–1860

6

The Prison House of Gender

Masculine Confinement and Escape in Southwest Humor

Gretchen Martin

Romance novels such as George Tucker's *The Valley of Shenendoah* and James Hungerford's *The Old Plantation,* which dominated the Southern literary landscape until the Civil War, idealized the plantation lifestyle by creating romantic character portraits that grew to become cultural ideals. At the top of the social hierarchy were wealthy white men, yet even this privileged position was vulnerable to economics, social opinion, and accepted cultural dictates. These novels became increasingly didactic. As the necessity for the defense of class and social hierarchy increased, so too did the rules of the game. Class distinctions and gender roles grew to be increasingly polarized, discipline grew onerous, and social form became methodically refined and esoteric. Burgeoning largely from southern literary romances, the "aristocratic myth would grow in precise proportion to the need of the South to justify itself in the eyes of the world" (Lynn 6). The tropes manipulated within the southern romantic tradition prominently signify dissimilarities among men based on cultural considerations such as social status, race, region, education, and economics in order to support and reinforce the South's social and political hierarchy. Southwest humor tales manage these same tropes, maintaining the patriarchal paradigm, yet do so by inverting them to signify and illuminate the commonalties between men, which offer very different interpretations of masculinity. The transposition of these tropes illustrate that despite cultural considerations, men are united by their shared understanding of the issues specific to masculinity, such as troublesome women, ideals of honor, and the adversarial relationship between man and nature, problems not specific to region, race, or economic definitions.

Of significant importance to the general critical understanding of the genre is Kenneth Lynn's assumption of the *cordon sanitaire*, an artistic structure that pits the author's narrator (and audience) above and apart from the dialect-speaking characters. The humor within this paradigm derives from the moral and cultural ineptitude of the comic characters revealed in juxtaposition to the superiority of the narrator. As Lynn explains, "the humorists of the Southwestern tradition by and large remained loyal to the Southern myth, and to the image of themselves as gentlemen" (18). Comedic characters "by being humorously 'low'" made "the aristocrats seem more grand by contrast" (54). This essay demonstrates that there is much greater understanding and interest between social groups than general scholarship has indicated and that through homosocial relationships in Southwest humor tales, men conspire in a united attack against the feminizing influences of America's more refined and polite literary productions. Southwest humor tales celebrate ideals of masculinity vastly different from the very uncompromising southern ideal featured in the romances.

The male southern aristocrat walked a fine line between "gentleman" and "dandy." The romances function to explain what a "gentleman" is, how to recognize one, and ultimately rationalize why southern gentlemen should continue to maintain control of the political and social power in the South. The definition became one of control over self, recognizable largely through the display of refinement and genteel behavior. Temper was channeled into the duel, hunting was relegated to sport, courting demanded strict adherence to the dictates of chivalry, and political opinion became increasingly prescribed. Southwest humor redeemed the vitality of masculinity from the debilitating effects of refinement by giving men an outlet to express their sense of manliness, which offered them the opportunity to form a masculine community of readers and artists.

Territorial expansion into Tennessee, Georgia, Alabama, Louisiana, Mississippi, Arkansas, and Missouri, reawakened the need for "manly" strength and reclaimed the playing field of brute survival; traits depicted as no longer necessary, indeed often detrimental, to the established Old Dominion community featured in the romances. The types illustrated in Southwest tales were crucial to territorial development because neither a "bar" nor an "injun" cared about social status or education, and the authors develop these portraits with a sense of respect for raw, unrestricted masculinity. Southwest humor literary devices celebrate masculinity by highlighting and creating criteria defining manliness, honor, and integrity very different from the aristocratic southern "gentleman."

Unlike the romance novels, Southwest humor sketches depict less restrictive social segregation; indeed, the viability of producing the narrative structure of these tales depends upon interaction between social groups, whereas the structure of the romances projects an illusion of "natural" differences. In James Hungerford's *The Old Plantation*, the novel's patriarch, Uncle Weatherby, throws a party. The narrator, Clarence, describes the party as a community event and praises the hospitality of his uncle and cousin: "Dear Uncle Weatherby! How full he was with the happiness which he was conferring upon others. Cousin Walter and I found him, with a face glowing with smiles, doing his best to shake hands with and welcome every body 'high and low, rich and poor'" (225). Uncle Weatherby condescends to shake everyone's hand, rich and poor, but there is no dialogue recorded, suggesting that little or none occurred worth notice, and Weatherby's hospitality does not extend to the blacks at the party at all. They, "male and female, who were engaged in waiting upon their masters and mistresses, hung around as near to the dancing-ground as proper respect for the white superiors would allow" (251). The social event is carefully structured but is presented as if separations occurred naturally rather than as an indication of power. Adjectives describing class groups are manipulated to suggest inherent qualities rather than social constructions. The lower classes are often described as inferior, irresponsible, childlike, and superstitious, suggesting irrationality; whereas, members of the upper class—particularly men—are described as superior, responsible, wise, fatherly, and logical. Character analyses and portraitures in Southwest humor sketches, however, undergo close and personal scrutiny, and descriptions are highly unique among various characters, often developed through lengthy personal relationships between social groups. Regarding Augustus Baldwin Longstreet's *Georgia Scenes,* Scott Romine observes that through social interaction, Hall, the narrator, is able to describe and categorize the collection's characters because "they are, in a deep sense, *familiar* to him" (21). And, it is through Hall's social interaction that his observations function as a learning process, which enlightens the reader as well. By the final sketch in *Georgia Scenes,* "The Shooting Match," Hall's observations indicate significantly greater participation: "No longer a mere moralizing spectator, he actively participates in communal ritual, gladly accompanying Billy to the shooting match when invited to do so. This physical act is significant, for here we see a negotiated settlement of potentially divisive class boundaries being effected—literally and figuratively—on common ground"(18). The process leads Hall to learn that common interests and problems between men are not limited to class, social, or economic concerns, but affect all men within the culture, which illustrates a bond Hall uncovers rather than creates.

The genuine interest illustrated in *Georgia Scenes* among men is similar to the narrative structure of Alexander G. McNutt's "Jim and Chunkey" tales. The narrator is a wealthy cotton planter, referred to as "the Captain" by Jim and Chunkey. What is unique about McNutt's tales is that there is another upper-class character depicted—the Governor—aside from the narrator, suggesting that the bond between the narrator and his characters is not the unique oddity of a specific individual but is instead a more common connection between men other literary devices have failed to notice. Jim and Chunkey have an economic relationship with the Governor, but they rarely defer to him. In "A Swim for a Deer," the Governor becomes exasperated with Chunkey's "whistlin," and "says he to Chunkey—"'Chunkey, you have kept me awake two nights a whistlin, and you must stop it tonight, or *you* or *me* must quit the plantation'" (82). Chunkey responds: "'Governor I don't want to put you to no trouble, but I *can't* stop in the middle of a chune, and as you have known the plantation longer than me, I expect you can leave it with lest trouble'" (82). Chunkey not only defies the Governor's authority, he exerts his own by informing the Governor that if he doesn't like it, he can leave his own property. The section also allows the reader to understand that the relationship between Jim and the Captain is not merely an economic situation but illustrates a personal attachment depicted through the tales the Captain solicits from Jim. Within the sketches there exists a comfortable and enjoyable camaraderie. Jim often refers to the Captain as "honey," which overtly suggests a very familiar (if not endearing) relationship between the two, and they happily "licker" together throughout their adventures.

In "Chunkey's Fight with the Panthers," while on a hunting excursion with Jim and the Captain, Chunkey relates a tale about a previous hunting excursion. The Captain's participation in the hunting trip involves him in an adventure that transgresses the boundaries of mere "sport." As the sketch proceeds, Chunkey offers hunting advice to the Captain that reveals that hunting for provisions is a very different endeavor than the upper class's rigidly constructed fox or deer hunt "sport." The tale concludes by returning the group of hunters from the story of the hunt to their present hunt, and Chunkey instructs the Captain: "'Look out, Capting! Here's the place! Make the skift fast to that cyprus log'" (92). The advice clearly signifies the expert in the situation and the student, which highlights the futility of social concerns in the woods, yet also works to allow the Captain an escape from the rigidity of rule-oriented "aristocratic" sport.

George Washington Harris's "Sut Lovingood" tales also function through a rather close relationship between men of distinctly different social groups. They often begin with the ignoble Sut greeting the upper-class George by bellowing "Hey Ge–orge!" (86). The unabashed eagerness and all-out glee expressed by Sut for a chat with George suggests a comfortable familiarity between the characters. George describes Sut in "Sut Lovingood's Daddy, Acting Horse" as a "queer looking, long legged, short bodied, small headed, white haired, hog eyed, funny sort of a genius" (19). He may not be pretty, but George seems to admire his particular type of wit and wisdom, and there exists a comfortable relationship between the two that is especially irreverent of class consciousness. George often calls Sut a fool, but Sut feels no reticence about returning barbs and chastising George for his refined naiveté. When George doesn't understand Sut's reference to the "'huggin place'" on Sicily, he bellows, "'the wais' yu durn oninisheiated gourd, yu'" (76). The deference of the lower classes paid to the upper classes depicted in the romance novels is significantly omitted in these tales, which suggests a sense of camaraderie and confederation for masculinity that subordinates social and cultural considerations; indeed, femininity is often a more treacherous antagonist of masculinity than even the dangers of the wild because the playing field is often inequitable due to the socialization of male and female relationships.

Courtship in the romances is never depicted as a private affair, and the conduct of men becomes governed by the institutionalization of propriety. The humor tales, however, function to rail against the acculturating power of women through a misogynistic tenor almost indicative of Southwest humor sketches. But the misogyny functions to allow masculinity an opportunity to escape social restrictions and critique gender ideals rather than reinforce the oppression of women. The tales battle the socializing power of femininity and allow men the opportunity to challenge the cultural restrictions enforced upon them by the "genteel tradition," openly expressing anger, lustiness, and vengeance, sometimes against women, which was particularly taboo for the southern gentleman. They could also "unmask" femininity, illustrating indelicacy, hostility, and greed—portraits that were severely at odds with the "magnolia myth."

David Shi explains that the "feminization" of culture, especially in literature, was not a problem men encountered exclusively in the South. "As early as the 1840s anxious men began to complain about the loss of 'manliness in thought.' By mid-century such complaints had formed a chorus" (17). Indeed, the feminization of culture flourished to such an extent that critic Fred Lewis Pattee illustrates its social saturation in his study of the decade by the title of his analysis: *The Feminine Fifties.* He writes: "The nation's most prominent writers, artists, architects, educators, ministers, and moral philosophers . . . shared refined tastes, delicate sensibilities, and magisterial demeanors . . . They viewed themselves as guardians of conventional religious belief, aesthetic standards, and moral values" (16).

The tradition had a profound effect upon the nation, and as Leslie A. Fiedler explains, "conventions of tenderness and courtesy; and literature, expressing and defining those conventions, tends to influence 'real life' more than such life influences it" (31). In retaliation against the conventions of refinement, the tales function not only to create an escape, but also to expose the superficial nature of the genteel tradition. Jesse Bier, in *The Rise and Fall of American Humor*, contends that the Southwest humorists were "a combined group in a psychic revolt they did not fathom" (63). Elements of revolt and retaliation may indeed have been somewhat subconscious to a minor extent, yet the recurring themes of rebellion throughout the tales and among these authors render complete unconscious coincidence illogical. The tales are often too scathing and specific to suggest an unintentional focus.

Augustus Baldwin Longstreet is particularly suspicious (and sometimes openly contemptuous) of women. In the tale "The 'Charming Creature,' as a Wife," his protagonist learns a difficult lesson regarding the myth of the "Southern Belle." His character George is taken with a "lovely, and charming, and beautiful little creature," and his affection is increased when her father reveals the sum of her twenty-thousand-dollar dowry. The portrait is juxtaposed with that of his mother, whose "order, neatness, and cleanliness prevailed everywhere" (83). Clues to Evelina's nature are overlooked and dismissed by George, who has fallen for the manipulative beauty, as is the advice from his mother, and they are married. Longstreet goes on to describe the deterioration of the marriage and of his character: "George now surrendered himself to drink and to despair, and died the drunkard's death" (109). The cautionary structure of this tale is vastly different from the idealization of femininity depicted by the romance novelists, and reveals images of the women's sphere conspicuously omitted from the romances. In Hungerford's *The Old Plantation*, Aunt Mary is a woman with "a very pleasant smile upon her countenance. She appeared, indeed, with that sweet and benign-looking face of hers, as if she had never been impatient in all her life" (59). As a typical day begins on the plantation, Old Delight, Uncle Weatherby is pictured "engaged in his study, and Aunt Mary in her household duties" (82). This is the only peek Hungerford allows into the woman's sphere in his novel. However, Catherine Clinton's analysis of plantation life in *The Plantation Mistress* offers a more thorough description about what these "household duties" involved. Clinton explains that "the planter's wife was in charge not merely of the mansion but of the entire spectrum of domestic operations throughout the estate from food and clothing to the physical and spiritual care of both her white family and her husband's slaves" (18). The plantation mistress' duties had been common since "the American colonies severed connection with the British, the southern plantations lost important sources of goods and services; for the first time, women were forced to manufacture their own cloth, and plantations had to become self-sufficient" (29). The duties of the mistress are much too numerous to list, but the chore of "putting up port" illustrates the harsh realities of the southern woman's sphere: "December was the month set aside for hog killing. The mistress supervised the long and complicated series of jobs that the process entailed . . . Male slaves did the dirty work of the slaughter . . . Once the carcass was prepared, however, the mistress took over. She emptied and scraped clean the small intestines . . . processed the fat into lard, and chopped and seasoned the back meat" (23).

As Clinton observes, "it was grueling, repetitious work for planters' wives, and but one of their numerous unromantic duties" (24). With that in mind, it is little wonder that George and Evelina's lives are so disordered. Longstreet is not only shedding a realistic light into the female arena, specifically after marriage, but also critiquing the culture of romance projected through plantation novels. Within these novels, young unmarried women are pictured being escorted to parties, gossiping together, writing love letters, singing, and reciting poetry. Yet, as frivolous as these scenes might appear, they are not unrealistic: "As young girls, southern women were seldom trained to keep house; education at home and in academies instead emphasized intellectual and artistic accomplishments" (19). As Clinton points out, these women were in for a rude awakening after marriage.

In "The Mother and Her Child," Longstreet illustrates a woman who openly expresses anger and treats her servant severely. Mrs. Slang often boxes her servant Rosa, but her hostility is not limited to her servant. She is a woman with a short fuse, and her child's distress provokes her: "'Hush! You little brat! I believe it's nothing in the world but crossness Hush!' (shaking it), 'Hush, I tell you'" (131). The image is an extreme deviation from the gentle and almost saintlike mother image touted by the genteel tradition, for example Aunt Mary. The critique of the ideal allows Longstreet to illustrate that dealing with troublesome women is not confined to a specific class but indicates a problem shared by all men.

Longstreet was not alone in choosing to satirize concepts of femininity. In "Megatherium's" tale "Fire in the Rear," published May 10, 1851, in the *Spirit of the Times*, the author, whose identity remains unknown, describes a young man spying on a group of girls swimming. He cuts two eyeholes in a gourd and swims down the stream to "have some fun out of the girls" (136). However, when he is discovered, the girls rush up the bank, but "turned on him, seized him and threw him on his face, twined his arms around a sapling, and bound his hands with a kerchief" (136). Their modesty is forgotten in their haste for revenge, and each "provided herself with a trim birch or willow rod" (136) and proceeded to beat her anger out on his backside. Fatigued, but not fully satisfied with the beating, they untie the naked Bill

Jones, and he was forced to "run the gauntlet" (136); each girl, armed with a fresh switch, delivered a final whack. At the end was "a stout country lass whose strength he had often tried in a wrestle" (136). The final blow "fell upon his rear that the sparks flew out of his eyes, and he bounded half across the stream at one leap. This rock has been known as "'Jones's Leap' ever since" (136). The author creates a group of girls whose anger and sense of vengeance is excessive and ruthless, which deviates intensely from the cultures' rhetoric regarding woman's "natural" refinement.

George Washington Harris's character Sut Lovingood is perhaps the most openly contemptuous representation of masculinity toward the rules of etiquette, refinement, and courtship, but he is also perhaps the greatest admirer of natural woman to be found in the tales. The world in which Sut lives is absurd, and he expresses no reluctance to critique it. Absurdity as an artistic trope is common in Southwest humor sketches, as Pascal Covici Jr. observes: "If there is any one pattern basic to the humor of the Southwest it is precisely this: a character is pushed by the author into a situation in which he either exposes the pretensions of others or himself" (327). The trope is manipulated in the romances as well; however, it is manipulated to expose the absurdity of, specifically, lower classes and different races to reinforce the white male ideal rather than to expose the artificial nature of culture. Harris's tales depict a newly formed settlement during a stage in which cultural, gender, and class roles are in their early stages and therefore more obviously "under construction" and as a result, often obviously absurd. The social roles in the Old Dominion community featured in the romances are much more practiced and acculturated, which creates the illusion that they are "natural" rather than traditional. By depicting newly established and developing communities, Southwest humor tales are able to expose the artifice of social and cultural roles because participants are learning and developing these roles.

In "Sut Lovingood's Sermon," Sut explains his "five pow'ful pints of karacter." By pointing out his own personal flaws, Sut is able to defuse character attacks by beating critics to the punch, while at the same time these "pints" give him the credibility of experience in his critique of the community. His opinions are based on personal dilemmas and observations and are delivered with outrageous humor, suggesting that he is just a fool and should not be taken seriously; however, there exists within his tales an undeniable logic, which when stripped of the humor, is surprisingly precise.

Sut's behavior with women depends upon the individual woman rather than cultural rules and courting requisites. In "Parson John Bullen's Lizards," Sut seeks revenge on Parson John for betraying a promise made to Sal to keep from her parents an affair the parson has discovered between Sut and Sal. Sut is furious with Parson John when he fails to keep his promise, and rails to George, "'He'd a heap better a stole sum *man's* hoss; I'd a tho't more ove 'im'" (51). Sut openly criticizes the hypocrisy he finds in organized religion, and his disgust for the betrayal illustrates his much less refined, but no less zealous, sense of honor in attempting to protect Sal's reputation.

There is a significant difference in the relationship between Sut and Sicily in "Sicily Burns's Wedding." Sut is avid about protecting Sal, yet when crossed by Sicily, she becomes fair game. When Sicily plays a rather harsh joke on Sut, tricking him into drinking soda that makes him violently ill, she yells: "'Hole hit down, Mister Lovingood! Hole hit down!'" (82) She is hardly expressing "ladylike" behavior and quite obviously enjoys Sut's dilemma. George, representing a southern gentleman, is restricted by his social position from avenging his gender from attacks by the other, but his less socially bound confidant is not. The continuous solicitation of Sut's stories suggests that George relishes hearing experiences forbidden to him, which through Sut he can enjoy while firmly maintaining his reputation, which he vehemently protects. When asked by Sut what he would do if Sut wandered into George's church, scantily clad "'a-aimin fur yure pew pen, an' hit chock full ove yure fine city gal friends, jus' arter the peopil hed sot down frum the fust prayer, an' the orgin beginnin tu groan,'" George replies, "'Why, I'd shoot you dead, Monday morning before eight o'clock'" (228). George and Sut are physically and ideologically restricted from one another within the limitations of convention, but their conversations, most often conducted on the outskirts of town, allow them to form an alliance that neither solicits nor desires social sanction. The relationship also illustrates George's need to occasionally escape the confinement of his social role.

As Sut continues his story, he explains to George that he finds his opportunity for revenge during Sicily's wedding. Her matrimonial choice also allows Sut to seek vengeance on "the suckit rider" as well because he is the groom. "'The very feller hu's faith gin out when he met me sending sody all over creashun. Suckit-riders am the surjestif things tu me. They preaches agin me, an' I hes no chance tu preach back at them'" (89). Published at a time in which personal, political, and social critiques were subjected to severe censor circumscription, Sut's complaints become an ingenious vehicle for critical freedom.

Sut avenges his injured pride by destroying Sicily's wedding, which seems excessive, but is it more so than Sicily's behavior? She purchases the powder, mixes it, uses Sut's attraction to her to get him to drink it, and thoroughly enjoys the results. Basically, Sut tips a basket over a cow's eyes. The results border on unusual cruelty, but Sut could not possibly have anticipated the excessive results, yet the chaos created by the angry bull further allows Harris to expose the artifices of femininity by illustrating the unreserved reaction of the women when bees are after them. Etiquette, manners, and refinement, literally, "loped outen windows, they rolled outen the doors in bunches, they clomb the chimbeys, they darted onder the hous jus' tu dart out agin" (95). And, Sicily's language is less than delicate as she chastises Sut: "'Yu jis' say bees agin, yu infunel gallinipper, an' I'll scab yer head wif a rock'" (96).

Sut holds himself bound to no laws but his own, and as Milton Rickels observes: "His life is a free choice he has made for himself; his existence is the product of his own will . . . His existence is not, like that of the average man, dead in the world of tradition, habit, and illusion" (116). Of significant importance in understanding this complex character is his open admiration for physical beauty and his determination to fulfill his quest for lust. In "Mrs. Yardley's Quilting" he unabashedly explains to George: "'Gals an' ole maids haint the things to fool time away on. Hits widders, by golly what am the rale sensiblil, steady-goin, never-skeerin, never-kicken, willin, sperrited, smoof pacers'" (141), which suggests that Sut has had some sexual success with "widders." Jane Curry makes an interesting observation in "The Ring-Tailed Roarers Rarely Sang Soprano" pointing out that "it is ironic that in the most masculine of humor traditions, we should find positive acknowledgment of healthy sensual satisfaction for women" (135). Curry explains that Harris illustrates positive female sexuality because "the widows have experienced sexual intercourse, and they like it! Not only does their experience heighten enjoyment for their partners and circumvent the need to play courting games—they enjoy and desire sexual activity for themselves . . . This is a far cry from the sentimental vision of the widow who is by virtue of her husband's death liberated from performing the necessary sexual duties of a wife" (134).

Indeed, nineteenth-century medical advice books often described female sexual arousal as dangerous, and Dr. Robert Gooch's *Practical Compendium of Midwifery* deems excessive female excitement a disease, to be treated by cold-water enema (47). Sut's interest in sexuality and Harris's rendition of female sexuality are presented as much more congenial components of human nature than the culture's restrictive and oppressive medical expertise. As many Southwestern tales illustrate in depicting the early stages of a developing community, social structures will inevitably form; but early on, these cultural divisions are less restrictive, and the authors of these tales capture this important distinction. The narrators, then, represent the sacrifices necessary for leadership in an established community; whereas, characters such as Dick Kelsy, Jim Doggett, and Sut Lovingood signify the freedom from convention the West offered to those who were willing to participate in the early stages of development. The appreciation of unrestricted masculinity illustrated in Southwest humor tales is apparent in the content of the sketches, their popularity, and in the quantity of the productions. A vast amount of Southwest humor sketches were published in William T. Porter's sporting journal the *Spirit of the Times*, largely in reaction to, as Porter biographer Norris W. Yates explains, "the bleak and crabbed aspects of New England morality, its academic garb, its rigid dogmatism and harsh judgments on human nature" (Yates 5). In 1831, editors Porter and Howe proclaim in a prospectus of the journal that the paper is designed to be devoted "to the pleasures, amusements, fashions, and divertissements of life . . . To paint 'life as it is,' without the artificial embellishments of romance" (1). The journal's early readers consisted of primarily upper-class sportsmen, but by 1856, readership burgeoned considerably and "it becomes plain that the bulk of his later readers belong to a new and larger economic and social class" (Yates 21). Through papers like the *Spirit of the Times*, the *St. Louis Reveille,* and *New Orleans' Delta*, men found common ground, regardless of social and cultural criteria.

The tales draw upon and develop the uniquely American desire for masculine escape. Leslie A. Fiedler explains that "Rip Van Winkle presides over the birth of the American imagination; and it is fitting that our first successful homegrown legend should memorialize, however playfully, the flight of the dreamer from the drab duties of home and town . . . the typical male protagonist of our fiction has been a man on the run . . . anywhere to avoid 'civilization,' which is to say, the confrontation of a man and woman which leads to the fall, to sex, marriage, and responsibility" (26). William E. Lenz observes that Southwest humor "writers understood that men in social situations entered what they perceived to be the province of women," which required men of "culture and breeding" to "uphold gentlemanly standards of decorum" (598). These cultural obligations demanded sacrifice, yet the tales suggest that but for the narrators' commitment to community duty, they were as adventurous, brave, and courageous as their less socially beholden characters.Territorial expansion required men who were willing and able to penetrate sections of unexplored and hostile wilderness. The endeavor required bravery, brute strength, and natural cunning merely to survive the daily natural hazards of the wild. The physical adversities of the wilderness became symbolically embodied in the great black bear. Encounters with this revered adversary emerged as a unique subgenre, "the big bear school," the greatest of these being Thomas Bangs Thorpe's "The Big Bear of Arkansas." The tale reveals the tremendous esteem these adventurers have for nature, as well as their distrust and hostility towards the city.

Jim Doggett, the great Arkansas bear hunter, explains to a group of men on a steamboat on the Mississippi, "'I never made *the first visit before* [New Orleans], and I don't intend to make another in a crow's life. I am thrown away in that ar place, and useless, that ar a fact'" (337). He is perhaps more critical of city men, telling the group: "'Some of the gentlemen thar called me *green*—well perhaps I am, said I, *but I aren't so at home*; and if I ain't off my trail much, the heads of them perlite chaps themselves weren't much the hardest; for according to my notion, they were *real no-nothings*, green as a pumpkin-vine—couldn't, in farming, I'll bet, raise a crop of turnips; and as for shooting, they'd miss a barn if the door was swinging, and that, too, with the best riffle in the country'" (337). Doggett is, however, perfectly suited for his life in the woods, which requires skill with a gun, farming knowledge, and other very practical accomplishments. His expertise is juxtaposed with the gentlemanly version of hunting. Doggett interprets the distinction as he explains the difference between "meat" and "game," which is the difference between hunting for survival and hunting for recreation. Doggett contemptuously argues that the necessity for mere survival in the wild renders mere "game" too trifling for him to waste his time on. Survival in the wilds of Arkansas requires "meat," and the hunting skills necessary for survival demands a healthy respect for nature. Doggett explains, "'Nature intended Arkansaw for a hunting ground, and I go according to nature'" (341). In fact, mosquitoes and other pests in the wild are merely elements of nature, and as Doggett contends, "'I never find fault with her'" (338).

Doggett begins the tale of a particularly memorable adventure with a bear in whom he has met his "match." He gains such respect for the bear's cunning, size, and "sassy" personality that he develops a deep regard for the bear and loves him "like a brother" (334). Yet the contest becomes so engrossing, Doggett determines "'to catch that bear, go to Texas, or die'" (345). He finally succeeds in catching the bear, but the death of this great adversary is ambiguous, and after his demise, Doggett deeply "missed him" (346). He reveals his deep esteem for the bear as he relinquishes his hunter's bragging rights and contends, "'My private opinion is, that that bear was an *unhuntable bear, and died when his time come*'" (346). Early suspicion of Doggett's tale crumbles as he acknowledges his inferiority to this unconquerable being, and Doggett "sat some minutes with his auditors, in a grave silence" (346). Regional, social, and economic differences are subordinated as the men coalesce in this moment of silent respect.

Early explorers like Doggett, laying the foundation of a future community, of course lack the polish of more established leaders; but they are not without their own sense of justice, honor, and social norms. In John Robb's "The Pre-emption Right," Dick Kelsy is "tall, raw-boned, good-natured and fearless," and he is also hospitable and generous. He is presented as the potential of the "ideal" but lacks the socialization of culture, yet he is perfectly suited in his role as the base on which a community will grow. Lacking the socialization of the cultural ideal (the southern gentleman), but maintaining important and valuable personal traits, he represents a natural ideal. This ideal is presented as no better or worse than the cultural ideal, such as the narrators; it is merely different and serves very different purposes. The sketch illustrates the need for unrestricted "prairie justice" in the wilderness and suggests that negative elements, such as the tale's stranger, will be weaned out of the community by the superiority of men like Dick Kelsy. When an emigrating couple, the stranger and his wife, visit Kelsy's area, he welcomes them into his home and "started to the settlement for some notions with which to entertain them more comfortably" (119). Like Jim Doggett, who extends an invitation to Thorpe's narrator "'to visit a month or two, or a year, if you like,'" Kelsy's hospitality lacks polish but not congeniality. Kelsy gathers a group of men to help the couple "raise a cabin" (120) near his settlement, but soon becomes outraged by the stranger's treatment of his wife.

Kelsy will not see a woman abused, he states, because "'the love I have for an old Kentucky mother won't permit me to see or hear one of her sex abused beneath my cabin roof, ef it is in the wilderness,—I don't like red skins, none of 'em, but even a *squaw* couldn't be abused here!'" (121) The overt racism in the statement, while offensive, firmly establishes Kelsy's code of honor and at the same time reiterates the established ideological binary split between the genders: women in need of protection and men providing protection. Kelsy and his friends protect the stranger's wife, and in doing so are purifying the settlement: "They moved with silence, for a deed of blood was to be enacted. The law of the wilderness was about to offer up a victim for common safety" (130). Within the rudimentary stages of this settlement, justice is dependent upon these early settlers, yet Robb presents a system of equity that is impartial, just, and although crude, illustrates a less refined, but no less important, system of honor. The men in this tale are laying the foundation upon which a community will be constructed and protecting it through the only means of justice available to them. Prairie justice is unrefined, yet it is effective and fair and, more importantly, is crucial to the viability of progress, which since the Revolution had become an American imperative.

The genre has often been criticized for its descriptions of physical brutality, especially the tales of fighting, yet the juxtaposition of newspaper accounts chronicling the aristocracy's deadly, although more socially respectable alternative, the duel, renders these humorous fight scenes mild in comparison. Yates explains that "tempers ran high in the antebellum South, and the back-country cavalier in particular kept his dueling pistols cleaned and ready. Albert Pike had fought at least one duel. Noland, also of Arkansas, had killed an opponent on the field of honor; a third Arkansas correspondent, Matt Flournoy Ward, had killed a school teacher for punishing his boy" (27). Bertram Wyatt-Brown observes in *Southern Honor*: "Although the occasions for duels differed somewhat, almost all arose because one antagonist cast doubt on the manliness and bearing of the other, usually through the recitation of ritual words—liar, poltroon, coward. The stigma had to be dealt with or the labels would haunt the bearer forever . . . Death and abandonment were all too often the outcome for the losers, and even some victors found themselves without the companionship that the duel was supposed to bring them" (360). In a dueling manual published in 1858 in Charleston, South Carolina, writer John Lyde Wilson explains that the only socially acceptable exemptions for declining a challenge were "from a minor, (if you have not made an associate of him); one that has been posted; one that has been publicly disgraced without resenting it; one whose occupation is unlawful; a man in his dotage and a lunatic" (19). To meet and participate on "the field of honor" was both a privilege and a mortal hazard; the outcome of this ritual could secure one's reputation but might also end in death.

Catherine Clinton reminds readers that due to the patriarchal structure of antebellum society the death of a patriarch had the potential of destroying many lives; indeed, the effects could reach into future generations. She also notes the devastation suffered by persons involved in a duel, indicating they had no other option but to participate. Clinton quotes from a letter between two women in Louisiana: "'Have you heard of Mrs. Pearson's misfortune in the Death of her youngest son, he was killed in a Duel—his adversary as soon as he had kill'd him blew his own brains out'" (108). Yet the practice continued throughout the South until the Civil War, and as Paul Finkelman explains in "Dueling," the list of duelists "reads like a 'who's who' of the antebellum South" (1503). Southwest humor fights, while unorganized and often vicious affairs, rarely left a corpse.

Given the personal dueling experiences of several *Spirit of the Times* contributors, it is little wonder such clashes are often ridiculed in the tales. Cohen and Dillingham comment upon Phillip B. January: "Beneath the level of rollicking masculine fun in stories like those printed here is a barb of satire—unusual in its sharpness—pricking the inflated code of behavior lauded on the surface. 'The Last

Duel in Loaferville' accepts the code of honor that motivates men to fight duels but proceeds then to make a farce of it" (246). A conflict arises over the issue of who is to maintain title to "the loafer of Loaferville" (247). True to the genre, the antagonists' skills at loafing are exaggerated claims to superiority, but also, like many of these tales, the brag comes to a crisis by outside influences. Due to the interference of others, it is determined that the dispute should be settled in a duel. Dueling was outlawed following the Hamilton-Burr affair in 1804, yet despite legal penalties it continued to flourish throughout the South until the Civil War; however, as January's tale illustrates, authorities often overlooked the crime. As the duel commences, the community turns out for the spectacle, "exceptin' Jim Truly, deputy sherrif, and he was a peepin'" (248).

The opponents meet on a mock "field of honor," yet the challenger (John) does not know that there are no balls in the pistols. Dummy, the current reigning loafer, feigns an injury. John "gazed in horror on Dummy; his pistol dropt." He cries: "'By jingo! Did I *do that*? Didn't think I was aimin' a nigh him'" (248). He then spots the sheriff and "tuck to the woods" (249). His flight from the community clearly indicates that he had no desire or intention of harming his opponent and is horrified by what he believes to be the outcome of the event, which sends him fleeing in fear of the law and his own actions. The duel is structured through a trick played on John yet also functions to shed a very contemptuous light on this highbrow ritual.

The tropes commonly used in Southwest humor sketches often directly invert those found in the romances; thus, they offer a very different interpretation of masculinity. The genre sheds the cumbrances of the genteel tradition and depicts social relationships in a much more natural and honest light. Many have credited the genre for being the first to show signs of literary realism in American writing. This certainly appears an accurate assertion in regard to the authors' boldness in tackling taboo subjects such as sensual females, overly refined gentility, organized religion, and unabashedly celebrating the fine masculine pursuits of swearing, drinking, hunting, fighting, and lusting, without apology. After Sicily's disastrous wedding, Sut tells George, "'They is huntin me tu kill me, I is fear'd,'" but the resurgence of the genre after the Civil War, and most notably Harris's Sut tales, informs the reader that Sut, and with him a healthy regard for Southwestern-style masculinity, was indeed able to secure an escape.

Works Cited

Bier, Jessie. *The Rise and Fall of American Humor*. New York: Holt, Rinehart and Winston, 1968.

Clinton, Catherine. *The Plantation Mistress*. New York: Pantheon, 1982.

Cohen, Hennig, and William B. Dillingham, eds. *Humor of the Old Southwest*. 3rd ed. Athens: Univ. of Georgia Press, 1994.

Curry, Jane. "The Ring-Tailed Roarers Rarely Sang Soprano." *Frontiers* 2 (1977): 129–40.

Fiedler, Leslie A. *Love and Death in the American Novel.* New York: Stein and Day, rev. ed., 1966.

Finkelman, Paul. "Dueling." *Encyclopedia of Southern Culture.* Chapel Hill: Univ. of North Carolina Press, 1989.

Gooch, Robert. *Practical Compendium of Midwifery.* 3rd ed. Philadelphia: Haswell, Barrington & Haswell, 1840.

Harris, George Washington. *Sut Lovingood Yarns Spun by a 'Nat'ral Born Durn'd Fool'.* New York: Dick & Fitzgerald, 1867.

Lenz, William E. "The Function of Women in Old Southwestern Humor: Re-reading Porter's *Big Bear* and *Quarter Race* Collections." *Mississippi Quarterly* 46 (1993): 598–600.

Longstreet, Augustus B. *Georgia Scenes: Characters, Incidents, &c. in the First Half Century of the Republic.* 1835. Savannah, Ga.: Beehive, 1975.

Lynn, Kenneth S. *Mark Twain and Southwestern Humor.* Boston: Little, Brown, 1959.

"Megatherium." "Fire in the Rear; or, Bill Jones Among the Girls." *Spirit of the Times,* May 10, 1851: 136.

Pattee, Fred Lewis. *The Feminine Fifties.* New York: D. Appleton-Century, 1940.

Porter, William T., and James Howe. "Prospectus." *Spirit of the Times,* December 1, 1831.

Rickles, Milton. "The Fool as Point of View." *Sut Lovingood's Nat'ral Born Yarnspinner.* Eds. James E. Caron and M. Thomas Inge. Tuscaloosa: Alabama Univ. Press, 1996.

Robb, John. *Streaks of Squatter Life, and Far-West Scenes.* Ed. John Francis McDermott. Gainesville: Scholars' Facsimiles & Reprints, 1962.

Romine, Scott. "Negotiating Community in Augustus Baldwin Longstreet's *Georgia Scenes.*" *Southern Literary Journal* 30 (1996): 1–27.

Shi, David E. *Facing Facts: Realism in American Thought and Culture 1850–1920.* New York: Oxford Univ. Press, 1995.

Wilson, John Lyde. *The Code of Honor; or Rules for the Government of Principles And Seconds in Duelling.* Kennesaw, Ga.: Continental, 1959.

Wyatt-Brown, Bertram. *Southern Honor: Ethics & Behavior in the Old South.* Oxford, UK: Oxford Univ. Press, 1982.

Yates, Norris W. *William T. Porter and the Spirit of the Times.* Baton Rouge: Louisiana State Univ. Press, 1957.

7

Augustan Nostalgia and Patrician Disdain in A.B. Longstreet's *Georgia Scenes*

Kurt Albert Mayer

Although they are usually allotted no more than a brief mention in most surveys of American literature, Augustus Baldwin Longstreet and his *Georgia Scenes* are regularly credited as having initiated Southwestern humor on which Twain and Faulkner were to feed copiously. Detailed examinations of Longstreet's only notable literary achievement are comparably scarce; moreover, they seem to be preoccupied with determining whether in fact the sketches may be regarded as social history—whether, in literary terms, the book is protorealist. Easy launches for arguments along those lines were provided by the inflated subtitle of the volume, *Characters, Incidents, &c. in the First Half Century of the Republic;* by a Native Georgian; and by the preface appended to the first edition, which appeared anonymously in 1835. As the secret of authorship was soon out, the assertions contained in the opening paragraph of the preface were duly rehearsed—that "some little art" was used in crafting the sketches, which were "nothing more than fanciful *combinations* of *real* incidents and characters," though "some of the scenes are as literally true as the frailties of memories would allow them to be" *(Georgia Scenes Completed* 3).[1]

Highlighting set phrases of authorial prefatory tiptoeing, the debate has gone wrong, misled by statements Longstreet made in later years. An 1836 letter, for instance, claimed: "The design of the 'Georgia Scenes' has been wholly misapprehended by the public. It has been invariably received as a mere collection of fancy sketches, with no higher object than the entertainment of the reader, whereas the aim of the author was to supply a chasm in history which has always been overlooked—the manners, customs, amusements, wit, dialect, as they appear in all grades of society to an ear and eye witness of them" (qtd. in Rachels, xlviii).

The question is not whether *Georgia Scenes* is social history, but how it is to be read as social history. Longstreet attempted a partial answer in the last paragraph of the preface: "I cannot conclude these introductory remarks without reminding those who have taken exception to the coarse, inelegant, and sometimes ungrammatical language which the writer represents himself as occasionally using, *that it is language accommodated to the capacity of the person to whom he represents himself as speaking*" (*GSC* 3–4, emphasis in the original).

The ambiguities culminating in the italicized passage are a final twirl of authorial prefatory tiptoeing. Repetition of the word "represent" invokes the political dimension of the sketches, and the pun on "to whom" makes clear that the pieces were meant as direct addresses to readers rather than as social history—that is, disinterested texts, accounts once removed. James M. Cox has noted that Longstreet's "weakness came from leaning too much toward refinement, politeness, and culture" (110). In other words, the clumsiness compounded in the final sentence of the preface results less from "ignorance of the implications of using frontier materials and oral narrative techniques" (Lenz 316) or an inadequately realized "aesthetic distance" (Holman 7) but, more fundamentally, from an uncertainty with respect to notions of social difference.[2]

This essay argues that when writing *Georgia Scenes,* Longstreet was a frustrated politician turned temporary artist by accident, rather than exemplifying "the drift from art to politics" Richard M. Weaver regards as characteristic of most antebellum Southern humorists (80; cf. Lynn, *Twain* 116). Social difference is a major determinant of Longstreet's *Georgia Scenes,* which originated as occasional items in the local press, while their author, a jack-of-all-trades but not really a writer, was hotly engaged in day-by-day politics. The sketches are held together mainly by their common setting; as Franklin J. Meine (xvi), Walter Blair (65), and Van Wyck Brooks (240) have remarked, they are provincial, wholly and intensely local. They are also intensely political, drawing on the context of the debates coming to the hilt in the 1830s. The region depicted, Middle Georgia, was a middle ground, contested economically, socially, culturally, and politically. There, the ways of the tidewater aristocracy crossed those of the yeomanry peopling the red hills of the upcountry. The area had experienced spectacular economic growth as the center of the cotton belt during the 1820s; but by the 1830s the boom was over, having moved west. As signs of stagnation were noticeable, the antagonism crested in controversies over the tariff, nullification and states' rights, the institution of slavery, and the urge for democratic reform of local and state governments.

"Georgia Theatrics," the sketch opening Longstreet's collection, stages that antagonism as an incongruous confrontation, a clash of cultures cast in part as a class conflict. A gentleman by the name of Hall remembers a foray into Lincoln County, thirty miles northwest of Augusta. Conscious of his social and moral superiority, he expends a good deal of rhetoric on creating the narrative distance he deems appropriate: "If my memory fail me not, the 10th of June, 1809, found me, at about 11 o'clock in the forenoon, . . . in what was called 'The Dark Corner' of Lincoln. I believe it took its name from the moral darkness which reigned over that portion of the county at the time of which I am speaking" (*GSC* 4).

The incident about to be related is tucked away safely in the past and in a far corner of the locale, not yet penetrated by the light of culture. Hall is hardly within, and much less of, the world he presents. His bland imitation of Augustan essayists contributes to opening a gap Longstreet himself identified unwittingly as "a chasm in history" and Kenneth S. Lynn termed a *"cordon sanitaire"* (*Twain* 64), set up against a tale of a brief encounter that happened long ago. Riding in that Dark Corner, Hall suddenly heard strange noises from a thicket, voices that seemed to emanate from a "band of ruffians" engaged in "Pandæmonian riots." Finally, a single youth emerges, embarrassed by the inadvertent witness. The young man is immediately classed by the vernacular put in his mouth, even if he seemingly has the punch line of the sketch. "'You needn't kick before you're spurr'd. There a'nt nobody there, nor ha'nt been nother. I was jist seein' how I could 'a' *fout*.'" The words take on portent in terms of class when the narrator realizes that the "Lincoln rehearsal" was staged in preparation for a fight in front of the courthouse, the sociopolitical center of the county. Even if it was just a rehearsal, the histrionics were all the more intimidating because of the social difference Hall established so deftly. "I went to the ground from which he had risen, and there were the prints of his two thumbs, plunged up to the balls in the mellow earth, about the distance of a man's eyes apart" (*GSC* 5–6).

The social polarization and the latent violence contained in the narrative invoke notions of class struggle—or at least the fear of it. Lynn cites "Georgia Theatrics" as evidence in support of his thesis that the antebellum humorists were mostly Whigs who wrote with a strongly aristocratic bias. In particular, he points to "the conservative political allegory inherent in the sketch," for the narrator "embodies a conservative political ideal," and "the violent boy represents what to the Whig mind was the central quality of Jacksonianism" (*Twain* 67–68). But the opposition of gentleman versus yokel, Georgia style, is too clear-cut. Longstreet cannot be tucked away as a Whig aristocrat. His political views, Lynn concedes, were "Whig *manqué*" (*Twain* 57); beyond those, Longstreet was a planter patrician only by marriage. Legend has it that upon his wedding he did not have money enough to buy proper clothes or pay the fee to the officiating minister. His parents had come from New Jersey a few years before their fourth son Gus was born in Augusta in 1790. They were yeoman farmers who struggled at times to make ends meet but managed to provide Gus with the best education that could be had. At age eighteen, he was sent to Moses Waddel's academy in Willington, South Carolina, then one of few schools of note in the whole South.

More profitable than the learning Longstreet acquired were the social connections gained. Waddel's institution was attended by many a future congressman, senator, and governor of Georgia and South Carolina. Boarding with a brother of John Calhoun, Gus shared a room with George McDuffie, who had already been a boarder of the Longstreets and who would become governor and U.S. senator of South Carolina, "perhaps the boldest of the loquatious tribe of Fire Eaters" (Parrington 2:62). Thus, it was early on when Gus Longstreet befriended the two men who were to be the leading figures in his political life. Recalling them four years after the end of the Civil War, he termed Calhoun "matchless" and regarded McDuffie as "hardly inferior to him in anything" (qtd. in Wade, 123).[3]

Gus followed the educational path of John Calhoun to Yale and on to Tapping Reeve's law school in Litchfield. In the fall of 1814, Gus returned to his home state, took the bar examination, and commenced riding the circuit as a lawyer on the western tier. The area was settled only recently; social stratification had not yet had time to consolidate. The introduction of cotton as the cash crop supplanting tobacco promised easy fortunes but entailed social upheaval, for the economic urge towards bigger farms demanded more and more slaves while driving out many dispossessed whites.

Longstreet was "a young man . . . looking to popular confidence as his sole means of advancement," writes John D. Wade, his biographer (51). And everybody, it seems, liked him. He soon married—"up." Eliza Parke's dowry amounted to a handsome fortune—two thousand dollars in cash and thirty slaves, whose renting out netted their owner another fifteen hundred dollars annually. Gus did well with his wife's money, as he bought six hundred acres of land near his in-laws at the prospering county seat of Greensboro. Greene County soon elected him captain of the militia, a hub of the social and intellectual life of the community. In 1821, he was chosen as a representative to the state assembly and elected Judge of the Superior Court in the following year. He had risen to chairman of the Judiciary Committee of the Georgia assembly when in 1824 he ran for Congress, but dropped out of the race after his first-born son and his mother-in-law died within two days of each other. When the states' righters suffered defeat in the 1825 state assembly elections, Longstreet fell victim to the spoils system; turned out of office, the judge was left with no more than the title he proudly retained until his death. The personal losses incurred a religious conversion—characteristically an undogmatic one—to Methodism. Conceivably, the ousting from politics nourished his radicalism as well as his increasing vindictiveness.

In 1827 the Longstreets moved to Augusta. He "commenced planting and lawing," as an autobiographical sketch for the Yale alumni paper has it (qtd. in Wade, 117). The residence purchased was ostentatious, located on a large tract of land not far from the city named Westover and built by one of the Byrds of Virginia. The oligarchic airs Longstreet affected scarcely concealed inherent contradictions; the pose resembled the pretensions of many a self-made planter aristocrat of Middle Georgia. Well-educated by the standards of his time, he was "not in any sense a cultured man," according to the estimate of a well-meaning acquaintance (qtd. in Hubbell, 667).[4] The judge, losing money on the plantation, soon sold all his slaves; more successful in auctioning off his land as real estate, he remained a fervent propagandist of slavery. In the 1840s he would advance the foundation of a separate Southern Methodist church and publish *Letters on the Epistle of Paul to Philemon or The Connection of Apostolical Christianity with Slavery*, a pamphlet calling upon the Bible to defend "the peculiar institution." On other grounds, Longstreet became active in the temperance movement even though he always liked his glass of wine with dinner.

Augusta was more inviting than the upcountry and its federalist yeomanry, for an advocate of states' rights could expect support from beyond the Savannah River, where the prophets of the creed had their home base. Longstreet leaned strongly towards the extreme tenets pronounced by McDuffie and eventually by Calhoun—he indeed preceded both of his idols in advancing those tenets—but the stance was precarious, for nullifiers found little backing outside South Carolina (cf. Cooper and Terrill 165). In summer 1832, as the dispute over nullification neared frenzy, Longstreet announced his bid for a seat in the state assembly but withdrew when he realized that the sentiment in Georgia was overwhelmingly pro-union and he had no chance of winning.

Dreams of office thwarted, he turned to the press. The move was propitious as the cultural climate of the South was ripe with a sudden flourish of periodical publications. The first eight of the sketches came out originally in the *Milledgeville Southern Recorder*, a paper historians consult chiefly as a lode of radical states' rights journalism. Drafts of scenes may have begun as early as 1830 but were only printed late in 1833, a few weeks before Longstreet acquired his own outlet for his writings. The takeover of a languishing federalist weekly was surely meant as a political gesture. The *Augusta North American Gazette*, promptly renamed *State Rights Sentinel*, became the mouthpiece of his opinions in editorials that, for Kenneth Lynn, "screamed political and moral outrage" ("Longstreet" 57). Wade, too, emphasizes the "extreme political view-point of the paper," which regularly and prominently featured "announcements about runaway slaves" (133, 135).

Since the collected *Georgia Scenes* are attributed to "A Native Georgian," the title of the opening sketch, "Georgia Theatrics," adverts to authorial theatrics as well. Elaborate guises accompanied the piecemeal publication of what in less than two years' time would surprisingly amount to a book. The sketches in the *Southern Recorder* were ascribed to two different authors whose pen names, Hall and Baldwin, recalled two early Georgia patriots. Lyman Hall signed the Declaration of Independence and served as governor in 1783–1784; Abra(ha)m Baldwin signed the Constitution and was the first Georgian to win recognition as a congressman. Once the scenes appeared in the *State Rights Sentinel*, the author's masks were upheld, though they were no longer urgent. The differentiation between Baldwin and Hall was subjected to the overall bent of the paper, which was voiced by a third pseudonymous spokesman—Bob Short, a diehard nullifier expounding his convictions in numerous squibs. "My friend Jack wishes to know at what age he should marry. Answer.—If he be a States' Rights man he should marry at twenty-five; but if he be a D.U. [Democratic Union] Republican he should not marry before he attain[s] the age of eighty-five" (qtd. in Rachels, xxiv).

The preface of the book concedes that the distinction between Hall and Baldwin is a leftover undermining the unity of the volume: "I was extremely desirous of concealing the author, and, the more effectually to do so, I wrote under two signatures. These have now become too closely interwoven with the sketches to be separated from them, without an expense of time and trouble which I am unwilling to incur. *Hall* is the writer of those sketches in which men appear as the principal actors, and *Baldwin* of those in which women are the prominent figures" (*GSC* 3).

A reminder that *Georgia Scenes* are gendered in awkward ways, the assertion makes too much of keeping the two narrators apart. Their notions of social difference, for one, diverge on irrelevant matters at best.[5] Baldwin, a respectable, stiff and prudish urbanite of indefinite interests, is always out on some unspecified business.

Hall is a judge riding the circuit, conscious of the gravity of his office and forever embarrassed by crudities. The two men meet on occasion and seem closer to each other than to anyone else in the book.

Two narrators allow for a certain latitude of presentation and variety of scenery, yet the perspective never varies. Looking down on practically all others, Longstreet's observers of "the 'civilizing' process" (Kibler xvi) perceive mainly differences between their caste and those below, while conflating the disparities among those dismissed as inferior. "The Fight" offers a case in point. Hall virtually disappears from the set he laid out so carefully. Ransy Sniffle, the epitome of the dirt eater, is all over the place to get the fight started yet does not associate with the narrator observing the scene from increasing distance. Early on, though, Sniffle is close enough for a detailed portrait that becomes a vicious caricature of a déclassé. Bill and Bob may be "the very *best men* in the county . . . , in the Georgia vocabulary" (*GSC* 33); the mutilations they inflict upon each other make them appear more grossly distorted than Sniffle. The graphic quality of the descriptions and the inherent verbal violence betray that, for all his efforts at dissociating himself from the scene, Hall is a voyeur, whose pangs of conscience are woven into the moralizing closure of the frame, an insufferable affirmation of low-to-middle-brow culture.

"The Gander Pulling," the last sketch to appear in the *Milledgeville Southern Recorder* and among the first to be printed in the *State Rights Sentinel*, combines Hall's social and political views most explicitly. Removed to a distant past, "the year 1798" (*GSC* 73), it opens with a lengthy digression on the prehistory of Augusta, declaring that then four villages competed for primacy in the region. Making his case "from conjecture" (*GSC* 74), the erstwhile resident of the city presents the rivalry as an extended analogy of national affairs in the early 1830s.[6] The account teems with catch-phrases of political doctrine of the day—*"single body," "public welfare," "Social Compact," "separate bodies," "private welfare"*—all italicized so as to make sure that the reader will not miss the point, and capped with the assertion that in due course one of the towns "was literally *nullified."* Advocating a confederacy, not a union, Hall bespeaks his commitment to states' rights, supposing that his audience share that position. As he introduces the central episode of the story proper, the gander-pulling contest, by quoting an "'*advurtyzement*' . . . to All woo mout wish to purtak tharof" (*GSC* 74), he does not even pretend to imitate speech but exaggerates the distance between himself and the objects of narration. When describing his arrival on the scene where the atrocious spectacle is to take place, he quickly sets himself apart from those who have gathered: "a considerable number of persons, of different ages, sexes, sizes, and complexions, . . . from the rival towns, and the country around. But few females were there however, and those few, were from the lowest walks of life." After some remarks on the gander—once "moving with patriarchal dignity," it was now reduced to "a fit object for 'cruelty'" (*GSC* 76)—the emphasis on social difference is maintained in the rendition of the participants, for they are reduced to mere names, owners of horses which in turn are depicted in mocking detail. In the end, the winner by luck turns out to be Fat John

Fulger, whose "own voice condemns him as a hopeless vulgarian" (Silverman 549); and Hall's concluding remarks bristle with unmitigated condescension for all involved. If, as Kenneth Silverman contends, "The Gander Pulling" posits "the crackers" as the "real enemies" of Longstreet's South (549), then *Georgia Scenes* must be seen as reflecting not so much "an interest in the common man," as Gretlund suggests (127), but a patrician disdain of poor-white ambitions.

Frankly self-congratulatory about his mission as a vanguard of civilization, Hall is less certain if the culture he imported has been beneficial in all respects. Rather than facing the present, he relishes nostalgic glimpses of the days when the frontier was still a presence on the western tier of Middle Georgia and the unpleasant realities of the contemporary world had not yet mushroomed. "The Turn-Out" reminisces about "the good old days," when a visit Hall paid to "my friend Captain Griffin . . . and his good lady" was met "with a *Georgia welcome* of 1790" (*GSC* 47). This dating of what is chronologically the first sketch marks the year of Governor Hall's death and Longstreet's birth as a seamless transition. The nostalgia blurs social differences as it limns an idealized harmony in Edenic surroundings. Yet, Griffin's idyll vanished with the illusion that the lands were inexhaustible. The Captain had boasted that "they will be as good fifty years hence as they are now." Hall records a return to the spot, "forty two years afterward," finding the place "barren, dreary and cheerless" (*GSC* 49–50). The reader is left to infer that soil erosion resulting from abuse of the land, the wastefulness of the plantation system, had a share in the destruction of the pastoral.[7]

Yearning for the good, simple country life is Hall's province, though Baldwin resorts to it as well. In "The Dance, A Personal Adventure of the Author," a nostalgic lens glorifies a county magistrate's family of five, who live content and happy in a one-room log cabin. They comport themselves with natural dignity and ease, unhampered by social etiquette. Even Billy Porter, the African American scratching the fiddle at the frolic, is awarded an approving nod, for he knows his assigned place and assumes it willingly. Baldwin's nod comes easily as it is granted to one who at the time of narration is already dead. The treatment of Porter and the marginalization of African Americans—who made up about one-third of the population in Middle Georgia but are hardly mentioned in the *Georgia Scenes*—suggest that in his thinking of race Longstreet upheld the dogma of the benevolent subservience of slave to master. He was about to make the turn from negro bondage as a necessary evil to slavery as a positive good.[8]

Baldwin is given only six pieces to Hall's twelve, but his sketches balance the distribution of rural and urban Georgia scenes. Nearly half of the sketches contained in the book have an urban setting, focusing largely on the upper segment of society. Baldwin is as prone to moralizing as Hall, while his insights in the dwellings of well-to-do burghers are more easily given to satire. Foppishness is targeted in "The Ball," where Misses Feedle, Deedle, Gilt, and Rhino congregate with gentlemen like Crouch, Flirt, Boozle, and Noozle. They pretend not "to ape the indecencies of Europe's slaves" and abstain from "mathematical cotillons . . . immodest waltzes . . . detestable, disgusting gallopades" (*GSC* 80); instead, Baldwin has them perform indigenous movements, "the three motions of a turkey-cock strutting, a sparrow-hawk lighting, and a duck walking" (*GSC* 86).

Baldwin's notions of social rank receive fullest treatment in "The 'Charming Creature,' as a Wife." The longest piece of the collection displays, according to Jessica Wegmann, "Longstreet's careful construction of what he considers correct social hierarchy" (19). Preachy and remonstrative, the sketch ends by recapitulating its moral, "a warning to mothers, against bringing up their daughters to be 'Charming Creatures'" (*GSC* 73). The note of caution is accentuated by personal connection. George Baldwin, the central character, is identified as the narrator's nephew. His parents are all modesty and moderation: the mother, "the repository of all feminine virtue"; the father, "a plain, practical, sensible farmer," bettered by no one of "those who move in his sphere of life" (*GSC* 53–54). George, an aspiring lawyer, deviates from the model path laid out by his elders when he falls for the "charming Evelina" (*GSC* 63). Her beauty blinds him to social difference—which the narrator expounds in a lengthy portrait of Evelina's father, a wealthy, unlettered cotton merchant. She is spoiled since she never received a proper domestic education; "pride and vanity became at an early age the leading traits of the child's character." She matures to "an accomplished hypocrite, with all her other foibles" (*GSC* 56). George insists on marrying her and finds an early grave.

The moral is unrelenting: Do not stray from your social roots. Beware of deception by superficial glamor. Virtue elevates, not wealth. Baldwin advocates benevolent paternalistic control and would have the proper position of women defined entirely by their subservience to fathers and husbands. Wegmann concludes, "when either wife or slave attempts to subvert the hierarchy of white male superiority, all lose and become miserable" (23). The observation is valid for issues of social difference as well.[9]

Toward the latter part of his career as an editor, political opponents accused Longstreet of having lost his old democratic faith (cf. Wade 137). His hardening conservatism, discernible in the progression of *Georgia Scenes,* resulted from the realization that nullification was a lost cause and further effort vain. Disenchanted with the course of affairs, his interest in journalism faded; in the summer 1836, he sold the paper that, as Longstreet would claim in his autobiographical sketch, had caused "much loss of time, and some loss of money" (qtd. in Wade, 138). The flow of scenes petered out once the book collection was printed in September 1835; only a few more sketches were published in the following years, not collected until 1998. Ascribed mostly to Baldwin, they were hastily written, sententious tracts rather than composed scenes, their flimsy story lines mere pretexts for sermonizing.

"Darby Anvil" is exemplary. In Wade's opinion, it "proclaims Longstreet's complete abandonment of any but the most conservative democracy" (205). Written late in 1838, when Longstreet decided to take up the ministry, it poses as an autobiographical obituary of Baldwin's life in politics—which, the sketch insinuates, was ended by the likes of Darby Anvil. Those populists appealing to the class from which they emerged were invited to usurp power when in 1835 Georgia opened floodgates by formally abandoning freehold suffrage.

"I well remember," Baldwin begins, "the first man who, without any qualifications for the place, was elected to the legislature of Georgia. He was a blacksmith by trade, and Darby Anvil was his name" (*GSC* 162). The title character turns into a negative image lacking in all that is deemed necessary and expedient for the tasks coming with public office. Social difference is a major distinctive category, defined by cultural prerogative rather than by ownership of property. Anvil's deficit is that he is unlettered, "ignorant in the extreme," the want squared by "some shrewdness, and much low cunning" (*GSC* 163). When he announces his candidacy, he cannot even comprehend the basics of states' rightism. "'I know I'm nothin' but a poor ign'ant blacksmith that dont know nothin' no how'" (*GSC* 167). The thick accent classes, and is classed; it is "to demonstrate," Kenneth S. Lynn has noted, "the social and political incapacities of the barbarous Democracy" (*Twain* 68–69). So as to make sure that the reader will not miss the point, Baldwin inserts a lengthy portrait of Darby Anvil as a Ransy Sniffle done over before he exposes the unabashed populism and "electioneering harangues" (*GSC* 165) that secure Darby's election.

Anvil's sudden political rise is propelled by overreaching ambition, the cause of his subsequent fall. He ends ignominiously, an alcoholic. The narrator, a captive of the worldview of his author, cannot muster any sympathy but castigates Darby for having set a detrimental precedent. The final paragraph of the sketch swells to a farewell address not easily surpassed in pathos. "The penalties of these acts are now upon our heads; and upon our children's children will they descend with unmitigated vigor. I forbear to follow the consequences farther—in charity to my native land I forbear" (*GSC* 178).

Baldwin's announcement that he will quit politics follows a pattern of vindictive withdrawals characteristic of Augustus Longstreet, in whose disposition there was an anticipation of the morbid sensitivity and touchy pride ascribed to southern politicians in the late antebellum.[10] Longstreet was moved by temper, not by intellect. The *Georgia Scenes* betray that shifty base in oscillations from queasiness to ebullience in diction. If the structural unity of the book is haphazard, a clear pattern can be made out with respect to social difference. The background of Longstreet's thought was vaguely, if fiercely, Jeffersonian agrarian; rural life was theoretically the best and most normal (cf. Parrington 2:170). In keeping with that particularly southern brand of conservatism that meandered from John Randolph to John Calhoun, his ideal society is patriarchal, biblical, as John D. Wade has noted (60). It subscribes fully to Calhoun's notions of a "white democracy," including all its contradictions.[11] Calhoun maintained he "had always been . . . a staunch supporter of the interests of his state, his class, and his region" (Niven 2). Intensely concerned with the South's social order, he was a Republican hostile to the democratic principle of numerical majority.

Eugene D. Genovese contends that "[e]ducated Southerners, as self-proclaimed heirs to medieval chivalry, understood true nobility to rest on virtue" (49). Politics becomes a question of morals, and on that, Longstreet was unrelenting, even if at times he propounded a rather hollow moralism. Devoted to Calhoun, he was not a vigorous intellectual or a profound thinker like the Carolinian. "His mind was of a literal cast" (Wade 93). A countryman at heart, he had a strong desire for social order. His *Georgia Scenes* attempted to fix that social order in writing. The result was a dirge for a world gone under, a prelapsarian pastoral, with planter society and slavery written out of the sketches. Longstreet is a realist only in that for him it is important that his writing establishes relations to an empirical reality. His negotiations of that reality more often than not give in to the prescriptive ordering of Augustan ideals.

Judge Longstreet comes remarkably close to James Henry Hammond, Calhoun's firebrand votary in the House of Representatives. An upwardly mobile lawyer, erstwhile schoolmaster and newspaper editor, Hammond became a plantation owner in 1831, when he married the heiress of Silver Bluff, an estate of over ten thousand acres located about a dozen miles southeast of Augusta. The diary he kept meticulously documented his learning of the ways of a planter politician; the book complements *Georgia Scenes* while sharing most premises. Hammond, an editor of the diary concludes, "seems to have succumbed to the myth of the Old South even before the South was old and before there was a myth" (Bleser 304).

Notes

1. When Sydnor (312ff.) and Hubbell (666ff.) elevated Longstreet to an early prototype of the local color writer, this was ostensibly to balance the portrait presented by Longstreet's first biographer, Bishop Oscar Penn Fitzgerald of the Methodist Episcopal Church, South, whose *Judge Longstreet, A Life Sketch* emphasized the career in education and the church while it barely mentioned political ambitions. The tag of "proto-local-colorist" became a catch phrase used by almost everyone writing on Longstreet; it indeed grew to the central argument of fairly recent works by Meriwether, Newlin, and Kibler, where a political dimension is explicitly denied. Only in the last few years have essays come out, notably the ones by Smith and Wegmann, that challenge those traditionalist views of Longstreet and *Georgia Scenes.*

2. I use the term "social difference" rather than "class" because of ideological implications. While I follow Althusser and Jameson in their belief that the perception of reality is always already an interpretive act that is prefigured by a collective discourse that is produced by the combination of material and social conditions, my disuse of the term "class" is to signal that I share the doubts Derrida phrased in *Specters of Marx.* There, Derrida claims he is "suspicious of the simple opposition of *dominant* and *dominated,* or even of the final determination of the forces in conflict" (55). Society is not necessarily defined by head-on antagonisms of rival groups; rather, oppositions are manifold, mostly gradual, and only rarely polar. And, to avoid an overload of ideological import, I have settled on the term "social difference," which has the advantage of denoting neither a binary opposition nor a hierarchic structure but a bundle of differences, albeit fundamental ones.

3. Longstreet's late assertion of his deliberately staking out his future course by following Calhoun and McDuffie exemplifies Derrida's tenet that social difference, as part of one's inheritance, is not received but assumed. "Inheritance is never *a given,* it is always a task. . . .

To be . . . means . . . to inherit[;] . . . the *being* of what we are *is* first of all inheritance, whether we like it or know it or not. . . . An inheritance is always the reaffirmation of a debt, but a critical, selective, and filtering reaffirmation" (54, 91–92).

4. Parrington's appellation of "so vigorous a plebeian" (2:167) diminishes Longstreet's patrician prepossessions. More to the point is Carr's summary: "enamored by wealth and power, [Longstreet] very early adopted, and throughout his life maintained, the conservative philosophy of those politicians with whom he was in constant association" (25).

5. Hamlin Hill regards Hall and Baldwin bluntly as "two sanctimonious halves of a single personality" (qtd. in Lilly, 278).

6. Silverman (548) offers a persuasive reading of the elaborate analogy.

7. Since "The Gander Pulling" alludes to the days of "Tobacco, then the staple of Georgia" (*GSC* 75), as an historical "other," "The Turn-Out" may well be read as an implicit criticism of the heedless expansion of the plantation system after cotton replaced tobacco as the leading cash crop.

8. For a detailed evaluation of Longstreet's condescending depiction of African Americans, see Wegmann (14–18), who picks up a remark made by Rachels: "readers will notice that the word 'slave' appears only once in the book [and 'slaves' once as well], and it does not refer to African-American slavery. Despite the obvious importance of slavery to Georgia social life, Longstreet discusses it nowhere in *Georgia Scenes*" (xcviii; the parenthetical addition is Wegmann's [14]).

9. The very title and didacticism of "The 'Charming Creature,' as a Wife" have the sketch appear as if it were a chapter of a gentleman's conduct book. That this may indeed have been part of Longstreet's intention—that the *Georgia Scenes* were to set examples by which young southern gentlemen in search of cultivation could orient themselves—can also be inferred from "The Character of a Native Georgian." That sketch portrays the central figure, Ned Brace, in less than commendable terms. He is anything but a gentleman, but rather a trickster "marked by a desire to put self above society regardless of the social costs of doing so" (Bruce 229).

10. Longstreet seems like a prototype of the southerner described by Tocqueville, who noted a "deep-seated uneasiness and ill agitation which are observable in the South," a region that, "peopled with ardent and irascible men, is becoming more and more irritated and alarmed" (1:418).

11. See Gray (34–45) for an evaluation of Calhoun's ability to talk in two ways at once.

Works Cited

Blair, Walter. *Native American Humor, 1800–1900*. New York: American Book Co., 1937.

Bleser, Carol, ed. *Secret and Sacred: The Diaries of James Henry Hammond, a Southern Slaveholder*. New York: Oxford Univ. Press, 1988.

Brooks, Van Wyck. *The World of Washington Irving*. New York: Dutton, 1944.

Bruce, Dickson D., Jr. *Violence and Culture in the Antebellum South*. Austin: Univ. of Texas Press, 1979.

Carr, Duane. *A Question of Class: The Redneck Stereotype in Southern Fiction*. Bowling Green, Ohio: Bowling Green State Univ. Popular Press, 1996.

Cooper, William J., Jr., and Thomas E. Terrill. *The American South. A History*. New York: McGraw-Hill, 1991.

Cox, James M. "Humor of the Old Southwest." *The Comic Imagination in American Literature*. Louis D. Rubin, ed. Voice of America Forum Series. Washington: USIA, 1974. 105–16.

Derrida, Jacques. *Specters of Marx. The State of the Debt, the Work of Mourning, and the New International*. Peggy Kamuf, tr. New York: Routledge, 1994.

Fitzgerald, Oscar Penn. *Judge Longstreet. A Life Sketch.* Nashville, Tenn.: Publishing House of the Methodist Church, South, 1891.

Genovese, Eugene D. *The Southern Tradition. The Achievement and Limitations of an American Conservatism.* Cambridge, Mass.: Harvard Univ. Press, 1994.

Gray, Richard. *Writing the South. Ideas of an American Region.* Cambridge, UK: Cambridge Univ. Press, 1986.

Gretlund, Jan Nordby. "1835: The First Annus Mirabilis of Southern Fiction." *Rewriting the South: History and Fiction.* Lothar Hönnighausen and Valeria Gennaro Lerda, eds. Tübingen, Germany: Francke, 1993. 121–30.

Holman, C. Hugh. *The Roots of Southern Writing.* Athens: Univ. of Georgia Press, 1972.

Hubbell, Jay B. *The South in American Literature, 1607–1900.* Durham, N.C.: Duke Univ. Press, 1954.

Kibler, James E., Jr. Introduction. Augustus Baldwin Longstreet. *Georgia Scenes.* Nashville, Tenn: J.S. Sanders, 1992. vii–xxii.

Lenz, William E. "Augustus Baldwin Longstreet (1790–1870)." *Fifty Southern Writers Before 1900. A Bio-Bibliographical Sourcebook.* Westport, Conn: Greenwood, 1987. 312–22.

Lilly, Paul R., Jr. "Augustus Baldwin Longstreet." *American Humorists, 1800–1950.* Part I: A–L. DLB 11. Stanley Trachtenberg, ed. Detroit, Mich.: Gale Research, 1982. 276–83.

Longstreet, Augustus Baldwin. *Georgia Scenes Completed.* David Rachels, ed. Athens: Univ. of Georgia Press, 1998. [GSC]

Lynn, Kenneth S. *Mark Twain and Southwestern Humor.* Westport, Conn.: Greenwood Press, 1976. (Boston: Little, Brown, 1960.)

———. "A.B. Longstreet." *The Comic Tradition in America.* New York: Norton, 1958. 55–58.

Meine, Franklin J., ed. *Tall Tales of the Southwest.* New York: Knopf, 1930.

Meriwether, James B. "Augustus Baldwin Longstreet: Realist and Artist." *Mississippi Quarterly* 35 (1982): 351–64.

Newlin, Keith. "Georgia Scenes: The Satiric Artistry of Augustus Baldwin Longstreet." *Mississippi Quarterly* 41 (1987–1988): 21–34.

Niven, John. *John C. Calhoun and the Price of Union.* Baton Rouge: Louisiana State Univ. Press, 1988.

Parrington, Vernon Louis. *Main Currents in American Thought.* 2 vols. New York: Harcourt, Brace, and Co., 1927.

Rachels, David. "Introduction." Augustus Baldwin Longstreet. *Georgia Scenes Completed.* David Rachels, ed. Athens: Univ. of Georgia Press, 1998. xi–lxvii.

Silverman, Kenneth. "Longstreet's 'The Gander Pulling.'" *American Quarterly* 18 (1966): 548–49.

Smith, Stephen A. "The Rhetoric of Southern Humor." *The Future of Southern Letters.* Jeffrey Humphreys and John Lowe, eds. New York: Oxford Univ. Press, 1996. 170–85.

Sydnor, Charles S. *The Development of Southern Sectionalism.* Baton Rouge: Louisiana State Univ. Press, 1949.

Tocqueville, Alexis de. *Democracy in America.* Henry Reeve and Francis Bowen, trans. Phillips Bradley, ed. 2 vols. New York: Knopf, 1945.

Wade, John Donald. *Augustus Baldwin Longstreet: A Study in the Development of Culture in the South.* M. Thomas Inge, ed. Athens: Univ. of Georgia Press, 1969. (New York: Macmillan, 1924.)

Weaver, Richard M. *The Southern Tradition at Bay: A History of Post-Bellum Thought.* George Core and M.E. Bradford, eds. New Rochelle, N.Y.: Arlington House, 1968.

Wegmann, Jessica. "'Playing in the Dark' with Longstreet's *Georgia Scenes*: Critical Reception and Reader Response to Treatments of Race and Gender." *Southern Literary Journal* 30 (1997): 13–26.

A Biographical Reading of A.B. Longstreet's *Georgia Scenes*

David Rachels

> Judge Longstreet was born on Monday, the 22d of September, 1790. Where he was born is not so easy to say. Duyckink, in his *Cyclopædia of American Literature*, says he was born in Richmond County, near Augusta, Georgia. Appleton's *New American Cyclopædia* says he was born in Augusta, Georgia. Judge Longstreet himself says he was born in Edgefield District, South Carolina.
>
> James Wood Davidson, *The Living Writers of the South* (1869)[1]

Whenever Augustus Baldwin Longstreet discussed the impetus behind *Georgia Scenes, Characters, Incidents, &c. in the First Half Century of the Republic* (1835), he insisted the work was more than "a mere collection of fancy sketches." His motivation, he claimed, was a "higher object than the entertainment of the reader." This object "was to supply a chasm in history which has always been overlooked—the manners, customs, amusements, wit, dialect, as they appear in all grades of society to an ear and eye witness of them."[2] Thus, Longstreet thought of *Georgia Scenes* not as humor but as social history.

One puzzling fact is that Longstreet found so much of this social history an embarrassment. *Georgia Scenes* is cluttered with his apologies for and condemnations of the very behaviors that he felt compelled to record for posterity. The first sketch in the book, "Georgia Theatrics," is set in Lincoln, Georgia, in 1809. At this time, Lincoln was a town of "[inconceivable] moral darkness," but Longstreet's narrator, Lyman Hall, assures his readers that Lincoln has since become "a living proof 'that light shineth in darkness.'"[3] The only "darkness" in "Georgia Theatrics" is a one-man fight in which an eighteen-year-old practices eye gouging by jamming his thumbs into the earth. Elsewhere, however, Hall describes and condemns an actual rough-and-tumble fight. In addition, he depicts lower-class Georgians swearing, gambling, and drinking to excess. Longstreet's other narrator, Abraham Baldwin, criticizes upper-class Georgians for impractical dress, bad marriages, poor taste in music, miseducation of their children, and a variety of pretentious behaviors. Why would Longstreet, a proud Georgian, have wanted to preserve these myriad faults for the ages?

The answer may be that the subject of *Georgia Scenes* is not only "characters, incidents, &c. in the first half century of the republic" but, more specifically, Longstreet himself. Like the young man in "Georgia Theatrics," Longstreet grew up in a lower-class world where social status was earned with one's fists. By virtue of his education at Willington Academy, Yale College, and Litchfield Law School, however, he was able to establish himself among the upper classes. *Georgia Scenes*, then, is Longstreet's attempt to negotiate a social position in keeping with his ambitions while not forgetting his origins.

The autobiographical elements of *Georgia Scenes* have been overlooked by critics who have accepted orthodox views of antebellum southern humorists. In his genre-defining anthology, *Tall Tales of the Southwest* (1930), Franklin J. Meine painted this group of writers in broad strokes: "They were not professional humorists, but debonair settlers engaged in various tasks: lawyers, newspaper editors, country gentlemen of family and fortune, doctors, army officers, travellers, actors—who wrote for amusement rather than for gain." Meine singles out Longstreet as "a prominent young lawyer and newspaper editor." In another important early anthology, *Native American Humor* (1937), Walter Blair expands Longstreet's résumé to "lawyer, legislator, judge, and editor."[4] These biographies are accurate as far as they go, but readers cannot appreciate Longstreet's work if they imagine that his birth was coincident with his bar exam.[5]

Meine and Blair gave currency to the belief that antebellum southern humorists, if not always "debonair," were professional men who described from a safe distance the strange behavior of the "crackers" around them. In his influential analysis of antebellum southern humor, Kenneth S. Lynn described this distance as a "*cordon sanitaire*" (quarantine line) provided by framed narratives:

> That the frame device eventually became the structural trademark of Southwestern humor is because it suited so very well the myth-making purposes of the humorists. For Longstreet and his successors found that the frame was a convenient way of keeping their first-person narrators outside and above the comic action, thereby drawing a *cordon sanitaire*, so to speak, between the morally irreproachable Gentleman and the tainted life he described. . . . However hot-tempered the author might be in private life, the literary mask of the Southwestern humorists was that of a cool and collected personality whose own emotions were thoroughly in hand.

Lynn singles out Hall of "Georgia Theatrics" as a "Self-controlled Gentleman" narrator. Then, in a summary of the story remarkable for its misleading omissions, Lynn obscures the fact that Hall becomes the butt of the story's joke precisely because he *lacks* self-control.[6] Rushing to the scene of the supposed fight, Hall commands the fleeing youth: "'Come back, you brute! and assist me in relieving your fellow mortal, whom you have ruined forever!'" The young man replies with a taunt that "'you need n't kick before you're spur'd. There an't nobody there, nor ha'nt been nother. I was jist seein' how I could 'a' *fout*'" (5). Lynn's "Self-controlled Gentlemen" now seems an impulsive fool.

As *Georgia Scenes* progresses, the dominant narrative and thematic threads are provided by the book's narrators, Hall and Baldwin, and the ways in which they react to and interact with the people around them. Though many critics of *Georgia Scenes* have taken Lynn's *cordon sanitaire* as a given, only oversimplification or misrepresentation can sustain the notion throughout a full reading of the book.[7] Unfortunately, widespread acceptance of Lynn's analysis has further obscured the connection between Longstreet's life and work. In a striking example, Hennig Cohen and William B. Dillingham, in their discussion of the frameworks employed by antebellum southern humorists, conclude that "[i]t is as hard to identify Longstreet with the lowly characters of *Georgia Scenes* as it is to link [Frank] Norris with his brute dentist [McTeague]."[8]

My argument is that it is not difficult to identify Longstreet with his "lowly characters" and that the reasons for doing so predate his legal career. Portrayals of Longstreet as a "gentleman" imply that he was born into his social position. This was not the case. Longstreet was born in Augusta, Georgia, in 1790 to William Longstreet and Hannah Randolph Longstreet who, circa 1784, had moved to Georgia from New Jersey in search of a better life. There is evidence that William Longstreet was a well-regarded member of his community: in 1794, he served as a justice of the peace; in 1794–1795, he served as a representative in the state legislature; and, when Augusta was incorporated in 1798, he was elected one of six city commissioners.[9]

It is not clear, however, how the elder Longstreet supported his family. In a brief biography that Augustus wrote of William, he identifies his father as "an American inventor."[10] Unfortunately, all of the inventions that Augustus describes were financial failures. His father devised a method of propelling a boat by steam, but Robert Fulton undercut him. He invented a new roller for ginning cotton, which "promised him a fortune," but his two steam-powered mills burned within a week. He later erected a new set of steam mills, but the British burned them during the War of 1812. Augustus concludes that "[t]hese disasters exhausted his resources and discouraged his enterprise, though he was confident that steam would soon supersede all other motive powers."[11]

William Longstreet's failed inventions, particularly his steamboat, made him something of a laughingstock. According to tradition, he was so obsessed with his boat that he "was ridiculed by his neighbors and friends." A letter that he wrote in 1790 to Edward Telfair, the governor of Georgia, hints that tradition may be near the truth. Hoping to win the governor's patronage, Longstreet first attempts to forestall the reaction to which he seems accustomed: "Sir:—I make no doubt but that you have often heard of my steamboat, and as often heard it laughed at." This was written four days after Augustus was born. Thus, given that William worked at his steamboat well into the next century, Augustus grew up with a father who was, paradoxically, a well-respected joke.[12]

William Longstreet's reputation could not have been helped by his support of the Yazoo Act, which one historian has called "the greatest fraud that Georgia was ever to know." This act, passed by the Georgia assembly in 1794, provided for the sale of at least 35 million acres of land to four companies for only $500,000. In return for their votes, legislators were to receive generous grants of land. Longstreet himself offered a bribe of 100 thousand acres to a fellow legislator. The act became law in 1795, and a political firestorm soon followed. Many legislators were voted out of office; at least one angry community forced its representative to leave the state. This may explain the brevity of William Longstreet's political career. The act was repealed in 1796; every mention of it was deleted from state records; and all paperwork associated with it was burned. Thus, William Longstreet failed in another attempt to support his family.[13]

Fortunately, Hannah Longstreet had the greater influence on the life of young Augustus. Longstreet's mother wrote to a relative that she was determined "to give [her children] a good education as it [was] all [they could] do for them." Longstreet's first school was Augusta's Richmond Academy, which had opened in 1785. At the end of 1798, however, decaying buildings and a lack of money forced the school to close.[14] Longstreet was eight years old and had no school. This may have been the family's motivation for moving a short distance away. About 1800, they crossed the Savannah River into Edgefield District, South Carolina.

According to Edgefield historian John A. Chapman, this was a period of "great demoralization" in the district. Chapman writes, "The great besetting sin was the too free use of whiskey or rum; and to this may be added their usual accompaniments, card-playing, profanity and the disregard of the Sabbath. Many persons now living [in 1897] can remember when there was a grog-shop at every cross road, and sometimes between, when the cross roads were too far apart." Chapman records that it was not until 1809—well after the Longstreets had returned to Georgia—that a religious revival swept through Edgefield and morals began to improve.[15]

With or without religion, murder was so common in the district that it earned the reputation of "Bloody Edgefield." One historian describes the "Edgefield tradition" as "[standing] for the syndrome of violence and extremism that until recent times was thought to epitomize the South Carolina spirit."[16] While Edgefield had less crime than average for South Carolina, it had nearly double the number of homicides. So violent was the district that Thomas Jefferson Mackey, a judge whose circuit included Edgefield, joked, "I am going to hold court in Edgefield, and I expect a somewhat exciting term, as the fall shooting is about to commence."[17]

But not all Edgefield deaths were shootings. Some doubtless came as a result of the backcountry's tradition of rough-and-tumble fighting. Fighting was such a problem in South Carolina that in 1786, following the lead of North Carolina and Virginia, the state made "premeditated mayhem" punishable by death. This law prohibited gouging out eyes and biting off fingers, but not the severing of ears and noses. Ears and noses remained fair game because their loss did not prevent hearing and smelling. A pair of eye gouges, on the other hand, would blind an opponent, and thus—legal codes notwithstanding—it became, according to Elliott J. Gorn, "the sine qua non of rough-and-tumble fighting, much like the knockout punch in modern boxing." The prevalence of eye gouging in South Carolina led an amazed judge to declare, "Before God, gentlemen of the jury, I never saw such a thing before in the world. There is a plaintiff with an eye out! A juror with an eye out! And two witnesses with an eye out!"[18]

In this environment Longstreet spent, in his words, "two or three happy years." So happy were these years that later in life he would sometimes claim to have been born in Edgefield. But his birth there was only spiritual. His departure from Augusta and school was "a joyous release." Longstreet records that in Edgefield his "highest ambition was to out-run, out-jump, out-shoot, throw down and whip, any man in the district."[19] This was no small ambition given that in 1790 Edgefield counted 2,333 free white male citizens aged sixteen and up.[20] Longstreet claims that when "the heart-sinking order" came that he must return to school in Augusta, "[he] was giving fair promise of attaining [his] ends."[21] Of course, "attaining his end" of whipping any man in Edgefield would have required proficiency in eye gouging, the very skill that the eighteen-year-old young man practices in "Georgia Theatrics." It is interesting to note that "Georgia Theatrics" is set in the spring of 1809—when Longstreet himself would have been eighteen.

But the ambitions of Longstreet's youth were squelched by his mother—it was she, Longstreet remembered, who "kept him resolutely to his tasks"—and he did not end up an eighteen-year-old rough-and-tumble fighter.[22] Longstreet returned to Richmond Academy sometime after it reopened on November 1, 1802, and the age of eighteen found him enrolled in Moses Waddel's academy in Willington, South Carolina. From there he attended Yale College and then Litchfield Law School. When he passed his bar exam in 1815, he became the gentleman familiar to students of southern literature. As a circuit-riding lawyer encountering citizens of all classes, Longstreet would have had opportunities to gather material for *Georgia Scenes*. Critics have also stressed the importance of the legal profession's tradition of oral storytelling, which provided method and material to Longstreet and other lawyer-humorists.[23]

In Longstreet's case, however, the telling of his stories predates law school. Longstreet recalled that he "projected [the Georgia Scenes] in Judge [Jonathan] Ingersoll's parlor in New Haven" while a student at Yale. Obviously, the sources for these stories must predate 1813, when Longstreet left New Haven. Given the intensity of life in Edgefield in combination with the joy that he experienced there, Longstreet would naturally have drawn on his years in the district when he regaled his Yankee friends with tales of the southern backcountry. As well, Longstreet would have had difficulty escaping the influence of Edgefield even when the ostensible subject of his storytelling was Georgia. Looking back on his life, Longstreet observed that "South Carolina and Georgia have been twin nurses of me and twin sisters in my affections."[24]

It has been easy to for critics to assume a cause-and-effect relationship between Longstreet's legal career and his fiction writing, as the first Georgia Scene was published in 1833, more than eighteen years after his bar exam. Longstreet had made a good marriage in 1817, and now, with careers in law and politics, he was solidly established in the upper class. To a casual observer, he would indeed have seemed a man apart from many of the lower-class characters about whom he wrote. Furthermore, another important change had taken place in his life: in 1827 he had joined the Methodist Church, and in 1829 he had become licensed to preach (though he would not become a full-time minister until 1838, more than three years after the publication of *Georgia Scenes*). Thus, while Longstreet might fondly remember sowing the wild oats of his youth, and while he might enjoy observing life in the Georgia backcountry, he now felt that he could describe these scenes only with disclaimers attached. He might relish the details of a rough-and-tumble fight, but those "peace officers who countenance them, deserve a place in the Penitentiary" (41). He might be amused by the inane banter of two drunken men, but he "hope[s] the day is not far distant, when drunkenness will be unknown in our highly favored country" (109).

Longstreet's uneasy relationship with his material led him to publish the Georgia Scenes anonymously. When he gathered them for a book, he offered this explanation: "From private considerations, I was extremely desirous of concealing the author, and the more effectually to do so, I wrote under two signatures. . . . *Hall* is the writer of those sketches in which *men* appear as the principal actors, and *Baldwin* of those in which *women* are the prominent figures" (3). Having adopted a pair of personae, Longstreet was able to play out contrasting scenarios as Hall and Baldwin negotiate their class relationships. Like Longstreet, Hall and Baldwin are upper-class men of lower-class origin. Hall, whose narratives explore mostly the masculine world of the frontier, manages to reestablish a relationship of mutual respect with the lower classes, while Baldwin, whose narratives explore mostly the feminized world of the upper classes, becomes a social outcast. In the end, Longstreet finds less to admire in his present station in life than in his humble origins.

When Longstreet published the first Georgia Scenes in the *Milledgeville Southern Recorder*, he began by running through the possibilities afforded by his narrators: Baldwin narrates "The Dance"; Baldwin narrates "The Song," with Hall appearing in the sketch; Hall narrates "The Horse Swap"; and Hall narrates "The Turf," with Baldwin appearing in the sketch.[25] But as sketches continued to appear, Hall became the dominant voice of the series. Thus, when Longstreet rearranged the sketches for *Georgia Scenes,* he used a sketch narrated by Hall—"Georgia Theatrics"—to open the book.

In "The Dance," we learn that Baldwin, like Longstreet, was a man of humble origin who aspired to a higher station. As a young man he quit farm life, and he appears to have become a professional, though the nature of his profession is never made clear. At the start of "The Dance," he has been "called by business to one of the frontier counties," where he must "enlist the services of . . . one of the magistrates of the county" (6). Lest readers should think Baldwin is a lawyer, in a later sketch he makes clear that he is not (55). Beyond this, information about his "business" is scarce. In any case, his aspirations, whatever they were, have turned out to be misguided. At a country dance, he encounters an old flame:

> I thought of the sad history of many of her companions and mine, who used to carry light hearts through the merry dance. I compared my after life with the cloudless days of my attachment to Polly. Then I was light hearted, gay, contented and happy; I aspired to nothing but a good name, a good wife, and an easy competency. The first and last were mine already, and Polly had given me too many little tokens of her favor, to leave a doubt now, that the second was at my command. But I was foolishly told that my talents were of too high an order to be employed in the drudgeries of a farm, and I more foolishly believed it. I forsook the pleasures which I had tried and proved, and went in pursuit of those imaginary joys which seemed to encircle the seat of Fame. From that moment to the present, my life had been little else than one unbroken scene of disaster, disappointment, vexation and toil—and now when I was too old to enjoy the pleasures which I had discarded, I found that my aim was absolutely hopeless, and that my pursuits had only served to unfit me for the humbler walks of life, and to exclude me from the higher. (10)

Baldwin suffers because he feels no sense of belonging to any class, high or low. Ostensibly, he may now belong to the upper class, but as we will see in his later sketches, his encounters with the upper class revolt him. In "The Dance," he tries to recapture, however briefly, "the pleasures which [he has] discarded." His attempt hinges upon a theatrical revelation of his identity to his old flame Polly. When Polly does not recognize his name, he joins the dance and attempts to perform "the double cross hop," a difficult dance step, which, in Baldwin's youth, "was almost exclusively [his] own" (11). Unfortunately for Baldwin, Polly leaves just before he dances. After she returns, he shares with her his memories of the friends of their youth. Polly remembers them all—but she does not remember Baldwin. Like Hall at the end of "Georgia Theatrics," Baldwin seems a fool.

Having failed to recapture his past, Baldwin spends most of the rest of *Georgia Scenes* languishing in the miserable present and satirizing the pretensions of the upper classes. While "The Dance" was set "[s]ome years ago" (6), his next sketch, "The Song," is set only "a few evenings ago" (43). "The Song" bears out Baldwin's claim that his "pursuits" have in some sense "exclude[d]" him from the higher classes. On the surface of things, this would not seem to be the case: he finds himself not at a country "frolick" but at a sophisticated party given by Mrs. B—. After tea and conversation, the entertainment is music, and two Georgia belles play the piano and sing. Mary Williams performs so beautifully that Baldwin cries. He cannot, however, abide the performance of the pretentious Aurelia Emma Theodosia Augusta Crump. Her performance drives Baldwin from the party "in convulsions" (46).

Also at the party is Hall. Ironically, Longstreet's narrator of the masculine frontier is better suited for the evening's entertainment. When he sees Baldwin crying, he comes to his aid by requesting that Miss Mary play "some lively air" (43), and he has no difficulty enduring the onslaught of Miss Crump. Though he wishes not to leave while Miss Crump is playing, he finally departs near midnight. Fittingly, Baldwin turns out to be his roommate, and Hall's arrival wakes him from a nightmare starring Miss Crump. When Baldwin learns that Miss Crump is still performing, he does something even more stereotypically feminine than cry—he swoons. It seems that Baldwin is too feminine even for the feminine world that he inhabits.

In "The Dance," Baldwin appears as a participant—albeit in some sense a failed participant—in the action of the story. In "The Song," Baldwin withdraws his participation from an already passive activity. In the remaining four sketches that he narrates, Baldwin participates even less. He plays no part at all in "The 'Charming Creature,' as a Wife" but to tell the cautionary tale of his nephew, George Baldwin.

The trajectory of George Baldwin's life resembles that of his uncle: the son of a successful though uneducated farmer, George shows great promise as a lawyer until his life is derailed by the "charming creature" whom he chooses for a wife. Miss Evelina Caroline Smith possesses a good mind and, what is infinitely more important to her nouveau riche parents, good looks. Such superficial priorities have led the Smiths to ruin their daughter. Between the ages of six and fourteen, Evelina received no education beyond praise for her beauty and instruction in exhibiting herself to best advantage. Then, when Evelina was fourteen, her parents—purely in an effort to keep up with the Joneses—sent her north for an education. When a solid education was grafted onto Evelina's superficial personality, the result was an upper-class nightmare: Longstreet describes her as proud, vain, and hypocritical (56).

By parroting the "modest, sensible" views that she has learned by rote, Evelina snares George without even trying (57). Beyond her beauty, however, she is nothing that she appears to be. Though formally educated, Evelina uses her knowledge only to manipulate others, and after she has married George, she proves wholly incapable of managing a household. George's mother, by contrast,

> was pious, but not austere; cheerful, but not light; generous, but not prodigal; economical, but not close; hospitable, but not extravagant. In native powers of mind, she was every way my brother's equal—in acquirements she was decidedly his superior.—To this I have his testimony, as well as my own; but it was impossible to discover in her conduct, any thing going to shew that she coincided with us in opinion. To have heard her converse, you would have supposed she did nothing but read—to have looked through the departments of her household, you would have supposed she never read. Every thing which lay within her little province, bore the impress of her own hand, or acknowledged her supervision. Order, neatness, and cleanliness prevailed every where. (54)

She seems to be Longstreet's ideal woman, a perfect balance of upper-class education and lower-class practicality.

While Longstreet's portrayal of Evelina is unsympathetic, even hostile, he sees George as the unfortunate victim of one bad decision. However, when Mr. Dawson, a dear old friend of the Baldwins, insults Evelina, readers may feel their sympathies begin to shift. When Evelina tries to defend herself, her father-in-law does not take up her case. Rather, he explains to Mr. Dawson, "'She is unused to our country manners, and therefore does not understand them'" (66). To Evelina, he tries to explain that Dawson's acerbic insults were actually jokes. George, for his part, does not utter a syllable in defense of his wife. Later, during their first evening in their new home together, when George tells Evelina that he wants her to become just like his mother, readers may feel their sympathies shift even more still. For the modern reader, the balance may finally tip in Evelina's favor when she defends her treatment of their slaves: "Well, really, I can't see any great harm in treating aged people with respect, even if their skins are black." George, unfortunately, may speak for Longstreet: "I wish you had thought of that when you were talking to old Mr. Dawson. I should think he was entitled to as much respect as an infernal black wench!" (69)

George eventually succumbs to alcoholism and dies, and the sketch concludes with his uncle's injunction to mothers "against bringing up their daughters to be 'Charming Creatures'" (73). Just as Abraham Baldwin is undone by "pursuit of those imaginary joys which seemed to encircle the seat of Fame," George Baldwin is undone by pursuit of those imaginary joys which seemed to encircle Evelina. As for Evelina's fate, Longstreet's sympathies rest with her husband—he does not bother to tell what becomes of her.

How, then, is a man to avoid marrying an Evelina? In 1817, Longstreet too had been a promising young barrister in search of a helpmate. What led him to propose to his wife, Frances Eliza Parke? In an 1842 letter, Longstreet, perhaps speaking from experience, advised the son of his wife's stepfather to "marry some handsome, intelligent, industrious girl; and if she should withal happen to be rich, why dont refuse her on that account." This could well describe Longstreet's wife, an attractive woman who had inherited a substantial dowry from a grandfather, her father, and a brother. Longstreet biographer James R. Scafidel cynically wonders, "Who could resist her (and her wealth)?" Evelina, like Longstreet's wife, was a beautiful, wealthy woman. Longstreet could easily have made the same mistake as George Baldwin, but he did not. He and Eliza were married, by Longstreet's own count, for "fifty years, seven months, and ten days."[26] Perhaps, then, "The 'Charming Creature,' as a Wife" is the literary equivalent of an extended sigh of relief.

In Baldwin's next sketch, "The Ball," our narrator again crosses paths with someone from his humble past. He is invited to the ball by Jack DeBathle, of whom he writes, "Jack had been the companion of my childhood, my boyhood, and my early manhood, and through many a merry dance had we hopt, and laughed and tumbled down together, in the morning of life" (80). His memories of Jack recall his embarrassing reunion with Polly Gibson in "The Dance." Though the two men are reunited for a different sort of dance, Baldwin's meeting with an old friend might afford him a chance to renew his interest in the business of living. Instead, Baldwin passively observes and reports what he sees: a superficial world in which the women are vain and the men are effete. It is the antithesis of "The Dance" and the world that he has lost.

Baldwin's penultimate sketch, "The Mother and Her Child," is his slightest. Again he passively reports what he sees. Here he is critical of baby talk, "the gibberish which is almost invariably used by mothers and nurses to infants" (87). The narrative—focusing as it does on a mother, her baby, *and* the baby's nurse—implies that this offensive "gibberish" is the domain of the upper classes. However, this is a difficult distinction to make, for we have seen that in *Georgia Scenes* upper class tends to go hand in hand with feminine.

"A Sage Conversation" is Baldwin's final and most interesting narrative. He begins the sketch as something of a participant. He is traveling with his friend Ned Brace—whose character Longstreet based in part on Edmund Bacon, a lawyer from Edgefield—when the men stop for the night at a house where three elderly women are keeping company. An inveterate joker, Brace decides to have some fun with the women; just before he and Baldwin retire for the evening, he tells of two men he knew "who became so much attached to each other that they actually got married" (129). Even more remarkably, he reveals that the two men raised children together. When Brace asks his friend if he knew these men and their children, Baldwin plays along with the joke. With the old women amazed and confused, Brace and Baldwin retreat to bed.

Now Baldwin resumes his role of passively observing and reporting, but his method of observation takes a new form. In four of his five previous sketches—"The Dance," "The Song," "The Ball," and "The Mother and Her Child"—Baldwin openly observed the activity about him. In "A Sage Conversation," by contrast, he is reduced to "casting an eye through the cracks of [a] partition." Baldwin explains, "I could not resist the temptation. . . . From my bed it required but a slight change of position to see any one of the group at pleasure" (130). Thus, Baldwin spends the majority of his last sketch as an emasculated Peeping Tom. He entered *Georgia Scenes* dancing with "fine bouncing, ruddy cheeked girls" in the morning (7). He exits peeping at three old women and eavesdropping on their conversation at night.

The women are unable to solve the riddle of the men who married and raised children together. Their best guess is that one of the men was a woman in disguise. In the morning they press Ned Brace for an explanation. He responds that the men were widowers who had children from their earlier marriages (presumably, to women). Thus, they were able to raise children together. But the original oddity remains unexplained: Did two men really want to marry one another—and was this actually allowed?

James B. Meriwether first noted that the themes of "A Sage Conversation" include homosexuality and transvestitism.[27] The juxtaposition of these themes with Baldwin the latter-day Peeping Tom is suggestive. Baldwin is a bachelor with no visible prospects, and as *Georgia Scenes* progresses, his chances of a relationship with a woman seem increasingly remote. With "The Dance," he begins the book with the hope of rekindling, in some small way, his relationship with the elder Polly Gibson. Though he fails, he does keep company with fine young women. He dances with the daughters of his contemporaries in "The Dance," and then he is deeply moved by the singing of Miss Mary Williams in "The Song." After the performance of Miss Aurelia Emma Theodosia Augusta Crump, however, Baldwin turns misogynistic. He shows nothing but contempt for the "charming creature" who ruined the life of his nephew George Baldwin and for the "charming creatures" who populate "The Ball." Mrs. Slang of "The Mother and Her Child" appears only in her role as the mother of another man's son, and in "A Sage Conversation" Baldwin is reduced to peeping at the oldest women in the book. Perhaps, then, Ned Brace's story of the married men is a dig at Baldwin. At this stage in his life, Baldwin's only meaningful relationships are with other men—Jack DeBathle in "The Ball," Mr. Slang in "The Mother and Her Child," and his roommate Hall in "The Turf" (narrated by Hall). In his final sketch, it is Ned Brace—a man—with whom he retires for bed. Thus, Baldwin stands as Longstreet's worst-case scenario for upward mobility. Indeed, we might consider him a worst-case scenario for what could have become of Longstreet himself.

Baldwin, however, is not the dominant voice of the book. Longstreet reserves that role for Lyman Hall, who narrates twelve sketches to Baldwin's six.[28] Hall has no relationships with women worth mentioning, nor does he seem to need any. His domain is the masculine world of the backcountry. In his last sketch in *Georgia Scenes*, he succeeds in doing what Baldwin failed to do in his first sketch: he recaptures his place among the common people of Georgia.

Like Baldwin, Hall appears to be a professional. Lynn, in his reading of "Georgia Theatrics," takes Hall to be a minister. But the evidence for this, which Lynn does not discuss, is only circumstantial. In the opening paragraph of the story, Hall refers to Judas and the apostolic ministry, and he quotes John 1:5 (4). In addition, he uses such phrases as "In Mercy's name" and "hellish deed," and he describes the setting as a "heavenly retreat, for such Pandæmonian riots" (5).[29] The most compelling evidence may be Hall's explanation that when he confronted the young fighter he felt "emboldened by the sacredness of [his] office" (5), but this passage is open to at least a pair of interpretations. Hall is traveling on horseback, and "the sacredness of [his] office" may confirm that he is, indeed, a circuit-riding minister. It seems equally plausible, however, that "the sacredness of [his] office" refers merely to the moral urgency of having encountered a "hellish deed." Meriwether takes Hall for a lawyer, though, like Lynn, he does not explain his deduction.[30] Either profession, minister or lawyer, would of course link Hall to his creator.

We have already seen that in "Georgia Theatrics" Hall begins *Georgia Scenes* on a shaky note. Like Baldwin, his initial brush with the lower classes leaves him looking foolish. Also like Baldwin, his reaction is to become more passive in his next sketches. It seems natural to trace the evolution of Hall just as we have done with

Baldwin, beginning with his first sketch and concluding with his last. But this strategy for interpreting *Georgia Scenes* has one serious problem. As Longstreet prepared to publish his sketches as a book, he arranged them for artistic effect. This arrangement, however, is not chronological. For example, "Georgia Theatrics," set in 1809, is not the earliest sketch that Hall narrates. Nor is his final sketch, "The Shooting Match," which is set "about a year ago," his most recent (136).[31]

Critics can defend the practice of giving interpretive precedence to the arrangement of Longstreet's sketches if they are willing to consider the circumstances under which he published *Georgia Scenes*.[32] The project of writing the sketches evolved haphazardly, and the collected and rearranged sketches were published in haste. Longstreet took the time to do some revision, though not as much as he would have preferred.[33] Indeed, it is surprising that Longstreet revised as much as he did, given, as he states in the book's preface, that he could not afford the time to read proof. If Longstreet had actually produced the revised edition of *Georgia Scenes* that he planned, he may well have harmonized the dating of the sketches with their arrangement.[34]

Appropriately, the earliest dateable sketch is set in 1790, the year of Longstreet's birth. Hall narrates "The Turn-Out," which is set at a country school. Scafidel suspects a link between this school and Willington Academy; he notes the similarities between the setting for "The Turn-Out" and Longstreet's later description of Willington in his 1841 eulogy for Moses Waddel.[35] In "The Turn-Out," the school is set near "the brow of a hill which descended rather abruptly to a noble spring, that gushed joyously forth." In Longstreet's eulogy for Waddel, he sets Willington Academy near "the brow of [a] gentle eminence . . . [that] descends, to a bold gushing fountain at its foot." Both idyllic descriptions give way to more somber thoughts. In "The Turn-Out," Captain Griffin opines, "These lands will never wear out. Where they lie level they will be as good fifty years hence as they are now." But Hall reports that when he returned to the site of the school in 1832, he found "many a deep washed gully met at a sickly bog, where gushed the limpid fountain" (49–50). Similarly, Longstreet describes that in Willington "the beautiful rivulet that laved [the students'] feet, now darkly flows through an artificial channel, bordered on either side with a treacherous morass."[36] Such similarities suggest that "The Turn-Out" may be a paean to the joy of Longstreet's youth. In "The Turn-Out," this joy takes a mischievous form: the schoolboys barricade themselves inside the schoolhouse before the schoolmaster arrives in hopes of winning a holiday. Neither Hall nor Captain Griffin condemns this troublemaking. Griffin, in fact, encourages it.

Longstreet's other tale of schoolboys is also narrated by Hall. "The Debating Society" is set in about 1812, and it is the most explicitly autobiographical *Georgia Scene,* as Longstreet explained in an 1836 letter: "'The Debating Society' is as literally true, as the frailty of memory would allow it to be. McDermot, is His Excellency George McDuffie, present Governor of South Carolina: and Longworth, is your humble servant. The scene of the debate, was Willington Academy, Abbeville District, So. Carolina; then under the superintendence of the Rev. Dr. Moses Waddel."[37] In this sketch, the young Longstreet and his accomplice McDuffie trick their debating society into arguing a nonsensical question. The sketch ends with the other boys "[laughing] heartily at the trick" (98). Thus, in both "The Debating Society" and "The Turn-Out," schoolboys thwart the upper-class business of education, and neither sketch condemns this behavior. These are the only sketches in *Georgia Scenes* that portray upper-class activity in a wholly positive light, and in both cases the activity in question succumbs to anarchy.

Here Longstreet remembers his education with fondness. He was being initiated into the upper classes, but the wildness of Edgefield had not yet been subdued. Longstreet's schoolboy sketches support Scott Romine's observation that "when Hall prefers the present, he is generally speaking about the lower class, while his preference for the past usually indicates that the upper class is the topic of discussion."[38] We can reduce this to a cliché: the grass is always greener on the other side. Longstreet's fondness for the upper class was strongest when he was young and still working to earn his place in the world, and his fondness for the lower class intensified when he was no longer one of them.

As strong as his feelings for the present-day lower class may have been, when Longstreet looked back in time—that is, when he looked back at his own history—his feelings were often ambivalent. "The Fight," for example, is set in "the younger days of the Republic" (33) and thus may predate "The Turn-Out." Its plot centers on Billy Stallings and Bob Durham and their long-anticipated battle to determine the "best man" in the county. Stallings and Durham represent the very type of man whom Longstreet idolized as a boy. Longstreet's ambition to "throw down and whip, any man in the district" meant that he wanted to be the victor in his own version of the Stallings-Durham fight: Longstreet wanted to be the "best man" in Edgefield. Many years removed from Edgefield, Longstreet still finds the spectacle of rough-and-tumble fighting fascinating—as much he may now claim to disapprove of "such scenes of barbarism and cruelty," he cannot look away. And when Longstreet offers his disclaimer at the end of the sketch, he refuses to single out his heroes, Stallings and Durham, for censure. Instead, he scapegoats the "peace officers" who look the other way (41).

Over the course of *Georgia Scenes,* Hall becomes more at home among the lower classes, and Meriwether traces a corresponding change in the violence he encounters: the savagery of man against man in "The Fight" gives way to the cruelty of man against animal in "The Gander Pulling," which in turn gives way to the bloodless sport of "The Shooting Match."[39] Remarkably, these sketches appear to fall in chronological order: "The Fight" occurs in the "younger days of the Republic"; "The Gander Pulling" takes place in 1798; and "The Shooting Match" concludes *Georgia Scenes* "about a year ago." Therefore, it seems that if Hall is to regain his place among the humbler classes, then they must meet him half way. Only when the revolting spectacle of a rough-and-tumble fight is a thing of the past—fascinating though the spectacle may be—can he recapture his place in that past.

"The Shooting Match" is Hall's triumph and Longstreet's best-case scenario for upward mobility. Hall holds his own in a friendly verbal sparring match with a "swarthy, bright-eyed, smerky little fellow" named Billy Curlew (136), and then he holds his own with a rifle as well. Hall's final sketch is an inversion of Baldwin's first. In "The Dance," Baldwin revealed his humble origins and then failed to recapture them. Hall, on the other hand, does not reveal his own humble origins until his final sketch, when he is able to recover the very skill that made him renowned as a boy:

> [Curlew:] "I reckon you hardly ever was at a shooting match, stranger, from the cut of your coat?"
> [Hall:] "Oh yes," returned I, "many a time. I won beef at one, when I was hardly old enough to hold a shot-gun off-hand."
> "*Children* don't go to shooting matches about here," said he, with a smile of incredulity. "I never heard of but one that did, and he was a little swinge-cat.—He was born a shooting, and killed squirrels before he was weaned."
> "Nor did *I* ever hear of but one," replied I, "and that one was myself." (137)

Further conversation confirms that Hall is indeed the prodigy whom Curlew has heard about.

"The Shooting Match" is the only sketch in *Georgia Scenes* that Longstreet did not first publish in his newspaper. He appears to have written it specifically to conclude his book. Hall ends *Georgia Scenes* with the moral victory of a second-place finish in the shooting match, a victory that Longstreet may well have imagined for himself. Hall's youthful talent was among Longstreet's youthful talents: Longstreet wrote that in his youth he was "expert as a cotton picker, a wrestler, and a marksman."[40] Neither Longstreet nor Hall could have held his own picking cotton or wrestling with Billy Stallings or Billy Curlew. Marksmanship, by comparison, offers an easy bridge to the past. Hall needs only one lucky shot, and his opponents recognize him as one of their own—yet they cannot overlook that he is a man above them. Should he ever run for office, they all swear to vote for him.

As Lyman Hall returns to his roots in "The Shooting Match," so did A.B. Longstreet return to his roots in *Georgia Scenes.* He never forgot how he loved the freedom of Edgefield. When he was forced to return to Richmond Academy, it became, in his words, his "hated penitentiary," where he was "considered by [his] preceptors a dunce . . . and treated accordingly." Longstreet's behavior on the dunce stool, as recorded by George W. Williams, may serve as a metaphor for his literary career:

> The teacher thought he would break the spirit of the fun-loving and mischief-making young man. . . . It was like the boy who attempted to punish the rabbit by turning it loose in a brier patch. . . .
>
> The six foot gawky boy enacted a monkey show that made the school boys wild. There the "dunce" sat with the side of his face exposed to the master's view, as quiet, placid and respectful as if he had been in a church.

> By some legerdemain he distorted the other side of his face. The school was thrown into uncontrollable confusion, so ridiculous was his appearance while grinning, winking and blinking at the boys; in spite of the anger and hickory switch of the master, they laughed, whooped, breaking up in a general stampede. There sat young Longstreet on the dunce box, quiet and calm, with only the school master for an audience.[41]

Just as there were two Longstreets as a youth—the serious façade offered his teacher and the devil-may-care cut-up revealed only to his classmates—there were two Longstreets as an adult. On the one hand, there was Longstreet of Yale, who argued a case before the Supreme Court and who published the *Augusta State Rights' Sentinel.* On the other, there was Longstreet of Edgefield, who recalled and rekindled the spirit of his wild youth in *Georgia Scenes.* And, just as Longstreet the youth hid half his face from his teacher, so did Longstreet the adult think it wise to hide half his face from the public. Thus, he published *Georgia Scenes* anonymously.

Notes

1. James Wood Davidson, *The Living Writers of the South* (New York: Carleton, 1869), 340.

2. Longstreet quoted in O.P. Fitzgerald, *Judge Longstreet: A Life Sketch* (Nashville: Publishing House of the Methodist Episcopal Church, South, 1891), 164.

3. A.B. Longstreet, *Augustus Baldwin Longstreet's Georgia Scenes Completed: A Scholarly Text,* ed. David Rachels (Athens: Univ. of Georgia Press, 1998), 4. Hereafter cited parenthetically in the text.

4. Franklin J. Meine, *Tall Tales of the Southwest: An Anthology of Southern and Southwestern Humor 1830–1860* (New York: Alfred A. Knopf, 1930), xvi, xvii; Walter Blair, *Native American Humor (1800–1900)* (New York: American Book Company, 1937), 63.

5. The standard anthology of recent decades, Hennig Cohen and William B. Dillingham's *Humor of the Old Southwest* (1964, 1975, 1994), continues in the same vein, asserting that the "typical Old Southwestern humorist . . . was a man of education and breeding." As for Longstreet himself, Cohen and Dillingham leapfrog from his birth in Augusta, Georgia, to his education at Willington Academy in South Carolina (*Humor of the Old Southwest*, 3rd ed. [Athens: Univ. of Georgia Press, 1994], xx, 29).

6. Kenneth S. Lynn, *Mark Twain and Southwestern Humor* (Boston: Little, Brown, 1959), 64, 66–67.

7. Lynn's reading of *Georgia Scenes* has been attacked most extensively (and successfully) by Scott Romine in "Negotiating Community in Augustus Baldwin Longstreet's *Georgia Scenes,*" *Style* 30.1 (1996): 1–27.

8. Cohen and Dillingham, *Humor of the Old Southwest*, xxx.

9. James R. Scafidel, unfinished Longstreet biography, James R. Scafidel Papers, South Carolina Historical Society, 3. Hereafter cited as Scafidel. Scafidel's manuscript, which carries Longstreet to 1835, is the best source available for information about Longstreet's early life. The only complete biographies of Longstreet are inadequate: O.P. Fitzgerald's *Judge Longstreet: A Life Sketch* (1891) and John Donald Wade's *Augustus Baldwin Longstreet: A Study of the Development of Culture in the South* (1924).

10. For the origins of this biographical sketch, see Fitzgerald, 199, and "The Letters of Augustus Baldwin Longstreet," ed. James R. Scafidel (Ph.D. diss., University of South Carolina, 1977), 581. The latter is hereafter cited as "Letters."

11. [A.B. Longstreet], "William Longstreet," in *The New American Cyclopædia: A Popular Dictionary of General Knowledge*, ed. George Ripley and Charles A. Dana (New York: D. Appleton, 1867), 646.

12. Joel Chandler Harris, *Stories of Georgia* (New York: American Book Company, 1896), 165; William Longstreet to Edward Telfair, September 26, 1790, quoted in Edward Mayes, *Genealogy of the Family of Longstreet* ([Jackson, MS?]: [Hederman Brothers?], [1893?]), 23.

13. Kenneth Coleman, *Georgia History in Outline* (Athens: Univ. of Georgia Press, 1978), 31; Scafidel, 7.

14. Hannah Longstreet to Rebekah Hendrickson, May 12, 1807, Augustus Baldwin Longstreet Papers, Manuscript Division, South Caroliniana Library, Univ. of South Carolina; Charles G. Cordle, "The Academy of Richmond County," *Richmond County History* 1.1 (1969): 26–27. Cordle's essay first appeared in the February 1939 issue of the *Southern Association Quarterly*.

15. John A. Chapman, *History of Edgefield County from the Earliest Settlements to 1897* (Newberry, S.C.: Elbert H. Aull, 1897), 73.

16. Fox Butterworth, *All God's Children: The Bosket Family and the American Tradition of Violence* (New York: Alfred A. Knopf, 1995), 7; Richard Maxwell Brown, *Strain of Violence: Historical Studies of American Violence and Vigilantism* (New York: Oxford Univ. Press, 1975), 83.

17. Jack Kenny Williams, *Vogues in Villainy: Crime and Retribution in Ante-Bellum South Carolina* (Columbia: Univ. of South Carolina Press, 1959), 3–4; Thomas Jefferson Mackey quoted in U.R. Books, *South Carolina Bench and Bar,* vol. 1 (Columbia, S.C.: The State Company, 1908), 199.

18. Williams, *Vogues in Villainy*, 33; Elliot J. Gorn, "'Gouge and Bite, Pull Hair and Scratch': The Social Significance of Fighting in the Southern Backcountry," *American Historical Review* 90 (Feb. 1985), 20; Judge Aedamus Burke, quoted in Gorn, 33.

19. A.B. Longstreet, "Old Things Become New," *The XIX Century*, April 1870, 839.

20. Bureau of the Census, *Heads of Families at the First Census of the United States Taken in the Year 1790: South Carolina* (Washington, D.C.: Government Printing Office, 1908), 9.

21. Longstreet, "Old Things Become New," 839.

22. [A.B. Longstreet], "Augustus Baldwin Longstreet," in *The New American Cyclopædia: A Popular Dictionary of General Knowledge*, ed. George Ripley and Charles A. Dana (New York: D. Appleton, 1867), 646. For the origins of this autobiographical sketch, see Fitzgerald, 199, and "Letters," 581.

23. See, for example, Blair, *Native American Humor*, 70ff.

24. "Letters," 145, 662.

25. These sketches appeared over four weeks in 1833: "The Dance" appeared on October 30; "The Song," on November 6; "The Horse Swap," on November 13; and "The Turf," on November 20.

26. "Letters," 135, 656; Scafidel IV–3.

27. James B. Meriwether, "Augustus Baldwin Longstreet: Realist and Artist," *Mississippi Quarterly* 35 (1982): 359–60.

28. The nineteenth sketch in *Georgia Scenes*, "The Militia Company Drill," was writ-

ten by Longstreet's friend Oliver Hillhouse Prince. For a discussion of Longstreet's motivations for including this sketch in his book, see David Rachels, "Oliver Hillhouse Prince, Augustus Baldwin Longstreet, and the Birth of American Literary Realism," *Mississippi Quarterly* 51 (1998): 603–19.

29. Though it is probably a coincidence, it is interesting to note that in 1816, eighteen years before Longstreet first published "Georgia Theatrics," another minister, Mason Locke Weems, compared Longstreet's old home Edgefield to Pandemonium: "Oh mercy! . . . Old Edgefield again! Another murder in Edgefield! . . . For sure it must be Pandemonium itself, a very District of Devils" (Mason Locke Weems, *The Devil in Petticoats or God's Revenge against Husband Killing* (1816; rep., Edgefield: Bacon and Adams, 1878), 3.

30. Lynn, *Mark Twain and Southwest Humor*, 66; Meriwether, "Augustus Baldwin Longstreet: Realist and Artist," 359.

31. The business of tracing Baldwin's evolution is also complicated by the fact that his sketches are not arranged chronologically. "The Dance," which is set "[s]ome years ago," is followed by "The Song," which is set only "a few evenings ago" (6, 43). Next, "The 'Charming Creature,' as a Wife," though given no specific date, is the earliest of Baldwin's sketches, as it traces the life of Baldwin's nephew, who is ten years younger than his middle-aged uncle and who died as a young man. Baldwin's fourth sketch, "The Ball," is set "about ten years ago," and his fifth, "The Mother and Her Child," only "[a] few days ago" (80, 88). Finally, his last sketch, "A Sage Conversation" is not his most recent, as it is set "many years since" (128).

32. Recent critics have focused mostly on the arrangement of the sketches while generally ignoring their chronological order. See, for example, Meriwether, "Augustus Baldwin Longstreet: Realist and Artist," 360–61; Patricia Beam, "The Theme and Structure of *Georgia Scenes*," *Journal of English* 15 (1987): 68–79; and Keith Newlin, "*Georgia Scenes*: The Satiric Artistry of Augustus Baldwin Longstreet," *Mississippi Quarterly* 41 (1987–1988): 24ff.

33. For a catalog of Longstreet's revisions, see *Georgia Scenes Completed* (279–331). Longstreet particularly regretted that he did not have a chance to thoroughly revise "The Character of a Native Georgian" ([William W. Mann], "Who Is 'Ned Brace?'" *Southern Field and Fireside*, October 8, 1859, 156).

34. Longstreet mentions his plans for a revised *Georgia Scenes* in an 1842 letter to James Barton Longacre ("Letters" 140). Years later, he may have been planning to revise and enlarge the book ([Mann], "Who Is 'Ned Brace?'" 156).

35. Scafidel, II–12.

36. A.B. Longstreet, *Eulogy on the Life and Public Services of the Late Rev. Moses Waddel* (Augusta, Ga.: Published at the Chronicle and Sentinel Office, 1841), 7–8.

37. "Letters," 98–99.

38. Romine, "Negotiating Community in Augustus Baldwin Longstreet's *Georgia Scenes*," 12.

39. Meriwether, "Augustus Baldwin Longstreet: Realist and Artist," 361. In his analysis, Meriwether includes "The Militia Company Drill," which I have omitted because it was not written by Longstreet and does not concern Hall.

40. [Longstreet], "Augustus Baldwin Longstreet," 646.

41. Longstreet, "Old Things Become New," 839; George W. Williams, *Advice to Young Men, and Nacoochee and Its Surroundings* (Charleston, S.C.: Walker, Evans & Cogswell Co., 1899), 108. Williams places the dunce-stool story *before* the Longstreets moved to Edgefield, but his chronology and dating of events is confused. See Scafidel, 9–13.

9

A Sadder Simon Suggs:

Freedom and Slavery in the Humor of Johnson Hooper

Johanna Nicol Shields

> "Well, mother-wit kin beat book-larnin, at any game! . . . Human natur' and the human family is my books, and I've never seed many but what I could hold my own with."
>
> Captain Simon Suggs

The variety of human experience in the Old South stands much more fully before us now than it did only decades ago. Today, however, while historians clearly perceive the complex relationships between white freedom and black slavery, they do not fully understand the alien mentality behind them. How could intelligent men and women have expected to perpetuate both slavery and freedom in a progressive world? Historians' efforts to answer this troubling question can be aided by a fresh look at old evidence: the abundant comic record left by popular southern humorists such as Johnson Hooper.[1] Humor had special use to people with deep potential conflicts among their values. Humor flows directly from the tension between what is and what ought to be—sometimes from conflicts so severe that they are tragic, as the twin faces of drama imply. But laughter has unique power to make all but the worst problems tolerable, if only by easing tensions or postponing resolutions. Johnson Hooper's famous comic saga, *Some Adventures of Captain Simon Suggs*, reflects the hopeful spirit of its Whig author in the early 1840s, when the stories were written, but it also reveals a strong undercurrent of anxiety. Thus Hooper's popular art demonstrates the instrumental relationship linking humor with freedom and slavery in southern society. His art provoked laughter that had tragic repercussions.

Hooper treated a southern problem while satirizing American social values. As a good Whig, he believed that the individual freedom that dissolved archaic forms of order would finally stimulate social progress but only when men worked together in a new spirit of cooperation.[2] In Suggs's ludicrous adventures, Hooper shows the crude results of unrestrained liberty on Alabama's frontier. With one eye on the future, he lampooned white men's ceaseless competition and savagely ridiculed the impact of their freedom on slaves. Ultimately, his jokes made slavery seem natural, even necessary, in an American jungle where "mother-wit" was a sine qua non for survival.

Simon Suggs was a predatory opportunist, a grotesque and bestial version of an American self-made man, but if his naturalistic traits derived from any explicit social theory, Hooper's humor hid it well. Hooper's understanding of the world drew instinctively from his experience as well as from formal ideas. "'Book larning spiles a man ef he's got mother-wit, and ef he aint got that, it don't do him no good,'" quipped Suggs, and the blue-blooded Hooper's career demonstrated the point. He claimed an ancient literary lineage that ran from Juvenal through Cervantes, Swift, and Addison to America. He read England's gentlemanly reviews, which reported intellectual life abroad. And he also knew the folk mythology that provided comic relief in the cabins and taverns of a dangerous frontier. But a newspaper editor's "mother-wit," a canny sense of ear and eye that captured the common tongue in a readable form, enabled Hooper to market his humor. First circulated in his Whig newspaper, the Suggs stories went through roughly a dozen antebellum printings issued mainly from northern presses. In a serious mood, Hooper used his newspaper's press to publish a proslavery tract in 1846 and agitated for southern nationalism in the late 1850s, but his humor betrayed no polemical intent. Instead, he buried his ideas so deeply in new images of "human natur' and the human family" that when readers laughed at Suggs's reckless freedom they may well have ignored how their amusement condoned slavery.[3]

Historians will not fail to see the ugly side of Hooper's humor, yet understanding why others laughed is important since it links slavery and freedom in an unfamiliar way. Historians like James Oakes and George M. Fredrickson have insisted that popular proslavery ideology used race rather than paternalism to justify a herrenvolk society. By making slaves outsiders in a liberal state, their status as property was guaranteed. These arguments, however, relegate paternalistic values to a minor, geographically restricted rôle, as if migrants left their ingrained habits behind when they moved westward from the coastal South. Such a view slights the force of memory, operating in the minds and upon the "manners"—to use the Jeffersonian word of the many people who were raised with the ethos by which patricians had long justified their moral right to dominate others.[4] In Hooper's humor, paternalistic standards covertly impugned the morality of a herrenvolk ethic. The spirit of freedom animated Suggs's world, creating a moral anarchy that naturally bred slavery, but such unstable freedom held no promise of equality since race quite imperfectly separated those people with "mother-wit" from those without it. For all of their brutish qualities, Hooper's black slaves are humans, while his free whites can be kin to animals—and witless, too.

At the same time, however, Suggs's inegalitarian society presented no case for planter dominance over plain folk. Eugene Genovese and Elizabeth Fox-Genovese have forcefully argued that slaveholders, "in but not of the capitalist world," were driven by the logic of paternalism to accept slavery in the abstract, implicitly renouncing the absolute value of freedom. Unquestionably, paternalistic values provided a coherent way to attribute morality to exploitative relationships. That many planters embraced an ideology enshrining themselves as Christian guardians for their benighted African wards is both logically consistent and historically demonstrable. It is much more difficult, however, to demonstrate that a paternalistic ideology pervaded southern white society. The notion that planters should rightfully be fatherly stewards for other free men sat poorly with many nonplanters—and Johnson Hooper thought it nonsense.[5]

Instead, Hooper made Suggs demonstrate again and again the comic futility of traditional conceptions of paternalism, hinting at a new moral order in which good men must earn the right to organize a progressive society. But Hooper's satire only hinted at moral standards he made explicit elsewhere, and therein lay its special suitability for joining freedom and slavery in popular thought. The apparent moral anarchy in Suggs's world stems from the literary model Hooper employed. In the underlying structure of satire, the targets of derisive laughter—Hooper's predators and their victims—stand judged by those who might be their opposites. Without the hopeful implicit standard, predators would not be funny. For thousands of amused readers, the pleasure of laughter affirmed hope without defining aspirations.

A contrast with George Fitzhugh readily illustrates the inherent advantage of the humorist over the polemicist. Simon Suggs's free society was quite like the harsh jungle that Fitzhugh attacked in *Cannibals All!* in 1857. But Fitzhugh's radical logic led him to denounce the freedom and equality that made human life precarious in the North. Hooper's competitive jungle was strangely attractive, its lure of freedom overwhelming, and humor required no explanation of how danger might be desirable. In the last analysis, Hooper helped his readers laugh away discomfort about the perils of freedom. On the one hand, then, his satire illustrates Genovese's longstanding insistence that free society's derogation of dependent relationships created a substantial ethical dilemma for southern slaveholders.[6] But on the other, Hooper's reliance upon satire relieved him from the pressures of logic. Through new images of human nature, not formally consistent ideas, he could meld opposing values into a common channel for popular hopes. His glee at the crafty chicanery of Simon Suggs reflected his hope that an order for the future South would emerge based on the natural potential for order in individual character. He hinted at a new future for slavery and freedom through the same naturalistic ethos.

Historians are of course aware of the incipient naturalism in proslavery thought, but they have generally failed to appreciate underlying similarities between scientific racialism, which had limited appeal, and southern humorous literature, which was nationally popular. Literary scholars, on the other hand, have for many years associated southwestern humorists like Hooper with darker tensions in popular culture, but they underestimate the historical significance of such writers in antebellum society. Some early critics treated the tall tales as "just fun." Others focused upon the stories' satiric form and stressed the transmutation of European influences. But since the time of Kenneth Lynn's influential work, *Mark Twain and Southwestern Humor,* scholars have recognized the comic writers' influence upon later American artists such as Twain and William Faulkner, and critics now have linked the antebellum influence with twentieth-century black humor and with the "cheerful nihilism" of existential writers. Scholars such as Susan Kuhlmann, Karen

Halttunen, and Gary Lindberg have identified confidence men as icons of expanding capitalism, and William E. Lenz has suggested that Suggs was the prototype for a whole series of fictional rogues, the most important being Herman Melville's Confidence Man.[7] The hidden meanings embedded in Hooper's satire have been illuminated by critics aided by anthropology, folklore, and postmodern critical theory, and a variety of alternative readings are available. Ironically, however, perhaps because Lynn years ago described the response of proslavery humorists to *Uncle Tom's Cabin* as reactionary, recent critics have failed to notice how deftly Hooper's earlier stories had fastened slavery to the future of American freedom.[8]

Some Adventures of Captain Simon Suggs is a provocative incarnation of the violent metamorphosis that occurred as the South moved West, "opening up," "opening out," in Robert H. Wiebe's suggestive phrases.[9] J. Mills Thornton III, whose work treats the "Hooperite" influence in Alabama's secession movement, characterized Hooper's neglected insights as "laughter through tears"; and contemporaries called the journalist's tales comic histories—exaggerated but honest at their core. Hooper believed that "truth is the foundation of all fame and honor—of all that is desirable in life," and his stories have the ring of truth, for all of their gross hyperbole.[10] That truth is drawn from Hooper's participation in historically important changes in southern society, and it also reflects a raw honesty about his personal life, which contained such extremes as to require a satiric treatment. Hooper created the fictional world of Simon Suggs from the real incongruities between his eastern childhood and western adulthood, experiences that were distinctly American and peculiarly southern.

Hooper was born in 1815 to the kind of advantages found among members of the South's upper classes. His coastal North Carolina family was part of a large kinship network distinguished by learning, piety, and wealth.[11] Johnson's father, Archibald Maclaine Hooper, was the nephew of a signer of the Declaration of Independence. He inherited slaves and property in the Cape Fear region, but his inheritance was dissipated by the time of Johnson's adolescence. The boy's mother, Charlotte deBerniere Hooper, was a zealous evangelical Episcopalian, who bemoaned her son's attraction to the "low" company that kept him on the streets at night. Affectionate, witty, and sociable, Johnson displayed little of the moral earnestness that marked his brothers and sisters. But he was a gifted youth with a "scribbling propensity" that showed early. So, like the others, he received private schooling with the aid of their extended family. And though he was sometimes an indifferent student, he acquired the rudiments of a classical education.[12] At eighteen, living in Charleston partly supported by prominent relatives, Johnson felt keenly the sting of the family's decline and his liminal relationship to the city's elite society. Unwilling to continue accepting largess for an uncertain educational future, in 1835 he followed his older brother George, a lawyer, to the eastern border of Alabama, where the Creek cessions had recently opened new lands.[13]

The Hoopers hoped that the frontier South presented opportunities for the talented brothers to regenerate the family's wealth. But Johnson, to his family's considerable dismay, seemed more inclined to act out the motto he soon attached to Simon Suggs: "IT IS GOOD TO BE SHIFTY IN A NEW COUNTRY!" He spent most of the next seven years drifting about the frontier, trying one occupation and another, getting trapped in the panic of 1837 by a disastrous business venture, and being bailed out by various relatives.[14] In 1842 he settled temporarily in the tiny border town of La Fayette with George, who had already assured their parents that "if he can be made steady, he is just the fellow to advance in the practice of law in this country where a fluent tongue and abundant assurance invariably succeed with any modicum of talent." Within a year's time, the newly reformed vagrant married and began establishing a place for himself in Alabama. He became an ardent Whig and editor of the party's local newspaper, the *La Fayette East Alabamian,* and he rather halfheartedly practiced law.[15] Enjoying the first modest security of his adult life, Johnson could laugh at his errant past and think about his future.

With considerable zest for his adventures, the novice editor almost immediately began writing his comic histories for the Whig readers of his little newspaper. A satiric story of his recent experience, "Taking the Census," was picked up by William Porter, Whig editor of the popular sporting paper the *New York Spirit of the Times*.[16] When the Suggs stories began to appear in 1844, Porter promoted them to national prominence through his paper and through the popular anthology entitled *The Big Bear of Arkansas*. With Porter's support, Hooper expanded the stories into a loose picaresque novel, and he published a new collection before the decade's end. His stories were widely pirated, and Hooper's originality even won recognition in England's gentlemanly reviews.[17]

Before his literary career began, Hooper's humor showed the corrosive effect of his family's decline and of his own scramble for financial success. With a critical edge derived from his marginal status, he satirized all classes of people in his adopted society. Like Juvenal, whom he once praised for "lashing snobs," Hooper saw patrician standards of honor subvened by greed. Like the Roman, he thought that in his society the first questions asked of a man were "How many slaves does he have?" and "How many acres does he own?" and the last was "What is his reputation?" In his newspapers, the "poor 'worm in the dust'—of a whig editor" almost perversely baited the "aristocracy" of Montgomery's Democratic Regency for their social pretensions.[18] Hooper bragged about his ancestry and plainly wished to be thought a gentleman, but his gestures toward gentility were always matched by impulses to what Bertram Wyatt-Brown has called "primal honor," a more violent form of self-assertion. A passionate man, he had a legendary generosity, was fond of drinking and gambling, and was noted for his conviviality. Money slipped through his fingers like water, by his own admission.[19] In later life, worn by repeated failures and enraged at the Yankee threat to a prosperous South, Hooper's bitterness equaled that of Juvenal. Then Hooper would violently affirm his endangered honor and that of his region. But in the 1840s, when honor, worldly ambition, and a booming economy seemed made for each other, the hopeful young satirist could laugh like Suggs at the fun of being shifty in a new country.

Indeed, *Some Adventures of Captain Simon Suggs* perfectly captures the spirit of opportunity the young Whig editor sensed before him as Alabama bounced back from the panic of 1837. The setting is the southern frontier, but the overriding theme is American, and a wild freedom gives birth to Suggs. The saga's narrative structure is a burlesque campaign biography penned by "Johns" Hooper, the "brittish feddul edditur" of the "La Fait eest Allybammyun." Elevated language separates Johns from Suggs's vulgar vernacular, in that sense providing a genteel frame for the low comedy, but the "edditur" cannot epitomize civilized virtue while selling the amoral captain.[20] Johns is promoting himself, too, just as Suggs would promote the real Hooper. At one level, then, Johns's blather about the "pious task of commemorating the acts, and depicting the character" of Suggs mocked the very role Hooper sought to play in Alabama's democratic politics.[21] Newspaper editors were critical tools for welding voters to mass-based panics, and talented writers like Hooper were in demand. But how much truth and honor did the job entail? Hooper strenuously advocated Whig candidates and policies, yet he knew that much of his writing was "hack" work, "setting up and knocking down of partisan politicians," as a worn-out Hooper would one day call it. Suggs put it more flatly: "ritin' lies." Hooper could hardly scorn the ladder he was climbing, but editing brought honor only if its crasser aspects could somehow be transformed. Johns, the Whig who "usetur to be as nisey a dirnmikrat as ever drinkt whiskey," perfectly epitomized opportunity's problems.[22]

Johns is quite obviously Johnson Hooper, thinly disguised, but Suggs is Hooper, too—an identification that underlines the writer's sympathy for his shifty man and the freedom that engendered his kind. Suggs is the common man writ large: dirty and disreputable but master of his world. More fundamentally, he is human nature in the raw. Hooper—later nicknamed "the Ugly Man"—resembled Suggs, whose physiognomy and spindly body are described in language that reveals the kinship.[23] Suggs, too, has just emerged from a "somewhat extended juvenility" and a long period of wandering without "authentic trace" of his whereabouts. Like Hooper, he is incurably fond of drinking and gambling. Suggs lives by his wits, making something out of nothing, needing no capital to "get along." He has something better: an infallible knowledge of human nature. He is "a sort of he-Pallas, ready to cope with his kind, from his infancy. . . ." If nature made Suggs a "beast of prey, she did not refine the cruelty by denying him the fangs and the claws." Simon Suggs is man as animal, his residence the jungle, not an abstract state of nature. Not only does no wrathful God intervene to punish Suggs for bestial behavior, but time and again the environment rewards it.[24]

Suggs's depraved world is too funny to be confused with Hell. In reflection of Hooper's dual allegiances—to the society which shaped his character and to that which promised his redemption—his genius made the freedom of Suggs's natural habitat both as frightening and as attractive as unbounded opportunity. Suggs roamed a frontier waiting for development, a jungle ready to be tamed, amusing because his wit was equal to the task. Although it bears some hints of a nightmare republic corrupted by unrestrained avarice, Hooper's vision was not retrogressive.[25] Order in the new society would have to take unfamiliar forms, tapping forces compatible with those unleashed by freedom. The license of satiric form did not require Hooper to explain precisely how the spirit of freedom might be retained as civilization advanced or exactly what moral glue would hold society together. A positivist by instinct, Hooper offered reality as he saw it. Decrying false visions defined by tradition or convention, he empowered Suggs, the scholar of human nature, to destroy them, suggesting the potentialities of freedom by what was left in ruins.[26]

The landscape of Suggs's world is littered with the victims of his destructive power, its creative strength purging the jungle of more venal predators. In story after story, Suggs defeats his fellow confidence men, who pose as false stewards while manipulating conventional standards to promote themselves. Suggs and Johns symbolize the great deception of Jacksonian politics, but Suggs also triumphs over land speculators robbing the Indians, members of the legislature and profligate "men of fortune" outwitting each other in card games, lawyers and judges bilking the people at large, and preachers extorting money from their congregations.[27] Suggs can victimize these would-be nabobs because they are too busy exploiting others' "soft spots" to see ruin approaching. No moral superiority separates these beasts from their intended prey; their status in society rests only upon pretense. By any standards of moral responsibility, they deserve the laughter their foibles provoke.

Simon Suggs also exploits ignorant, gullible, and seemingly harmless poor whites, but only at first glance are most of them innocents.[28] The frontiersmen elevate Suggs to their captaincy for an Indian war he has conjured wholly from rumor, through feeding their prejudice and fear. These commoners are sorted out by wit, however, and significantly, it is their lowliest representative, a din-eating, "spindlelegged young man" called Yellow Legs, who sees right through Suggs's charade. He is too young and powerless to depose the captain, so Yellow Legs proclaims the truth to his fellows over Suggs's dire threats. Like knowledge unfettered, he bounces in and out of the plot, challenging Suggs with "a gesture expressive of the highest contempt."[29] When the dirt-eater's elders fail to act upon the truth he reveals, they become victims of the faulty order they have created. Hooper's satire has a kind of primitive moral truth: given freedom, men must be responsible for their own "soft spots."

But the nihilism inherent in Hooper's naturalism is more brutally revealed by the exploitation of those who do not seem to deserve their fate at all: slaves, whose weaknesses come directly from nature, in Hooper's view. They are perpetual victims, captives of their inferiority. Relative innocents, however deficient in wit, they are exploited by Suggs and by his other victims as well. Cruel laughter about slaves was important to the meaning of both the first and last stories in Simon Suggs's biography, and brief but grim jokes about slaves mark the center of Hooper's most effective piece of satire, "The Captain Attends a Camp-Meeting." Hooper cannily shifted his narrative from American white freedom to southern Negro slavery, confident that racism would allow his readers to share his amusement at slavery's ugly features, some of which could not be changed, even in a tamer world. The laughter of white people demeaned the black slaves, assuaging unease and fixing their place as victims with natural finality, as the same freedom that empowered whites forever entailed blacks to slavery.[30]

Black slavery first defines white freedom in the opening escapade of Simon Suggs, when he acquired the liberty that created his adult character. The story of Simon's escape from his parents drew power from Hooper's conviction that external restraints upon the anarchic impulses of human nature were useless. Simon's father, Jedediah Suggs, is a hard-shell Baptist preacher, avaricious and something of a hypocrite, but he believes himself duty-bound to save his son from gambling. While trying to do so, he is tricked by the precocious sharpster into a card game that costs Jedediah a horse and all control over young Simon. Jedediah's greed and his moral tyranny warrant his loss, but Simon's mother's self-deception seems quite minor: she merely entertains a sentimental view of her son. As the boy puts it: "'There's some use in mammies—I kin poke my finger right in the old 'oman's eye, and keep it thar, and if I say it aim thar, she'll say so too.'" Still, Suggs takes a parting shot at her, loading her favorite pipe with gunpowder. He rides away from home on his father's horse, laughing at the picture of the pipe exploding in his mother's face. False piety and sentiment were no match for Suggs's wit and his powerful thirst for freedom.[31]

Jedediah Suggs is no more a loving patriarch to his slave Bill than he is to his son. The slave cannot escape, however, and his punishment is essential to Simon's getaway. When Jedediah first catches his son and young Bill playing cards in a field, he declares that they both deserve a beating. Bill, already being beaten at poker, goes first, and as Simon watches in horrified expectation, "Bill was swung up a-tiptoe to a limb, and the whipping commenced, Simon's eye followed every movement of his father's arm; and as each blow descended upon the bare shoulders of his sable friend, his own body writhed and 'wriggled' in involuntary sympathy."[32] The shifty white boy vicariously felt the slave child's pain, but it gave him extra time to invent the card trick that wins his freedom. Simon triumphantly escapes both a beating and his confining home; Bill can avoid neither. The story begins with the two young men as playmates. It ends with their futures in sharp contrast.

The multiple meanings of this complicated parable touch upon the most basic human relations, conveying Hooper's sense that in free society the dissolution of familial order might be pervasive. The story bears witness to the rising influence of the cash nexus, and it heralds the arrival of a new era of oedipal tensions aggravated by the lure of recurring flush times. The competitive frontier seduced eastern sons to western freedom, to the irresistible promise of a future gained by wit, not given by family. Hooper assailed with equal enthusiasm the futile authority of patriarchy and the more manipulative order of sentimental families like his own. Both gave way before the appetite for self-determination. So if, like proslavery intellectuals, Hooper compared the moral obligations within families to the responsibilities of power over dependent slaves, he found that new and deeply felt tensions made the family an unusable model for slavery.[33] The loose ties of affection might "refine the cruelty" of nature, preventing fathers from whipping sons or slaves, but they would be inadequate to restrain slaves. With the same brutal frankness that would lead him later to defend burning alive a slave accused of murder as a wrong justifiably committed by respectable people, Hooper affirmed what he thought had to be.[34]

Jedediah Suggs points toward other predatory stewards whom Hooper, through Simon, punishes for creating social order false to nature's own. This moral is outrageously invoked in "The Captain Attends a Camp-Meeting," a stunning satire of enthusiastic religion. In a scene dominated by nearly pornographic imagery, Simon steals the meeting's offering from impious preachers by posing as a "saved" sinner. The hedonism unveiled by Hooper's coarse humor lies in human nature, but its eruption at the meeting is the work of greedy preachers, whose bad faith exposes whites to petty theft and blacks to worse. The opening scene describes the emotional turmoil the preachers stir up among white and black people, who mix "promiscuously," though the "negroes sang and screamed and prayed" more wildly than the whites: "'Gl-o-ree!' yelled a huge, greasy negro woman, as in a fit of the jerks, she threw herself convulsively from her feet,"—falling all over a tiny white man in her ecstasy. In the middle of this biracial uproar, Suggs captivates the excited crowd with his theatrically sexual account of being born again. His "load o' sin" that had been "'a-mashin down on my back'" lifts as soon as Suggs relates his vision of the threatening jaws of a dreadful alligator: "'I jist pitched in a big rock which choked him to death, and that minit I felt the weight slide off, and I had the best feelins—sorter like you'll have from good sperrits—any body ever had!'" Throughout Suggs's spellbinding "discourse" the ministers, recognizing no difference between his theatrics and the conduct of other converts, maintain a steady flow of exhortations about the "'sperience" and its spiritual meaning, their commentary demonstrating the tools with which Suggs will soon defraud them all.[35]

But Hooper more ominously punctuates Suggs's performance with the exclamations of a hysterical old white woman dressed in black silk. Three times Mrs. Dobbs shrieks at her slave Sukey to fetch Mr. Dobbs so he can hear Simon "talk sweet":

> "Whar's John Dobbs? You Sukey!' screaming at a negro woman on the other side of the square—'ef you don't hunt up your mass John in a minute, and have him here to listen to his [Suggs's] 'sperience, I'll tuck you up when I get home and give you a hundred and fifty lashes, madam!—see if I don't!'" "'Blessed Lord!'"—referring again to the Captain's relation, "'aint it a *precious* 'scource!'"[36]

Aroused by Simon and the preachers, the frustrated old woman threatens her slave with a violence that underscores the mistress's animal qualities. Mrs. Dobbs's threats appear as a dark counterpoint to her supposed religious enthusiasm. Yet like the murky "krick swamp" that adjoins the camp ground and provides shelter for Suggs's eventual escape, her shrill exclamations warn of the natural wildness never far removed from human experience.

Suggs's wild spirit and his licentious humor completely dominate the camp meeting story, hinting that the necessity for liberty warrants the risk of license. But Hooper, like many religious critics, was genuinely bothered by the tactics of revivalists, and like the conservatives in his family, he was openly skeptical about the possibilities for mass redemption. Nonetheless, he found the camp meeting's confusion of passions and spiritual experience more funny than tragic; his objections were ethical but not religious. Even if his mother's repeated laments about Johnson's lost soul are ignored, it is plain that Hooper's spirituality was at best underdeveloped and that he was wholly lacking in the kind of piety from which many of his fellow Whigs thought self-discipline emanated.[37] Unwilling to apply external controls upon the passions of human nature and unable to place faith in religious appeals, Hooper saw the only hope of restraint in humans' natural capacity for self-knowledge, a message obliquely conveyed by his frank treatment of sex. Honest confrontation of the sexuality in all humans (acknowledgement such as his humor prompted) would bar sexual manipulation; neither blacks nor whites would be driven to violent frenzy. White self-restraint might flow from the knowledge of human nature found beneath the shams of social forms, so the possible perils of releasing the wild human energies of white men could provoke laughter through tears. But Hooper believed that the gross animal instincts of slaves were such as to endanger the very foundations of civilization if they could freely be unleashed by unscrupulous whites. And Hooper presumed his readers shared his views well enough to laugh that possibility away.

In the final escapade of Simon Suggs, slaves become commodities, the uniquely southern feature in a typical frontier scheme. More starkly here than in any of Suggs's other adventures, the natural freedom of the Southwest stood in implicit opposition to the civilized restraints of the coastal South. As a fitting finale for Johns's biography, Simon describes his conquest of schemers bent on floating worthless paper to rob the public. Having hired Suggs to promote their money, the proprietors of the "Wetumpky Trading Kumpiny" direct him to pose as a respectable planter going to "Urwintun . . . to buy niggars to stock my plantashun." To gain credibility for the fraudulent notes, Suggs flamboyantly "buys" valuable slaves from a fellow conspirator, hoping that use of the notes in such an important transaction will prompt others to take the worthless paper. His attempt to spread the "Kumpiny" notes fails, however, because "even the niggers knowd they warn't no 'count." So Suggs truly sells the slaves, for "state money" with which he absconds, cheating the "institushun" out of its slaves and foiling the proprietors' corrupt scheme. The slaves vanish into the market, their perception of the scam only serving to heighten the stupidity of the directors of the "Trading Kumpiny."[38]

Hooper's images captured what James Oakes has described: the flux of people and commodities in the capitalistic society of the Southwest. There was no decent credit system in Alabama, but rapid development demanded a medium of exchange, with or without specie backing. "Institushuns" and "plantashuns" were both necessary elements of prosperity, and if the frontier was to contain opportunities for ambitious men of little means, traditional values would have to be abandoned. Land speculation (the subject of two of Suggs's adventures), like trade in slaves, actively eroded conservative ideals, undermining whatever attachments to place and persons survived the westward movement.[39] Moreover, slave labor had to be moved freely at the wish of white masters, belying any pretensions to seigneurial attachments. Honest banks, honest money, honest planters would slow the social flux, but stopping it altogether was unthinkable.

The freedom Hooper prescribed for the "ruling race" did not, however, mandate a fully egalitarian society, even for whites. In the primitive ethical order bred by freedom, he found lurking new and unstable forms of inequality, as white men preyed upon each other. In his rejection of the liberal ethos that extolled enlightened self-interest, Hooper was slowly abandoning a priori principles and "abstractions" in favor of truth based on experience. In the spirit of a nascent naturalism, he was separating biblical absolutes from the positivist truth of human history.[40] His free men are more compulsively competitive than rationally calculating, and they compete to extract wealth from their fellow humans, both white and black. In spite of these predatory traits, Hooper abjured the fixity that might confine human beasts within hierarchy and dependence. Implacably, the same natural law that visibly decreed slavery required freedom for whites to demonstrate their true worth, whatever that was. The instinctive positivist found honor and wit distributed among white people without regard to class—a finding confirmed as much in the depravity of those who falsely claimed aristocracy as in the talents of the poor. Nonetheless, the aristocratic values Hooper derived from his class origins covertly sustained a naturalistic code of honor that would constantly reorganize society in honest recognition of innate inequality. Innate wit required freedom in which to prove who should rule by right.

Thus freedom and slavery stood justified in the same comic images. Although Hooper probably had a darker view of human nature than most members of his Whiggish audience, he too hoped that a free society's cultivation of human wit would engender progress. He hoped—one cannot say believed—that honorable, honest men with self-knowledge would have enough self-restraint to check their predatory instincts, to curb might with right. So even after northern antislavery politics had destroyed his nationalism, Hooper remained a Whiggish advocate of education and public improvement and an avid promoter of state aid for economic development. Moreover, he wanted slavery's cruelties, like those of other human relationships, to be meliorated, to make all "institushuns" consistent with a social order he later described as a "true, permanent, and homogeneous condition, in which a steady, well-regulated public sentiment is a powerful influence to direct and correct in every department of life."[41] He saw black slavery as a necessary cost of civilized freedom in a biracial society, but it was not to be confused with the goal of progress. During the long process, in order to sustain the effort, how much better to laugh than cry at every inevitable failure?

Johnson Hooper was not, then, an atavistic remnant of bygone patriarchy, nor was he an apologist for a tyrannical ruling class in the making. He belonged in a sense to a southern elite that never emerged. On the one hand, he drew his ideas from the larger currents of the Anglo-American world, as Mills Thornton has suggested for other Alabama fire-eaters of a decade later.[42] In his zeal for progress, his pragmatic naturalism, and his deep-seated racism, Hooper foreshadowed the laissez-faire ideology of the latter half of the nineteenth century. Yet he would have attacked the greed of industrial robber barons as strongly as he did the reigning planters of Alabama's senatorial aristocracy or, as Suggs did, the predatory false stewards of frontier Alabama. In 1845, in his thirtieth year, he at least hoped that strong southern whites would also be good men, democratically responsible to their peers and protective of their black charges. But then he also hoped that his own strengths would come to outweigh his youthful weaknesses. As it turned out, he was tragically wrong about both.[43]

At the spontaneous level from which humor springs, most of what was funny in *Some Adventures of Simon Suggs* stemmed from Johnson Hooper's fond toleration of his own shortcomings. It was the toleration of a young man, still expecting to succeed, writing for a new world, waiting to be civilized. Hooper's resistance to self-control—his reluctance to pay all of the psychological costs of becoming civilized, if you will—is reflected in the energies of Suggs's unbounded world. For all of his bestial nature, Simon Suggs was funny because civilized readers could take comfort in their expectation that his kind would be tamed with the frontier itself. Suggs is thus an emblem of the creative and destructive possibilities inherent in the American freedom that sustains his life, as air does fire. His energies, his wit, and his predatory instinct for human weaknesses required self-control but not elimination. Like Hooper himself, his readers could laugh at the excesses of their ambitions without ceasing to aspire.[44]

It seems worthwhile to underscore what may already be obvious: in the 1840s, Hooper had many national readers who, if they attended at all to the place of slaves in his stories, seem to have found it proper.[45] Hooper's slave characters were not really actors in his comedy. They were acted upon, forced into social passivity by the aggressiveness of the whites around them. Hooper hoped that this combination of human power—white wit and black brute force—would build a great society. That view was not explicit in Suggs, but the writer's hopes provided the contrast that made his stories funny rather than sad. Ironically, Hooper's covert standards contributed to Suggs's popularity across classes and regions, fitting the aspirations of men with quite differing notions of society but similar instincts for order and freedom. Some found his coarse humor vulgar; others perhaps despised his racial slurs; but in the decade before *Uncle Tom's Cabin* laid bare the connections between competitive freedom and slavery, Hooper found many amused readers.[46] His success compels modern readers to contemplate nineteenth-century white Americans so entranced by what they wanted to become that they could laugh at the slaves who might become hapless victims of white freedom. It also suggests that we reflect upon the popular foundations for their amusement: weaknesses in human nature that bound slavery with freedom and pervasive racial prejudice that cut across geographical lines. The world of Simon Suggs is sometimes vulgar, always coarse, but it is still alive with an energy that was not to be restrained. Hooper's images reflect the force of a southern mind fixed on the future, its outlines all the more ominous for their national appeal.

Notes

1. The best modern edition of Hooper's first and most famous book is *Adventures of Captain Simon Suggs, Late of the Tallapoosa Volunteers*, intro. by Manly Wade Wellman (Chapel Hill, N.C., 1969); all subsequent page references to Hooper, *Adventures of Captain Simon Suggs*, are to this edition, and the quoted headnote is from pages 49–50. The first edition was published in 1845 by Carey and Hart of Philadelphia. While recent historians have neglected southern white humor, there is a steadily growing body of criticism by literary scholars of the humorous tradition. For historians' purposes, the criticism is marred by insensitivity to social context and by a lumping together of humorists whose views of society are substantially different. Still, much of it is invaluable for placing Hooper in the proper literary context. Particularly helpful in this attempt to chart unfamiliar literary territory are four collections of essays: Louis D. Rubin Jr., ed., *The Comic Imagination in American Literature* (New Brunswick, N.J., 1973); M. Thomas Inge, ed., *The Frontier Humorists: Critical Views* (Hamden, Conn., 1975); William Bedford Clark and W. Craig Turner, *Critical Essays on American Humor* (Boston, 1984); and Ronald Paulson, ed., *Satire: Modern Essays in Criticism* (Englewood Cliffs, N.J., 1971). Edward A. Bloom and Lillian D. Bloom, in *Satire's Persuasive Voice* (Ithaca, N.Y., 1979), emphasize the reformist nature of satiric literature, but in Chapter I, entitled "Intention," cogently warn against "dogmatic" interpretations. See also Charles E. Davis and Martha B. Hudson, comps., "Humor of the Old Southwest: A Checklist of Criticism," *Mississippi Quarterly*, XXVII (Spring 1974), 179–99. Historical studies that specifically treat the subject of humor about blacks in the antebellum period include Jean H. Baker, *Affairs of Party: The Political Culture of Northern Democrats in the Mid-Nineteenth Century* (Ithaca, N.Y., 1983); and Joseph Boskin, *Sambo: The Rise and Demise of an American Jester* (New York, 1986). Research for this essay was undertaken with the support of grants from the National Endowment for the Humanities Program for Travel-to-Collections and the University of Alabama in Huntsville. The author wishes to thank Thomas B. Alexander, Ann Boucher, Vicki Johnson, Larry Kohl, Michael O'Brien, Stephen Waring, Carolyn White, John White, and Bertram Wyatt-Brown for their helpful comments and suggestions.

2. The standard biography of Hooper is W. Stanley Hoole, *Alias Simon Suggs: The Life and Times of Johnson Jones Hooper* (University, Ala., 1952), which is outdated in some respects, including its interpretation of Hooper's Whiggish views. A newer critical study by Paul Somers Jr., *Johnson J. Hooper* (Boston, 1984), treats Hooper's partisan ideas more effectively, though it repeats some of Hoole's errors.

3. Quoted passages from *Adventures of Captain Simon Suggs*, 49 (second quotation), 50 (first quotation). Among the growing number of studies about the market's influence upon nineteenth-century writers most useful for understanding Hooper are Shelley Fisher Fishkin, *From Fact to Fiction: Journalism and Imaginative Writing in America* (Baltimore, 1985); Michael T. Gilmore, *American Romanticism and the Marketplace* (Chicago, 1985); and David S. Reynolds, *Beneath the American Renaissance: The Subversive Imagination in the*

Age of Emerson and Melville (New York, 1988). John McCardell has briefly related Hooper's work to larger themes in southern culture in *The Idea of a Southern Nation: Southern Nationalists and Southern Nationalism,* 1830–1860 (New York, 1979), 160–61. Essential to understanding the role Hooper played in the secession crisis is J. Mills Thornton III, *Politics and Power in a Slave Society: Alabama, 1800–1860* (Baton Rouge, 1978). The proslavery tract is Matthew Estes, *A Defence of Negro Slavery, as it Exists in the United States* (Montgomery, Ala., 1846).

4. The most cogent interpretations emphasizing the liberal character of southern society are those of George M. Fredrickson in *The Black Image in the White Mind: The Debate on Afro-American Character and Destiny, 1817–1914* (New York and other cities, 1971), and *The Arrogance of Race: Historical Perspectives on Slavery, Racism, and Social Inequality* (Middletown, Conn., 1988); and James Oakes in *The Ruling Race: A History of American Slaveholders* (New York, 1982), and *Slavery and Freedom: An Interpretation of the Old South* (New York, 1990). The "outsiders" usage is prominent in *Slavery and Freedom,* while *The Ruling Race* stresses coastal paternalism. That emphasis is also reflected in some scholarship in social and political history. See, for example, Michael P. Johnson, *Toward a Patriarchal Republic: The Secession of Georgia* (Baton Rouge, 1977); Orville Vernon Burton, *In My Father's House are Many Mansions: Family and Community in Edgefield, South Carolina* (Chapel Hill, N.C., 1985); and William H. Pease and Jane H. Pease, *The Web of Progress: Private Values and Public Styles in Boston and Charleston, 1828–1843* (New York, 1985). Lawrence Shore's *Southern Capitalists: The Ideological Leadership of an Elite, 1832–1885* (Chapel Hill, N.C., 1986), which stresses continuity between Old South and New South, treats with considerable sensitivity the flexibility of southern ideologues in addressing tensions between the values of liberal capitalism and aristocratic paternalism, especially as those were revealed in theories of labor; see especially Chap. 2, "Nonslaveholders in Slaveholders' Capitalist World." Among literary critics, Louis D. Rubin Jr. insists upon the similarities between North and South as part of an emerging industrial capitalist world, but his observation that the South produced no satiric "self-scrutinizing critique" is puzzling; see the opening chapter to *The Edge of the Swamp: A Study in the Literature and Society of the Old South* (Baton Rouge, 1989), 46 (quotation).

5. Much of the recent scholarship emphasizing paternalism has been stimulated by Genovese's influential work *The World the Slaveholders Made: Two Essays in Interpretation* (New York, 1969). A more comprehensive treatment is Elizabeth Fox-Genovese and Eugene D. Genovese, *Fruits of Merchant Capital: Slavery and Bourgeois Property in the Rise and Expansion of Capitalism* (New York, 1983), 16 (quoted passage). Also important have been a series of books by Drew Gilpin Faust, *The Sacred Circle: The Dilemma of the Intellectual in the Old South, 1840–1860* (Baltimore, 1977); *The Ideology of Slavery: Proslavery Thought in the Antebellum South. 1830–1860* (Baton Rouge, 1981); and *James Henry Hammond and the Old South: A Design for Mastery* (Baton Rouge, 1982). For related interpretations in literary criticism, see the influential work of Lewis P. Simpson, especially *The Man of Letters in New England and the South: Essays on the History of the Literary Vocation in America* (Baton Rouge, 1973); his brief study, *The Dispossessed Garden: Pastoral and History in Southern Literature* (Athens, Ga., 1975); and his recent prizewinning *Mind and the American Civil War: A Meditation on Lost Causes* (Baton Rouge, 1989); and Elizabeth Fox-Genovese and Eugene D. Genovese, "The Cultural History of Southern Slave Society: Reflections on the Work of Lewis P. Simpson," in J. Gerald Kennedy and Daniel Mark Fogel, eds., *American Letters and the Historical Consciousness: Essays in Honor of Lewis P. Simpson* (Baton Rouge, 1987). Other recent works stressing patriarchal themes are Kenneth S. Greenberg, *Masters and Statesmen: The Political Culture of American Slavery* (Baltimore, 1985); and Larry E. Tise, *Proslavery: A*

History of the Defense of Slavery in America, 1701–1840 (Athens, Ga., 1987). The difficulty of explaining how slaveholders' views were accepted by nonslaveholders is discussed in Fox-Genovese and Genovese, "Yeoman Farmers in a Slaveholders' Democracy," in *Fruits of Merchant Capital, 249–64*. Also relevant are the summary comments of Greenburg in *Masters and Statesmen*, 102–3.

6. For a more recent edition of Fitzhugh's work see *Cannibals All! or, Slaves without Masters*, edited by C. Vann Woodward (Cambridge, Mass., 1960). The slaveholders' dilemma is thoughtfully placed in the context of a Marxist view of Western history in Fox-Genovese and Genovese, *Fruits of Merchant Capital*, Chap. 13, "Slavery: The World's Burden," which concludes that "despite their honest protestations of respect for freedom and even democracy, the exigencies of their social system were dragging them irresistibly toward political and social policies flagrantly tyrannical, illiberal, and undemocratic, at least by American standards" (p. 401). Fox-Genovese's incisive analysis of Louisa McCord's effort to "bind the liberal free trade principles of bourgeois political economy to apparently contradictory particularistic and hierarchical proslavery convictions" illustrates that these tensions ran across gender in the intellectual elite; see *Within the Plantation Household: Black and White Women of the Old South* (Chapel Hill, N.C., 1988), especially Chap. 5, p. 282 (quoted passage).

7. Lynn first identified the humorists as Whiggish gentlemen critical of the frontier spirit, and he, perhaps more than any other critic, was responsible for redirecting scholarship about the antebellum humorists away from a Turnerian fascination with their optimistic, individualistic "Americanness." Lynn comments extensively upon slavery, but since his emphasis in that regard was on the period after the publication of *Uncle Tom's Cabin, or, Life Among the Lowly* (Boston, 1852; rev. ed., New York, 1965), he did not include Hooper. See Kenneth S. Lynn, *Mark Twain and Southwestern Humor* (Boston, 1960; rpt. ed., Westport, Conn., 1972), especially pp. 46–88, 100–104. The "just fun" interpreters celebrated vernacular influences upon American literature with an unabashed enthusiasm, for western influences reminiscent of the frontier thesis of Frederick Jackson Turner. A balanced early interpretation in this vein was Constance Rourke, *American Humor: A Study of the National Character* (New York, 1931); for more explicitly conservative political comments see Mody C. Boatright, *Folk Laughter on the American Frontier* (New York, 1949). For the relationship between contemporary black humor and the antebellum humorists, useful essays are in Sarah Blacher Cohen, ed., *Comic Relief: Humor in Contemporary American Literature* (Urbana, Ill., 1978); continuities with existential themes are explored in Richard Boyd Hauck, *A Cheerful Nihilism: Confidence and "The Absurd" in American Humorous Fiction* (Bloomington, Ind., 1971), especially pp. 70–74. Karen Halttunen has treated middle-class anxieties about a commercialized society in *Confidence Men and Painted Women: A Study of Middle-class Culture in America, 1830–1870* (New Haven, Conn., 1982). Literary studies include Susan Kuhlmann, *Knave, Fool, and Genius: The Confidence Man as He Appears in Nineteenth-Century American Fiction* (Chapel Hill, N.C., 1973); Gary Lindberg, *The Confidence Man in American Literature* (New York, 1982); and William E. Lenz, *Fast Talk and Flush Times: The Confidence Man as a Literary Convention* (Columbia, Mo., 1985). An appreciative essay review that relates Lenz's study to the others is Edward J. Piacentino, "A Confidence Study of Confidence Men," *American Quarterly*, XXXVIII (Spring 1986), 152–57. David Reynolds in *Beneath the American Renaissance* ties Hooper and other humorists directly to the major literary works of the antebellum period more broadly than have other scholars.

8. Without treating Hooper in detail, several studies of American culture have discussed the relationships among capitalism slavery, and literature; see, for example, William

R. Taylor, *Cavalier and Yankee: The Old South and the American National Character* (New York, 1961); Richard Slotkin, *Regeneration through Violence: The Mythology of the American Frontier, 1600–1860* (Middletown, Conn., 1973); Larzer Ziff, *Literary Democracy: The Declaration of Cultural Independence in America* (New York, 1981); and Annette Kolodny, *The Lay of the Land: Metaphor as Experience and History in American Life and Letters* (Chapel Hill, N.C., 1975). The differences in tone between the genre studies of humor and the historicist approaches to literature are especially striking in their treatments of slavery. Since the students of the genre of humor (or the subgenre of what is often called southwestern humor) begin with the assumption that their subject is funny, they may be understandably shy about confronting slavery, a humorless subject to most modern Americans.

9. Wiebe, *The Opening of American Society: From the Adoption of the Constitution to the Eve of Disunion* (New York, 1984), xv.

10. Thornton, *Politics and Power*, 479–80; Johnson Hooper to William deBerniere Hooper, October 21, 1861, reproduced in Edgar E. Thompson, "The Literary Career of Johnson Jones Hooper: A Bibliographical Study of Primary and Secondary Material (With a Collection of Hooper's Letters)" (Master's thesis, Mississippi State University, 1971), 103–4.

11. Accurate biographical material about Hooper is difficult to collect. Hoole's biography, *Alias Simon Suggs*, was done without benefit of those family papers now available. Somers's *Johnson J. Hooper* draws its biographical material from Hoole's work, but it is more critically useful. The more important family papers are those of Johnson's brother deBerniere, who was a noted professor of classics at the University of North Carolina. The deBerniere name appears in various forms in the papers and in later sources. John deBerniere Hooper was usually addressed in writing by his family as D.B., although Johnson wrote him as deB. in the 1850s. Also quite helpful are the papers of Caroline Mallet Hooper, the wife of Johnson's brother George. See John deBerniere Hooper Papers and Caroline Mallet Hooper Papers in the Southern Historical Collection (University of North Carolina at Chapel Hill [papers hereinafter referred to respectively as JDBH Papers and CMH Papers]. Some helpful information concerning the family lineage is in related articles-biographical sketches of William (the signer) Hooper by Archibald Maclaine Hooper, taken from his *Hillsboro Recorder* of November and December 1822, and a family history by Fanny deBerniere Hooper Whitaker (deBerniere's daughter) reprinted in *The North Carolina Booklet*, V (July 1905), 39–71. Hooper's pride in his family is probably indicated by the name of his first son, William deBerniere Hooper, whose birth date Hooper recorded in a family Bible now located in the small Johnson Jones Hooper Collection (Evans Memorial Library, Aberdeen, Miss.), which contains an early paperback edition of *Adventures of Captain Simon Suggs*.

12. Johnson's character and his family's poverty and concern for his education are discussed in family correspondence between 1832 and 1834; see especially Charlotte to D.B., August 22 [1832]; George to D.B., February 3, 1833; Charlotte to D.B., March 29 and December 30, 1833; A.M (the family's common usage for Johnson's father Archibald) to D.B., June 12, 1834; all in JDBH Papers. Hoole's account of these years is largely inaccurate; he asserts, for example, that Hooper's education consisted of "the meagre offerings of the Wilmington public schools" and tutoring at home by his family (*Alias Simon Suggs,* 13). See also Edward McCrady to William Porcher Miles, January 28, 1861, recommending Johnson for a position in the Confederate government, in which he comments that "my wife's cousin and my late uncle John Johnson educated him in this place [Charleston]" (William Porcher Miles Papers, Southern Historical Collection). McCrady's wife was a deBerniere, and her sister was married to another Hooper cousin, John Johnson, brother of Associate Justice

William Johnson of the U.S. Supreme Court. Hoole argued that the story of Johnson's residence in Charleston cited in earlier biographical sketches was "difficult to believe" (*Alias Simon Suggs,* 189–12). Hooper's sense of honor was intense; his character seems to illustrate how a child raised to standards of "gentility" would, in his young adulthood, evince more "primal honor," as this is described in Bertram Wyatt-Brown, *Southern Honor: Ethics and Behavior in the Old South* (New York, 1982). The essential work for family patterns in North Carolina is Jane Turner Censer, *North Carolina Planters and Their Children, 1800–1860* (Baton Rouge, 1984). Although the Hoopers no longer belonged to the planter class, much of Censer's description seems relevant for the relations between the Hooper parents and children. Paul D. Escott has commented upon the continuities between the gentry and professional classes in his *Many Excellent People: Power and Privilege in North Carolina, 1850–1900* (Chapel Hill, N.C., 1985), especially pp. 4–7.

13. According to Charlotte, Johnson wrote her from Charleston late in 1833 arguing that if he must become a clerk "without any hope of going to college," the family should "let him go at once" (the "go" referring to ongoing family discussions about western migration), but his letter to D.B. from Tuscaloosa, Alabama, three years later refers still to "Ma's question about entering college"; see Charlotte to D.B., December 30, 1833; and Johnson to D.B., August 23, 1836, both in JDBH Papers. Many passages in the former letter, apparently containing negative comments about Johnson, have been cut, but the letter still provides evidence of Johnson's dissatisfaction and the family's differences with him about his future. Family plans for migration notwithstanding, Johnson followed George to eastern Alabama in 1835 but did not actually "join" him there (Hoole, *Alias Simon Suggs,* 14) until 1842; for one of numerous comments about Johnson's future, see a letter from Charlotte to D.B., March 5, 1835, in which she writes that Johnson has not even seen George lately (JDBH Papers).

14. On the family's hopes for migration see Charlotte to D.B., September 20, 1831, and May 9, 1833; George to D.B., February 2 and June 10, 1833. Family letters that woefully chronicle Johnson's wanderings, include Mary Hooper (sister) to D.B., October 22, 1834; Charlotte to D.B., March 5 and May 5, 1835; A.M. to D.B., July 11, 1835; Charlotte to D.B., June 10, 1836; George to Charlotte, December 20, 1837; George to A.M., April 16, 1838; George to Charlotte, August 12 and December 30, 1839; all in JDBH Papers. See also George to Caroline, January 10 and 27, 1835; March 27, April 4, and April 15, 1838; all in CMH Papers. In Hoole's account, Johnson during this period was with George, laboring "day after day" reading law (*Alias Simon Suggs,* 15–17, 31 [quoted phrase in note]). The business failures may be traced through the Circuit Court Trial Dockets and Minutes, Tallapoosa County, 1839–1841 (Tallapoosa County Courthouse, Dadeville, Ala.).

15. Quoted passage is from George to Charlotte, December 30, 1839, in JDBH Papers. Records of Hooper's business dealings, especially those with his father-in-law, Greene Brantley, are in Chambers County Deed Books 1–9 and Will Book I (Chambers County Courthouse, Lafayette, Ala.). There are only a few surviving copies of the *La Fayette East Alabamian,* ten in the Alabama Department of Archives and History in Montgomery. One of these contains the notice that Hooper was practicing law alone at the newspaper office; see the *La Fayette East Alabamian,* October 21, 1843.

16. See Norris W. Yates, *William T. Porter and the Spirit of the Times: A Study of the BIG BEAR School of Humor* (Baton Rouge, 1957); Eugene Current-Garcia, "Alabama Writers in the Spirit," *Alabama Review,* X (October 1957), 243–69; and a helpful reprinting of the comments about Hooper that Porter published by Edgar E. Thompson in James L. West III,

ed., *Gyascutus: Studies in Antebellum Southern Humorous and Sporting Writing* (Atlantic Highlands, N.J., 1978), 223–34. There are no reliable accounts of the sales of Porter's paper, which was specifically designed for the tastes of gentlemen who had (or aspired to have) wealth and leisure. Copied from English models, it apparently had a large southern and western audience outside of Porter's home base in New York. Critics, beginning with Lynn, have identified the humorous tradition with Whig writers, although Hooper's stories were widely pirated in both Democratic and Whig newspapers. Yates emphasizes the importance of the southern audience for shaping editorial policy in *William T. Porter*, 13–34; Negroes, he asserts, rarely appeared in the humor of the sporting paper (p.157). On the complex interplay of class, region, and culture in antebellum writers' perceptions of their audience see Bertram Wyatt-Brown, "Proslavery and Antislavery Intellectuals: Class Concepts and Polemical Struggle," in Lewis Perry and Michael Fellman, eds., *Antislavery Reconsidered: New Perspectives on the Abolitionists* (Baton Rouge, 1979), 308–36. See also two additional articles by Current-Garcia, "'Mr. Spirit' and The Big Bear of Arkansas: A Note on the Genesis of Southwestern Sporting and Humor Literature," *American Literature*, XXVII (November 1955), 332–46; and "'York's Tall Son' and His Southern Correspondents," *American Quarterly*, VII (Winter 1955), 371–84.

17. The various printings of Hooper's works are described in Thompson, "The Literary Career of Johnson Jones Hooper." In addition to the eleven known book-length printings of the Suggs stories, Hooper also wrote *A Ride with Old Kit Kuncker, and Other Sketches, and Scenes of Alabama* (Tuscaloosa, 1849), which was reissued three times in slightly modified form as *The Widow Rugby's Husband, A Night at the Ugly Man's, and Other Tales of Alabama* (Philadelphia, 1851, 1853, 1856). For the English reception, see Louis Fraiberg, "The *Westminster Review* and American Literature, 1824–1885," *American Literature*, XXIV (March 1953), 310–29; and Milton Rickels, "The Humorists of the Old Southwest in the London *Bentley's Miscellany*," ibid., XXVII (May 1956), 557–60. Hooper contributed one story' to Porter's collection; see William T. Porter, ed., *The Big Bear of Arkansas, and Other Sketches, Illustrative of Characters and Incidents in the South and South West* (Philadelphia, 1845). There are extant rare copies of a printing of this collection by T.B. Peterson of Philadelphia that carries the publication date of 1843, and AMS Press published a reprint of that edition (New York, 1973). In that reprint, however, Porter's preface appears to be dated 1845 (p. xii), although the type is broken. Norris Yate's biography, *William T. Porter*, gives the date of Porter's publication as 1845 (p. 42), which seems generally accepted. Obviously, however, if there was an 1843 printing, Hooper began writing the stories of Simon Suggs earlier than 1844, which is plausible but impossible to verify in the absence of letters about their composition, dated manuscript versions of a story, or newspapers containing a Suggs story prior to Porter's first publication.

18. The commentary on Juvenal appears in an article from the "Editor's Table" in Hooper's *Montgomery Weekly Mail*, March 29, 1855. Between 1845 and 1849 Hooper moved from La Fayette—first to nearby Wetumpka, then to Montgomery, and then back to La Fayette. In each of the three places, he edited a newspaper; see Hoole, *Alias Simon Suggs*, 62–67. Hooper's three children were, however, all born (and one died) in La Fayette between 1844 and 1847; recorded in his hand in the family Bible (Evans Memorial Library, Aberdeen, Miss.). He returned to Montgomery in 1854 to edit the *Mail*. Hooper's attitudes toward the wealthy may profitably be compared to those of his father, contrasting the "good taste" of George's home with the "vulgar and commonplace" houses of Augusta, Georgia, "the showy and noisy residence of a rowdy aristocracy" (A.M. to Fanny Hooper [his grand-

daughter], July 3, 1850, JDBH Papers). For references to the family status, see Hooper's *Montgomery Weekly Mail,* September 28, 1854, and February 11, 1857. The kinship that Hooper felt with Juvenal and other satirists deserves more attention than it can receive here; the paraphrased questions are from Juvenal's third satire ("Against the City of Rome"), reprinted in Rolfe Humphries, trans., *The Satires of Juvenal* (Bloomington, Ind., 1958), 38. See also Gilbert Highet, *Juvenal the Satirist* (London, 1954), especially Chap. 9. One of many references to the Democratic "aristocracy" can be found in a superb example of Hooper's satiric political invective in the *Montgomery Weekly* [Alabama] *Journal,* September 20, 1847.

19. Wyatt-Brown, *Southern Honor,* chaps. 2 and 3, "Primal Honor: Valor, Blood, and Bonding" and "Primal Honor: The Tensions of Patriarchy." For conflicting views of Hooper's conviviality, see William Garrett, *Reminiscences of Public Men in Alabama for Thirty Years* (Atlanta, 1872), who insists that "the association of Mr. Hooper, and his great fund of wit and humor, which made his society much sought and enjoyed by the lovers of fun, had never tended to a very moral course of life" (p. 527); and a Whig colleague's warm declaration: "Ask us to point out a whole-souled fellow, devoted to his friends, liberal in his views, generous to a fault, and we will show you Hooper," in the *Montgomery Weekly* [Alabama] *Journal,* February 26, 1850.

20. Quoted passages appear in Hooper, *Some Adventures of Captain Simon Suggs,* 134–35. See Robert Hopkins, "Simon Suggs: A Burlesque of Campaign Biography," *American Quarterly,* XV (Fall 1963), 459–63; Charles Martin Kerlin Jr., "Life in Motion: Genteel and Vernacular Attitudes in the Works of the Southwestern American Humorists, Mark Twain, and William Faulkner" (Ph.D. dissertation, University of Colorado, 1968); Joseph O'Beirne Milner, "The Social, Religious, Economic and Political Implications of the Southwestern Humor of Baldwin, Longstreet, Hooper, and G.W. Harris" (Ph.D. dissertation, University of North Carolina, 1971); and Howard Winston Smith, *Johnson Jones Hooper: A Critical Study* (Lexington, 1963). In addition, there are pertinent observations on the role of the genteel frame in southwestern humor from noted critics Louis Rubin Jr. and James Cox; see Rubin's introduction and conclusion to *The Comic Imagination in American Literature,* especially pages 5, 12, 385; and in the same collection, Cox's essay "Humor of the Old Southwest," 105–7.

21. Quoted passage appears in Hooper, *Adventures of Captain Simon Suggs,* 3. For the role and significance of editors in Alabama's politics, see Thornton, *Politics and Power,* 128–31. William J. Cooper Jr. stresses the modernization of southern politics in *The South and the Politics of Slavery, 1828–1853* (Baton Rouge, 1978); and *Liberty and Slavery: Southern Politics to 1860* (New York, 1983). Two other studies with special relevance for Hooper's experience, both of which treat with considerable subtlety the counterpoints of continuity and change in political evolution, are Marc W. Kruman, *Parties and Politics in North Carolina, 1836–1865* (Baton Rouge, 1983); and Harry L. Watson, *Jacksonian Politics and Community Conflict: The Emergence of the Second American Party System in Cumberland County, North Carolina* (Baton Rouge, 1981).

22. Hooper refers to himself as an "old hack . . . worn out and without a hope" in an extraordinary letter to D.B. written on Christmas night, 1860, JDBH Papers. Somers cites the "setting up and knocking down" passage from a biographical sketch in *Magnum Opus, The Great Book of the University of Comus . . .* (Louisville, Ky., 1886), a satire on Masonry to which Hooper contributed; see Somers, *Johnson J. Hooper,* 110. Suggs's comment on Johns's affiliation with the drinking Democracy is quoted in Hooper, *Adventures of Captain Simon Suggs,* 135; his quip that Johns's work is "'ritin lies" appears on page 139.

23. In Hoole's account, Suggs is patterned after Bird H. Young, a notorious resident of Tallapoosa County, who was a likely source for many of Suggs's characteristics; *Alias Simon Suggs*, 51–60; see also Somers, *Johnson J. Hooper*, 26–28, a more balanced evaluation. Suggs is described at length by Johns in Hooper, *Adventures of Captain Simon Suggs*, 6–7. Hooper's appearance was a standing joke in journalistic circles in Alabama, as his biographers have noted. The picture of him in the Alabama Department of Archives and History makes the resemblance to Suggs evident. One Alabamian who called himself "Captain Cuttle" in a series of articles about writers commented with typical insight: "Jonce Hooper is indeed a lucky man. Nature in marring his 'face divine,' conceived that she was clipping his wings and precluding his rise to fame, but she was grieviously [*sic*] at fault in her calculation, as his homeliness has contributed fully as much to his success as his mental resources and efforts. He is always on the look out for eccentricities of manner, thought, and expression, and when once detected, he transfers them to his canvass, and gives a portrait which would provoke a hearty laugh from the bedridden." See the *Livingston Sumter Democrat*, July 3, 1852; "Captain Cuttle" was not identified, but he seems to have been a resident of Livingston, Alabama, where the articles were published. Bertram Wyatt-Brown has pointed to the emphasis placed upon proper appearance in *Southern Honor*, noting (like "Captain Cuttle") that physical shortcomings could stimulate compensatory ambitions, (pp. 48–49).

24. Mrs. Suggs reflects on Suggs's "juvenality" on page 153; Suggs's wandering is described on page 28; and his character on pages 8–9; all in Hooper, *Adventures of Captain Simon Suggs*. Elliott Gorn in "'Gouge and Bite, Pull Hair and Scratch': The Social Significance of Fighting in the Southern Back Country," *American Historical Review*, XC (February 1985), 18–43, demonstrated how the frontier folklore of individualism "buttressed the emergent ideology of equality" (p.30) at the same time it affirmed the older ethos of honor. Interestingly, Hooper himself wrote a "gouging" story, but in it the genteel frame is dominant, perhaps because the piece was written for New England's humorous magazine *The Yankee Blade*. The story was reprinted with the notation that it was "from *The Yankee Blade*" in the *Montgomery* [*Alabama*] *Journal*, July 9, 1850. See also David E. Sloane's introduction to Sloane, ed., *The Literary Humor of the Urban Northeast, 1830–1890* (Baton Rouge, 1983); reference to *The Yankee Blade* as one of a number of New England publications is on page 315.

25. The political manipulation of republican themes is satirized by Hooper in *Adventures of Captain Simon Suggs*. A corrupt office seeker comments, for example, on one of Suggs's deceptions: "Yes, sir, it was a sublime moral spectacle, worthy of a comparison with any recorded specimens of Roman or Spartan magnanimity, sir. How nobly did it vindicate the purity of the representative character, sir!" (p. 43).

26. As David Reynolds notes in *Beneath the American Renaissance*, "Suggs is the first figure in American literature who fully manipulates Conventional values—piety, discretion, honesty, entrepreneurial shrewdness—for purely selfish ends. The Conventional becomes fully relativized in the world of subversive humor" (p.454).

27. See, for example, chapters entitled "Simon Speculates," "Simon Starts Forth to Fight the 'Tiger' [faro], and Falls in with a Candidate whom he 'Does' to a Cracklin'," and "Simon Fights 'the Tiger' and Gets Whipped-but Comes out Not Much the 'Worse for Wear'," all in Hooper, *Adventures of Captain Simon Suggs*.

28. These stories, in which Suggs manipulates poor whites, are parodies of Andrew Jackson's supporters' exploitation of his 1814 victory at Horseshoe Bend (in Tallapoosa County, thus Suggs's company of Tallapoosa Volunteers) and of the hysteria that seized Alabama during the Creek War of 1836. The three stories relating to the phony war and how Simon

earned his rank are "Simon Becomes Captain," "Captain Suggs and Lieutenant Snipes 'Court-Martial' Mrs. Haycock," and "The 'Tallapoosy Volluntares' Meet the Enemy"; all in Hooper, *Adventures of Captain Simon Suggs*. Johnson's location during the Creek episode is questionable, but George wrote about the local uproar in reassuringly funny letters to Caroline Mallet before their marriage; see his letters of February 21 and 28, May 11 and 22, 1836, in CMH Papers.

29. Yellow Legs is another disguise for the author, as is indicated by his appearance and wit and by Suggs's comments that he earned his stained legs as "the mark of the huckleberry ponds . . . whar the water come to when he was a-gatherin 'em in his raisin' in Northkurliny"; Hooper, *Adventures of Captain Simon Suggs*, 84. The young man is described by Johns as "spindle-legged" (p. 82) and by Suggs as "dirt eatin'" (p. 84). He flees contemptuously (quoted passage) on page 100 and "contumaciously" on page 103; he suggests that he is only a child and Suggs is a coward for mistreating him on page 83. In one sense, because he is like Hooper, the youth cannot be taken as low-born, despite appearances to the contrary. But as in the case of Suggs, what matters is not the circumstance of Yellow Legs's birth but the presence of his wit. The character appears on pages 82–84, 88–89, 100, and 102–3. There are comments relevant to Hooper's portrayal of frontier commoners in Dickson Bruce Jr., *Violence and Culture in the Antebellum South* (Austin, Tex., 1979), 224–32, although Bruce's emphasis on the distance established between the humorists and their frontier subjects and his insistence on their affinities for social control seem more relevant for Augustus Baldwin Longstreet, whom he discusses at some length, than for Hooper, whom he treats only incidentally. I would make the same criticism of Richard Gray's application of contemporary literary theory to the humorists, in which he asserts (p.74) that they achieved a comfortable distance from their subjects by encoding the "rough beast" in an inherited populist vocabulary rather than seeing them freshly; see his *Writing the South: Ideas of an American Region* (Cambridge, Eng. 1986), 62–74.

30. The use of white racial humor as a device to demean blacks is a major theme in Boskin's *Sambo*, which also explores the national popularity of the derogatory stereotype. Thornton discusses the symbiotic relationship between white freedom and black slavery in *Politics and Power*, xviii; their psychological interdependence is also stressed in Orlando Patterson, *Slavery and Social Death: A Comparative Study* (Cambridge, Mass., 1982), especially sharply in his concluding remarks, 340–42. Also relevant is Bertram Wyatt-Brown. "The Mark of Obedience: Male Slave Psychology in the Old South," *American Historical Review*, XCIII (February 1988), 1228–52. Although Suggs himself is for Hooper the "shameless trickster"(as Wyatt-Brown described that role on p. 1242) and slaves are shamed, there are intriguing hints of affinities between white and black tricksters.

31. Suggs's departure from home runs across the first three chapters in Hooper, *Adventures of Captain Simon Suggs*: "Introduction—Simon Plays the 'Snatch' Game," "Simon Gets a 'Soft Snap' Out of his Daddy," and "Simon Speculates." The father's description is on page 9. "Daddies," who exist "jist to beat 'em [boysj and work 'em," are compared to the "use in mammies," who are more inclined to spoil their sons, on page 16. By way of comparison, see Johnson's father's letter to D.B. about his "anxieties . . . in respect to Johnson. He is at a critical period of life, and your mother's fondness has countenanced too much his scribbling propensity," A.M. to D.B., July 1, 1835, JDBH Papers, written after the time Johnson fled Charleston for Alabama. Hooper's crude humor here bears comparison with that of George Washington Harris in the Sut Lovingood stories; see the analysis of Sut's social significance in Ziff, *Literary Democracy*, 185–94. Dickson Bruce describes Suggs's leave-taking as a "virtual paradigm for a life spent skirting violence and convention for profit"; *Violence and Culture*, 230.

32. Hooper, *Adventures of Captain Simon Suggs,* 16.

33. Relevant analyses of the changing relationships between white southern parents and children are Jane Turner Censer, *North Carolina Planters and Their Children;* and Ann Williams Boucher, "Wealthy Planter Families in Nineteenth-Century Alabama" (Ph.D. dissertation, University of Connecticut, 1978). See also Bertram Wyatt-Brown's observations about oedipal and other tensions in family life associated with changes in southern society in "Fathers, Mothers, and Progeny" *(Southern Honor*, Chap. 5); and those of Steven M. Stowe in *Intimacy and Power in the Old South: Ritual in the Lives of the Planters* (Baltimore, 1987), which emphasize especially the celebration of hierarchy by planters and the social tensions fostered by sex and gender differences that were emphasized in the planter ethos. The tensions of authority and gender in Hooper's family warrant more attention than they have been given in previous biographies or can be given here.

34. Comments about the burning of the slave at nearby Mt. Meigs (*Montgomery Weekly Mail*, August 31, 1859) made by Hooper when fear had gripped him tightly, should be compared with his earlier and somewhat less immoderate views in the *Montgomery Weekly Mail*, May 31, 1855. When Nature made Suggs bestial, "she did not refine the cruelty by denying him the fangs and the claws," and in his case, neither the tyranny of his father nor the affectionate tolerance of his mother had any meliorative influence; quoted passage in Hooper, *Adventures of Captain Simon Suggs*, 9.

35. Suggs refers to the salvation of sinners as "saving" on page 116. The description of the "promiscuous" audiences and the preachers' sexual motives and methods begins on page 112 and concludes with the black woman's falling upon the little white man on page 114; quoted passages on pages 112 and 114. Suggs's graphic account of his supposed salvation appears on pages 118 through 121; quoted passages on pages 119 and 121. Suggs commonly refers to the falsities by which he entraps his victims as "discourses" (see, for example, p. 72), but the minister Bela Bugg calls the salvation story a "discorse" (p. 123); and Mrs. Dobbs, a key observer, calls the narrative of Suggs's "'sperience" a "'scource" (p. 119); all quotations and page numbers from Hooper, *Adventures of Captain Simon Suggs.* The camp meeting episode was imitated by Twain in *Adventures of Huckleberry Finn* (New York, 1884), an imitation Bernard DeVoto finds inferior to the original; see his *Mark Twain's America* (Boston, 1932), 253. See Hooper, *Adventures of Captain Simon Suggs*, 111–26.

36. The whipping threat appears first on pages 118–19 (where "'scource" may suggest scourge) and is repeated by implication on page 120 ("I'll settle wi' you!"). Mrs. Dobbs's excitement interrupts the narrative from pages 118 to 121. Quoted passages and page numbers from Hooper, *Adventures of Captain Simon Suggs*. For relevant comments on sexuality in George Washington Harris's humor, see Ziff, *Literary Democracy*, 186–88; in "subversive" literature, see Reynolds, *Beneath the American Renaissance,* 211–24; in the humor of the "reverend rake," *ibid.*, 476; and in frontier humor, *ibid.*, 454–57.

37. Daniel Walker Howe emphasizes religious influences on Whig ideas in *The Political Culture of the American Whigs* (Chicago, 1979), but he slights southern Whiggery, as have most students of the parry's ideas. Although he does not deal with regional differences (and specifically not with slavery), Lawrence Frederick Kohl's very fine recent analysis of the Whig worldview is as persuasive for southern Whigs as it is for their northern colleagues; see especially Chap. 2, "The Whig World," in *The Politics of Individualism: Parties and the American Character in the Jacksonian Era* (New York, 1989), which places Whig concerns about self-control in a broad context of religious, social, and psychological influences. Also relevant is Anne C. Loveland's discussion of revivalism in Chap. 3 of *Southern Evangelicals and the Social*

Order, 1800–1860 (Baton Rouge, 1980). Hooper's mother's unhappiness about her son's lack of piety is a constant theme of her letters; see, for example, those from Charlotte Hooper to D.B., December 30, 1833, and March 22, 1851 ("I have to lament in my Poor Johnson, utter indifferences to religion."), JDBH Papers; from her to Caroline Hooper, December 1, 1849, and December 26, 1850, CMH Papers.

38. Quoted passage about the proprietors' hiring of Suggs from pages 135–36; about buying slaves who knew the money was not as good as "state money" on page 137; "institushun" recurs repeatedly from pages 135–39, as if Hooper wished to call attention to its artificial nature; all in Hooper, *Adventures of Captain Simon Suggs*, 135–39. Hooper commented on the sale of a family slave in a letter to Mrs. T.R. Heard, August 22, 1850, reproduced in Marion Kelley, "The Life and Writings of Johnson Jones Hooper" (M.A. thesis, Alabama Polytechnic Institute, 1934), 324–26:

> I requested Joe to see Muse promptly on the subject of buying Lucinda. But the poor fellow is just now in bad plight for buying negroes in consequence of proceedings which, unluckily enough, it was my duty to institute to annul certain orders in his favor, on the county treasury, amounting to some 800 and which were illegally (but I think not fraudulently) obtained. It will be months before a decision can be had, most probably; and when had, will be against Muse, according to all *"human probability."* This, I am afraid, throws him out of the market as a purchaser, but I will nevertheless urge the matter, and sell her if it can be done at the price—*which is low.*

The details of his letter, written while Hooper was circuit solicitor, are unclear, but his attitude toward Lucinda and the sale of slaves is not.

39. Oakes's depiction is drawn with broad strokes throughout part two "The Market Culture," in *The Ruling Race*. For an excellent view of the transforming power of the Alabama frontier, see Daniel Dupre, "Ambivalent Capitalists on the Cotton Frontier: Settlement and Development in the Tennessee Valley of Alabama," *Journal of Southern History*, LVI (May 1990), 215–40.

40. In his shift to a positivistic understanding of human nature, Hooper may have been influenced by the emerging scientific racism of the 1840s, particularly that espoused by Josiah Nott of Mobile, whose ideas the newspaper editor Hooper undoubtedly knew by 1845. But to repeat, Hooper was neither scientific nor theoretical nor even systematic in the exposition of his views. See Reginald Horsman, *Josiah Nott of Mobile: Southerner, Physician, and Racial Theorist* (Baton Rouge, 1987), 88–92, for a description of Nott's belief that the Bible was an imperfect source for understanding human nature, as stated in his lectures in Mobile during the winter of 1843–1844; see also Horsman, *Race and Manifest Destiny: The Origins of American Racial Anglo-Saxonism* (Cambridge, Mass., 1981), 116–57, for a more general discussion of the influence of antebellum scientific racism.

41. *Montgomery Weekly Mail*, August 31, 1854; compare with the sentiments of Daniel Webster discussed in Kohl, *Politics of Individualism*, 85.

42. Thornton, *Politics and Power*, 337. For a discussion of the implications of Thornton's study for southern intellectual history, see Michael O'Brien, "Modernization and the Nineteenth-Century South," in *Rethinking the South: Essays in Intellectual History* (Baltimore, 1988), 115–18.

43. Hooper's later difficulties were barely mentioned by Hoole in *Alias Simon Suggs*,

but they are referred to in family letters, which suggest quite serious financial problems at the very least. See, for example, Charlotte Hooper to D.B., March 22, 1851, in which she mentions Johnson's "set back 4 years ago [that] cost him dearly," a line followed by a cut passage, a phenomenon that appears more than once in the family papers when negative references to Johnson were apparently the subject. Johnson's own letters refer to poverty, ill health, and hard work. See, for example, his letters to D.B., August 15 [?], 1855, and December 25, 1861; all in JDBH Papers. In the latter, a highly charged commentary on Alabama's secession and the family's personal trials, Johnson wrote his older brother: "When I think of your labors, however, and of your uncomplaining endurance, I feel ashamed both of my weakness and egotism. With more delicate health and harder work, you have fought the world even longer than land without whining." See also a very funny letter in which Hooper acknowledges his gambling and drinking; letter written to his business associate E. Sanford Sayre in the winter of 1846 [?] in the Sayre file, Thomas Hill Watts Papers (Alabama Department of Archives and History). The Sayre file also contains evidence relating to the financial problems of the *Montgomery* [*Alabama*] *Journal* between 1846 and 1848, when Hooper was its co-owner.

44. Both Hauck and Slotkin have commented in their literary studies on the extent to which laughter at the humor of the confidence men legitimized the exploitative tendencies in American society; see Hauck, *Cheerful Nihilism,* 71; and Slotkin, *Regeneration through Violence,* 416–17.

45. Given what little is known about book marketing and purchasers in the 1840s, this assessment rests on inference, but most recent scholars have treated Hooper's audience as national. Ronald J. Zboray, "The Transportation Revolution and Antebellum Book Distribution Reconsidered," *American Quarterly,* XXXVIII (Spring 1986), 53, 71, argues persuasively that most scholarly evaluations of the relationship between market tastes and book sales have failed to allow for the influence of regional differences in transportation upon marketing. Even with accurate figures for the total sales of Hooper's books, which surely numbered in the thousands, it would be impossible to say where they sold. See Hoole, *Alias Simon Suggs,* 58–59, 203–5, 207, 212–13, for figures on the printings of Carey and Hart, Hooper's publisher in Philadelphia.

46. The influence of Harriet Beecher Stowe's book has recently been evaluated by Thomas F. Gossett. *"Uncle Tom's Cabin" and American Culture* (Dallas, 1985); and Moira Davison Reynolds, *"Uncle Tom's Cabin" and Mid-Nineteenth Century United States: Pen and Conscience* (Jefferson, N.C., and London, 1985). The similarities between Stowe's slave character Sam and Hooper's Simon Suggs are sufficiently strong to suggest that Stowe knew Hooper's racist humor; see especially Stowe, *Uncle Tom's Cabin,* 75–79; and Hooper, *Adventures of Captain Simon Suggs,* 76, 103.

10

Revising Southern Humor

William Tappan Thompson and the Major Jones Letters

David C. Estes

In the same year that William Tappan Thompson died—1882—Henry Watterson published an anthology of humorous sketches entitled *Oddities in Southern Life and Character,* containing the work of more than ten well-known southern humorists of the preceding fifty years. Fifteen of Thompson's Major Jones letters comprise one hundred pages—more than twenty percent of the total and also more than is allowed for any other author. Although Thompson wrote numerous sketches that do not employ the Major Jones persona, the presence of only these letters in this popular anthology reflects the close identification between Thompson and the major in the public's mind. Originally printed in the 1840s, versions of the two collections of Major Jones letters continued to be marketed by several publishers up into the 1890s. Of the humorists of the Old Southwest who collected their newspaper sketches into books, Thompson seems to have reached the widest contemporary audience and to have remained in print the longest. However, in our century, what Louis Budd has termed the "gentlemanly" humor of Thompson has received less attention than the raucous backwoods humor found in pieces by George Washington Harris, Johnson Jones Hooper, and Thomas Bangs Thorpe.

Despite Thompson's contemporary obscurity, the textual history of the Major Jones letters sheds light on antebellum southern journalistic humor, a genre that has been too often examined on the basis of sketches as revised for book publication. Thompson reworked the letters for several editions, successfully reshaping a humorous persona popular among local southern readers into one that would also appeal to a national, book-buying audience. The Major Jones who wrote for Georgia newspaper readers from 1842 to 1844 is not the same one who appears as correspondent in the final 1872 edition of *Major Jones's Courtship*. That the new readership was largely northern quite possibly motivated the ardent southerner Thompson in many of his changes. Furthermore, despite the predominant domestic quality of the humor, the differences in the letters suggest the greater freedom in choosing incidents allowed a journalistic humorist in the antebellum South as opposed to one trying to publish a book in the North in the middle decades of the nineteenth century. Such a reading of the Major Jones letters goes beyond the approach typically taken by previous scholars, who have tended to value Thompson for "faithfully record[ing] the manners and customs of rural antebellum Georgia" (Shippey 334).

A look at the letters in their original journalistic context shifts their value as documents away from being examples of protorealism in American literary history and foregrounds them as part of the dynamic, self-reflexive public discourse antebellum southerners were conducting about their culture.

The narrative thread unifying Major Jones's letters is his courtship of Mary Stallins throughout 1842, their marriage the next year, and the birth of a son in 1844. Complicating this naive planter's progress toward capturing the heart of his beloved are the tricks played on him by her sisters and the competition from an itinerant northern music teacher and the local braggart, his cousin Pete. They finally become engaged at Christmas, when the major gives himself to her as a present by hiding in a large bag hanging from the porch rafter so to surprise her at dawn. The letter describing this ploy, which backfires when the curious family dog barks and nips at him all night, is probably the best known in the series. Besides courting Mary, the major also leads Pineville's militia, goes coon hunting, and visits both Macon and Madison—activities that provide much material for gentle satire of both contemporary fashions as well as human nature. The eight letters from the honeymoon up to the birth of their boy recount incidents that, for the most part, relate to the major's growing literary fame since they were written after the first collection had been issued in the spring of 1843.

Altogether thirty-three letters appeared during these two years. The first is in the *Augusta Family Companion and Ladies' Mirror*, a monthly Thompson edited for several months in 1842. All of the others were first printed in the *Madison Southern Miscellany*, except for the last two. While the original appearance of one has not been discovered, the last in the series was originally addressed to William T. Porter of the *New York Spirit of the Times.* The first collection entitled *Major Jones's Courtship* was issued in 1843 by the owner of the *Southern Miscellany* as a subscription premium. The sixteen letters in the collection conclude at the wedding and are accompanied by another sketch by Thompson, "Great Attraction!" which had been carried in the paper previously. A year later, in the spring of 1844, Carey and Hart issued a second edition of *Major Jones's Courtship*, this one containing an additional ten letters and ending with the birth of the baby. It does not include "Great Attraction!" The next revised edition in 1847, which was volume six in Carey and Hart's "Library of Humorous American Works," includes two more letters, making a total of twenty-eight and leaving five uncollected from the pages of the *Southern Miscellany.* Over the next twenty-five years, ownership of the plates passed to the firm of Getz and Buck and then to T.B. Peterson, who continued to keep the book in print. Possibly because of its popularity, it became volume one in Peterson's "Library of Humorous American Works." In 1872, upon the expiration of the copyright, which Thompson had signed over to Carey and Hart twenty-eight years previously, he brought out a revised edition of the letters that includes a selection of thirteen sketches unrelated to Major Jones's exploits.

Thompson reshaped the Major Jones persona in each of the four editions in which he had a hand—1843, 1844, 1847, and 1872. As is so often the case in the real world, literary fame influenced the major to become more urbane and less rustic, so that his style eventually belied his naiveté and lack of schooling, which are essential to the humor. Furthermore, he started to take a less active interest in the journalistic life of his region and assumed more fully the role of successful southern planter. His satisfaction with managing his estate is explicit in the first of his several travel letters from the North published in the *Baltimore Western Continent* beginning in January 1846, and it is also implied through revisions in the *Courtship* series of letters.

Prefatory remarks in the volumes indicate Thompson's original intentions in composing the letters and the commercial reason they were first collected. In the 1844 edition, Major Jones tells readers that "this book of letters was rit jest to oblige a frend, and to give variety to a weekly newspaper. They was rit off and on . . . without any rangement, or any notion that they would ever be red out of Georgia. But ther was such a call for 'em, that the papers soon gave out, and the printer turned in and printed a edition in pamphlet form—but a thousand copies wasn't a primin—they was all gone in no time" (7). Speaking to readers in his own voice in 1872, Thompson again emphasizes that the letters were originally intended for "home circulation and an ephemeral existence" (6). The seventy-six-page pamphlet that is the 1843 edition "was made jest to get subscribers to the 'SOUTHERN MISCELLANY'" (iii), according to the original version of the preface. And under those circumstances, it is understandable that little revision occurred. According to a letter printed after the volume's release, the one exception greatly amused Pineville readers. It was the addition of a practical joke Mary played on cousin Pete—a party trick that led to his dunking. The audience for this pamphlet was the same as that of the weekly, and they in turn met the same Major Jones who had been entertaining them for seven months.

The most interesting changes in the 1843 printing are found by comparing it not to the original in the *Southern Miscellany*, but rather to the opening letter as it appeared initially in the *Family Companion* two months before Thompson changed editorial chairs. Quite possibly, he felt free to develop the character more realistically after he ceased appearing in the pages of a literary monthly. In any case, numerous spelling changes reflect a desire to make Jones sound less like a refined reader of the *Family Companion* and more like one of Georgia's small farmers. Dropping the initial syllable of such words as "about," "among," and "because" suggests pronunciation. Frequently, misspellings have the same effect. But an equal number of misspellings do not reflect local pronunciation; they point merely to a lack of education. "Deth," "dore," "rite," "ses," and "ther" are the kinds of words to become a staple of the Phunny Phellows in later decades, and Thompson's controlled use of them contributes to the major's characterization without detracting from the intelligibility of the prose. Thompson continued to use misspelling as a humorous device throughout the 1840s. But curiously, the 1872 revisions suggest that the major spent the intervening decades reading back issues of the *Family Companion*, for in it the number of misspellings is greatly reduced and those that remain generally reflect pronunciation.

Thompson continued to give careful attention to matters of spelling in the 1844 edition, trying to suggest more of the Georgia dialect. The decision to change the spelling of Mary's surname from "Stallions" to "Stallins" is one that he did not later reject. But much more important reworkings of published material occurred in this first national publication in order to make the major popular with anticipated new readers. While all sixteen letters in the 1843 pamphlet remained, he selected only ten of the fourteen he had published in the *Southern Miscellany* during the interval since it was issued. Those rejected are primarily political in content and would undoubtedly have offended some of the book-buying northerners he hoped to attract.

In revising the manuscript, Thompson gave far greater attention to necessary deletions than to additions. And very few additions are more than a couple of words in length. For example, in the letter recounting his Christmas proposal, the only comment added is that Mrs. Stallins had "her nittin in her hand" as she nodded off to sleep before the fire (96). On the other hand, the one important change in that letter is the omission in the postscript of the major's reply to a request from Thompson to edit a new paper: "I should like to blige you if it won't be no more trouble than you say, but Mary ses she thinks I better not, cause editors dont never make nothin, and are always poor as Jobe's turky" (51). He goes on about the difficulty of collecting from subscribers, recalling a comment from the second letter in the series also deleted in that edition: "I'm monstrous glad you's formed a connection with that paper [*Southern Miscellany*], and it can't help but exceed, cause all Pineville is gwine to scribe for it, and if you've a mind to I'll be agent down in these parts, which will be a mighty help" (6). Such omissions as these strip Major Jones of his ambitions for a career in journalism and establish him as a planter content with merely corresponding occasionally with an editor. The two men are more distant from each other in the 1844 version. They no longer consider collaborating in business ventures, and Major Jones shows no desire to leave the plantation.

While many references to the *Southern Miscellany* are omitted— especially those which tend to puff the publication—readers of the 1844 book do still find its name in the letters. But they no longer come across references to other Pineville sketches by Thompson and the characters in them. While such allusions would have been understood by a local audience regularly reading the same weekly newspaper in which all these humorous works appeared, readers outside that community would have been confused. Yet in excising these allusions for the sake of clarity, Thompson diminished the readers' sense of Major Jones's participation in his own town. Since his reactions to subjects of national prominence such as the Millerites remain, he seems in some ways to have become more involved in the life of the nation and less interested in the small events and local characters of Pineville. Similarly, he no longer takes time in a postscript to complain about the South's slow reception of his 1843 edition. The original letter to the *Spirit of the Times*, printed in the issue of 10 February 1844, concludes sarcastically: "Our people's monstrous loud about Southern genus, and Southern institutions, and Southern feelin, and

Southern literature, and all that, but they never find out they've got anything good at home, until the Northern people tell 'em of it" (589). Although most certainly still a southerner, the 1844 Major Jones is less interested in writing to and for southerners than previously. In order to attract a national audience, his relationship to his locality and region had to become less prominent.

Thompson deleted other abusive and ungenteel comments that he had previously deemed suitable for a local audience. The few curse words that do appear are carefully omitted, but it is the disappearance of the major's attacks against others that significantly alters his persona. In one instance the itinerant music teacher Crotchett is exposed as a bigamist and quickly leaves town. About a month later, Major Jones writes in the 1844 text: "I was monstrous riled tother day when I got a letter from Crotchett, callin me all sorts of hard names, and abusin me for every thing he could think of" (90). The newspaper and local 1843 versions, however, are more emphatic and colorful: "I was monstrous riled when I read that letter of Crotchett's in your paper. The imperent cus! If he thinks I care for contempt or commisery either, he's mighty mistaken, and if he'll just cum back to Pineville and tell me I'm a liar to my face, I'll shake him out o' the gates of life afore he can say peas" (44). Thompson seems eager to hide his character's mean streak and to disassociate him from the violence of the region conventional in the writing of most of the other southern humorists.

The illustrations for the 1844 volume reinforce the effect of the textual revisions I have been discussing. They depict a well-to-do planter who seems refined and almost boyishly gentle. In each one he is dressed as he is for his wedding—in a coat with long tails, a vest, and bow tie. Clean-shaven, he no longer resembles the portrait on the cover of the 1843 pamphlet. After seeing that one, Mary exclaimed that the book was ruined because that "mean old thing with his big whiskers, and his mouth screwed up like he had been eatin a peck of green simmons . . . don't look no more like you, Joseph, than you does like a cow. I declare if anybody would go and make picter like that for me, I'd prosecute 'em for it" (1872 ed., 182).

In 1844, then, Thompson transformed this humorously naive character into a less local and more urbane figure who, under the author's guidance, was beginning to show signs of the refinement readers would expect of a southern planter bearing a military title. Yet this was not the persona of Major Jones in the journalistic world at that time. For in spring 1844 he was sending his most viciously angry letters to newspapers. One became, rather curiously, the final letter, number twenty-eight, in the 1847 edition. The other was never reprinted. Both were responses to attacks on the major's character by other newspaper humorists after they read about the birth of his son. Because the *New York Spirit of the Times* printed the three engagement, wedding, and birth announcement letters within a month of each other, a certain John Smith, choosing to ignore their dates and telescope the intervals between them, posed this question in the pages of the *Spirit*: "Now, Major Jones of Pineville, was that night you swung in the bag the first night you passed on the premises?" In a fiery postscript to the only one of his letters printed originally in that sporting weekly, the Georgian replied that Mary "ses he's a nasty, mean wretch, to be . . . castin slurs on decent people; and if she only know'd who he was she'd scald his 'bominable ugly eyes out of him." He continued: "we're decent Christian white people out here in Georgia, [and] we is a little smarter than his people, what live up thar in the fork [at Pittsburgh], whar they swaller more coal smoke in a year than would bust a balloon, and whar they're so black and dirty that it would take six month's bleachin to make 'em pass for white folks." He closes by threatening Jones to "keep clear of my track" when he takes a journey to the North the next summer.[1] It is surprising to find this postscript still attached to the letter in the 1847 edition. Its vague references to "some insinewations on my wif's character" would leave readers wondering what they had missed in the pages of the *Spirit* where Major Jones states they appeared. But even more remarkable is that Thompson closes the book with this paragraph so greatly at odds with his characterization of the major as established in the 1844 revisions and retained in the 1847 version, to which it was one of two letters added. This is the edition that circulated widely and that Thompson had to wait until the expiration of the copyright to revise. As one would expect, in 1872 he struck the postscript.

The other vicious newspaper letter was never reprinted in book form. It is a sustained attack against a Louisiana humorist, Pardon Jones, who claimed that the major was an old enemy of his from when they both lived in Massachusetts. Pardon charged the major with adopting his name after moving to Georgia to make a fortune dishonestly. According to Major Jones, he intended to treat this attack "with silent contempt," until Mary convinced him that his "character would be tetotaciously ruinated among people as don't know me, if I don't sue him for a lie-bill, or shut him up some way." The major chooses to silence this attacker by misreading comments in Pardon's earlier letters in much the way John Smith misread his own. Wittily, he defends himself from the charge of roguery by picturing his accuser as a bachelor not smart enough to keep his whereabouts a secret after deserting his pregnant girlfriend. This exchange of humorous letters was typical in the local press, and in fact, the editor of the *Southern Miscellany* had printed Pardon's letter along with a request that his friend vindicate himself. This uncollected Major Jones letter is one further indication that in preparing the book versions Thompson consciously distanced his character from the stream of local, southern life in which he felt free to swim when writing for a smaller, more homogeneous newspaper audience. Gone, in particular, is the sense of the interaction between Major Jones and his audience, which was a valuable source of his humor.

Thompson clearly explains his primary revisions in the 1872 text in the prefatory remarks, which for the first time are in his own, not the major's, voice: "Many verbal and orthographic changes, not inconsistent with the general character of the story, have been made. . . . Where . . . bad spelling was unnecessary to the 'cracker' pronunciation, and the change did not involve too glaring an inconsistency with the style of composition, it has been modified" (6–7). Thompson seems to have labored over making the purposeful misspellings consistent and at representing the peculiarities of local dialect faithfully. Compared to the previous editions, this one more successfully imitates the sound of Major Jones talking. Yet choosing to correct all misspellings unrelated to pronunciation, he transformed the major's persona once again because of the fact that in letters the appearance of the written word greatly influences judgments about character. Now able to spell accurately his standard closing "Your friend till death" as well as numerous other simple words, Major Jones appears more worthy of respect, and the humorous incidents depending on his lack of formal schooling are no longer appropriate. It is fitting that this major, who has become more refined and polished in behavior as well as in literary style, must wait until "after tea" to go courting Mary on Christmas Eve; however, this new detail makes his crawling into a bag hanging from the porch rafters seem even more ludicrous than it did in 1842 when he was still just a country boy.

Over the years Major Jones probably became increasingly uncomfortable with the humor at his expense that predominates in the letters. Characterization and incidents began to diverge when he stopped writing on newsprint and put his letters between hard covers. And by 1872 Thompson was no longer the master of his material, despite his increased mastery over dialect. I would argue that the best way to preserve Thompson's place in the history of American humor is to revive the original Major Jones, who was interested in making newspapers—not books. That resurrection will help us understand more about American humor as a journalistic phenomenon and will also correct our misperceptions of the Old Southwest's reputedly most "gentlemanly" humorist.

Notes

1. For a discussion of this exchange, see Estes.

Works Cited

Budd, Louis J. "Gentlemanly Humorists of the Old South." *South Folklore Quarterly* 17 (1953): 232–40.

Estes, David C. "Major Jones Defends Himself: An Uncollected Letter." *Mississippi Quarterly* 33 (1980): 79–84.

Shippey, Herbert. "William Tappan Thompson," in *Antebellum Writers in New York and the South.* Ed., Joel Myerson. *Dictionary of Literary Biography*. Vol. 3. Detroit: Gale Research, 1979. 332–35.

Thompson, William Tappan. [Major Jones Letter Dated 28 May 1842]. *The Family Companion and Ladies' Mirror* (June 1842): 191–92.

———. [Major Jones Letter dated 5 Jan. 1844]. *Spirit of the Times* 13 (10 Feb. 1844):589.

———. *Major Jones's Courtship*. Madison, Ga.: Hanleiter, 1843.

———. *Major Jones's Courtship*. Philadelphia: Carey and Hart, 1844.

———. *Major Jones's Courtship*. Philadelphia: Carey and Hart, 1847.

———. *Major Jones's Courtship*. New York: Appleton, 1872.

Watterson, Henry. *Oddities in Southern Life and Culture*. Boston: Houghton-Mifflin, 1882.

11

Backwoods Civility, or How the Ring-Tailed Roarer Became a Gentle Man for David Crockett, Charles F.M. Noland, and William Tappan Thompson

James E. Caron

A familiar view held by scholars about comic writings in the tradition of the Old Southwest begins with a claim for the prominence of the framed story. This device presents a story told by a backwoods, vernacular-speaking character that is framed by introductory and closing remarks made from a cultured perspective. The importance of the frame story as a vehicle to highlight vernacular voices from the backwoods was first articulated by Walter Blair, when he carefully analyzed the device to note the salient points of the humor of the Old Southwest (1960, 156). Since then, critics have fastened onto this type of story as representative of the Old Southwest's comic writings because it dramatizes a conflict seen as essential to the history of the region. This conflict pits the upper-class, moral gentleman speaking the frame of the story in correct—even refined—language against the lower-class, morally suspect, vulgar man speaking the inside or framed portion of the story in an ungrammatical dialect.

The origin of critical perception of class and/or moral conflict in the frame story can be found in Kenneth Lynn's *Mark Twain and Southwestern Humor* (1959). Lynn elaborated the values, especially the political values, of both the outside and inside voices found in the frame story, voices he calls the "Self-Controlled Gentleman" and the "Clown." Lynn then connects these values to Sam Clemens. Blair's highlighting of a semiliterate voice evocative of the frontier becomes for Lynn a set of upper-class attitudes about the common folk. Both critics are utilizing an idea of "vernacular" that signifies historical people as well as literary representations firmly anchored in the specific context of the antebellum period. Lynn, however, emphasizes an antagonism between the writers and the folk about whom they write. The frame in Lynn's analysis thus becomes a "*cordon sanitaire*" (64) meant to indicate the moral and social superiority of the writers.

A weakness of the argument stems from Lynn's generalizations about the prevalence of the frame story and about the social and political attitudes of the Old Southwest writers. In particular, the generalization about social and political attitudes is a problem because it reflects an incorrect assumption about the nature of society in the antebellum South. This false image projects a society that had only two classes of whites: the planters and the poor. Ultimately, this image of southern society can be traced back at least as far as the publication of Frederick Law Olmsted's *The Cotton Kingdom* (1861). Based on Olmsted's view of southern society, Lynn's articulation of conflict between the two voices of the framed story—a conflict entailing manners and morality—has exerted a continuing influence on scholars of American humor.[1]

Nevertheless, Lynn's analysis has been challenged on both historical and literary grounds. Even before Lynn's book was published, a counterimage of southern society was being presented by Frank Owsley and Clement Eaton, one that insisted upon a more complex set of classes among white southerners. John Q. Anderson (1963) had also taken this position early on. Such a complex view had been originally promulgated in Daniel H. Hundley's *Social Relations in Our Southern States* (1860), which differentiated between poor whites and different classes of plain folks. The most recent historical scholarship has confirmed the Hundley-based analysis by Owsley. Distinguishing between poor whites and plain folks can no longer be an option. Insofar as the Old Southwest comic writers attempted to render a realistic social portrait, the implication of the historical scholarship is that these writers made distinctions among white southerners that went beyond poor folk and rich planter. Thus, insofar as literary critics wish to understand how comic images of the common man in the writings of the Old Southwest authors interacted with contemporary social dynamics, they too must make these distinctions.[2]

On literary grounds, the challenge to Lynn consists of different interpretations of the frame story technique. Jesse Bier (1968) inverts the idea of *cordon sanitaire* by asserting that the frame was actually a covert sign of rebellion against social values. However, the more widespread alternative interpretation of the meaning of the frame has followed from the position of James Cox (1973), who argues that the frame is a sign of collaboration between the gentleman, who speaks proper English, and the backwoodsman, who speaks in dialect. The gentleman's ambivalence toward the backwoodsman implied by Cox's analysis has become a significant alternative to Lynn's notion of antagonism. One still has to be careful about characterizing how scholarship on the subject has proceeded since Lynn was challenged, however, because the strength of a sense of ambivalence claimed by a critic depends upon how careful he or she is when distinguishing between plain folks and poor whites. Lorne Fienberg, Leo Lemay, and Michael Pearson, for example, seem to lump these classes together like Lynn, yet nevertheless find ambivalence. To the extent that poor whites and plain folks have been carefully differentiated (e.g. Sylvia Cook, Michael Fellman, Robert Jacobs), one can assert that Lynn's idea of *cordon sanitaire* works well for representations of the poor folk, while images of the plain folk reveal complex attitudes that sometimes include positive elements (e.g. Sonia Gernes, Richie Watson).

The idea that comic portraits of the common folk can be measurably positive, that one can laugh with instead of at *dēmos* (i.e. the people), is critical to the complex nature of the comic tradition of the Old Southwest I wish to elaborate. In Lynn's view, Mark Twain "solves" the problem of the conflict of the Self-Controlled

Gentleman and the Clown by combining the two voices of the frame story (148). This solution, however, can occur only when the analysis focuses on conflict in the frame story, conflict resulting from an upper-class, urbane attitude toward the vernacular voice featured within the frame. If instead that superior attitude is only one part of a spectrum of comic representations, and if this spectrum already includes a more complex attitude such as the one implied by combining the voices, then Clemens through his Mark Twain persona did not create a hitherto unheard-of solution. Rather, the Old Southwestern tradition already contained such a combination of voices. Moreover, this combination does not develop as the nineteenth century progresses but is a technique present at the very outset of the tradition. The writings of Charles F.M. Noland and William Tappan Thompson, for example, do not have the gentleman's perspective insisted on by Lynn and his followers, writings in print at roughly the same time as Augustus B. Longstreet's and Johnson J. Hooper's, whose works remain the standard evidence for the conventional opinion about comic writings from the Old Southwest.

The complexity of the Old Southwest comic tradition I am insisting upon in part reflects the complicated nature of popular representations of backwoods settlers, hunters, and keelboatmen. Well before the Old Southwest writers began in 1830 to sketch their comic views of the common man, the customs and manners of such men had contributed to the first widespread comic stereotype of the poor white, the Backwoods (or Ring-Tailed) Roarer. Based to an extent on actual frontier conditions found even in colonial times, by the beginning of the nineteenth century this image had captured the popular imagination of America and established the tradition of a "comic barbarian" (Blair 1953). The image fomented a swirl of ridiculing laughter that caught up the real David Crockett and created his popular culture counterpart, Davy Crockett of the almanacs. To the extent that writers like Longstreet saw the Roarer stereotype in poor whites and plain folk alike, their satiric condescension is clear. And to the extent that antebellum audiences continued to enjoy variations on the stereotype, many comic writers obliged. The stories written about such wild comic figures are among the best evidence for Lynn's thesis about Mark Twain and the comic tradition of the Old Southwest. Popular as these comic figures were in the antebellum period, however, they were much less noteworthy than the attempt by some comic writers to reshape the Roarer into a roughneck who was nevertheless a Gentle Man. By transforming the theme of the comic barbarian, with its easy laughter of condescension, to a theme of backwoods civility, antebellum comic writers from the Old Southwest generated a much more complex laughter in their audience.

The background for the Roarer as a Gentle Man is a fascinating entanglement of politics, history, and popular images about antebellum common man that results primarily from mythmaking by and about David Crockett. This skein of representations is important because it tangles competing ideologies about dēmos—one that rendered an individual as a beastlike man in a wilderness; the other that pictured a pastoral world inhabited by a natural gentleman, a cross between *le bon sauvage* and an Arcadian shepherd (cf. Caron). Thus James K. Paulding could take the stereotypical Backwoods Roarer and create *The Lion of the West* (1831), a popular play featuring a relatively tame version, despite the fact the Roarer stereotype was largely based on a very brutal behavior, rough-and-tumble fighting. A most interesting aspect of American antebellum comic writers is the way that some of their comic figures, like Paulding's Nimrod Wildfire, effect a strange amalgamation of these two ideological, apparently irreconcilable, images of *dēmos*. The boast of these comic figures should be that they are half horse, half alligator, with a "leetle" touch of aspiring gentleman. The David Crockett of the *Narrative* as well as of *The Life of Colonel David Crockett* and the Davy Crockett of the almanacs wonderfully encapsulates this oxymoronic figure, the Roarer as Gentle Man.

When Kenneth Lynn sketches David Crockett, he presents a caricature of the actual man, painting him as merely ruthless and hard, full of rage and revenge despite his gift for humor (32–36). Because he portrays Crockett as having a savage nature, Lynn is surprised that Paulding presents Nimrod Wildfire as a natural gentlemen as much as a lampoon of the congressman (40). *The Lion of the West,* Lynn declares, is an aberration from Paulding's southern sympathies and aristocratic politics. Joseph J. Arpad, however, renders a very different picture of David Crockett, one who fought for squatters' rights and who also had a rare sympathy for Indians' rights (12–16), one who possessed a gentility that was "basic, something inherent in his nature [and whose] backwoods eccentricity was superficial, a masquerade" (18–19). Richard Boyd Hauck demonstrates that the masquerade functioned for political as well as comic purposes, noting that Crockett humorously cultivated an image of "the gentleman from the cane" in the 1822 session of the Tennessee legislature. Moreover, Crockett's 1827 electioneering tactics for Congress were designed to play up a contrast between new settlers (or squatters) and the rich, educated politicians who then controlled Tennessee politics (Hauck 1985, 2–7).

Arpad's rendition of Crockett is based on the experience of John Chapman, an artist who in 1834 over a period of a month and a half painted two oil portraits of Crockett. Given Chapman's testimony about Crockett's natural civility, Arpad concludes that Nimrod Wildfire catches the essential David Crockett, a man possessing an inner goodness that is masked by the crudities of being a backwoods bear hunter. In the logic of Lynn's analysis, Wildfire might conjure Jonathan Swift's bestial Yahoo; for Arpad, Nimrod Wildfire evokes Roger de Coverly, Uncle Toby, and Deitrich Knickerbocker (25). David Crockett, it would seem, did not mind drinking whiskey, did his share of bragging about his prowess as a hunter, and admitted to a fight in which he attacked his opponent "like a wild cat [and] scratched his face all to a flitter jig" (*Narrative* 30)—all requisite credentials for a Roarer. Yet Chapman, who had a six-week close-up of Crockett, underscores the gentle man. This contradiction distinguishes the strand of antebellum comic writing highlighted in this essay, for it generates an oxymoron—the Roarer as Gentle Man. The contradictory attitudes that create the Roarer-as-Gentle-Man figure can be found everywhere in antebellum culture. A major reason for the force of the myth of David Crockett is his embodiment of those attitudes.

According to Catherine Albanese (1978, 1985), the contradictory figure also informs the semiliterary, half-folklore representations of Crockett, autobiography and pseudo-biographies as well as almanacs. At the core of these representations is a projection of "civilized savagery" that resonated with the collective mental world of Crockett's contemporary Americans (Albanese 1985, 81). Crockett is both the man from the woods, representative of the wilderness of the natural world, and the man from Congress, representative of *polis* and politics, of civilization and civility (Albanese 1978, 249). The almanacs in particular present this contradiction in a caricatured manner, but one that nevertheless captures an important cultural debate about the definitions of savage and civilized while reflecting antebellum Americans' fear and fascination with the wildness of the frontier. Americans first of all were fearful about the lack of civilized refinement found in their culture, a lack dramatized by frontier wilderness but discernible even in the cities when behavior was compared to European cultures. Nevertheless, Americans were also fascinated by an ideology of newness, which transformed the untamed natural world into a democratic antidote against a decadent Europe (Albanese 1985, 83). The figure of Crockett in his *Narrative,* but especially in the almanacs, functioned as an expression for both sides of the question, providing an opportunity for Americans to identify ambiguously with wildness. Given the popularity of the *Narrative* (at least seven editions the first year) and other stories supposedly by Crockett, the identification was widespread. With the almanacs alone, the identification is enormously widespread, for they are the first true popular literature in the United States. Printed for twenty years in several editions, the almanacs commanded an audience that knew no boundaries, encompassing adults and juveniles, middle-class city and rustic dwellers, yeoman farmers and mechanics, eastern seaboard as well as western frontier folk.[3]

In Albanese's analysis, Davy Crockett of the almanacs exhibits a mastery of nature, a control that symbolizes the order of civilization, but the power of that mastery comes from a complete union with the wildness he ultimately tames. By becoming more savage than the savages he encounters in the wilderness, Davy Crockett ironically ensures the triumph of civilized values and behavior. He is thus a figure both of cultural degeneracy—the ultimate backwards man from the backwoods—and a figure of cultural progress—the pioneer who trailblazes for the civilization that follows. The crudities attributed to Crockett therefore can be read either as the signs of a loss of civility or as merely the rough manners that necessarily mediate the prospective wilderness and the subsequent civilization.

This uncertainty can be found when tracing the historical career of what might be taken as the epitome of the backwoodsman—the rough-and-tumble fighter—because the single most important fact about the major antebellum comic American writers is the way they manipulated stereotypes of actual frontier folk to create their comic figures. The Backwoods Roarer is undoubtedly the most enduring literary representation of the stereotyped backwoodsman. He is certainly one of the more dramatic. Moreover, the distortion in Lynn's analysis of Old Southwest comic writers happens because he narrowly conceives of the voice of the Clowns as essentially the voice of the Roarer, the stereotypical representation of the actual rough-and-tumble fighter.[4]

Some dispute exists among scholars about just how often actual examples of Backwoods Roarers might have been found in the frontier territories. Michael Fellman argues that the material reality of such men was far less important than the psychological or emblematic reality (n. 2, 321–22). Psychological reality certainly had much to do with the creation of a cycle of stories about Mike Fink, the most famous early historical example of a Backwoods Roarer. In any case, Fink's actual career is clearly a model for the historical men whose behavior was the basis for the type in popular writings. Fink started his career in the west as a scout for Fort Pitt during the border wars with Indians along the Ohio River during the 1780s and 1790s. In this capacity Fink acquired a reputation for courage, daring, and skilled shooting with his "Kentucky" rifle. Once the Indians were decisively defeated at the battle of Fallen Timbers, these scouts were no longer needed. By then, however, many were unsuited for farming, and they turned to the river for a living. These scouts, said an historian in 1845, "had imbibed in their intercourse with the Indians a . . . contempt as well as a disrelish for regular and steady labor. A boatsman's life was the very thing for such individuals. From the nature of their movements, they felt themselves scarcely responsible to the laws, as indeed they were not, except at New Orleans"(qtd. in Blair and Meine, 7). Mike Fink became one of these frontier scouts turned keelboatman.

Though the backwoodsman in his horrific incarnation as the Roarer might be found in almost any frontier setting, circumstances surrounding keelboating apparently made this form of river commerce a focal point for rough-and-tumble fighting. The difficulty in bringing a keelboat back upriver meant that its crew were among the hardiest to be found anywhere in the frontier areas. In the slang of the backwoods, however, the "best" man meant more than mere strength. Within the hierarchy of riverboats, with rafts at the bottom and keelboats at the top, physical prowess meant fights to maintain the pecking order. Moreover, physical prowess and the courage to fight no-holds-barred spawned rivalries among the keelboat crews to establish preeminence at the top, sometimes one champion bully meeting another in a wrestling match with no rules. The brutality of these fights was noted by travelers in their books, and when combined with the keelboatman's habits of excessive drinking and boasting, these travelers' descriptions helped create the lawless profile upon which the literary figure of the Backwoods Roarer was predicated.[5]

The majority opinion of scholars focused on the comic writers of the Old Southwest perceives the writers' upper-class gentlemen narrators as antagonistic toward their vernacular clowns because the gentlemen wish to preserve a social ideal about behavior—or wish to lament the fact that the ideal is disappearing. In this view, the new men from the frontier, the folks who gave Andrew Jackson his presidential victories, are the dregs of society at the worst or a parody of gentlemen at best (Fienberg 118), upstarts who degrade a social propriety. The worst fears were embodied by the grotesquely comic figure commonly known as a Roarer.

One of the writers said to hold this view was Charles F.M. Noland, whose Pete Whetstone letters were published in William T. Porter's *New York Spirit of the Times*. These letters were so popular in the late 1830s and early 1840s that racing horses and steamboats were named after the character (Williams 50, 204). Pete Whetstone, however, represents not the antagonism of the gentlemen writers toward the frontiersmen but their ambivalence. The ambivalence comes in part because the common folk pioneers, though rude and ignorant, uncouth and even violent, were also hard-working as well as hardy and understood to be educable. In short, Noland and his class could be ambivalent about the common man because they recognized their potential to be the Roarer as Gentle Man. Like David Crockett and Nimrod Wildfire, Pete Whetstone is another early example of this oxymoronic comic figure.

In one of the few extended analyses of the Pete Whetstone letters, Lorne Fienberg points to Noland's ambivalence toward his creation by suggesting that Pete has two roles: one as Noland's social antagonist, the other as Noland's alter ego. Part of this antagonism is political, says Fienberg: Noland is thoroughly Whig in his politics, while Pete represents frontier-style Jacksonian Democrats. When Pete runs for the Arkansas legislature, however, he is elected as a Whig who supports sound monetary policy, even though he has complained earlier about having to buy government land with coin and not paper money.[6] Pete's party affiliation is not explicit during the election but is unmistakable when he reports after the election that his opponent, Lawyer McCampbell, is "'turning Whig'": "I tell you he is warm in our cause . . . and I told him I would give way to him next time" (86). In subsequent letters (e.g. #13, #15), McCampbell espouses Whig monetary policy too. Indeed, as Pete Whetstone developed, Noland obviously felt comfortable using the character as a mouthpiece for his political views. In one letter to the *Spirit,* Noland created a substitute, Sam Grindstone, to report the news in Arkansas without transgressing Porter's rules about not discussing politics. Noland creates this second voice because Pete was being used to publish his political views in an Arkansas paper (Williams 183–85). Far from representing Noland's political foes, Pete in part functioned as Noland's attempt to beat the Democrats at their own electioneering tactics, paralleling the Whigs' use of Crockett before the election of 1836 (Blair 1940). Pete's vernacular voice, when discussing politics, was meant to convince whatever plain-folk audience he had that Whig policies were good for them. Noland's upper-class audience should be convinced that Whig policies could be embraced by the masses.

Pete Whetstone, then, reflects not only Noland's habitual pastimes of horse racing, hunting, gambling, and drinking, but his political habits as well; he very much is the comic alter ego of Noland, not his fictional antagonist. Yet, if Pete does not represent political foes, then what about Fienberg's point that Pete's attempt to be a gentleman is perceived by Noland and his class as a social threat (117)? If the boast of the Roarers as Gentle Men should be that they are half horse, half alligator, with a "leetle" touch of aspiring gentleman, should not men like Noland be alarmed? In this arena Noland's ambivalence is profound. On the one hand, Pete's comic foibles are presented to the upper-class readers of the *Spirit* every time he speaks in his rustic dialect full of bad grammar and spoonerisms. Pete as clown cannot escape the prevailing attitude that vernacular always signals a cause for laughter.[7] Pete's cultural deficiency is also a standard target for scornful laughter. His ignorance of pianos, his inability to dance a cotillion, and his rustic remarks about tragic drama and the opera are all examples of moments when the better folks in the audience are sure to laugh with a superior attitude. When Pete's letters with such moments are considered alongside those Noland published in the same issues of the *Spirit* and signed "N of Arkansas," letters which comment knowingly on the same tragic plays or operas, Fienberg's reworking of Lynn's concept of *cordon sanitaire* into laughter as a strategy for containing the upstart frontiersman works well. There can be little doubt that for Noland and his educated class, the folk represented by Pete Whetstone are distinctly inferior.

However, for Noland those folk are inferior mostly in ways that can be corrected. Thus Pete is hilarious because he cannot dance properly at a fancy ball (Letter #17), but at a subsequent upscale affair he has learned the fashionable dance (Letter #19). Pete may be a rustic clown, but he is capable of learning what high society requires. Noland, in fact, portrays Pete even more favorably. When Pete meets women at dress balls or country frolics, his behavior invariably polite and proper in substance whatever may be the risibility of his style, suggesting that Pete is a natural-born gentleman, who needs only education to come up to Noland's own level. Like David Crockett, Pete Whetstone is a "gentleman from the cane." In some measure, then, Noland could see the backwoods folk that Pete represents as people he could respect socially, people who might not yet be polished in manners but who could learn such niceties. Moreover, these backwoods folk were potential political allies. This potential explains why Pete and Lawyer McCampbell and Jim Cole could all be portrayed as Whigs: Noland must have believed that at least some individuals could be taught correct political views as well as social manners just as Crevecoeur in his famous third letter, "What is An American?," depicted some frontier folk as rising in the world despite their contact with wilderness. In the meantime, Pete and comic figures like him remain capable of generating a range of laughing responses.

One letter in particular (#29) illustrates how Noland's concept of Pete combines elements an audience can laugh *with* as well as laugh *at*. Pete attends a fancy party wearing new pants that are too big for him because he was in too great a hurry to try them on before the party starts and he has no other to substitute. Though an object of ridicule as a result, Pete demonstrates that his backwoods dress and manner are not completely out of place at the gathering. His rustic wit makes a lady laugh and induces her to continue singing when other polite requests fail. And when at the dinner table he spits out a chile he has mistaken for a pickle, he does so with a witty apology, punning on the name of his hometown. "'Excuse me, ladies, if I have done wrong,' says I, 'but that pickle is too hot for the Devil's Fork'" (126). Pete goes on to say that except for one chap, everybody "seemed to take the thing in good part," but Pete silences him quickly: "'Look here, Mister, if you don't like the smell of fresh bread, you had better quit the bakery'" (126). Pete's retort to the charge of rude behavior wonderfully captures his comic ambivalence, for the fresh bread analogy acknowledges that his manners are out of place in the parlor yet implies a basic goodness to his nature.

The incident with the chile raises the issue of how rustic manners, though laughable, come to represent behavior preferable to an aristocratic snobbishness. A few years later, Noland writes a letter about Pete going to New Orleans that more explicitly considers this issue. In New Orleans, Pete once again shows his mix of rustic politeness and social miscues guaranteed to raise laughter with an upper-class audience. He orders an unsavory game bird unintentionally because he does not recognize it on the menu written in French, and he declares an opera in Italian to be "'Injun to me'" (172). When a "dandy looking fellow" comments "'How vulgar'" and seems ready to duel, however, Pete responds with a country phrase underscoring the dandy's artificial manners: "'If you don't like the smell of the apples, you had best quit the cider press.'" Pete then goes on to question the opera itself, wondering if people attend opera because they like it or "'because it is the hight of quality?'" (173) In such instances as these, Noland uses Pete and his speech in a way that is different from Kenneth Lynn's idea of vernacular. In this case, "vernacular" functions as a badge for democratic values, the way Seba Smith had often used it earlier in the 1830s with Jack Downing, the way Henry Nash Smith (1962) argues Sam Clemens uses it with Mark Twain after the Civil War. If Charles Noland's portrayal of Pete Whetstone's manners clearly demonstrates an ambivalence rather than an antagonism he felt about the folk Pete represents, even more obvious in its ambivalence is his rendering of Pete as Backwoods Roarer.

In the very first letter signed "Pete Whetstone," Noland portrays "the boys" from Devil's Fork as Backwoods Roarers. When they meet a rival group of men from Raccoon Fork, boasting about the speed of their horses ensues, and they agree to a race immediately. When they all begin to drink whiskey in anticipation of the event, the real boasting quickly starts—and so does the fighting. The melee is general and includes Squire Woods; Noland's first sketch of the Arkansas frontier implies that almost everyone is ready to fight just for the fun of it. Moreover, though he does not provide details of the action, Noland clearly indicates the rough-and-tumble nature of the fighting when Pete reports that "'bit noses and fingers were plenty'" (62). In subsequent letters during the first year that Noland is creating the adventures of Pete Whetstone, the character remains hair-trigger ready to fight when he thinks someone has slandered him (Letter #20) or when he drinks too much champagne and hears someone speaking Latin (Letter #21). In the first instance, Pete as vernacular clown seems to be a foolishly violent embodiment of a gentleman's honor. He is no better in the second, for his reaction to Latin clearly does not represent a democratic comment on aristocratic snobbishness that a reasonable person can support; rather, his violent and ungovernable temper suggests how "vernacular" can refer to behavior that antebellum gentlemen writers might symbolically contain with their frame narratives. In yet another letter, which echoes and elaborates this theme (#22), Pete and his backwoods comrades fight after a dispute about the outcome of a horse race.[9] Here again, Fienberg's thesis that Pete represents a parody of gentlemanly behavior works well, for the backwoodsmen are grappling with each other minutes after the race ends, without even hearing what the judges are saying. Such men may ape their betters in betting on horses, but their true nature as barbaric Roarers quickly asserts itself. Once again the melee is general, and this time Pete slashes a man "right across the face, cutting his nose in two" (112) when he mistakenly thinks a comrade has been stabbed to death.

What makes Pete Whetstone most interesting, then, is Noland's willingness to portray him both as Roarer and gentleman, for the examples cited above create a composite image, a man unafraid in a backwoods encounter with a bear but naturally polite to women, capable of wielding a knife in a melee or learning a cotillion for a society ball. One suspects that Colonel Pete Whetstone and Colonel David Crockett would have been bosom friends. These odd junctures of courage and manners are the last elements in Noland's fictional alter ego, added to Pete's sound judgment in political as well as horse races. Noland is therefore ambivalent about Pete not because he represents an antagonist but because he represents his own less-civilized impulses. This composite image of Roarer and gentleman gains a sharper outline when other Pete Whetstone letters telling about fights and near-fights over horses and politics are also considered.[10] These accounts of brawling imply that Arkansas folks are people who resort to fisticuffs and worse when anything is disputed. In this general picture, the behavior of his friends Jim Cole and Dan Looney and Bill Spence are crucial in creating Pete's composite image because they "outroar" him. Pete is belligerent at times, but he never starts a fight: the two fights that involve him begin with either Dan Looney or Jim Cole. When Pete draws his knife, it is only after another man has drawn his and has stabbed one of Pete's compatriots. Finally, Pete is never depicted as using no-holds-barred tactics; nor is his brother-in-law Jim Cole, though he almost loses an eye when he gets into a brawl because he drinks too much (49). Dan Looney from Raccoon Fork, however, has two fights in which he eye-gouges (Letters 40, 63). Noland distances Pete, his family, and all of Devil's Fork from this quintessential bestial act of the backwoods.

Pete also emerges as Roarer and gentleman when the letters are read as a whole because all of his belligerency occurs the first year in which the letters are published. In subsequent letters, Noland shifts whatever portrayal of fighting and excessive drinking he presents away from Pete and toward his friends. Moreover, after the first year, Pete sounds moderate in political matters. When Van Buren's vice president, Richard Johnson, visits Little Rock, Pete calls him "a mighty good man" (151) even though he clearly was not impressed with him. When Pete meets Van Buren in an earlier letter, Noland passes up the chance to be violently partisan, as he also does when he imagines Pete exchanging letters with another Democrat in the White House, Franklin Pierce (Letters 31, 60). As the letters proceed, this moderation can also be seen in Pete's comments about Thomas H. Benton, the famous Democratic Senator from Missouri. Benton starts off as a figure of ridicule, whose pomposity is symbolized by his habit of wearing stiff cravats, but earns admiring remarks after the political campaign of 1852 (Letter 57). In the hostile sectional atmosphere brewing in the 1850s, Pete's ability to see merit in the political opposition is a clear indication of his gentleman aspect. Perhaps the ultimate example of Charles Noland's ambivalence toward the vernacular-speaking folk of his day is his use of Dan Looney to defend against talk by abolitionists about breaking up the union, for Dan beats his opponent when he gouges his eyes (Letter 63). With the ultimate gesture of frontier violence, a Roarer ironically defends a moderate political position, a structure that echoes Albanese's view of Davy Crockett's embrace of savagery to tame savages and the wilderness.

The Roarer as Gentle Man represents the most interesting part of antebellum humor because the figure embodies an ambivalence in American culture about *dēmos*. A final instance of this proposition is William Tappan Thompson. If the character Pete Whetstone suggests that the faults of the vernacular-speaking folk might be remedied by education, Thompson's Major Joseph Jones demonstrates it. Major Jones, in effect, completes a movement toward backwoods gentility, for the major, in comic country fashion, wins his ladylove. However, if the major is domesticated, even to the point of abjuring tobacco and whiskey, he nevertheless does not lose all of the Roarer's features. Instead, Major Jones suggests an idealized image of *dēmos*, losing the Roarer's brutality but not his courage, transforming hardiness into an ethic of hard work, displaying as much common sense as naiveté and bumptiousness. Though readers can laugh at him as a slapstick figure, country oaf, and lovesick swain, they can also laugh with his vernacular-rendered, homespun philosophy about education, people, politics, fashions, and manners. He is held up for admiration as much as for ridicule.

In a thorough discussion of Thompson, Henry Prentice Miller (1946) sums up Major Jones by calling him a middle-Georgia farmer, a cracker-box philosopher representative of plebeian attitudes, and a politician. Though this summary leaves out the comic elements in the way Thompson presents Joseph Jones, Miller does discuss how *Major Jones's Courtship* creates laughter, noting the major's country-bumpkin ignorance and the repeated presence of practical joking in the letters. Miller also states that much of the book's humor is to be found in "the accurate representation of the Georgia cracker dialect" (295). Indeed, the major's vernacular speech at times succinctly captures his country-bumpkin quality, with his predilection for spoonerisms, poor spelling, and bad grammar. A particularly good example of how the speech of Joseph Jones reveals his rustic ignorance is a misunderstanding involving Mary Stallins, whom he courts and eventually marries. When Joe asks Mary if she has any beaux at college, Mary jokingly says "yes" and names the subjects she is studying. Jones misses the joke Mary makes about devotion to her studies, hearing "Matthew Matix" for mathematics, for example, and becoming jealous. Thompson also shows the major's backwoods upbringing by portraying his fear of riding trains, his misunderstanding of Macon's masked procession staged as part of its civic festivities during a college graduation, and his anxieties while in a big town. In these instances, the laughter generated would presumably come from a superior attitude taken by an educated and/or urban reader.

Though Miller mentions the horseplay of practical joking that easily creates laughter from any sort of reader, he does not discuss how Thompson uses slapstick incidents to color a reader's perception of Major Jones's character. In the third letter of *Major Jones's Courtship*, Thompson portrays the comic qualities of a country militia muster, a favorite comic topic since Oliver Prince's 1807 sketch "The Militia Drill," so popular that Longstreet included it in *Georgia Scenes* (1835). Though Thompson follows Prince in showing how a militia company's clumsiness at drill is exacerbated by an inexperienced officer, his Major Jones is not the fool that Prince's Captain Clodpole is. For Jones, the trouble begins with his tailor, not the military manual. Proud of his new uniform made expressly for his first muster as Major, Joseph Jones discovers that the clothes are ill-fitting. Moreover, his horse acts skittish when he tries to mount, not recognizing its master, who has been transformed by new clothes as well as a saber and hat, complete with feather. The major's pride demands a salute, and he orders his slave to tell the men to be ready to provide it when he rides into view. The skittishness of the horse turns to panic when the company, misunderstanding Jones's order, salutes him by firing its guns. Jones fails to remain in the saddle and his uniform is ruined.[11] A second incident that ends in slapstick begins with a spontaneous contest. When a group of young men try to pick grapes from a vine tangled high in a tree for the young women they are escorting home from church, Jones again finds that pride comes before a literal fall. In this case, the major not only attempts to pick the grapes highest from the ground but decides to impress the women further by performing an acrobatic maneuver he calls "skin the cat" (44) while hanging from a tree limb. He ends up ruining his Sunday clothes when he falls in the creek.

Thompson also uses slapstick to represent Joseph Jones as comically lovesick for Mary Stallins. In Letters 8, 9, and 10, Thompson creates an out-of-town rival for Mary, a Yankee music teacher named Crochett. Worried and jealous because Mary seemed to favor the rival, Major Jones is relieved when Crochett is discovered as "a bigamy" (77) and Mrs. Stallins tells him Mary was never interested in but only being polite to the stranger. Joe has deliberately not visited Mary during the false courting by the Yankee. When he finally returns just to say hello and leave, Mary insists he stay and help her and her sisters with pulling molasses. So bewitched is the major by Mary's renewal of attention to him that he inadvertently sticks his hand into a bowl of molasses still too hot for pulling into candy (88). In all of these instances, Thompson uses slapstick to create incidents that allow a reader to laugh at Major Jones for his temporary foibles.

Jones burns his hand in slapstick style because he is absent-minded to everything but his love for Mary, indicating that *Major Jones's Courtship* has its foundation in pastoral. Thus to the list of roles Miller attributes to the major should be added the comically lovesick swain. Thompson uses the role to illustrate his perception of the domestic manner of Americans, middle-Georgia style. Though there is no doubt that Mary will accept the major, what dramatic conflict exists in the original group of sixteen letters occurs because of the comic contrast between Mary's and Joe's manners: hers have been polished into those of a belle by attendance at the Female College in Macon, while his remain those of a rustic farmer. He is confused by her sudden formality, referring to him as "Mr. Jones" and "Joseph" when he visits the Stallins household in the letter that begins the series. He may pretend to be visiting an old friend, but Mary the college student now treats him as a gentleman caller. The major's rustic manners are revealed in the clumsy attempt to discover if she might care for him, climaxed by accidentally putting out the fire in the fireplace with a stream of tobacco juice. The incongruity between his romantic intentions and his vile rudeness in dousing the fire as he does leads to the first use of slapstick by Thompson in the letters. Deprived of the only light and unable to coax a response to his gaucherie from the presumably horrified Mary, Joe attempts to leave the darkened house, running into the door and knocking over chairs and the spinning wheel in the process. Once outside, the inevitable pack of hunting dogs adds insult to his injured dignity. His abandoned hat is returned ignominiously to him the next day (17–19). Though his rustic quality depicts him as ridiculous in contrast to polite behavior and points to the pastoral nature of the Major Jones letters, his comic behavior stems from circumstance not character. Moreover, when in the second letter the major reveals that he has quit chewing tobacco as a result of the incident, Thompson indicates the fundamentally positive nature of Joe Jones's character, for quitting the use of tobacco suggests a capacity for learning. Like Pete Whetstone, Joe Jones is crude but educable.

In fact, many clues exist in the letters to indicate that Major Jones, though possessed of little formal education, is nevertheless much more than a country simpleton. For instance, in the first letter Jones compares Mary to the pictures of pretty women found in *Graham's Magazine* (12), indicating his level of literacy as well as his awareness of fashions more sophisticated than Pineville's and the manners they represent. Taken together, Joe Jones and Mary Stallins in fact suggest the relatively high level of literacy possible in the antebellum middle classes, quoting Shakespeare more than once (Letters 3, 6, 14, 16, 26), and alluding to Byron (Letter 5) and Dickens (Letters 11, 18).

If the major's literacy helps to move his character past that of a country simpleton, it also adds to his credibility when, on more than one occasion, he demonstrates the cracker-box philosopher's blending of educated and natural wit. One moment of such homespun philosophizing involves the topic of how education and natural abilities can or cannot be yoked together. Typically, the major expresses himself in terms drawn from his farmer's life:

> I use to think human nater was jest like the yeath bout cultivation. Everybody knows thar's rich land, pore land what can be made tolerable good, and some bominable shaller, rollin truck what all the manure in creation wouldn't make grow cow peas. Well, there's some men whose nateral smartness helps 'em along first rate, some what takes a mighty site of skoolin, and some that all the edecation in the world wouldn't do no manner of good—they'd be nateral fools any way you could fix it. Ther minds is too shaller and rollin; they haint got no foundation, and all the skoolin you could put on 'em wouldn't stay no longer nor so much manure on the side of a red sandhill. (31)

However one assesses the literacy and education of Major Jones, he knows "larnin ain't sense" (*Chronicles of Pineville* 99). Given that formal education is figured as manure in his analogy, one can conclude that the major is wary of it. Thompson deliberately intends his character to be less than the well-educated and wealthy high class, a country clown at times, yet nevertheless a symbol of how a wise and good man from the middling classes of backwoods settlements thinks.

Major Joseph Jones's character, then, is a classic frontier type, a compound of book learning and common sense. Such amalgamation is congruent with my claim that the major is an example of the Roarer as Gentle Man, for Jones is not only a man of action but also a man of feeling. James Paulding's comic character Nimrod Wildfire had suggested how the extravagance of the Backwoods Roarer speech and behavior could be laughably combined with the noble instincts of a "natural gentleman." Charles Noland's Pete Whetstone also illustrates this comic compound of wildness and civility, for he is handy wielding a knife in a free-for-all and adept dancing cotillions at a fancy ball. With Major Jones, William Tappan Thompson manages to blend to a considerable degree the two elements of the compound. To be sure, the major starts off as a farmer, not a bear hunter or keelboatman, and thus the net effect of the blending is such that one might wonder if any of the wildness of the Roarer remains beneath the domesticity of the major's courtship, marriage, and fatherhood.

The question is a good once inasmuch as the major from the beginning is a teetotaler and thus lacks the most obvious trait of the Roarer—his hard-drinking, which leads to his hard fighting. Indeed, one of the important themes in *Major Jones's Courtship* is the advantages of temperance. The major attempts to keep his men away from liquor at the militia muster (Letter 3), convinces a man to give up drinking (Letter 7), has an alcohol-free wedding (Letter 16), and sponsors an alcohol-free Fourth of July festival (Letter 21). Because Thompson does not narrate the event, presumably the major's decision to be a teetotaler results from observing all the sorts of trouble engendered by the nearly universal frontier habit of drinking whiskey, and making such a decision must have been very much like the way in which the major decides to quit chewing tobacco—his common sense telling him that the harm outweighs the pleasure.[12]

However, while common sense surely played its role in the major giving up tobacco, the remarkable aspect of the change is the role that embarrassment plays in it, for the slapstick of the major tripping over chairs and spinning wheels and running into doors not only comically represents the enormity of his social clumsiness but also the depth of the chagrin he feels at dousing the fire by spitting on it—a feeling only expelled by giving up tobacco. The ability of the major to feel deeply is also demonstrated when he reads newspaper reviews of his book of letters and blushes because they are so favorable. When his cousin Pete, standing in the crowd of men near the major as he reads the reviews, notices the blush, he mistakenly thinks that Jones blushes because they are critical. Pete's demand that the reviews be read out loud completes the major's triumph by making it public and sharpens the contrast between Pete Jones's mean-spirited and Joe Jones's modest behaviors (129–30). In effect, Major Jones's blush signals his emotional side, an aspect Joe demonstrates in particular toward his cousin Pete, feeling sorry for him on two occasions even though Pete gets what he deserves. In one case, Joe has thrown his cousin into a creek because he was rude to Mary but feels sorry about it later. In the second, Pete attempts to repeat with Mary's sister Keziah Joe's trick of proposing by pretending to be a gift in Keziah's Christmas stocking. Everyone but Pete knows that Keziah has substituted a slave woman's stocking for hers, and as Pete endures the cold and the barking dogs, just as Joe did, the major feels a bit sorry for his arrogant and foolish cousin.

Though Major Jones might be called a man of feeling, a role that accords well with his lovesick swain behavior, Thompson makes sure that Jones is not to be thought of as a "Miss Nancy sort of young gentleman" (*Chronicles of Pineville* 87) but as a man of action, too. Hints of the major's pugnacity readily surface in connection with his courtship of Mary Stallins. Thus he is ready to kick one rival in the pants (Letter 8) or knock another into "a greas-spot" (17), and cousin Pete only has to be rude to Mary to be bodily picked up and thrown into a creek (Letter 5). The major's quick temper and his physical strength echo the Roarer stereotype. After his marriage, however, occurs the incident that demonstrates that Thompson's conception of Major Jones, though decidedly civil, includes typical Roarer behavior. Cousin Pete again stirs up trouble, this time by trumping up a warrant for the major's arrest that charges him with harming young women from Macon with his book of letters. When Jones rides into town to discover what is behind the trouble, Pete and a crowd led by a man named Snipe attempt to arrest the major, literally, by tying him up with a rope:

> That was more'n I could stand from [Pete], and I jest brung my hand round and tuck him spang in the mouth. I spose it must [have] been pretty much of a lick, for it sounded jest like hittin a piece of raw beef with the flat side of a meet-axe, and it drawed considerable blood and a tooth or two. Peter kivered his mouth with his hand and sort o' backed out of the crowd. But little Snipe stood off and hollered "help! rescue!

> help" as loud as he could, and the fellers grabbled hold of me like they was gwine to tear me to pieces. My dander was up and I couldn't help slingen 'em a little, and after I piled five or six of 'em on top of one another and put two or three of their noses out of jint, I told Snipe I was ready to go.[13] (140–41)

Given the major's ability in a fight, his earlier restraint with cousin Pete is noteworthy—not only being content with a simple ducking when Pete is rude to Mary but also refraining from acting when Pete, under cover of a parlor game, more than once hits Joe hard with a book. Restraint is noticeable too in the above quote: Major Jones whips everyone and then surrenders. All of this restraint suggests that Major Joseph Jones has the courage of the Backwoods Roarer tempered with the civility of a Self-Controlled Gentleman. Indeed, his readiness to defend Mary's character is part of his natural-born gentleman's behavior, and so too is his restraint with Pete during the parlor game, for Joe defers to Mary's plan of revenge. No full-fledged Roarer would have restrained himself after realizing Pete's cowardly trick, and when the major does hit Pete during the attempted arrest, a definite sense exists that the major has been pushed beyond a reasonable man's limit. Jones shows the same balance at the militia muster, which ends in a drunken brawl. He is ready beforehand to fight at the muster if the men attempt to play practical jokes on him as they did on the previous commanding officer, but he stays out of the senseless fray once it begins on a political pretext, though certainly not from a sense of fear.

While Major Jones is a vernacular-speaking example of *dēmos*, his is very far from Lynn's notion of how the Old Southwest writers portrayed their vernacular characters. Retaining the bumptiousness of the Jacksonian folk and even a significant measure of the Roarer's fighting ability, Major Jones is nevertheless clearly held up for the admiration of the audience as well as its ridicule. The height of admiration for the major comes with his speech at a liquor-free Fourth of July celebration. His theme is the inferior behavior of contemporary men compared to the founding fathers, a standard antebellum rhetorical tactic on such occasions. Major Jones, however, is meant to be taken as an exception to that decline and more like the mythical founding fathers: a sober and loving husband, hard-working, with enough education not to act foolish yet not to take on aristocratic airs, too. Major Jones is a republican in the non-party sense of the word, and, like Colonel Pete Whetstone, he advocates Whig politics, naming his son Henry Clay in a symbolic gesture. Major Jones is thus an idealized yet comic portrait of *dēmos*. The curious mixture found in the idea of the Roarer as Gentle Man also extends to the major's political partisanship when he declares that he goes for Clay "tooth and toenail" (189), evoking the rough-and-tumble fight in defense of sober Whig principles. Finally, no frame exists around the major's letters to contain his bumptiousness in the name of a gentleman's point of view, for Joe Jones is that gentleman—albeit cast in comic terms and drawn from the middle classes.

Even if one takes into account Thompson's other book of comic sketches about antebellum Georgia, *Major Jones's Chronicles of Pineville (*1843), the most remarkable features of Thompson's fictional world are 1) its lack of portraits of the upper-class, wealthy, and well-educated planters and 2) its relative lack of the superior viewpoint said to mirror that class's attitude toward the common folk. In the preface to *Chronicles,* Thompson says that his intention was to present "a few interesting specimens of the genus 'Cracker,'" and the portraits he draws present a remarkable range of such characters if the term is understood to designate the plain folk of the Old South, people from the lower and middle classes.

In *The Plain Folk of the Old South* (1949), Frank Owsley uses tax records to divide antebellum society into no fewer than nine groups. Five groups were slaveholders, four were not, and the range begins at the top with the great planters and ends with renters and squatters, who not only do not own slaves but also do not own the few acres they farm. Scholarship subsequent to Owsley on this topic has added at least one more group—drovers who may or may not have owned land but made a good living with their cattle and hogs—and scholars have also demonstrated the complicated nature of relationships (political as well as economic) among all of these groups of white southerners.[14] Though in his first letter Major Jones implies that his farm is a "plantation" (12), in a subsequent letter Thompson pictures him working in the fields with his slaves (Letter 19), which suggests that the major is either a small planter or a large slaveholding farmer in Owsley's taxonomy. These groups are just above Owsley's designation of plain folks, and Jones's election as major in the militia as well as his literary endeavors seem to confirm his status as just above those plain folks. Yet, he also could be a small slaveholding farmer, and calling his farm a plantation could be read as a comic hint at Jones's pride. His homespun point of view and his vernacular way of expressing it suggest that conceptualizing him as plain folk, right in the middle of Owsley's groupings, has a firm basis.

If more than a little plausibility exists for placing the major within two or even three groups from Owsley's social strata, that range indicates on a most basic level the realism of Thompson's sketches, suggesting the fluid nature of the frontier and semi-frontier back settlements of antebellum southern society. Joseph Jones as successful author and farmer, married to a woman with a college education, represents a rising middle class. In "How to Kill Two Birds with One Stone," part of Thompson's second book, he portrays another example of an enterprising young man rising in the world, this time in one of the professional fields available to such young men. However, as an ambitious lawyer, Thomas Jefferson Jenkins provides a contrast to Joseph Jones in terms of method. Jenkins's law practice flourishes only after he plays a trick that starts two lawsuits, then argues both sides and wins both cases. In the context of an environment in which practical jokes flourished, Jenkins's trick seems as much enterprising as underhanded, making him an odd blend of Horatio Alger and Simon Suggs, and perhaps most readers of the sketch—then as well as now—would expect nothing less of a lawyer anyway. Jenkins's surname of Thomas Jefferson, however, suggests that Thompson sees such chicanery as part and parcel of Democrats' behavior and not typical of a Whig like Major Jones. Here

Lynn's political analysis works. Taking Jones and Jenkins together, however, one might say that the issue is not Whigs versus Democrats or upper-class gentlemen versus lower-class clowns. Rather, the issue is a moral one, and so categories of reputable and subversive work better (as Walter Blair and Hamlin Hill suggest) to analyze antebellum comic writers: Jones is reputable, and Jenkins, though apparently respectable and certainly capable, is subversive of moral order.

Thompson's perspective, then, is not so much that of a Whig who scorns and fears the lower classes but that of a satirist who attacks evil behavior. "The Duel," another sketch from *The Chronicles of Pineville*, readily makes the point, for the character laughed at is the upper-class gentleman, Major Bangs, who has a habit of becoming a particularly nasty *mīlēs glōriōsus* when fortified with whiskey. When Bangs insults some of the plain folk he encounters in a tavern, the inevitable fight with one of the men, Ned Jones, begins as a rough-and-tumble encounter might—bragging first, with coats coming off when an endurable limit has been passed—but it quickly moves to a duel, "the most genteel way of settling the difficulty" (141). This phrase is freighted with irony, for Ned is obviously not genteel but neither has the major been acting like a gentleman, and in any case, the gentility attached to the cold-blooded killing in a duel can only exist vis à vis the savagery of the rough-and-tumble fight.[15]

The major is obviously a coward, and when Ned and the boys are through playing tricks on him, he has demonstrated his cowardice. More importantly for Thompson the satirist, Major Bangs reveals the main target for ridicule—alcohol—when he forswears drink. The reader is told early in the sketch that Major Bangs is a fool only when drinking (151), and thus the reader laughs at him, joining in with the plain folks like Ned Jones. Drunkenness is also a problem for the plain folks, as Josiah Perkins ("How to Kill Two Birds with One Stone"), John Borum ("The Anti–Rail-Rode Man"), and Boss Ankles ("Boss Ankles, the man what got blowed up with a sky-racket") demonstrate. Perkins, possibly a small, nonslaveholding farmer, seems to be a man of very modest means, who is respectable until he is drunk. His wife claims to save him an eye when she prevents his fighting when drunk (107–8), the only reference to the most brutal part of rough-and-tumble fighting in Thompson's two books. The dirty and disheveled Boss Ankles appears as a poor white version of Major Bangs—a vain and loud-talking man, who turns foolish when drunk. In producing these characters, Thompson writes not as a political or class-conscious satirist but as a moral satirist. The implication is that all of these characters may be good men when they do not drink. If that is not true for the repugnant Boss Ankles, Thompson distances him from all of his contemporary readers by placing him in an earlier generation.

A character from the contemporary generation and thus closer to Thompson's first audience of readers has foibles that seem more bound to his class status—Sammy Stonestreet ("The Mystery Revealed"). Sammy is a physically ugly and not-so-bright clay eater, whose insistence to the other town idlers that two women passing through town in a wagon are really disguised bank robbers is reminiscent of Ransy Sniffle in Longstreet's "The Fight." Both men are eager to stir something up among their neighbors. Thompson's satiric target here seems to be the changeable nature of public opinion, but this general jab at *dēmos* is offset by the usually favorable picture of plain folks like old Uncle Hearly, Ned Jones, Bill Peters, Bob Eschols, and Billy Wilder.

Sammy Stonestreet and Boss Ankles, then, are Thompson's versions of the negative view of *dēmos* that Lynn sees as typical of the Old Southwest comic writers. However, if those two characters confirm Lynn's thesis while John Borum and Josiah Perkins seem equivocal, Sam Sikes from "Fire Hunt" suggests how even the portrait of an apparently shiftless poor white can be drawn with sympathy. Sikes is "one of the most inveterate hunters" around Pineville, a man who "pretended to cultivate a small spot of ground, [whose] few acres of corn and . . . small patch of potatoes [stand] greatly in need of the hoe" (161). In Owsley's social groupings, Sikes is probably a renter or squatter, though other scholars have suggested that such men were possibly part-time drovers who might not be as poor as they looked, because their wealth was their cattle and hogs mostly out of sight in the woods. These men were not farmers but part-time farmers, part-time drovers, and part-time hunters. Possibly Sikes is all of the above, but he is certainly passionate about hunting. The degrees of economic wealth in such places as middle Georgia were more rather than less, as Lynn's analysis has it, a variety commensurate with the attitudes expressed in such stories as "Fire Hunt." Thompson makes Sikes look foolish for being keen on showing the proper-speaking narrator (addressed as "Major") how to fire hunt and then shooting his own mule in his eagerness. However, Sikes's philosophical reaction to the error—"what can't be cured must be indured" (178)—and his worry about what his wife will say renders his reasonable side and indicates the part-time nature of his hunting. Readers then and today can agree with the narrator and regard Sikes "as an object of sympathy rather than ridicule" (177). Sikes in fact is a wonderfully humorous character in a classic, Ben Jonson sense—a man possessed by a passion that renders him ridiculous and thus one who is not always in charge of his behavior. The reader laughs at his foible, but because it is a foible rather than a vice like drunkenness, the laughter can easily be tempered with sympathy. Though Sikes is far less than respectable and fits the profile that is supposed to elicit a ridiculing, satiric laughter from an upper-class perspective, Thompson creates instead a more complex comic portrait of a common man.

William Tappan Thompson was a very popular writer in the 1840s and 1850s. The popularity of *Major Jones's Courtship* alone was enormous and began even before the letters were printed as a book. So many people in Madison, Georgia, asked for back copies of the *Southern Miscellany*, where the letters were first printed, that the newspaper's owner published the first sixteen letters in a pamphlet that was offered free to anyone who would subscribe to the paper for a year and pay in advance. Then a wealthy citizen of Madison named Colonel Jones told Thompson he would pay to have the letters printed in book form. While Thompson was inquiring for the colonel about costs, the Philadelphia publishing firm Carey and Hart proposed to publish the letters. The new book sold fifteen thousand copies the first year

(1842), and within eighteen months six editions had been issued (Miller 287–88). By 1852 twelve editions existed, and Thompson would say later that eighty thousand copies were eventually sold. When T.B Peterson and Company published its "Library of Humorous American Works" in the 1850s, *Major Jones's Courtship* was the first and most popular volume in the series (Miller 289).

In his analysis of Mark Twain and the Old Southwest writers, Kenneth Lynn sees all the writers as representative of a Whig, upper-class perspective—what might be called the "sporting crowd." The sporting crowd was interested in horse racing, hunting, and the theater; would likely subscribe to the *New York Spirit of the Times;* and was made up of people who either were from or aspired to the planter class. The brief circuit between Whig authors and this sporting-crowd audience is precisely what Lynn and Covici describe in their books (cf. Blair 1953). Given the continuing influence of Lynn's thinking about the Old Southwest writers and the nature of their connection to Mark Twain, there is much significance in the popularity of Thompson's work, which rivaled the popularity of the Colonel Pete Whetstone letters, the Crockett materials, and *The Lion of the West.* The enormous popularity of all these comic stories suggests that Lynn's argument at best captures the intent of some Old Southwestern writers to convey a Whig-oriented, upper-class perspective while ignoring the varied audience of antebellum comic writings and the import of what happened in the book-buying market. The huge sales figures for these comic materials indicates that the audience for comic stories was much bigger and more diverse than a narrow socioeconomic class with specific political views.

Thompson's original audience in middle Georgia, however, was "chiefly the hard-working, half-educated, rough-and-ready Scotch-Irish cotton farmers" (Miller 269), an audience Thompson throughout his career courted in his books and his own newspaper and from which he received approval over the years (Osthaus 240). Joseph Jones more or less mirrored these folks. Using Major Jones, Thompson could gently make fun of those folks but also praise them, hold them up for ridicule and for admiration, too. Indeed, Thompson's audience actually wrote the same sort of letters to the *Southern Miscellany*, half-literate with poor spelling and bad grammar (Miller 270), and thus the Major Jones letters parodied real letters. Yet, they also idealized the people who wrote them. Moreover, the enormous sales of the letters collected into book form demonstrates that the original middle-class audience, Southern and mostly rustic, expanded into the middle-class in all corners of the book-buying market. No doubt the success of *Major Jones's Courtship* went both higher and lower than middle-class on the socioeconomic scale. The first five letters at least of the original series were reprinted in the *New York Spirit of the Times* (Miller 290), suggesting that they were popular with the "sporting crowd," too. Porter himself said that the letters were equal in popularity to the famous Jack Downing letters of the 1830s, by the Maine writer Seba Smith, and he compared Thompson to a popular contemporary satiric writer from England, William Thackeray.

William Tappan Thompson's cast of characters in his two most important books, *Major Jones's Courtship* and *Major Jones's Chronicles of Pineville*, represents the range of middle-class plain folks that historical scholarship has confirmed actually existed in America in the 1830s and 1840s. In this respect his comic sketches demonstrate the realism at the foundation of much of antebellum America's comic writing. His characters no doubt elicited a range of contemporary audience attitudes about the common man and woman of the 1830s and 1840s, with tolerant attitudes possible even in the comic context. Taken together, these two points argue that the work of William Tappan Thompson is the strongest evidence for the flawed nature of Kenneth Lynn's still influential thesis about the comic writers grouped as the frontier humorists of the Old Southwest. Lynn's analysis falters in assuming a one-to-one correspondence between the psychological reality of the Roarer figure and the material reality of antebellum social strata. The first national image for the southerner/westerner was the Roarer, courtesy of David Crockett and James K. Paulding. The image was based in reality but was essentially exaggerated, a literary stereotype more than a description of actual people. The psychological reality of the rough-and-tumble fighter and its literary representation in the Roarer Lynn equates to political attitudes and social classes: the frame story and the ridiculing attitude it projects equals two classes of southern whites, even though society was much more complicated. The antebellum political arena was also more complicated, Whig political rhetoric attempting to court the plain and poor folks as it kept them at a social distance.

The humorists or comic frontier writers from the Old Southwest are better described not as "gentlemen," with that term's connotations of the upper-class planter, but rather as "men of moderation." Literary equivalents of this fundamentally moderate position include Moliere's *homme raisonnable* or Joseph Addison's persona in his essays. Thus the distance from certain characters found in the voices of the Old Southwestern writers and in their framing technique is more one of behavior, attitude, or temperament than economic class or political affiliation. Whatever satire these writers direct at behavior would be targeted at excess no matter who practiced it—gentleman, yeoman, or poor white. Moreover, historians have shown that the excessive gambling, drinking, fighting, and boasting that coalesces into the Roarer figure was part of all social strata in the Old Southwest. In this sense, the comic Roarer functioned as a satire of a masculine ideal gone awry. Thus to call the narrators of the Old Southwestern frame stories "Self-Controlled Gentlemen" because they ridicule excessive behavior in the lower orders and to assume that those narrators should be aligned with the upper-classes against the lower-classes is to misunderstand the social dynamics of the Old Southwest. Intemperance was endemic on the frontier and semi-frontier conditions of backwoods settlements, not confined solely to the lower classes of people (Cashin 109; cf. Bruce, Tyrrell).

William Tappan Thompson's vision of the folk is quite different from the model of conflict used by many scholars when discussing how humor and laughter operates in the Old Southwest comic tradition. Along with David Crockett, Davy Crockett, Nimrod Wildfire, and Pete Whetstone, Thompson's most popular character, Major Joseph Jones, embodies an oxymoron instead: the Roarer as Gentle

Man. This comic representation of the positive possibilities of frontier folk by definition is a contradictory figure who exemplifies an important theme of the Old Southwest writers—backwoods civility. This theme is important because it dramatizes in comic ways a cultural nexus of ideas and feelings in the antebellum American mind: How is it that the physical wilderness of the continent evoked both the fears and hopes of society as it pursued its experiment with democracy? This theme of backwoods civility and its representative figure, the Roarer as Gentle Man, should be seen as the most portentous aspects of the Old Southwest comic tradition, for they are the fabric from which Sam Clemens tailors the early Nevada phase of the most famous literary persona that comically portrays the common man in the United States of the nineteenth-century, Mark Twain.

The Washoe version of Mark Twain, a combination of admirable wit and regrettably poor manners, follows in the tradition of the Roarer as Gentle Man, a figure worthy of satire's ridicule and humor's sympathy. Within the circumstances generated by Virginia City's urban yet mining-camp atmosphere, the Roarer for Clemens becomes the uncouth Comstock miner. Insofar as the Washoe Mark Twain and his sidekick, the Unreliable, parodied the behavior of a stereotypical ill-mannered miner, Clemens was elaborating the theme of backwoods civility so prominent in antebellum comic materials: Mark Twain as a character is comically uncouth yet humorously fallible and even shrewdly witty. In his newspaper persona, Clemens creates an ambiguously laughable portrait, one akin to that trio of comic colonels—Wildfire, Crockett, and Whetstone. However, because Mark Twain sheds a significant portion of the Roarer image exhibited by the colonels, Major Joseph Jones should be counted his nearest comic kin from the pens of the Old Southwest writers.

Notes

1. A good example of how old and firmly entrenched the false image of southern culture is can be found in an 1867 article entitled "The Poor Whites of the South," written by E.B. Seabrook. Critics who followed in Lynn's wake include Covici, McHaney, Ridgely, and Spengemann.

2. Eaton argued the Hundley position both before and after Lynn's and Covici's books on Mark Twain and the Old Southwest writers, and Merrill Skaggs elaborated the idea. See M. Thomas Inge for another critic who urges caution for generalizations about the Old Southwest writers. Owsley's book is the most detailed of the earlier scholarship. For two more recent overviews of historical scholarship on the subject, see Randolph B. Campbell and Lacy K. Ford. Tommy W. Rogers discusses Hundley's class analysis in sociological terms.

3. Albanese (1978), 230–31. For the publication information of *Narrative,* see Shackford and Folmsbee, ix–x. For publication of the almanacs, see Seeyle.

4. Cf. Cohen and Dillingham, who claim that the Roarer figure "provides the origins of old Southwestern humor" (xvi).

5. Despite the plausibility that actual circumstances added to the portrait of the typical keelboatmen being a Roarer, the image is almost assuredly more invented than real. Even contemporaries objected that the Backwoods Roarer was far from typical within the western population (see Blair 1960, 31). The process from actual frontiersman to emblematic backwoodsman, as much folkloric as literary, is discernible with Mike Fink. Blair and Meine

show how oral tales about Fink circulated during his lifetime, and after his death in 1823, how tales continued to be told as written accounts added to the image. See Gorn for quotes from travelers about the brutality of actual fights.

6. See letters #1 and #8 in Leonard Williams. Further references to the Whetstone letters use Williams's edition and will appear in the text.

7. Cf. Schmitz, ch. 2.

8. Noland shared this attitude with Longstreet and Thompson. Cf. Longstreet at the end of "The Fight" and Thompson in his preface to *Chronicles of Pineville*. Kibler's analysis of *Georgia Scenes* (1996) casts doubt on Longstreet's easy inclusion in Lynn's gentlemen category.

9. This scene approximates a situation Captain Meriweather Lewis encountered near St. Louis in 1803: see Ambrose, 122.

10. Fights and disputes are shown in Letters 7, 9, 13, 15, 19, 23, 40, 42, 49, 60, 63.

11. See pages 21–24 in Thompson (1844). Further references will hereafter appear in the text.

12. Thompson does have Jones identify Mary's family as "Washingtonians" (Letter 16), a reference to a temperance group of the 1840s. Of interest because vernacular speech is associated with the uneducated lower classes, the Washingtonian societies were largely composed of artisans of the lower and lower-middle classes (Tyrrell, ch. 7; Miller 272, n. 42). They were enormously successful for temperance efforts from 1840 to 1843 when William Tappan Thompson was writing the Major Jones letters.

13. Bartlett's *Dictionary of Americanisms* notes "dander" as scruff or dandruff and says the phrase "my dander was up" means to "get into a passion" (108). Bartlett's first quote for the phrase is from Crockett's *Down East Tour*; the third is from Thompson's *Courtship*. Clearly the phrase echoes Crockett's *Narrative* (73, 89), and the link of dander to scalp and hair suggests animal fur—perhaps more hints of Major Jones's link to the famous boast of the Roarer. In any case, the major's account of his fight reads more than a little like a tall-tale boast.

14. For drovers as a class, see McDonald and McWhiney. Owsley's groupings are as follows. Slaveholders are divided up into great planters with thousands of acres and hundreds of slaves; planters, with a thousand or fewer acres and scores of slaves; small planters, with about five hundred acres and ten to fifteen slaves; large farmers, with three to four hundred acres and five to ten slaves; and small farmers, with two hundred or fewer acres and one or two slaves. The nonslaveholding groups begin with large farmers who own two hundred to a thousand acres; farmers, with one to two hundred acres; small farmers, with fewer than one hundred acres; and finally renters or squatters who farm a very small acreage. The nonslaveholders plus small slaveholding farmers are the groups Owsley calls "plain folk" (8).

15. Gorn notes that dueling replaced the rough-and-tumble fight among upper-class men who wanted to distinguish themselves from their inferiors. See also Dickson Bruce. Thompson himself once refused to fight a duel (Osthaus).

Works Cited

Albanese, Catherine. 1978. "King Crockett: Nature and Civility on the American Frontier." *Proceedings of the American Antiquarian Society* 88 (Oct.): 230–31.

———. 1985. "Davy Crockett and the Wild Man; Or, the Metaphysics of the *Longue Durée*." 80–101 in Lofaro 1985.

Ambrose, Stephen J. 1996. *Undaunted Courage: Meriweather Lewis, Thomas Jefferson, and the Opening of the American West.* New York: Simon and Schuster.

Anderson, John Q. 1963. "Scholarship in Southwestern Humor—Past and Present." *Mississippi Quarterly* 17 (winter): 67–86.

Arpad, Joseph J. 1972. Introduction. *A Narrative of the Life of Colonel David Crockett.* New Haven, Conn.: College and University Press.

Barlett, John Russell. 1848 *A Dictionary of Americanisms.* New York: Barlett and Welford.

Bier, Jesse. 1968. "Southwestern Humor." 52–76 in *The Rise and Fall of American Humor.* New York: Holt, Rinehart, and Winston.

Blair, Walter. 1937. Rpt. with new material 1960. *Native American Humor*. New York: Harper and Row.

———. 1940. "Six Davy Crocketts." *Southwest Review* 25 (July): 443–62.

———. 1953. "Traditions in Southern Humor." *American Quarterly* 5 (summer): 132–42.

Blair, Walter and Hamlin Hill. 1978. *America's Humor: From Poor Richard to Doonesbury.* Oxford, UK: Oxford Univ. Press.

Blair, Walter and Franklin J. Meine. 1956. "Mike Fink in History, Legend, and Story." 3–40 in *Half Horse, Half Alligator: The Growth of the Mike Fink Legend.* Eds. Blair and Meine. Chicago: Univ. of Chicago Press.

Bruce, Dickson D., Jr. 1979. *Violence and Culture in the Antebellum South*. Austin: Univ. of Texas Press.

Campbell, Randolph B. 1987. "Planters and Plain Folks: The Social Structure of the Antebellum South." 48–77 in *Interpreting Southern History: Historiographical Essays in Honor of Sanford Higginbotham*. Eds. John B. Boles and Evelyn Thomas Nolen. Baton Rouge: Louisiana State Univ. Press.

Caron, James E. 1988. "Laughter, Politics, and the Yankee Doodle Legacy in America's Comic Tradition." *Thalia* 10: 3–13.

Cashin, Joan E. 1991. *A Family Venture: Men and Women on the Southern Frontier*. Oxford, UK: Oxford Univ. Press.

Chapman, John Gadsby. 1959. "A Legend at Full-Length: Mr. Chapman Paints Colonel Crockett—and Tells About It." Introduced by Curtis Carroll Davis. *Proceedings of the American Antiquarian Society* 69 (Oct.): 155–74.

Cohen, Hennig, and William B. Dillingham. 1994. Introduction. xv–xl in *Humor of the Old Southwest*. 3rd ed. Athens and London: Univ. of Georgia Press.

Cook, Sylvia Jenkins. 1976. "The Development of the Poor White Tradition." 3–17 in *From Tobacco Road to Route 66: The Southern Poor White in Fiction*. Chapel Hill: Univ. of North Carolina Press.

Covici, Pascal, Jr. 1962. *Mark Twain's Humor: The Image of a World.* Dallas: Southern Methodist Univ. Press.

Cox, James. 1973. "Humor of the Old Southwest." 101–12 in *The Comic Imagination in American Literature*. Ed. Louis D. Rubin Jr. New Brunswick, N.J.: Rutgers Univ. Press.

Crockett, David. 1834. Rpt. 1973. *A Narrative of the Life of Colonel David Crockett.* Facsimile ed. Knoxville: Univ. of Tennessee Press.

De Crèvecouer, Hector St. John. 1782. Rpt. 1945. "What is an American?" 39–86 in *Letters From an American Farmer.* Everyman's Library. London: J.M. Dent and Sons, Ltd.

Eaton, Clement. 1941. "The Humor of the Southern Yeoman." *Sewanee Review* 49: 173–83.

———. 1967. "The Southern Yeoman: The Humorists' View and the Reality." *The Mind of the South*. Rev. ed. Baton Rouge: Louisiana State Univ. Press.

Fellman, Michael. 1986. "Alligator Men and Cardsharpers: Deadly Southwestern Humor." *Huntington Library Quarterly* 49 (autumn): 307–23.

Fienberg, Lorne. 1984. "Laughter as a Strategy of Containment in Southwestern Humor." *Studies in American Humor* 3 [n.s.] (summer/fall): 107–22.

Ford, Lacy K. 1997. "Popular Ideology of the Old South's Plain Folk: The Limits of Egalitarianism in a Slaveholding Society." 205–27 in *Plain Folk of the South Revisited*. Ed. Samuel C. Hyde Jr. Baton Rouge: Louisiana State Univ. Press.

Gernes, Sonia. 1982. "Artists of Community: The Role of Storytellers in the Tales of the Southwest Humorists." *Journal of Popular Culture* 15 (spring): 114–28.

Gorn, Elliott J. 1985. "'Gouge and Bite, Pull Hair and Scratch': The Social Significance of Fighting in the Southern Backcountry." *American Historical Review* 90 (Feb.): 18–43.

Hauck, Richard Boyd. 1985. "The Man in the Buckskin Hunting Shirt: Fact and Fiction in the Crockett Story." 3–20 in Lofaro 1985.

Hundley, Daniel H. 1860. Rpt. 1973. *Social Relations in Our Southern States*. New York: Arno.

Inge, M. Thomas. 1975. Introduction. In *The Frontier Humorists: Critical Views*. Ed. M. Thomas Inge. Hamden, Conn.: Archon.

Jacobs, Robert D. 1980. "*Tobacco Road*: Lowlife and the Comic Tradition." 206–26 in *The American South: Portrait of a Culture*. Ed. Louis D. Rubin Jr. Baton Rouge: Louisiana State Univ. Press.

Kibler, James E., Jr. 1992. Introduction. *Georgia Scenes*. Nashville: J.S. Sanders.

Lemay, J.A. Leo. 1991. "The Origins of the Humor of the Old South." *Southern Literary Journal* 23 (spring): 3–13.

Lofaro, Michael A., ed. 1985. *Davy Crockett: The Man, The Legend, The Legacy, 1786–1986*. Knoxville: Univ. of Tennessee Press.

Longstreet, Augustus B. *Georgia Scenes*. 1835. Rpt. 1971. Facsimile ed. Atlanta: Cherokee.

Lynn, Kenneth S. 1959. Rpt. 1972. *Mark Twain and Southwestern Humor*. Westport, Conn.: Greenwood.

McDonald, Forrest and Grady McWhiney. 1975. Rpt. 1980. "The Antebellum Southern Herdman: A Reinterpretation." 119–37 in *The Southern Common People; Studies in Nineteenth-Century Social History*. Eds. Edward Magdol and Jon L. Wakelyn. Westport, Conn.: Greenwood.

McHaney, Thomas. 1985. "The Tradition of Southern Humor." *Chiba Review* 7: 51–72.

Miller, Henry Prentice. 1946. "The Background and Significance of *Major Jones's Courtship*." *Georgia Historical Quarterly* 30 (Dec.): 267–96.

Olmsted, Frederick Law. 1861. Rpt. 1953. *The Cotton Kingdom: A Traveller's Observations on Cotton and Slavery in the American Slave States*. New York: Knopf.

Osthaus, Carl R. 1976. "From the Old South to the New South: The Editorial Career of William Tappan Thompson of the *Savannah Morning News*." *Southern Quarterly* 14 (April): 237–60.

Owsley, Frank. 1949. *Plain Folk of the Old South*. Baton Rouge: Louisiana State Univ.

Paulding, James K. 1831. *The Lion of the West*. Rpt. 1954. *The Kentuckian, or, A Visit to New York*. Ed. and intro. James N. Tidwell. Stanford, Calif.: Stanford Univ. Press.

Pearson, Michael. 1986. "Pig Eaters, Whores, and Cowophiles: The Comic Image in Southern Literature." *Studies in Popular Culture* 9: 1–10.

Ridgely, J.V. 1980. "The Southern Way of Life: The 1830s and '40s." 50–61 in *Nineteenth-Century Southern Literature*. Lexington: Univ. Press of Kentucky.

Rogers, Tommy W. 1970. "D.R. Hundley: A Middle-Class Thesis of Social Stratifications in the Antebellum South." *Mississippi Quarterly* 23 (spring): 135–54.

Seabrook, E.B. 1867. "The Poor Whites of the South." *New York Galaxy* 6 (Oct.): 681–90.
Seeyle, John. 1985. "A Well-Wrought Crockett: Or, How the Fakelorists Passed through the Credibility Gap and Discovered Kentucky." [rev. vers.] 21–45 in Lofaro 1985.
Schmitz, Neil. 1983. *Of Huck and Alice: Humorous Writing in American Literature.* Minneapolis: Univ. of Minnesota Press.
Shackford, James A., and Stanley J. Folmsbee. 1973. Introduction. ix–xx in *A Narrative of the Life of David Crockett.* Annotated facsimile ed. Knoxville: Univ. of Tennessee Press.
Skaggs, Merrill Magire. 1972. "The Beginning: Southwest Humor." 25–35 in *The Folk of Southern Fiction.* Athens: Univ. of Georgia Press.
Smith, Henry Nash. 1962. *Mark Twain: Development of a Writer*. Cambridge, Mass.: Harvard Univ. Press.
Smith, Seba. 1859. *My Thirty Years Out of the Senate. By Major Jack Downing*. New York: Oaksmith.
Spengemann, William C. 1966. *Mark Twain and the Backwoods Angel: the Matter of Innocence in the Works of Samuel L. Clemens.* Kent, Ohio: Kent State Univ. Press.
Thompson, William Tappan. 1843. Rpt. 1969. *Major Jones's Chronicles of Pineville.* Facsimile ed. Upper Saddle River, N.J.: Gregg.
———. 1844. *Major Jones's Courtship*. 2nd ed., greatly enlarged. Philadelphia: Carey and Hart.
Tyrrell, Ian. 1979. *Sobering Up: From Temperance to Prohibition in Antebellum America, 1800–1860.* Westport, Conn.: Greenwood.
Watson, Richie Devon, Jr. 1993. "Southwest Humor, Plantation Fiction, and the Generic *Cordon Sanitaire.*" 56–69 in *Yeoman Versus Cavalier: The Old Southwest's Fictional Road to Rebellion.* Baton Rouge: Louisiana State Univ. Press.
Williams, Leonard. 1979. Introduction. 1–54 in *Cavorting on the Devil's Fork: The Pete Whetstone Letters of C.F.M. Noland.* Ed. Leonard Williams. Memphis, Tenn.: Memphis State Univ. Press.

12

Bench and Bar

Baldwin's Lawyerly Humor

Mary Ann Wimsatt

The time is more than ripe for a reassessment of the contributions that Joseph Glover Baldwin (1815–1864) made to the humor of the Old South and of his unique accomplishments in the field of southern or Southwestern humor. Despite a recent gentle upswing of interest in his writing, Baldwin remains the most neglected, and as a result the most unfairly underrated, of the antebellum southern humorists. Though generally grouped with A.B. Longstreet, T.B. Thorpe, W.T. Thompson, and G.W. Harris as one of the major writers in the mode, he is the only one on whom no standard scholarly book has yet been published, a fact that may help to explain the relative paucity of critical essays about him. His single volume of humor, *The Flush Times of Alabama and Mississippi* (1853), sold well; there were ten editions in the nineteenth century (Justus, "A Note on The Text"). It also earned him considerable contemporary acclaim: William Makepeace Thackeray, lecturing in America, remarked that Baldwin's essays "were of the right stuff," and Abraham Lincoln, no mean humorist himself, told Baldwin that "he slept with a copy . . . under his pillow" (Stewart 230, 379). What then accounts for the relative neglect into which *Flush Times* has fallen?

The answer to this question is not difficult to find. It is rooted in the changing nature of nineteenth- and twentieth-century interpretive communities, which, at least where scholarly study of the humorists is concerned, has with some exceptions increasingly worked to Baldwin's disadvantage. A chronological sampling of commentary on Southwest humor and Baldwin in particular makes the situation plain at the same time that it reveals Baldwin's distinctive gifts, which critics have either appreciated or decried. Of all the Southwest humorists, Baldwin, whose models included Joseph Addison, Oliver Goldsmith, and Charles Lamb, shows the greatest preference for the patrician voice and the essay mode; and of them all, he is the one least given to scenes of violence, bawdry, and grotesquerie. Critics and reviewers near Baldwin's time, who were perhaps more attuned to his methods than we are, understood and valued his procedure: as already indicated, *Flush Times* made its debut to an almost universal chorus of praise. It was warmly commended in the influential *Southern Quarterly Review* in a notice probably written by the editor, William Gilmore Simms, a renowned author who was both highly knowledgeable about Southwestern humor and a noteworthy contributor to the mode. In the volume for April 1854, Simms styles *Flush Times* "[f]ull of fun and spirit; a lively picture of the salient and racy, in a rough unsophisticated society." "But," Simms observes in a comment that later reviewers would echo, the work is "not all fun. The author gives us some really brilliant sketches of prominent persons, and shows himself capable of an excellent analysis of character" (555). A writer for the *North American Review* similarly praised the volume, calling *Flush Times* "a series of pictures, for the most part intensely comic, yet hardly overdrawn, of life and manners in the Southwest, when . . . that region was new and manners in the Chesterfieldian sense were not" (266). And a reviewer for *Graham's Magazine*, commending both content and style, called *Flush Times* "a brilliant book. . . . full of acuteness, animation, humor and vigor. The writer, while he excels in the broadest and most rollicking fun, and loves for the mirth of the thing, to push character to the verge of caricature, is an analyst as well as a humorist. . . . The interest of the sketches, is enhanced by the peculiar elasticity of the style. There is an off-hand elegance, a reckless grace, a dashing, daring, defiant sportiveness in the movement of the sentences, very captivating to the reader" (Moses 236).

After Baldwin's death, *Flush Times* continued to garner acclaim. His former law partner T.B. Wetmore observed that Baldwin "wrote as he talked" and that the "result of this great capacity of his to form without effort his sentences" was "to render all that he said enjoyable without having to be studied" (69). Attorney Reuben Davis, in *Recollections of Mississippi and Mississippians*, praises Baldwin as a lawyer and calls *Flush Times* "a book replete with the richest anecdote and unsurpassed humor" (63). George Frederick Mellen, writing in *The Sewanee Review* at the turn of the century, remarks that *Flush Times* has "not a dull or commonplace page" in it, commends its "excellence and variety of rich humor," and insists, in phrases twentieth-century readers would do well to remember, that in "the or[i]ginality of its characters and scenes and in the excellence of its style and narrative, it is worthy to rank with Longstreet's 'Georgia Scenes' and Thompson's 'Major Jones's Courtship,' as a faithful transcript of past conditions" (179, 180).

Similar praise continued into the early twentieth century. Montrose J. Moses, for example, in *The Literature of the South* (1910) deplored the fact that certain antebellum southern humorists "sink into low wit based upon rough, uncouth falsification of incident and character." Absolving *Flush Times* of this practice, Moses remarks that "even though it is comical, it is also true; even though it is rollicking, it is not irreverent." He praises Baldwin's "exceptional" characterizations, says beneath "the crust of external peculiarity lies the rich substratum of social history," and maintains that Baldwin "saw fully, and he laughed with effect" (230, 231, 232). And in the influential *Cambridge History of American Literature*, issued during World War I, Will D. Howe, after treating the work of Longstreet, Thompson, Johnson Jones Hooper, and others, declares that *Flush Times* was "[p]erhaps the most significant volume of humour by a Southerner before the Civil War." Howe accurately notes that, although "chiefly concerned with the Flush-time bar, Baldwin described as well most of the sharpers, boasters, liars, spread-eagle orators," and others "in the newly rich and rapidly filling South," and observes that "unlike some of the books" of the time, *Flush Times* "does not degenerate into mere horse-play or farce" (I, 153–54).

But with the increasing dominance of realism as a literary mode, and the related emergence of twentieth-century interpretive communities that value dialect, horseplay, and bawdy comedy in Southwest humor over polished manner and elegant diction, critics began to find some fault with the manner that Baldwin had deliberately set about to create. Walter Blair, for example, whose *Native American Humor* (1937) set the tone for many later studies, seems to have misunderstood or undervalued Baldwin's aims—at least to some degree. Though Blair observes that Baldwin is "a highly readable contemporary historian," he complains that Baldwin "is influenced by the older essay style" and finds the writing in *Flush Times* "at times too leisurely, too polished, for an account of the brisk frontier" (78, 79). Jay B. Hubbell in *The South in American Literature* (1954) likewise sees some difficulties in Baldwin's manner—"[T]he dialogue is scanty and the digressions are numerous"—but commends his "gusto, whimsy, and keen eye for incongruity" (676). Recent surveys of Baldwin's work tend to echo the strictures of Blair and Hubbell. Thus in *Fifty Southern Writers Before 1900,* (1987), the author of the essay on Baldwin, while attributing merit to his work, claims that he fails to achieve "the racy vigor that characterizes some of the best Southwestern humorists" (Moseley 31).

Until lately, the twentieth-century voices raised in Baldwin's favor have praised his work because it advances a certain view of American politics and culture. Notable here is Kenneth Lynn, who in *The Comic Tradition in America* (1958) observes that the Virginia-born Baldwin saw and experienced "the gulf separating the ideal of the Declaration of Independence from the reality of life in the American Southwest," where the legal profession was riddled with "chicanery, fraud, bribery, corruption of judges and juries, the fixing of evidence," and other crimes. Lynn also says that in *Flush Times,* Baldwin "satirizes this social chaos in an attempt to impose a coherence upon it, to accommodate raw, wide-open Mississippi to the social structure and the cultural traditions of the Old Dominion. Written in a vocabulary of considerable elegance and in a highly finished style, the book effectively marks off the author from his material, thereby defining his superiority" to the seedy operators with whom he was forced to associate (193, 194). Lynn takes this argument further in *Mark Twain and Southwestern Humor* (1960). Here he pits the generic Whig conservative against what he calls the Democratic Clown and employs Baldwin as the type of educated, polished, anti-Jacksonian Whig who tried to stem the viciousness and ignorance made possible by Jacksonian democracy. With "the fluency of his style and the elegance of his wit," Baldwin, says Lynn, "spoke with an unusual eloquence" and thereby helped to stage "the most urbane comedy in the history of the Southwestern tradition" (115).

In Lynn's view it is therefore no accident that Baldwin's patrician voice dominates *Flush Times.* For implicit in the volume, despite its comedy, "are a vigorous defense of the planter aristocracy's achievement in stabilizing a lawless and violent society and a warning to all the gentleman of America as to what sort of people would come to power in the South if outside interference should succeed in overturning the *status quo*." Hence in *Flush Times*, "the vernacular is seldom allowed to muddy a prose the incontestable gentlemanliness of which was so vital to the argument that Baldwin was advancing." Through his patrician manner, Baldwin makes "the 'I' who is the historian of the *Flush Times* a strongly felt and unmistakable presence. To this Self-controlled Gentleman, the style everywhere implies, went all the credit for saving the Southwest, and by extension the nation, from anarchy" (*Mark Twain* 118, 119, 120).

Lynn's analyses accurately describe Baldwin's literary methods while indicating his intense dislike of the social, moral, and economic chaos that Jackson's financial practices unleashed. To understand the bases of Baldwin's attitudes, it is necessary to glance briefly at the background and experiences of Baldwin himself. He was born into a good family in Winchester, Virginia, and was ably trained in law. But because there was a superabundance of legal talent in the state, at age twenty-one he moved to the trans-Appalachian frontier—urged, he would later waggishly remark, "'by hunger and request of friends'" (*Flush Times* 47). In Mississippi and Alabama he made a considerable name for himself as lawyer and politician; and in the early 1850s, his reputation secure, he began sending humorous sketches of his youthful days in the region to *The Southern Literary Messenger*. The editor, John R. Thompson, urged him to collect the sketches in book form. Tellingly, the resulting volume is dedicated "To 'The Old Folks at Home,' My Friends In the Valley of the Shenandoah," revealing that Baldwin had not lost his Virginia allegiances. More tellingly, perhaps, at least for certain portions of the book, is Baldwin's outright disdain for President Andrew Jackson and his fiscal policy.

To some extent Baldwin's attitude towards Jackson was linked to his Whig support for the patrician South, to his fervent belief in states' rights, and to his dislike of the United States Bank (Stewart, Ch. 4). But when Jackson, who likewise opposed the bank, ordered in his second term that government funds from it be withdrawn and deposited in state banks, Baldwin, like other fiscal conservatives, grew concerned. In language appropriate to his dismay, he rightly observed that the state banks were "shin-plaster concerns that had sprung up, like frog-stools, all over the Union" (*Party Leaders* 337). And he saw that Jackson's moves enabled the state banks to indulge in orgies of imprudent practices—for example, printing far more paper money than was justified by their specie or coin reserves. After the alarmed president issued the Specie Circular in 1836, state banks, unable to meet the demand for specie, closed; and the following year saw the recession known as the Panic of 1837, which would have far-reaching consequences for the country and many of its citizens.

Baldwin described and condemned this economic chaos in some of the most memorable passages in *Flush Times*. In essay after essay, he scathingly denounces the ills he felt Jackson had brought upon the country—paper money, an unstable economic climate, and the general havoc wrought by uncontrolled financial speculation. His book opens with ironic condemnations of the "history of that halcyon period, ranging from the year of Grace, 1835, to 1837; when bank-bills were 'as thick as Autumn leaves in Vallambrosa' and credit was a franchise" ([1]). Somewhat later in the book, in sentences dripping with sarcasm, Baldwin styles the flush times "the era of the second great experiment of independence: the experiment, namely, of credit without capital, and enterprise without honesty"; when "[l]ots in obscure villages were held at city prices; lands, bought at the minimum cost of government, were sold at from thirty to forty dollars per acre, and considered dirt cheap at that"; and when, in sum, "the country had got to be a full ante-type of California, in all except the gold." Financial and social ethics vanished; "[s]ociety was wholly unorganized: there was no restraining public opinion: the law was well-nigh powerless." In consequence, the "man of straw, not worth the buttons on his shirt, with a sublime audacity, bought lands and negroes, and provided times and terms of payment which a Wall-street capitalist would have had to re-cast his arrangements to meet" (81, 83–84, 86).

Small wonder that when Andrew Jackson, the "Jupiter Tonans of the White House," saw "the monster of a free credit prowling about like a beast of apocalyptic vision, and marked him for his prey" that "the Specie Circular was issued without warning, and the splendid lie of a false credit burst into fragments." Confirming Lynn's remarks, Baldwin claims that the much-heralded flush times actually constituted in economic terms "the reign of humbug, and wholesale insanity, just overthrown in time to save the whole country from ruin." Using vivid personifications to enforce his point, he charges that the "old rules of business and the calculations of prudence were alike disregarded, and profligacy, in all the departments of the *crimen falsi*, held riotous carnival. Larceny grew not only respectable but genteel, and ruffled it in all the pomp of purple and fine linen. Swindling was raised to the dignity of the fine arts. Felony came forth from its covert, put on more seemly habiliments, and took its seat with unabashed front in the upper places of the synagogue" (90, 91, 85).

Baldwin discusses some very unpretty results of this general economic havoc in an essay entitled "The Bar of the South-West." He admits that he distrusts the moral influence of the new region upon those who emigrated there: many were "mere gold-diggers"; nearly all were speculators or traders. The litigation growing out of land claims furnished field for unbridled speculation. "[M]any land titles were defective; property was brought from other States clogged with trusts, limitations, and uses, to be construed according to the laws of the State from which it was brought; claims and contracts made elsewhere [were] to be enforced here; . . hard and ruinous bargains; . . an elegant assortment of frauds constructive and actual . . . in short, all the flood-gates of litigation were opened and the pent-up tides let loose upon the country" (236, 237). Then, in memorable dramatic fashion, Baldwin unleashes a torrent of scathing rhetoric at practices he considers intolerable:

> What country could boast more largely of its crimes? What more splendid rôle of felonies! What more terrific murders! What more gorgeous bank robberies! . . . Such superb forays on the treasuries, State and National! . . . Such flourishes of rhetoric on ledgers auspicious of gold

> which had departed for ever from the vault! And in INDIAN affairs! . . . What sublime conceptions of super-Spartan roguery! Swindling Indians by the nation! . . . Stealing their land by the township! . . . Conducting the nation to the Mississippi river, stripping them to the flap, and bidding them God speed as they went howling into the Western wilderness. (238)

In much the same vein, Baldwin demonstrates in his essay "The Bench and the Bar" how sham counselors and their equally sham clients manipulate the law through ignorance and chicanery. Quoting *Othello*, "Chaos had come again," he remarks, "or rather, had never gone away. Order, Heaven's first law, seemed unwilling to remain where there was no other law to keep it company." Older lawyers appear to think "that judicature was a tanyard—clients skins to be curried—the court the mill . . . the idea that justice had any thing to do with trying causes, or sense had any thing to do with legal practices, never seemed to occur to them once, as a possible conception." Younger ones could "'entangle justice in such a web of law,' that the blind hussey could never have found her way out again" (53, 55, 61). Things, in short, were considerably less than desirable to one schooled in the ethics and traditions of the Old Dominion and in essentially eighteenth-century notions of law and politics (Grammer 137).

Elsewhere in *Flush Times*, Baldwin employs his urbane manner to describe honest backwoods clients as well as sharpsters, rogues, and dupes, in the process offering crisp sketches of anomalous legal proceedings involving himself and others. In "My First Appearance at the Bar," he portrays himself as a fledgling attorney who finds himself haplessly in charge of a case because the original attorney, Frank Glendye, had been "suddenly taken dangerously drunk" (21). The principals in the case are a farmer, Caleb Swink, who has accused a butcher, Stephen Higginbotham, of stealing hogs. Baldwin derives considerable merriment from the incongruities inherent in the situation by alternating pungent dialect and cultivated legal phrasing:

> [S]hortly after I obtained license to practise law in the town of H———, State of Alabama, an unfortunate client called at my office to retain my services in a celebrated suit for slander. The case stands on record, *Stephen O. Higginbotham* vs. *Caleb Swink*. The aforesaid Caleb, "greatly envying the happy state and condition of said Stephen," . . . said, "in the hearing and presence of one Samuel Eads and other good and worthy citizens," . . . "you" (the said Stephen meaning) "are a noted hog thief, and stole more hogs than all the wagons in M——— could haul off in a week on a turnpike road." (20)

In the absence of Glendye, Higginbotham asks Baldwin to defend him, and Baldwin, though concerned about his relative inexperience, takes on the case.

The opposing lawyer is the elderly, renowned, and splenetic Caesar Kasm, known for his dislike of new laws, books, and men. Kasm, Baldwin notes, "had a talent for vituperation which would have gained him distinction" in any theater; when "he argued a case, you would suppose he had bursted his gall-bag"; therefore, it is with good reason that the younger lawyers have styled him "Sar Kasm." Before describing his encounter with Kasm, Baldwin conscientiously describes his own greenness: "My conscience—I had not practised it away then—was not quite easy. I couldn't help feeling that it was hardly honest to be leading my client, like Falstaff his men, where he was sure to be peppered. But then it was my only chance; my bread depended on it" (25, 27, 28).

Baldwin then admits that had he modestly acknowledged his inexperience he might have fared better at Kasm's hands. "But the evil genius that presides over the first bantlings of all lawyerlings, would have it otherwise." Fancy got the better of judgment; "[a]rgument and common sense grew tame"; Baldwin waxed poetic, pathetic, and plethoric. "I spoke of the woful sufferings of my poor client, almost heart-broken beneath the weight of the terrible persecutions of his enemy: and, growing bolder, I turned on old Kasm, and congratulated the jury that the genius of slander had found an appropriate defender in the genius of chicane and malignity." Kasm, understandably furious, demolishes Baldwin's "'flatulent bombast and florid trash'" and then mocks Baldwin, Higginbotham, and Higginbotham's occupation: "There was something exquisite in [Baldwin's] picture of the woes, the wasting grief of his disconsolate client, the butcher Higginbotham"—who, Kasm charges, far from wasting away, "weighs twelve stone *now!* He has three inches of fat on his ribs this minute! He would make as many links of sausage as any hog that ever squealed . . . and has lard enough in him to cook it all" (31, 32, 35, 37–38). Not surprisingly, Baldwin loses the case. He flees to Natchez, where he eventually learns that Glendye, finally sober, had got a new trial that Higginbotham had won. But, concluding the essay with tongue in cheek, Baldwin observes: "Reader! I eschewed *genius* from that day. I took to accounts; did up every species of paper that came into my office with a tape string . . . read law, to fit imaginary cases, with great industry; dunned one of the wealthiest men in the city for fifty cents . . . associated only with skin-flints . . . and thus, by this course of things, am able to write from *my sugar plantation*, this memorable history of the fall of *genius* and the rise of solemn humbug!" (45–46)

Several essays in *Flush Times* that are usually either labeled social history or dismissed as mere character sketches actually serve as launching pads for humorous anecdotes. In "The Bench and the Bar," for example, Baldwin describes the mishaps of a schoolmaster who, shot in the buttocks, claps his hands on the afflicted place while "bellowing out that the murderer had blown out his brains" (65). And in "An Affair of Honor," he demonstrates how rustic characters employ the patrician custom of dueling to ludicrous effect. The essay centers on boastful, cowardly Jonas Sykes and "quiet, demure" Samuel Mooney. Jonas, being drunk, sees fit to denounce Mooney's "liver, soul and eyes." Mooney, says Baldwin, "stood it for some time, but at length, like a terrapin with coals on his back . . . began to retort." Sykes challenges him to a duel, but when Mooney strikes a button off of Sykes's drawers and cuts his skin, the coward falls, shouting "Murder! Murder! he's knocked off all the lower part of my ab*do*men. . . . Oh! Lordy! Oh! Lordy!" (193, 195).

Aside from "Ovid Bolus" and "Cave Burton," two essays that have attracted a considerable amount of commentary, the two pieces in *Flush Times* that perhaps best repay detailed analysis indicate Baldwin's knowledge of, and his intertextual connections with, characters and situations prominent in the humor of the time. The first of these essays, "Simon Suggs, Jr., Esq.; A Legal Biography," pays tribute to the famous creation of Baldwin's friend and fellow Southwesterner Johnson Jones Hooper, whose *Adventures of Captain Simon Suggs* (1845) had become one of the most celebrated works of southern humor. The other, "Justification After Verdict," gives some unexpected twists to the well-known topic of the greenhorn in the city.

To relish the skill and wit of Baldwin's Suggs essay it is necessary to glance at Hooper's book. *Adventures of Captain Simon Suggs* is a mock campaign biography that parodies the political biographies of Andrew Jackson and others both in its exceedingly pompous rhetoric and in its portrayal of one of southern humor's most famous scoundrels as a candidate for public office. For the work, Hooper creates an obsequious, wordy, and pretentious authorial persona who describes in elevated phrasing the difficulties of his task: "It is not often that the living worthy furnishes a theme for the biographer's pen. The pious task of commemorating the acts, and depicting the character of the great or good is generally and properly deferred until they are past blushing, or swearing—constrained to a decorous behaviour by the folds of their cerements" (7). Hooper then proceeds to contrast both Suggs's deeds and Suggs's language with the author's. After filling his mother's pipe with gunpowder, for instance, Suggs muses, "that he'll 'be damned if it didn't blow the old woman within a foot, or a foot and a half of kingdom come.'" The author notes that some people think Suggs will not escape "the clutches of the old gentleman with the cloven hoof" for such an act and then observes, "On this point, *we*, of course, have nothing to say. . . . On so delicate a question, propriety will barely allow us the single remark, that should the Captain fail to slip past St. Peter, none but the 'duly qualified' need thereafter attempt to effect an entrance" (31–32).

In "Simon Suggs, Jr.," Baldwin cleverly imitates both the language and the characterization of Hooper's masterpiece. Beginning in the epistolary mode, he creates a pretentious editor who has "established, at great expense, and from motives purely patriotic and disinterested, a monthly periodical for . . . the commemoration and perpetuation of the names, characters, and personal and professional traits and histories of American lawyers and jurists." After telling Suggs Jr. "that such true merit as yours might find a motive for your enrolment [*sic*] among the known sages and profound intellects of the land," the editor inquires, "May we rely upon your sending us the necessary papers, viz., a sketch of your life, genius, exploits, successes, accomplishments, virtues, family antecedents, personal pulchritude, professional habitudes, and whatever else you deem interesting" and also "a good daguerreotype likeness of yourself[?]" *(Flush Times* 114, 116, 117) To this language Baldwin carefully counterpoints the salty dialect of Suggs's reply:

Dear Sir—I got your letter dated l8 Nov., asking me to send you my life and karackter for your Journal. Im obleeged to you for your perlite say so, and so forth. I got a friend to rite it—my own riting being mostly perfeshunal. He done it—but he rites such a cussed bad hand I cant rede it: I reckon its all korrect tho'. As to my doggerrytype I cant sent it there aint any doggerytype man about here now. . . . You can take father's picter on Jonce Hooper's book —take off the bend in the back, and about twenty years of age off en it . . . and it'll suit me but dress it up gentele in store close. (118–19)

The editor thanks Suggs for the sketch but adds: "We fear . . . the suggestion you made of the use of the engraving of your distinguished father will not avail; as the author, Mr. Hooper, has copyrighted his work." Then, in a postscript that reveals his true intentions, the editor observes, "Our delicacy caused us to omit, in our former letter, to mention what we suppose was generally understood, viz., the fact that the cost to us of preparing engravings, &c., &c., for the sketches or memoirs is one hundred and fifty dollars, which sum it is expected, of course, the gentleman who is perpetuated in our work, will forward to us before the insertion of his biography." To this postscript Suggs Jr. craftily rejoins: "*Dear Mr. Editor*—In your p.s. which seems to be the creem of your correspondents you say I can't get in your book without paying one hundred and fifty dollars. . . . I believe I will pass. . . Jewhillikens!" (119, 120).

Still using the editorial persona, Baldwin then appends a biography of Suggs Jr., inflating the bombast even more than Hooper's to make his parodic purposes clear. The editor either describes Suggs's misdoings in gilded rhetoric or explains them away as youthful pranks. At school, for instance, the incorrigible Simon receives numerous "flagellations and cuffings" from the schoolmaster that lead him to retaliate, in a manner reminiscent of the gunpowder prank in Hooper, by blowing off one ear and three fingers of the man's hand. Forced to leave school, Suggs Jr. obtains a law license in settlement of a debt, forges his name to it, presents it to the court, "and was duly admitted an attorney and counsellor at law and solicitor in chancery." In important cases, "he always managed to have his friends in the court room, so that when any of the jurors were challenged, he might have their places filled by good men and true." In comparably tricky fashion, by "the most insinuating manners," Suggs persuades his landlady to divorce her husband and then marries her himself, in the process gaining money by appropriating her property. He extricates a client from a forfeiture "by having the defaulting defendant's obituary notice somewhat prematurely inserted in the newspapers," and he similarly saves another client from the death sentence by pretending he is dead and then smuggling him out of prison in a coffin (125, 133, 136, 135, 139). If imitation is indeed the sincerest form of flattery, then Baldwin paid Hooper high compliment by his portrait of Simon Suggs's inimitable son.

"Justification After Verdict," one of the most memorable narratives in *Flush*

Times, uses to great advantage the time-honored motifs of the greenhorn in the city, the gull duped by the sharpster, and the bumpkin bemused by polite social customs. At the beginning of the narrative, Baldwin is retained by the defendant, Paul Beechim, who has unaccountably caned his erstwhile friend Phillip Cousins in the public square while demanding "'How d—n you, how do you like *that* pine-apple sop?'" (178) Beechim refuses to divulge the facts of the case, but the highly inquisitive judge, struck by the phrase "'pine-apple sop,'" encourages Baldwin to unravel the mystery. In doing so, Baldwin reveals that Beechim, who had previously lived in Knoxville, Tennessee, considers what Baldwin describes as that "out-of-the-way, not-to-be-gotten-to, Sleepy-Hollow town" the "Athens and Paris of America" by which all social behavior is to be judged (185, 184). After moving to the Southwest, Beechim accompanies his friend Phillip Cousins to New Orleans. When Beechim worries that his manners may be rusty, Cousins, who knows the city well, offers to act as cicerone, thus setting the stage for the climactic incident.

At dinner in the hotel, Beechim has just put a piece of pineapple onto his plate when the waiter places "a green-colored bowl before every guest's plate with water and a small slice of lemon in it." Beechim asks Cousins what it is, and the waggish Cousins replies that it is "'Sop for the pine-apple.'" Claiming, "'That's the way it used to be served . . . in Knoxville," Beechim "took the bowl and put it in his plate, and then put the pine-apple into the bowl, and commenced cutting up the apple, . . and ate it, piece after piece" while people on either side of the table stare at him in wonder. Cousins asks Beechim "'how he liked the pine-apple?'" and Beechim replies, "'I think the pine-apple very good, but don't you think the sauce is rather insipid?'" Immoderate laughter ensues, and an Englishman informs Beechim that he "'had been making an ass of himself—he had been eating out of the finger-bowl'" (188, 189). The chagrined Beechim returns home, and when next he sees Cousins licks him "'within an inch of his life with a hickory stick'." (189) The judge, absorbed in the story, unexpectedly announces, "'Yes . . . and served him right. Justification complete!'. . . . Most men would have seized their gun, or bowie, . . . but this young gentleman has set an example which older heads might well copy: he has contented himself with taking a club and giving [Cousins] a good, sound, constitutional, conservative licking" (190–91). Thus the "justification" ("a good, sound, constitutional, conservative licking") follows the verdict that Beechim's behavior has "served [Cousins] right."

With reference to an author's literary aims and intentions, Simms once astutely observed, "Just criticism should be intrinsic, not comparative," and a review of Baldwin's procedures in *Flush Times* supports Simms's statement (*Letters* I, 88). Too many twentieth-century critics nourished on the "Big Bear" school of humor have blamed Baldwin for doing the very thing he set out to do: to enclose vernacular dialect and portray questionable legal proceedings in the Old Southwest within his own amused, aloof, and elegant language in order to assert the superiority of civilized over frontier values. Two late twentieth-century critics analyze and commend what Baldwin attempted to accomplish. In the introduction to his edition of *Flush*

Times, James Justus praises Baldwin's "Tidewater urbanity," which "makes his narrating voice one of the most cultivated of the era," and observes that critics who view this voice as anomalous overlook the fact that "Big Bears are not the only inhabitants of the literary Southwest, and neither are their rhetorical fireworks the stylistic norm" (xxxiii, xxxvii). And John Grammer rightly commends Baldwin's balanced, ironic manner; chastises critics who, "valuing frontier humor according to the amount of space it concedes to vernacular speech, have found this voice to be the major flaw in Baldwin's work"; and insists that with its "unfailingly urbane" tone, Baldwin's "is the most distinctive narrative voice in the tradition of southwestern humor" (145). Such comments suggest that discriminating students of Southwestern humor may eventually achieve a sensible revaluation of Baldwin that is based on the author's own standards for his work. For Baldwin's creation of his narrative persona, with its elegance, its sophisticated allusiveness, and its ironic condemnation of the sham, fraud, and crimes found on the frontier is an accomplishment of which his sympathetic readers can deservedly be proud.

Works Cited

Baldwin, Joseph Glover. *The Flush Times of Alabama and Mississippi. A Series of Sketches.* New York: D. Appleton, 1853. Rpt. ed. James H. Justus. Baton Rouge: Louisiana State Univ. Press, 1987.

———. *Party Leaders.* New York: D. Appleton, 1854.

Blair, Walter. *Native American Humor (1800–1900).* New York: American Book Co., 1937. Rev. ed. New York: Harper and Row, 1960.

Davis, Reuben. *Recollections of Mississippi and Mississippians.* Boston: Houghton Mifflin, 1889.

Grammer, John M. *Pastoral and Politics in the Old South.* Baton Rouge: Louisiana State Univ. Press, 1996.

Hooper, Johnson Jones. *Adventures of Captain Simon Suggs.* Philadelphia: Carey and Hart, 1845. Rpt. with intro. by Johanna Nicol Shields. Tuscaloosa: Univ. of Alabama Press, 1993.

Howe, Will D. "Early Humorists." *The Cambridge History of American Literature.* Ed. William Peterfield Trent et al. 4 vols. New York: G.P. Putnam's Sons, 1918.

Hubbell, Jay B. *The South in American Literature 1607–1900.* Durham, N.C.: Duke Univ. Press, 1954.

Lynn, Kenneth, ed. *The Comic Tradition in America.* Garden City, N.Y.: Doubleday, 1958.

———. *Mark Twain and Southwestern Humor.* Boston: Little, Brown, 1960. Rpt. Westport, Conn..: Greenwood, 1972.

Mellen, George Frederick. "Joseph G. Baldwin and the 'Flush Times';" *The Sewanee Review* 9 (April 1901): 171–184.

Moseley, Merritt W., Jr. *Fifty Southern Authors Before 1900.* Eds. Robert Bain and Joseph M. Flora. New York: Greenwood, 1987.

Moses, Montrose J. *The Literature of the South.* New York: Thomas Y. Crowell, 1910.

Review of *The Flush Times of Alabama and Mississippi. Graham's Magazine* 44 (Feb. 1854): 236.

Review of *The Flush Times of Alabama and Mississippi* and *Party Leaders. North American Review* 80 (Jan. 1855): 266.

[Simms, William Gilmore.] Review of *The Flush Times of Alabama and Mississippi*. *The Southern Quarterly Review* 25 (April 1854): 555.

Simms, William Gilmore, *The Letters of William Gilmore Simms*, Eds. Mary C. Simms Oliphant, Alfred Taylor Odell, and T.C. Duncan Eaves. 5 vols. Columbia: Univ. of South Carolina Press, 1952–1956. Vol. 6, eds. Mary C. Simms Oliphant and T.C. Duncan Eaves. Columbia: Univ. of South Carolina Press, 1982.

Stewart, Samuel Boyd. *Joseph Glover Baldwin*. Diss. Vanderbilt University, 1941.

Wetmore, Thomas Badger. "Joseph Glover Baldwin." *Transactions of the Alabama Historical Society* 2 (1897–1898): 67–73.

13

The Good Doctor

O.B. Mayer and "Human Natur'"

Edwin T. Arnold

Medical doctors make for good humorists, and why not? They see their fellows as patients, in the most pathetic and abject of circumstances, weak and ailing, begging or bargaining for ease, well-being, escape from death. We shed our clothes and our pretensions for doctors and allow them, engage them, to probe and peer into the most private of recesses, both physical and psychic. Naked, we tell them the secrets and fears kept hidden from others. Moreover, doctors, if they are blessed with self-awareness, recognize how tenuous and temporary their position of authority is, realize that time and physiological inevitability will one day make patients of them all as well.

How they react to this knowledge can be telling. Someone like Henry Clay Lewis, the Louisiana frontier doctor who wrote sketches under the pen name of "Madison Tensas" in the mid-nineteenth century, revealed his fear and despair by creating scenes of outlandish cruelty and grotesquerie: his works are darkly funny in the most awful fashion, as he recounts scenes of intense physical suffering, often inflicted by the doctor himself. Disease was for him an image of the ugliness and outrageousness of life, and grinning death was always at the doctor's elbow. Others develop a more accepting view and achieve a kind of genial comedic understanding, albeit often touched by pensive melancholy: Anton Chekhov comes to mind. It is among these physician-humorists that we might situate Orlando Benedict Mayer, the doctor of the old Dutch Fork area of upland South Carolina. As Mayer scholars James E. Kibler Jr. and Edward J. Piacentino have observed, "Mayer's love of humanity is never in doubt. As a physician, he was always praised for his kind-heartedness, patience, and unselfishness, and these qualities show through his warm humor" (Kibler and Piacentino 317). Largely unknown today, despite recent publications of his nineteenth-century writings, O.B. Mayer offers us rare glimpses at a forgotten world as found in this antebellum German settlement. Drawing on such writers as Henry Fielding, Jonathan Swift, Laurence Sterne, and Washington Irving, as well as southern frontier humorists such as A.B. Longstreet, Johnson Jones Hooper, and William Tappan Thompson, Mayer created his own small universe: an isolated community, drawn with both affection and satire, that exists on its own terms, speaks its own language, follows its own customs, and yet unerringly reflects the world of its outside readers. The Dutch Fork can be found on the same map as Frenchman's Bend, Mississippi; Dogpatch, Kentucky; and Stay More, Arkansas, the fictive landscapes of William Faulkner, Al Capp, and Donald Harington. And, like these places, the Dutch Fork provides an intriguing mixture of the actual and the imaginative.

The real O.B. Mayer and the real Dutch Fork have been carefully exhumed and examined largely through the scholarly work of Kibler, who has seen to it that the majority of Mayer's significant writing is now in print, and Piacentino, who has argued strongly for a greater appreciation of these writings.[1] As both scholars have related, Mayer was born (in 1818) and raised in a part of South Carolina settled in the mid-eighteenth century by a group of German and Swiss Protestants, a "Teutonic island" situated some thirty miles in distance from the state capital of Columbia but much farther in custom, dress, language, and superstition from its largely English or Scotch-Irish neighbors.[2] In the first of his "historical" sketches of the Dutch (*Deutsch*) Fork, written near the end of his life for publication in the local *Newberry Herald and News*, Mayer recalled, "Here, the offspring of the pioneer settlers went to school, learning the same lessons, and prattling in the same language as did the children away over in the Fatherland" (*Dutch Fork* 4). During Mayer's childhood, however, the settlement changed, and English became the language selected for both church and school, although the older people especially might still use German in their everyday conversations. Indeed, much of Mayer's comedic success comes from his representation of community elders speaking heavily accented English or switching from one language to another in attempts to express their (often exasperated) feelings. Although we probably should allow for humorous exaggeration, Mayer constantly maintains that he will "endeavor to imitate" or "respectfully attempt to imitate" (*Punterick* 38, 13) the language of his people without mocking them in the process.

Mayer wrote about the Dutch Fork primarily in three ways. He first made it the setting for a series of tales produced largely during the 1840s and 1850s. He then examined the fictional place in greater detail in his novel *John Punterick*, written sometime around 1860; and finally he returned to the old Dutch Fork in a series of newspaper sketches and reminiscences intended to record for later generations his memories of this unusual and bygone world.

A number of the humorous tales were initially published in the *Columbia South Carolinian*, "a weekly agricultural newspaper" edited by Mayer's friend Adam G. Summer and modeled to some extent on William T. Porter's *Spirit of the Times* (Kibler and Piacentino 316). Kibler collected five of Mayer's works in his volume *Fireside Tales: Stories of the Old Dutch Fork*. Four of these—"The Innocent Cause," "Snip," "The Easter Eggs," and "The Corn Cob Pipe"—were first written in the late 1840s under the pseudonym "Obadiah Haggis" (Mayer revised the last two for additional publication later in his career). Each of these stories deals with the major themes of love, courtship, and marriage, and each in its own distinct way. "The Innocent Cause, or How Snoring Broke Off a Match. A Tale of Hog Killing Time" is an accomplished version of the "Sut Lovingood" genre of frontier humor, in which prankster-fools relate to a friend the results of some mischievous (or worse) misdeed that usually causes the temporary breakdown of social order. In this case the story itself is related in a letter written by "my esteemed friend, Belt: Seebub, or Belzebub, as he was more generally known"[3] to "Haggis," who then relates it to his friend the "Colonel" (Summer himself) with the humorous warning, "What he records may be true, or it may not: my opinion is, that there is something in it" (*Fireside Tales* 35). After this brief framing device, the story then is told in Belzebub's own written words. Belzebub is thus somewhat educated and literate, although his spelling reveals his frontier dialect: "After spendin an agreeable time among you down there, jest as I was mountin my hoss to bid you adiew, you requested me to write to you a long letter narratin some adwenture of my own personal occurrunce," he begins his letter (35).

Belzebub is in love with Michael Ann Hull and hopes to ingratiate himself with her mother by supervising the hog killing at their farm. His reputation is such that he needs all the goodwill he can muster. As he explains to Michael Ann after she sits on his lap, "[I]t was predestyned from infinity that at times I should make a fool of myself: and it seems to me that tonight I am so full of devil that it chokes me" (39). Indeed, Belt is a self-portrayed rascal, a sexually profligate scoundrel who has apparently fathered at least one child out of wedlock, although he maintains that "I never was ashamed of any thing in all my life" and "I call God to witness that I am as innosent of it as the child itself. . . . All babies are as much alike as all the pattridge eggs as ever was laid." After this disclaimer, he and Michael Ann "drew nearer to the fire and eat sawsudges out of one another's mouth until two o'clock, when I axed her where I was to sleep" (40).

The jest of the tale revolves around a stranger, a Kentucky hog drover with whom Belt is to bed. The "Kaintuckian" is already asleep and loudly snoring when Belt enters the room. "He lay flat upon his back, with his hed berried in the piller, his eyes sot and half open, and his under jaw hung down tel his tung could be seen as dry as a swinged pig tail. In fact, his mouth looked like a steel trap set for a otter and baited with a piece of dried beef. The diffikulty of respuration under which he labered made my flesh crawl" (41), Belt recalls, capably employing the grotesque physical imagery so common in Southwest humor. In an attempt to escape the terrible noise, Belt removes the exhaust pipe from the stove and places it over the man's mouth, only to discover the next morning that the excessive snoring has spewed soot all over the clean laundry in the yard and has caused other accidents as well. The mother runs Belt off from the farm, and he pleads with Haggis for advice, but the tale ends in proper comic resolution, with reconciliation, marriage, and children.

"Snip——A Tale" is set in 1838 and is told by Dr. Haggis himself. "Snip" is a horse, "a pet . . . spoilt by good treatment" (61) and used by young Joe Wimple in his courtship of Polly Pumpernickle, member of a German family in the Dutch Fork. In this tale, Mayer is less interested in story than in establishing the world of these people. Much of the narrative is devoted to contrasting customs and dialects ("'I got married about twenty years ago, to cure the histurrics,'" one country woman says, "but I let you know, I didn't git rid on 'em ontel I got to be a widder"; while Mr. Pumpernickle speaks with marked German accent: "'Vy, 'owdy Dogder! vare de tevil tid you gum vrom?'" [63]). Again there is a strong affirmation of sexuality in this tale of courtship and marriage, as when Joe promises Dr. Haggis that "'I'll set some galls at you who will jest kiss you to deth'" (62). And again the story ends in celebration, although muted somewhat by the passage of ten years, during which time some older members of the community have died, "summoned to eternal judgment, with nothing but their honesty and generosity to plead for the forgiveness of the sins to which the flesh is heir, and of which there were none on earth to accuse them" (72).

"The Easter Eggs: A Tale of Love, Poetry, and Prose" is a more ambitious piece than the other two, as its title suggests. Closer in tone to "The Innocent Cause" than to "Snip," it begins with an establishing set piece that describes both the world of the story and the conflicted desires of its protagonist, a young man named David Hartman who is in love with Bekky Towns. There is no framing device in this tale, and Haggis appears neither as narrator nor participant. Instead, Mayer ambitiously employs the omniscient narrator—and to good effect. David has become infatuated with Bekky, especially after accidentally touching her bare foot as he helped her onto her horse: "'Her shoe had to cum off too jest as I took hold of it, and while I was a puttin it on again she accused me of ticklin her in the bottom of her foot: a thing I wouldn't a'done for all the world. There is no use o' resistin for I am clean gone'" (102). The Hartman family further complicates David's hopes, for his sister is "an irretrievable old maid, as bitter as her own weight in aloes" who has "forbidden him to fall in love with the girls"; and his father, "who had been vanquished by his mother in several domestic rencontres," habitually warns him, "'David my son, beware of the wimming'" (103).

David Hartman woos Bekky by copying verses of poetry from the wrappings of candy sugar kisses, but in his courtship he must contend with his best friend Martin Sawyer, who is also courting Bekky (a similar conflict is hinted at in "Snip," when Dr. Haggis tries to make Joe jealous by his attentions to Polly, but Haggis is being playful rather than seriously competitive). When they come to fight, Mayer brings in some of his few black characters, "two negro fellows," apparent slaves or hands of Bekky's father, who are commanded to serve as "seconds" to the two young men. Mayer relates their speech in comic black dialect: "'Massa Martin,' one says, 'I hab only few words to say. Nebber you mind enny ting Massa Dave can do to you, but trow your hed forruds and but 'um in de pit ob de stummick. You see dat will knock all de bret out, and he 'bliged to holler'" (113). Nevertheless, this tale also ends in forgiveness and marriage, with handshakes all around and a "hymenial notice" in the local paper (115).

These previous stories can be read as comic, rustic epithalamia, for each celebrates love and concludes in connubial happiness, despite the complications found within them. However, Mayer's best story, "The Corn Cob Pipe: A Tale of the Comet of '43," reveals a darker view.[4] Modeled on Washington Irving's "The Legend of Sleepy Hollow" (the schoolmaster Samuel Burns is compared to Ichabod Crane, "the pedagogue of Sleepy Hollow," at one point [*Dutch Fork,* 59]), "The [Corn] Cob Pipe" is a remarkable work in a number of ways. Kibler and Piacentino note that the story line is "appropriate to situation comedy" (317). But underneath its genial manner, this is a tale of attempted patricide and contains all the elements (albeit disguised) of what would later become "hard-boiled" or *noir* fiction: a murder plot, a scheming beautiful woman, a naïve young man entrapped in the plan, the intention to blame the murder on an innocent party, a strong sense of fate running the show. This description, of course, is at odds with the experience of reading the story itself, for the tone is both playful and moral due to the voice and perspective of the narrator. Even so, stripped of that mediating voice, the outline of the tale remains surprising in its violence and duplicity.

The story is told in three parts: "The Comet," "The Pipe," and "The Chopping, Log-Rolling, and Carding" (or what could have been called "The Party" or even "The Attempted Assassination"). In earlier versions of this story, Mayer again assumed the persona of "Obadiah Haggis," but in the final revision this frame narrator has disappeared. However, there is still an identifiable authorial voice telling the tale. Kibler and Piacentino observe that "the modern reader may condemn the frame narrator's editorializing as antiquated" (317), but there is much to be said for the humor and invention of the narration, especially in the final version of the tale. Here the narrator, the self-acknowledged author of the story, comments on his role as writer, his relationship to his characters, his difficulty in controlling them or making their desires conform to his own. For example, once Yetta Elfins determines to "blow daddy up" (*Dutch Fork* 45) by packing gunpowder in his pipe, so that she can marry Abram Priester rather than the suitor chosen by her father, the pompous schoolteacher Samuel Burns, the narrator stops the story in exasperation:

> What a disclosure! The pretty, black-eyed Yetta engaged in a gunpowder plot against her father! No, no, Yetta Elfins, that must not be. From this moment I abandon you and Abram Priester to your fate; for I plainly perceive he will yield to your persuasions, as Adam did to Eve's. Blow up your father, who has told me so many anecdotes of the olden time! Murder Thomas Elfins, at whose fire-side I have spent so many merry winter evenings! No, Yetta, though you explode a mine under his split-bottomed chair, no harm shall befall him: and mark me! you shall marry Samuel Burns, if I am able to hold my pen! (45)

At another point he exclaims, "Foolish girl! Will you provoke me to make Abram Priester's execution, and likewise your own, the denouement of this story?" (47); and yet again he attempts to negotiate with his character, observing, "There is a spark of goodness yet remaining in your heart. Come, now, do not let us murder your old father,—he is deluded; but rather let us elope with Abram Priester, and save our consciences from the pangs of guilt!" (51). By the time the story ends with an apparent "moral"—"Now, Yetta, I hold you up to the world as a warning to all undutiful daughters" (60)—the narrator himself has become a comic figure full of bluster and indignation, an impotent god who has revealed all his own foibles while detailing those of his "creations."

Clearly there is another author who stands behind the nameless narrator of this story, and it is this artist who constructs such a finely wrought tale. As previously noted, the subtitle of the story is "A Tale of the Comet of '43," and this image becomes the connection among all three sections of the narrative. The "fire" of the marvelous comet is repeated by the "fire in [Yetta's] dark eye" (43) when, inspired by stories of Guy Fawkes, she plots to "blow daddy up with gunpowder" (47). Mark Moyer, who first spots the comet, recounts his discovery as if it were a vision or dream: "'I suddently see'd de frightfulest white streak in de sky wat was ever hearn tell of . . . and jest den I disciver'd dat de ting was alive; for it commenced to move itself like a surpunt, and it darted out o' its head a forky tongue what reetch'd away up in de fermamint of Job's coffin, and a sting out o' its tail as tetch'd de top of a high pine-tree'" (39).

In the second part of the story, "The Pipe," Yetta uses the comet as a warning for her father, telling him, "'Wy, daddy, I've had a dream; and I've dreamt it t'ree nights, one arter de odder. Ef I was you, daddy, I'd run dis here schoolmaster off, and I'd never let him come anigh me agin; for, take my word for it, he's got evil designs agin you; and dis here ting, wat we sees every night in de sky, is sent for a warnin'" (45). Later she describes the comet in Moyer's terms as "a dreadful fiery dragon wat licked out its tongue at Mark Moyer, and tried to run its sting trough him"; and she then tells her father, who reads it as a "warnin' agin all ondutiful children," that "it's more likely a sign dat somethin' dreadful is a goin' to happen to you, daddy" (52).

The third section is set at the home of Captain Joshua Grimm, who has invited his neighbors to a land-clearing and cotton-carding party. In the fields, "blazing lightwood stumps" burn with a bright roar. "Such a tumbling about of logs, amidst the crash of falling trees will never again be seen and heard in Dutch Fork," the narrator tell us, "nor will there ever be repeated such jokes followed by such laughter as went the rounds, that day" (53). It is at this community gathering that Yetta attempts to kill her father. Samuel Burns (his name in the earlier version was Isom Jones; the change to "Burns" as further example of the fire imagery is significant) had earlier made as a gift for the old man a pipe "'fantastically carved' out of a red cob, and having attached to it a stem of unusual length" (47). Yetta induces Burns, unknowingly, to finish filling the pipe with powder and hand it to her father so that he will be the direct cause of the old man's death; and it is while Abram is entertaining the crowd by singing "Yes, hold them lights 'til the moon gits higher" that Mr. Elfins lights the pipe that then explodes in his face. "'Guy Fawkes! Guy Fawkes! daddy! Didn't I know it, daddy, dat dis here schoolmaster was a plottin' agin' your life!'" Yetta cries (58), and Burns races away from the angry group, eluding also Abram and Mark Moyer, who had been placed outside as a final guard against either Mr. Elfins or Samuel Burns escaping.

In addition to the underlying violence of this story, Mayer again imbeds a strong current of sexuality in the narrative, also linked to the image of fire. When Mark Moyer first spots the comet, he runs in panic to the home of the Widow

Halberdoppels and her daughter Nancy. "'It frighten'd de old woman and her dorter so much dat day could n't speak; but wen I made 'em look out o' doors tow'rds sunset and day cotch'd sight of de fiery dragon, day took to screamin' and barrin' up de house ontel I got wuss skeer'd dan ever. Nancy was so overtook wid de histurricks dat she sot on my lap de whole of de blessed livelong night; and I hain't had a wink o' sleep,'" Moyer claims (41). At the later party, another man jokes with Mark, asking "'if it was possible he could think of doing a day's work so soon after holding Nancy Halberdoppels on his lap a whole night'"; and another suggests that "'it was *him* wat sot on *Nancy's* lap instid of her settin' on his'n'" (54). Later, Nancy asks Mark to "sing a song, 'wat was her delight'"; but Samuel Burns objects, "declaring that such a song should not be tolerated in elegant society." "'Neffer mind, Mark,'" Nancy tells him, "'you shall sing it for me weneffer you comes to see me'" (56). Our narrator at one point refers to Nancy and Mark as "wicked young people" (41), but the Dutch Fork, in all of Mayer's writings, is a highly sexed place,[5] and Yetta's influence over Abram is, to no small degree, fueled by sexual desire and manipulation. Indeed, the proposed method of patricide—the daughter (who is twice called a "hussy" by her parents) killing the father by tampering with his pipe (a provocatively described symbol of patriarchy, as we have seen)—is worthy of its own further exegesis.

Mayer's novel *John Punterick, A Novel of Life in the Old Dutch Fork,* in many ways serves as a culmination of the characters and ideas examined in the tales written in the decade leading up to it. Mayer's emphasis on local color, his care in documenting or explaining in footnote some of the more exotic sayings, customs and beliefs, make it clear that, as in the stories, the narrator wishes to recreate a reality in this novel, a world that no longer exists. When we consider the time in which the book was written—the nation on the verge of Civil War—it is not difficult to imagine that some of Mayer's concerns for his country and heritage are reflected in his portrayal of this fragile, isolated "island" of the Dutch Fork. Nevertheless, Mayer's view is essentially a comic one. There is, it is true, a strong sense of loss in the novel. Indeed, James Kibler has revealed that the novel as published represents only part of what Mayer had planned, that "Part 1/Mirthful," which makes up the novel as we have it, was possibly to be followed by a "Part 2/Mournful" section, a "companion piece to fill out a longer volume" (Introduction, *Punterick* x). However, as Kibler also notes, the "Mirthful" section stands quite satisfactorily on its own.

Punterick begins with an introductory frame in which six friends join together on a summer's day at Pomaria Plantation (an actual place, just as at least some of these six characters have historical references). The present time of the frame is 1847, and Mayer himself seems to be represented in "a young physician whom they addressed by the name of Ernest" (1). It is Ernest who is "preparing a story of mournfulness founded upon events recorded in his journal" to be read to the group "on the next New Year's eve" (2). The emphasis in the frame, however, is on his companion Fritz, who is associated with mirth and good spirits. "The contagiousness of his laugh, the concentrated attention directed to his remarks, and the eagerness with which his arrival was ever expected pointed to the fact that Fritz was a dear fellow, beloved by every body" (2). Fritz also has a manuscript, and it is that document that forms the heart of the "novel" put before us—the story of John Punterick.

The frame, however, serves purposes other than merely to introduce this story of Punterick. The frame allows Mayer, through the character of Herman, to comment on the nature of humor and its place in our lives. Herman holds that "mirthfulness is the preparatory state for soberness . . . it is only after we have made sensible progress in life, and have been influenced by experience in morals, that our seasons of gaity become feebler and shorter, and the reign of sedateness firmer and more enduring" (17). He continues: "Sorrow is better than laughter. Happy and deserving of veneration is the man, who near the close of life can remember that the regrets of his youth for intemperate merriment never cost him more than profitable pensiveness; and the jovial struggles of his manhood against the inevitable bleakness of old age, only established him in dignified cheerfulness" (18).

This "happy seriousness, which excludes the dread of death" (18), also allows Herman to enjoy "the pleasures of life, without fear of being seduced by them, or regret at the prospect of speedily leaving them" (19). It is this "dignified cheerfulness," this "happy seriousness" that best describes the comic tone of much of Mayer's work. As in "The [Corn] Cob Pipe," underneath the humor often lies a wry ruefulness about the human condition, a realization that people act badly, are foolish, may sometimes be evil. But this information is presented to us as a medicine to counteract such inclinations, if possible.

In the story of John Punterick, Mayer uses a comic trio of secondary characters—a chorus of sorts—to comment on human nature and to illustrate the very flaws they intend to condemn. HonWindel Himmelschau, the leader of this group, often proclaims these truths, while his companions Rückblick, and Bodenstarr act them out. "A man dat is not honesht wid himself, cannot be honesht wid his nabors," Himmelschau says (59). "'If folks can pe always a quarrellin', and fightin', and yet pe goot friends, unbeknowin' to demselves, I'm of de obinion dat two men can pe de besht of friends, and go on a pein' so, to de besht of deir knowletch, for year after year, wen after all dere is sumtink hid in deir hearts, dat would make dem cut one annoder's troats, if ennyting should come along to traw it out;—and dat mought happen when dey leasht egsbected it'" (60). This is exactly what happens shortly thereafter when HonYokkel and HonAdam begin to fight over some forgotten injury. "'I told you to examine your hearts, and see wat was dere,'" HonWindel cries as he comes between them. "'If you had done so, dere would haf pin none of dis. Dere is sometink evil in your hearts, dat you do n't know apout. Wat does de Prophet Cheerymiar say? 'De heart is deceitful apove effery ting; and deshperitly wicked'"" (69), at which point the two men turn on HonWindel himself. Godfrey, one of the men to whom the story of John Punterick is read, comments in the prologue to the story, "That's a mighty bad doctrine to teach—that what's born in a man can't be corrected. There would, then, be but little hope, for such of us, as were conceived in sin, and shaped in iniquity" (20). But, essentially, this is the human condition as Mayer sees it, although he mitigates it through humor and compassion.

It is important to keep this view in mind while reading Mayer; otherwise we might fall into the misapprehension that Mayer portrays the Old Dutch Fork simply as a prelapsarian world sorrowfully corrupted and destroyed by the intrusion of evil outside forces. It is true that Mayer, or his characters, view change with suspicion. In *John Punterick*, for example, the IOU presented to Christian Stoudenmyer by Gabriel Süssinger, "the first note of hand, that was ever given in the Dutch Fork" (22), is seen as a sad transaction that substitutes a piece of paper for an honest word and handshake. It is also true that strangers who come into the Dutch Fork are often presented as suspicious or sinister characters, like the outsider "travelling with a brand-new pair of saddlebags through the neighborhood" (41) whose counterfeit silver dollar destroys the magic of Enoch Staubig's "Purse of Odin": "'wen dis tamt rashkul of a shtranger comes along, you takes money from him, widout tryin' it at all; and you ruins de Detch Fork,'" as Bodenstarr accuses Staubig (68). Moreover, those Dutch Forkers who leave the community for the outside world either come running back, like Hiob Staubig, or arrive at bad ends, like Punterick himself.

But Mayer's view is a bit more complicated than this reading would indicate. A figure like Christian Stoudenmyer, who "was imperious in his domestic sway; and could not brook contradiction, nor disobedience. . . . His stern resistance to anything like innovation, was not likely to be irritated, in so secluded a community as the Dutch Fork" (23), is essentially comic, an obvious focus of Mayer's satire in his hatred of change. Moreover, the Dutch Fork has its share of superstitious, greedy, arrogant, muddle-headed, duplicitous, and violent native folk, quite without the intrusion of outside forces. Stoudenmyer's opposition to the keeping of musical time by "crooking and straightening the fore-finger" causes him "to break forth, one day, into an unseemly fit of anger, and drive from his usually hospitable home, an innocent and accomplished young man. He even went so far in his violence as to assault the unoffending stranger with a blunderbuss" (23). John Punterick's gluttony—his favorite dish, known as "Punterick's Delight," consists of apple dumplings, seventeen or which are for him and three apiece for the others—serves as one of the slowly unfolding jokes throughout the book (the full title to the book is *John Punterick; or The Apple Dumplings. A Chronicle of the Dutch Fork*), and eventually leads to his death, at least according to Molly Munter's narrative, which brings the novel to its end. "'Well, he burshted!'" she claims, in a fit, after he has eaten twelve dumplings, thinking them his favorite apple variety, only to discover that his wife had substituted "bertaters" (141). Mayer surely remembers the Old Dutch Fork and its people with great fondness, but like any good humorist, he emphasizes their flaws for comic effect rather than sentimentally extolling their virtues.

It should also be noted just how skillfully this "mirthful" novel is constructed for comic effect, how carefully it leads us as readers into unexpected and sometimes remarkably absurd places and conclusions. Although the title indicates that Punterick will be the main subject of the story, his leaving from the Dutch Fork is only one of several ongoing narratives that make up the book. Indeed, Punterick is far from the most significant character in the work except as catalyst for other incidents. One thread of this story, for example, explains how Gabriel Süssinger's IOU to Christian Stoudenmyer led to Punterick's removal from the Dutch Fork and the end of the old ways of doing things. Another concentrates on Enoch Staubig and his oafish son Hiob, who becomes a comic hero undertaking a mock epic journey in search of Punterick and his family (specifically his daughter Happy). Still another revolves around Molly Munter's account of Punterick's mysterious death and the narrator's later efforts to discover the truth.

Each of these stories is essentially a shaggy-dog tale in which the joy of telling is more important than the thing eventually told. The *point* of a narrative is often carefully withheld while the speaker works through all manner of secondary information. Chapter 2, for example, ends with Bodenstarr, Rückblick, and Himmelschau mulling over the question: "'Ah . . . dere was sometink not right in Punterick's heart. Wat made him go away, ennyhow?'" The mysterious answer is "'Schmitt!'" "Wy, Schmitt was de cause of it." They walk away, "each one nodding his head, and muttering: 'Schmitt! Schmitt! Schmitt!'" (72) The next chapter, however, evades the question of "Schmitt" and details instead Hiob Staubig's journey and return for some twenty-five pages, until the very end of the section when the trio reappears. Then Himmelschau speaks to Hiob: "'I haf a question to ax Hiob, sence he is willin' to shpeak, at lasht,' said Himmelschau, 'and I will beg him not to use enny brofane lankwitch. You all haf shust seen what effeck brofanity, comink from oldt men, has upon yunk beeples. Yunk men will foller de example of old ones. Wat I wants to ax you, Hiob, is dis. Did you hear Punterick say enny tink, wen you saw him de lasht time?'"

"'Shust pefore he fired off his rifle . . . he shtomp'd his foot and said: 'Schmitt!'" Hiob answers. "They separated as they did once before, muttering with contemptuous gestures, the name 'Schmitt'" (98–99), the chapter ends. Mayer then imposes yet another break in the action, this time with a fourth chapter innocuously entitled "*Description of an old-time Dutch Fork domicile*" (100), before beginning Chapter 5 with a sudden and disdainful exclamation "Schmitt!" (109) and finally explaining to the reader the story behind the controversial Dr. Schmitt and his role in Punterick's removal.

Indeed, Mayer's most complete comic character in the work is not John Punterick but Hiob Staubig, whose journey away from and back to the Dutch Fork serves as the central event of the novel. Hiob comes from a long line of comic heroes like Tom Jones or, closer to home, Sut Lovingood, and he clearly anticipates such later variations as Li'l Abner, whom Al Capp regularly dispatched from Dogpatch into the outer world for satirical purposes, and Will Stockdale, the Abner-like hillbilly hero of *No Time for Sergeants*. Like both of them, Hiob is "a bushy-headed broad-shouldered youngster, of wonderful bodily strength," about whom his father says, "'Hiob is a right shmairt yunk man; but he knows nottink; and he is goot for nottink. If I hadt proke his headt wid my shtick oftener, wen he was yunkerer and tenderer, he mought haf pin wort sumtink;—but, now, he is got to pe so tuff, and his headt is so tamt hardt, dat nottink can pe done wid him ennymore, in dat wa'" (42). Hiob is also a drinker of renown as well as the besotted lover of Happy Punterick, whose quitting Dutch Fork with her family causes Hiob to venture forth in search of her. But ultimately more important to Hiob is his relationship to the plough horse Futterfresser ("fodder-eater"), whom Hiob abuses one moment and caresses the next. When Hiob leaves, his father wails, "'Oh, Hiob! Hiob! . . . wat is pecome of him? I don't care so much for him, myself; but Futterfresser will go crazy, if Hiob do n't soon come home. De poor oldt creeter does nottink but whicker and whicker and whicker, de plessed night, so dat I can't shleep for him'" (59). And when Hiob does return, after much confusion and fright, Old Enoch Staubig tells his friends that the boy is "'down in de horse-lot, wid Futterfresser. Dey haf pin a gryin' and a huggin' of one anodder, effer sence Hiob came home'" (79), and Hiob later notes "'dat Futterfresser was de only berson dat receif'd him like a gentleman'" (89).

Hiob's journey is an inspired mock epic. The people of the Dutch Fork are certain that he has circled the world, since he returns in the opposite direction from which he leaves (Mayer's chapter description grandly announces "*Hiob's mysterious return, by which the evidence of the earth's rotundity afforded by circumnavigation is somewhat strengthened*" [73]). He passes through "enchanted" lands and is "bestridden by witches." He sees strange people with "red hair and speckled faces, as well as children not three years old whose hair was as white as that upon the heads of the oldest patriarch in Dutch Fork" (86). He spends time at the home of a farmer whose daughter is named "Penelope": "'dat was de gal's name, and it was sich a shtrange name, dat it made him feel, more dan enny tink else wat a great dishtance he was from home.'" She "looked tenderly upon him" and tries to seduce him; Hiob is later threatened by her brother, who accuses him of "trifling with her" (88), and he must flee for his life. When he returns to the Dutch Fork, his odyssey over, his stories are mistrusted and questioned in part, like Rip Van Winkle's, but no one totally disbelieves his description of the bizarre lands beyond the boundaries of their secluded, hermetic home. Although the book ends with our narrator offering rational explanations for Hiob's experiences and observations, the people of the Dutch Fork remain ignorant and safe in their own beliefs.

Certainly there is more to Mayer than the works briefly discussed in this essay. Inspired by his own travels abroad (he lived and studied for three years in Europe, primarily Germany), he, like Irving before him, wrote a series of sketches and stories with European settings and sometimes tried his hand at mysteries and Gothic tales. As Kibler and Piacentino observe, "There is little humor or no in them, and as good as they are, they fall short of the fiction in which Mayer utilizes this strength" (315). He was an amateur poet, kept an extensive journal, and late in life started another novel, *Malladoce, the Briton, His Wanderings from Druidism to Christianity*, which was completed after his death by a friend. He also wrote the series of Dutch Fork reminiscences that appeared in the *Newberry News and Herald* in 1891, the year he died, with the intention of gathering them into a collection. James Kibler's introduction to *The Dutch Fork* carefully discusses Mayer's plan to combine these personal recollections with some of his earlier tales in order to capture a feeling of these long-gone days. "The tone is at times elegiac, at times warmly humorous, occasionally filled with regret, but always intensely personal," Kibler writes. "Mayer does not write a 'bookish' book. Instead, he practices an essentially preliterary tradition; that is, a tradition stemming from and growing out of a culture in which art is not yet cut off from its roots in the ballad, oral tale, and yarn—hence the inclusion of a wealth of folk ballads, folk tales, superstitions, dialect, and folk customs" (*Dutch Fork* ix). The genial character of these sketches imbues them with great charm, and the very real sense of times passed and passing once again evokes the "dignified seriousness" and "happy cheerfulness" that is the hallmark of Mayer's best work.

This attitude is perhaps best revealed in Mayer's last story, "Little Dassie, or 'The Burning Pine-Knot's Fitful Flare'," published in the *Newberry Herald and News* after his death. It begins with Mayer's simple declaration, "I am a doctor" (*Fireside Tales* 141). The introduction to the story explains what it means to be a country doctor. He speaks of good horses and of wise people and of his experiences of many years. "Of diaries, this is what I have to say. Oh, the wi[s]dom and the humor that is lost to the country doctor, and perhaps to the world, by his not keeping a diary!" (142) he tells us, and the subsequent story comes from entries recorded some fifty years earlier. "Little Dassie" is a story of death, loss, and sorrow. The doctor is called to the distant home of Dave, a countryman who believes his wife is dying. The doctor travels at night, through dark forest, fearful and lost (this part of the story draws comparison with Henry Clay Lewis's "Valerian and the Panther" in its sense of dread). Once arrived, he discovers that Nancy is pregnant and about to give birth; the child is a girl and Dave, asking the doctor's advice, names her "Hadassah" or "Dassie." But the baby dies and "there was a ferocious grief in that dark, dingy, pine-log cabin; and . . . it was dangerous to approach Dave" (151), the doctor relates. The second part of the story tells of Dave's meeting an old friend, based on Adam Summer, of whom he asks to buy an arbor vitae to plant at his daughter's grave. "Adam," once he understands that Dave's child is dead, is so overcome by his own grief that he turns away from Dave after ordering that "the finest arber [*sic*] vitae" and a "cryptomeria" be dug up and given to the man. "Addrum, what's poor Dave done to make you angry with him?" Dave cries in pitiful astonishment (153), failing to comprehend that Adam's fury is directed towards a world in which innocence is so fragile and sorrow so constant. "They are all dead," Mayer concludes the narrative. "Adam sleeps with his people; and Dave and Nance lie side by side, with Little Dassie slumbering between them, as she did before she died. I visited their graves, not long ago" (153). Thus, Mayer's last story ends with the passing of life, the loss of friends and family, the gentle acknowledgement of death's finality.

A man of taste, a man of decorum, a man of affection, O.B. Mayer displays a wisdom and acceptance concerning the human condition that escaped his fellow doctor-humorist Henry Clay Lewis. Lewis, of course, died a very young man, while

Mayer lived into his seventies, and perhaps Lewis would have matured into the old, resigned, stoic physician he created as his literary persona in "Madison Tensas." But it seems unlikely. Mayer reveals in his writings a compassion for humanity in all its foolishness that in Lewis engendered bitterness and rage. When Lewis attempted sympathy, it came out as self-pity; when he sought for understanding, he produced bathos instead. Lewis is ultimately more fascinating and perhaps more worthy of our study than Mayer—darkness continues to attract more than light—but Mayer is the more surprising. His combination of propriety and absurdity, of melancholy and merriment, of commiseration and comedy sets him apart from most of his fellow humorists in a manner that is much to be admired. For George Washington Harris's Sut Lovingood, "human nater" was best represented by a "blind bull" ("Taurus in Lynchburg Market"), but Mayer had a different opinion: "'Human natur, Doc, is more amazin' than the seasins,'" Dave says in "Little Dassie" (150). O.B. Mayer's kind and generous acceptance of "human natur" in all its varied manifestations remains one of the rarities of nineteenth-century southern humor.

Notes

1. The chief publications are *John Punterick, A Novel of Life in the Old Dutch Fork.* Spartanburg, S.C.: Reprint Co., 1981; *The Dutch Fork.* Columbia, S.C.: Dutch Fork Press, 1982; and *Fireside Tales: Stories of the Old Dutch Fork.* Columbia, S.C.: Dutch Fork Press, 1984. All of these publications are edited by James E. Kibler Jr., the scholar most responsible for bringing Mayer to the reading public today. Piacentino's call for greater attention is found in his essay "Backwoods Humor in Upcountry South Carolina: The Case for O.B. Mayer," *South Carolina Review* 30 (fall 1997): 79–85.

2. See Kibler and Piacentino, "Orlando Benedict Mayer." *Encyclopedia of American Humorists.* Ed. Steven H. Gale. New York: Garland (1988), 315–20, for a full biographical sketch. Also see Kibler, "O.B. Mayer." *Antebellum Writers in New York and the South.* Vol. 3. *Dictionary of Literary Biography.* Ed. Joel Myerson. Detroit: Gale Research (1979), 213–18.

3. "You know my name is Belton Seebub, or Belt. Seebubb, as the boys hereabouts call me; but Mr. Dukes, the Universalist preacher, calls me Belzebub, becase, ses he, I am the only devil the existence of which he is convinced of," Belt later explains in the letter (36).

4. The story first appeared in the *South Carolinian* in December 1848, was revised for publication in *Russell's* magazine in 1858, and revised yet again for final publication in the *Newberry Herald and News* in 1891. The earliest version is the one included in *Fireside Tales,* 117–31; the version discussed in this essay is Mayer's final revision, "The Cob Pipe," found in *The Dutch Fork,* 39–60.

5. For example, in the prologue to *John Punterick,* Dr. Koon recalls the sexual playfulness that occurred during harvest time in the Dutch Fork, when the men and women would cut wheat together in the fields. When a grasshopper flies down Christian Stoudenmyer's shirt, "Pritzilly" Putzerick "puts her hand down de pack of his neck; and sure enough, after feelin' apout a goot deal, she prings up a grasshopper. . . . Christian had pin a gittin' foolish for some time . . . and wen Ageneses went on to take de tip of his ear between her fore-finger and tumb and say to him: A leetle to de right or a leetle to de left, Chreestian, he losht his mind combletely, and did not know what he was a doin'. But we all know'd wat we was apout . . . and we all got married pefore de settin in of de colt wetter" (15).

The Literary Legacy

14

An Old Southwesterner Abroad

Cultural Frontiers and the Landmark American Humor of J. Ross Browne's *Yusef*

Joseph Csicsila

For more than a decade between the mid-1850s and 1870, J. Ross Browne was as widely read and celebrated as any American travel writer of his generation. During those years, Browne published six successful books with Harper and Brothers and regularly contributed to *Harper's Monthly*, where his work almost always ran as lead articles. But today, unfortunately, he is remembered for little more than exerting a minor influence on Herman Melville and Mark Twain. Browne's *Etchings of a Whaling Cruise* (1846), for instance, has long been considered by critics to have inspired aspects of *Moby Dick* (1851). Readers since the latter nineteenth century have also recognized more than a few striking similarities between several of Browne's travel narratives written in the 1850s and 1860s and Twain's *The Innocents Abroad* (1869), *Roughing It* (1872), and *A Tramp Abroad* (1880). While such distinctions have no doubt proved helpful in sustaining limited interest in his writings over the last century, Browne clearly deserves recognition for more than furnishing other writers with story line ideas. A nascent realist, Browne crusaded against romantic literature a generation before American writers collectively took up the cause of literary realism. And though Browne utilized the travel book format throughout his career, he approached his craft as a writer of humorous prose fiction, introducing the styles, techniques, and characters of American frontier humor to the one of the most conventional and popular genre of his times.

A case in point is Browne's first success as a writer, his 1853 travel book *Yusef; Or the Journey of the Frangi, a Crusade in the East.* The events of the book—a six-month tour through Southern Europe and the Middle East—are related in the first person by Browne himself, and the narrative consists essentially of two halves. The first part recounts Browne's trip through Italy, Greece, and Turkey. The second part commences at the book's midpoint as Browne arrives in Syria and meets Yusef, the young, charismatic guide who escorts him through the Holy Land. At this moment the book really transforms—it becomes a different story altogether. Here the focus of the narrative shifts dramatically from the humorous (but standard) tour book descriptions of foreign lands to the skillful development of the title character and the folk culture he comes to represent.

Though Browne's *Yusef* might initially appear to be a conventional travel book in its documentation of one man's tour of foreign countries, it stands as a veritable milestone in American humorous literature for at least two reasons. First, consciously playing off the sort of blind adoration of things exotic that had become a fundamental component of the travel book genre, *Yusef* satirizes that tradition by subtly ridiculing practically everything its narrator encounters—landmarks, customs, and local inhabitants. Of course, American writers—particularly American humorists—had always felt comfortable mocking European manners when they were exhibited by a visitor to the United States, but rarely before Browne had an American writer dared to deride Europeans in Europe. Moreover, *Yusef* eventually became the model for *The Innocents Abroad*, the book that effectively launched the career of Mark Twain more than a decade and a half later.

Second, Browne hit his stride with *Yusef* not just as an original American humorist but also as a literary craftsman. The portrayal of the narrative's central character Yusef, the wily Syrian guide who supplies the second half of the story with so much of its vitality, is singularly masterful. Yusef is a Jim Doggett-like braggart of Old Southwestern proportions. He purports to be known throughout the East as "the destroyer of robbers," and he continually boasts of his exploits to the apparently naive narrator and his fellow travelers, who in turn gullibly accept the dragoman's tall tales of having single-handedly fought, maimed, and killed incredible numbers of Bedouin marauders. Consider, for example, Yusef's spirited introduction to Browne and his fellow American tourists (and the reader) as the dragoman attempts to hawk his services as a guide:

> "Gentlemen, I am YUSEF SIMON BADRA, the dragoman for Syria. This is my book of recommendations. I have taken a thousand American gentlemen through Syria. Yes sir; the Americans like me; I like Americans! I hate Englishmen; I won't take an Englishman; they don't suit me; can't get along together; I know too much for 'em. But the Americans suit me; always ready; up to everything—fun, fight, or frolic. There are other dragomans here, gentlemen. Emanuel Balthos is my friend; I won't interfere, if you wish to take him. I don't say he's afraid of robbers; I don't say he hires guards in all the bad places on that account. I speak only of myself. The robbers know me. The name Yusef Badra is guard enough in any part of Syria. Courage is a great thing in this country; courage will carry a man through where a thousand guards daren't show their faces. The last time I was out I killed six Bedouins. I sometimes kill such fellows for fun. They know me; they know it's a habit I have, and they always keep clear when they can. But you can choose for yourselves, gentlemen; there's my book; look over it." (177)

In addition to the obvious hyperbole of Yusef's claims for himself—guiding thousands of Americans, killing six Bedouins last time he was out, slaying such types for fun and out of habit—much of the humor of the passage eventually arises from the disparity between Yusef's self-proclaimed ferocity and the facts. Any time the deadpan narrator of the book actually witnesses Yusef confronted by real danger, the ridiculous and cowardly guide conveniently manages to disappear or somehow otherwise escape jeopardizing his own safety.

When discussed or analyzed at all by scholars, Browne's title character has been all too casually labeled something of a garden-variety picaro.[1] However, something more may be at work here. Yusef seems to match Walter Blair's descriptions of a particular class of Southwestern hero—the tall talker.[2] Blair and other critics of American frontier literature have, of course, traced the origins of the Southwestern hero to the picaro. But they eventually point out key differences between the two character classifications. Generally, the picaro (a distinctly European character type) is a rogue, a borderline criminal, whose main function is to expose some form of social injustice during the course of the story. On the other hand, the Southwestern hero (a distinctly American character type), in particular the tall talker, is more often a sympathetic, basically good-natured individual, whose chief vice is the tall tale and whose exaggerated claims function to supply humor to the narrative.[3]

Given these definitions, Yusef is no picaro.[4] Yet he does fit Blair's description of the Davy Crockett-like frontier tall talker. Yusef's dialogue is marked continuously by vernacular contractions and expressions, hyperbole, exaggeration, and from the reader's perspective, incredulity. Additionally, at its core, the second half of the book possesses a hallmark feature of frontier humor: a fundamental incongruity between the frame narrative and the comic fantasy world created by a tall talker.[5] As readers we come to understand that there is a great disparity between the reality of the frame and the tall-tale world of Yusef. The dramatic tension created by this disparity is what Blair, M. Thomas Inge, Carolyn Brown, and others have identified as a defining element of Old Southwestern humor.

Browne's *Yusef* was written and published between 1850 and 1853, years that fall comfortably within the high period of American frontier humor. Browne lived and worked as a journalist in Louisville in the 1840s, and the *Louisville Courier* was one of the half-dozen major southern newspapers of the mid-1800s that regularly published the work of major Southwestern humorists.[6] It seems completely plausible, then, that Browne, whether consciously or unconsciously, employed the techniques of frontier humor in his portrayal of Yusef and his fantastic adventures. Indeed, careful consideration of the narrative setting of the second half of the book yields further evidence of Browne's use of Old Southwestern materials in the construction of *Yusef.*

On the surface, Browne presents the Holy Land as an untamed frontier territory, one that closely resembles the mid-nineteenth-century American West. For example, like the American frontier, Browne's interpretation of the Holy Land is an unsettled wilderness populated by isolated grangers, wide-eyed tenderfoot travelers, sage old-timers, horses, mules, and wandering herds of livestock. Browne even supplies the Holy Land with its own version of American Indians—the Bedouins—who are, after all, characterized as a savage indigenous people considered hostile to immigrant settlers and travelers alike. What's more, Browne engages this cast of characters in episodes immediately familiar as typical of American frontier humor. Throughout the narrative, for example, Browne and the unsuspecting "greenhorn" travelers are swindled by the seemingly charitable local guides, traders, and merchants—in a word, they are continuously hoaxed.

Equine humor, another staple of the Old Southwestern tradition, also accounts for much of the amusement in *Yusef.* At one point Browne is audience to the tall tale of Syed Sulemin, "a horse that must be known even in America, for Syed had leaped a wall twenty feet high, and was trained to walk a hundred and fifty miles a day, and kill the most desperate robbers by catching them up in his teeth and tossing them over his head" (183). In other parts of *Yusef,* Browne develops comic scenes around horses that are maimed. Among the most macabre is the so-called "genuine Syrian" that Yusef furnishes Browne, a horribly disfigured animal reminiscent of the images out of Longstreet's *Georgia Scenes* (1835):

> That there were some points of some kind about him was not to be disputed. His back must have been broken at different periods of his life, in at least three places; for there were three distinct pyramids on it, like miniature pyramids of Gizeh; one just in front of the saddle, where his shoulder-blade ran up to a cone; another just back of the saddle; and a third, a kind of spur of the range, over his hips, where there was a sudden breaking off from the original line of the backbone, and a precipitous descent to his tail. The joints of his hips and the joints of his legs were also prominent, especially those of his forelegs, which he seemed to be always trying to straighten out, but never could, in consequence of the sinews being too short by several inches. His skin hung upon this remarkable piece of frame-work as if it had been purposely put there to dry in the sun, so as to be ready for leather at any moment after the extinction of the vital functions within. But, to judge him from the eye (there was only one), there seemed to be no prospect of a suspension of vitality, for it burned with great brilliancy, showing that a horse, like a singed cat, may be a good deal better than he looks.
>
> "A great horse that," said Yusef, patting him on the neck kindly; "no humbug about him general. Fifty miles a day he'll travel fast asleep. He's a genuine Syrian." (184)

As Thomas Tenney has pointed out, readers acquainted with Twain's *Roughing It*—a book often praised for integrating features of Old Southwestern humor into popular travel literature—might recognize in Browne's "genuine Syrian" spoof a probable source for Twain's self-effacing horse-swap burlesque involving the "Genuine Mexican Plug."

Browne even devotes an entire chapter in the second half of *Yusef* to a Middle Eastern version of an Old Southwestern yarn-spinner named Ben-Hozain, "the

King of Talkers" (193). Note how Browne's sketch of this individual could just as readily describe the most prototypical of personas in the American frontier humor tradition:

> By profession and inclination Ben-Hozain is a story-teller. I do not mean to say that he is given to willful lying, or to any malicious misrepresentation of facts; but the business of his life is to entertain the public of Beirut with traditional romances of the country. Where people read but little, they make up in some measure for the deficiency by talking and listening a good deal. . . . In the absence of a general circulation of newspapers, of printed histories of wars, philosophical essays on man, and books of travel, they must have professional story-tellers; that is to say, men whose regular business it is to deal in tradition or fiction. Throughout the whole East there is not a more important personage than the story-teller, or one who wields a greater influence on the public mind. He is a walking newspaper, a living history, a breathing essay, a personified book of travels, which evolves its stores of knowledge on self-acting principles. . . . Men who have listened for years to the same stories and the same jokes, continue to listen for years again with undiminished delight, and always applaud at the same points and laugh at the same strokes of wit. (193)

That is not to say Browne could not have actually met a storyteller named Ben-Hozain while traveling through Syria as recounted in *Yusef.* Perhaps he did. But even if he had, his characterization of the Arab old-timer here is clearly reminiscent of, interchangeable with, and arguably based on that of the nineteenth-century American yarn-spinners Browne had certainly encountered earlier in his life on the riverboats of the Ohio and Mississippi Rivers and around the camps of California, those individuals who practiced what Walter Blair has aptly called "the greatest American folk art—the art of oral story-telling" (70).

Beyond such cosmetic similarities between the setting for the second half of *Yusef* and aspects of the nineteenth-century American West, Browne's version of the Holy Land appears to exhibit a profound cultural correspondence with the American frontier. In her comprehensive study of the American tall-tale tradition, *The Tall Tale in American Folklore and Literature* (1987), Carolyn Brown discusses at great length the folk culture milieu in which American frontier humor necessarily operates. She observes that at the heart of this tall-tale folk culture is the opposition of insider and outsider. The tall talker, Brown continues, functions as mediator between these two spheres by virtue of being an insider who comes into intimate contact with the outsider and who ultimately guides the outsider through the unfamiliar world of his culture. If one considers the basic ingredients of the travel book format—a foreign culture as setting, a curious reader who is more than likely a newcomer to that setting, and a narrator who serves as tour guide for the unfamiliar reader—the genre would seem rife with potential for consolidation with the American tall-tale tradition.

Indeed, J. Ross Browne seems to have intuitively recognized the aesthetic possibilities for combining the two literary modes with his 1853 travel book. In *Yusef,* Browne presents the Holy Land as operating according to the precepts of a frontier folk culture, replete with indigenous myths, rites, and codes (even though most as they are presented are merely transplanted American frontier myths, rites, and codes) that must be tendered to the outsider by the tall talker. Like the American tall-tale hero, Yusef is an insider in this Holy Land folk culture, who interacts and communicates with the outsider visitors (Browne the narrator, his companions and, again, even the reader), typically through the tall tale. That Browne and the tourists of *Yusef* remain outsiders during the course of the narrative probably owes much to the fact that Browne adopted a naive narrative point of view for his book. For as Carolyn Brown suggests: "In folk culture, the tall tale challenges the listener to prove himself clever or dull, in or out of the group to which the tale belongs, through his ability to recognize and appreciate the fiction" (77).

Browne as narrator is perhaps not entirely dull, but he is a newcomer and will often attempt to salvage his dignity in an embarrassing situation for humorous effect by appearing to accept the exaggerated claims of Yusef's tall tales as truth. In either case, whether dull or merely pretending to be dull, Browne's narrative persona delivers the comic moment over and over again—ultimately with Browne the author's principal objective, of course—but never penetrates the culture of Yusef and, therefore, remains an outsider to the end.

J. Ross Browne deserves to be recognized for having introduced indigenous forms of American humor to the travel book format, not just because his *Yusef* later served as a model for Mark Twain, but also—and more importantly—because he provided unprecedented exposure for the techniques of American frontier humor in well-circulated books and in the pages of enormously popular monthly periodicals a full generation before Twain and other more celebrated authors would employ them in their own full-length writings. J. Ross Browne merits further study in his own right and for the full range of his contributions to American humorous literature.

Notes

1. Franklin Walker's *Irreverent Pilgrims: Melville, Browne, and Mark Twain in the Holy Land* identifies Yusef as a "picaro."

2. See Walter Blair, *Native American Humor*, 80–ff.

3. See, for example, M. Thomas Inge's discussion of the importance of humor and "amusement" in American frontier literature in his introduction to *The Frontier Humorists.*

4. Admittedly, Yusef does regularly "visit" what he calls his pretty little "nieces" (who are inevitably married to older men) along the travel route, which often leads to the entire party's hasty departure from that particular locale. And at the end of the book, in an attempt to live up to his self-proclaimed ferocious reputation, Yusef assaults a man, after which he is jailed. But these actions would hardly qualify the young guide as a criminal or a picaro.

5. See, for example, Walter Blair's classic discussion of the "three types of incongruities" of frontier humor in *Native American Humor*, 92–99.

6. See M. Thomas Inge's *The Frontier Humorists*, 27.

Works Cited

Blair, Walter. *Native American Humor*. New York: Chandler, 1960.

Brown, Carolyn. *The Tall Tale in American Folklore and Literature*. Knoxville: Univ. of Tennessee Press, 1987.

Browne, J. Ross. *Yusef; Or The Journey of the Frangi, a Crusade in the East*. New York: Harper and Brothers, 1853.

Inge, M. Thomas, ed. *The Frontier Humorists*. Hamden, Conn.: Archon, 1975.

Rock, Francis J. *J. Ross Browne: A Biography*. Washington, D.C.: Catholic University of America, 1929.

Walker, Franklin. *Irreverent Pilgrims: Melville, Browne, and Mark Twain in the Holy Land*. Seattle: Univ. of Washington Press, 1974.

15

Mark Twain

The Victorian of Southwestern Humor

Leland Krauth

When Mark Twain moved into the New England culture—first in 1870 to its edge at Buffalo, and then in 1871 to one of its centers at Hartford's Nook Farm—he came doubly disguised. Truly from the South, he came to New England as a man from the West, and even his Western identity was itself partially concealed by his fame as the all-American traveler of *The Innocents Abroad.* While it is hyperbolic to say, as Van Wyck Brooks once did, that the New England Twain entered was "emasculated by the Civil War," the war, together with Westward migration, had reduced the male population of the region, changing somewhat its cultural tone.[1] Many of the remaining writers and public figures were unwittingly participating in the process of Victorianization that Ann Douglas has recently called the "feminization of American culture."[2] In this context, as the deeper layers of Mark Twain's personality expressed themselves, his presence was notably—to use an old-fashioned term in a conventional way—masculine. To genteel society he brought free drinking and smoking; to morality he added humor; to sentiment, burlesque; to seriousness, play. (Only Mark Twain's *study* had a billiards table.) He was in part, as James M. Cox has observed, "an invader" of the dominant culture of New England.[3]

While occupying New England, a secret Southerner in the North, a man in a feminized world, Mark Twain extended himself imaginatively back into the world of his true origin—the Old Southwest. And in this context, his presence was quite different. Twain's absorption of and contributions to the traditions of Southwestern humor have been extensively studied, but certain important aspects of his performance as a Southwestern humorist in *Adventures of Huckleberry Finn* have not, I think, been fully perceived. For as he entered the territory of his past to create his finest fiction, Twain brought to bear upon it a refinement more characteristic of New England than of the Old Southwest.

That Twain was steeped in the humorous traditions of the Old Southwest goes without saying these days. He owned personal copies of works by Augustus Baldwin Longstreet, Joseph M. Field, William Tappan Thompson, George Washington Harris, Johnson Jones Hooper, and Joseph G. Baldwin, and he planned to include most of these writers in *Mark Twain's Library of Humor.*[4] His knowledge of the tradition goes well beyond this, however, for as various critics have shown, the comic tradition of the Old Southwest was, in Bernard De Voto's words, the "matrix of Mark Twain's humor."[5] The scholarly investigation of his relationship to this tradition has thus established specific sources as well as the general influence of milieu, and the result is the widespread recognition that in Mark Twain, "Southwestern humor reached its climax."[6] What kind of a climax was it?

The tensions that inform his masterpiece of Southwestern humor *Huckleberry Finn* were defined by Twain himself as he moved between his frontier days in the West and South and his genteel days to come in New England. Writing from New York in May 1867 as the Traveling Correspondent for the *Alta California*, Twain posted a now well-known notice of George Washington Harris's work. He praised a collection of Sut Lovingood's yarns, saying that the book "abounds in humor," and then he speculated that while it would "sell well in the West," the "Eastern people" would "call it coarse and possibly taboo it."[7] At the time of his report, Twain was clearly in sympathy with Harris's humor, free from genteel taboos, but by the time he came to write *Huckleberry Finn* he was more firmly governed by a strong innate sense of propriety. And this is, I think, the key to understanding what he accomplishes within the tradition he employed. Twain reshapes the tradition of Southwestern humor by writing within it as a Victorian.[8]

To describe him as the Victorian of Southwestern humor is unfortunately to raise the specter of the long regional war waged so brilliantly by Brooks and De Voto (and often so dully by their followers) over Twain's "ordeal."[9] But I am not suggesting that the Wild Humorist of the Pacific Slope sold out to New England gentility at the cost of his artistry or that his art was fully nourished by the frontier he left behind him. On the contrary, I am emphasizing an innate propriety that was always a part of Mark Twain, a propriety that, if anything, marked him off from frontier life in the first place and finally led him to settle in New England. It was after all, to summon a single representative example, Twain himself, not those "sensitive & loyal subjects of the kingdom of heaven," Howells, Livy, and Livy's mother, who cleaned up the perceived impropriety of Huck's saying "they comb me all to hell."[10]

Twain's propriety, what I am calling his Victorianism, expressed itself in *Huckleberry Finn* in several ways. First, it led him to reshape some of the stock situations and characters common to the tradition of Southwestern humor. Second, it caused him to select from the raw materials of that tradition only certain subjects and, more important, to discard others. And third, it governed his creation of character, leading to the formation of a hero whose nature not only transcends the tradition but still challenges us today. Writing as a Victorian, Twain reformed Southwestern humor.

Four elements of *Huckleberry Finn* have repeatedly been singled out as particularly common to the tradition of Southwestern humor: the con-men (the Duke and the King), the camp meeting, the circus, and the Royal Nonesuch. But Twain's presentation of these traditional motifs is significantly different from the way they are treated by other Southwestern humorists. His greater complexity and seriousness have often been suggested, and in one of the most extended commentaries on his relation to Southwestern humor, Pascal Covici Jr. has pointed out—as a distinguishing difference—a "preoccupation" in Twain "with revealing a discrepancy between seeming and reality."[11] This is certainly true, but what has been overlooked is the fact that Twain transforms the reality of such situations and characters even as he exposes their seeming. The camp meeting is a case in point.

Camp meetings were of course both realities of backwoods life and stock episodes in the humorous fiction that fastened onto that life. The differences between Twain's camp meeting and that of Johnson Jones Hooper in *Some Adventures of Captain Simon Suggs*, the literary work most often cited as a source, illustrate how Twain Victorianizes the tradition of Southwestern humor.[12] Hooper's camp meeting is at once an orgy, a fleecing, a thrill-filled happening, and a staged melodrama. The religious longings presumably informing the meeting are transparently bogus; the impulses that actually animate the gathering are sexual, monetary, sensational, and theatrical. Hooper is insistent upon the sensual aspect of the action. "Men and women," he writes, "rolled about on the ground, or lay sobbing or shouting in promiscuous heaps."[13] He exposes the sexual urgencies underlying the crowd's frenzy in a highly suggestive language:

> "Keep the thing warm!" roared a sensual seeming man, of stout mould and florid countenance, who was exhorting among a bevy of young women, upon whom he was lavishing caresses. "Keep the thing warm, breethring!—come to the Lord, honey!" he added, as he vigorously hugged one of the damsels he sought to save.
>
> "Gl-o-ree!" yelled a huge . . . woman, as in a fit of the jerks, she threw herself convulsively from her feet, and fell 'like a thousand of brick,' across a diminutive old man in a little round hat, who was squeaking consolation to one of the mourners.
>
> "Good Lord, have mercy!" ejaculated the little man. (pp. 120–21)

In his punning, Hooper is daring as well as amusing. He writes here very much in the so-called strong masculine vein of Southwestern humor.

In his camp meeting, Twain preserves the sense of the meeting's monetary, sensational, and theatrical impulses, but he all but eliminates the sexual. Huck gives us this description:

> The women had on sun-bonnets; and some had linsey-woolsey frocks, some gingham ones, and a few of the young ones had on calico. Some of the young men was barefooted, and some of the children didn't have on any clothes but just a tow-linen shirt. Some of the old women was knitting, and some of the young folks was courting on the sly.[14]

This is far from the sexual antics of Hooper's fanatics, and it is far indeed from his ribald language. In fact, Huck's acknowledgment of covert play between the sexes is phrased in such a way as to suggest its essential innocence: "the young folks was courting on the sly." Twain does come somewhat closer to the sensual when he has

Huck describe the crowd's response to the King's outlandish tale of conversion from piracy to missionary work, but again a transformation of the raw material of Southwestern humor is apparent:

> So the king went all through the crowd with his hat, swabbing his eyes, and blessing the people and praising them and thanking them for being so good to the poor pirates away off there; and every little while the prettiest kind of girls, with the tears running down their cheeks, would up and ask him would he let them kiss him, for to remember him by; and he always done it; and some of them he hugged and kissed as many as five or six times— (p.112)

The King is a bit of a lecher, though finally more interested in cash than kissing, and the young girls could be said to be sublimating their sexual urges, but what Twain invites us to laugh at them for is not their sublimated desires but their misplaced sentimentality.

Twain's expurgation of the traditional camp meeting is representative of the way he Victorianizes the material of Southwestern humor. He effects similar changes in presenting his con men, the circus, and the Royal Nonesuch—his version of Gyascutus, that favorite exhibition of Southwestern lewdness. (Huck says the performance was enough to make "a cow laugh" [p. 127, but he characteristically declines to describe it.) In discussing Twain's ties to George Washington Harris (Harris of course creates a camp meeting that is almost as lascivious as Hooper's), one critic has suggested that they share a sense of "man's predisposition to dehumanize himself."[15] But more often than not in *Huckleberry Finn,* Twain refuses to let his characters debase themselves by being the fully carnal, somewhat bestial creatures of their tradition.

Even more important than his virtual bowdlerizing of specific episodes common to Southwestern humor is Twain's selection of material from that body of writing. The traditional subjects of Southwestern humor have often been defined and even itemized. In the introduction to their fine collection, Hennig Cohen and William B. Dillingham offer this set of categories:

(1) The hunt
(2) Fights, mock fights, and animal fights
(3) Courtings, weddings, and honeymoons
(4) Frolics and dances
(5) Games, horse races, and other contests
(6) Militia drills
(7) Elections and electioneering
(8) The legislature and the courtroom
(9) Sermons, camp meetings, and religious experiences
(10) The visitor in a humble home
(11) The country boy in the city

(12) The riverboat
(13) Adventures of the rogue
(14) Pranks and tricks of the practical joker
(15) Gambling
(16) Trades and swindles
(17) Cures, sickness and bodily discomfort, medical treatments
(18) Drunks and drinking
(19) Dandies, foreigners, and city slickers
(20) Oddities and local eccentrics[16]

While no single work of Southwestern humor contains all these, some come close; *Huckleberry Finn* does not. What is revealing, however, is not the number of these conventional topics absent from *Huckleberry Finn* but the particular kinds that are absent. It ignores, first of all, those subjects—like courtings, frolics, dances, weddings, and honeymoons—that naturally involve adult sexuality. And secondly, it omits entirely or else skims over those activities—like hunting, fighting, gambling, gaming, horse racing, heavy drinking, and military maneuvering—that are the traditional pastimes of manly backwoods living. (Whenever such activities do appear briefly, they are targets of ridicule.) In short, Twain purges from the Southwestern tradition its exuberant celebration of rough-and-tumble masculinity.

D.H. Lawrence's famous dogmatic summary of the essential American "soul" may not do justice to the heroes of classic American fiction, but the summary is a fitting description of the recurrent hero of Southwestern humor: "hard, isolate, stoic, and a killer."[17] When Twain appropriates the type, he disparages it far more than his predecessors do, and unlike his forerunners in Southwestern humor, he reveals the pernicious traits in gentleman and commoner alike. The adult white males in *Huckleberry Finn* are indeed hard, isolate, stoic, and lethal. From the new Judge who threatens to reform the drunken Pap "with a shot-gun" to Colonel Sherburn, who does reform the drunken Boggs with a "pistol," the men in the novel are aggressive and destructive (pp. 21, 121). The book is surcharged with an atmosphere of imminent violence, whose source is simply the nature of white males. The ferocity they embody erupts in the antics of Pap, in the search of the slave hunters, in the feud between the Grangerfords and Shepherdsons, in the relationship of the Duke to the King, in the mob that rides them out of town on a rail, and in the acts of the *Walter Scott* gang, as well as in the gunning down of Boggs. The terror of masculine violence is intensified by its arbitrariness. When Huck is seeking information about Cairo the day after he has found the pair of slave hunters, he meets a nameless man setting a trotline from his skiff. Their encounter is emblematic of the male world of the novel:

> "Mister, is that Cairo?"
> "Cairo? No. You must be a blame fool."
> "What town is it, mister?"

> "If you want to know, go and find out. If you stay here botherin' around me for about a half a minute longer, you'll get something you won't want."[18] (p. 79)

Twain's imagination seems haunted by the memory of a gratuitous hostility in men that borders on violence. The memory is partly of literature, of the rough men who people Southwestern humor, but it is also a recollection of life, of his life in Hannibal, on the river, and in the West. And no doubt this image of man has something to do with the father, John Marshall Clemens, the Judge and Southern gentleman of whom Mark Twain once secretly recorded: "Silent, austere, of perfect probity and high principle; ungentle of manner toward his children, but always a gentleman in his phrasing—and never punished them—a look was enough, and more than enough."[19] Although Twain is sixty-two when he makes this notation, the remembrance of fear is still strong—"a look was enough, and more than enough." Hamlin Hill has recently suggested that "fear" was in fact "the controlling emotion" of Mark Twain's life.[20] Certainly fear is the dominant emotion in Huck Finn's experience, and it is most often a fear engendered by the men of his world (Huck is never afraid of women).

In their verbal and physical aggressions, the men in *Huckleberry Finn* express their pride, uphold their honor, and assert their manhood—all of which seem for them somehow in question. Pap's raging complaint is that "*a man* can't get his rights" (p. 24, my italics), and Colonel Sherburn's philippic turns precisely upon the question of what makes "a *man*" (p. 124, Twain's italics). The issue for Twain is far-reaching. Oddly, although it is central to his life, cropping up as a question of courage in his youth, his river piloting, his brief Civil War experience, his days in the West, and in particular in his abortive duel, Twain's sense of manliness has never been fully explored.[21] Yet from his Western sketches, on through *Huckleberry Finn* and *Simon Wheeler, Detective*, to the late essay "The United States of Lyncherdom," to mention only a few obvious examples, he was preoccupied with the idea of manliness. Significantly, it was bound up for him with two issues that are central to *Huckleberry Finn*: the sense of freedom and the concept of the gentleman. In an 1866 letter to his boyhood friend Will Bowen (a part of which was later to emerge in "Old Times on the Mississippi"), Twain conflated manliness, independence, and gentlemanliness (all the italics are his):

> I am sorry to hear *any* harm of any pilot—for I hold those old river friends above all others, & I know that in genuine *manliness* they assay away above the common multitude. You know, yourself, Bill—or you *ought* to know it—that *all* men,—kings & serfs alike—are *slaves* to other men & to circumstances—save, alone, the pilot—who comes at no man's beck or call, obeys no man's orders & scorns all men's suggestions. . . . It is a strange study—a singular phenomenon, if you please—that the only real, independent & genuine *gentlemen* in the world go quietly up &

> down the Mississippi river, asking no homage of anyone, seeking no popularity, no notoriety, & not caring a damn whether school keeps or not.[22]

Huck goes quietly down the Mississippi, asking "no homage of any one, seeking no popularity, no notoriety, & not caring a damn whether school keeps or not." It is no accident that when Huck struggles with his conscience, trying to bring himself to turn Jim in, Twain specifically has Huck denounce himself for his failure to do the "right" thing in the language of manhood. "I warn't," Huck says, "man enough—hadn't the spunk of a rabbit" (p. 76). On the contrary, of course. In resisting the pressures of his society, the norms that dictate Jim's return to slavery, Huck demonstrates not only his freedom but also his true manhood. Like the pilot of Twain's vision, Huck assays above the multitude in genuine manliness. His fortitude in determining to free Jim at whatever cost to himself stands in stark contrast to the self-vaunting courage of the other white males of the novel—and of their prototypes in previous Southwestern humor. Twain recreates the hero of that tradition in Huck, replacing the aggressive, violent male with a passive, loving one. Further, through Jim, Twain ascribes to Huck an additional status. As a recent critic has pointed out, a number of "labels" are imposed on Huck, none of which fits the reality of his character.[23] Thus to the Widow Douglas he is a "poor lost lamb," and to Pap he is "a good deal of a big-bug," while to Miss Watson he is simply a "fool" (pp. 3, 18,11). Only Jim, who comes to know Huck intimately on the raft, really apprehends the essence of Huck's character. He articulates for us the significance of Huck. On the most intimate level, Huck is "de ole true Huck," Jim's "bes' fren'," but Huck is for Jim also something more: he is a "white genlman" (p. 76).

Huck is the true man and gentleman of the novel, Twain's most radical departure from the tradition that nurtured him. Before Twain, the gentleman was trapped in the frame of the Southwestern tale, reduced to moralizing about the action in polite language, while the free and the manly were represented by the unfeeling, amoral, violent vulgarians of the story itself.[24]. But in Huck the free, the manly, and the moral coalesce. In order to create Huck—to recreate the conventional hero of the tradition—Twain altered the formal tactics of Southwestern humor in two important ways. First, he changed the frame, that structural division between the conventional gentleman narrator and his vulgar heroes, which created a separation between the author's world of order, reason, and morality, and the actor's life of disorder, violence, and amorality. Twain eliminated this division by fusing, in the words of Kenneth Lynn, "the Gentleman and the Clown" into a "single character," into Huck himself.[25] Second, Twain profoundly changed the tradition of Southwestern humor by changing the language of its narrative; he transformed, as James M. Cox has put it, the traditional "dialect" into "vernacular."[26] These changes gave birth to Huck, but their implications have not been fully understood.

The union of gentleman and vulgarian suggests, on the face of it, a re-alignment of sympathies—away from the conventional and elite toward the radical and common. This is in fact how Twain's achievement is frequently described. But I would suggest that the effect of the formal fusion is just the reverse: instead of committing himself to the common person through his union of gentleman and vulgarian, Mark Twain elevates the common beyond itself. The second formal act operates even more clearly in the same way. For to transform dialect into vernacular is to raise the crude language of a restricted region to the broader plain of a more versatile and more nearly universal speech.

Huck has, as recent critics have emphasized, a dual role in his novel: he is, in Alan Trachtenberg's terms, both "the verbalizer of the narrative" and "a character within the narrative."[27] As verbalizer of the narrative, although his language is vernacular, Huck preserves a linguistic decorum—a decorum that would have puzzled the likes of, say, Sut Lovingood, but pleased almost any of the Southwestern authors. Huck reports that the speech of Pap "was all the hottest kind of language" (p. 25), and he tells us that while he himself had "stopped cussing" living at the Widow Douglas's because "the widow didn't like it," he "took to it again" (p. 22) living in the woods with Pap. But of course Huck never uses the words, his or Pap's. Huck's propriety of language within the vernacular is one sign of the infusion of the gentleman into Huck—of his more Victorian character. Another is Huck's treatment of sexual material. Here the verbalizer and the character become identical, for not only does Huck as narrator shy away from sexual or sexually suggestive language, but Huck as actor also shuns the erotic. The most striking example of Huck's modesty occurs when he and Jim enter the floating house that contains the dead Pap. To the reader it is clear that the house—with its "naked" dead man, "old whisky bottles," "bed," "two old dirty calico dresses," and "some women's underclothes" (pp. 43–44—is either a bawdy house or a house where bawdy activities have been pursued. Huck's narrative gives no sign of whether he has taken this in, but what it does reveal is his response to the graffiti on the walls. Huck says, "all over the walls was the ignorantest kind of words and pictures, made with charcoal" (p. 44). His condemnation of such writings as "ignorantest" is more than a joke; it is indicative of the delicacy in Huck that leads him to keep his own narrative language free from crudity. Further, incorrect as it is, Huck's use of "ignorantest" draws some of its force from the recent conflict in his life between the widow Douglas, who would educate him in the ways of civilization, and Pap, who would keep him as ignorant as he is in order to insure that he is not "better'n" his father (p. 18). But Huck is clearly more civilized than Pap in speech as well as action (as verbalizer as well as character). Although Jim conceals the fact of Pap's death from Huck, Huck's rejection of the pornographic is tantamount to a rejection of the world of his father at its deepest core.[28]

Huck's avoidance of profanity and his disapproval of the pornographic point to his character as authentic gentleman, just as his courage in behalf of Jim points to his manliness. Transformed as he is from the crude, violent, and amoral hero of Southwestern humor, Huck can be seen as the unlikely representative of true civilization. Twain's novel thus presents more than a simple conflict between a debased society and a primitive goodness; it reveals in Huck the foundation of a genuine civilization. That foundation is nicely summed up in Ortega y Gasset's insistence that the human root of civilization is "the desire on the part of each individual to take others into consideration."[29] In these terms, Huck, the most considerate free person in the novel, is clearly the most civilized.

Henry Nash Smith has called attention to the presence in the novel of "a residue of the eighteenth-century cult of sensibility,"[30] but no one to my knowledge has made the obvious connection between this cult of sensibility and Huck himself. The historical emphasis upon sensibility carried well beyond the eighteenth century, of course, becoming a prominent feature of nineteenth-century Victorian life and art, especially the "feminized" American version of it. In attending to such emotionalism, Twain was not only being true to his novel's setting in the 1830s or 1840s; he was also commenting on current postures in his own society. The sentimental was, in short, very much with Mark Twain. It was also in him. Twain's burlesque of the cult in *Huckleberry Finn* is in part I believe, a check against his own susceptibility, and in part a diversion calculated to deflect our attention away from Huck's own overabundance of emotion. A further disguise of "de ole true Huck" is provided by Huck's role as critic of the sentimental. Huck memorably dismisses emotional outpourings as "tears and flapdoodle," "soul-butter and hogwash," "rot and slush" (p. 138). But Huck himself is governed by intense feeling, and at times he gives voice to his emotions in fairly sentimental ways. Unlike the various impostors in the novel who call themselves gentlemen, weeping soulful tears only to perpetrate violent acts, Huck is always a gentle-man. His tenderness is extraordinary. For he is, I suggest, Mark Twain's version of the eighteenth-century Man of Feeling.

The ideas that generated the Man of Feeling may be summarized as follows: first, the identification of virtue with acts of benevolence and with feelings of universal good will; second, the assumption that good affections, benevolent feelings, are the natural outgrowth of the heart of man; third, the conviction that tenderness is manly; and fourth, the belief that benevolent emotions, even anguished ones, result in pleasant, self-approving feelings.[31] The first three of these, I suggest, fit Huck's character perfectly. He is virtuous in his predisposition to aid virtually everyone he encounters, from the Widow Douglas to the *Walter Scott* gang, from the Grangerfords to the Shepherdsons, from Aunt Sally to Jim, from Mary Jane Wilks to the con-men who would defraud her. This universal good will in Huck is indeed rooted in his heart, the one Twain praised as "sound."[32] And without question Huck's tenderness is manly; his tears are strong and genuine. Twain's departure from the archetype of the Man of Feeling lies in his rejection of the fourth engendering idea: the notion that pleasure can be derived from painful benevolent emotions. This is a crucial variation, one that saves Twain's character from absurd postures of self-approving joy, and more important, one that makes Huck a comic Man of Feeling. Huck never feels good about his goodness; his altruistic emotions—with the possible exception of his aid to Mary Jane—never give him egoistic satisfaction. For of course Huck always thinks that in following his fine feelings he is acting immorally.

His confusion is the source of our laughter. "I cried a little," Huck says, "when I was covering up Buck's face" (p. 98), and when he learns that Jim has been sold by the Duke and the King, he reports, "then I set down and cried; I couldn't help it" (p. 177). In his narrative Huck is recurrently tearful, but most often it is the refusal to set forth his feelings—"I ain't agoing to tell all that happened" (p. 97)—that persuades us of the depth and authenticity of his emotions. Huck's mode of narrating—in both its language and its flat, matter-of-fact style—conveys his tenderness without sentimental excess. Nothing is more persuasive in just this way than the moment when Huck, accompanied by Tom, who is for once silent and forgotten, first sees Jim in the privacy of the Phelps cabin after their forced separation: "We crept in under Jim's bed into the cabin, and pawed around and found the candle and lit it, and stood over Jim a while, and found him looking hearty and healthy, and then we woke him up gentle and gradual" (p. 207). At times, however, Huck's account, in style and language, flirts with the "rot and slush" of sentimental piety: "It was only a little thing to do, and no trouble; and it's the little things that smoothes people's roads the most, down here below" (p. 160). Only the fact that the "it" here is a lie (one that "wouldn't cost nothing" [p. 160]) saves Huck's utterance from emotional stickiness. What the remark reveals is how bound together in *Huckleberry Finn* humor and sentiment are.

Twain, who said surprisingly little about humor for a humorist, once insisted that "a man can never be a humorist, in thought or deed, until he can feel the springs of pathos."[33] It is often the pathos of Huck's experience as gentle Man of Feeling that creates the humor in the book. And this too is something new in the tradition of Southwestern humor. What is generally thought to be Huck's finest moment—his decision to steal Jim out of slavery and go to hell—is both his greatest moment of pathos and one of the most humorous moments in the entire book. The pathos emerges as Huck faces his dilemma:

> I went to the raft, and set down in the wigwam to think. But I couldn't come to nothing. I thought till I wore my head sore, but I couldn't see no way out of the trouble. After all this long journey, and after all we'd done for them scoundrels, here was it all come to nothing, everything all busted up and ruined, because they could have the heart to serve Jim such a trick as that, and make him a slave again all his life, and amongst strangers, too, for forty dirty dollars. (pp. 177–78)

Huck's language remains steadfastly colloquial, and its earthy incorrectness checks against sentimentality at the same time it provokes amusement. But his style significantly veers away from its characteristic pattern. Huck most often writes run-on sentences that lack subordination and so equalize the events he strings together.[34] Here, however, emotion begins to build in the fourth sentence as Huck registers in two subordinates the catastrophe of Jim's return to slavery as a betrayal of a shared past: "After all this long journey, and after all we'd done for them scoundrels, here was it all come to nothing." The inversion, "here was it," is a further departure from Huck's usually natural speech, one designed to focus and intensify feeling. His emotion breaks into a moral indignation at the end that is realized in the language of feeling hearts and in a syntax that bespeaks compounding emotion: "because they could have the heart to serve Jim such a trick as that, and make him a slave again all his life, and amongst strangers, too, for forty dirty dollars."

The climax of Huck's feeling comes in the full recollection of his time with Jim, one of the most admired passages in the novel:

> I felt good and all washed clean of sin for the first time I had ever felt so in my life, and I knowed I could pray now. But I didn't do it straight off, but laid the paper down and set there thinking—thinking how good it was all this happened so, and how near I come to being lost and going to hell. And went on thinking. And got to thinking over our trip down the river; and I see Jim before me, all the time, in the day, and in the night-time, sometimes moonlight, sometimes storms, and we a floating along, talking, and singing, and laughing. But somehow I couldn't seem to strike no places to harden me against him, but only the other kind. I'd see him standing my watch on top of his'n, stead of calling me, so I could go on sleeping; and see him how glad he was when I come back out of the fog; and when I come to him again in the swamp, up there where the feud was; and such-like times; and would always call me honey, and pet me, and do everything he could think of for me, and how good he always was; and at last I struck the time I saved him by telling the men we had small-pox aboard, and he was so grateful, and said I was the best friend old Jim ever had in the world, and the only one he's got now; and then I happened to look around, and see that paper. (p. 179)

The pathos here is worthy of Dickens. Huck's style becomes rather conventionally poetic, as he employs repetition, alliteration, assonance, and artfully balanced rhythms. He is in fact writing in the cadences of gentility, evoking refined gentlemanly sentiment: "all the time, in the day, and in the night-time, sometimes moonlight, sometimes storms, and we floating along, talking, and singing, and laughing."[35] This is a touching, idealized image of the times on the raft, more lyric than any on-the-spot descriptions of them. This welling of pathetic emotion makes unbelievable, moving, and comic Huck's desperate resolution—"All right, then, I'll go to hell" (p. 180)—for of course we know that no one of such fine and tender feeling can be damned. Twain achieves here precisely: what he once praised in William Dean Howells' fiction as the power to make the reader "cry inside" and "laugh all the time."[36]

Jesse Bier has explained one impetus behind Southwestern humor as a reaction against the "prettification" of American writing in the nineteenth century.[37] Twain was in turn reacting against the coarseness of the Southwestern tradition.

While exerting to one degree or another his rowdy side within the New England culture he invaded, Twain expressed his own propriety while writing within the tradition of Southwestern humor. (The impulse to run counter to the norm was always strong in this man who contained within himself so many contrary selves.) Far from being a simple bowdlerizing, Twain's Victorian reformation on the material and hero of Southwestern humor enacted a profound concept whose cultural implications are still challenging. In its tradition and beyond it to our time, *Huckleberry Finn* is a radical novel.

Huckleberry Finn is still challenging today because of its portrayal of a Man of Feeling whose degree of tenderness defies not only the sexual stereotypes of Southwestern humor but also the still-prevailing values of our own times. Huck's delicacy and tenderness exceed, even today, the popular sense of what constitutes a man's feelings. Leslie Fiedler's now-famous perception of a secret "male love" at the center of *Huckleberry Finn* both points accurately to a core of feeling and misconstrues it into a "homoerotic" bond.[38] More recently, Harold H. Kolb Jr. has reviewed Huck's "seemingly motiveless benignity" and ended by calling him a "seven dollar Friendship's Offering moral idealist."[39] Apparently, it is only by employing provocatively a skewed language of love, as Fiedler does, or by using ironically the sentimental language of nineteenth-century women's books, as Kolb does, that we can come to terms with Huck's fineness of feeling. His kind of manliness seems to elude our language for it,—even today.

Notes

1. *The Ordeal of Mark Twain*, rev. ed. (1933; rpt. New York: Dutton, 1970), p. 91.
2. *The Feminization of American Culture* (New York: Knopf, 1977).
3. "Humor and America: The Southwest Bear Hunt," *Sewanee Review* 83 (1975): 596.
4. For a listing of Twain's personal copies of Southwestern humorists, see Alan Gribben, *Mark Twain's Library: A Reconstruction*. 2 vols. (Boston: G.K. Hall, 1980); for the plans for *Mark Twain's Library of Humor*, see *Mark Twain's Notebooks & Journals*, II, eds. Frederick Anderson, Lin Salamo, and Bernard I. Stein (Berkeley: Univ. of California Press, 1975), 361–65.
5. "The Matrix of Mark Twain's Humor," *Bookman* 74 (1931): 172–78.
6. M. Thomas Inge, Introduction. *The Frontier Humorists: Critical Views* (Hamden, Conn.: Archon, 1975), p. 8.
7. "Sut Lovingood," *Mark Twain's Travels With Mr. Brown*, eds. Franklin Walker and Ezra Dane (New York: Knopf, 1940), p. 221.
8. Used casually in Twain scholarship for years, the term "Victorian" is general but apt. Many of his attitudes and values correspond remarkably with the ethos defined in such standard studies as Walter E. Houghton's *The Victorian Frame of Mind, 1830–1870* (New York: Yale Univ. Press, 1957) and Jerome H. Buckley's *The Victorian Temper: A Study in Literary Culture* (Cambridge: Harvard Univ. Press, 1951).
9. See Brooks, *The Ordeal* and Bernard De Voto, *Mark Twain's America* (Boston: Little, Brown, 1932).
10. *Mark Twain–Howells Letters*, eds. Henry Nash Smith and William M. Gibson. 2 vols. (Cambridge: Harvard Univ. Press, 1960), I, 122.

11. *Mark Twain's Humor: The Image of a World* (Dallas: Southern Methodist Univ. Press, 1962), p. 15.

12. Hooper is cited as a source in *The Art of "Huckleberry Finn,"* eds. Hamlin Hill and Walter Blair (San Francisco: Chandler, 1962), p. 453, and in *Adventures of Huckleberry Finn*, eds. Sculley Bradley et al., 2nd ed. (New York: Norton, 1977), p. 253. For conflicting assessments of how successfully Twain uses Hooper, see De Voto, *Mark Twain's America*, p. 225, and Walter Blair, *Mark Twain & "Huck Finn"* (Berkeley: Univ. of California Press, 1960), pp. 279–81.

13. *Some Adventures of Captain Simon Suggs* (Philadelphia: Carey and Hart, 1845), p. 119. Subsequent references to this edition are given parenthetically in my text. The camp meetings of both Hooper and Twain should be read in light of such accounts of the "real thing" as those given in the *Autobiography of Peter Cartwright, The Backwoods Preacher*, ed. W.P. Strickland (Cincinnati: Cranston and Stowe, 1856).

14. *Adventures of Huckleberry Finn*, ed. Henry Nash Smith (Boston: Houghton Mifflin, 1958), p. 110. Subsequent references to this edition are given parenthetically in my text.

15. Hennig Cohen, "Mark Twain's Sut Lovingood," in *The Lovingood Papers*, ed. Ben McClary (Knoxville: Univ. of Tennessee Press, 1962), p. 21.

16. *Humor of the Old Southwest*, 2nd ed. (Athens: Univ. of Georgia Press, 1975), p. xvii.

17. *Studies in Classic American Literature* (1922; rpt. Garden City, New York: Doubleday, 1951), p. 73.

18. In "The Raft Episode in *Huckleberry Finn*," *Modern Fiction Studies* 14 (1968): 11–20, Peter Beidler suggests that some of the meaning of Huck's encounter with the fisherman has been lost by the deletion of the raftsman's passage. If, as Beidler believes, the omitted passage makes it clear that Huck and Jim have already passed Cairo, then its inclusion would explain why the fisherman thinks Huck is a "blame fool." But there is still no explanation for his hostility and gratuitous threat of violence.

19. Mark Twain, "Villagers of 1840–3," *Hannibal, Huck & Tom*, ed. Walter Blair (Berkley: Univ. of California Press, 1969), p. 39.

20. *Mark Twain: God's Fool* (New York: Harper & Row, 1973), p. 269.

21. The sexual dimension of the issue is raised provocatively by G. Legman, *Mark Twain: the Mammoth God* (Milwaukee: Maledicta, 1976), pp. 1–17; but see also my very different "Mark Twain Fights Sam Clemens's Duel," *Mississippi Quarterly* 33 (1980): 141–53.

22. *Mark Twain's Letters to Will Bowen*, ed. Theodore Hornberger (Austin: Univ. of Texas Press, 1941), pp. 13–14.

23. Louise K. Barnett, "Huck Finn: Picaro as Linguistic Outsider," *College Literature* 6 (1979): 225.

24. The seminal discussion of the frame device, a hallmark of Southwestern humor, is Walter Blair, *Native American Humor* (New York: American Book Co., 1937), pp. 90–92. Two useful yet differing perspectives on the humor generated by the frame are provided by Louis J. Budd, "Gentlemanly Humorists of the Old South," *Southern Folklore Quarterly* 17 (1953): 232–40, who emphasizes the elite outlook of these humorists, and James M. Cox, "Humor of the Old Southwest," *The Comic Imagination in American Literature*, ed. Louis D. Rubin Jr. (New Brunswick: Rutgers Univ. Press, 1973), pp. 101–12, who acknowledges their gentility but nonetheless stresses their "cooperation" with the vulgar heroes.

25. *Mark Twain and Southwestern Humor* (Boston: Little, Brown, 1959), p. 148.

26. *Mark Twain: The Fate of Humor* (Princeton: Princeton Univ. Press, 1966), p. 167. While describing Huck's language as dialect rather than vernacular, David Carkeet, "The

Dialects of *Huckleberry Finn*," *American Literature* 51 (1979): 315–32, points out that among the various dialects, Huck's is the least like the speech employed by traditional Southwestern humorists.

27. "The Form of Freedom in *Adventures of Huckleberry Finn*," *Southern Review*, NS 6 (1970): 960.

28. If we take into account the distinction insisted upon by Watson Branch, "Hard-Headed Huck: 'No Time to Be Sentimentering,'" *Studies in American Fiction* 6 (1978): 212–18, between the past when the events of the narrative occurred and the present in which Huck writes of them, then Huck's description of the scene of Pap's death can be said to be informed by Huck's knowledge of the death.

29. Jose Ortega y Gasset, *The Revolt of the Masses* (1932; rpt. New York: Norton, 1957), p. 76. For Ortega's barbarism becomes the deposition "not" to "take others into account," a formulation that fits well the other free white men in the novel.

30. Henry Nash Smith, *Mark Twain: The Development of A Writer* (Cambridge: Harvard Univ. Press, 1962), p. 117.

31. I follow closely here R.S. Crane, "Suggestions Toward a Genealogy of the 'Man of Feeling'," *ELH,* 1 (1934): 205–30.

32. Notebook #28a [1], TS, p. 35 (1895), Mark Twain Papers, as quoted in Smith "Introduction," *Huckleberry Finn*, p. xvi.

33. "Visit of Mark Twain/Wit and Humour," *Sydney (Australia) Morning Herald,* 17 September 1895, pp. 5–6, as reproduced in Louis J. Budd, "Mark Twain Talks Mostly About Humor and Humorists," *Studies in American Humor* 1 (1974): 11.

34. For an extended examination of Huck's style and its implications, see Janet H. McKay, "'Tears and Flapdoodle': Point of View and Style in *The Adventures of Huckleberry Finn*," *Style* 10 (1976: 41–50.

35. In *Democracy and the Novel* (New York: Oxford Univ, Press, 1978), pp. 109–14, Henry Nash Smith also calls attention to Huck's shift into a more conventional language and style. For Smith this betrays the moral contamination of Huck's consciousness by the dominant culture. I would add that it reveals as well the impress of the cult of sensibility. As he slides into a more or less conventionally poetic style, Huck voices the delicacy of feeling espoused, though seldom attained, by the dominant culture; writing for a moment in the cadences of gentility, he in effect authenticates the ideal of feeling so spuriously upheld by the culture.

36. *Twain–Howells Letters,* II, 533.

37. *The Rise and Fall of American Humor* (New York: Holt Rinehart & Winston, 1968), p. 63.

38. Leslie Fiedler, "Come Back to the Raft Ag'in, Huck Honey!" *Partisan Review* 15 (1948): 666–67.

39. Harold H. Kolb Jr. "Mark Twain, Huck Finn, and Jacob Blivens: Gilt-Edged Tree-Calf Morality in *The Adventures of Huckleberry Finn*," *Virginia Quarterly Review* 55 (1979): 663.

16

Jason Compson and Sut Lovingood

Southwestern Humor as Stream of Consciousness

Stephen M. Ross

> And then I like Sut Lovingood from a book written by George Harris about 1840 or 50 in the Tennessee mountains. He had no illusions about himself, did the best he could; at certain times he was a coward and knew it and wasn't ashamed; he never blamed his misfortunes on anyone and never cursed God for them.[1]

Faulkner's admiration for the long-legged prankster Sut Lovingood hints at how deeply the roots of his own art strike into the soil of the Southwest. Sut is, after all, not necessarily an easy character to like; Edmund Wilson calls him "malignant" and "a peasant squatting in his own filth," and Harris's *Sut Lovingood's Yarns* "by far the most repellent book of any real literary merit in American literature."[2] Faulkner's and Wilson's reactions to Sut, when set side by side, point up the paradoxical nature of frontier humor. Many American tall tales are "repellent" in their violence, grotesquery, and exaggeration; yet they are simultaneously funny and exuberantly joyful, a shouting down of hostile reality. That he could respond to Sut as a character worthy of respect suggests how fully Faulkner, like Twain before him, absorbed the contradictory spirit of Southwestern Humor into his own art.

Contemplating the relationship between Southwestern Humor and Faulkner's fiction is a considerably more complicated process than pointing to authors and works from which Faulkner may have gathered material. To be sure, there is much "gathering" evident in Faulkner's writings: the dialects of his hill people, the schemes of Flem Snopes, the overblown voluptuousness of Eula Varner, the bear that Ike McCaslin hunts—these naturally harken back to Longstreet, Thorpe, Hooper, and Harris.[3] But behind such borrowing lies the assimilation by Faulkner of an entire sense of felt life; he could at times adopt the vision of man and the world endemic to frontier humor, treating it as one viable—though in no sense final or always admirable—version of human existence. Instead of proving bothersome, the contradictions inherent in the tall tale offered Faulkner another lens through which to project certain truths of the human spirit; Faulkner could "like" Sut Lovingood because he could imaginatively apprehend the world Sut runs through.

I want to consider here one instance of Faulkner's revitalization of Southwestern Humor: the resemblance Jason Compson's world and character bear to Sut

Lovingood's. If we explore Jason's section of *The Sound and the Fury* alongside *Sut Lovingood's Yarns*, we can sense a convergence of tone, of kind of event, of mentality that reaches far deeper than the mere fact that Faulkner knew Harris's book and liked Sut. Sut, in fact, may be Jason's closest ancestor in American literature, not so much because of specific parallels in event or image, but because of a basic similarity of spirit, stripped in Jason's case of the exuberance and occasional decent feeling that keeps Harris's *Yarns* from being (Edmund Wilson notwithstanding) totally repellent. In Jason, Faulkner creates a comic fool much like Sut—like him in forms of expression, in patterns of behavior and motive, in perceptions of self. Faulkner incorporates both the humor and the darkness of Sut's Tennessee hill country into Jason's mental world; and he creates in Jason's monologue a version of stream of consciousness that grows directly out of the vernacular narrative mode in which Harris wrote.

I

Jason's monologue has been discussed, at some length by James Mellard, as belonging to the broad tradition of oral narrative.[4] As Mellard points out the intensely oral qualities of Jason's talk make his section the most accessible of the three Compson monologues. Far more than either Benjy's or Quentin's, Jason's voice creates the illusion of a story being told publicly. Faulkner explores Jason's deepest psychic impulses in a language that reproduces the rhythms of audible, colloquial speech with its fillers, its digressions and sudden jumps in subject or logic, its slight alterations in grammar, word order, or usage. Jason is very much the colloquial storyteller speaking an externally directed idiom, talking at the reader, joking, complaining, voicing his opinions. For all its bitterness, Jason's talk still evinces those qualities that make a storyteller like Thorpe's Arkansas hunter or the furniture salesman who narrates the last chapter of *Light in August* such delights to listen to. Humor, wit, farce, fantastic metaphors, exaggeration, pithy aphorisms of small-town wisdom—these are all part of Jason's idiom; we can easily imagine him spinning his "yarn" on the gallery of a store, suddenly starting up, banging his fist on the porch railing, and launching into, "Once a bitch always a bitch, what I say."

Mellard does not undertake to find particular predecessors of Jason in American oral narrative, although he does mention *Huckleberry Finn* as the tradition's most important literary manifestation, and Faulkner naturally turned to Twain for lessons in evoking the colloquial storyteller. Especially in style, Twain improved on the writing of earlier frontier humorists by creating spoken narration without relying on cumbersome eye-dialect; and he was the master of mingling humor with the more somber realities of Huck's life. But Huck himself is a young boy, an innocent, hardly a suitable forerunner of the character Faulkner called his "most vicious."[5] Just behind Huck in the frontier tradition, however, stands Sut Lovingood, a character-narrator more appropriate to Faulkner's purpose, and in some extensive and complex way, the experience we hear in Jason's voice gets its energy from the same sources that set Sut in motion.

Sut Lovingood's Yarns (1867), the collection of tales Harris had been publishing in newspapers since 1854, is the most carefully crafted product of frontier humor before Mark Twain, bringing to a head the strange brew of comedy and horror always present in the American tall tale, and advancing the movement toward increased reliance on vernacular storytelling.[6] Harris's special legacy to American literature is his almost total use of the yokel as narrator. He lets Sut do virtually all the talking, moving the authority of a "reported" tale away from the educated "frame" to the rustic himself: not some sophisticated and stuffy traveler from the East (like the narrator of Longstreet's *Georgia Scenes*), not even Harris's sparsely used persona "George," but the hillbilly Sut is the real source of the world portrayed. In *Yarns* the colloquial narrator talks to us as a personality in his own right, commenting on and reacting to himself and the events he relates: Sut reveals himself in his storytelling, through his own voice. As Faulkner's comment suggests, it is Sut that we respond to, that we care about. When his heavy Tennessee vernacular became the norm of a fictional world, became not a quaint mannerism to be exhibited but a literary medium to be heard, the way was opened for Huck Finn and the affirmation of oral colloquial narration as an artistic virtue.

By using Sut as narrator and chief character, Harris all but eliminates the heroic overtones of the tall tale. The comic fool steps in where the mighty hunter, fighter, boaster, and even unscrupulous con man once stood. Sut's only two "heroic" traits are his long legs and his ingenuity for practical jokes. As Milton Rickles has elaborated, Sut is directly in the line of the Shakespearian fool, a kind of backwoods court jester delighting and edifying with his stories, his wit, and his fantastic pranks.[7] Like the traditional fool, Sut is naturally a coward, surviving by his wit, and his "laigs long" as "litnin rods." If many of his anecdotes pit himself against someone who has done him wrong, nearly as many show Sut the victim of his own foolishness—in "Taurus in Lynchburg Market," he literally cannot resist taking the bull by the tail and bringing near destruction down around his ears ("'Thar I wer, froze tu a savidge bull's tail, no frien's, an' hed begun hit mysef'"[8]). Sut's world, the one he creates in his own talking, is one of disorder, one of constant chaos and confusion, set swirling by the impetus of his revenge, kept going by the spur of his wit, and discolored by the discomfort he invariably inflicts on his victims or on himself. Sut knows all this, of course, calling himself again and again a "'nat'ral born durn'd fool.'" In this he is like his Shakespearian counterparts, a wise fool after all. He serves the fool's office of exposing lies and escaping unscathed (though he is occasionally caught by his own foolishness), instigating pranks against pretenders of all kinds, tearing off the masks of respectability behind which Yankees, circuit riders, sheriffs, and even literary critics hide.[9]

It is mainly in his talk that Sut transcends his own foolishness. He gives us the wisdom of his wit in passing images, in long tirades (and one "sermon" on corrupt innkeepers), and in exchanges with the inevitable hecklers. Except for the eye-dialect, Harris's style surpasses that of any other Southwestern Humorist in brilliance and consistency of image. Like the events in Sut's stories, the language is in constant motion, coming at us in a closely packed rush of descriptions, metaphors, complaints, and aphorisms. Sut's presence as a *wise* fool is felt most strongly on the linguistic level—here perhaps he does regain something of the frontier hero's stature.

Jason is very much a comic fool in the Sut Lovingood mold, evoking a world of chaos and frantic motion through the rush of his talk. His caustic wit entertains in much the way Sut's does, as Jason too tries to "top" everyone with insults; he often launches into long tirades filled with all the grotesquery of Harris's writing: "He's going to keep on running up and down that fence and bellowing every time they come in sight until first thing I know, they're going to begin charging me golf dues, then Mother and Dilsey'll have to get a couple of china door knobs and a walking stick and work it out, unless I play at night with a lantern. Then they'd send us all to Jackson, maybe. God knows, they'd hold Old Home week when that happened."[10] While we naturally are repelled by the viciousness of Jason's actions and insults, he should be seen as a comic figure as well as a villain, a buffoon who does incredibly stupid things, and perhaps it is his stupidity that finally entertains us the most.[11] Just as Sut's victims thrash around wildly fleeing hornets, bulls, etc., and just as Sut is always running from trouble, Jason spends his day rushing from one frustration to another, chasing his niece, the market reports, a peaceful meal. Even the most mundane decisions turn out to be blunders: he decides not to take camphor in his car this one afternoon; he refuses to put the spare tire on the car because it is not his job; he declares that he'd never bet on a team "that fellow Ruth played on"; he ignores the market advice he pays for and buys when he should sell. Jason rushes frantically about victimizing himself as well as others.

Bungling of this kind sets Jason apart from another possible counterpart in Southwestern Humor—the con man. Like Hooper's Simon Suggs, Twain's the King and the Duke, and like Faulkner's own Flem Snopes, Jason devises elaborate schemes to dupe the unwary. But Suggs, the King and the Duke, and certainly Flem are more successful rogues: even though justice is finally meted out to Twain's con men and to Flem (in *The Mansion*), in their particular schemes they demonstrate a cleverness Jason cannot quite seem to manage. His persistent ineptitude trips him up, turning his villainy into a kind of slapstick comedy, best exemplified by his futile pursuit of Quentin, when he catches only a flat tire, poison oak, and a headache. His actions, for all the fury they evoke in Jason and in the reader, are the stuff farce is made of—near misses, confusion, discomfort, frustration. Nonetheless Jason still has pretensions to cleverness, and in this he differs from Sut, taking himself seriously in a way the traditional fool never does. Sut knows he's a "'nat'ral born durn'd fool,'" Jason thinks he is a "different breed of cat." Faulkner does, though, have Jason inadvertently call himself a fool at least three times in the monologue (pp. 288, 292, 307), and old Job quips that Jason "'fools a man whut so smart he cant even keep up wid hisself . . . Mr. Jason Compson'" (pp. 311–12).[12]

Yet Jason does play a "wise" fool in certain ways. Though he is not as clever as he thinks he is, and though his wit reveals mainly his own hypocrisy and malice, he does provide a perspective on his family different from that we have gained in the novel's first two sections, a corrective to our sympathies that exposes a kind of common-sense truth about the Compsons. Helpless Benjy becomes the Great American Gelding, and the confused Quentin is reduced to a Harvard student who could not learn to swim. Objectionable as such wisecracks are, they serve the same function as Sut's insults by revealing another side to people we have seen only in one way, tipping the balance of our sympathy back—just a bit—toward objectivity. The most effective of these correctives is Jason's picture of Mr. Compson, for he clearly saw and deeply resented his father's weaknesses, his favoritism for Quentin, his cynicism, his escape into drink: "'Like I say, if he had to sell something to send Quentin to Harvard we'd all been a damn sight better off if he'd sold that sideboard and bought himself a one-armed strait jacket with part of the money'" (p. 245).

II

That Jason performs like a comic fool of the Sut Lovingood variety, that he is at times funny as well as vicious, that he entertains us the way Sut does, does not reduce the intense tone of anger and bitterness that pervades his monologue. The world that emerges through the filter of Jason's mind has an emotional brutality that no amount of humor can finally mitigate. In Jason's internal talking, the traditional vernacular narrative habits go sour—the aphorisms, the digressions, the humor all turn into personal diatribe and complaint, revealing him a man as much trapped in bitterness as his brothers are in idiocy and despair.

As the foolishness of Jason's behavior reminds us of Sut's, so too the bitterness of Jason's world reflects the dark undercurrent of Sut's existence. Sut's yarns are often funny, and Sut as a wise fool can often transcend his own foolishness and his threatening world, but he is still a very bitter fool indeed. Pain, discomfort, embarrassment, and most disturbingly, genuine malice are too much a part of Sut's life to be washed away by any spirit of frolic behind his pranks. Real hatred tinges nearly everything Sut does and says—he hates hypocrites, of course, but he also hates Negroes, women, young lovers, any authority figure, and even himself. With the possible exception of drinking whiskey, Sut enjoys little that does not in some way involve hurting others. If Edmund Wilson's judgment that Sut is "malignant" and Harris's book "repellent" seems a bit humorless, it does point to the overall absence of affirmative values that blackens Sut's world.

It can be argued that brutality runs through all folk humor and that its victims are usually such caricatures—more like dolls losing their stuffing than humans suffering pain—that the violence stays within the bounds of comedy. But this argument does not quite suffice in Sut's case, for Harris changed the impetus of Southwestern Humor toward a more deeply felt pessimism, toward a dark tone that Faulkner captures so powerfully in the mind of Jason.

A central strand running through all Southwestern Humor is a desire to conquer, an expressed impulse to defeat or destroy others in some way. Whether through overt physical violence, through trickery, or through verbal reduction of people to grotesque objects, the frontier hero assaults the world "out there." Mythical beasts like Thorpe's big bear exist to be hunted and killed; other men exist to be fought, gouged, ripped, and torn, or at least to be frightened by ritualistic boasts. Others exist to be swindled out of their money and self-respect by a Simon Suggs in horse swaps, at camp meetings, everywhere, and in any way. Life is a contest and the world is filled with opponents, natural or human. Much of the humor of the tall tale, of course, grows directly out of this impulse to overwhelm the opposition through exaggerated prowess: contests are not inherently malicious. One saving grace of the tall tale is its mythical quality, which pits man against a harsh frontier and allows him to rise above it through his strength or wit. If the world is harsh, it can still be laughed at as one fights back.

Harris, however, through the figure of Sut, alters the nature of this impulse to conquer. He removes the mythical quality inherent in hunting stories or boasts, reducing the contest against life to a more malicious desire to hurt others. The struggle for survival becomes the playing of practical jokes. Opponents become enemies and victims. Sut does not battle nature so much as he attacks specific, often innocent, persons. His world is the most social in all Southwestern Humor writing, pitting man against man in an environment that is no longer the frontier. The Tennessee hill country is a relatively settled community, and it is indicative that the majority of Sut's pranks are instigated against social gatherings like quiltings, camp meetings, funerals, or dances. The hostile nature against which Sut defines himself is human nature, and he views humanity cynically indeed

> I hates ole Onsightly Peter, jis' caze he didn't seem tu like tu hear me narrate las' night; that's human nater the yeath over, an' yere's more univarsal onregenerit human nater: ef ever yu dus enything tu enybody wifout cause, yu hates em allers arterwards, an' sorter wants tu hurt em agin. An' yere's anuther human nater: ef enything happens [to] sum feller, I don't keer ef he's yure bes' frien, an' I don't keer how sorry yu is fur him, thar's a streak ove satisfackshun 'bout like a sowin thread a-runnin' all thru yer sorrer.[13]

Paranoia runs beneath the swirling surfaces of Sut's life. His world, as he wills it, is peopled with hypocrites, swindlers, and fools; Sut himself is at best a hero by default, and he tells us often that "'I'm no count, no how.'" He lives in an antagonistic world, and he is its chief antagonist: even in his role as wise fool he resigns himself to frustration and pain, which he usually causes. But he stoically accepts his existence, saying often "'I don't keer a durn, I kin stand hit.'" And his answer to this horror show of life is simply to "Jis run over ur thru everthing yure durndest, till yu gits cumfort, that's hit'" (*Yarns*, p. 169).

Sut's world becomes Jason's mentality, raised to a shriller pitch. Jason certainly wants to conquer everyone, and there is no one he cannot hate. His talk is filled, as is Sut's, with tirades against this or that segment of humanity—Yankees, Jews, his family, Negroes, women—Jason hates them all. The mechanical and animal imagery of Jason's talk reduces humans to objects: Benjy is a gelding or a sideshow freak; Caddy is some kind of a toy that is wound too tight; his niece Quentin has "eyes hard as a fice dog's" and "her nose looked like a porcelin insulator."

Like Sut, Jason is essentially a prankster, whose main weapon against the hostile world is a kind of serious practical joke ranging from the spontaneous taunting of Luster with the show tickets to the elaborately planned fraud he perpetrates with Caddy's money. Jason's language and actions are those of assault, prompted by the same cynicism that underlies Sut's world.[14] Linda Wagner has argued that Jason does act on affirmative values as a responsible breadwinner with a strong sense of family honor.[15] But these values become transmuted by Jason's bitterness into selfish obsessions, less values than self-justification. He feels, for example, that he deserves his niece's money because her mere existence cost him a bank job and his schemes to steal it have taken brains and work. The darkness of Jason's world is largely of his own making, as he brings chaos into his life in much the way Sut does, by not being able to leave anything alone. Ironically, Jason echoes Sut's stoic resignation to this largely self-created fate, declaring "I can stand it" in the face of his antagonistic existence.

III

We must never forget that Jason's section of *The Sound and the Fury,* like his brother Quentin's, is an interior monologue. Faulkner seeks to take us as deeply into the psychological sources of Jason's bitterness as he does into the causes of Quentin's despair. Indeed, one of Faulkner's real triumphs with Jason is that he can capture such strident emotions over such outwardly mundane concerns. Nowhere is his mastery of the Southern oral-literary heritage more evident than in the way he modulates Jason's external sounding narrative into stream of consciousness: he causes Jason to lose control of his own "storytelling," to reveal those experiences that have shaped his personality.

Jason's personality bears, again, an interesting resemblance to Sut's. *Sut Lovingood's Yarns* begins and ends with stories about Sut's father, tricks Sut plays on "Dad," the true king of fools. These stories reflect the adolescent quality in Sut's existence; he seems trapped in a single point of time between childish freedom and adult fulfillment, too old and too aware of adult needs (especially sexual) to really be childlike, yet too protective of his freedom to be an adult. He instigates many of his pranks against authority figures (Dad, circuit riders, sheriffs), as if the mere existence of such people threatened him. He has a childish fascination with sexuality, especially with nakedness; a large number of his tricks strip somebody of his or her clothes, or turn some woman upside down. A beautiful girl like Sicily Burns Sut sees as an untouchable being put on earth to frustrate and tantalize, but certain, like any woman, to be unfaithful. Both his playfulness and his malice are those of the eternal adolescent prancing his way through life yearning for the rewards of adulthood but fearing its restraints.

Jason suffers from the same kind of truncated development. For all his egotism, he does not respect himself; he respects only what he believes he could become if the restraints on his life were removed. He is unfulfilled, arrested in emotional adolescence, and consequently he must engage in never-ending self-justification. His is the defensive self-centeredness of the child seeking proof of his own worth, of the teen-ager expecting to be scolded; once when he returns to the store and Earl looks at his watch, Jason assumes a lecture is forthcoming and tries to head it off by taking the offensive. Wagner has pointed to the childish stridency of the phrases (like "just for that") Jason uses when he is angry.[16] He drinks Coke all the time, and fantasizes about his manhood even "if I don't drink." He resents being sent on errands; he childishly will not take the medicine his mother wants him to; he hides from a barking dog.

Jason shares Sut's fascination with sex and nakedness, calling obsessive attention to his niece's sexuality: "I stood there and watched her go on past, with her face painted up like a damn clown's and her hair all gummed and twisted and a dress that if a woman had come out doors even on Gayso or Beale street when I was a young fellow with no more than that to cover her legs and behind, she'd been thrown in jail. I'll be damned if they dont dress like they were trying to make every man they passed on the street want to reach out and clap his hand on it" (p. 289). He despises women and fears their judgment of him, and brags that he knows how to handle them—with a bust in the jaw. In this sense, Jason is as much trapped in time as Benjy and Quentin are, and for the same reason; his sister Caddy lost her innocence. None of the brothers can bear Caddy's growth into adulthood. To Benjy it means the loss of Caddy the loving child, who "smelled like trees." To Quentin her lost innocence equals corruption and sullied honor. To Jason Caddy's fall, besides proving that all women are whores, means a lost bank job. When he lost that chance, he stopped maturing because the adult image he projected of himself crumbled; now he could not become a banker, now he could not become a man. Instead he remains stuck in what is a kind of "after-school" clerk's job, pretending to be a big financial wheeler and dealer, pulling off his petty thievery.

The degree of Jason's entrapment is revealed through his memories, particularly the memories of the night Mr. Compson brought Caddy's baby home and of Mr. Compson's funeral. Faulkner brilliantly modulates oral narration into stream of consciousness by turning the complaints and tirades that fill Jason's section into reveries on the past. All of Jason's memories begin as complaints against others (Quentin, his father, Uncle Maury). Jason as vernacular storyteller loses control of his "public" narration, willy-nilly reverting to private rumination on the past. Tirades, which are similar in form to Sut Lovingood's, turn into associative meditations, similar to if less intricately woven than Quentin's reveries in the novel's second section. Like Quentin, Jason begins in the present, slowly drifting deeper and deeper into the past, losing narrative control as he "talks."[17] In the longest such revery, which occurs while Jason is working in the store and complaining about having to wait on people for trivial items, he first complains about his lost "opportunities" (p. 243), moves to a specific memory about his father's funeral (p. 244), then drifts further back in time to the arrival of Caddy's baby (p. 245). This is Jason's deepest involvement in the past, this moment of his arrested development—"'Well, they brought my job home tonight'" (p. 246). He then returns to the present, in Earl's store, for a brief complaint about Uncle Maury (p. 250) before once again returning to the funeral and the long conversation with Caddy at the cemetery. Like Quentin before him, Jason literally relives his memories.

Jason's reveries are never separated from his storytelling but emerge from it; the illusion of vernacular narration is never destroyed, though the "talk" blends into and finally becomes thought. The loss of narrative control signalling Jason's involvement in memory takes the form of accelerated talking; a passage beginning with controlled narrative statement builds to a high pitch of memory as the sentences lengthen and run together, moving faster and faster through Jason's mind:

> I went on to the street but they were out of sight. And there I was, without any hat, looking like I was crazy too. Like a man would naturally think, one of them is crazy and another one drowned himself and the other one was turned out into the street by her husband, what's the reason the rest of them are not crazy too. . . . Selling land to send him to Harvard and paying taxes to support a state University all the time that I never saw except twice at a baseball game and not letting her daughter's name be spoken on the place until after a while Father wouldn't even come down town anymore but just sat there all day with the decanter I could see the bottom of his nightshirt and his bare legs and hear the decanter clinking until. . . . (p. 290)

While the idiom remains that of the oral storyteller, the talking flows in and out of stream of consciousness.

Jason frequently recalls conversations with members of his family, especially exchanges in which he emerges (at least as he remembers them) the victor by "topping" someone, saying something clever and insulting. But remembered talking most often reveals Jason's relationship with his mother. If Quentin is his father's son, Jason is clearly his mother's, for his adolescent perversity can be traced to his role as her favorite, her last hope among her lost brood, the only real Bascomb of all the children. It becomes evident, in fact, that most of what Jason says throughout his monologue is directed at Mrs. Compson. He not only reports present conversations with her, but much of what he seems to be merely stating turns out to be something he has said or would like to say to his mother—the section's opening paragraph, for example, is directed at her. Time and again a tirade which begins on some other subject reverts to Mrs. Compson: "I might have been a stranger starving to death, and there wasn't a soul in sight to ask which way to town, even. And she trying to get me to take aspirin. I says when I eat bread I'll do it at the table. I says. . ." (p. 298). In one instance the remembered talking actually breaks into quoted dialogue, literally being relived by Jason, not merely reported. After a complaint against Benjy, Jason continues

> I says, 'You've done your duty by him: you've done all anybody can expect of you and more than most folks would do, so why not send him there and get that much benefit out of the taxes we pay.' Then she says 'I'll be gone soon. I know I'm just a burden to you,' and I says 'You've been saying that so long that I'm beginning to believe you,' only I says you'd better be sure and not let me know you're gone because I'll sure have him on number seventeen that night. (p. 276)

But for all his tough talk to Mrs. Compson, Jason spends his entire monologue—and we can assume his entire life—trying to prove himself a man in her eyes. Her notions of Bascomb respectability have become his own, and just as Quentin could not deal with his father's skepticism, Jason cannot find comfort in his mother's pride; like Sut Lovingood, he can only keep on running.

Linda Wagner, in her defense of Jason as a man trying to fulfill the "demands of honor," quotes Faulkner's praise of Sut to suggest that Faulkner could have sympathy for cowardly fools like Sut and Jason.[18] But if Sut finally cannot be taken so seriously as to be called a villain, Jason can; no matter how thoroughly Faulkner grants us insight into the causes of Jason's viciousness, causes rooted in the loveless antagonism in his family, no matter how ludicrous his actions sometimes are or how witty his wisecracks, Jason evinces a moral depravity frightening in its implications for the American "folk" character. Jason the comic fool, after all, lacks Sut's most redeeming trait—the ability to laugh at himself—and without this, the spirit of Southwestern Humor that Faulkner incorporates so brilliantly into Jason's portrayal turns genuinely malignant.

Notes

1. James B. Meriwether and Michael Millgatre, eds. *Lion in the Garden: Interviews with William Faulkner, 1926–1962* (New York: Random House, 1968), p. 251.

2. Edmund Wilson, *Patriotic Gore: Studies in the Literature of the American Civil War* (New York: Oxford Univ. Press, 1962), pp. 509, 510.

3. The most thorough summary of Faulkner's relation to Southwestern Humor is Hans Bungert's *William Faulkner und die humoristische Tradition des amerikanischen Sudens* (Heidelberg: Carl WinterUniversitatsverlag, 1971). Thomas Inge in "William Faulkner and George Washington Harris: In the Tradition of Southwestern Humor," *Tennessee Studies in Literature* 7 (1962): 47–59 discusses Harris as a source for various Faulkner stories and characters other than *The Sound and the Fury* and Jason Compson.

4. James Mellard "Faulkner's Jason and the Tradition of Oral Narrative," *Journal of Popular Culture* 2 (Fall 1968): 192–210.

5. Bungert argues that, except for the absence of eye-dialect, Faulkner's "robust and masculine" vernacular style is closer to Harris than to Twain (p. 134).

6. Milton Rickels, in *George Washington Harris* (New York: Twayne, 1965), pp. 121–22, shows the crucial influence Harris's book had on Mark Twain.

7. Ibid., pp. 95–106.

8. George Washington Harris, *Sut Lovingood's Yarns* (New York: 1867), p. 130. Hereafter cited as *Yarns*.

9. Sut on literary critics: "'Then thar's the book-butchers, orful on killin an' cuttin up, but cud no more perjuce a book, than a bull-butcher cud perjuce a bull'" (*Yarns*, p. x).

10. *The Sound and the Fury*, p. 232. All references to the novel are to the Vintage edition, a photographic reproduction of the original, 1929, edition published by Random House.

11. For an excellent summary of Jason's incompetence, see Donald M. Kartiganer, "*The Sound and the Fury* and Faulkner's Quest for Form," *ELH* 37 (Dec. 1970), 613–39.

12. One of Sut's comments on foolishness, even in its reference to banking, seems a perfect description of Jason: "'Ef I wer jis' as smart as I am mean, an' ornary, I'd be President ove a Wild Cat Bank in less nor a week'" (*Yarns,* p. 97). In another of Sut's yarns ("Hen Bailey's Reformation"), there is an image of a man chasing himself: "'He went so fas' he looked like three or four fellers arter each uther, groanin, hollerin, an' remarkin 'Hell-fire' all roun thar. He's a pow'ful activ injurin man, when ondor stiumulses, that's a fact'" (*Yarns,* p. 203).

13. *Yarns,* p. 245. In another story, Sut tells George "'Whar thar ain't enuf feed, big childer roots littil childer outen the troff, an' gobbils up thar part. Jis' so the yeath over: bishops eats elders, elders eats common peopil; they eats sich cattil es me, I eats possums, possums eats chickins, chickins swallers wums, an' wums am content to eat dus, an the dus am the aind ove hit all. Hit am all es regilur es the souns from the tribil down tu the bull base ove a fiddil in good tchune an' I speck hit am right, ur hit wudn't be 'lowed'" *(Yarns*, p. 228).

14. Jason is like Sut, too, in that his most gratuitous prank is directed at a Negro (Luster) with no apparent revenge motive. In "Sut Assists at a Negro Night Meeting," Sut decides to disrupt a Negro camp meeting simply for the fun of it—not even seeming to feel the need for justifying the prank to George as he does justify almost all his other pranks.

15. Linda Wagner, p. 570. "Jason Compson, The Demands of Honor," *Sewanee Review* 79 (1971): 554–75.

16. Wagner, p. 570. For examples, see *The Sound and the Fury,* pp. 256, 265.

17. For a discussion of the loss of narrative control in Quentin's monologue, see Stephen M. Ross, "The Loud World of Quentin Compson," *Studies in the Novel* 7 (Summer 1975): 245–57.

18. Wagner, p. 574.

17

Southwestern Humor, Erskine Caldwell, and the Comedy of Frustration

R.J. Gray

Erskine Caldwell enjoys what is perhaps one of the most dubious distinctions possible for a writer: he is popular—one of the most, if not *the* most, popular of all modern Southern writers. This has brought him money, security, even fame (who, after all, hasn't heard of him?), but also a great deal of obloquy. It is usual, for example, to claim that Caldwell is a sensationalist posing as a journalist—a historian, of a kind, who tends to forget facts and concentrate instead upon bizarre, intriguing details. The assumption, somehow, is that Caldwell is really after verisimilitude, and that only another, more important ambition—namely, his wish to be successful in the accepted meaning of that term—has prevented him from ever properly fulfilling his desire.

Few things could, I think, be further from the truth. Certainly, there is a journalistic aim implicit in most of Caldwell's work, in a sense that he was in a way trying to tell us what it is like to live in the South now. But with him this aim assumes new dimensions because (as he himself has more than once suggested) he is not so much interested in verisimilitude as in special pleading: the kind of report that tends to emphasize certain chosen aspects of its subject. He has a number of observations, important observations as he sees it, to make about the South, and he makes them to the exclusion of almost everything else. The result is something which is perhaps closer to the art of the caricaturist than to the comparatively objective account of the reporter; particular aspects of the described situation are continually being exaggerated in the interests of theme.

What is Caldwell's theme? Stated simply, it is one of degeneracy—the reduction of the human being to the lowest possible levels of his experience. In appearance, at least, his rural characters bear no resemblance at all to Jefferson's idea of the noble tillers of the earth. Grotesques responding only to a basic physical urge, they represent an abstraction not merely from the human to the animal but from the complete animal to a single instinct: . . "Ellie May got down from the pine stump and sat on the ground. She moved closer and closer to Lov, sliding herself over the hard white sand . . . 'Ellie May's acting like your old hound used to when she got the itch,' Dude said to Jeeter. 'Look at her scrape her bottom on the sand. That old hound used to make the same kind of sound Ellie May's making too. It sounds just like a little pig squealing, don't it?'"[1] The difference of perspective, when we compare this description of Ellie May in *Tobacco Road* with, say, most of William Faulkner's portraits of poor whites, is a radical one. Faulkner tends, usually, to take us inside the consciousness of his "peasants," to share the death of their inner life as well as the poverty of their condition. Caldwell, however, nearly always insists, as he does here, on keeping his readers at a distance—in other words, on presenting his characters entirely in terms of externals and in the process dehumanizing them.

This distancing, dehumanizing approach is responsible among other things, I think, for the nature of Caldwell's comedy. Nearly all of his country folk operate between the poles of greed and sexual desire—they are the slaves of appetite— and such humor as his novels possess is generally the result of the violence which these appetites provoke. In fact, the comic note is at its wildest in his fiction when the two appetites actually clash, throwing the victim of the subsequent cross-fire into confusion. The description of Ellie May quoted above, for instance, is part of a much longer sequence in which Ellie's father, Jeeter Lester, uses Ellie to distract his son-in-law Lov while he steals a bag of turnips from him. To summarize the complicated interplay of hunger and lust which follows is hardly to do justice to the Grand Guignol effects of the situation. As soon as Jeeter does grab the bag of turnips, Lov turns to recover it, but he is immediately pulled to the ground by his would-be seducer. Jeeter makes off into the woods with his capture and meanwhile his son, his wife Ada, and his grandmother all keep beating Lov down whenever he tries to rise up in pursuit, until Ellie May can crawl on top of him. With a mixture of excitement and desolation, Lov then resigns himself to his fate; while Dude, the son, goes off to find his father before all the turnips are eaten, and Ada and her mother-in-law sit whimpering over their inability to participate in either the eating session or the rutting. The scene is, as I have said, a long one and throughout it is presented as a *spectacle*, something to be watched with detached amazement. That perhaps is why Caldwell places three Negro passersby at the gate to the Lester farm, to witness the occasion and register appropriate reactions to it: We share with them, as it were, the role of a self-conscious audience. And that also is why he permits even the participants in the action an occasional note of commentary, as if they too were able to stand back from what they were doing and so become their own spectators. Jeeter, for instance, pauses midway in his flight to expatiate on the possible quality of the turnips and on the relationship between this and his own social condition: "'Has these turnips got them damn-blasted green-gutted worms in them, Lov?' Jeeter said. 'By God and by Jesus, if they're wormy, I don't know what I'm going to do about it. I been so sick of eating wormy turnips, I declare I almost lost my religion. It's a shame for God to let them damn-blasted green-gutted worms bore into turnips. Us poor people always gets the worse end of all deals, it looks like to me.'"[2] Here, as when Dude supplies us with a system of deliberate comparisons for Ellie May's behavior, the character seems to be emphasizing the illustrative quality of his own actions—their representative status as part of a series of Georgia Scenes.

The phrase, "Georgia Scenes," is not chosen at random. For it points to one aspect of his Southern inheritance on which Caldwell leans heavily—an aspect that is symptomatic of the radical differences obtaining between him and such other celebrants of the Southern farmer as Ellen Glasgow and Elizabeth Madox Roberts. More than a hundred years ago—in 1835 to be precise—a lawyer and academic named Augustus Baldwin Longstreet published a book with the imposing title of *Georgia Scenes: Characters, Incidents, etc., in the First Half-Century of the Republic.* To the extent that it was imposing, though, the title was a misleading one since a major purpose of the book was comedy. In a series of sketches, which varied in approach from the purely descriptive to the dramatic, Longstreet presented his readers with illustrations of life in the remoter parts of the state. The sketches were linked by the appearance in nearly all of them of a narrator bearing a suspicious resemblance to the author himself: a kindly, generous, but rather pompous and patronizing man, who tended to treat his subjects as if they were specimens of some alien form of life, with a mixture of curiosity and amusement. A healthy distance was maintained from characters who were presented not so much as individuals as in terms of their common behavioral patterns; and the combined effect of the detachment, the condescension, and the generalising tendency was to create an effect of caricature. Here is a typical passage, where the narrator is describing the aftermath of a fight:

> I looked and saw that Bob had entirely lost his left ear, and a large piece from his left cheek. His right eye was a little discolored, and the blood flowed profusely from his wounds. Bill presented a hideous spectacle. About a third of his nose, at the lower extremity, was bit off, and his face so swelled and bruised that it was difficult to discover in it anything of the human visage. . . .
>
> . . . Durham and Stallings [the fighters] kept their beds for several weeks, and did not meet again for two months. When they met, Billy stepped up to Bob and offered his hand, saying. "Bobby you've licked me a fair fight; but you wouldn't have done it if I hadn't been in the wrong—I oughtn't have treated your wife as I did; and I felt so through the whole fight; and it sort o' cowed me." "Well, Billy," said Bob, "let's be friends. Once in the fight, when you had my finger in your mouth, I was going to halloo; but I thought of Betsy, and knew the house would be too hot for me if I got whipped when fighting for her, after always whipping when I fought for myself . . ."
>
> . . . Thanks to the Christian religion, to schools, colleges, and benevolent associations, such scenes of barbarism and cruelty as that which I have been just describing are now of rare occurrence, though they may still be occasionally met with in some of the new counties.[3]

In the preface to his book, Longstreet claimed proudly that he was filling in "a chasm in history which has always been over-looked"; and this passage illustrates well, I think, how he reconciled such a claim with the exigencies of comedy. The tone of the description is humorous, but the writer clearly hopes that by means of this humor he will demonstrate something significant about the backwoods character as well—its simplicity and its capacity for violence. That is to say, the simplification and exaggeration which create the comic note are there because they enable Longstreet to locate what is different about the boy and emphasize it at the expense of any qualities he may share, in a Wordsworthian sense, with the rest of humanity.

This is not the place to go into Longstreet's further motives for emphasizing the specific qualities of the Georgia folk that he did. The virtual impossibility of resolving the problem, anyway, is indicated by the fact that the critical field is about equally divided between those who argue that Longstreet admired his subjects for their "free and active simplicity" and those who say that as a gentleman and a Whig, he loathed and feared them for the threat they offered to his own lifestyle![4] What *does* matter, though, and needs to be mentioned here is that whatever his ulterior motives, Longstreet offered his readers a portrait of the poor farmer which was characterized by three things: detachment, a claim to historical accuracy, and a tendency towards comic exaggeration. These were the strategies that gave *Georgia Scenes* much of its drive and contemporary appeal, and these were the ones also that were variously adopted by the writers following Longstreet, who are now referred to generally as the "Southwestern humorists"—"Southwestern" because nearly all of them were interested in the younger states of the interior (such as Alabama, Mississippi, Tennessee). Of course, their approach was never uniform. Apart from anything else there was a tendency in later years to reduce the status of the dramatized narrator altogether: the story was then told impersonally or given to the rural character himself to tell. But the qualities I have mentioned continued to supply a point of departure, a common basis, as it were, upon which the individual writer could improvise. And one result of this is that in the work which certainly represents the culmination of Southwestern humor, the *Adventures of Huckleberry Finn*, we can find the same combination of historical and comic intention recurring. The portrait that Mark Twain develops in his book, of old times on the Mississippi, is presented via a technique of violent exaggeration which makes it simultaneously elegiac and critical, a humorous masterpiece and a piece of social history; and that exaggeration is itself symptomatic of a detachment which enables us to place every character—including Huckleberry Finn himself—even while we may sympathize with them.[5]

Time (and the sheer complexity of the subject) may prevent us from examining Southwestern humor in any great detail. But as a way of indicating some of its further implications, and in particular its relevance for Erskine Caldwell, I would like to look briefly at a writer who stands somewhere in between Longstreet and Twain in terms of achievement and chronology; and that is George Washington Harris. The choice is not meant to be an obscurantist one, since apart from the fact that Harris did exercise enormous personal influence on Caldwell (and William Faulkner as well), there can be no doubt that he represents an important moment in the history of American humor—a time when, in opposition to the dominant climate of prissiness and gentility, it could still be pungent, incisive, and above all, broad. Just how broad it could be is indicated by the controlling belief Harris attributes to his major character, Sut Lovingood—that "'Men were made a-purpus jis' to eat, drink, an' fur stayin' awake in the yearly part of the nites.'"[6] A native of rural Tennessee, Sut is in effect another example of the creature who tended to become an obsession with the humorists—the primitive or natural man, who stands on the periphery of conventional society and yet can still offer significant comments on it. His life, circumscribed by the animal functions, is a continual drag on our own pretensions, about the nature of our personalities and the efficacy or security of the social system we have organized for ourselves. At one point in his narrative, Sut Lovingood admits that he has "'nara a soul, nuffin but a whiskey proof gizzard'" and Harris's habitual strategy of making us share Sut's life and experience the connection between what he is and how he lives leads us to suspect that in similar conditions we might be forced to say exactly the same.

It will be clear already that Harris's intentions and techniques are rather different from Longstreet's. For while both share the claim to historical accuracy and the device of comic exaggeration, they differ in the sense that the placing of their subject (the way they invite us to look on rural folk as a demonstration) is based upon almost contrary premises. Longstreet, as I have suggested, offers us the portrait of a world quite different from our own, which may provoke amusement, perhaps even the occasional tremor of apprehension, but nothing more than that. Harris, by contrast, presents us with a kind of test case, which paradoxically derives its impact, the sense of its relevance to our own lives, from the distance it establishes between the literate reader and the illiterate protagonist. Suppose, Harris seems to be saying, we had been brought up in surroundings similar to those of Sut Lovingood: would we be that different from him? Would we not perhaps speak the same language and live upon the same level of comic but grotesque animalism? And if this is the case, does it not tend to undermine our pretensions: the belief in our dignity as God-given rather than acquired as a matter of special privilege? Sut Lovingood is detached from us—certainly the use of an almost impenetrable dialect sees to that—but he is detached from us only in the way that a mirror image of ourselves is. We watch him and in doing so, witness a curious aping and a criticism of our own behavior.[7]

The criticism is made all the more effective because of Harris's capacity for reminding us, in the middle of Sut's various scrapes, that his protagonist does possess traces of what we are pleased to call virtue, waiting for the appropriate conditions to bring them into life. There is his extraordinary pride and independence of judgment, for instance, which prompts him to consider himself "the very best society" and to punish those who he feels have insulted him in any way. More telling still is the ability which Harris endows him with for sensing who his enemies are, regardless of whether they have slighted him personally or not. They are, he realizes, the preachers and the pedagogues, the politic and educated leaders of society who are there not simply to supply a butt for Sut's fooling, although they certainly do that, but to remind us of the kind of people—*people like ourselves*—who are indirectly responsible for his condition. For their privileges, we must realize, have been bought at his expense; they, and we, are the beneficiaries of a system from which he is excluded and by which he is deprived. The mirror is being held up to the readers as a group, in other words, as well as to the reader as an individual. We see in Sut Lovingood a reflection of possibilities existing in ourselves—and we are forced to acknowledge our complicity in the creation of circumstances which, in Sut's case, have translated possibility into fact. And just in case we should continue to miss the point, denying Sut a germ of sensitivity even after all this, there are occasions in the narrative when more energetic hints of his potential are allowed to appear. Instead of a cursory reference to some dormant virtue, we may then be confronted with a passage of extraordinary lyrical beauty—not denying the comic framework but actually growing out of it—which serves as the most incisive reminder possible of those aspects of Sut Lovingood's character that remain mostly unexercised. Here, by way of illustration, is what is deservedly the most famous moment in all of Sut Lovingood's yarns, set characteristically enough at a mealtime:

> Wirt's wife got yearly supper, a rale suckit-rider's supper, whar the 'oman ove the hous' wer a rich b'lever. Thar wer chickens cut up, an' fried in butter, brown, white, flakey, light, hot biskit, made wif cream, scrambil'd aigs, yaller butter, fried ham, in slices es big es yure han, pickil'd beets, an' cowcumbers, roas'in ears, shaved down and fried, sweet taters, baked, a stack ove buckwheat cakes . . . I gets dang hongry every time I see Wirt's wife, ur evan her side-saddil, ur her frocks a-hangin on the closeline. Es we sot down, the las' glimmers ove the sun crep thru the histed winder, an' flutter'd on the white tabil-cloth and play'd a silver shine on her smoof black har, es she sot at the head ove the tabil, a-pourin out the coffee, wif her sleeve, push'd tight back on her white roun' arm, her full throbbin neck wer bar to the swell ove her shoulders, an' the steam ove the coffee made a movin vail afore her face, es she slowly brush'd hit away wif her lef han', a-smilin an' a flashin her talkin eyes lovingly at her hansum husbun.[8]

The occasion being described here is mundane enough, admittedly, but what matters about it is not so much the occasion itself as all that Harris allows his protagonist to make out of it. Sut, we are forced to recognize, has a sensitivity—a capacity for recognizing the beauty and value of a particular experience which will emerge at the least available opportunity—although all too often it is left to waste uncultivated. The waste is articulated in the rest of the narrative, in the scene of comic violence and degeneracy that illustrate the actual conditions of his existence; and placed in this context it becomes unarguable, I think, that Harris even more than Longstreet has used his humor to reinforce a serious social and historical point. If we are willing to simplify for a moment, we can say that the comedy in Sut Lovingood defines the given situation, the occasional moments of lyricism and commentary imply the possibilities which have been more or less frustrated, and the activity taking place between these two poles helps to locate the core meaning of the sketches.

Nearly half a century separates the creator of Sut Lovingood from the creator of Jeeter Lester, but perhaps this gap in time may serve only to emphasize the relevant connections between the two writers. The difference of historical situation may, after all, help to isolate what is similar in their purposes and techniques and so concentrate our attention upon it. Be that as it may, it is patently clear I think, once we look at him in this light, that Caldwell owes a profound debt to the Southwestern humorists and to George Washington Harris in particular; a debt which is betrayed among other things by their common dependence on a broad and grotesque type of comedy. The specific borrowings from Harris are at their most obvious in *Georgia Boy*, published in 1943, in which the boy of the title recounts the antics of his "old man," and in the process draws us the portrait of a delightful and impoverished scapegrace not unlike Sut Lovingood himself.[9] But these are less interesting, I believe, than the kind of understanding of Harris and his methods which can be inferred from Caldwell's more important fiction, by which I mean from *Tobacco Road*, *God's Little Acre*, and perhaps *Tragic Ground* as well.[10] In such cases it is not merely the surface structure of Southwestern humor which is recovered but the relationship obtaining between that structure and the ulterior purposes of the writer. Comic these books may be, but the comedy is all the sharper, the wit all the more pungent, and the characters that much more striking, because (just as in *Sut Lovingood*) everything is unambiguously attached to an underlying and genuinely serious series of intentions.

Exactly how these intentions manifest themselves is (again as in *Sut Lovingood*) as much a matter of context as anything else, the total situation in which the humorous moments are played out. The comedy is still a comedy of waste, of human potential denied and frustrated, and that fact is communicated to the reader in part by Caldwell's barren landscapes—whether it be the decayed rural landscape where his farmers are described living in reluctant exile or the urban scene, to which they may retreat occasionally in pursuit of an illusory alternative. The description in *God's Little Acre* of mill towns populated by farmers looking for some way of making a living is typical of what I mean:

> Up and down the valley lay the company towns and the ivy-walled cotton mills . . . the men stood on the hot streets looking at each other while they spat their lungs into the deep yellow dust . . . In the rear of the houses . . . tight-lipped women sitting at kitchen windows with their backs to the cold cooking-stoves. In the streets in front of the houses . . . the bloody-lipped men spitting their lungs into the yellow dust . . . The grass and weeds melted in the sun, and the dust that blew down from the . . . uplands settled on the ground and on the buildings like powdered paint.[11]

Even from this comparatively brief passage it is clear, I think, that Caldwell sees the hopelessness of the rural landscape penetrating the town, to make it unavailable as a resource for impoverished farmers. A common dust (similar, perhaps, to the dust which floats in the wake of the Great Gatsby) settles over city and adjacent countryside alike, so creating a pervasive sense of fruitlessness. And this is the stage on which the Lesters, the Waldens in *God's Little Acre,* and all their kind must act out their comedies of frustration; or, to be more accurate, this is the environment which prescribes their frustrated lives.

That it is a comedy of frustration we are concerned with here; a series of appropriate responses to a thwarting environment is witnessed by the habitual activity of Caldwell's characters. For the gestures that make them comic have nothing at all to do with intrinsic evil, however violent and grotesque they may appear to be. On the contrary, Jeeter Lester and Ty Ty Walden (in *God's Little Acre*) are exactly like Sut Lovingood in that they are presented as the victims of evil, whose strange behavior demonstrates the response of the innocent to circumstances he cannot control.[12] The whole trouble with Caldwell's characters, as with Harris's, is that they have no relevant connection with the emergent social structure and so are at best anomalies in that structure and at worst encumbrances to it. And Caldwell, *unlike* Harris, makes sure that the reader is aware of this by explaining, very early on in most of his novels, how people like the Lester family and the Waldens have become the way they are. Both the Lesters and the Waldens were, we learn, once well-to-do landowners. But they fell upon hard times, partly as a result of natural fluctuations in the cotton and tobacco markets, and partly thanks to the machinations of the financiers, the bankers, and the Wall Street brokers. In the event, they—like so many of their class, Caldwell reminds us—lost their land and had to resort to cropping on shares, a ruinous system whereby they placed themselves heavily in debt to the landowner, and the landowner in turn remained solvent by borrowing at a high rate of interest from the merchant banks. This was bad enough perhaps, but (Caldwell goes on) matters have since become worse because the sharecropping system has itself collapsed, and land has now to be cultivated in very large units or—as in most cases—not at all. In effect, big business has assumed direct control of farming rather than working through the power of its credit and in doing so has created a new, large-scale agricultural system in which the Jeeter Lesters and Ty Ty Waldens of this world have no place. Jeeter, Ty Ty, and their kind have been turned into anachronisms, an irrelevant nuisance to the present owners of the land; and the most they can hope for, really, is that they will be left alone on the farms they occupy, to eke a meagre existence out of them.[13]

This, more or less, is the starting point for nearly all of Caldwell's fiction and certainly the basis of his finest novels. The farmer, he argues, has been "robbed of his livelihood by the downfall of the old systems of agriculture,"[14] and this in turn has led to the physical deterioration which we now see and to his moral collapse. Treated like an animal he has become an animal; excluded from the human community in an economic sense, he has degenerated into a kind of moral leper as well, whose humanity is more a matter of biology than of character. The argument is an utterly deterministic one, of course. But, then, so also is the argument implicit in most stories of the old Southwest. More to the point, the determinism is not I think objectionable because it can be seen as part of a total strategy of caricature. Life is simplified and character is distorted in Caldwell's fiction, it may be true; but this is done in a conscious and valuable way—so as to isolate certain specific aspects of the author's given experience and, in isolating them, to explain them.

Given this self-conscious determinism of approach and the tendencies towards caricature and generalization which accompany it, it becomes less surprising, I think, that Caldwell should impose the status of a demonstration on every aspect of his character's behavior: the reader is, after all, being summoned to witness what is likely to happen when a certain type of social and historical situation exists. There is a profoundly illustrative quality, for instance, not just about particular scenes in *Tobacco Road* but about its major source of comedy—. This is Jeeter Lester's belief that one year, next year perhaps, he will be able to plant a tobacco crop. Under the influence of this belief he is forever burning the ground in preparation for the planting until eventually at the end of the novel he sets fire to his own house, killing himself and his wife in the process. The belief is an idiosyncratic one, certainly, leading to situations that range from the ludicrous to the macabre, but not so idiosyncratic that it cannot act as a gauge of Jeeter's innocence and the desperate nature of a situation which imposes such desperate remedies on its victims. Similarly, Ty Ty Walden's habitual activity of digging up his land in search of gold—absurd though it may appear to be—is founded on the supremely illogical and revealing logic of the helpless naïf. He cannot live on what he gets out of the land, Ty Ty reasons, so why not try to live on what he finds in it? There is perhaps a hint of blasphemy in his behavior too, of the kind familiar to readers of *Go Down, Moses*: the idea that rooting about in the land for gold, oil, or whatever represents a despoliation, an act of rape which is the very opposite of the enrichment offered to the soil by the agricultural activity.[15] But whether this is part of Caldwell's intention or not, there can be little doubt I think that he does intend Ty Ty's behavior, like Jeeter's, to achieve the apparently paradoxical feat of being representative by virtue of its idiosyncrasy. Its illustrative quality, that is—as an indication of rural decline and the despair to which this decline leads—is made to depend for its impact on the comic absurdity of the illustration.

The humor is not left in isolation, though, to carry the entire freight of meaning of the book unaided. As in *Sut Lovingood*, the dominant strain of comedy is punctuated by an occasional lyric note, which reminds us of what might have been in more favorable circumstances—of how people like Jeeter Lester and Ty Ty Walden could have developed, given the proper opportunity. The few times that Jeeter is allowed to express his "inherited love of the land" offer us some beautiful instances of this:

> "I think more of the land than I do of staying in a durn cotton-mill. You can't smell no sedge fire up there, and when it comes time for planting, you feel sick inside but you don't know what's ailing you . . . But when a man stays on the land, he don't get to feeling like that this time of the

> year, because he's right there to smell, the smoke of burning broom-sedge and to feel the wind fresh off the ploughed fields going down inside of his body . . . out here on the land a man feels better than ever he did. The Spring-time ain't going to let you fool it by hiding away inside a durn cotton-mill. It knows you got to stay on the land to feel good."[16]

This passage deserves comparison with Sut Lovingood's hymn to the good life which I quoted earlier, and not just because it helps us to recognize and to accept the latent dignity of the speaker. It does this, of course, but what it does as well is contribute a new dimension of feeling to the narrative—a sense of pathos which depends upon our seeing that within the limits established by the comedy, the desires expressed here are destined to remain unconsummated. Jeeter Lester will never really live up to the ideal of the farming experience he is describing, nor will Sut Lovingood ever be able to develop his sensibilities and sensitivity to the full; and that, as their creators see it, is a cause for our honest sympathy as much as our amusement— or, rather, something to give depth and direction to our laughter.

It is only a step beyond this strategy of contrast between the comic episode and the lyric moment to that of placing active commentary in the mouths of the characters—commentary, that is, which does not simply *imply* a criticism of the given situation but insists upon it. Needless to say, Caldwell frequently takes this step. His characters suddenly pause—as Jeeter does when he is stealing the bag of turnips—and turn upon their own grotesque attitudes in order to explain them. And not only the attitudes but the context of victimization in which they occur as well; for Caldwell differs from Harris in the sense that he makes his characters articulate their own sufferings, so that we are never left in any doubt as to where to place the blame. Thus, when Ty Ty Walden describes the iniquities of the speculative system to his daughter-in-law, and in particular the depredations of the cotton broker, he seems as much as anything else to be offering an explanation of himself to the reader—supplying the kind of direct analysis of the dramatic situation, and its origins, which is normally assigned to a chorus rather than the protagonist: "You know what a cotton broker is, don't you? Do you know why they're called cotton brokers? . . . Because they keep the farmers broke all the time. They lend a little money, and then they take the whole damn crop. Or else they suck the blood out of a man by running the price up and down, forcing him to sell. That's why they call them cotton brokers!"[17] Statements like this may offer a special problem to some readers. After all, it might be argued, can they be reconciled with the deterministic premises of the rest of the narrative, which require the characters to behave like automatons? Ty Ty betrays a clear understanding of his situation here, as much understanding, in fact, as would be necessary for him to exercise some measure of control over it; and how does this jibe with an action which elsewhere tends to reduce him to the status of a Pavlovian dog?

The problem is only an apparent one, though (at least, in the case of Caldwell's major fiction it is), because it is based on the assumption that the writer is aiming at verisimilitude. And the plain fact, as we have seen, is that he is not. Like Harris, Longstreet, and all the other humorists, Caldwell has complicated the function of reporter by adding to it that of the caricaturist, a creator of the grotesque. On top of that, he has forced on the reader an attitude of radical detachment. Statements such as the one Ty Ty makes about cotton brokers, or Jeeter's comment on the turnips, are part of the pattern of demonstration I mentioned earlier, in which the characters as well as the audience seem to be made aware of the illustrative quality of the action. As a resource this attitude of detachment is, of course, just as much of an inheritance from Southwestern humor as the strategy of caricature is. But Caldwell develops it much further than any previous humorist ever did—so much further, in fact, that perhaps to explain and justify it we need to draw a comparison from a very different field of literature. I mean by this the programme for an "epic" theatre formulated more than forty years ago by the German dramatist Bertolt Brecht. For the distance placed between reader and character in Caldwell's best fiction is, I think, significantly related—both in its purposes and its effects—to Brecht's core idea of "Vermfremdung," or audience alienation.[18] The idea, stated simply, is this: that in an "epic" play, the audience, instead of being invited to involve themselves in the action, should be forced to adopt an attitude of clinical detachment towards it. Consequently, what happens on stage will be witnessed as an explicable social phenomenon with its own definite causes and room for subsequent maneouvre. The sense of an experience participated in is forfeited, according to this theory, but what (hopefully) is gained in its place is a new certainty—the knowledge which comes from having located the dramatic action firmly in its historical time and social place. The events the writer describes become part of an explicable series: their origins understood, the problems they pose carefully defined, and solutions to these problems offered, ready and waiting, for the audience to act upon. This is very much the notion of playwright—or novelist, or poet—as scientific historian, and committed scientific historian at that. And regardless of whether or not Brecht entirely adhered to his theories when it came to the actual writing of plays, there can be little doubt, I think, that they encouraged him to develop certain specific literary devices. Among these was the device of permitting someone to comment on events of which he was elsewhere shown to be the victim. Time and again in Brechtian theatre, a character will slip into the role of surrogate spectator, to emphasize moments in the drama (or links in the series) which other spectators may have missed. No one worries about this when it occurs in *Mother Courage* or *The Caucasian Chalk Circle,* because it is part of the denial of surface realism which is integral to the action—as well as something which helps to place that action within a context of possible remedies. No one should worry about it when it occurs in *Tobacco Road* or *God's Little Acre* either, and for precisely the same reasons.[19]

The sense of problem solving—the feeling that we are being asked to look at the action in very much the same spirit as a scientist looks at an experiment—is in fact as pronounced in books like *Tobacco Road* as it could be in any "epic" play—

more pronounced, even, since Caldwell likes to add his own comments to those he puts in the mouths of his characters. Asides from the author occasionally supplement asides from his creations, so as to make the didactic intention of the story perfectly clear. This, admittedly, has some use simply because it helps to settle any doubts that may be left in the reader's mind—both about what Caldwell is trying to do and what he is trying to say. But, on the whole, I think it is a mistake. At such moments, it is very difficult for him not to sound like a schoolmaster talking to an exceptionally dull pupil:

> Jeeter could never think of the loss of his land and goods as anything but a man-made calamity . . . he believed steadfastly that his position had been brought about by other people. He did not blame Captain John [his landlord] to the same extent that he blamed others . . . Captain John had always treated him fairly . . . But the end soon came. There was no longer any profit in raising cotton under the Captain's antiquated system, and he abandoned the farm and moved to Augusta. . . . An intelligent use of his land, stocks, and implements would have enabled Jeeter, and scores of others who had become dependent on Captain John to raise crops to be sold at a profit.[20]

Caldwell never tires of offering direct advice like this; and as any reader of *Tobacco Road* or *God's Little Acre* will testify, the specific proposals he makes are pretty various—ranging as they do from pleas for more government aid to the occasional invocation of the principle of self-help, and taking in agricultural schools, crop rotation, and land recovery along the way. The variety of his proposals, however, should not prevent us from seeing that everything he says stems ultimately from one core belief, a single premise. This is how Caldwell states that premise in one of his books: "Until the agricultural worker commands his own farm, either as an individual or as a member of a state-allotted farm group, the Southern tenant-farmer will continue to be bound hand and foot in economic slavery."[21] Caldwell, as I think this brief passage indicates, is finally a traditional writer. His characters are traditional; his humor is traditional (although certainly it is broader and wilder than the Southwestern humorists' ever was); above all, the social and political program implicit in his work is traditional. For what that program boils down to is a belief in the pieties of the small farm. The dream of a chosen people tilling their own fields in perfect freedom: that is the dream Caldwell expresses here—and that also is the dream which dictates nearly all of his problem solving. No matter how little we may realize it while we are enjoying some of the surface details of his comedy, Caldwell—in everyone of his finest stories—is trying to draw us back steadily into the world of Jeffersonian myth.

Once we realize this—that the ideal of the good farmer hovers as an admonitory image at the back of Caldwell's best novels and tales—then, I think, the principal reason for the almost apocalyptic violence of his work becomes clear. All the events that occur in books like *Tobacco Road* and *God's Little Acre* are wild and grotesque, ultimately, because they represent for their creator such a radical departure from the Jeffersonian norm. Jeeter Lester and Ty Ty Walden are not the noble farmers of regional legend, and the fact that they are not, the fact that they stand for *a dream or an ideal betrayed*, is I believe meant to be the real measure of their absurdity. No blame attaches to Teeter or Ty Ty for their plight, far from it, but that only makes it the more difficult to bear: the more difficult for them to bear, that is, for their author to bear—and, most important of all, for us to bear as well. For it would be putting matters in their right perspective, I think, to say that Caldwell insists on the difference between Jefferson's tillers of the earth and his own Georgia crackers and then imposes full responsibility for this difference upon a corrupt social machine, precisely so as to arouse our anger and encourage our demands for change. He is not the only humorist to do this, of course; George Washington Harris, as we have seen, tried to do something similar. But he is, as far as I know, the only one to supplement this by talking about the brave new world which may emerge when the machine is reprogrammed; to make tentative moves, in other words, towards turning from the dream betrayed to the dream fulfilled.

This, anyway, is what I take Caldwell to be doing when (as in the passage I quoted just now) he refers to the mistakes made by Captain John and his class; he is beginning to talk about an alternative environment. And elsewhere, in some of the stories that he wrote after *Tobacco Road* and *God's Little Acre*, these beginnings are carried through to a detailed portrait of that alternative. Caldwell then shows us the reorganization of farm management and the restructuring of rural society actually taking place and being succeeded in turn by a revival of spirit among his characters. Obviously, the intended effect of these stories is one of uplift; the author wants us to experience a sense of release because the oppressive circumstances, and with them the claustrophobic atmosphere, of the earlier narratives have been dissolved. Their actual effect is a lot less exhilarating than that, however, and the reasons for this take us right back to the virtues of that earlier work; we can define why Caldwell succeeded in *Tobacco Road* and *God's Little Acre* by understanding why he is failing now. For what Caldwell does as a preliminary to drawing his portrait of a better life is to take his rural folk out of the grotesque, comic world of the Lesters and the Waldens, which is a necessary step certainly, but one which deprives him of his previous excuses for the simplifications and determinism of his argument. The one-sided portrait can no longer be defended as part of a satirical strategy. And having done this, he does not really know what to do with his people, because he does not have any other satisfactory approach available to him—one which would make them meaningful and at the same time vivid and believable, too. His characters have lost the power of a Jeeter Lester—the power, that is, deriving from the deliberately isolating and exaggerating tendencies of the comic method—without acquiring any of the more complicated interest, or more sophisticated contact with their time and place, which the participants in a more strictly "realistic" fiction should possess. To adopt E.M. Forster's useful terms for a moment, they have no imaginative life of their own either as "flat" characters or as "round" ones. They are merely mouthpieces for utopian attitudes—as two-dimensional and as unprepossessing as some of the less successful heroes of Elizabeth Madox Roberts or Ellen Glasgow are. In *A House in the Uplands,* for instance, a novel published in 1946, the protagonist—who is, of course, a simple farmer—talks to his aristocratic fiancée in this way. It tells us a lot, I think, about the strained, self-consciously heroic posture of much of Caldwell's later work: "I'm just as good as you or anybody else who lives up . . . in the big house, and you know it. If I lived in one of those rotting old houses and loafed all the time and borrowed money to live on you'd marry me . . . quick . . . I'm going to amount to something in life and I can give you a lot more than any other man will ever give you, and money won't be the only thing either."[22] This is pure melodrama, horribly appropriate to a story which is only a slightly regionalized version of the Horatio Alger dream, and it represents a sad decline from the comic inventiveness of *Tobacco Road.* Admittedly, it is based on the same values as *Tobacco Road* is. The difference, however—and it is a crucial difference—is that what constitutes a background to comedy in the earlier narrative has now been carried into the foreground. The values, previously implied, have been allowed to occupy centre stage; and—unfortunately for Caldwell—they have not benefited in the process either from an involvement in credible experience or from contact with the sort of vivifying literary medium that the comic tradition of the old Southwest represents.

What has occurred in the later fiction is really very simple; and one useful way of summarizing it, within the context of Caldwell's total achievement, might go something like this: In stories like *Tobacco Road* or *God's Little Acre,* Caldwell's success depends largely upon two factors. These are his acquaintanceship with, and his use of, the methods of comic journalism which had been perfected by the humorists of the old Southwest; and his commitment to a dream of the rural landscape which he had also learnt from his region. The factors are not just coincidental, of course. On the contrary, they complement and enhance each other here just as they do in the stories of George Washington Harris: with the dream giving power and coherence to the journalism, and the journalism in turn appropriating some sense of urgency and possibility for the dream. Idea and event are made to interact so as to produce a thoroughly traditional reading of the environment—a reading, that is to say, which depends on the earlier history of that environment without being circumscribed by it. But in later novels like *A House in the Uplands* this interaction more or less ceases. The idea remains unenlivened by any contact with experience; or, on those occasions when Caldwell does return to journalism—a comic account of things as they are—that journalism does not seem to have an ulterior motive anymore. It no longer radiates the kind of significance that would come from its being placed within the framework of a controlling idea. Idea or event, dream or journalistic report: the two things exist separately, even if they both occur within the covers of one book. And what we are left with, consequently, is either heroic posturing of the sort I have just illustrated—or a descent into episodes of comic violence and degeneracy which have no purpose beyond themselves, which are, in a word, sensationalistic. We are not being asked to register the gap between fact and potential any longer, only to indulge in daydreaming about what might happen in the best of all possible worlds, or to enjoy the cheaper thrills offered by a random and meaningless enumeration of some of the sordid facts of life. The strategy of detachment is, in sum, replaced by one of vicarious excitement. This is a sad end for somebody like Caldwell who started off so well. But even if it does nothing else, it helps us, I think, by suggesting what happens when the functions of journalist (that is, a reporter of things as they are) and caricaturist or mythologizer (that is, a reporter of things as they might be) are separated for a writer; and history is then translated by him into a refuge for some dormant principle or, alternatively, into a series of disconnected happenings.

Notes

1. Erskine Caldwell. *Tobacco Road* (New York: Grosset & Dunlap, 1932), p.23.

2. Ibid., p. 39.

3. "The Fight," in Augustus Baldwin Longstreet, *Georgia Scenes* (New York: Harper Bros., 1835), pp. 50, 52–53. Caldwell's debt to the Southwestern humorists is mentioned in passing by Carl Van Doren, "Made in America. Erskine Caldwell," *Nation*, CXXXVII (Oct. 1937), 444.

4. For different opinions of Longstreet's aims and achievement, see: Constance Rourke, *American Humor A Study of the National Character* (New York: Harcourt, Brace, 1931); Walter Blair, *Horse Sense in American Humor From Benjamin Franklin to Ogden Nash* (Chicago, Ill.: Univ. of Chicago Press, 1942): Kenneth Lynn, *Mark Twain and Southwestern Humor* (Boston: Little, Brown, 1960).

5. The complexity of Mark Twain's purposes in the book and the various levels of interest on which it consequently operates are brought out well in Walter Blair, *Mark Twain and Huck Finn* (Berkeley, Calif.: Univ. of California Press, 1960).

6. "Sut Lovingood's Sermon," in *Sut Lovingood: Yarns Spun by a "Natural Born Durn'd Fool"* (New York: Dick and Fitzgerald, 1867), p. 88; also p. 172.

7. I am aware that this is an unorthodox interpretation of Harris, but I think it can be reconciled at least with the expressed opinions of Lynn and Tony Tanner, *The Reign of Wonder* (Cambridge University Press, 1956), pp. 100–03. They argue that Harris is in sympathy with Sut Lovingood and that this is one reason why he adopts Sut as narrator. 1 am essentially in agreement with this but feel that the sympathy is as much for Sut's potential as for what he actually is. The kinds of values expressed by this potential, it need hardly be added, have nothing at all to do with the genteel culture which Sut criticizes.

8. "Trapping a Sheriff," in *Sut Lovingood's Yarns*, pp. 261–62.

9. See, for example, the stories entitled "The Day We Rang the Bell for Preacher Hawshaw," "My Old Man and the Gypsy Queen," and "Handsome Brown's Day Off."

10. *God's Little Acre* (New York: Grosset & Dunlap, 1933); *Tragic Ground* (Boston: Little, Brown, 1944).

11. *God's Little Acre*, pp. 99–102. Compare *Tragic Ground*, pp. 17, 236.

12. "Ty Ty is irascible and indestructible, but above all innocent." R. Hazel, "Notes on Erskine Caldwell," in *South: Modern Southern Literature in its Cultural Setting*. Eds. Louis D. Rubin Jr. and Robert D. Jacobs (Garden City, N.Y.: Doubleday, 1961), p. 325.

13. For the clearest and most succinct description of this entire process, see *You Have Seen Their Faces* (New York: Modern Age Books, 1937), pp. 32–33.

14. "Tenant Farmers," in *Some American People* (New York: R.M. McBride, 1935), p. 212.

15. See "The Fire and the Hearth," in *Go Down, Moses* (New York: Random House, 1942).

16. *Tobacco Road*, p. 28.

17. *God's Little Acre*, p. 108.

18. The theory of the "epic" theatre was given its most elaborate and schematic expression in a statement written by Brecht in 1931 and cited by Ronald Gray, *Brecht* (Edinburgh: Oliver & Boyd, 1961), pp. 62–63.

19. Of course, this device would not be very different from the choric methods of more traditional drama were it not that its purpose is specifically to detach the audience from the action (rather than to explicate an action in which it is otherwise involved) and to apprise it of the social nature of the problems being confronted.

20. *Tobacco Road*, pp. 82–83.

21. *Tenant Farmers*, p. 259.

22. *A House in the Uplands* (New York: Duell, Sloan & Pearce, 1946), pp. 182–83.

Humor of the Old South: A Comprehensive Bibliography

Ed Piacentino

The following bibliography incorporates all the relevant information (excluding unpublished dissertations other than a few indispensable scholarly works) contained in the following earlier bibliographies: Charles E. Davis and Martha B. Hudson's "Humor of the Old Southwest: A Checklist of Criticism," *The Frontier Humorists: Critical Views*. Ed. M. Thomas Inge. Hamden, Conn.: Archon, 1975, 303–23; Nancy Snell Griffith, *Humor of the Old Southwest: An Annotated Bibliography of Primary and Secondary Sources*. New York: Greenwood, 1989, 1–47; and the "Bibliography" in *Humor of the Old Southwest*. Ed. Hennig Cohen and William B. Dillingham. Athens: Univ. of Georgia Press, 1994, 465–95. This compilation also includes all editions of primary texts of antebellum southern humor published since 1950 and all additional secondary materials about this humor published since 1993. All essays reprinted in this volume are identified with an asterisk (*).

The bibliography contains five sections: 1) Editions and reprints of collections of Old Southwestern humor published since 1975; 2) General Studies: Books; 3) General Studies: Articles; 4) Individual Authors; and 5) the influence of Southwestern humor on modern literature and popular culture.

In addition to writers who have long been recognized as practitioners in the southern backwoods humorous school, I have also included in the Individual Authors section J. Ross Browne, Marcus Lafayette Byrn, Joseph Gault, Orlando Benedict Mayer, Francis James Robinson, and William Gilmore Simms, all of whom wrote works in this tradition.

Readers who would like to stay informed about the continuing scholarship on the humor of the Old South should likewise consult the "Checklist of Scholarship On Southern Literature," published annually in the *Mississippi Quarterly*, *American Literary Scholarship: An Annual;* and *The MLA International Bibliography of Books and Articles on the Modern Languages and Literatures*.

Humor of the Old South: Selected Anthologies, Editions, and Reprints

Baldwin, Joseph Glover. *The Flush Times of Alabama and Mississippi: A Series of Sketches*. Gloucester, Mass.: Peter Smith, 1974.

———. *The Flush Times of Alabama and Mississippi: A Series of Sketches*. 1853. Rpt. ed. James H. Justus. Baton Rouge: Louisiana State Univ. Press, 1987.

Barr, John Gorman. *Rowdy Tales from Early Alabama: The Humor of John Gorman Barr*. Ed. G. Ward Hubbs. Tuscaloosa: Univ. of Alabama Press, 1981.

Cohen, Hennig, and William B. Dillingham, eds. *Humor of the Old Southwest*. 3rd ed. Athens: Univ. of Georgia Press, 1994.

Craig, Raymond C., ed. *The Humor of H.E. Taliaferro*. Knoxville: Univ. of Tennessee Press, 1987.

Crockett, David. *A Narrative of the Life of David Crockett of the State of Tennessee . . . Written by Himself*. Ed. Joseph A. Arpad. New Haven, Conn.: College and University Press, 1972. Reprint, St. Clair Shores, Mich.: Scholarly Press, 1978. Reprint, Lincoln: Univ. of Nebraska Press, 1987.

Harris, George Washington. *High Times and Hard Times: Sketches and Tales by G.W. Harris*. Ed. M. Thomas Inge. Nashville, Tenn.: Vanderbilt Univ. Press, 1967.

———. *Sut Lovingood's Yarns*. Ed. M. Thomas Inge. New Haven, Conn.: College and University Press, 1966.

———. *"Sut Lovingood's Yarns": A Facsimile of the 1867 Dick and Fitzgerald Edition*. Ed. M. Thomas Inge. Memphis, Tenn.: Saint Lukes, 1987.

Hooper, Johnson Jones. *Adventures of Captain Simon Suggs, Late of the Tallapoosa Volunteers*. Southern Literary Classics Series. Chapel Hill: Univ. of North Carolina Press, 1969.

———. *Adventures of Captain Simon Suggs*. Nashville, Tenn.: Sanders, 1993.

———. *Some Adventures of Captain Simon Suggs, Late of the Tallapoosa Volunteers*. Tuscaloosa: Univ. of Alabama Press, 1993.

Hudson, Arthur Palmer. *Humor of the Old South*. New York: Macmillan, 1936.

Jones, Hamilton C. *Ham Jones, Ante-Bellum Southern Humorist: An Anthology*. Eds. George Hendrick and Willene Hendrick, eds. Hamden, Conn.: Archon, 1990.

Kibler, James Everett, Jr., ed. *Fireside Tales: Stories of the Old Dutch Fork*. Columbia, S.C.: Dutch Fork, 1984.

Lewis, Henry Clay. *Louisiana Swamp Doctor: The Writings of Henry Clay Lewis*. Ed. John Q. Anderson. Baton Rouge: Louisiana State Univ. Press, 1962.

———.*Odd Leaves from the Life of a Louisiana Swamp Doctor*. 1850. Rpt. ed. Edwin T. Arnold. Baton Rouge: Louisiana State Univ. Press, 1997.

Lofaro, Michael A., ed. *The Tall Tales of David Crockett. The Second Nashville Series of Crockett Almanacs 1839–1841*. Knoxville: Univ. of Tennessee Press, 1987.

Longstreet, Augustus Baldwin. *Augustus Baldwin Longstreet's Georgia Scenes Completed*. Ed. David Rachels. Athens: Univ. of Georgia Press, 1998.

———. *Georgia Scenes: Characters, Incidents, &c. in the First Half Century of the Republic*. Atlanta: Cherokee, 1971. Reprint, Savannah, Ga.: Beehive, 1975. Reprint, Nashville, Tenn.: Sanders 1992.

Mayer, Orlando Benedict. *John Punterick: A Novel of Life in the Old Dutch Fork*. Ed. James E. Kibler Jr. Spartanburg, S.C.: Reprint Co., 1981.

Meine, Franklin J., ed. *Tall Tales of the Southwest: An Anthology of Southern and Southwestern Humor 1830–1860*. New York: Knopf, 1930.

Noland, C.F.M. *Cavorting on the Devil's Fork: The Pete Whetstone Letters of C.F.M. Noland*. Ed. Leonard Williams. Memphis, Tenn.: Memphis State Univ. Press, 1979.

———. *Pete Whetstone of Devil's Fork: Letters to the "Spirit of the Times"*. Ed. Ted R. Worley and Eugene A. Nolte. Van Buren, Ark.: Press-Argus, 1957.

Oehlschlaeger, Fritz, ed. *Old Southwest Humor from the St. Louis Reveille, 1844–1850*. Columbia: Univ. of Missouri Press, 1990.

Porter, William T., ed. *The Big Bear of Arkansas and Other Sketches Illustrative of Characters and Incidents in the South and South-West*. Philadelphia: T.B. Peterson, 1843.

———, ed. *A Quarter Race in Kentucky and Other Sketches Illustrative of Scenes, Characters and Incidents Throughout "The Universal Yankee Nation"*. Philadelphia: Carey and Hart, 1846.

Rattlehead, David [Marcus Lafayette Byrn]. *The Life and Adventures of an Arkansas Doctor.* Ed. W.K. McNeil. Fayetteville: Univ. of Arkansas Press, 1989.
Robb, John S. *Streaks of Squatter Life, and Far-West Scenes.* Ed. John Francis McDermott. Gainesville: Scholars' Facsimiles & Reprints, 1962. Reprint, Delmar, N.Y.: Scholars' Facsimiles & Reprints, 1978.
Thompson, William Tappan. *Major Jones's Courtship: Detailed, with Other Scenes, Incidents, and Adventures, in a Series of Letters by Himself.* Rev. and enlarged. Atlanta: Cherokee, 1973.
Thorpe, Thomas Bangs. *Mysteries of the Backwoods; Or Sketches of the Southwest, Including Character, Scenery and Rural Sports.* Upper Saddle River, N.J.: Literature House/Gregg Press, 1970.
———. *A New Collection of Thomas Bangs Thorpe's Sketches of the Old Southwest.* Ed. David C. Estes. Baton Rouge: Louisiana State Univ. Press, 1989.
Warren, Kittrell J. *The Life and Public Services of an Army Straggler.* Ed. Floyd C. Watkins. Athens: Univ. of Georgia Press, 1961.
———. *Ups and Downs of Wife Hunting.* Ed. Floyd C. Watkins. Atlanta: Emory Univ. Library, 1957.
Watterson, Henry, ed. *Oddities in Southern Life and Character.* Boston: Houghton-Mifflin, 1883.

General Studies: Books, Sections From Books

Alderman, Edwin Anderson, et al., eds. *Library of Southern Literature.* Atlanta: Martin and Hoyt, 1907–1923. 17 vols.
Anderson, John Q. *With the Bark On: Popular Humor of the Old South,* Nashville, Tenn.: Vanderbilt Univ. Press, 1967.
Arac, Jonathan. "Southwestern Humor." *The Cambridge History of American Literature.* Ed. Sacvan Bercovitch. Vol. 2. New York: Cambridge Univ. Press, 1995. 630–41.
Austin, James C. *American Humor in France: Two Centuries of French Criticism of the Comic Spirit in American Literature.* Ames: Iowa State Univ. Press, 1978.
Babcock, C. Merton, ed. *The American Frontier.* New York: Holt, Rinehart, and Winston, 1965. 391–92 and passim.
Bain, Robert, et al., eds. *Southern Writers: A Biographical Dictionary.* Baton Rouge: Louisiana State Univ. Press, 1979.
Baldwin, Oliver P., ed. *Southern and South-Western Sketches.* Richmond: J.W. Randolph, 1855. 3–4.
Beidler, Philip D., ed. *The Art of Fiction in the Heart of Dixie.* University: Univ. of Alabama Press, 1986. 1–50.
Bier, Jesse. *The Rise and Fall of American Humor.* New York: Holt, Rinehart, and Winston, 1968. 52–76.
Blair, Walter. "A German Connection: Raspe's Baron Munchausen," *Critical Essays on American Humor.* Eds. William B. Clark and W. Craig Turner. Boston: Hall, 1984. 123–39.
———. *Horse Sense in American Humor.* Chicago: Univ. of Chicago Press, 1942. v–ix and passim.
———. "'A Man's Voice Speaking': A Continuum of American Humor." *Veins of Humor.* Ed. Harry Levin. Cambridge, Mass.: Harvard Univ. Press, 1972. 185–204.
———. *Native American Humor.* New York: American Book Co., 1937. 62–101, 163–96.
———. *Tall Tale America.* New York: Coward McCann, 1944.
——— and Hamlin Hill. *America's Humor: From Poor Richard to Doonesbury.* New York: Oxford Univ. Press, 1978.
——— and Raven I. McDavid Jr., eds. *The Mirth of the Nation: America's Great Dialect Humor.* Minneapolis: Univ. of Minnesota Press, 1983.

Boatright, Mody C. *Folk Laughter on the American Frontier*. New York: Macmillan, 1949.

Blount, Roy, Jr., ed. *Roy Blount's Book of Southern Humor.* New York: Norton, 1994.

Botkin, B.A., ed. *A Treasury of American Folklore*. New York: Crown, 1944. 2–9, 272–73.

———, ed. *A Treasury of Southern Folklore*. New York: Crown, 1949. 418–20.

Brewer, Willis. *Alabama: Her History, Resources, and Public Men, from 1540–1872.* Montgomery, 1872. Spartanburg, S.C.: Reprint Co., 1975. 465–529.

Brevard, Carolina M. *Literature and the South*. New York: Broadway, 1908. 35, 40–41.

Bridgman, Richard. *The Colloquial Style in America*. New York: Oxford Univ. Press, 1966. 23–30 and passim.

Brown, Carolyn S. *The Tall Tale in American Folklore and Literature*. Knoxville: Univ. of Tennessee Press, 1987. 41–60, 63–70, 74–88, 122–23.

Bruce, Dickson D., Jr. *Violence and Culture in the Antebellum South*. Austin: Univ. of Texas Press, 1979. 212–32.

Budd, Louis, and Edwin H. Cady. *On Humor: The Best from "American Literature."* Durham, N.C.: Duke Univ. Press, 1992.

Carr, Duane. *A Question of Class: The Redneck Stereotype in Southern Fiction*. Bowling Green, Ohio: Popular Press, 1996. 25–31.

Chittick, V.L.O., ed. *Ring-Tailed Roarers: Tall Tales of the American Frontier, 1830*–1860. Caldwell, Idaho: Caxton Printers, 1946. 13–25, 305–11, and passim.

Clark, Thomas D. *The Rampaging Frontier: Manners and Humors of Pioneer Days in the South and the Middle West*. Indianapolis: Bobb-Merrill, 1939.

Clark, William Bedford, and W. Craig Turner, eds. *Critical Essays on American Humor*. Boston: Hall, 1984.

Clemens, Samuel Langhorne, comp. *Mark Twain's Library of Humor.* New York: Charles L. Webster, 1888.

Cohen, Hennig, and William B. Dillingham, eds. *Humor of the Old Southwest*. Athens: Univ. of Georgia Press, 1994. xv–xl.

Cohen, Sandy. "South and Southwest." *American Humorists, 1800–1950*. Ed. Stanley Trachtenberg. Vol. 11. *Dictionary of Literary Biography*. Detroit: Gale Research, 1982. 597–605.

Cook, Sylvia Jenkins. *From Tobacco Road to Route 66: The Southern Poor White in Fiction*. Chapel Hill: Univ. of North Carolina Press, 1976. 5–11.

Covici, Pascal, Jr. *Mark Twain's Humor: The Image of a World.* Dallas: Southern Methodist Univ. Press, 1962. 3–91.

Cox, James. M. "Humor of the Old Southwest." *The Comic Imagination in American Literature,* Ed. Louis D. Rubin Jr. New Brunswick, N.J.: Rutgers Univ. Press, 1973. 101–12.

Current-Garcia, Eugene. *The American Short Story Before 1850: A Critical History*. Boston: Twayne, 1985. 99–118.

DeVoto, Bernard. *Mark Twain's America*. Boston: Little, Brown, 1932. 92–99, 240–45, 252–60, 335–39.

Dorson, Richard M. *American Folklore*. Chicago: Univ. of Chicago Press, 1959. 49–73, 203–14.

Downs, Robert B. *Books That Changed the South*. Chapel Hill: Univ. of North Carolina Press, 1977. 63–73, 74–81.

Eaton, Clement. "The Southern Yeoman: The Humorists' View and the Reality." *The Mind of the Old South*. 2nd ed. Baton Rouge: Louisiana State Univ. Press, 1967. 130–51.

Ellison, Rhonda C. *Early Alabama Publications: A Study in Literary Interests*. University: Univ. of Alabama Press, 1947. 74–77, 167–69.

Flanagan, John T. "Western Sportsmen Travelers in the New York *Spirit of the Times*." *Trav-*

elers on the Western Frontier. Ed. John Francis McDermott. Urbana: Univ. of Illinois Press, 1970. 168–86.

———, and Arthur P. Hudson, eds. *Folklore in American Literature.* Evanston, Ill.: Row, Peterson, 1958. 236–37 and passim.

Flanders, Bertram H. *Early Georgia Magazines: Literary Periodicals to 1865.* Athens: Univ. of Georgia Press, 1944. 30–36, 64–66, 89–90, 191–94.

Flautz, John T. "The Dialect Sermon in American Literature." *Popular Literature in America: A Symposium in Honor of Lyon N. Richardson.* Eds. James C. Austin and Donald A. Koch. Bowling Green, Ohio: Bowling Green Univ. Popular Press, 1972. 129–45.

Fowler, Bill F. "Hell-Fire and Folk Humor on the Frontier." *Tire Shrinker to Dragster.* Ed. W.M. Hudson. Austin, Tex.: Encino, 1968. 51–62.

Fussell, Edwin. *Frontier: American Literature and the American West.* Princeton, N.J.: Princeton Univ. Press, 1965. 133–34.

Gale, Steven H., ed. *Encyclopedia of American Humorists.* New York: Garland, 1988.

Garrett, William. *Reminiscences of Public Men in Alabama for Thirty Years.* Atlanta: Plantation, 1872. 358–59, 526–29.

Gohdes, Clarence, ed. *Hunting in the Old South: Original Narratives of the Hunters.* Baton Rouge: Louisiana State Univ. Press, 1967. 113–14 and passim.

Gray, Richard. *The Literature of Memory: Modern Writers of the American South.* Baltimore: Johns Hopkins Univ. Press, 1977. 114–25, 214–15.

———. *Writing the South: Ideas of an American Region.* Cambridge, UK: Cambridge Univ. Press, 1986. 62–74.

Gretlund, Jan Nordby. "1835: The *Annus Mirabilis* of Southern Fiction." *Rewriting the South: History and Fiction.* Ed. Lothar Honnighausen and Valeria Gennaro Lerda. Tübingen, Germany: Franke Verlag, 1993. 121–30.

Gribben, Alan. "Mark Twain Reads Longstreet's *Georgia Scenes.*" *Gyascutus: Studies in Antebellum Southern Humorous and Sporting Writing.* Ed. James L.W. West III. Atlantic Highlands, N.J.: Humanities, 1978. 103–11.

Halliburton, Thomas C. *The Americans at Home; or Byeways, Backwoods, and Prairies.* Vol. 1. London: Hurst and Blackett, 1854. v–ix.

Hall, Wade. *The Smiling Phoenix.* Gainesville: Univ. of Florida Press, 1965. 1–18, 357–68.

Harris, Isabella Deas. *The Southern Mountaineer in American Fiction, 1824–1910.* Lexington: Univ. Press of Kentucky, 1956. 59–92, 239–73.

Harris, Joel Chandler. *Stories of Georgia.* New York: American Book Co., 1896. 240–51.

Hauck, Richard Boyd. *A Cheerful Nihilism: Confidence and "the Absurd" in American Humorous Fiction.* Bloomington: Indiana Univ. Press, 1971. 40–76.

Hill, Hamlin, ed. *Essays on American Humor: Blair Through the Ages.* Madison: Univ. of Wisconsin Press, 1993.

Hoffman, Daniel G. *Form and Fable in American Fiction.* New York: Oxford Univ. Press, 1961. 53, 57, 62–78.

Holliday, Carl. *A History of Southern Literature.* New York: Neale, 1906. 117–355.

Howe, William D. "Early Humorists." *The Cambridge History of American Literature.* Ed. William P. Trent. Vol. 2. New York: Macmillan, 1933. 148–59.

Hubbell, Jay B. *The South in American Literature, 1607–1900.* Durham, N.C.: Duke Univ. Press, 1954. 658–86.

———. *Southern Life in Fiction.* Athens: Univ. of Georgia Press, 1960. 71–78.

Hudson, Arthur Palmer. *Humor of the Old Deep South.* New York: Macmillan, 1936.

Inge, M. Thomas. *Perspectives on American Culture: Essays on Humor, Literature, and the Popular Arts.* West Cornwall, Conn.: Locust Hill, 1994.

———, ed. *The Frontier Humorists: Critical Views*. Hamden, Conn.: Archon, 1975.

Jacobs, Robert D. "*Tobacco Road:* Lowlife and the Comic Tradition." *The American South: Portrait of a Culture*. Ed. Louis D. Rubin Jr. Baton Rouge: Louisiana State Univ. Press, 1980. 206–26.

Jerdan, William, ed. *Yankee Humor and Uncle Sam's Fun*. London: Ingram, Cook, 1859.

Jones, Anne G. "Humor of the Old Southwest." *The Heath Anthology of American Literature.* eds. Paul Lauter et al. 3rd ed. Vol. 1. Boston: Houghton Mifflin, 1998. 1537–41.

Joost, Nicholas. "Reveille in the West: Western Travelers in the *St. Louis Weekly Reveille*." *Travelers on the Western Frontier*. Ed. John Francis McDermott. Urbana: Univ. of Illinois Press, 1970. 203–40.

Justus, James H. "The Lower South: Space and Place in Antebellum Writing." *Southern Landscapes*. Eds. Tony Badger, Walter Edgar, and Jan Nordby Gretlund. Tubingen, Germany: Stauffenburg-Verlag, 1996. 3–13.

———. "The Unheard Reader in the Writing of the Old Southwest." *Discovering Difference: Contemporary Essays in American Culture*. Ed. Christoph K. Lohmann. Bloomington: Indiana Univ. Press, 1993. 48–64.

———. "Poe's Comic Vision and Southwestern Humour." *Edgar Allan Poe: The Design of Order*, Ed. A. Robert Lee. Totowa, N.J.: Barnes and Noble, 1987. 66–87.

Krapp, George P. *The English Language in America.* New York: Century, 1925. 1:261, 300–14.

Kuhlmann, Susan. *Knave, Fool and Genius: The Confidence Man as He Appears in Nineteenth-Century American Fiction.* Chapel Hill: Univ. of North Carolina Press, 1973. 13–19, 22–31.

Lenz, William E. "Confidence and Convention in *Huckleberry Finn*." *One Hundred Years of Huckleberry Finn: The Boy, His Book, and American Culture*. Eds. Robert Sattelmeyer and J. Donald Crowley. Columbia: Univ. of Missouri Press, 1985. 186–200.

———. *Fast Talk and Flush Times: The Confidence Man as a Literary Convention*. Columbia: Univ. of Missouri Press, 1985. 42–56, 65–121+.

Link, Samuel Albert. "Southern Humorists: Longstreet, Baldwin, Hooper, W.T. Thompson, Davy Crockett, and Others." *Pioneers of Southern Literature*. 2 vols. Nashville, Tenn.: M.E. Church South, 1900. 2:465–545.

Lofaro, Michael A. "Riproarious Shemales: Legendary Women in the Tall Tale World of the Davy Crockett Almanacs." *Crockett at Two Hundred: New Perspectives on the Man and the Myth*. Eds. Michael A. Lofaro and Joe Cummings. Knoxville: Univ. of Tennessee Press, 1989. 114–52.

Lynn, Kenneth S. *Mark Twain and Southwestern Humor*. Boston: Little, Brown, 1959.

———. "Violence in American Literature and Folklore." *Violence in America: Historical and Comparative Perspectives.* Eds. Hugh D. Graham and Ted R. Gurr. Beverly Hills, Calif.: Sage, 1979. 133–43.

McKee, Kathryn Burgess. "Writing in a Different Direction: Women Authors and the Tradition of Southwestern Humor, 1875–1910." Diss. University of North Carolina at Chapel Hill, 1996.

McIlwaine, Shields. "Southern Comic Portraits of Crackers, Wool-hats, and Dirt-eaters." *The Southern Poor White from Lubberland to Tobacco Road*. Norman: Univ. of Oklahoma Press, 1939. 40–74.

———, ed. *The Comic Tradition in America.* Garden City, N.Y.: Doubleday, 1958.

McNair, Donald. "Backwoods Humor in the *Pendleton, South Carolina Messenger*, 1810–

1851." *South Carolina Journals and Journalists.* Ed. James B. Meriwether. Spartanburg, S.C.: Reprint Co., 1975. 225–32.

Major, Mabel, and T.M. Pearce. *Southwest Heritage: A Literary History with Bibliographies.* 3rd ed. Albuquerque: Univ. of New Mexico Press, 1972. 58–63.

Masterson, James R. *Tall Tales of Arkansas.* Boston: Chapman and Grimes, 1943. 299–305 and passim.

Meats, Stephen E. "South Carolina Writers in the *Spirit of the Times. Gyascutus: Studies in Antebellum Southern Humorous and Sporting Writing.* Ed. James L.W. West III. Atlantic Highlands, N.J.: Humanities, 1978. 185–207.

Meine, Franklin J. *Tall Tales of the Southwest: An Anthology of Southern and Southwestern Humor, 1830–1860.* New York: Knopf, 1930. xv–xxxii.

Messenger, Christian K. *Sport and the Spirit of Play in American Fiction: Hawthorne to Faulkner.* New York: Columbia Univ. Press, 1981. 65–82.

Mims, Edwin, ed. *History of Southern Fiction: The South in the Building of the Nation.* Vol. 8. Eds. J.A.C. Chandler et al. Richmond, Va.: Southern Historical Publication Society, 1909. xl–xlvii.

The Mississippi Writers Page, 18 Feb. 1999. University of Mississippi Department of English. 28 Jan. 2000. <http://www.olemiss.edu/depts/english/>.

Morris, Christopher. "'What's So Funny?' Southern Humorists and the Market Revolution." *Southern Writers and Their Worlds.* College Station: Texas A & M Univ. Press, 1996. Baton Rouge: Louisiana State Univ. Press, 1998. 9–26.

Morris, Linda A. *Women Vernacular Humorists in Nineteenth-Century America.* New York: Garland, 1988.

Moses, Montrose J. *The Literature of the South.* New York: Thomas Y. Crowell, 1910. 230–38.

Myerson, Joel, ed. *Antebellum Writers in New York and the South.* Vol. 3. *Dictionary of Literary Biography.* Detroit: Gale Research, 1979.

Paine, Gregory, ed. *Southern Prose Writers: Representative Selections.* New York: American Book Co., 1947. lxxiv–lxxix and passim.

Parks, Edd Winfield. "The Intent of the Humorists." *Ante-Bellum Southern Literary Critics.* Athens: Univ. of Georgia Press, 1962. 60–65.

Parrington, Vernon L. *Main Currents in American Thought: The Romantic Revolution in America, 1800–1860.* New York: Harcourt Brace, 1927. 166–79.

Phillips, Robert L., Jr. "The Novel and the Romance in Middle Georgia Humor and Local Color." Diss. University of North Carolina at Chapel Hill, 1971.

Porter, William T. *The Big Bear of Arkansas and Other Sketches.* Philadelphia: Carey and Hart, 1845. vii–xii.

Quinn, Arthur H. *American Fiction: An Historical and Critical Survey.* New York: D. Appleton-Century, 1936. 100–1 and passim.

———, et al. *The Literature of the American People: An Historical and Critical Survey.* New York: Appleton-Century-Crofts, 1951. 235–36 and passim.

Railton, Stephen. "The Democratic Nonesuch: Southwestern Humor." *Authorship and Audience: Literary Performance in the American Renaissance.* Princeton, N.J.: Princeton Univ. Press, 1991. 90–106.

Reynolds, David S. *Beneath the American Renaissance: The Subversive Imagination in the Age of Emerson and Melville.* Cambridge, Mass.: Harvard Univ. Press, 1989. 449–57.

Rickels, Milton. "The Grotesque Body of Southwestern Humor." *Critical Essays on American Humor.* Eds. William Bedford Clark and W. Craig Turner. Boston: Hall, 1984. 155–66.

Ridgely, J.V. *Nineteenth-Century Southern Literature*. Lexington: Univ. Press of Kentucky, 1980. 56–61.

Rose, Alan Henry. "Blackness in the Fantastic World of Southwestern Humor." *Demonic Vision: Racial Fantasy in Southern Fiction*. Hamden, Conn.: Archon, 1977. 19–38.

Roth, Martin. Introduction. *Some American Humorists*. Ed. Napier Wilt. New York: Johnson Reprint, 1970. v–xlv.

Rourke, Constance M. "The Gamecock in the Wilderness." *American Humor: A Study of the National Character*. New York: Harcourt Brace, 1931. 33–76.

Rubin, Louis D., Jr., ed. *The Literary South*. New York: John Wiley & Sons, 1979. 72–76.

———. *The Writer in the South: Studies in a Literary Community*. Athens: Univ. of Georgia Press, 1972. 62 and passim.

Rutherford, Mildred L. *The South in History and Literature: A Hand-Book of Southern Authors*. Atlanta: Franklin Turner, 1906. 153–59, 304–5, and 372–78.

Schmitz, Neil. "Forms of Regional Humor." *Columbia Literary History of the United States*. Ed. Emory Elliott. New York: Columbia Univ. Press, 1988. 306–23.

Skaggs, Merrill Maguire. *The Folk in Southern Fiction*. Athens: Univ. of Georgia Press, 1972. 25–35.

Sloane, David E.E. *American Humor Magazines and Comic Periodicals*. Westport, Conn.: Greenwood, 1987. 271–78, 558–59.

Slotkin, Richard. *Regeneration Through Violence: The Mythology of the American Frontier, 1660–1860*. Middletown, Conn.: Wesleylan Univ. Press, 1973. 412–17, 479–84.

Smith, Henry Nash. "Origins of a Native American Literary Tradition." *The American Writer and the European Tradition*. Ed. Margaret Denny. Minneapolis: Univ. of Minnesota Press, 1950. 63–77.

Spiller, Robert E., et al. *Literary History of the United States*. 4th ed. rev. New York: Macmillan, 1974. 738–41.

Steadman, Mark. "Humor." *Encyclopedia of Southern Culture*. Eds. Charles Reagan Wilson and William Ferris. Chapel Hill: Univ. of North Carolina Press, 1989. 855–56.

Tandy, Jeanette. "The Development of Southern Humor." *Crackerbox Philosophers in American Humor and Satire*. New York: Columbia Univ. Press, 1925. 65–102.

Thorp, Willard. *American Humorists*. Minneapolis: Univ. of Minnesota Press, 1964. 11–17.

Trent, William P., ed. *Southern Writers: Selections in Prose and Verse*. New York: Macmillan, 1905. 75–76 and passim.

Trachtenberg, Stanley, ed. *American Humorists, 1800–1950*. Vol. 11. *Dictionary of Literary Biography*. Detroit: Gale Research, 1982.

Turner, Arlin, ed. *Southern Stories*. New York: Holt, Rinehart and Winston, 1960. xi–xl and passim.

Veron, Enid, ed. *Humor in America: An Anthology*. New York: Harcourt, 1976.

Wade, John Donald. "Southern Humor." *Culture in the South*. Ed. W.T. Couch. Chapel Hill: Univ. of North Carolina Press, 1934. 159–82.

———. "Southern Humor." *A Vanderbilt Miscellany*. Ed. Richard Croom Beatty. Nashville, Tenn.: Vanderbilt Univ. Press, 1944. 188–204.

Walker, Nancy, ed. *What's So Funny? Humor in American Culture*. Wilmington, Del.: Scholarly Resources, 1998.

Walker, Nancy A. *A Very Serious Thing: Women's Humor and American Culture*. Minneapolis: Univ. of Minnesota Press, 1988.

Watson, Ritchie Devon, Jr. "Southwest Humor, Plantation Fiction, and the Generic *Cordon*

Sanitaire." Yeoman Versus Cavalier: The Old Southwest's Fictional Road to Rebellion. Baton Rouge: Louisiana State Univ. Press, 1993. 56–69.
Watterson, Henry, ed. *The Compromises of Life.* New York: Fox, Duffield, 1903. 59–101.
———, ed. *Oddities in Southern Life and Character.* Boston: Houghton Mifflin, 1882. v–ix, 1–2, and passim.
Weber, Brom, ed. *The Art of American Humor: An Anthology.* Foreword, Lewis Leary. New York: Thomas Y. Crowell, 1962. Passim.
Wendel, A.S, ed. "Another New Mock Sermon." In *Gyascutus: Studies in Antebellum Southern Humorous and Sporting Writing.* Ed. James L.W. West III. Atlantic Highlands, N.J.: Humanities, 1978. 215–18.
Wimsatt, Mary Ann, and Robert L. Phillips. "Antebellum Humor." *The History of Southern Literature.* Ed. Louis D. Rubin Jr. Baton Rouge: Louisiana State Univ. Press, 1985. 136–56.
Yates, Norris W. *William T. Porter and the "Spirit of the Times": A Study in the Big Bear School of Humor.* Baton Rouge: Louisiana State Univ. Press, 1957.
Zanger, Jules. "The Frontiersman in Popular Fiction, 1820–1860." *Frontier Re-examined.* Ed. John Francis McDermott. Urbana: Univ. of Illinois Press, 1967. 141–53.

General Studies: Articles

Allen, Michael. "'Sired by a Hurricane': Mike Fink, Western Boatman and the Myth of the Alligator Horse." *Arizona and the West* 2 (1985): 237–52.
Allen, G. Wilson. "Humor in America." *Sewanee Review* 40 (1932): 111–13.
Anderson, John Q. "Folkways in Writing about Northeast Louisiana before 1865." *Louisiana Folklore Miscellany* 1 (1960): 67–86.
———. "Scholarship in Southwestern Humor—Past and Present." *Mississippi Quarterly* 17 (1964): 67–86.
———. "Some Migratory Anecdotes in American Folk Humor." *Mississippi Quarterly* 25 (1972): 447–57.
Arnold, St. George Tucker, Jr. "The Twain Bestiary: Mark Twain's Critters and the Tradition of Animal Portraiture in Humor of the Old Southwest." *Southern Folklore Quarterly* 41 (1977): 195–211.
Arpad, Joseph J. "The Fight Story: Quotation and Originality in Native American Humor." *Journal of the Folklore Institute* (1973): 141–72.
Austin, James C. "Cycle of American Humor." *Papers on English Language and Literature* 1 (1965): 83–91.
Baptist, Edward E. "Accidental Ethnographer in an Antebellum Newspaper: Snell's Homecoming Festival." *Journal of American History* 84 (1998): 1355–83.
Baskervill, W.M. "Southern Literature." *Publications of the Modern Language Association* 7 (1892): 89–100.
Beidler, Philip D. "'The First Production of the Kind, in the South': A Backwoods Literary Incognito and His Attempt at the Great American Novel." *Southern Literary Journal* 24 (1992): 106–24.
Bettersworth, John K. "The Humor of the Old Southwest: Yesterday and Today." *Mississippi Quarterly* 17 (1964): 87–94.
Betts, John R. "Sporting Journalism in Nineteenth-Century America." *American Quarterly* 5 (1953): 39–56.

Blair, Walter. "Americanized Comic Braggarts." *Critical Inquiry* 4 (1977): 331–49.

———. "Burlesques in Nineteenth-Century American Humor." *American Literature* 2 (1930): 236–47.

———. "Inquisitive Yankee Descendants in Arkansas." *American Speech* 14 (1939): 11–22.

———. "The Popularity of Nineteenth-Century American Humorists." *American Literature* 3 (1931): 175–94.

———. "Traditions in Southern Humor." *American Quarterly* 5 (1953): 132–42.

Boatright, Mody C. "The Art of Tall Lying." *Southwest Review* 34 (1949): 357–63.

———. "Frontier Humor: Despairing or Buoyant?" *Southwest Review* 27 (1942): 320–34.

Bolton, Theodore. "The Book Illustrations of Felix Octavius Carr Darley." *Proceedings of the American Antiquarian Society*, n.s., 61 (1951): 137–82.

Bradley, Sculley. "Our Native Humor." *North American Review* 242 (1937): 351–62.

Brashear, Minnie M. "The Missouri Short Story as It Has Grown Out of the Tall Tale of the Frontier." *Missouri Historical Review* 43 (1949): 199–219.

Brown, Sarah. "*The Arkansas Traveller*: Southwestern Humor on Canvas." *Arkansas Historical Quarterly* 46 (1987): 348–75.

Bryant, John. "Melville, Twain, and Quixote: Variation in the Comic Debate." *Studies in American Humor*, n.s., 3.1 (1994): 1–27.

Budd, Louis J. "Gentlemen Humorists of the Old South." *Southern Folklore Quarterly* 17 (1955): 232–40.

Bukoski, Anthony. "The Lady and Her Business of Love in Selected Southern Fictions." *Studies in the Humanities* 5 (1976): 14–18.

Calhoun, Richard J. "Southwestern Humor, Tar Heel Humor, and the Vernacular Perspective in the American Comic Imagination." *Emerson Society Quarterly: Journal of the American Renaissance* 22 (1976): 183–86.

Cardwell, Guy A. "The Duel in the Old South: Crux of a Concept." *South Atlantic Quarterly* 66 (1967): 50–69.

Carlisle, Henry. "The Comic Tradition." *American Scholar* 28 (1958–1959): 96–108.

Caron, James E. "Laughter, Politics, and the Yankee Doodle Legacy in America's Comic Tradition." *Thalia: Studies in Literary Humor* 10 (1988): 3–13.

———. "The Violence and Language of Swapping Lies: Towards a Definition of the American Tall Tale." *Studies in American Humor* 5, n.s. (1986): 27–57.

Chamberlain, Bobby J. "Frontier Humor in *Huckleberry Finn* and Carvalho's *O Coronel e o Lobisomen*." *Comparative Literature Studies* 21 (1984): 201–16.

Chittick, V.L.O. "Ring-Tailed Roarers." *Frontier* 13 (1933): 257–63.

Clark, Thomas D. "The American Backwoodsman in Popular Portraiture." *Indiana Magazine of History* 42 (1946): 1–28.

———. "The Common Man Tradition in the Literature of the Frontier." *Michigan Alumnus Quarterly Review* 63 (1957): 208–17.

———. "Humor in the Stream of Southern History." *Mississippi Quarterly* 13 (1960): 176–88.

———. "Manners and Humors of the American Frontier." *Missouri Historical Review* 35 (1940): 3–24.

Collins, Carvel. "Nineteenth-Century Fiction of the Southern Appalachians." *Bulletin of Bibliography* 17 (1942–1943): 186–87, 217–18.

———. "The *Spirit of the Times*." *Papers of the Bibliographical Society of America* 40 (1946): 164–68.

Colville, Derek. "History and Humor: The Tall Tale in New Orleans." *Louisiana Historical Quarterly* 39 (1956): 153–67.

———. "A Rich Store of Southern Tall Tales." *Bibliographical Society of the University of Virginia Society News Sheet* No. 33 (1955).
Cox, James E. "Humor and America: The Southwestern Bear Hunt, Mrs. Stowe, and Mark Twain." *Sewanee Review* 85 (1975): 573–601.
Current-Garcia, Eugene. "Alabama Writers in the *Spirit*." *Alabama Review* 10 (1957): 243–69.
———. "Mr. Spirit and *The Big Bear of Arkansas*: A Note on the Genesis of Southwestern Sporting and Humor Literature." *American Literature* 27 (1955): 332–46.
———. "Newspaper Humor in the Old South, 1835–1855." *Alabama Review* 2 (1949): 102–21.
———. "'York's Tall Son' and His Southern Correspondents." *American Quarterly* 7 (1955): 371–84.
Curry, Jane. "The Ring-Tailed Roarers Rarely Sang Soprano." *Frontiers* 2 (1977): 129–40.
Dillingham, William B. "Days of the Tall Tale." *Southern Review* 4 (1968): 569–77.
Dondore, Dorothy A. "Big Talk! The Flyting, the Gabe, and the Frontier Boast." *American Speech* 6 (1930): 45–55.
Dorson, Richard M. "The Identification of Folklore in American Literature." *Journal of American Folklore* 70 (1957): 1–8, 21–23.
Durham, Frank. "The Southern Literary Tradition: Shadow or Substance?" *South Atlantic Quarterly* 67 (1968): 455–68.
Eastman, Max. "Humor in America." *Scribner's* 100 (1936): 9–13.
Eaton, Clement. "The Humor of the Southern Yeoman." *Sewanee Review* 49 (1941): 173–83.
Eberstadt, Lindley. "The Passing of a Noble 'Spirit.'" *Papers of the Bibliographical Society of America* 44 (1950): 372–73.
Ellis, Michael. "Literary Dialect as Linguistic Evidence: Subject-Verb Concord in Nineteenth-Century Southern Literature." *American Speech: A Quarterly of Linguistic Usage* 69.2 (1994): 128–44.
Fellman, Michael. "Alligator Men and Cardsharpers in Deadly Southwestern Humor." *Huntington Library Quarterly* 49 (1986): 307–23.
Ferguson, J.D. "On Humor as One of the Fine Arts." *South Atlantic Quarterly* 38 (1939): 177–86.
———. "The Roots of American Humor." *American Scholar* 4 (1935): 41–49.
Fienberg, Lorne. "Laughter as a Strategy of Containment in Southwestern Humor." *Studies in American Humor* 3, n.s. (1984): 107–22.
Fisher, Benjamin Franklin IV. "Devils and Devilishness in Comic Yarns of the Old Southwest." *Emerson Society Quarterly* 36 (1990): 39–60.
Flanders, B.H. "Humor in Ante-Bellum Georgia." *Emory University Quarterly* 1 (1945): 149–56.
Foster, Ruel E. "Kentucky Humor: Salt River Roarer to Ol' Dog Tray." *Mississippi Quarterly* 20 (1967): 224–30.
Freeman, D.S. "The Tonic of Southern Folklore." *American Scholar* 19 (1950): 187–93.
Gernes, Sonia. "Artists of Community: The Role of Storytellers in the Tales of the Southwest Humorists." *Journal of Popular Culture* 15 (1982): 114–28.
Gilmer, Gertrude. "A Critique of Certain Georgia Ante-Bellum Literary Magazines Arranged Chronologically and a Checklist." *Georgia Historical Quarterly* 18 (1934): 293–334.
Gorn, Elliott J. "'Gouge and Bite, Pull Hair and Scratch': The Social Significance of Fighting in the Southern Backcountry." *American Historical Review* 90 (1985): 18–43.
Hansen, Arlen J. "Entropy and Transformation: Two Types of American Humor." *American Scholar* 43 (1974): 405–21.

Hauck, Richard Boyd. "'Let's Licker'—Yarnspinning as Community Ritual." *American Humor: An Interdisciplinary Newsletter* 5 (1978): 5–10.

———. "Predicting a Native Literature: William T. Porter's First Issue of *The Spirit of the Times*." *Mississippi Quarterly* 22 (1968–1969): 77–84.

———, and Dean Margaret Hauck. "Panning for Gold: Researching Humor in the *Spirit of the Times*." *Studies in American Humor* 3 (1977): 149–57.

Havard, William C. "Mark Twain and the Political Ambivalence of Southwestern Humor." *Mississippi Quarterly* 17 (1964): 95–106.

Hayne, William H. "Georgia Humorists." *The American* 5 (1882): 23–24.

Higgs, Robert J. "The Solemn Burial of Dialect Humor." *Appalachian Journal* 10 (1985): 379–85.

———. "Southern Humor: The Light and the Dark." *Thalia: Studies in Literary Humor* 6 (1983): 17–27.

Hill, Hamlin. "The Durability of Old Southwestern Humor." *Mississippi Quarterly* 29 (1975–1976): 119–23.

———. "Modern American Humor: The Janus Laugh." *College English* 24 (1963): 171–76.

Hubbell, Jay B. "The Frontier in American Literature." *Southwest Review* 10 (1925): 86–92.

———. "The Old South in Literary Histories." *South Atlantic Quarterly* 48 (1949): 452–67.

Hyde, Stuart W. "The Ring-Tailed Roarer in American Drama." *Southern Folklore Quarterly* 19 (1955): 171–78.

Inge, M. Thomas. "Literary Humor of the Old Southwest: A Brief Overview." *Louisiana Studies* 7 (1968): 132–43.

Ives, Sumner. "A Theory of Literary Dialect." *Tulane Studies in Literature* 2 (1950): 137–82.

Johnston, Charles. "Old Funny Stories of the South and West." *Harpers Weekly* 57 (1913): 21.

Jones, Howard M. "The Generation of 1830." *Harvard Library Bulletin* 13 (1959): 401–14.

Jordan, P.D. "Humor of the Backwoods, 1820–1840." *Mississippi Valley Historical Review* 25 (1938): 25–38.

Keller, Mark. "'The Big Bear of Maine'???: Toward the Development of American Humor." *New England Quarterly* 51 (1978): 565–74.

*Krauth, Leland. "Mark Twain: The Victorian of Southwestern Humor." *American Literature* 54 (1982): 368–84.

Kummer, George. "Who Wrote 'The Harp of a Thousand Strings'?" *Ohio Historical Quarterly* 67 (1958): 221–31.

Leisy, Ernest J. "Folklore in American Literature." *College English* 8 (1946): 122–29.

———. "Folklore in American Prose." *Saturday Review of Literature* 34 (1951): 6, 7, 32.

*Lemay, J.A. Leo. "The Origins of Humor of the Old South." *Southern Literary Journal* 23.2 (1991): 3–13.

*Lenz, William E. "The Function of Women in Old Southwestern Humor: Re-reading Porter's *Big Bear* and *Quarter Race* Collections. *Mississippi Quarterly.* 46 (1993): 589–600.

Loomis, C. Grant. "The American Tall Tale and the Miraculous." *California Folklore Quarterly* 4 (1945): 109–28.

———. "A Tall Tale Miscellany, 1830–1866." *Western Folklore* 6 (1947): 28–41.

Lukens, Henry C. "American Literary Comedians." *Harper's Magazine* 80 (1890): 783–97.

Maclachlan, John M. "Southern Humor as a Vehicle of Social Evaluation." *Mississippi Quarterly* 13 (1960): 157–62.

McHaney, Thomas L. "The Tradition of Southern Humor." *Chiba Review* 7 (1985): 51–71.

Meine, Franklin J. "American Folk Literature." *Amateur Book Collector* 1 (1951): 3–4.

Mendoza, Aaron. "Some 'Firsts' of American Humor, 1830–1875." *Publisher's Weekly*, 21 Mar. 1931, 1603–5.
Miller, H. Prentice. "Antebellum Georgia Humor and Humorists." *Emory University Quarterly* 5 (1949): 84–100.
Moore, Arthur K. "Specimens of the Folktales from Some Ante-Bellum Newspapers of Louisiana." *Louisiana Historical Quarterly* 32 (1949): 723–58.
Moses, M.J. "The South in Fiction: The Trail of the Lower South." *Bookman* 33 (1911): 161–72.
Niesen de Abruna, Laura. "Sources of Humor and Aggression in Mark Twain's *Adventures of Huckleberry Finn*." *Mid-Hudson Language Studies* 9 (1986): 39–53.
Oehlschlaeger, Fritz. "A Bibliography of Frontier Humor in the *St. Louis Daily Reveille*, 1844–1846." *Studies in American Humor* 3 (1984–1985): 267–89.
———. "A Bibliography of Frontier Humor in the *St. Louis Daily Reveille*, 1847–1850." *Studies in American Humor* 4 (1985–1986): 262–76.
Oriard, Michael. "Shifty in a New Country: Games in Southwestern Humor." *Southern Literary Journal* 12.1 (1980): 3–28.
Otto, John Solomon. "'On a Slow Train Through Arkansas': Creating an Image for a Mountain State." *Appalachian Journal* 14 (1984): 70–74.
Parks, Edd Winfield. "The Intent of Antebellum Southern Humorists." *Mississippi Quarterly* 13 (1960): 163–68.
———. "The Three Streams of Southern Humor." *Georgia Review* 9 (1955): 147–59.
Pearce, James T. "Folk Tales of the Southern Poor White, 1820–1860." *Journal of American Folklore* 63 (1950): 398–412.
Pearson, Michael. "Pig Eaters, Whores, and Cowophiles: The Comic Image in Southern Literature." *Studies in Popular Culture* 9 (1986): 1–10.
Penrod, James H. "Characteristic Endings of Southwestern Yarns." *Mississippi Quarterly* 11 (1961–1962): 27–55.
———. "The Folk Hero as Prankster in the Old Southwestern Yarns." *Kentucky Folklore Record* 2 (1956): 5–12.
———. "The Folk Mind in Early Southwestern Humor." *Tennessee Folklore Society Bulletin* 18 (1952): 49–54.
———. "Folk Motifs in Old Southwestern Humor." *Southern Folklore Quarterly* 19 (1955): 117–24.
———. "Military and Civil Titles in the Old Southwestern Yarns." *Tennessee Folklore Society Bulletin* 19 (1953): 13–19.
———. "Minority Groups in Old Southern Humor." *Southern Folklore Quarterly* 22 (1958): 121–28.
———. "Teachers and Preachers in the Old Southwestern Yarns." *Tennessee Folklore Society Bulletin* 18 (1952): 91–96.
———. "Two Aspects of Folk Speech in Southwestern Humor." *Kentucky Folklore Record* 5 (1957): 145–52.
———. "Two Types of Incongruity in Old Southwest Humor." *Kentucky Folklore Record* 4 (1958): 163–73.
———. "Women in Old Southwestern Yarns." *Kentucky Folklore Record* 1 (1955): 41–47.
*Piacentino, Ed. "Contesting the Boundaries of Race and Gender in Old Southwestern Humor." *Southern Literary Journal* 32.2 (2000): 116–40.
*———. "'Sleepy Hollow' Comes South: Washington Irving's Influence on Old Southwestern Humor." *Southern Literary Journal* 30.1 (1997): 27–42.

Reaver, J. Russell. "From Reality to Fantasy: Opening–Closing Formulas in the Structures of American Tall Tales." *Southern Folklore Quarterly* 36 (1972): 369–82.

Rees, John O. "Some Echoes of English Literature in Frontier Vernacular Humor." *Studies in American Humor* 1, n.s. (1983): 153–62.

Rickels, Milton. "Elements of Folk Humor in the Literature of the Old Southwest." *Thalia: Studies in Literary Humor* 4 (1981): 5–9.

———. "The Humorists of the Old Southwest in the London *Bentley's Miscellany.*" *American Literature* 27 (1956): 557–60.

———. "Inexpressibles in Southwestern Humor." *Studies in American Humor* 3 (1976): 76–83.

Romine, Scott. "Text, Types, and Southwest Humor." *Mississippi Quarterly* 49 (1995–1996): 99–108.

Rourke, Constance M. "Examining the Roots of American Humor." *American Scholar* 4 (1935): 249–52.

———. "Miss Rourke Replies to Mr. Blair." *American Literature* 7 (1931): 207–10.

———. "Our Comic Heritage." *Saturday Review of Literature* 21 (Mar. 1931): 678–79.

Rutherford, Mildred Lewis. "The Humorists of the South." *Miss Rutherford's Scrap Book* 4 (1926): 1–27.

Schmitz, Neil. "Tall Tale, Tall Talk: Pursuing the Lie in Jacksonian Literature." *American Literature* 48 (1977): 471–91.

Sederberg, Nancy B. "Antebellum Southern Humor in the *Camden Journal*: 1826–1840." *Mississippi Quarterly* 27 (1973–1974): 41–74.

Shepherd, Esther. "The Tall Tale in American Literature." *Pacific Review* 2 (1921): 402–14.

Shields, Johanna Nichol. "A Social History of Antebellum Alabama Writers." *Alabama Review* 42 (1989): 165–91.

Simms, William G. "Southern Literature: Its Conditions, Prospects and History." *Magnolia* 3 (1841): 1–6, 69–74.

Simpson, Lewis P. "The Humor of the Old Southwest." *Mississippi Quarterly* 17 (1964): 63–66.

Smith, Charles F. "Southern Dialect in Life and Literature." *Southern Bivouac* 1, n.s. (1885): 343–51.

Snyder, H.N. "The Matter of Southern Literature." *Sewanee Review* 15 (1907): 218–26.

Spotts, C.B. "The Development of Fiction of the Missouri Frontier (1830–1860)." *Missouri Historical Review* 28 (1934): 195–205, 275–86; 29 (1934–1935): 17–26, 100–8, 186–94, 279–94.

Stein, Allen F. "Return to the Phelps Farm: *Huckleberry Finn* and the Old Southwestern Framing Device." *Mississippi Quarterly* 24 (1971): 111–16.

Stewart, Randall. "Tidewater and Frontier." *Georgia Review* 13 (1959): 296–307.

Tanner, Stephen L. "The Art of Self-Deprecation in American Literary Humor." *Studies in American Humor,* n.s., 3.3 (1996): 54–65.

Thompson, W.F. "Frontier Tall Talk." *American Speech* 9 (1934): 187–99.

Tilford, John E. "Literary Traditions in Southwest Humor: 1830–1860." *Emory University Quarterly* 4 (1948): 239–45.

Togni, Mario L. "'Preachin's My Line, Too': Trasformazioni della figura letteraria del confidence man,' dagli umoristi dell' Old Southwest a Mark Twain. *Annali di Ca' Foscori: Rivista della Facolta di Letterature Straniere dell' Universita di Venezia.* 35.1–2 (1996): 303–42.

Trent, W.P. "A Retrospect on American Humor." *Century* 63 (1901): 45–64.

Turner, Arlin. "Realism and Fantasy in Southern Humor." *Georgia Review* 12 (1958): 451–57.

———. "Seeds of Literary Revolt in the Humor of the Old Southwest." *Louisiana Historical Quarterly* 39 (1956): 143–51.

Turner, W. Craig. "Southwestern Humor." *The Mark Twain Encyclopedia*. Eds. J.R. LeMaster and James D. Wilson. New York: Garland, 1993. 705–7.

W., H. "Slick, Downing, Crockett, etc." *London and Westminster Review* 32 (1838): 136–45.

Watts, Edward. "The Changing Critical Placement of Humor of the Old Southwest." *Mississippi Quarterly* 44 (1990–1991): 95–103.

Weaver, R.M. "Scholars or Gentlemen?" *College English* 7 (1945): 72–77.

Weber, Brom. "American Humor and American Culture." *American Quarterly* 14 (1962): 503–7.

West, James L.W. III. "Early Backwoods Humor in the *Greenville Mountaineer*, 1826–1840." *Mississippi Quarterly* 25 (1971): 69–82.

Whiting, B.J. "Guyuscutus [*sic*], Royal Nonesuch, and Other Hoaxes." *Southern Folklore Quarterly* 8 (1944): 251–75.

Wilkinson, C.W. "Backwoods Humor." *Southwest Review* 24 (1929): 164–81.

Wolfe, Charles K. "Southwestern Humor and the Old-Time Music: Lunsford's 'Speaking the Truth.'" *John Edwards Memorial Foundation Quarterly* 10 (1974): 31–34.

Wonham, Henry. "Character Development of the Ring-Tailed Roarer in American Literature." *Southern Folklore* 46 (1989): 265–79.

———. "In the Name of Wonder: The Emergence of Tall Narrative in American Writing." *American Quarterly* 41 (1989): 284–307.

Wright, Lyle H. "A Statistical Survey of American Fiction, 1774–1850." *Huntington Library Quarterly* 2 (1939): 309–18.

Yates, Norris W. "Antebellum Southern Humor as a Vehicle of Class Expression." *Bulletin of the Central Mississippi Valley American Studies Association* 1 (1958): 1–6.

———. "'The Spirit of the Times': Its Early History and Some of Its Contributors." *Papers of the Bibliographical Society of America* 48 (1954): 117–48.

Individual Authors

Joseph Glover Baldwin

Alderman, Edwin A., et al., eds. *Library of Southern Literature*. Vol. 1. Atlanta: Martin and Hoyt, 1907–1908. 175–81.

Amacher, Richard E., and George W. Pohemus. Introduction. *The Flush Times of California*. Athens: Univ. of Georgia Press, 1966. 1–10, 65–78.

Bain, Robert. "Joseph Glover Baldwin." *Antebellum Writers in New York and the South*. Ed. Joel Myerson. Vol. 5. *Dictionary of Literary Biography*. Detroit: Gale Research, 1979. 7–10.

Beidler, Philip D. *First Books: The Printed Word and Cultural Formation in Early Alabama*. Tuscaloosa: Univ. of Alabama Press, 1999. 87–101.

Blanck, Jacob. "Joseph Glover Baldwin." *Bibliography of American Literature*. New Haven: Yale Univ. Press, 1955. I:116–17.

Braswell, William. "An Unpublished Letter of Joseph Glover Baldwin." *American Literature* 2 (1935): 292–94.

Current-Garcia, Eugene. "Joseph Glover Baldwin: Humorist or Moralist?" *Alabama Review* 5 (1952): 122–41.

———. "Poor-Ben O. and *The Flush Times of Alabama and Mississippi*." *Alabama Review* 45 (1992): 26–37.

Dillon, Richard H. "The Flush Times of California." *Journal of the West* 5 (1966): 423.

Farish, H.D. "An Overlooked Personality in Southern Life." *North Carolina Historical Review* 12 (1935): 341–53.

Grammer, John. "The Republican Historical Vision: Joseph Glover Baldwin's *Party Leaders.*" *Southern Literary Journal* 25 (1993): 3–13.

Griffith, Nancy Snell. *Humor of the Old Southwest: An Annotated Bibliography of Primary and Secondary Sources.* Westport, Conn.: Greenwood, 1989. 48–57.

Hubbell, Jay B. *The South in American Literature, 1607–1900.* Durham, N.C.: Duke Univ. Press, 1954. 675–78.

Justus, James H. Introduction. *The Flush Times of Alabama and Mississippi: A Series of Sketches.* Baton Rouge: Louisiana State Univ. Press, 1987. xiii–l.

Keller, Mark A. "The Transfiguration of a Southwestern Humor Sketch: Joseph Glover Baldwin's 'Jo, Heyfron.'" *American Humor* 8 (1981): 19–22.

Lenz, William E. *Fast Talk and Flush Times: The Confidence Man as a Literary Convention.* Columbia: Univ. of Missouri Press, 1985. 97–106.

Link, Samuel Albert. *Pioneers of Southern Literature.* Nashville, Tenn.: M.E. Church, 1899. 486–504.

Lynn, Kenneth S. *Mark Twain and Southwestern Humor.* Boston: Little, Brown, 1959. 115–24.

McDermott, John Francis. "Baldwin's 'Flush Times of Alabama and Mississippi'—A Bibliographical Note." *Papers of the Bibliographical Society of America* 45 (1951): 251–56.

McMillan, Malcolm C., ed. "Joseph Glover Baldwin Reports on the Whig National Convention of 1848." *Journal of Southern History* 25 (1959): 366–82.

Mellen, George F. "Joseph G. Baldwin and the 'Flush Times.'" *Sewanee Review* 9 (1901): 171–84.

Moseley, Merritt W., Jr. "Joseph Glover Baldwin (1815–1864)." *Fifty Southern Writers Before 1900: A Bio-Bibliographical Sourcebook.* Eds. Robert Bain and Joseph M. Flora. Westport, Conn.: Greenwood, 1987. 29–37.

Paul, Rodman W. "*The Flush Times of California.*" *Pacific Northwest Quarterly* 57 (1966): 133.

Rubin, Louis D., Jr. "The Great American Joke." *South Atlantic Quarterly* 72 (1973): 82–94.

Saunders, James Edmonds. *Early Settlers of Alabama with Notes and Genealogies.* New Orleans: L. Graham and Son, 1899. Baltimore: Genealogical Publishing, 1982. 55–56.

Schmitz, Neil. "Mark Twain, Henry James, and Jacksonian Dreaming." *Criticism* 27 (1985): 155–73.

Simms, L. Moody, Jr. "Joseph G. Baldwin's 'General Gymm and Colonel Burrows': An Uncollected 'Flush Times' Sketch." *Mid-South Folklore* 5 (1977): 31–37.

———. "Joseph Glover Baldwin." *American Humorists, 1800–1950.* Ed. Stanley Trachtenberg. Vol. 11. *Dictionary of Literary Biography.* Detroit: Gale Research, 1982. 12–17.

Stewart, Thomas H. "Baldwin, Joseph Glover." *Encyclopedia of American Humorists.* Ed. Steven H. Gale. New York: Garland, 1988. 23–24.

Watson, Charles S. "Order Out of Chaos: Joseph Glover Baldwin's *The Flush Times of Alabama and Mississippi.*" *Alabama Review* 45 (1992): 257–72.

Wetmore, T.B. "Joseph Glover Baldwin." *Transactions of the Alabama Historical Society, 1897–1898,* 2 (1898): 67–73.

Williams, Benjamin Buford. "Joseph Glover Baldwin, Droll Historian of 'Flush Times.'" *A Literary History of Alabama: The Nineteenth Century.* Cranbury, N.J.: Associated University Presses, 1979. 82–95.

Wilson, James D. "Joseph Glover Baldwin: 1815–1864." *Lives of Mississippi Authors, 1817–1967.* Ed. James B. Lloyd. Jackson: Univ. Press of Mississippi, 1981. 18–19.

Wimsatt, Mary Ann. "Baldwin's Patrician Humor." *Thalia: Studies in Literary Humor* 6.2 (1983): 43–50.

———. "Thrice-Told Tales: Or, Several Ways of Drinking from a Fingerbowl." *Postscript: Publication of the Philological Association of the Carolinas* 11 (1994): 35–41.

John Gorman Barr

Beidler, Philip D. *The Art of Fiction in the Heart of Dixie.* University: Univ. of Alabama Press, 1986. 3–4, 328.

Hoole, W. Stanley. "John Gorman Barr: Forgotten Alabama Humorist." *Alabama Review* 4 (1951): 83–116.

Hubbs, G. Ward. "Letters from John Gorman Barr." *Alabama Review* 36 (1983): 271–84.

———. Introduction. *Rowdy Tales from Early Alabama: The Humor of John Gorman Barr.* University, Ala.: Univ. of Alabama Press, 1981. 1–10.

William Penn Brannon

Kummer, George. "Who Wrote 'The Harp of a Thousand Strings'?" *Ohio Historical Quarterly* 67 (1958): 221–31.

West, James L.W. III, ed. "A New Mock Sermon." *Gyascutus: Studies in Antebellum Southern Humorous and Sporting Writing.* Ed. James L.W. West III. Atlantic Highlands, N.J.: Humanities, 1978. 209–14.

J. Ross Browne

Browne, Lisa Fergusson. "J. Ross Browne in the Apache Country." *New Mexico Quarterly* 35 (1965): 5–28.

———, ed. *J. Ross Browne: His Letters, Journals, and Writings.* Albuquerque: Univ. of New Mexico Press, 1969.

Csiscila, Joseph. "J. Ross Browne." *DLB 202: Nineteenth-Century American Fiction Writers.* Ed. Kent P. Ljungquist. Detroit: Gale Research, 1999. 57–64.

Dillon, Richard H. *J. Ross Browne, Confidential Agent in Old California.* Norman: Univ. of Oklahoma Press, 1965.

Goodman, Michael David. *A Western Panorama, 1849–1875, the Travels, Writings, and Influence of J. Ross Browne.* Glendale, Calif.: Arthur H. Clark, 1966.

Rock, Francis J. *J. Ross Browne.* Washington, D.C.: Catholic University of America, 1929.

Walker, Franklin. *Irreverent Pilgrims: Melville, Browne, and Mark Twain in the Holy Land.* Seattle: Univ. of Washington Press, 1974.

Marcus Lafayette Byrn

Masterson, James R. "The Arkansas Doctor." *Annals of Medical History.* 3rd ser., 2 (1940): 30.

———. *Arkansas Folklore: The Arkansas Traveler, Davey Crockett, and Other Legends.* Boston: Chapman and Grime, 1942. Little Rock: Rose, 1974. 88–91, 334–35, 400–1.

McNeil, W.K. Introduction. *The Life and Adventures of an Arkansas Doctor.* By David Rattlehead. Fayetteville: Univ. of Arkansas Press, 1989. ix–xxi.

Pettengell, Michael J. "Marcus Lafayette Byrn: Southwest Humorist in New York City." *University of Mississippi Studies in English* 7 (1989): 85–97.

Joseph Beckman Cobb

Anderson, Hilton. "A Southern Sleepy Hollow." *Mississippi Folklore Register* 3 (1969): 85–88.

Buckley, George T. "Joseph B. Cobb: Mississippi Essayist and Critic." *American Literature* 10 (1938): 166–78.

Hendricks, George, and Fritz Oehlschlaeger. "Some Additions to the Bibliography of Joseph Beckman Cobb." *Notes on Mississippi Writers* 18.1 (1986): 53–63.

Hubbell, Jay B. *The South in American Literature, 1607–1900.* Durham, N.C.: Duke Univ. Press, 1954. 637–39.

Mohr, Clarence L. "Candid Comments from a Mississippi Author." *Mississippi Quarterly* 25 (1972): 83–93.

Phillips, Robert L., Jr. "Cobb, Joseph Beckman: 1819–1858." *Lives of Mississippi Writers, 1817–1967.* Ed. James B. Lloyd. Jackson: Univ. Press of Mississippi, 1981. 95–98.

———. "Joseph B. Cobb and the Evangelicals in the Old South." *Thalia: Studies in Literary Humor* 6.2 (1983): 128–32.

Rogers, Tommy W. "The Folk Humor of Joseph B. Cobb." *Notes on Mississippi Writers* 3 (1970): 13–35.

———. "Joseph B. Cobb: Antebellum Humorist and Critic." *Mississippi Quarterly* 22 (1969): 131–46.

———."Joseph B. Cobb: Continuation of a Distinguished Lineage." *Georgia Historical Quarterly* 56 (1972): 404–14.

———. "Joseph B. Cobb: The Successful Pursuit of Belles Lettres." *McNeese Review* 20 (1971–1972): 70–83.

David Crockett

Albanese, Catherine L. "Citizen Crockett: Myth, History, and Nature Religion." *Soundings* 61 (1978): 87–104.

———. "David Crockett." *Antebellum Writers in New York and the South.* Ed. Joel Myerson. Vol. 5. *Dictionary of Literary Biography*. Detroit: Gale Research, 1979. 94–96.

———. "King Crockett: Nature and Civility on the American Frontier." *Proceedings of the American Antiquarian Society* 88 (1979): 225–49.

———. "Savage, Sinner, and Saved: Davy Crockett, Camp Meetings, and the Wild Frontier." *American Quarterly* 33 (1981): 482–501.

Arpad, Joseph J., ed. *A Narrative of the Life of David Crockett.* New Haven, Conn.: College and University Press, 1972.

Baugh, Virgil E. *Rendezvous at the Alamo: Highlights in the Lives of Bowie, Crockett and Travis.* New York: Pageant, 1960. Lincoln: Univ. of Nebraska Press, 1985.

Beck, Horace P. "The Making of the Popular Legendary Hero." *American Folk Legend: A Symposium.* Ed. Wayland D. Hand. Berkeley: Univ. of California Press, 1971. 121–32.

Blair, Walter. "Americanized Comic Braggarts." *Critical Inquiry* 4 (1977): 331–49.

———. *Horse Sense in American Humor from Benjamin Franklin to Ogden Nash.* Chicago: Univ. of Chicago Press, 1942. 24–50, 102–22.

———. "Six Davy Crocketts." *Southwest Review* 25 (1940): 443–62.

Boatright, Mody C. *Folk Laughter on the American Frontier.* New York: Macmillan, 1949.

Boorstin, Daniel J. *The Americans: The National Experience.* New York: Random House, 1965. 327–33.

Bright, Verne. "Davy Crockett Legend and Tales in the Oregon Country." *Oregon Historical Review* 51 (1950): 207–15.

Cawelti, John G. *Apostles of the Self-made Man.* Chicago: Univ. of Chicago Press, 1965. 68–71.

Chittick, V.L.O. "Haliburton Postscript I: Ring-tailed Yankee." *Dalhousie Review* 37 (1937): 19–36.

Clark, William Bedford. "*Col. Crockett's Exploits and Adventures in Texas*: Death and Transfiguration." *Studies in American Humor,* n.s., 1 (1982): 66–76.

Davis, Curtis Carroll. "A Legend at Full-Length: Mr. Chapman Paints Colonel Crockett—And Tells About It." *Proceedings of the Antiquarian Society* 69 (1959): 155–74.

Davis, William C. *Three Roads to the Alamo: The Saga and Fortunes of Davy Crockett, James Bowie, and William Barret Travis.* New York: HarperCollins, 1998.

Derr, Mark. *The Frontiersman: The Real Life and the Many Legends of Davy Crockett.* New York: William Morrow, 1993.

Dorson, Richard M. "America's Comic Demigods." *American Scholar* 10 (1941): 389–401.

———. Introduction. *Davy Crockett: American Comic Legend.* New York: Rockland Editions, 1939. xi–xvi.

———. "Davy Crockett and the Heroic Age." *Southern Folklore Quarterly* 6 (1942): 95–102.

———. "Davy Crockett the Backwoodsman." *America in Legend: Folklore from the Colonial Period to the Present.* New York: Random House, 1973. 64–79.

———. "The Sources of *Davy Crockett, American Comic Legend.*" *Midwest Folklore* 8 (1958): 143–49.

Downing, Marvin. "Davy Crockett in Gibson County, Tennessee: A Century of Memories." *West Tennessee Historical Society Papers* 37 (1983): 54–61.

Downs, Robert B. "Folk Hero." *Books That Changed the South.* Chapel Hill: Univ. of North Carolina Press, 1977. 63–73.

Flood, Royce E. "Rhetoric in Defense of the Dispossessed: David Crockett and the Tennessee Squatters." *Rhetorical Movement: Essays in Honor of Leland M. Griffin.* Ed. David Zarefsky. Evanston, Ill.: Northwestern Univ. Press, 1994. 34–54.

Folmsbee, Stanley J. "David Crockett and His Autobiography." *East Tennessee Historical Society's Publications* 43 (1971): 3–17.

———, and Anna Grace Cartron. "David Crockett: Congressman." *East Tennessee Historical Society's Publications* 29 (1957): 40–78.

———. "David Crockett in Texas." *East Tennessee Historical Society's Publications* 30 (1958): 48–74.

———. "The Early Career of David Crockett." *East Tennessee Historical Society's Publications* 28 (1956): 58–85.

Foreman, Gary L. *Crockett: The Gentleman from the Cane: A Comprehensive View of the Folkhero Americans Thought They Knew.* Dallas: Taylor, 1986.

Foster, Austin P. "David Crockett." *Tennessee Historical Magazine* 9 (1925): 166–77.

French, Janie P.C., and Zella Armstrong. *Notable Southern Families: Vol. 5, The Crockett Family and Connecting Lines.* Bristol, Tenn.: 1928. Baltimore: Genealogical Publishing, 1974.

Griffith, Nancy Snell. *Humor of the Old Southwest: An Annotated Bibliography of Primary and Secondary Sources.* Westport, Conn.: Greenwood, 1989. 58–82.

Harper, Herbert L., ed. *Houston and Crockett: Heroes of Tennessee and Texas: An Anthology.* Nashville: Tennessee Historical Commission, 1986.

Harrison, Lowell H. "David Crockett." *American History Illustrated* 6 (1971): 23–30.

———. "Davy Crockett: The Making of a Folk Hero." *Kentucky Folklore Record* 15 (1969): 87–90.

Hauck, Richard Boyd. *Crockett: A Bio-bibliography.* Westport, Conn.: Greenwood, 1982. Rpt. *Davy Crockett: A Handbook.* Lincoln: Univ. of Nebraska Press, 1986.

———. "The Man in the Buckskin Hunting Shirt: Fact and Fiction in the Crockett Story." *Davy Crockett: The Man, the Legend, the Legacy, 1786–1986.* Ed. Michael A. Lofaro. Knoxville: Univ. of Tennessee Press, 1985. 3–17.

Heale, M.J. "The Role of the Frontier in Jacksonian Politics: David Crockett and the Myth of the Self-Made Man." *Western Historical Quarterly* 4 (1973): 405–23.

Hoffman, Daniel G. "The Deaths and Three Resurrections of Davy Crockett." *Antioch Review* 21 (1961): 5–13.

———. *Form and Fable in American Fiction.* New York: Oxford Univ. Press, 1961. 70–78.

Hutton, Paul Andrew. "Davy Crockett, Still King of the Wild Frontier." *Texas Monthly* 14 (1986): 122–30, 244–48.

———. "'Going to Congress and making allmynack is my trade': Davy Crockett: His Almanacks and the Evolution of a Frontier Legend." *Journal of the West* 37.2 (1998): 10–22.

———. Introduction. *A Narrative of the Life of David Crockett.* Lincoln: Univ. of Nebraska Press, 1987. v–lvii.

Jones, Jesse Aquillah. "Say It Ain't True, Davy! The Real David Crockett versus the Backwoodsman in Us All." *Appalachian Journal* 15 (1987): 45–51.

Krupat, Arnold. "American Autobiography: The Western Tradition." *Georgia Review* 35 (1981): 307–17.

Leach, Joseph. "Crockett's Almanacs and the Typical Texan." *Southwest Review* 35 (1950): 88–95.

Lofaro, Michael A. "Davy Crockett, David Crockett, and Me: A Personal Journal Through Legend into History." *Tennessee Folklore Society Bulletin* 56 (1994): 96–106.

———, ed. *Davy Crockett: The Man, The Legend, The Legacy, 1786–1986.* Knoxville: Univ. of Tennessee Press, 1985.

———. "Davy Crockett, Tall Tale Humor, and the Second Nashville Series of Crockett Almanacs." *The Tall Tales of Davy Crockett: The Second Nashville Series of Crockett Almanacs, 1839–1841.* Ed. Lofaro, Knoxville: Univ. of Tennessee Press, 1987. xv–xl.

———. "From Boone to Crockett: The Beginnings of Frontier Humor." *Mississippi Folklore Register* 14 (1980): 57–74.

———. "The Hidden 'Hero' of the Nashville Crockett Almanacs." *Davy Crockett: The Man, The Legend, The Legacy, 1786–1986.* Ed. Lofaro. Nashville: Univ. of Tennessee Press, 1985. 46–75.

Lofaro, Michael A., and Joe Cummings, eds. *Crockett at Two Hundred: New Perspectives on the Man and the Myth.* Knoxville: Univ. of Tennessee Press, 1989.

Loomis, Grant C. "The American Tall Tale and the Miraculous." *California Folklore Quarterly* 4 (1945): 109–28.

———. "Davy Crockett Visits Boston." *New England Quarterly* 20 (1947): 396–400.

Masterson, James R. *Tall Tales of Arkansas.* Boston: Chapman and Grimes, 1943. 21–28.

Meine, Franklin J. Introduction. *The Crockett Almanacks: Nashville Series 1835–1838.* Chicago: Caxton Club, 1955. v–xxxvi.

Miles, Guy S. "David Crockett Evolves, 1821–1824." *American Quarterly* 8 (1956): 53–60.

O'Connor, Robert H. "Crockett, David [Davy]." *Encyclopedia of American Humorists.* Ed. Steven H. Gale. New York: Garland, 1988. 104–8.

Pettengell, Michael J. "Crockett, David [Davy]." *Encyclopedia of American Literature.* Ed. Steven R. Serafin. New York: Continuum, 1999. 238–39.

Porter, Kenneth W. "Davy Crockett and John Horse: A Possible Origin of the Coonskin Story." *American Literature* 15 (1943): 10–15.

Reynolds, Louise Wilson. "The Pioneer Crockett Family in Tennessee." *DAR Magazine* 55 (1921): 186–91.

Rourke, Constance M. *Davy Crockett.* New York: Harcourt, Brace, 1934.

———. "Davy Crockett: Forgotten Facts and Legends." *Southwest Review* 19 (1934): 149–61.

Seelye, John. "A Well-Wrought Crockett: Or, How the Fakelorists Passed Through the Credibility Gap and Discovered Kentucky." *Toward a New American Literary History.* Eds. Louis Budd et al. Durham, N.C.: Duke Univ. Press, 1980. 91–110.

Shackford, James Atkins. "The Author of Davy Crockett's Autobiography." *Boston Public Library Quarterly* 3 (1951): 294–303.

———. "David Crockett and North Carolina." *North Carolina Historical Review* 28 (1951): 298–315.

———. *David Crockett, The Man and the Legend.* Chapel Hill: Univ. of North Carolina Press, 1956.

———, and Stanley J. Folmsbee. Introduction. *A Narrative of the Life of David Crockett of the State of Tennessee . . . Written by Himself.* Knoxville: Univ. of Tennessee Press, 1973. ix–xx.

Shapiro, Irwin. "The All-American Hero: Davy Crockett Was a Cut from the Whole Cloth." *Saturday Review of Literature* (1 Apr. 1944): 10–11.

Shribman, David. "King of the Great Unwashed." *The Wall Street Journal,* 26 Jan. 1988: 34.

Slotkin, Richard. "Houston, Crockett, and the Return of the Frontiersman." *The Fatal Environment: The Myth of the Frontier in the Age of Industrialization, 1800–1890.* New York: Atheneum, 1985. 162–73.

Smith-Rosenberg, Carroll. "Davey Crockett as Trickster: Pornography, Liminality and Symbolic Inversion in Victorian America." *Journal of Contemporary History* 17 (1982): 325–50.

Stiffler, Stuart. "Davy Crockett: The Genesis of a Heroic Myth." *Tennessee Historical Quarterly* 16 (1957): 134–40.

Stout, S.H. "David Crockett." *The American Historical Magazine* (Jan. 1902): 3–21.

Thorne, Creanth S. "The Crockett Almanacs: What Makes a Tall Tale Tall?" *Southern Folklore Quarterly* 44 (1980): 93–104.

Torrence, Robert M., and Robert L. Wittenburg. *Colonel "Davy" Crockett.* Washington, D.C.: Homer Fagan, 1956.

Voss, Frederick S. "Portraying an American Original: The Likenesses of Davy Crockett." *Southwestern Historical Quarterly* 91 (1988): 457–82.

Wade, J.D. "The Authorship of David Crockett's 'Autobiography.'" *Georgia Historical Quarterly* 6 (1922): 265–68.

Woodward, Robert W. "Davy Crockett: Whitman's 'Friendly and Flowing Savage.'" *Walt Whitman Review* 6 (1960): 48–49.

Wright, General Marcus J. "Colonel David Crockett of Tennessee." *Magazine of American History* (July–Dec. 1883): 484–89.

Zanger, Jules. "The Frontiersman in Popular Fiction, 1820–1860." *The Frontier Re-examined.* Ed. John Francis McDermott. Urbana: Univ. of Illinois Press, 1967. 141–53.

William Elliott

Alderman, Edwin A., et al., eds. *Library of Southern Literature*. Vol. 4. Atlanta: Martin and Hoyt, 1907–1908. 1569–71.

Anderson, Charles R. "Thoreau Takes a Pot Shot at *Carolina Sports*." *Georgia Review* 22 (1968): 289–99.

Hubbell, Jay B. *The South in American Literature, 1607–1900*. Durham, N.C.: Duke Univ. Press, 1954. 564–68.

Jones, Lewis Pinckney. "Carolinians and Cubans: The Elliotts and Gonzales, Their Work and Their Writings." Diss. University of North Carolina, 1952.

———. "William Elliott: South Carolina Non-Conformist." *Journal of Southern History* 17 (1951): 361–81.

Marks, Stuart A. *Southern Hunting in Black and White: Nature, History, and Ritual in a Carolina Community*. Princeton, N.J.: Princeton Univ. Press, 1999. 18–23.

Rubin, Louis D., Jr. "William Elliott Shoots a Bear." *William Elliott Shoots a Bear: Essays on the Southern Literary Imagination*. Ed. Louis D. Rubin Jr. Baton Rouge: Louisiana State Univ. Press, 1975. 1–27.

Sanderlin, Reed. "William Elliott (1788–1863)." *Fifty Southern Writers Before 1900*. Eds. Robert Bain and Joseph M. Flora. Westport, Conn.: Greenwood, 1987. 205–11.

Scafidel, Beverly. "William Elliott, Planter and Politician: New Evidence from the Charleston Newspapers, 1831–1856." *South Carolina Journals and Journalists*. Columbia: Southern Studies Program, 1975. 109–19.

C.N.B. Evans

Hubbell, Jay B. "Charles Napoleon Bonaparte Evans: Creator of Jesse Holmes the Fool-Killer." *South Atlantic Quarterly* 36 (1937): 431–46.

Joseph M. Field

Keller, Mark. "*St. Louis Reveille*." *American Humor Magazines and Comic Periodicals*. Ed. David E.E. Sloane. Westport, Conn.: Greenwood, 1987. 244–48.

Oehlschaeger, Fritz. "Field, Joseph M." *Encyclopedia of American Humorists*. Ed. Steven H. Gale. New York: Garland, 1988. 154–58.

———. Introduction. *Old Southwest Humor from the "St. Louis Reveille," 1844–1850*. Columbia: Univ. of Missouri Press, 1990. 11–19.

Smith, Sol. *Theatrical Management in the West and South for Thirty Years*. New York: Harper & Brothers, 1868.

Spotts, Carle Brooks. "The Development of Fiction on the Missouri Frontier."*Missouri Historical Review* 29, pts. 4–6 (1935): 100–8, 186–94, 279–94.

Matthew C. Field

Carson, William G.B. "The Diary of Mat Field, St. Louis, April 2–May 16, 1839." *Missouri Historical Society Bulletin* 5 (1949): 91–94.

Cox, Leland H., ed. "T.B. Thorpe's Far West Letters." *Gyascutus: Studies in Antebellum Southern*

Humorous and Sporting Writing. Ed. James L.W. West III. Atlantic Heights, N.J.: Humanities, 1978. 115–57.
Gregg, Kate L., and John Francis McDermott, eds. *Prairie and Mountain Sketches by Matthew C. Field*. Norman: Univ. of Oklahoma Press, 1957.
Joost, Nicholas. "Reveille in the West: Western Travelers in *the St. Louis Weekly Reveille*, 1844–50." *Travelers on the Western Frontier*. Ed. John Francis McDermott. Urbana: Univ. of Illinois Press, 1970. 205, 209–12.
McDermott, John Francis. "T.B. Thorpe's Burlesques of Far West Sporting Travel." *American Quarterly* 10 (1958): 175–80.
Oehlschlaeger, Fritz. Introduction. *Old Southwest Humor from the "St. Louis Reveille," 1844–1850*. Columbia: Univ. of Missouri Press, 1990. 4–11.
Sunder, John E., ed. *Matt Field on the Santa Fe Trail*. Norman: Univ. of Oklahoma Press, 1960.

Joseph Gault

Meats, Stephen. "Joseph Gault, Cobb County Humorist." *Studies in American Humor*, n.s., 4.4 (1985–1986): 290–304.
———. "Joseph Gault, an Unknown Georgia Humorist." *Mississippi Quarterly* 51 (1998): 589–602.

William C. Hall

Anderson, John Q. "Mike Hooter: The Making of a Myth." *Southern Folklore Quarterly* 19 (1955): 90–100.
Bowman, Robert. "Yazoo County's Contribution to Mississippi Literature." *Publications of the Mississippi Historical Society* 10 (1909): 501–2.
DeCell, Harriet, and JoAnne Pritchard. *Yazoo: Its Legends and Legacies*. Yazoo City, Miss.: Yazoo Delta Press, 1976. 199–200.
Keller, Mark. "The Cowardly 'Lion of the [Old South] West': Mike Hooter of Mississippi." *Mississippi Folklore Register* 18 (1984): 3–18.
———. "How Mike Shouter 'Cotch the Bar': Another 'Yazoo Sketch.'" *Southern Folklore Quarterly* 41 (1977): 65–72.
———. "'Yazoo:' Reporter of Antebellum Mississippi Life." *Notes on Mississippi Writers* 14.1 (1981): 1–11.
Polk, Noel E., and James R. Scafidel, eds. *An Anthology of Mississippi Writers*, Jackson: Univ. Press of Mississippi, 1979. 9–12.

George Washington Harris

Armitage, Shelley. "Seeing Sutly: Visual and Verbal Play in the Work of George Washington Harris." *Sut Lovingood's Nat'ral Born Yarnspinner: Essays on George Washington Harris*. Eds. James E. Caron and M. Thomas Inge. Tuscaloosa: Univ. of Alabama Press, 1996. 228–45.
Arnold, St. George Tucker, Jr. "Sut Lovingood, The Animals, and the Great White Trash Chain of Being." *Thalia: Studies in Literary Humor* 1 (1978–79): 33–41.
Bain, Robert. "George Washington Harris." *Antebellum Writers in New York and the South*.

Ed. Joel Myerson. Vol. 3. *Dictionary of Literary Biography*. Detroit: Gale Research, 1979. 138–43.

Bass, William W. "Sut Lovingood's Reflections on His Contemporaries." *Carson-Newman College Faculty Studies* 1 (1964): 33–48.

Bier, Jesse. "Southwestern Humor." *The Rise and Fall of American Humor*. New York: Holt, Rinehart, and Winston, 1968. 52–76.

Blair, Walter. *Native American Humor, 1800–1900*. New York: Knopf, 1937. Rpt. as *Native American Humor* (with some new material). New York: Harper and Row, 1960. 96–101.

———. "Sut Lovingood," *Saturday Review of Literature* 7 (Nov. 1936): 3–4.

———, and Hamlin Hill. *America's Humor: From Poor Richard to Doonesbury*. New York: Oxford Univ. Press, 1978. 213–21.

Blount, Roy Jr., ed. *Roy Blount's Book of Southern Humor*. New York: W.W. Norton, 1994. 235–41.

Boykin, Carol. "Sut's Speech: The Dialect of a 'Nat'ral Borned' Mountaineer." *The Lovingood Papers*. Ed. Ben Harris McClary. Knoxville: Univ. of Tennessee Press, 1965. 36–42.

Bridgman, Richard. *The Colloquial Style in America*. New York: Oxford Univ. Press, 1966. 23–31.

Brown, Carolyn S. "Sut Lovingood: A Nat'ral Born Durn'd Yarnspinner." *Southern Literary Journal* 18 (1985): 89–100. Rev. for *The Tall Tale in American Folklore and Literature*. Knoxville: Univ. of Tennessee Press, 1987. 74–88.

Brown, J. Thompson, Jr. "George Washington Harris." *Library of Southern Literature*. Vol. 5. Eds. Edwin A. Alderman, Joel Chandler Harris, and Charles W. Kent. Atlanta: Martin and Hoyt, 1907–1908. 2099–102.

Camfield, Gregg. "George Washington Harris: Howl in the Family." *Necessary Madness: The Humor of Domesticity in Nineteenth-Century American Literature*. New York: Oxford Univ. Press, 1997. 121–35.

Caron, James E. "An Allegory of North and South: Reading the Preface to *Sut Lovingood, Yarns Spun by a Nat'ral Born Durn'd Fool*." *Studies in American Humor,* n.s., 3.2 (1995): 49–61.

———. "Playin' Hell Sut Lovingood as Durn'd Fool Preacher." *Sut Lovingood's Nat'ral Born Yarnspinner: Essays on George Washington Harris*. Eds. James E. Caron and M. Thomas Inge. Tuscaloosa: Univ. of Alabama Press, 1996. 272–98.

———, and M. Thomas Inge, eds. *Sut Lovingood's Nat'ral Born Yarnspinner: Essays on George Washington Harris*. Tuscaloosa: Univ. of Alabama Press, 1996.

Casey, James G. "Newly Discovered Reprintings of George W. Harris's Tales and Letters." *Studies in American Humor* 5 (1986): 89–91.

Cohen, Hennig. "Mark Twain's Sut Lovingood." *The Lovingood Papers*. Ed. Ben Harris McClary. Knoxville: Univ. of Tennessee Press, 1962. 19–24.

———, and William B. Dillingham, eds. *Humor of the Old Southwest*. 3rd ed. Athens: Univ. of Georgia Press, 1994. 193–246.

Covici, Pascal, Jr. "Propriety, Society, and Sut Lovingood: Vernacular Gentility in Action." *Sut Lovingood's Nat'ral Born Yarnspinner: Essays on George Washington Harris*. Eds. James E. Caron and M. Thomas Inge. Tuscaloosa: Univ. of Alabama Press, 1996. 246–60.

———. *Mark Twain's Humor: The Image of a World*. Dallas: Southern Methodist Univ. Press, 1962.

Current-Garcia, Eugene. "Sut Lovingood's Rare Ripe Southern Garden." *Studies in Short Fiction* 9 (1972): 117–29.

Day, Donald. "George Washington Harris." *Encyclopedia Britannica.* Vol. 11. Chicago: Encyclopedia Britannica, 1960. 217.

———. "The Humorous Works of George Washington Harris." *American Literature* 14 (1943): 391–406.

———. "The Life of George Washington Harrris." *Tennessee Historical Quarterly* 6 (1947): 3–38.

———. "The Political Satires of George W. Harris." *Tennessee Historical Quarterly* 4 (1945): 320–28.

———. "Searching for Sut." *The Lovingood Papers*. Ed. Ben Harris McClary. Knoxville: Univ. of Tennessee Press, 1965. 9–15.

Eddings, Dennis W. "The Emergence of Sut Lovingood." *Essays in Arts and Sciences* 26 (1997): 85–89.

Estes, David C. "Sut Lovingood at the Camp Meeting: A Practical Joker Among the Backwoods Believers." *Southern Quarterly* 25 (1987): 53–65.

Fisher, Benjamin Franklin, IV. "George Washington Harris and Supernaturalism." *Publications of the Mississippi Philological Association* 1 (1982): 18–23.

Gardiner, Elaine. "Sut Lovingood: Backwoods Existentialist." *Southern Studies: An Interdisciplinary Journal of the South* 22 (1983): 177–89.

Griffith, Nancy Snell. *Humor of the Old Southwest: An Annotated Bibliography of Primary and Secondary Sources.* Westport, Conn.: Greenwood, 1989. 83–109.

Hansen, Arlen J. "Entropy and Transformation: Two Types of American Humor." *American Scholar* 43 (1974): 405–21.

Hauck, Richard Boyd. *A Cheerful Nihilism: Confidence and "The Absurd" in Humorous American Fiction.* Bloomington: Indiana Univ. Press, 1971. 74–76.

Howell, Elmo. "Timon in Tennessee: The Moral Fervor of George Washington Harris." *Georgia Review* 24 (1970): 311–19.

Howland, Hewitt H. "The Selection of Irvin C. Cobb: Sut Lovingood's Daddy, Acting Horse." *Humor By Vote.* New York: Laugh Club, 1933. viii, 22–31.

Inge, M. Thomas. "A Bibliography of George Washington Harris." *Sut Lovingood's Nat'ral Born Yarnspinner: Essays on George Washington Harris.* Eds. James E. Caron and M. Thomas Inge. Tuscaloosa: Univ. of Alabama Press, 1996. 315–22.

———. "Early Appreciations of George Washington Harris by George Frederick Mellen." *Tennessee Historical Quarterly* 30 (1971): 190–204.

———. *Faulkner, Sut, and Other Southerners.* West Cornwall, Conn.: Locust Hill, 1992. 51–104.

———, ed. *The Frontier Humorists: Critical Views.* Hamden, Conn.: Archon, 1975. 69–74, 118–69, 266–80, 315–17.

———. "George Washington Harris." *American Literature to 1900.* Ed. James Vinson. New York: Saint Martin's, 1980. 149–50.

———. "George Washington Harris." *Fifty Southern Writers Before 1900.* Eds. Robert Bain and Joseph M. Flora. Westport, Conn.: Greenwood, 1987. 220–26.

———. "George Washington Harris." *Reference Guide to American Literature.* Ed. D.L. Kirkpatrick. Chicago: Saint James, 1987. 260–61.

———. "George Washington Harris." *The Mark Twain Encyclopedia.* Eds. J.R. LeMaster and James D. Wilson. New York: Garland, 1993. 349–50.

———. "George Washington Harris's 'The Doctor's Bill: A Tale About Dr. J.G.M. Ramsey." *Tennessee Historical Quarterly* 24 (1965): 185–94.

———. "George Washington Harris and Southern Poetry and Music." *Mississippi Quarterly* 17 (1963–1964): 36–44.
———. Introduction. *Sut Lovingood's Yarns.* New Haven, Conn.: College & University Press, 1966. 9–24.
———. Introduction. *"Sut Lovingood's Yarns": A Facsimile of the 1867 Dick and Fitzgerald Edition.* Memphis, Tenn.: St. Lukes, 1987. 1–8.
———. "A Personal Encounter with George Washington Harris." *The Lovingood Papers.* Ed. Ben Harris McClary. Knoxville: Univ. of Tennessee Press, 1963. 9–12.
———. "The Satiric Artistry of George W. Harris." *Satire Newsletter* 4 (1967): 63–72.
———. "Sut Lovingood: An Examination of the Nature of a 'Nat'ral Born Durn'd Fool.'" *Tennessee Historical Quarterly* 19 (1960): 231–51.
———. "Sut and His Illustrators." *The Lovingood Papers.* Ed. Ben Harris McClary. Knoxville: Univ. of Tennessee Press, 1965. 26–35.
Keller, Mark. "That George Washington Harris 'Christmas Story': A Reconsideration of Authorship." *American Literature* 54 (1982): 284–87.
Knight, Donald R. "Sut's Dog Imagery." *The Lovingood Papers.* Ed. Ben Harris McClary. Knoxville: Univ. of Tennessee Press, 1965. 59–60.
Leary, Lewis. "The Lovingoods: Notes Toward a Genealogy." *Southern Excursions: Essays on Mark Twain and Others.* Baton Rouge: Louisiana State Univ. Press, 1971. 111–30.
———. "The Satiric Artistry of George W. Harris." *Satire Newsletter* 4 (1967): 63–72.
Lenz, William E. *Fast Talk and Flush Times: The Confidence Man as a Literary Convention.* Columbia: Univ. of Missouri Press, 1985. 106–17.
———. "The Identity of George Washington Harris's 'Man in the Swamp.'" *Notes on Mississippi Writers* 13 (1981): 14–17.
———. "Sensuality, Revenge, and Freedom: Women in *Sut Lovingood's Yarns* [*sic*]." *Studies in American Humor,* n.s., 1 (1983): 173–80.
Long, Hudson. "Sut Lovingood and Mark Twain's *Joan of Arc.*" *Modern Language Notes* 64 (1949): 37–39.
Lynn, Kenneth S. *Mark Twain and Southwestern Humor.* Boston: Little, Brown, 1959. 130–39.
McClary, Ben Harris. "George and Sut: A Working Bibliography." *The Lovingood Papers.* Ed. Ben Harris McClary. Knoxville: Univ. of Tennessee Press. 1962. 5–9.
———. "George W. Harris's New York *Atlas* Series: Three New Items." *Studies in American Humor,* n.s., 2 (1983): 195–99.
———. George W. Harris's 'Special Vision': His *Yarns* as Historical Sourcebook." *No Fairer Land: Studies in Southern Literature Before 1900.* Eds. J. Lasley Dameron and James W. Mathews. Troy, N.Y.: Whitson, 1986. 226–41.
———. "On Quilts." *The Lovingood Papers.* Ed. Ben Harris McClary. Knoxville: Univ. of Tennessee Press, 1965. 61–62.
———. "The Real Sut." *American Literature* 27 (1955): 105–6.
———. "Sanky and Sut." *Southern Observer* 9 (1962): 13.
———. "Sut Lovingood's Country." *Southern Observer* 3 (1955): 5–7.
———. "Sut Lovingood Views 'Abe Linkhorn.' *Lincoln Herald* 56 (1954): 44–45.
McKeithan, D.M. "Mark Twain's Story of the Bull and the Bees." *Tennessee Historical Quarterly* 11 (1952): 246–53.
———. "Bull Rides Described by 'Scroggins,' G.W. Harris, and Mark Twain." *Southern Folklore Quarterly* 17 (1953): 241–43.

Matthiessen, F.O. *American Renaissance: Art and Expression in the Age of Emerson and Whitman.* New York: Oxford Univ. Press, 1941. 641–45.
Meine, Franklin J. "George Washington Harris." *Dictionary of American Biography*. Vol. 4, pt. 2. New York: Scribner, 1932. 309.
———, ed. *Tall Tales of the Southwest: An Anthology of Southern and Southwestern Humor, 1830–1860.* New York: Knopf, 1930. xxiii–xxiv.
Mellen, George F. "George W. Harris." *Knoxville Sentinel,* 13 Feb. 1909.
———. "Lovingood's Settings." *Knoxville Sentinel,* 7 Mar. 1911.
———. "Sut Lovingood." *Knoxville Sentinel,* 8 Jan. 1914.
———. "Sut Lovingood's Yarns." *Knoxville Sentinel,* 11 Feb. 1909.
Micklus, Robert. "Sut's Travels with Dad." *Studies in American Humor*, n.s., 1 (1982): 89–101.
"New Books." *Nashville Union and American*, 25 Apr. 1867.
"New Publications." *New York Times,* 8 Apr. 1867.
Nilsen, Don L.F. "Linguistic Humor in Western Literature." *Southwest Folklore* 5 (1981): 15–51.
Parker, Hershel. "A Tribute to Harris's Sheriff Doltin Sequence." *Sut Lovingood's Nat'ral Born Yarnspinner: Essays on George Washington Harris.* Tuscaloosa: Univ. of Alabama Press, 1996. 217–27.
Parks, Edd Winfield. *Segments of Southern Thought.* Athens: Univ. of Georgia Press, 1938. 215–22.
Penrod, James. "Folk Humor in *Sut Lovingood's Yarns* [*sic*]." *Tennessee Folklore Society Bulletin* 16 (1950): 76–84.
Pettengell, Michael J. "Harris, George Washington." *Encyclopedia of American Literature*. Ed. Steven R. Serafin. New York: Continuum, 1999. 488.
Pinsker, Sanford. "Uneasy Laughter: Sut Lovingood—Between Rip Van Winkle and Andrew Dice Clay." *Sut Lovingood's Nat'ral Born Yarnspinner: Essays on George Washington Harris*. Eds. James E. Caron and M. Thomas Inge. Tuscaloosa: Univ. of Alabama Press, 1996. 299–313.
Plater, Ormonde. "Before Sut: Folklore in the Early Works of George W. Harris." *Southern Folklore Quarterly* 34 (1970): 104–15.
———. "The Lovingood Patriarchy." *Appalachian Journal* 1 (1973): 82–93.
Polk, Noel. "The Blind Bull, Human Nature: Sut Lovingood and the Damned Human Race." *Gyascutus: Studies in Antebellum Southern Humorous and Sporting Writing*. Ed. James L.W. West III. Atlantic Highlands, N.J.: Humanities, 1978. 13–49.
Ragan, David Paul. "At the Grave of Sut Lovingood: Virgil Campbell in the Work of Fred Chappell." *Mississippi Quarterly* 37 (1983): 21–30.
Rickels, Milton. "Elements of Folk Humor in the Literature of the Old Southwest." *Thalia: Studies in Literary Humor* 4 (1981): 5–9.
———. *George Washington Harris*. New York: Twayne, 1965.
———. "George W. Harris." *American Humorists, 1800–1950*. Part 1, Vol. 11. *Dictionary of Literary Biography*. Ed. Stanley Trachtenberg. Detroit: Gale Research, 1982. 180–89.
———. "George W. Harris's Newspaper Grotesques." *University of Mississippi Studies in English* 2 (1981): 15–24.
———. "The Grotesque Body of Southwestern Humor." *Critical Essays on American Humor*. Eds. William Bedford Clark and W. Craig Turner. Boston: Hall, 1984. 155–66.
———. "The Imagery of George Washington Harris." *American Literature* 31 (1959): 173–87.
———. "Sut Lovingood's Yarns." *Mississippi Quarterly* 21 (1967): 80–82.

Rose, Alan Henry. "Characteristic Ambivalence in the Yarns of George Washington Harris." *Tennessee Folklore Society Bulletin* 41 (1975): 115–16.

———. "A Plan to Wake the Devil: Race and Aesthetics in the Tales of George Washington Harris." *Demonic Vision: Racial Fantasy and Southern Fiction*. Hamden, Conn.: Archon, 1976. 63–71.

Rourke, Constance M. *American Humor: A Study of the National Character*. 1931. Rpt., New York: Harcourt, Brace, Jovanovich, 1959. 311.

Royot, Daniel. "A Nat'ral Born Durn'd Fool: L'Irresistible decheance de Sut Lovingood." *Caliban* 26 (1989): 57–64.

Schmitz, Neil. *Of Huck and Alice: Humorous Writing in American Literature*. Minneapolis: Univ. of Minnesota Press, 1983. 30–64.

———. "Forms of Regional Humor." *Columbia Literary History of the United States*. Ed. Emory Elliott. New York: Columbia Univ. Press, 1988. 306–23.

Starr, Randall. "An Unknown Tale by George Washington Harris." *Gyascutus: Studies in Antebellum Southern Humorous and Sporting Writing*." Ed. James L.W. West III. Atlantic Highlands, N.J.: Humanities, 1978. 159–72.

Stewart, Randall. "Tidewater and Frontier." *Georgia Review* 13 (1959): 296–307.

Tandy, Jeannette. *Crackerbox Philosophers in American Humor and Satire*. New York: Columbia Univ. Press, 1923. 93–94.

Twain, Mark. "Sut Lovingood." *San Francisco Daily Alta California,* 14 July 1867.

Walker, Nancy A. "Sut and His Sisters: Vernacular Humor and Genteel Culture." *Sut Lovingood's Nat'ral Born Yarnspinner: Essays on George Washington Harris*. Eds. James E. Caron and M. Thomas Inge. Tuscaloosa: Univ. of Alabama Press, 1996. 261–71.

Watterson, Henry. *Oddities in Southern Life and Character*. Boston: Houghton Mifflin, 1883. 415.

———. *The Compromises of Life*. New York: Fox, Duffield, 1903. 66.

Weber, Brom. "A Note on Edmund Wilson and George Washington Harris." The *Lovingood Papers*. Ed. Ben Harris McClary. Knoxville: Univ. of Tennessee Press, 1962. 47–53.

Wenke, John. "*Sut Lovingood's Yarns* [*sic*] and the Politics of Performance." *Studies in American Fiction* 15 (1987): 190–210.

Williams, Cratis. "Sut Lovingood as a Southern Mountaineer." *Appalachian State Teacher's College Faculty Publications* 44 (1966): 1–4.

Wilson, Edmund. "Poisoned." *New Yorker,* 7 May 1955. 136–46. Rpt. *Patriotic Gore: Studies in the Literature of the American Civil War*. New York: Oxford Univ. Press, 1962. 507–19.

Young, Thomas Daniel. *Tennessee Writers*. Knoxville: Univ. of Tennessee Press, 1981. 5–11.

———. "A Nat'ral Born Durn'd Fool." *Thalia: Studies in Literary Humor* 6 (1983): 51–56.

Ziff, Larzer. "The Fool Killer: George Washington Harris and Sut Lovingood." *Literary Democracy: The Declaration of Cultural Independence in America*. New York: Viking, 1981. 181–94.

Johnson Jones Hooper

Alderman, Edwin A., et al., eds. *Library of Southern Literature*. Vol. 6. Atlanta: Martin and Hoyt, 1907–1908. 2489–91.

Anderson, John Q. "For the Ugliest Man: An Example of Folk Humor." *Southern Folklore Quarterly* 28 (1964): 199–209.

Bain, Robert. "Johnson Jones Hooper." *Antebellum Writers in New York and the South*. Ed. Joel Myerson. Vol. 5. *Dictionary of Literary Biography*. Detroit: Gale Research, 1979. 161–65.

Beidler, Philip D. *First Books: The Printed Word and Cultural Formation in Early Alabama.* University: Univ. of Alabama Press, 1999. 87–101.

Brannon, Peter A. "Hooper's Influence in Early State Literature." *Montgomery Advertiser.* Centennial Edition, 15 Mar. 1928.

Current-Garcia, Eugene. "Alabama Writers in the *Spirit.*" *Alabama Review* 10 (1957): 245–69.

Garrett, William. *Reminiscences of Public Men in Alabama for Thirty Years.* Atlanta: Plantation, 1872.

Griffith, Nancy Snell. *Humor of the Old Southwest: An Annotated Bibliography of Primary and Secondary Sources.* New York: Greenwood, 1989. 110–27.

Harkey, Joseph H. "*Some Adventures of Captain Simon Suggs*: The Legacy of Johnson Jones Hooper." *No Fairer Land: Studies in Southern Literature Before 1900.* Eds. J. Lasley Dameron and James W. Mathews. Troy, N.Y.: Whitston, 1986. 200–10.

Hauck, Richard Boyd. *A Cheerful Nihilism: Confidence and "The Absurd" in American Humorous Fiction.* Bloomington: Indiana Univ. Press, 1961. 70–74.

Hollingsworth, Annie Mae. "Johnson Jones Hooper, Alabama's Mark Twain, Champion of the Creeks." *Montgomery Advertiser,* 23 Mar. 1931, 3.

———. "Johnson Jones Hooper: Statesman and Humorist." *Alabama Historical Quarterly* 1 (1930): 257–60.

Hoole, W. Stanley. *Alias Simon Suggs: The Life and Times of Johnson Jones Hooper.* University, Ala.: Univ. of Alabama Press, 1952.

Hopkins, Robert. "Simon Suggs: A Burlesque Campaign Biography." *American Quarterly* 15 (1963): 459–63.

Hubbell, Jay B. *The South in American Literature, 1607–1900.* Durham, N.C.: Duke Univ. Press, 1954. 672–75.

Justus, James H. "Hooper, Johnson Jones." *Encyclopedia of American Humorists.* Ed. Steven H. Gale. New York: Garland, 1988. 227–31.

Keller, Mark A. "Johnson Jones Hooper." *American Humorists, 1800–1950.* Ed. Stanley Trachtenberg. Vol. 11. *Dictionary of Literary Biography.* Detroit: Gale Research, 1982. 211–19.

Lenz, William E. *Fast Talk and Flush Times: The Confidence Man as a Literary Convention.* Columbia: Univ. of Missouri Press, 1985. 65–96.

Link, Samuel Albert. *Pioneers of Southern Literature.* Vol. 2. Nashville, Tenn.: M.E. Church, 1899. 505–24.

Longest, George. "Hooper, Johnson Jones." *Encyclopedia of American Literature.* Ed. Steven R. Serafin. New York: Continuum, 1999. 535.

Lynn, Kenneth S. *Mark Twain and Southwestern Humor.* Boston: Little, Brown, 1959.

Phillips, Robert L. "Johnson Jones Hooper (1815–1862)." *Fifty Southern Writers Before 1900: A Bio-Bibliographical Sourcebook.* Eds. Robert Bain and Joseph M. Flora. Westport, Conn.: Greenwood, 1987. 250–56.

Rachal, John. "Scotty Briggs and the Minister: An Idea from Hooper's Simon Suggs?" *Mark Twain Journal* 17 (1974): 10–11.

Shields, Johanna Nicol. Introduction. *Adventures of Captain Simon Suggs, Late of the Tallapoosa Volunteers; Together with "Taking the Census" and Other Alabama Sketches.* Tuscaloosa: Univ. of Alabama Press, 1993. vii–lxix.

*———. "A Sadder Simon Suggs: Freedom and Slavery in the Humor of Johnson Hooper." *Journal of Southern History* 56 (1990): 641–64.

———. "White Honor, Black Humor, and the Making of Southern Style." *Southern Cultures* 1 (1995): 421–30.

Smith, Howard Winston. "An Annotated Edition of Hooper's *Some Adventures of Captain Simon Suggs.*" Diss. Vanderbilt University, 1964.

———. "Simon Suggs and the Satiric Tradition." *Essays in Honor of Richebourg Gaillard McWilliams*. Ed. Howard Creed. Birmingham, Ala.: Birmingham Southern College Press, 1970. 49–56.

Somers, Paul, Jr. *Johnson Jones Hooper*. Boston: Twayne, 1984.

Thompson, Edgar E., ed. "The Porter-Hooper Correspondence." *Gyascutus: Studies in Antebellum Southern Humorous and Sporting Writing*. Ed. James L.W. West III. Atlantic Highlands, N.J.: Humanities, 1978. 219–34.

Thorpe, T.B. "The Spectator and Simon Suggs." *Daily Commercial Times* (New Orleans), Nov. 1845. Rpt. in *Spirit of the Times,* 29 Nov. 1845, 471.

Togni, Mario L. "Flush Times/Hard Times in Alabama: Aspetti della vita e dell'opera di Johnson Jones Hooper, umorista dell' Old Southwest (1815–1862)." *Annali di Ca' Foscari: Rivista della Facolta di Lingue e Letterature Straniere dell' Universita di Venezia* 31.1–2 (1992): 329–55.

———. "Simon Suggs, picaro americano." *Annali de Ca' Foscari: Rivista della Letterature Straniere dell' Universita di Venezia* 33.1–2 (1994): 429–59.

Treadway, James L. "Johnson Jones Hooper and the American Picaresque." *Thalia: Studies in Literary Humor* 6 (1983): 33–42.

Wellman, Manly Wade. Introduction. *Adventures of Captain Simon Suggs, Late of the Tallapoosa Volunteers.* Chapel Hill: Univ. of North Carolina Press, 1969. ix–xxiv.

West, Harry C. "Simon Suggs and His Similes." *North Carolina Folklore Journal* 16 (1968): 53–57.

West, James L.W., III, ed. "Johnson Jones Hooper's 'The Frinnolygist at Fault.'" *Gyascutus: Studies in Antebellum Southern Humorous and Sporting Writing*. Ed. James L.W. West III. Atlantic Highlands, N.J.: Humanities, 1978. 173–84.

Whitaker, Fanny Hooper. "The Hooper Family." *The North Carolina Booklet,* July 1905, 39–71.

Williams, Benjamin Buford. "Johnson Jones Hooper, 'Alias Simon Suggs.'" *A Literary History of Alabama: The Nineteenth Century*. Cranbury, N.J.: Associated University Presses, 1979. 69–82.

Wilson, Clyde N. Foreword. *Adventures of Captain Simon Suggs*. Nashville, Tenn.: Sanders, 1993. v–xix.

Phillip B. January

Bureau of the Census, National Archives, Seventh Census (1850). Gam Publications, Compiler. *Index to Southern District 1840 Census, State of Mississippi*. Hope, Ark., 1976.

Keller, Mark Alan. "P.B. January," in "Mississippi Contributors to the 'Spirit of the Times.'" Diss. Auburn University, 1979. 245–61.

Hamilton C. Jones

Battle, Kemp, ed. "Letter of Hamilton C. Jones the Elder." *North Carolina University Magazine* 23 (Apr. 1893): 212–20.

Hendrick, Willene, and George Hendrick. Introduction. *Ham Jones, Antebellum Southern Humorist: An Anthology*. Hamden, Conn.: Archon, 1990. 1–27, 33–43, 81–82, 111–12.

———. "Jones, Hamilton C." *Encyclopedia of American Humor*. New York: Garland, 1988. 243–46.

The Heritage of Stokes County, North Carolina. Germanton, N.C.: Stokes County Historical Society, 1981. 362–63.

Jones, Paul C. "Hamilton C. Jones." *American National Biography.* Vol. 12. Ed. John Garraty. New York: Oxford Univ. Press, 1999. 196–97.

Walser, Richard. "Ham Jones: Southern Folk Humorist." *Journal of American Folklore* 78 (1965): 295–316.

George Wilkins Kendall

Brown, Harry James, ed. *Letters from a Texas Sheep Ranch*, Urbana: Univ. of Illinois Press, 1959.

Canaday, Nicolas, Jr. "Letters from the West: A Survey of Reports by Travelers in the *New Orleans Picayune*, 1857–60." *Travelers on the Western Frontier.* Ed. John Francis McDermott. Urbana: Univ. of Illinois Press, 1970. 241–44.

Copeland, Fayette. *Kendall of the Picayune.* Norman: Univ. of Oklahoma Press, 1943.

Coulter, Merton E., ed. *The Other Half of Old New Orleans: Sketches of Characters and Incidents from the Recorder's Court of New Orleans in the Eighteen Forties as Reported in the 'Picayune.'"* Baton Rouge: Louisiana State Univ. Press, 1939. 1–8.

Kendall, John S. "George Wilkins Kendall and the Founding of the *New Orleans Picayune. Louisiana Historical Quarterly* 11 (1928): 261–85.

Thomas Kirkman

Owen, Thomas McAlory. "Samuel Kirkman." *History of Alabama and Dictionary of Alabama Biography.* Vol. 3. Chicago: Clarke, 1921.

"Samuel Kirkman." *Northern Alabama: Historical and Biographical.* Birmingham, Ala.: Smith & De Land, 1888. 313.

Henry Clay Lewis

Anderson, John Q. "Folklore in the Writings of 'the Louisiana Swamp Doctor.'" *Southern Folklore Quarterly* 19 (1955): 243–51.

———. "Folkways in Writing About Northeast Louisiana Before 1865." *Louisiana Folklore Miscellany* 1 (1960): 18–32.

———. "Henry Clay Lewis, Alias 'Madison Tensas,' M.D., the Louisiana Swamp Doctor." *Bulletin of the Medical Library Association* 45 (1955): 58–73.

———. "Henry Clay Lewis, Louisville Medical Institute Student, 1844–1846." *Filson Club Historical Quarterly* 32 (1958): 30–37.

———. "Louisiana Swamp Doctor." *McNeese Review* 5 (1953): 45–53.

———. *Louisiana Swamp Doctor: The Life and Writings of Henry Clay Lewis, Alias 'Madison Tensas, M.D.'"* Baton Rouge: Louisiana State Univ. Press, 1962. v–viii, 3–70, 259–79.

———. "Mike Hooter: The Making of a Myth." *Southern Folklore Quarterly* 19 (1955): 90–100.

Arnold, Edwin T. Introduction. *Odd Leaves from the Life of a Louisiana Swamp Doctor.* Baton Rouge: Louisiana State Univ. Press, 1997. xi–xlviii.

Griffiths, Nancy Snell. *Humor of the Old Southwest: An Annotated Bibliography of Primary and Secondary Sources.* New York: Greenwood, 1989. 128–35.

Hauck, Richard Boyd. *A Cheerful Nihilism: Confidence and "The Absurd" in American Humorous Fiction*. Bloomington: Indiana Univ. Press, 1971. 44–48.

Israel, Charles. "Henry Clay Lewis's *Odd Leaves*: Studies in the Surreal and Grotesque." *Mississippi Quarterly* 28 (1974–75): 61–69.

Keller, Mark A. "'Aesculapius in Buckskin'—The Swamp Doctor as Satirist in Henry Clay Lewis's *Odd Leaves*." *Southern Studies: An Interdisciplinary Journal of the South* 18 (1979): 425–48.

Mace, Jennings R. "Henry Clay Lewis." *Antebellum Writers in New York and the South*. Ed. Joel Myerson. Vol. 5. *Dictionary of Literary Biography*. Detroit: Gale Research, 1979. 202–3.

Piacentino, Edward J. "Lewis, Henry Clay." *Encyclopedia of American Humorists*. Ed. Steven H. Gale. New York: Garland, 1988. 280–84.

"Reviews: Leaves from the Note Book of a Louisiana Swamp Doctor." *Literary World* (New York), 30 Mar. 1850, 326.

Rose, Alan H. *Demonic Vision: Racial Fantasy and Southern Fiction*. Hamden, Conn.: Archon, 1976. 25–38

———. "The Image of the Negro in the Writings of Henry Clay Lewis." *American Literature* 41 (1960): 255–63.

Watts, Edward. "In the Midst of a Noisome Swamp: The Landscape of Henry Clay Lewis." *Southern Literary Journal* 22.2 (1990): 119–28.

Bartow Lloyd

Figh, Margaret G. "Bartow Lloyd, Humorist and Philosopher of the Alabama Back Country." *Alabama Review* 5 (1952): 83–99.

Augustus Baldwin Longstreet

Alderman, Edwin A., et al., eds. *Library of Southern Literature*. Vol. 7. Atlanta: Martin and Hoyt, 1907–1908. 3241–44.

Beam, Patricia. "The Theme and Structure of *Georgia Scenes*." *Journal of English* 15 (1987): 68–79.

Bridgers, Emily. *The South in Fiction*. Chapel Hill: Univ. of North Carolina Press, 1948. 8–10.

Brooks, Cleanth. *The Language of the American South*. Athens: Univ. of Georgia Press, 1985. 18–20.

Cabaniss, Allen. "A Forgotten Poem by Augustus Baldwin Longstreet." *North Carolina Folklore* 10 (1962): 14–16.

Castel, Albert. "Mars and the Reverend Longstreet; Or, Attacking and Dying in the Civil War." *Civil War History* 33 (1987): 103–14.

Davidson, James Wood. *The Living Writers of the South*. New York: Carleton, 1869. 337–42.

Dillard, A.W. "William Gilmore Simms and A.B. Longstreet." *The XIX Century* 3 (1870): 425–30.

Downs, Robert B. "Yarns of Frontier Life." *Books That Changed the South*. Chapel Hill: Univ. of North Carolina Press, 1977. 74–81.

Evans, Lawton B. "Augustus Baldwin Longstreet." *Men of Mark in Georgia; A Complete Elaborate History of the State From Its Settlement to the Present Time, Chiefly Told in Biogra-*

phies and Autobiographies of the Most Eminent Men of Each Period of Georgia and Progress and Development. Ed. William J. Northen. Vol. 2. Atlanta: A.B. Caldwell, 1907–1912. 264–72. Spartanburg, S.C.: Reprint Co., 1974.

Fitzgerald, Oscar Penn. *Judge Longstreet: A Life Sketch.* Nashville: Publishing House of the Methodist Episcopal Church, South, 1891.

Ford, Thomas W. "Ned Brace of *Georgia Scenes.*" *Southern Folklore Quarterly* 29 (1965): 220–27.

Gilbert, Creighton. "Emory Portrait II: Four Figures of the College Campus." *Emory University Quarterly* 4 (1948): 40–54.

Gribben, Alan. "Mark Twain Reads Longstreet's *Georgia Scenes.*" *Gyascutus: Studies in Antebellum Southern Humorous and Sporting Writing.* Atlantic Highlands, N.J.: Humanities, 1978. 103–11.

Griffith, Nancy Snell. *Humor of the Old Southwest: An Annotated Bibliography of Primary and Secondary Sources.* New York: Greenwood, 1989. 136–47.

H., G.M. "Old Times in Georgia." *Bookman* 6 (1897): 67–68.

Hamilton, Kristie. "Toward a Cultural Theory of the Antebellum Literary Sketch." *Genre* 23 (1990): 297–323.

Harkey, Joseph H. "A Note on Longstreet's Ransy Sniffle and Brackenridge's *Modern Chivalry.*" *Western Pennsylvania Historical Magazine* 52 (1969): 43–45.

Harwell, Richard. Introduction. *Georgia Scenes.* Savannah, Ga.: Beehive, 1975. i–xix.

Hutton, Laurence. "Literary Notes." *Harper's Lost Reviews.* Ed. Clayton L. Eichenberger. Millwood, N.Y.: KTO, 1976. 567.

Jacobs, Charles P. "Will Mr. Hardy Explain?" *The Critic,* 28 Jan. 1882: 25–26; correction in *The Critic,* 25 Feb. 1882: 55.

Jansen, William Hugh. "Georgia Scenes." *Southern Folklore Quarterly* 22 (1958): 159.

Johnson, Glen M. "Longstreet, Augustus Baldwin." *Encyclopedia of American Literature.* Ed. Steven R. Serafin. New York: Continuum, 1999. 701.

Johnson, John W., and Dr. F.A.P. Barnard. "Biographical Sketches of Judge A.B. Longstreet." *Mississippi Historical Society Publications* 12 (1912): 122–47.

Justus, James H. "Longstreet, Augustus Baldwin." *Encyclopedia of American Humorists.* Ed. Steven H. Gale. New York: Garland, 1988. 289–92.

Kibler, James E., Jr. Introduction. *Georgia Scenes.* Southern Classics Series. Nashville, Tenn.: Sanders, 1992. vii–xxii.

King, Kimball. *Augustus Baldwin Longstreet.* Boston: Twayne, 1984.

Knight, Lucian Lamar. *Reminiscences of Famous Georgians.* Vol. 2. Atlanta: Franklin-Turner, 1908. 174–84.

Lenz, William E. "Augustus Baldwin Longstreet (1790–1870)." *Fifty Southern Writers Before 1900: A Bio-Bibliographical Sourcebook.* Eds. Robert Bain and Joseph M. Flora. Westport, Conn.: Greenwood, 1983. 312–22.

———. *Fast Talk and Flush Times: The Confidence Man as a Literary Convention.* Columbia: Univ. of Missouri Press, 1985. 65–96.

———. "Longstreet's *Georgia Scenes*: Developing American Characters and Narrative Techniques." *Markham Review* 11 (1981): 5–10.

Lilly, Paul R., Jr. "Augustus Baldwin Longstreet." *American Humorists, 1899–1950.* Ed. Stanley Trachtenberg. Vol. 11. *Dictionary of Literary Biography.* Detroit: Gale Research, 1982. 276–83.

Link, Samuel Albert. *Pioneers of Southern Literature.* Vol. 2. Nashville, Tenn.: M.E. Church, 1899. 471–85.

Lynn, Kenneth S. *Mark Twain and Southwestern Humor*. Boston: Little, Brown, 1959. 61–72.

McElderry, B.R., Jr. Introduction. *Georgia Scenes*. Gloucester, Mass.: Peter Smith, 1970. v–x.

Mayfield, John. "The Theatre of Public Esteem: Ethics and Values in Longstreet's *Georgia Scenes*." *Georgia Historical Quarterly* 75 (1991): 566–86.

Meriwether, James B. "Augustus Baldwin Longstreet: Realist and Artist." *Mississippi Quarterly* 35 (1982): 351–64.

Newlin, Keith. "*Georgia Scenes*: The Satiric Artistry of Augustus Baldwin Longstreet." *Mississippi Quarterly* 41 (1987–1988): 21–37.

Parrington, Vernon L. *The Romantic Revolution in America, 1800–1860*. New York: Harcourt, Brace & World, 1927. Vol. 2. *Main Currents of American Thought*. 3 vols. 1927–30. 166–72.

Pearson, Michael. "Rude Beginnings of the Comic Tradition in Georgia Literature." *Journal of American Culture* 11 (1988): 51–54.

Poe, Edgar Allan. "Georgia Scenes." *Southern Literary Messenger* 2 (1836): 287–92.

Rachels, David. Introduction. *Augustus Baldwin Longstreet's Georgia Scenes Completed*. Athens: Univ. of Georgia Press, 1998. xi–lxvii.

———. "Oliver Hillhouse Prince, Augustus Baldwin Longstreet, and the Birth of American Literary Realism." *Mississippi Quarterly* 51 (1998): 603–19.

Romine, Scott. "Negotiating Community in Augustus Baldwin Longstreet's *Georgia Scenes*." *Style* 30.1 (1996): 1–27. Rpt. and rev. version in Romine's *The Narrative Forms of Southern Community*. Baton Rouge: Louisiana State Univ. Press, 1999. 24–64.

Scafidel, James R. "A.B. Longstreet and Secession: His Contributions to Columbia and Charleston Newspapers, 1860–1861." *South Carolina Journals and Journalists*. Ed. James B. Meriwether. Columbia, S.C.: Southern Studies Program, 1975. 77–87.

———. "Augustus Baldwin Longstreet: Native Augustan." *Richmond County History* 11 (1979): 19–29.

———. "Augustus Baldwin Longstreet: 1790–1870." *Lives of Mississippi Authors, 1817–1967*. Ed. James B. Lloyd. Jackson: Univ. Press of Mississippi, 1981. 300–2.

———. "Georgia Scenes." *Mississippi Quarterly* 29 (1975–1976): 136–42.

———. "A Georgian in Connecticut: A.B. Longstreet's Legal Education." *Georgia Historical Quarterly* 61 (1977): 222–37.

———. "The Letters of Augustus Baldwin Longstreet." Diss. University of South Carolina, 1976.

Shaw, Arthur Marvin. "A.B. Longstreet's Brief Sojourn in Louisiana." *Louisiana Historical Quarterly* 32 (1949): 222–32.

Silverman, Kenneth. "Longstreet's 'The Gander Pulling.'" *American Quarterly* 18 (1966): 548–49.

Smith, Gerald J. "Augustus Baldwin Longstreet and John Wade's 'Cousin Lucius.'" *Georgia Historical Quarterly* 61 (1972): 276–81.

Snipes, Wilson. "The Humor of Longstreet's Persona Abram Baldwin in *Georgia Scenes*." *Studies in American Humor*, n.s., 4 (1985–1986): 277–89.

Swanson, William J. "Fowl Play on the Frontier." *West Georgia College Review* 1 (1968): 12–15.

"An Unreprinted *Georgia Scene*." *Emory University Quarterly* 2 (1946): 100–101.

Wade, John Donald. "Augustus Baldwin Longstreet, A Southern Cultural Type." *Southern Pioneers in Social Interpretation*. Ed. Howard W. Odum. Chapel Hill: Univ. of North Carolina Press, 1925. 119–40.

———. *Augustus Baldwin Longstreet: A Study of the Development of Culture in the South*, 1924. Ed. M. Thomas Inge. Athens: Univ. of Georgia Press, 1969.

———. "Old Books: *Georgia Scenes*." *Georgia Review* 14 (1960): 444–47.

Weber, C.J. "A Connecticut Yankee in King Alfred's Country." *Colophon* 1 (1936): 525–35.

Wegmann, Jessica. "'Playing in the Dark' with Longstreet's *Georgia Scenes*: Critical Reception and Reader Response to Treatments of Race and Gender." *Southern Literary Journal* 30.1 (1997): 13–26.

Alexander G. McNutt

Craig, Raymond C. "McNutt, Alexander Gallatin." *Encyclopedia of American Humor*. Ed. Steven H. Gale. New York: Garland, 1988. 308–9.

Davis, Reuben. *Recollections of Mississippi and Mississippians*. Boston: Houghton, Mifflin, 1889. 83–85.

Foote, Henry S. *Casket of Reminiscences*. Washington, D.C.: Chronicle, 1874. 198–215.

Howell, Elmo. "Governor Alexander G. McNutt of Mississippi: Humanist of the Old Southwest." *Journal of Mississippi History*. 55 (1973): 153–65.

Keller, Mark A. "'Th' Guv'ner Wuz a Writer'—Alexander G. McNutt of Mississippi." *Southern Studies: An Interdisciplinary Journal of the South* 20 (1981): 394–411.

Lowry, Robert and William H. McCardle. "The Administration of Governor McNutt." *A History of Mississippi*. Jackson, Miss.: R.H. Henry, 1891. 298. Spartanburg, S.C.: Reprint Co., 1978.

Lynch, James D. "Alexander Gallatin McNutt" *The Bench and Bar of Mississippi*. New York: Hale & Son, 1881. 133–35.

Moss, Warner. "Governor Alexander G. McNutt (1802–1848)." *Journal of Mississippi History* 42 (1980): 244–57.

Summers, Cecil L. "Alexander Gallatin McNutt." *The Governors of Mississippi*. Gretna, La.: Pelican, 1980. 53, 57–58, 61.

Yates, Norris W. *William T. Porter and the "Spirit of the Times": A Study of the Big Bear School of Humor*. Baton Rouge: Louisiana State Univ. Press, 1957. 81–82.

Orlando Benedict Mayer

Cox, Leland. "Realistic and Humorous Writings in Ante-Bellum Charleston Magazines." *South Carolina Journals and Journalists*. Ed. James B. Meriwether. Spartanburg, S.C.: Reprint Co., 177–205.

Kibler, James E., Jr. Introduction. *The Dutch Fork*. By O.B. Mayer. Spartanburg, S.C.: Reprint Co., 1982. vii–xv.

———. Introduction. *John Punterick: A Novel of Life in the Old Dutch Fork*. By O.B. Mayer. Spartanburg, S.C.: Reprint Co., 1981. ix–xix.

———. "The Dutch Fork of Mayer's Fiction." *Names in South Carolina* 30 (1983): 24–31.

———. "O.B. Mayer."*Antebellum Writers in New England and the South*. Vol. 3. *Dictionary of Literary Biography*. Ed. Joel Myerson. Detroit: Gale Research, 1979. 213–18.

———. Preface. *Fireside Tales: Stories of the Old Dutch Fork*. Ed. Kibler. Columbia, S.C.: Dutch Fork, 1984. 1–4.

———, and Edward J. Piacentino. "Mayer, Orlando Benedict." *Encyclopedia of American Humorists*. Ed. Steven H. Gale. New York: Garland, 1988. 315–20.

O'Neall, John B. *The Annals of Newberry*. Newberry, S.C.: Aull and Houseal, 1892. 567–68.

"Orlando Benedict Mayer." *Cyclopedia of Eminent and Representative Men of the Carolinas of the Nineteenth Century*. Vol. 1. Madison, Wis.: Brant and Fuller, 1892. 323–24.

Piacentino, Ed. "Backwoods Humor in Upcountry South Carolina: The Case for O.B. Mayer." *South Carolina Review* 30 (1997): 79–85.

———. "Letter from O.B. Mayer to Paul Hamilton Hayne: Some Notes on Literary Relationships." *Mississippi Quarterly* 50 (1996–1997): 117–23.

Charles F.M. Noland

Ainsworth, Albert C. "Sayings and Doings in New Orleans." *Spirit of the Times,* 26 Mar. 1842, 37.

Arrington, Alfred. "Fent Noland." *The Lives and Adventures of the Desperadoes of the South-West Containing an Account of the Duelists and Duelling.* New York: William H. Graham, 1849.

Bickley, R. Bruce, Jr. "From North Carolina to Nova Scotia: On the Bibliographical Trail of the Fool Killer." *Southern Folklore Quarterly* 45 (1981): 163–71.

Fienberg, Lorne. "C.F.M. Noland." *American Humorists, 1800–1950.* Ed. Stanley Trachtenberg. Vol. 11. *Dictionary of Literary Biography.* Detroit: Gale Research, 1982. 360–63.

———. "Colonel Noland of the *Spirit*: The Voices of a Gentleman in Southwest Humor." *American Literature* 53 (1981): 232–45.

Griffith, Nancy Snell. *Humor of the Old Southwest: An Annotated Bibliography of Primary and Secondary Sources.* New York: Greenwood, 1989. 148–69.

Masterson, James R. "The Arkansas Colonel" and "Col. Pete Whetstone." *Tall Tales of Arkansas.* Boston: Chapman and Grimes, 1943. 29–54.

Metarie. "Death of Charles Fenton Mercer Noland." *Spirit of the Times,* 31 July 1858, 291.

Milner, Joseph O. "Noland, Charles Fenton Mercer." *Encyclopedia of American Humorists.* Ed. Steven H. Gale. New York: Garland, 1988. 337–40.

Pope, William F. *Early Days in Arkansas: Being for the Most Part Recollections of an Old Settler.* Ed. Dunbar H. Pope. Little Rock, Ark.: F.W. Allsopp, 1895. 119–23, 125–26.

Ross, Margaret Smith. "Pete Whetstone of Devil's Fork." *Arkansas Historical Quarterly* 16 (1957): 407–9.

Shinn, Josiah H. "The Life and Public Services of Charles Fenton Mercer Noland." *Publications of the Arkansas Historical Association* 1 (1906): 330–43.

White, Lonnie J. "The Pope-Noland Duel of 1831: An Original Letter of C.F.M. Noland to His Father." *Arkansas Historical Quarterly* 22 (1963): 117–23.

Williams, Garner Leonard. "An Early Arkansas 'Frolic': A Contemporary Account." *Mid-South Folklore* 2 (1974): 39–42.

———. "Charles F.M. Noland: One Aspect of His Career." *The Independence County Chronicle* 10 (1969): 52–58.

———. "Introduction: C.F.M. Noland and the Roots of Southwestern Humor." *Cavorting on the Devil's Fork: The Pete Whetstone Letters of C.F.M. Noland.* Memphis, Tenn.: Memphis State Univ. Press, 1979. 1–54.

———. "Lingering in Louisville: Impressions of an Early Visitor." *Filson Club Historical Quarterly* 52 (1978): 191–295.

Wimsatt, Mary Ann. "Gyascutus and the The Devil's Fork." *Mississippi Quarterly* 34 (1981): 123–34.

Worley, Ted R. "An Early Arkansas Sportsman: C.F.M. Noland." *Arkansas Historical Quarterly* 11 (1952): 25–39.

———, and Eugene A. Nolte. Introduction. *Pete Whetstone of the Devil's Fork: Letters to the Spirit of the Times, by Charles F.M. Noland.* Van Buren, Ark.: The Press Argus, 1957. i–xxxvi.

James Kirke Paulding

Aderman, Ralph M. "James Kirke Paulding." *Antebellum Writers in New York and the South.* Ed. Joel Myerson. Vol. 3. *Dictionary of Literary Biography.* Detroit: Gale Research, 1979. 246–49.
———. "James Kirke Paulding's Contributions to American Magazines." *Studies in Bibliography: Papers of the Bibliographical Society of the University of Virginia* 17 (1964): 141–51.
———. "James K. Paulding on Literature and the West." *American Literature* 27 (1955): 97–101.
———, ed. *The Letters of James Kirke Paulding,* Madison: Univ. of Wisconsin Press, 1962.
Adkins, Nelson F. "James Kirke Paulding's *Lion of the West.*" *American Literature* 3 (1951): 249–58.
Arpad, Joseph J. "John Wesley Jarvis, James Kirke Paulding, and Colonel Nimrod Wildfire." *New York Folklore Quarterly* 21 (1965): 92–106.
Conklin, Willet Titus. "Paulding's Prose Treatment of Types and Frontier Before Cooper." *University of Texas Studies in English* 19 (1939): 163–71.
Faherty, Duncan. "Paulding, James Kirke." *Encyclopedia of American Literature.* Ed. Steven R. Serafin. New York: Continuum, 1999. 873–74.
Fisher, Benjamin F., IV. "Paulding, James Kirke." *Encyclopedia of American Humorists.* Ed. Steven H. Gale. New York: Garland, 1988. 349–53.
Henry, Joyce. "Five More Essays by James Kirke Paulding." *Papers of the Bibliographical Society of America* 66 (1972): 310–21.
Herold, Amos L. *James Kirke Paulding: Versatile American,* New York: Columbia Univ. Press, 1926. 98–99, 105, 148–60.
Hodge, Francis. "Biography of a Lost Play: *Lion in the West.*" *Theatre Annual* 12 (1954): 48–61.
Lynn, Kenneth S. *Mark Twain and Southwestern Humor.* Boston: Little, Brown, 1959. 37–41.
McDonough, Michael John. "James Kirke Paulding: A Bibliographical Survey." *Resources for American Literary Study* 15 (1985): 145–61
Mason, Melvin Rosser. "'The Lion of the West': Satire on Davy Crockett and Frances Trollope." *South Central Bulletin* 29 (1969): 143–45.
Owens, Louis D. "James Kirke Paulding and the Foundations of American Realism." *Bulletin of the New York Public Library* 79 (1975): 40–50.
Parrington, Vernon L. *Main Currents in American Thought: The Romantic Revolution in America, 1800–1860.* Vol. 2. New York: Harcourt, Brace, 1927. 212–21.
Pattee, Fred L. *The First Century of American Literature, 1770–1870.* New York: D. Appleton-Century, 1935. 289–93.
Paulding, William Irving. *The Literary Life of James K. Paulding.* New York: Charles Scribner, 1867. 216–33.
Person, Leland S., Jr. "James Kirke Paulding: Myth and the Middle Ground." *Western American Literature* 16 (1981): 39–54.
Reynolds, Larry J. *James Kirke Paulding.* Boston: Twayne, 1984.
Taylor, William R. *Cavalier and Yankee: The Old South and American National Character.* New York: G. Braziller, 1961. 225–59.

Tidwell, James N. Introduction. *The Lion of the West*, by James Kirke Paulding. Stanford, Calif.: Stanford Univ. Press, 1954. 7–14.

Turner, Arlin. "James K. Paulding and Timothy Flint." *Mississippi Valley Historical Review* 34 (1947): 105–11.

Watkins, Floyd C. *James Kirke Paudling, Humorist and Critic of American Life*. Nashville, Tenn.: The Joint University Libraries, 1952. 10–12.

———. James Kirke Paulding and the South." *American Quarterly* 5 (1953): 219–30.

———. "James Kirke Paulding's Creole Tale." *Louisiana Historical Quarterly* 33 (1950): 364–79.

———. "James Kirke Paulding's Early Ring-Tailed Roarer." *Southern Folklore Quarterly* 15 (1951): 183–87.

Wegelin, Oscar. "A Bibliography of Separate Publications of James Kirke Paulding, Poet, Novelist, Humorist, Statesman, 1779–1860." *Bibliographical Society of America Papers* 12 (1918): 34–40.

William T. Porter

Betts, John R. "Sporting Journalism in Nineteenth-Century America." *American Quarterly* 5 (1955): 39–56.

Brinley, Francis. *Life of William T. Porter*. New York: D. Appleton, 1860.

Collins, Carvel. "The Spirit of the Times." *Papers of the Bibliographical Society of America* 40 (1946): 164–68.

Cox, Leland H., Jr. "Porter's Edition of Instructions to Young Sportsmen." *Gyascutus: Studies in Antebellum Humorous and Sporting Writing*. Ed. James L.W. West III. Atlantic Highlands, N.J.: Humanities, 1978. 81–102.

Current-Garcia, Eugene. "'Mr. Spirit' and *The Big Bear of Arkansas*: A Note on the Genesis of Southwestern Sporting and Humor Literature. *American Literature* 27 (1955): 332–46.

———. "'York's Tall Son' and His Southern Correspondents." *American Quarterly* 7 (1955): 371–84.

Dasher, Thomas E. "William T. Porter." *Antebellum Writers in New York and the South*. Ed. Joel Myerson. Vol. 5. *Dictionary of Literary Biography*. Detroit: Gale Research, 1979. 298–300.

Flanagan, John T. "Western Sportsmen Travelers in the *New York Spirit of the Times*." *Travelers on the Western Frontier*. Ed. John Francis McDermott. Urbana: Univ. of Illinois Press, 1970. 168–86.

Fienberg, Leonard. "The *Spirit of the Times*." *American Humor Magazines and Comic Periodicals*. Ed. David E.E. Sloane. Westport, Conn.: Greenwood, 1987. 271–78.

Hauck, Richard Boyd. "Predicting a Native Literature: William T. Porter's First Issue of the *Spirit of the Times*." *Mississippi Quarterly* 22 (1968–1969): 77–84.

Keller, Mark. "The *New York Spirit of the Times*." *American Literary Magazines: The Eighteenth and Nineteenth Centuries*, Ed. Edward E. Chielens. Westport, Conn.: Greenwood, 1986. 284–89.

Lynn, Kenneth S. *Mark Twain and Southwestern Humor*. Boston: Little, Brown, 1959. 73–76.

Thompson, Edgar E., ed. "The Porter-Hooper Correspondence." *Gyascutus: Studies in Antebellum Southern Humorous and Sporting Writing*. Ed. James L.W. West III. Atlantic Highlands, N.J.: Humanities, 1978. 219–34.

Yates, Norris W. *William T. Porter and the "Spirit of the Times": A Study of the Big Bear School of Humor*. Baton Rouge: Louisiana State Univ. Press, 1977.

John S. Robb

Joost, Nicholas. "Reveille in the West: Western Travelers in the *St. Louis Weekly Reveille*, 1844–1850." *Travelers on the Western Frontier*. Ed. John Francis McDermott. Urbana: Univ. of Illinois Press, 1970. 212–14, 235–38.

McDermott, John Francis. "Gold Fever: The Letters of 'Solitaire,' Goldrush Correspondent of '49." *Missouri Historical Bulletin* 5 (1949): 115–26, 211–23, 316–31; 6 (1949): 34–45.

———. Introduction. *Streaks of Squatter Life and Far-West Scenes*. By John S. Robb. Delmar, N.Y.: Scholars' & Facsimile Reprints, 1978. v–xvi.

Oehlschlaeter, Fritz. Introduction. *Old Southwest Humor from the St. Louis Reveille, 1844–1850*. Columbia: Univ. of Missouri Press, 1990. 23–26.

———. "Robb, John S." *Encyclopedia of American Humorists*. Ed. Steven H. Gale. New York: Garland, 1988. 371–74.

Spotts, Carle Brooks. "The Development of Fiction of the Missouri Frontier." *Missouri Historical Review* 29, pt. 4 (1935): 100–8.

Francis James Robinson

Hubbell, Jay B. *The South In American Literature, 1607–1900*. Durham, N.C.: Duke Univ. Press, 1954. 660, 671.

"Francis James Robinson." *Humor of the Old Southwest*. Ed. Hennig Cohen and William B. Dillingham. Athens: Univ. of Georgia Press, 1994. 376–77.

*Piacentino, Ed. "Contesting the Boundaries of Race and Gender in Old Southwestern Humor." *Southern Literary Journal* 32.2 (2000): 116–42 [extended analysis of "'Old Jack' C—," 121–25].

*———. "'Sleepy Hollow' Comes South: Washington Irving's Influence on Old Southwestern Humor." *Southern Literary Journal* 30.1 (1997): 27–42 [brief treatment of "The Frightened Serenaders," 37–38].

William Gilmore Simms

Arnold, Edwin T. "'Facing the Monster: William Gilmore Simms and Henry Clay Lewis." *William Gilmore Simms and the American Frontier*. Ed. John Caldwell Guilds and Caroline Collins. Athens: Univ. of Georgia Press, 1997. 179–91.

Boyd, Molly. "Southwestern Humor in *The Wigwam and the Cabin*." *William Gilmore Simms and the American Frontier*. Ed. John Caldwell Guilds and Caroline Collins. Athens: Univ. of Georgia Press, 1997. 165–78.

Guilds, John Caldwell. *Simms: A Literary Life*. Fayetteville: Univ. of Arkansas Press, 1992.

Kibler, James E., Jr. "Simms's Indebtedness to Folk Tradition in 'Sharp Snaffles.'" *Southern Literary Journal* 4.2 (1972): 55–68.

———. "Simms, William Gilmore." *Encyclopedia of American Literature*. Ed. Steven R. Serafin. New York: Continuum, 1999. 1039–43.

Marshall, Ian. "The American Dreams of Sam Snaffles." *Southern Literary Journal* 18.2 (1986): 96–107.

Meats, Stephen E. "Bald-Head Bill Bauldy: Simms' Unredeemed Captive." *Studies in American Humor* 3, 4, n.s. (1985): 321–29.

Meriwether, James B. "Simms's 'Sharp Snaffles' and 'Bald-Head Bill Bauldy': Two Views of Men—and of Women." *South Carolina Review* 16 (1984): 66–71.

Piacentino, Ed. "Echoes of the 'Sleepy Hollow' Courtship in Simms's 'Sharp Snaffles.'" *Simms Review* 4.2 (1996): 21–24.

———. "Simms, 'Bill Bauldy,' and Alligator Horses." *Simms Review* 7.2 (1999): 28–35.

———. "Simms and Major Henry." *Simms Review* 7.1 (1999): 3–11.

"*Tales of the South*. By William Gilmore Simms." Storylines Southeast. Nat'l Public Radio. WUNC, Chapel Hill, N.C., 10 Oct. 1999.

Wimsatt, Mary Ann. "The Evolution of Simms's Backwoods Humor." *Long Years of Neglect: The Work and Reputation of William Gilmore Simms*. Ed. John Caldwell Guilds. Fayetteville: Univ. of Arkansas Press, 1988. 148–65.

———. "Frontier Humor and the 'Arkansas Traveler' Motif in *Southward Ho!*" *William Gilmore Simms and the American Frontier*. Ed. John Caldwell Guilds and Caroline Collins. Athens: Univ. of Georgia Press, 1997. 147–64.

———. *The Major Fiction of William Gilmore Simms: Cultural Traditions and Literary Form*. Baton Rouge: Louisiana State Univ. Press, 1989. 85–119, 194–210, 236–51.

———. "Native Humor in Simms's Fiction and Drama." *Studies in American Humor* 3 (1977): 158–65.

———. "Simms and Southwest Humor." *Studies in American Humor* 3 (1976): 118–30.

Solomon Franklin Smith

Oehlschlaeger, Fritz. Introduction. *Old Southwest Humor from the St. Louis Reveille, 1844–1850*. Columbia: Univ. of Missouri Press, 1990. 19–23.

———. "Smith, Solomon Franklin." *Encyclopedia of American Humorists*. Ed. Steven H. Gale. New York: Garland, 1988. 405–8.

Spotts, Carle Brooks. "The Development of Fiction on the Missouri Frontier." *Missouri Historical Review* 29, pts. 4–5 (1935): 100–8, 186–94.

Tees, Thomas Arthur. Introduction. *Theatrical Management in the West and South for Thirty Years*. New York: B. Blom, 1968. i–xii.

Hardin E. Taliaferro

Anderson-Green, Paula Hathaway. "Folktales in the Literary Work of Harden [*sic*] E. Taliaferro: A View of Southern Appalachian Life in the Early Nineteenth Century." *North Carolina Folklore Journal* 31 (1983): 65–75.

Boggs, Ralph S. "North Carolina Folktales Current in the 1820s." *Journal of American Folklore* 47 (1934): 269–88.

Coffin, Tristram P. "Harden [*sic*] E. Taliaferro and the Use of Folklore by American Literary Figures." *South Atlantic Quarterly* 64 (1965): 241–46.

Craig, Raymond C. Introduction. *The Humor of H.E. Taliaferro*. Knoxville: Univ. of Tennessee Press, 1987. 3–59.

———. "Taliaferro, H[ardin] E[dwards]." *Encyclopedia of American Humorists*. Ed. Steven H.Gale. New York: Garland, 1988. 422–24.

Curry, J.L.M. "H.E. Taliaferro." *History of the Baptists in Alabama*. Ed. B.F. Riley. Birmingham, Ala.: Roberts, 1896. 340–44.

Ficken, Carl. "Making Taliaferro Famus." *Review* 10 (1988): 137–47.

Guernsey, A.H. "Surry County, North Carolina." *Harper's New Monthly Magazine* 25 (1962): 178–85.

Higgs, Robert J. "The Humor of H.E. Taliaferro." *Appalachian Journal* 15 (1988): 372–82.

Jackson, David K., ed. *Carolina Humor: Sketches by Harden [sic] E. Taliaferro*. Richmond, Va.: Dietz, 1938.

Penrod, James H. "Harden [*sic*] Taliaferro, Folk Humorists of North Carolina." *Midwest Folklore* 6 (1956): 147–53.

Piacentino, Ed. "H.E. Taliaferro (Skitt)." *Nineteenth-Century American Fiction Writers*. Ed. Kent P. Ljungquist. Vol. 202. *Dictionary of Literary Biography*. Detroit: Gale Research, 1999. 251–58.

Walser, Richard. "Biblio-biography of Skitt Taliaferro." *North Carolina Historical Review* 55 (1978): 375–95.

———. "Skitt Taliaferro: Facts and Reappraissal." *American Humor* 4 (1977): 7–10.

Whiting, B.J. "Proverbial Sayings from Fisher's River, North Carolina." *Southern Folklore Quarterly* 11 (1947): 173–85.

Williams, Cratis D. "Mountain Customs, Social Life, and Folk Yarns in Taliaferro's *Fisher's River Scenes and Characters*." *North Carolina Folklore Journal* 16 (1968): 143–52.

William Tappan Thompson

Alderman, Edwin A., et al., eds. *Library of Southern Literature*. Vol. 12. Atlanta: Martin and Hoyt, 1907–1908. 5283–86.

Ellison, George R. "William Tappan Thompson and the *Southern Miscellany*, 1842–1844." *Mississippi Quarterly* 23 (1970): 155–68.

Estes, David C. "Major Jones Defends Himself: An Uncollected Letter." *Mississippi Quarterly* 33 (1979–1980): 79–84.

———. "Thompson, William Tappan." *Encyclopedia of American Literature*. Ed. Steven R. Serafin. New York: Continuum, 1999. 1140–41.

Flanders, Bertram H. *Early Georgian Magazines: Literary Periodicals to 1865*. Athens: Univ. of Georgia Press, 1944. 30–35 and passim.

Griffith, Nancy Snell. *Humor of the Old South: An Annotated Bibliography of Primary and Secondary Sources*. New York: Greenwood, 1989. 170–90.

Hubbell, Jay B. *The South in American Literature, 1607–1900*. Durham, N.C.: Duke Univ. Press, 1954. 669–72.

Lilly, Paul R. "William Tappan Thompson." *American Humorists, 1800–1950*. Ed. Stanley Trachtenberg. Vol. 11. *Dictionary of Literary Biography*. Detroit: Gale Research, 1982. 485–90.

Link, Samuel Albert. *Pioneers of Southern Literature*. Vol. 2. Nashville, Tenn.: M.E. Church, 1899. 525–33.

McKeithan, Daniel M. "Mark Twain's Letters of Thomas Jefferson Snodgrass." *Philological Quarterly* 32 (1953): 353–65.

Miller, Henry P. "The Authorship of *The Slave-Holder Abroad*." *Journal of Southern History* 10 (1944): 92–94.

———. "The Background and Significance of *Major Jones's Courtship*." *Georgia Historical Quarterly* 25 (1946): 267–96.

Osthaus, Carl R. "From the Old South to the New South: The Editorial Career of William Tappan Thompson of the *Savannah Morning News*." *Southern Quarterly* 14 (1976): 237–60.

Owens, Mary C. *Memories of the Professional and Social Life of John E. Owens, by His Wife*. Baltimore: John Murphy, 1892. 48–49.

Rutherford, Mildred L. *The South in History and Literature*. Atlanta: Franklin Turner, 1906. 372–75.

Shippey, Herbert. "William Tappan Thompson." *Antebellum Writers in New York and the South*. Ed. Joel Myerson. Vol. 3. *Dictionary of Literary Biography*. Detroit: Gale Research, 1979. 332–35.

———. *Fifty Southern Authors Before 1900: A Bio-Bibliographical Sourcebook*. Ed. Robert Bain and Joseph M. Flora. Westport, Conn.: Greenwood, 1987. 440–51.

———. "William Tappan Thompson as Playwright." *Gyascutus: Studies in Antebellum Southern Humorous and Sporting Writing*. Ed. James L.W. West III. Atlantic Highlands, N.J.: Humanities, 1978. 51–80.

Simms, L. Moody, Jr. "Thompson, William Tappan." *Encyclopedia of American Humorists*. Ed. Steven H. Gale. New York: Garland, 1988. 434–36.

Suttler, Bernard. "William Tappan Thompson." *Men of Mark in Georgia; a Complete and Elaborate History of the State From Its Settlement to the Present Time, Chiefly Told in Biographies and Autobiographies of the Most Eminent Men of Each Period of Georgia Progress and Development*. Vol. 3. Ed. William J. Northen. Atlanta: A.B. Caldwell, 1911. 16–20. Spartanburg, S.C.: Reprint Co., 1974.

Thompson, Maurice. "An Old Southern Humorist." *The Independent*, 20 Oct. 1898, 1103–5.

Williford, W.B. Biographical Note. *Major Jones Courtship*. Facsimile reprint of 1872 revision of the 1840 edition. Atlanta: Cherokee, 1973. 1–3.

Thomas Bangs Thorpe

Bain, Robert. "Thomas Bangs Thorpe." *Antebellum Writers in New York and the South*. Ed. Joel Myerson. Vol. 3. *Dictionary of Literary Biography*. Detroit: Gale Research, 1979. 335–39.

Blair, Walter. "The Technique of the 'Big Bear of Arkansas.'" *Southwest Review* 28 (1943): 426–35.

Callow, James. *Kindred Spirits: Knickerbocker Writers and American Artists, 1807–1835*. Chapel Hill: Univ. of North Carolina Press, 1967. 9–10, 171, 235.

Cox, Leland H., Jr., ed. "T.B. Thorpe's Far West Letters." *Gyascutus: Studies in Antebellum Southern Humorous and Sporting Writing*. Ed. James L.W. West III. Atlantic Highlands, N.J.: Humanities, 1978. 115–57.

Current-Garcia, Eugene. "Thomas Bangs Thorpe (1815–1878)." *Fifty Southern Writers Before 1900: A Bio-Bibliographical Sourcebook*. Ed. Robert Bain and Joseph M. Flora. Westport, Conn.: Greenwood, 1987. 452–63.

———. "Thomas Bangs Thorpe and the Literature of the Ante-Bellum Southwestern Frontier." *Louisiana Historical Quarterly* 39 (1956): 199–222.

Estes, David C. Introduction. *A New Collection of Thomas Bangs Thorpe's Sketches of the Old Southwest*. Baton Rouge: Louisiana State Univ. Press, 1989. 3–79.

———. "The Rival Sporting Weeklies of William T. Porter and Thomas Bangs Thorpe." *American Journalism* 2 (1985): 135–43.

———. "Thomas Bangs Thorpe's Backwoods Hunters: Culture Heroes and Humorous Failures." *University of Mississippi Studies in English* 5, n.s. (1984–1987): 158–71.

Garner, Stanton. "Thomas Bangs Thorpe in the Gilded Age: Shifty in a New Country." *Mississippi Quarterly* 36 (1982–1983): 35–52.

Griffith, Nancy. Snell. *Humor of the Old South: An Annotated Bibliography of Primary and Secondary Sources*. New York: Greenwood, 1989. 191–208
Hayne, Barrie. "Yankee in the Patriarchy: T.B. Thorpe's Reply to *Uncle Tom's Cabin*." *American Quarterly* 20 (1968): 180–95.
Hauck, Richard Boyd. *Cheerful Nihilism: Confidence and "The Absurd" in American Humorous Fiction*. Bloomington: Indiana Univ. Press, 1971. 56–60.
Higgs, Robert J. "The Sublime and the Beautiful: The Meaning of Sport in Collected Sketches of Thomas B. Thorpe." *Southern Studies: An Interdisciplinary Journal of the South* 25 (1986): 235–56.
Keller, Mark. "T.B. Thorpe's 'Tom Owen, The Bee-Hunter': Southwestern Humor's 'Origin of Species.'" *Southern Studies: An Interdisciplinary Journal of the South* 18 (1979): 89–101.
———. "Thomas Bangs Thorpe." *American Humorists, 1800–1950*. Ed. Stanley Trachtenberg. Vol. 11. *Dictionary of Literary Biography*. Detroit: Gale Research, 1982. 497–505.
———. "Thorpe, Thomas Bangs." *Encyclopedia of American Humorists*. Ed. Steven H. Gale. New York: Garland, 1988. 442–45.
Lemay, J.A. Leo. "The Text, Tradition, and Themes of 'The Big Bear of Arkansas.'" *American Literature* 47 (1975): 321–42.
Lenz, William E. *Fast Talk and Flush Times: The Confidence Man as a Literary Convention*. Columbia: Univ. of Missouri Press, 1985. 118–21.
Littlefield, Daniel F., Jr. "Thomas Bangs Thorpe and the Passing of the Southwestern Wilderness." *Southern Literary Journal* 11 (1979): 56–65.
Lynn, Kenneth S. *Mark Twain and Southwestern Humor*. Boston: Little, Brown, 1959. 88–99.
McDermott, John Francis. "T.B. Thorpe's Burlesque of Far West Sporting Travel." *American Quarterly* 10 (1958): 175–80.
Petry, Alice Hall. "The Common Doom: Thorpe's 'The Big Bear of Arkansas.'" *Southern Quarterly* 21 (1983): 24–31.
Rickels, Milton. "A Bibliography of the Writings of Thomas Bangs Thorpe." *American Literature* 29 (1957–1958): 171–79.
———. *Thomas Bangs Thorpe: Humorist of the Old Southwest*. Baton Rouge: Louisiana State Univ. Press, 1962.
———. "Thomas Bangs Thorpe in the Felicianas, 1836–1842." *Louisiana Historical Quarterly* 39 (1956): 169–97.
Simoneaux, Katherine G. "Symbolism in Thorpe's 'The Big Bear of Arkansas.'" *Arkansas Historical Quarterly* 25 (1966): 240–47.
Weber, Brom. "American Humor and American Culture." *American Quarterly* 14 (1962): 503–7.

Kittrell J. Warren

Hauck, Richard Boyd. *A Cheerful Nihilism: Confidence and "The Absurd" in American Humorous Fiction*. Bloomington: Univ. of Indiana Press, 1971. 66–70.
"Kit Warren Dead." *Atlanta Constitution,* 29 Dec. 1889, 17.
Lenz, William E. "The Failure of Conventional Form: The Civil War, Southwest Humor, and Kittrell Warren's *Army Straggler*." *University of Mississippi Studies in English* 5, n.s. (1984–1987): 120–30.
———. *Fast Talk and Flush Times: The Confidence Man as a Literary Convention*. Columbia: Univ. of Missouri Press, 1985. 136–46.
Piacentino, Edward J. "Kittrell Warren's *Ups and Downs of Wife Hunting*: A Hybrid of Two

Humorous Traditions." *Southern Studies: An Interdisciplinary Journal of the South* 26 (1987): 154–61.
———. "Warren, Kittrell J." *Encyclopedia of American Humorists*. Ed. Steven H. Gale. New York: Garland, 1988. 458–62.
Watkins, Floyd C. Introduction. *Life and Public Services of an Army Straggler*. Athens: Univ. of Georgia Press, 1961. ix–xiv.
———. "A Tale of the Civil War." *Emory University Quarterly* 13 (1957): 48.
———. Introduction. *Ups and Downs of Wife Hunting*. Atlanta: Emory University Library, 1957. v–viii.

Mason Locke Weems

Adams, R.G. "It Was Old Parson Weems Who Began It." *New York Times Magazine,* 5 July 1931, 10.
Alderman, Edwin A., et al., eds. *Library of Southern Literature*. Vol. 13. Atlanta: Martin and Hoyt, 1907–1908. 5731–37.
Crawford, T. Hugh. "Images of Authority, Strategies of Control: Cooper, Weems, and George Washington." *South Central Review* 11.1 (1994): 61–74.
Dawson, Hugh J. "Mason Locke Weems." *American Writers of the Early Republic*. Ed. Emory Elliott. Vol. 37. *Dictionary of Literary Biography*. Detroit: Gale Research, 1985. 298–303.
Downs, Robert B. "History Versus Legend." *Books That Changed the South*. Chapel Hill: Univ. of North Carolina Press, 1977. 51–62.
Green, James N. "'The Cowl Knows Best What Will Suit in Virginia': Parson Weems on Southern Readers." *Printing History* 17.2 (1995): 26–34.
Hall, Dean G. "Mason Locke Weems." *American Writers Before 1800*. Ed. James A. Levernier and Douglas R. Wilmes. Westport, Conn.: Greenwood, 1983. 1543–46.
Harris, Christopher L. "Mason Locke Weems's *Life of Washington*: The Making of a Bestseller." *Southern Literary Journal* 19 (1987): 92–101.
Hart, A.B. "American Historical Liars." *Harper's* (Oct. 1915), 732–34.
Ingraham, C.A. "Mason Locke Weems: A Great American Author and Distributor of Books." *Americana* (Oct. 1931), 469–85.
Kellock, Harold. *Parson Weems of the Cherry Tree*. New York: Century, 1928.
Lawson-Peebles, Robert. "On First Looking Into Cunliff's Weems's Washington: Or, The Story of America." *American Studies: Essays in Honour of Marcus Cunliffe*. Ed. Brian Holden Reid and John White. New York: St. Martin's, 1991. 21–43.
Leary, Lewis. *The Book-Peddling Parson: An Account of the Life and Works of Mason Locke Weems*. Chapel Hill: Univ. of North Carolina Press, 1984.
Moore, R. Laurence. "Religion, Secularization, and the Shaping of the Culture Industry in Antebellum America." *American Quarterly* 41 (1989): 216–42.
Purcell, James S., Jr. "A Book Pedlar's Progress in North Carolina." *North Carolina Historical Review* 29 (1952): 8–23.
Rosenblum, Joseph. "Weems, Mason Locke." *Encyclopedia of American Literature*. Ed. Steven R. Serafin. New York: Continuum, 1999. 1199–1200.
Skeel, Emily E.F. "Mason Locke Weems: A Postscript." *New Colophon* 3 (1950): 243–49
———. *Mason Locke Weems: His Works and Ways*. 3 vols. New York: n.p., 1929
Sorrentino, Paul. "Authority and Genealogy in Mason Locke Weems's *Life of Washington*."

Early American Literature and Culture: Essays Honoring Harrison T. Meserole. Ed. Kathyrn Zabelle Derounian-Stodola. Newark: Univ. of Delaware Press, 1992. 227–39.
Van Tassel, David D. "The Legend Maker." *American Heritage* 13 (1962): 58–59, 89–94.
Wills, Garry. "Mason Weems, Bibliopolist." *American Heritage* 32 (1981): 66–69.
Wroth, Lawrence C. *Parson Weems: A Biographical and Critical Study.* Baltimore: Eichelberger, 1911.
Zboray, Ronald J. "The Book-Peddler and Literary Dissemination: The Case of Parson Weems." *Publishing History: the Social, Economic and Literary History of Book, Newspaper and Magazine Publishing* 25 (1989): 27–44.

Modern Literature and Popular Culture

Arnold, St. George Tucker, Jr. "Stumbling Dogtracks on the Sands of Time: Thurber's Less-than-Charming Animal and Animal Portraits in Earlier American Humor." *Markham Review* 10 (1981): 41–47.
Bennett, Barbara. "Introduction: Southern Laughter and the Woman Writer." *Comic Visions, Female Voices: Contemporary Women Novelists and Southern Humor.* Baton Rouge: Louisiana State Univ. Press, 1998. 1–15.
Blair, Walter and Hamlin Hill. *America's Humor: From Poor Richard to Doonesbury.* New York: Oxford Univ. Press, 1978. 465–70.
Brown, Jerry Elijah. "Southern Humor and Roy Blount's Genius." *The Vanderbilt Tradition: Essays in Honor of Thomas Daniel Young.* Ed. Mark Royden Winchell. Baton Rouge: Louisiana State Univ., 1991. 139–50.
Bungert, Hans. "Re: Stark Young's Sut Lovingood." *The Lovingood Papers.* Ed. Ben Harris McClary. Knoxville: Univ. of Tennessee Press, 1965. 53–54.
———. *William Faulkner und die humoristische Tradition des amerikanischen Sudens.* Heidelberg: Carl WinterUniversitatsverlag, 1971.
Clark, John R., and William E. Morris. "Ah Similitudo! Notes on Southern Humor." *Mississippi Folklore Register* 17.2 (1983): 67–80.
Collins, Carvel. "Faulkner and Certain Earlier Southern Fiction." *College English* 16 (1954): 92–97. Revised version in *The Frontier Humorists: Critical Views.* Ed. M. Thomas Inge. Hamden, Conn.: Archon, 1975. 259–65.
Cox, Rosemary. "James Dickey, Humorist." *James Dickey Newsletter* 8 (1992): 19–26.
Davis, Charles E. "Eudora Welty's *The Robber Bridegroom* and Old Southwest Humor: A Doubleness of Vision." *A Still Moment: Essays on the Art of Eudora Welty.* Ed. John F. Desmond. Metuchen, N.J.: Scarecrow, 1978. 71–81.
Eby, Cecil D., Jr. "Faulkner and the Southwestern Humorists." *Shenandoah* 11 (1959): 13–21.
Edwards, C.H. "A Conjecture on the Name Snopes." *Notes on Contemporary Literature* 8 (1978): 9–10.
Ellis, Nancy S. "Kickin' up Dust on the Natchez Trace." *Publications of the Missouri Philological Association* 1993: 13–21.
Estes, David C. "Gaines's Humor: Race and Laughter." *Critical Reflections on the Fiction of Ernest J. Gaines.* Ed. David C. Estes. Athens: Univ. of Georgia Press, 1994. 228–49.
Foster, Ruel E. "The Modes and Functions of Humor in Faulkner. *Thalia: Studies in Literary Humor* 6.2 (1984): 9–16.
Froehlich, Peter Alan. "Faulkner and the Frontier Grotesque: *The Hamlet* as Southwestern Humor." *Faulkner in Cultural Context.* Faulkner and Yoknapatawpha Series. Eds. Donald M. Kartiganer and Ann J. Abadie. Jackson: Univ. Press of Mississippi, 1995. 218–40.

Gray, Richard. "The Comedy of Frustration: Erskine Caldwell." *The Literature of Memory: Modern Writers of the American South*. Baltimore: Johns Hopkins Univ. Press, 1977. 112–28.

*———. "Southwestern Humor, Erskine Caldwell, and the Comedy of Frustration." *Southern Literary Journal* 8.1 (1975): 3–26.

———. *Writing the South: Ideas of an American Region*. Cambridge: Cambridge Univ. Press, 1986. 62–74.

Grimwood, Michael. *Heart in Conflict: Faulkner's Struggles with Vocation*. Athens: Univ. of Georgia Press, 1987. 167–85.

Gwynn, R.S. "Ghostlier Demarcations, Taller Tales: Humor of the Old Southwest in the Poetry of Rodney Jones and Leon Stokesbury." *Lamar Journal of the Humanities* 23 (1997): 5–16.

Havard, William C. "Southwest Humor: Contemporary Style." *Southern Review* 6 (1970): 1185–90.

Hess, Judith W. "Traditional Themes in Faulkner's 'The Bear.'" *Tennessee Folklore Society Bulletin* 40 (1974): 57–64.

Hoadley, Frank M. "Folk Humor in the Novels of William Faulkner." *Tennessee Folklore Society Bulletin* 23 (1957): 75–82.

Holman, C. Hugh. "Detached Laughter in the South." *Comic Relief: Humor in Contemporary American Literature*. Ed. Sarah Blacher Cohen. Urbana: Univ. of Illinois Press, 1978. 87–104.

Inge, M. Thomas. "Al Capp's South: Appalachian Culture in *Li'l Abner*." *Li'l Abner Dailies* by Al Capp. Vol. 26: 1960. Northampton, Mass.: Kitchen Sink Press, 1997. 5–26.

———. "The Appalachian Backgrounds of Billy DeBeck's Snuffy Smith." *Appalachian Journal* 4 (1977): 120–32.

———. "Sut, Scarlet and Their Comic Cousins: The South in the Comic Strip." *On the Culture of the American South: Essays Celebrating the Twenty-Fifth Anniversary of the Popular Culture Association in the South and the American Culture Association in the South*. Ed. Dennis Hall. 19.2 (1996): 153–66

———. "Sut Lovingood and Snuffy Smith." *Comics as Culture*. Jackson: Univ. Press of Mississippi, 1990. 68–77.

———, ed. "Urban Rednecks and Genteel Rowdies: A New Generation of Southern Humorists." Special issue of *Kennesaw Review* 1.2 (1988): 37–85.

———. "William Faulkner and George Washington Harris: In the Tradition of Southwestern Humor." *The Frontier Humorists: Critical Views*. Ed. M. Thomas Inge. Hamden, Conn.: Archon, 1975. 266–80.

Insoe, John C. "Faulkner, Race, and Appalachia." *South Atlantic Quarterly* 86 (1987): 244–53.

Jacobs, Robert D. "Faulkner's Humor." *The Comic Tradition in American Literature*. Ed. Louis D. Rubin Jr. New Brunswick, N.J.: Rutgers Univ. Press, 1973. 305–18.

———. "The Humor of 'Tobacco Road.'" *The Comic Tradition in American Literature*. Ed. Louis D. Rubin Jr. New Brunswick, N.J.: Rutgers Univ. Press, 1973. 285–94.

———. "*Tobacco Road*: Lowlife and the Comic Tradition." *The American South: Portrait of a Culture*. Ed. Louis D. Rubin Jr. Baton Rouge: Louisiana State Univ. Press, 1980. 206–26.

Krauth, Leland. "Sherwood Anderson's Buck Fever; or, Frontier Humor Comes to Town." *Studies in American Humor* 3, 4 (1984–1985): 298–308.

McHaney, Thomas L. "What Faulkner Learned from the Tall Tale." *Faulkner and Humor*. Ed. Doreen Fowler and Ann J. Abadie. Jackson: Univ. Press of Mississippi, 1986. 110–35.

Messenger, Christian. "Southwestern Humor and Ring Lardner—Sport and Frontier." *Illinois Quarterly* 39 (1976): 5–21.

Moreland, Richard C. "Antisemitism, Humor, and Rage in Faulkner's *The Hamlet.*" *Faulkner Journal* 3.1 (1987): 52–70.

Richardson, H. Edward. "Faulkner, Anderson, and Their Tall Tale." *American Literature* 34 (1962): 287–91.

Rideout, Walter B., and James B. Meriwether. "On the Collaboration of Faulkner and Anderson." *American Literature* 27 (1963): 85–87.

*Ross, Stephen M. "Jason Compson and Sut Lovingood: Southwestern Humor as Stream of Consciousness." *Studies in the Novel* 8.1 (1976): 278–90.

Rouberol, Jean. "Southwestern Humor and Faulkner's View of Man." *William Faulkner: Materials, Studies, & Criticism* 7.1 (1985): 38–46.

Rubin, Louis D., Jr. "Flannery O'Connor's Company of Southerners Or, 'The ArtificialNigger' Read as Fiction Rather Than Theology." *Flannery O'Connor Bulletin* 6 (1977): 47–71. Rpt. in *A Gallery of Southerners*. Louis D. Rubin Jr. Baton Rouge: Louisiana Univ. Press, 1982. 115–34.

Schroeder, Patricia R. "The Comic World of *As I Lay Dying.*" *Faulkner and Humor*. Eds. Doreen Fowler and Ann J. Abadie. Jackson: Univ. Press of Mississippi, 1986. 34–46.

Silver, Andrew. "Laughing Over Lost Causes: Erskine Caldwell's Quarrel with Southern Humor." *Mississippi Quarterly* 50 (1996–1997): 51–68.

Skaggs, Merrill Maguire. "The Uses of Enchantment in Frontier Humor and *The Robber Bridegroom.*" *Studies in American Humor* 3.2 (1976): 96–102.

Terrie, Henry. "Erskine Caldwell's *Journeyman*: Comedy as Redemption." *Pembroke Magazine* 11 (1979): 21–30.

Thorp, Willard. "Suggs and Sut in Modern Dress: The Latest Chapter in Southern Humor." *Mississippi Quarterly* 13 (1960): 169–75. Rpt. in *The Frontier Humorists: Critical Views*. Ed. M. Thomas Inge. Hamden, Conn.: Archon, 1975. 292–99.

Turner, W. Craig. "Faulkner's 'Old Man' and the American Humor Tradition." *University of Mississippi Studies in English* 5 (1984–1987): 149–57.

Tyner, Troi. "The Function of the Bear Ritual in Faulkner's *Go Down, Moses.*" *Journal of the Ohio Folklore Society* 3 (1968): 19–40.

Utley, Francis Lee, et al., eds. *Bear, Man and God: Eight Approaches to William Faulkner's 'The Bear.'* New York: Random House, 1971.

VanSpanckeren, Kathryn. "Pop Anthropology as Humor: The Works of Florence King." *Kennesaw Review* 1.2 (1988): 50–58.

Wheeler, Otis B. "Some Uses of Folklore by Faulkner." *Mississippi Quarterly* 17 (1964): 107–22.

Contributors

Edwin T. Arnold is professor of English at Appalachian State University in Boone, N.C. He has published widely on southern writers in such works as *Conversations with Erskine Caldwell, Reading Faulkner: Sanctuary* (with Dawn Trouard), and *Perspectives on Cormac McCarthy* (with Dianne Luce). He wrote the introduction to LSU Press's reprinting of Henry Clay Lewis's *Odd Leaves From the Life of a Louisiana Swamp Doctor* (1997) is presently co-editing with Luce a collection of essays on Cormac McCarthy's Border Trilogy for the *Southern Quarterly,* and is editing a special issue of the *Faulkner Journal* devoted to "Faulkner and Film/Television."

James E. Caron is an associate professor of English and Director of the Undergraduate Honors Program at the University of 'Hawai'i at Manoa. He is co-editor with M. Thomas Inge of *Sut Lovingood's Nat'ral Born Yarnspinner: Essays on George Washington Harris* (University of Alabama Press, 1996). He has published articles on the American comic tradition as well as on various comic writers, including George Washington Harris, Mark Twain, Frank Norris, Hunter S. Thompson, and Bill Watterson.

Joseph Csicsila is an assistant professor of English Language and Literature at Eastern Michigan University. He is a specialist in late nineteenth- and early twentieth-century American literature and has published essays on many American writers, among them J. Ross Browne, Mark Twain, Mary Wilkins Freeman, and William Faulkner. At present, he is completing a book that studies the influence the classroom literature anthology has exerted on American criticism and the American canon of authors in the twentieth century.

David C. Estes is an associate professor of English at Loyola University New Orleans. He has edited two books on Louisiana authors, *A New Collection of Thomas Bangs Thorpe's Sketches of the Old Southwest: A Critical Edition* and *Critical Reflections on the Fiction of Ernest J. Gaines.* Currently, he is the editor of the *Louisiana Folklore Miscellany.*

Richard Gray is a professor in the Department of Literature at the University of Essex. He is the author of *The Literature of Memory: Modern Writers of the American South, Writing the South: Ideas of an American Region* (which won the C. Hugh Holman Award from the Society for the Study of Southern Literature), *American Poetry of the Twentieth Century, The Life of William Faulkner: A Critical Biography,* and *Southern Aberrations: Writers of the American South and the Problems of Regionalism.* He has edited two anthologies of American poetry, two editions of the poetry of Edgar Allan Poe, a collection of original essays on American fiction, and a collection of essays on Robert Penn Warren; and he has written a number of essays and articles on American literature of the last two centuries. He is currently editing a companion to the literature and culture of the American South and writing a history of American literature, both for Blackwell Publishers. A regular reviewer for various newspapers and journals, including the *Times Literary Supplement,* he is editor of the *Journal of American Studies* and the first specialist in American literature to be elected a Fellow of the British Academy.

M. Thomas Inge is the Robert Emory Blackwell Professor of English and Humanities at Randolph-Macon College in Ashland, Virginia. He edited the works of George Washington Harris and has written extensively on American humor, southern literature and culture, comic art, and William Faulkner. His recent publications include *William Faulkner: The Contemporary Reviews* (Cambridge 1995), *Conversations with William Faulkner* (Mississippi 1999), *Charles M. Schulz: Conversations* (Mississippi 2000), and new editions of Mark Twain's *A Connecticut Yankee* (Oxford 1997) and Sam Watkins's *Company Aytch* (Penguin 1999).

James H. Justus, who hails from Sut Lovingood country, did his undergraduate work at the University of Tennessee, where he also earned the M.A., with a thesis on the adaptations of the Beauchamp case in frontier Kentucky by William Gilmore Simms and Robert Penn Warren. After receiving his Ph.D. at the University of Washington in 1961, he joined the English Department at Indiana University, from which he retired as Distinguished Professor in 1993. He is the author of *The Achievement of Robert Penn Warren* (1981) and editor of Baldwin's *Flush Times of Alabama and Mississippi* (1987). He is currently completing a study of the humor of the Old Southwest.

Leland Krauth is an associate professor of English at the University of Colorado at Boulder. He has taught at the Universite Paul Valery in Montpellier, France, and the University of Kent in Canterbury, England. Specializing in nineteenth- and twentieth-century American literature, he has published numerous articles on novelists, poets, and humorists, including Walt Whitman, William Dean Howells, Mark Twain, Stephen Crane, Hamlin Garland, Sherwood Anderson, Edgar Lee Masters, William Stafford, and James Wright. He has recently published a critical study, *Proper Mark Twain* (University of Georgia Press, 1999), and is currently working on a study of Twain in relation to six other writers, three American—Bret Harte, William Dean Howells, and Harriet Beecher Stowe—and three British—Matthew Arnold, Robert Louis Stevenson, and Rudyard Kipling.

J.A. Leo Lemay, H.F. du Pont Winterthur Professor of English at the University of Delaware, specializes in early American literature but occasionally ventures into the nineteenth century. He is currently writing a seven-volume biography of Benjamin Franklin.

William E. Lenz is chair and professor of English at Chatham College. His most recent book, *The Poetics of the Antarctic* (1995), initiated his interest in nineteenth-century American exploration. Having taken five groups of Chatham women to Belize and Guatemala, he has redirected his research and is currently at work on a study tentatively called *The Construction of Central America in Nineteenth-Century American Travel Narratives.*

Gretchen Martin is currently working on a Ph.D. at the University of North Carolina, Greensboro. She received her bachelor's degree from the University of Iowa and her master's from Northern Michigan University. Her major scholarly interests are early American, and especially southern literature and culture, late American, and eighteenth-century British literature.

Kurt Albert Mayer is associate professor of American Studies at Vienna University (Austria). Educated at Vienna and, as a two-year Fulbright student, at SUNY-Buffalo, he wrote his dissertation on "Jack Kerouac, Ken Kesey, and Richard Brautigan: Popular Culture and Literary Aspiration" and his *Habilitationschrift* on "Henry Adams and the German-Speaking World, 1858–1905/7." Interested in the manifold interrelations between story and history, between literature, culture, and politics, he has published on Henry Adams, Charles Francis Adams Jr., John Hay, Gore Vidal, Ken Kesey, and William Faulkner. Currently, he is mainly at work on a multimedia project for the Internet, entitled "Roads in/of American Culture," of which the essay on Longstreet is a product.

Ed Piacentino is a professor of English at High Point University in North Carolina. He has published numerous essays on southern literature and culture, including Southwestern humor, in reference books and in such scholarly journals as the *Mississippi Quarterly*, the *Southern Literary Journal*, *Southern Studies*, *Studies in American Humor*, *Studies in Short Fiction*, and the *Simms Review*. His most recent book is *T.S. Stribling: Pioneer Realist in Southern Literature* (1988).

David Rachels is a member of the Department of English and Fine Arts at Virginia Military Institute. He is the editor of *Augustus Baldwin Longstreet's Georgia Scenes Completed: A Scholarly Text* (University of Georgia Press, 1998) and the co-editor of the *Classics of Civil War Fiction* reprint series (University of Alabama Press).

Scott Romine is an assistant professor of English at the University of North Carolina at Greensboro. In addition to his interest in Southwestern humor, he has published essays on such writers as John Crowe Ransom, Lillian Smith, William Alexander Percy, and Harry Crews. His work has appeared in *Style*, *Southern Quarterly*, *Mississippi Quarterly*, *Critical Survey*, *South Atlantic Review*, and in several collections of essays. His first book, *The Narrative Forms of Southern Community*, was published by Louisiana State University Press.

Stephen M. Ross is the author of *Fiction's Inexhaustible Voice: Speech and Writing in Faulkner* (Athens: Univ. of Georgia Press, 1989); *Reading Faulkner: The Sound and the Fury*, co-authored with Noel Polk (Jackson: Univ. Press of Mississippi, 1996); and *Unflinching Gaze: Morrison and Faulkner Re-envisioned*, co-edited with Carol Kolmerten and Judith Wittenberg (Jackson: Univ. Press of Mississippi, 1997). He has taught at Purdue University and the United States Naval Academy, and he is currently the director of the Office of Challenge Grants at the National Endowment for the Humanities in Washington, D.C.

Johanna Nicol Shields is professor emerita of history at the University of Alabama in Huntsville, where she also serves as director of the UAH Humanities Center. In addition to studies of antebellum American politics and political culture, she has published articles on southern humor. She wrote the biographical introduction to the Alabama Classics series edition of Johnson Hooper's *Adventures of Captain Simon Suggs* (1993). Currently, she is working on a book about writers in the Old Southwest, a study that will treat humorists Hooper and Joseph Baldwin, domestic writers Augusta Evans and Caroline Hentz, and other writers of popular fiction and history.

Mary Ann Wimsatt, McClintock Professor of Southern Letters at the University of South Carolina, is the author of *The Major Fiction of William Gilmore Simms*, the editor of *Tales of the South by William Gilmore Simms*, the senior editor of *Southern Women Writers*, and contributing editor to *The History of Southern Literature*. She has also written many essays on southern authors.

Index